Contents

Poststructuralist Challenges

Representational Challenges

Conclusion

List of Contributors

Ben Agger

Department of Sociology
State University of New York
Buffalo

Joel Best

Department of Sociology
Southern Illinois University
Carbondale

David Bogen

Humanities and Social Science
Emerson College

Richard Harvey Brown

Department of Sociology
University of Maryland

Avery F. Gordon

Department of Sociology
University of California
Santa Barbara

Jaber F. Gubrium

Department of Sociology
University of Florida

Lawrence Hazelrigg

Department of Sociology
Florida State University

James A. Holstein

Department of Social and
    Cultural Sciences
Marquette University

Peter R. Ibarra

Sociology Board
University of California
Santa Cruz

John I. Kitsuse

Sociology Board
University of California
Santa Cruz

Michael Lynch   Department of Sociology
                                 Boston University

Courtney L. Marlaire   Department of Social and
                                     Cultural Sciences
                                 Marquette University

Douglas W. Maynard   Department of Sociology
                                 Indiana University

Raymond J. Michalowski   Department of Criminal Justice
                                 Northern Arizona University

Gale Miller   Department of Social and
                                     Cultural Sciences
                                 Marquette University

Leslie J. Miller   Department of Sociology
                                 University of Calgary

Jackie Orr   Department of Sociology
                                 University of California
                                 Berkeley

Stephen Pfohl   Department of Sociology
                                 Boston College

Melvin Pollner   Department of Sociology
                                 University of California
                                 Los Angeles

Laurel Richardson   Department of Sociology
                                 Ohio State University

Joseph W. Schneider   Department of Sociology
                                 Drake University

Dorothy E. Smith   Ontario Institute for Studies in
                                     Education

Ronald J. Troyer   Department of Sociology
                                 Drake University

Carol A. B. Warren   Department of Sociology
                                 University of Kansas

Preface

This volume reconsiders the directions that the social constructionist perspective has taken in social problems theory and research. The approach has been both provocative and controversial since its introduction by John Kitsuse and Malcolm Spector during the 1970s. This volume reexamines constructionist theorizing and considers alternative possibilities for its future. The centerpiece of the book is a paper by John Kitsuse and Peter Ibarra which sets a new tone and agenda for constructionist studies. The paper is a point of departure for further developments and debates in social problems theory.

This is a unique group of essays. The authors of this collection—and its companion volume *Constructionist Controversies: Issues in Social Problems Theory* (Aldine de Gruyter 1993) represent a diversity of perspectives, but they share an interest in what the constructionist perspective on social problems has to offer. While the essays present a wide range of opinions, each offers a healthy dose of constructive criticism. Consequently, the debates may raise more questions than they resolve. But we hope the commentaries, criticism, and controversies that appear in this book will continue to animate discussions of social problems theory.

The volume is organized around recent debates in social problems. Part I begins with Ibarra and Kitsuse's bold pronouncement on the state of constructionism and the directions it should pursue in the future. More or less congenial commentaries are then offered in sections titled "Constructionist Responses" and "Ethnomethodological Concerns." Part II engages controversies that emanate from outside the constructionist perspective. These discussions are organized as "Critical Challenges," "Poststructural Challenges," and "Representational Challenges."

Throughout the volume, our intent is to articulate alternative points of view on the constructionist project, using the arising tensions as opportunities for theoretical clarification and growth. Some of the perspectives represented here are not generally associated with the constructionist program. We hope that by bringing disparate approaches to bear on a common theme we might provoke new ways of looking at, and doing, the sociology of social problems.

John Kitsuse has been at the forefront of the sociology of deviance and social problems since he arrived at Northwestern University in 1958.

There, and later at the University of California at Santa Cruz, Kitsuse pursued a consistently radical program of constructionist studies that has transformed American sociology. While his work has clear affinities for what has come to be known as "labeling theory," Kitsuse's analysis has been distinguished by its uncompromising constitutive emphasis. His early collaborations with Aaron Cicourel and, later, with Malcolm Spector, represent foundational pieces in the constructionist program that challenged the dominant sociological paradigms of the mid-twentieth century. Generations of sociologists are indebted to his clear and forceful articulations of the approach.

We are very much indebted to John for his work over the years, and for his contribution to this collection. Perhaps no higher tribute can be paid to a scholar than for his friends, colleagues, and detractors to get riled up over what he has to say. We think this collection is evidence that John Kitsuse can still provoke a good argument.

We have many people besides John and his coauthor, Peter Ibarra, to thank for making this project possible. Ron Troyer organized a social problems colloquium at the meetings of the Society for the Study of Social Problems in 1989 that sparked many of the debates that we have pursued in this collection. Some of the papers in the volume began at that session. We are deeply indebted to all the contributors to this book for their superb essays.

Getting a project of this magnitude into print is not an easy task. Joel Best, editor of Aldine de Gruyter's series in "Social Problems and Social Issues" was enthusiastic about the project from the start. Executive Editor Richard Koffler has been a tremendous help in working out the details and making it possible to publish the two volume set. They deserve our special thanks. Finally, Arlene Perazzini and Mike Sola have done a superbly professional job in pulling this difficult project together into a final product.

PART I
Debates Within Social Constructionism

Revising the Constructionist Project

1

Reconsidering Social Constructionism

Gale Miller and James A. Holstein

The social constructionist perspective has been the most controversial—
if not the most influential—development in social problems theory in
the past twenty-five years. *Constructing Social Problems* (Spector and
Kitsuse [1977] 1987) offered what is generally regarded as the quintessential statement of the approach, both transforming and revitalizing
the sociology of social problems. In the book and a series of articles
published in *Social Problems* (Kitsuse and Spector 1973, 1975; Spector and
Kitsuse 1974), Kitsuse and Spector challenged conventional approaches
to the field with their vision of social problems as social constructions,
that is, as the products of claims-making and constitutive definitional
processes.

While the constructionist approach quickly produced a flurry of empirical studies (see Schneider 1985a; Maynard 1988; Best 1989), it just as
quickly became the focus of a variety of debates. Objections from the
more conventional or "realist" orientations insisted that there is an objective reality to social problems, which should be the topic of sociological studies and which constructionists stubbornly deny. Charges of unacknowledged objectivism and "ontological gerrymandering" (Woolgar
and Pawluch 1985) resounded from the opposite direction. Most recently, the constructionist camp finds itself divided, some arguing for the
"strict" constitutive reading of *Constructing Social Problems*, while others
argue for a "contextual" constructionism that focuses on the claims-
making process, but acknowledges assumptions about objective conditions (Best 1989).

The purpose of this book is to reconsider the social constructionist
perspective in light of new developments and emerging debates in social
problems theory. Although they all express appreciation for the constructionist approach, the essays that follow offer a variety of orientations to the study of social problems. They critique previous constructionist formulations, make suggestions for advancing, expanding, or

5

diversifying the constructionist agenda, and challenge the perspective and agenda. The book is divided into two parts.

Part I addresses contemporary debates within the constructionist camp. Its focal point is the essay by Ibarra and Kitsuse, which refocuses and redefines Spector and Kitsuse's original programmatic position. It then considers constructionist responses to the revised position and introduces a variety of ethnomethodological concerns relating to the construction of social problems. Part II focuses on new challenges to social constructionism that emanate from a variety of related, though not wholly sympathetic, perspectives. Critical, poststructural, and representational challenges provide the basis for a wide-ranging discussion of the prospects and possibilities for the constructionist approach and social problems theory.

The Challenge of Social Constructionism

The social constructionist perspective has been controversial since its inception. Most notably, the approach breaks with conventional and commonsensical conceptions of social problems by analyzing them as a *social process* of definition. In their seminal paper, Kitsuse and Spector define social problems as "the activities of groups making assertions of grievances and claims with respect to some putative conditions" (1973, p. 415). Construed in this fashion, social problems are not objective conditions to be studied and corrected; rather, they are the interpretive processes that constitute what come to be seen as oppressive, intolerable, or unjust conditions like crime, poverty, and homelessness.

From this point of view, social problems are not distinctive and inherently immoral conditions; they are definitions of and orientations to *putative* conditions that are *argued* to be inherently immoral or unjust (Spector and Kitsuse [1977] 1987). The constructionist position emphasizes that the activities through which social problems are constructed are both implicitly and intentionally rhetorical. Public rhetoric and the politics of claims-making are analyzed in the myriad circumstances in which social problems construction takes place, including "demanding services, filling out forms, lodging complaints, filing lawsuits, calling press conferences, writing letters of protest, passing resolutions, publishing exposes, placing ads in newspapers, supporting or opposing governmental practice or policy, setting up picket lines or boycotts" (Spector and Kitsuse [1977] 1987, p. 79). The result is a constructionist sociology of social problems that attempts to "account for the emergence and maintenance of claim-making and responding activities" (Kitsuse and Spector 1973, p. 415).

Initially, the constructionist approach was a response and alternative to the structural functionalist approach to social problems. Structural functionalists assume that social conditions exist separately from persons' interpretations of them. They believe that objective knowledge of social conditions is obtainable through the scientific method and that the scientific study of social conditions will demonstrate that some social conditions are truly social problems. Sociologists use the assumptions as a warrant for defining problems as real and observable social conditions, portraying their studies as objective analyses, and describing themselves as experts on social problems.

Spector and Kitsuse's claims-making approach undercuts these fundamental assumptions by questioning the possibility of knowing the objective status of conditions. Indeed, their challenge is almost ironic because they take structural functionalists' definitions of social problems seriously, even as they undermine them. For example, in a classic functionalist statement, Merton contends that *"a social problem exists when there is a sizeable discrepancy between what is and what people think ought to be"* (1976, p. 7, emphasis in original). Spector and Kitsuse appreciate several questions implicit in this definition by asking, How do people know what is and what ought to be? How do persons know that there is a sizeable discrepancy between what is and ought to be? Spector and Kitsuse's answers to the questions emphasize the ways in which social conditions, cultural ideals, and discrepancies between them are socially constructed.

Spector and Kitsuse also challenge structural functionalists by analyzing how professional sociologists' conventional theories of social problems involve claims-making about putative social conditions. Like Merton, authors of social problems texts use their portrayals of "real" aspects of everyday life to justify their interest in analyzing the pervasiveness, social organization, and consequences of the conditions that they describe as manifest and latent social problems. Sociologists also act as expert consultants to policymakers, who assume that social problems exist as objective conditions and that sociologists are experts on them.

Thus, Spector and Kitsuse use the social constructionist perspective to subvert other sociologists' claims to objective knowledge about social problems and expert status. They also point to the theoretical advantages of studying sociologists as claims-makers by arguing that constructionism provides the basis for developing a distinctively sociological approach that focuses on the social processes through which social problems are constructed. Such a sociology would examine the diverse claims-making groups and activities, and avoid its own claims-making activities. Specifically, Spector and Kitsuse's ([1977] 1987) approach to

constructionism would avoid defining "real" social problems, or distinguishing between "real" and "spurious" social problems.

One indicator of the skill with which Spector and Kitsuse have argued
their position is the substantial literature on the social construction of
social problems that has developed since 1973. As Schneider (1985a)
states in his review and assessment of the perspective, social constructionism has influenced a wide range of theoretical and empirical studies,
including those concerned with the micropolitics of trouble, institutional
processing of social problems, competition between interest groups over
the "ownership" of social problems, and claims-making activities by
members of the news media. Taken together, the studies point to the
pervasiveness of social problems construction in contemporary Western
societies.

Contemporary Debates About Social Constructionism

Some contemporary controversies surrounding social constructionism
recast old issues raised in Spector and Kitsuse's debate with structural
functionalists. Questions still arise concerning sociologists' responsibilities to point out "real" social problems that are ignored by political
leaders and the public. Some critics argue that definitions of social problems are important, but there is a "reality" behind them that is paramount. As Eitzen states,

> [T]here is an objective reality to social problems. There are structures that
> induce material or psychic suffering for certain segments of the popula-
> tion; there are structures that ensure the maldistribution of resources with-
> in a society and across societies; there are structures that prevent certain
> societal participants from developing and realizing their full human poten-
> tial; there are corporate and political organizations that waste valuable
> resources, that pollute the environment, that are imperialistic, and that
> increase the gap between the "haves" and the "have-nots." (1984, p. 10)

Another set of debates involves Spector and Kitsuse's contention that
the examination of social problems claims-making is a distinctive field of
sociological study. For example, Mauss et al. (1975) and Mauss (1989,
1992) argue that social problems claims-making is a type of collective
behavior, and social constructionist studies of social problems can be
subsumed within the substantive field of social movements. Mauss insists that social problems theory would be enriched by the diverse theories that make up the latter field. Hilgartner and Bosk (1988) offer a
related challenge by analyzing social problems claims-making from an
ecological perspective. They treat social problems claims as aspects of

arenas of public discourse, and claims-making groups as engaged in competition for scarce public attention. Hilgartner and Bosk question social constructionists' emphasis on studying the natural histories of claims-making movements, and justify their use of organization network and resource mobilization theory to analyze such movements.

Finally there are debates that raise new questions about the fundamental assumptions and goals of social constructionism. Many of the new critics argue that the constructionist perspective actually invokes a selective "objectivism" because it assumes that social construction processes are observable aspects of social worlds that exist separately from social constructionists' descriptions of them. Social constructionists, then, act as "objective" analysts of and experts on the "real" social processes through which social problems are constructed. Perhaps the most influential of the new critics are Woolgar and Pawluch (1985), who analyze social constructionist theorizing as ontological gerrymandering.

Woolgar and Pawluch suggest that social constructionist arguments can generally be broken out into three parts. First, the analyst identifies particular conditions or behaviors. Then he or she identifies various definitions or claims made about these conditions or behaviors. Finally, the analyst highlights the variability of the definitions or claims relative to the constancy of the conditions to which they relate. The implication is that since the condition is invariant, changes in the definition of the conditions must result from the social circumstances of the definers rather than from the condition itself.

Woolgar and Pawluch note that this sort of analysis depends upon the "objective" statement about the constancy of the condition under consideration in order to justify claims about the shifting definitional process. Assumptions must be made regarding the actual existence and status of the condition if apparent change in the condition or problem is to be considered a definitional artifact. Woolgar and Pawluch argue that this selective "objectivism" represents a theoretical inconsistency in the definitional approach since it manipulates an analytic boundary to make certain phenomena problematic while leaving others unquestioned. Ontological gerrymandering thus glosses over the ways in which constructionist analysts' descriptions of conditions are themselves definitional claims.

Woolgar and Pawluch draw two very different implications from their analysis. First, they suggest that ontological gerrymandering may be a necessary aspect of the social constructionist project. It is not a practice that can be avoided; rather, it sets constructionist theorizing apart from other interpretive approaches to social problems. The response justifies the theoretical status quo, even taking an appreciative stance toward social constructionists' writing practices. A second and very different implication is that social constructionists should examine and reconsider their own writing and rhetorical practices. Woolgar and Pawluch suggest that constructionists "search for forms of argument which go beyond the current impasse between proponents of objectivism and of relativism" (1985, p. 224). The suggestion assumes that it is possible to write about social life and experience in ways that do not objectify the phenomena under discussion.

Responses to the Ontological Gerrymandering Critique

Woolgar and Pawluch's critique has raised a variety of responses among social constructionists concerning the essential claims and assumptions of the perspective, and the purposes of their studies. These involve both assessments of and responses to Woolgar and Pawluch's critique, and portrayals of social constructionism as a complex intellectual movement that includes diverse and somewhat opposed orientations to social problems theory. For example, in this volume, Ibarra and Kitsuse react to Woolgar and Pawluch by distinguishing between the assumptions and claims of the social constructionist perspective—as it was initially formulated by Spector and Kitsuse—and the ways in which it has been explained and applied by other social constructionists (see Schneider 1985b).

Ibarra and Kitsuse state that while Woolgar and Pawluch's critique is appropriate for much contemporary research on social problems that is called social constructionist, it is an inappropriate description of Spector and Kitsuse's formulation of the perspective because they express little interest in the sociohistorical circumstances associated with social problems definitions. Rather, they focus on how claims-making activities are organized and accomplished. Thus, Spector and Kitsuse analyze social problems as real to the extent that claims-makers are able to convince others to honor their claims, and state that it is sociologically counterproductive to ask whether claims-makers' definitions are accurate or warranted.

Other social constructionists, however, have responded to the ontological gerrymandering critique by emphasizing the implications noted by Woolgar and Pawluch. An important response acknowledges that social constructionist analyses do involve ontological gerrymandering, but maintains that this is not a problem. The argument is central to Best's (1989) articulation of the *contextual constructionist* perspective, which he contrasts with Spector and Kitsuse's *strict constructionist* position. A second response to Woolgar and Pawluch emphasizes the importance of avoiding ontological gerrymandering. It involves developing new ways of writing social constructionist texts. We briefly outline these responses in the following sections.

Contextual Constructionist Response

Contextual constructionists argue that Woolgar and Pawluch's critique is counterproductive to the development of an adequate social constructionist theory of social problems. They state that the critique diverts attention away from the study of the social worlds within which and social processes through which social problems are constructed. For example, Gusfield (1985) rejects the critique because it only focuses on the logic of social constructionists' theorizing and writing. It does not consider what it is that social constructionists are theorizing and writing about or, as Gusfield states, the substance of the social constructionist project.

The contextual constructionists' position derives from their orientation to sociological research and analysis. They argue that the object of research and theory should be to offer information about and insights into the organization and workings of social problems movements, and the social conditions that claims-makers describe as social problems. While not denying that their analyses are social constructions, contextual constructionists argue that a *primary* focus on such matters makes sociologists' studies of social problems irrelevant to most audiences within and outside the field.

Contextual constructionists also emphasize the theoretical usefulness of ontological gerrymandering in explaining why and how social problems claims emerge within sociohistorical contexts. Best (1989) justifies the practice in two major ways. First, he states that it may be impossible for social constructionists to avoid ontological gerrymandering, no matter how hard they try. It is a necessary aspect of writing about social worlds and definitional processes as existing separately from writers' portrayals of them. Second, efforts to avoid ontological gerrymandering may undermine the social constructionist project, because social constructionists may quit asking important questions about claims-making activities.

Finally, where strict constructionists try to avoid ontological gerrymandering by refusing to evaluate the accuracy of claims-makers' claims, contextual constructionists treat the evaluation of social problems claims as an important part of their analyses. It is one way in which they contribute to public and academic debates about social problems. According to Best, any social problems claim can be evaluated with reasonable confidence by using available statistical and other information about the condition that the claim describes. It is irrelevant that the information used to make the evaluation is itself a social construction and rhetorical claim. As Best states, "calling a statement a claim does not discredit it" (1989, p. 247).

Contextual constructionist analyses turn on distinguishing between "warranted" and "unwarranted" social problems claims, a distinction that implicitly involves treating some putative conditions as "real" social problems and others as "false" social problems. Real social problems are those putative conditions about which appropriate claims are being made and claims-makers are recommending responses that are assessed by contextual constructionists as likely to be successful. For example, Scritchfield analyzes recent claims-making about infertility as a false social problem because the claims are "unlikely to result in any major decreases in the incidence of such impairments" and "actually may contribute to an increase" (1989, p. 111).

Contextual constructionists also use their assessments of social problems claims to construct new and previously "unrecognized" social problems. For example, Bauman (1989) uses her review of studies of elder abuse to challenge the popular image of old people as victims of their children. The image emphasizes old persons' dependence on their caregiving children, and the children's failure to fulfill their responsibilities to their parents. Bauman counters this "false" image by stating that government officials' and others' treatment of elder abuse as a parent-child problem has diverted attention from the ways in which it is a form of wife abuse. Thus, Bauman constructs a new social problem centered in social relations involving the elderly, and casts it as a largely unrecognized problem.

New Writing Response

The second implication Woolgar and Pawluch (1985) draw from their critique involves developing new ways of writing social problems texts. They state that the purpose of the new writing forms is to get beyond the fruitless debates between advocates for objectivist and relativist positions. Such debates are fruitless because they are unresolvable within the writing forms typically used by sociologists to formulate and express their positions. An example of how new writing forms might be developed is Hughes's (1961) study of a drug addict. The research is based on extensive, tape-recorded conversations between Janet (a drug addict) and Howard S. Becker.

Hughes edited the tapes to produce a story that might be read as Janet's autobiography. Thus, Hughes's study gets beyond the objectivist-relativist debate by allowing Janet to tell her story without submitting it to external, sociological analysis. Similar concerns and themes are central to McCall and Becker's (1990) experiment with performance science, which is intended to show how the "findings" of field studies may be recast as theatrical performances. Among the advantages of such a mode of presentation are the organization of the findings as dialogues between actors, and opportunities to show the complexities of others' orientations to and responses to diverse situations and issues.

Other social constructionists have experimented with reflexive writing forms. Such texts are organized to remind readers that authors are aware of the rhetorical devices that they use to construct textual realities, and that they offer understandings that are partisan and potentially contestable by others. While social constructionists' interest in developing reflexive writing practices may be seen as an attempt to become more self-aware and sophisticated theorists and writers, it promises more than this. It is a possible bridge between social constructionism and related but very different poststructuralist perspectives. The introductory essay to Part II of this volume offers a more detailed and fuller treatment of these perspectives and their implications for social problems theory.

Ethnomethodology and Social Problems

While it remained for Woolgar and Pawluch to point out some of the major theoretical inconsistencies in the application of Spector and Kitsuse's initial formulations, ethnomethodologists anticipated Woolgar and Pawluch's argument, most specifically in early critiques of labeling theory. For example, in commenting on Becker's (1963) theory of deviance, Pollner (1974, 1978) distinguishes between "mundane" and "constitutive" versions of labeling theory. He states that mundane labeling theorists, like Becker, analyze the labeling process by assessing whether persons and/or acts have been accurately labeled as deviant. Making such assessments necessarily involves making privileged judgments about the "real" or "factual" character of the phenomena in question, and the objective character of acts and/or conditions retains its importance as the determinant of the accuracy of the labeling process.

For example, Becker takes this position when he suggests that "the degree to which an act will be treated as deviant depends on who commits the act" (1963, p. 12). He then illustrates the point by documenting the differential fates of middle-class versus lower-class boys, or white versus black youth when confronted by the criminal justice system for committing the "same" act. Establishing the "sameness" of the act, Pollner argues, requires reference to a criterion other that the actual disposition of and reaction to the cases under consideration. The independent criterion is necessary to establish that similar acts have elicited differential responses. Thus, some inherent feature of the act, not societal reaction or the labeling process itself, is treated as defining the act's character.

Pollner contrasts mundane labeling theory with an ethnomethodological or constitutive version, which assumes that the labeling process *constitutes* the phenomenon. There is no need to assess the "objective" characteristics of persons or events labeled as deviant because their deviant status is an interpretive accomplishment. Labelers accomplish deviance by applying deviant labels to themselves, others, activities, and/or events. Thus, the ethnomethodological approach is radically different from mundane labeling theory.

The Ethnomethodological Focus

Ethnomethodology attends to the commonsense practices, procedures, and resources that persons use to produce and recognize mutually intelligible objects and actions in the life world (Garfinkel 1967; Heritage 1984). It emphasizes locally managed, ongoing practices of reality construction and maintenance, and treats the social construction of social realities as an ongoing accomplishment. Talk and interaction are the focus of ethnomethodological studies of social problems. Aspects of the ethnomethodological perspective are clearly evident in Spector and Kitsuse's initial formulation of the social constructionist project. As Troyer states, Spector and Kitsuse emphasize ethnomethodological assumptions and concerns when they argue for

> suspending the issue of whether or not there is an external world and argued that social problems researchers should look at how the agreement arises that there is a "social problem." . . . . Spector and Kitsuse ask that researchers examine the methods people use in creating a sense that there is a bad condition. The definition itself is secondary: the primary concern is the methods (activities) used to create the "problem." (1989, p. 44)

Aspects of ethnomethodology resonate with Wittgenstein's (1953, 1969) analysis of language games and forms of life. For Wittgenstein, language games are the diverse, concrete, and culturally shared ways in which actors use language to organize situations and achieve practical ends. They include asking questions, telling stories, giving orders, and describing objects. Further, each of these language games is related to other activities in everyday life, including other language games. For example, asking questions is typically associated with the language game of answering questions, telling stories with laughter, and describing objects with questions about them. In associating language games with other activities, actors construct social contexts for assigning meaning to their own and others' actions (Wittgenstein 1967).

Thus, language games are aspects of patterns of behavior and relationship to which actors orient. Wittgenstein analyzes the patterns as forms of life. They are "the substratum of conventional behavior that underlies meaning and implication" (Bloor 1983, p. 137). Wittgenstein's analysis challenges individualistic and mentalistic theories, which treat language, meaning, and knowledge as the products of individual intention. He counters this tendency in philosophy and the human sciences by analyzing the ways in which meaning and intention are socially organized. They are embedded in shared linguistic and cultural connections that link actions into meaningful patterns, and are social contexts for establishing what the actions (and related states of mind) could mean:

> That is why a speaker can "mean" something of which he is ignorant at the time . . . . [O]ur language and our culture make the connections between what he says and what he means (can mean). And that is why the teacher can mean, or intend, for the pupil to write 1,002 after 1,000, even if he did not think about those numbers. . . . . The circumstances make possible the intention. (Pitken 1972, pp. 73–74)

Ethnomethodology complements Wittgenstein's analysis of language games and forms of life in at least two major ways. First, it is a radically social approach to everyday life that focuses on the ways in which actors descriptively construct and assign meanings (including intentions). Ethnomethodologists analyze actors' interpretive practices as reflexively implicated in situations; that is, they are constitutive aspects of the situations in which they occur. Meaning construction and assignment is a multifaceted process that simultaneously involves defining the events, objects, or issues under consideration, as well as the situations in which the considerations are made. The analyses may be further extended to consider the methods used by ethnomethodologists to describe and analyze situations (Mehan and Wood 1975; Pollner 1991; Wieder 1988).

Ethnomethodology also complements Wittgenstein's analysis in its concern for the practical assumptions and practices associated with meaning construction and assignment. Ethnomethodologists often express the concern as a problem of analyzing the taken-for-granted and "seen but unnoticed" aspects of everyday life (Garfinkel 1967). This partly involves analyzing the assumptions that underlie the natural attitude (Schutz 1970) and mundane reasoning (Pollner 1987) through which everyday life is organized.

Ethnomethodology and Social
Problems Theory

Ethnomethodology is a diverse mode of inquiry, composed of a variety of research methodologies and analytic techniques (Holstein and Gubrium forthcoming; Maynard and Clayman 1991). Ethnomethodological studies include in-depth, ethnographic studies of interaction in social institutions, highly detailed analyses of transcripts of conversations, and abstract studies of such issues as the natural attitude, the documentary method of interpretation, and reflexivity. This section is an overview of how ethnomethodological methods and analytic techniques may be used to study the social construction of social problems. We first consider how ethnomethodological studies have adopted and adapted the constitutive point of view by focusing on the organized application of social problems designations.

One way in which the ethnomethodological perspective has been applied within social problems theory is by analyzing the situated interactional and interpretive procedures used by claims-makers to describe aspects of everyday life as social problems. Such analyses are central to studies of the micropolitics of trouble in institutional settings (Emerson and Messinger 1977), which focus on the concrete ways in which interactants describe and orient to aspects of their own and others lives as troublesome (Emerson 1969; Gubrium and Holstein 1990; Holstein 1993; Loseke 1989, 1992; Miller 1983, 1991). The studies differ from those criticized by Woolgar and Pawluch because the analysts do not assume that troublesome conditions exist separately from interactants' descriptions of them. Both the trouble categories used by interactants and conditions that they describe as troublesome are analyzed as social constructions.

Where Spector and Kitsuse specified the processes by which social problems categories are made culturally prominent, ethnomethodologically informed analyses have attempted to describe the practices by which the categories are assigned to concrete cases. The reality-assigning practices that link public interpretive structures to aspects of everyday life can be called *social problems work* (Miller and Holstein 1989; Miller 1992). Studies of social problems work consider the culturally available labeling resources while maintaining the ethnomethodological focus on the ways that actors apply labels in relation to commonsense methods for handling experiences that come to be portrayed as troubles or problems (Maynard and Clayman 1991).

Many of the pioneering ethnomethodological studies of achieved social order involve social problems categorization. For example, Bittner's (1967a, 1967b) studies of police work and peacekeeping describe the variegated and complex interpretive practices used to establish and maintain order in the community. Integral to the process is police officers' use of social problems categories like crime and mental illness as both definitional and practical resources. Similarly, Sudnow (1965) shows how attorneys employ commonsense models of typical offenders, offenses, problems, and solutions to make plea bargaining arrangements that assign persons to social problems and criminal categories. Unofficial categorization practices have also been analyzed.

Cicourel's (1968) study of the policing of juveniles also elucidates several important aspects of social problems work. He analyzes the processes involved in classifying "juvenile delinquents" and the reflexivity of the categorization process. The study demonstrates how police activities were informed by commonsense theories of delinquency. For example, offenses by juveniles from "broken homes" were treated more seriously by officers than were actions by juveniles from stable families. As a consequence, offenders from broken homes were more likely to be officially apprehended and processed as delinquents—made formal occupants of the category. This practice, in turn, provided concrete documentary evidence in the form of crime statistics that verified the commonsense theory. Thus, the officers' commonsense theories reflexively produced and reproduced the evidence of their own validity.

Conversation analysis is a distinctive variant of ethnomethodology that is concerned with the social competencies that underpin social interaction, the procedures through which interaction is produced and understood (Heritage 1987). Although tensions exist concerning the relationship between conversation analysis and ethnomethodology (e.g., Lynch and Bogen forthcoming), the connection is most commonly underscored by their mutual interest in the local, methodical construction of intelligible and analyzable social action and activity (see Maynard and Clayman 1991). Conversation analytic studies of social problems have taken a variety of forms, most notably addressing how parties engaged in interaction routinely and procedurally produce and experience forms of "trouble" that may be characterized as social problems (Maynard 1988).

Some of the studies focus on the socially organized features of "telling" troubles, problems, and complaints. They analyze the ways individuals interactionally offer candidate problems for consideration and reaction (Jefferson 1988; Jefferson and Lee 1981). Several interesting parallels emerge from the microanalytic examinations of everyday conversation and larger-scale social problems rhetoric. For example, aspects of Drew and Holt's (1988) discussion of the use of idiomatic expressions in interpersonal complaint-making resonate with Ibarra and Kitsuse's discussion of the use of vernacular resources in the collective claims-making process.

Conversation analysis has also focused on institutions where social problems work is likely to occur. While one ethnomethodological strategy is to focus on the institutional context and its influence on social problems discourse, conversation analysts are primarily concerned with how institutional interactants accomplish or reveal the institutional context and their orientation to it (Maynard 1988). The concern is for the sequential organization of talk in the settings, focusing on how settings are organized as recognizable occasions for considering social problems. For example, conversation analysts have examined a variety of human service and social control settings where social problems work takes place, including telephone requests for police services (Whalen and Zimmerman 1987; Zimmerman 1984), criminal trials (Atkinson and Drew 1979), plea bargaining sessions (Maynard 1984), and educational testing (Marlaire and Maynard 1990).

Conversation analysts have also studied social problems construction in the mass media, particularly the routine sequencing of conversations that produce public knowledge or awareness. For example, conversation analysts study how reporters and their interviewees involved in television broadcasts open, elaborate, and close news interviews. The studies show how interactional practices produce the perceived character of news events, rather than merely eliciting or reporting them (Heritage, Clayman, and Zimmerman 1988; Maynard 1988). Such studies are important because public perceptions of social problems like homelessness, poverty, and crime are shaped by the social organization of media presentations of social problems.

Another provocative ethnomethodological theme is an ongoing concern for reflexivity. Pollner (1991) argues that as ethnomethodology has settled down in the "suburbs" of sociological inquiry, it has become increasingly committed to interactional, conversational, and scientific practices of reality construction. The emphasis on radical reflexivity—the appreciation of all analysis as constitutive activity—has been set aside. Woolgar and Pawluch's (1985) critique of social constructionism highlights aspects of the neglect. Pollner (1991) has gone further in calling for the resurrection of ethnomethodology's early emphasis on reflexivity. He states that studies of reflexive processes reveal to "epistemologically settled communities" the grounds on which their claims about social reality are built, including those underlying social constructionist and ethnomethodological studies.

A final set of ethnomethodological concerns involves Garfinkel and his close associates' studies of doing science (Heritage 1987). Conceived as "studies of work," their examinations focus on the embodied conceptualizations and practices that practitioners within a particular domain of work activities recognize as belonging to that domain (Garfinkel 1988;

Garfinkel, Lynch, and Livingston 1981; Livingston 1986; Lynch, Livingston, and Garfield 1983). The studies show how scientists' competencies are reflexively described *in situ*, the competencies being recognized and acted on in locally reasoned and temporally organized sites of the activity. The major implication of this program for social problems theory and research is the recommendation that social problems analysts generate detailed descriptions of highly localized, temporally bound practices through which social problems are accomplished in specific and historical circumstances.

Organization of Part I

While some old controversies simmer, new debates are animating a reconsideration of the constructionist perspective on social problems. The following sections in Part I of the volume undertake this reconsideration from standpoints that are sympathetic to the constructionist approach. Each also offers new ways of pursuing a revised constructionist agenda. In the first section, "Revising the Constructionist Project," Ibarra and Kitsuse offer an important clarification and expansion of Spector and Kitsuse's constructionist theory of social problems. They assert that their revised approach answers the most significant questions raised in Woolgar and Pawluch's critique. Warren then provides an example of how Ibarra and Kitsuse's proposal might be used to analyze "Radical Right" and "New Left" claims-making.

"Constructionist Responses" to Ibarra and Kitsuse and other recent debates comprise the next section. Each of the essays provides a reaction from constructionists who seek further elaboration and clarification of the constructionist approach. Gubrium notes that the focus of much constructionist theorizing and research on social problems (including Ibarra and Kitsuse's paper) has been on large-scale claims-making— "publicity" as he calls it. He recommends a similar emphasis on mundane interpretive practice in everyday interaction. Schneider's and Troyer's papers are reactions to the ontological gerrymandering critique and Ibarra and Kitsuse's response to it. Best takes a very different position on the issue in his paper. He argues that the "strict constructionist" concern with epistemological consistency is both misguided and counterproductive. Best encourages constructionists to "worry a little less about how we know what we know, and worry a little more about what, if anything, we do know about the construction of social problems."

The third section of Part I presents a variety of "Ethnomethodological Concerns" relating to the construction of social problems. Each in its own way reflects the ethnomethodological interest in reality constructing practice. Holstein and Miller suggest that the articulation of social problems categories with concrete cases can be understood as "social problems work." Marlaire and Maynard also focus on social problems as interactional interpretive work by emphasizing the need to examine the real-time, conversational accomplishment of troubles and problems. Next, Pollner discusses the ethnomethodological concern for reflexivity by reflecting on issues central to the ontological gerrymandering debate. He challenges constructionists to make reflexivity into a topic for analysis, rather than simply treating it as a problem to be managed. Finally, Bogen and Lynch question the desirability of a general theory of social problems. As an alternative, they suggest that researchers aim to produce rich, detailed, and interesting descriptions of unique ensembles of discursive routines and practices.

References

Atkinson, J. Maxwell and Paul Drew. 1979. *Order in Court*. Atlantic Highlands, NJ: Humanities Press.

Bauman, Eleen A. 1989. "Research Rhetoric and the Social Construction of Elder Abuse." Pp. 55–74 in *Images of Issues*, edited by Joel Best. Hawthorne, NY: Aldine de Gruyter.

Becker, Howard S. 1963. *Outsiders*. New York: Free Press.

Best, Joel. 1989. "Afterward." Pp. 243–54 in *Images of Issues*, edited by Joel Best. Hawthorne, NY: Aldine de Gruyter.

Bittner, Egon. 1967a. "Police Discretion in Emergency Apprehension of Mentally Ill Persons." *Social Problems* 14:278–92.

_____. 1967b. "The Police on Skid Row." *American Sociological Review* 32:699–715.

Bloor, David. 1983. *Wittgenstein*. New York: Columbia University Press.

Cicourel, Aaron V. 1968. *The Social Organization of Juvenile Justice*. New York: Wiley.

Drew, Paul and Elizabeth Holt. 1988. "Complainable Matters." *Social Problems* 35:398–417.

Eitzen, D. Stanley. 1984. "Teaching Social Problems." *SSSP Newsletter* 16:10–12.

Emerson, Robert M. 1969. *Judging Delinquents*. Chicago: Aldine.

Emerson, Robert M. and Sheldon L. Messinger. 1977. "The Micro-Politics of Trouble." *Social Problems* 25:121–35.

Garfinkel, Harold. 1967. *Studies in Ethnomethodology*. Englewood Cliffs, NJ: Prentice-Hall.

_____. 1988. "Evidence for Locally Produced, Naturally Accountable Phenomena of Order, Logic, Reason, Meaning, Method, etc. in and as of the Essential Quiddity of Immortal Ordinary Society." *Sociological Theory* 6:103–9.

Garfinkel, Harold, Michael Lynch, and Eric Livingston. 1981. "The Work of a Discovering Science Construed with Materials from the Optically Discovered Pulsar." *Philosophy of Social Science* 11:131–58.

Gubrium, Jaber F. and James A. Holstein. 1990. *What Is Family?* Mountain View, CA: Mayfield.

Gusfield, Joseph R. 1985. "Theories and Hobgoblins." *SSSP Newsletter* 17:16–18.

Heritage, John. 1984. *Garfinkel and Ethnomethodology.* Cambridge: Polity Press.

———. 1987. "Ethnomethodology." Pp. 224–72 in *Social Theory Today,* edited by Anthony Giddens and Jonathan H. Turner. Stanford, CA: Stanford University Press.

Heritage, John, Steven E. Clayman, and Don H. Zimmerman. 1988. "Discourse and Message Analysis." Pp. 77–109 in *Advancing Communication Science,* edited by Robert Hawkins, Suzanne Pingree, and John Weimann. Beverly Hills, CA: Sage.

Hilgartner, Stephen and Charles L. Bosk. 1988. "The Rise and Fall of Social Problems." *American Journal of Sociology* 94:53–78.

Holstein, James A. 1993. *Court-Ordered Insanity.* Hawthorne, NY: Aldine de Gruyter.

Holstein, James A. and Jaber F. Gubrium. Forthcoming. "Phenomenology, Ethnomethodology, and Interpretive Practice." In *Handbook of Qualitative Research,* edited by Norman Denzin and Yvonne Lincoln. Newbury Park, CA: Sage.

Hughes, Helen MacGill. 1961. *The Fantastic Lodge.* Greenwich, CT: Fawcett.

Jefferson, Gail. 1988. "On the Sequential Organization of Troubles-Talk in Ordinary Conversation." *Social Problems* 35:418–41.

Jefferson, Gail and John Lee. 1981. "The Rejection of Advice." *Journal of Pragmatics* 5:399–422.

Kitsuse, John I. and Malcolm Spector. 1973. "Toward a Sociology of Social Problems." *Social Problems* 20:407–19.

———. 1975. "Social Problems and Deviance." *Social Problems* 22:584–94.

Livingston, Eric. 1986. *The Ethnomethodological Foundations of Mathematics.* London: Routledge and Kegan Paul.

Loseke, Donileen R. 1989. "Creating Clients." Pp. 173–93 in *Perspectives on Social Problems,* Vol. 1, edited by James A. Holstein and Gale Miller. Greenwich, CT: JAI Press.

———. 1992. *The Battered Woman and Shelters.* Albany, NY: SUNY Press.

Lynch, Michael, Eric Livingston, and Harold Garfinkel. 1983. "Temporal Order in Laboratory Work. Pp. 205–38 in *Science Observed,* edited by Karin Knorr-Cetina and Michael Mulkay. Beverly Hills: Sage.

Lynch, Michael and David Bogen. Forthcoming. "Harvey Sacks' Primitive Natural Science." *Theory, Culture, and Society.*

Marlaire, Courtney L. and Douglas W. Maynard. 1990. "Standardized Testing as an Interactional Phenomenon." *Sociology of Education* 63:83–101.

Mauss, Armand L. 1989. "Beyond the Illusion of Social Problems Theory." Pp. 19–39 in *Perspectives on Social Problems,* Vol. 1, edited by James A. Holstein and Gale Miller. Greenwich, CT: JAI Press.

———. 1992. "Social Problems." Pp. 1916–21 in *Encyclopedia of Sociology,* Vol. 4, edited by Edgar F. Borgatt and Marie L. Borgatta. New York: Macmillan.

Mauss, Armand L. et al. 1975. *Social Problems as Social Movements.* Philadelphia: Lippincott.

Maynard, Douglas W. 1984. *Inside Plea Bargaining.* New York: Plenum Press.

————. 1988. "Language, Interaction, and Social Problems." *Social Problems* 35:311–34.

Maynard, Douglas W. and Steven E. Clayman. 1991. "The Diversity of Ethno-methodology." *Annual Review of Sociology* 17:385–418.

McCall, Michal and Howard S. Becker. 1990. "Performance Science." *Social Problems* 37:117–32.

Mehan, Hugh and Houston Wood. 1975. *The Reality of Ethnomethodology.* New York: Wiley.

Merton, Robert K. 1976. "The Sociology of Social Problems." Pp. 3–43 in *Contemporary Social Problems*, 4th ed., edited by Robert K. Merton and Robert Nisbet. New York: Harcourt Brace Jovanovich.

Miller, Gale. 1983. "Holding Clients Accountable." *Social Problems* 31:139–51.

————. 1991. *Enforcing the Work Ethic.* Albany, NY: SUNY Press.

————. 1992. "Human Service Practice as Social Problems Work." Pp. 3–21 in *Current Research on Occupations and Professions*, Vol. 7, edited by Gale Miller. Greenwich, CT: JAI Press.

Miller, Gale and James A. Holstein. 1989. "On the Sociology of Social Problems." Pp. 1–16 in *Perspectives on Social Problems*, Vol. 1, edited by James A. Holstein and Gale Miller. Greenwich, CT: JAI Press.

Pitken, Hanna Fenichel. 1972. *Wittgenstein and Justice.* Berkeley: University of California Press.

Pollner, Melvin. 1974. "Sociological and Common Sense Models of the Labeling Process. Pp. 27–40 in *Ethnomethodology*, edited by Roy Turner. Middlesex, England: Penguin.

————. 1978. "Constitutive and Mundane Versions of Labeling Theory." *Human Studies* 31:285–304.

————. 1987. *Mundane Reason.* Cambridge: Cambridge University Press.

————. 1991. "Left of Ethnomethodology." *American Sociological Review* 56:370–80.

Schneider, Joseph W. 1985a. "Social Problems Theory." *Annual Review of Sociology* 11:209–29.

————. 1985b. "Defining the Definitional Perspective on Social Problems." *Social Problems* 32:232–34.

Schutz, Alfred. 1970. *On Phenomenology and Social Relations.* Chicago: University of Chicago Press.

Scritchfield, Shirley A. 1989. "The Social Construction of Infertility." Pp. 99–114 in *Images of Issues*, edited by Joel Best. Hawthorne, NY: Aldine de Gruyter.

Spector, Malcolm and Kitsuse, John I. 1974. "Social Problems." *Social Problems* 21:145–58.

————. [1977] 1987. *Constructing Social Problems.* Hawthorne, NY: Aldine de Gruyter.

Sudnow, David. 1965. "Normal Crimes." *Social Problems* 12:255–76.

Troyer, Ronald J. 1989. "Are Social Problems and Social Movements the Same Things?" Pp. 41–58 in *Perspectives on Social Problems*, Vol. 1, edited by James A. Holstein and Gale Miller. Greenwich, CT: JAI Press.

Whalen, Marilyn R. and Don H. Zimmerman. 1987. "Sequential and Institutional Contexts in Calls for Help." *Social Psychology Quarterly* 50:172–85.

Wieder, D. Lawrence. 1988. *Language and Social Reality.* Landham, MD: University Press of America.

Wittgenstein, Ludwig. 1953. *Philosophical Investigations.* Translated by G. Anscombe. Oxford: Basil Blackwell.

———. 1967. *Zettel.* Edited by G. Anscombe and G. von Wright. Translated by G. Anscombe. Oxford: Basil Blackwell.

———. 1969. *The Blue and Brown Books.* Oxford: Basil Blackwell.

Woolgar, Steve and Dorothy Pawluch. 1985. "Ontological Gerrymandering." *Social Problems* 32:214–27.

Zimmerman, Don H. 1984. "Talk and Its Occasion." Pp. 210–28 in *Meaning, Form, and Use in Context,* edited by Deborah Schiffrin. Washington, DC: Georgetown University Press.

2

Vernacular Constituents of Moral Discourse: An Interactionist Proposal for the Study of Social Problems

Peter R. Ibarra and John I. Kitsuse

Introduction

As a preface to this paper, we would like review the ongoing commentaries and critiques that bear upon the constructionist formulation of social problems, especially as presented in Spector and Kitsuse's *Constructing Social Problems* ([1977] 1987, hereafter *CSP*), suggest how some of the conceptual problems might be resolved, and identify some central issues worth clarifying for the further development of a sociological theory of social problems.

The statement in *CSP* was directed toward the consolidation of a particular perspective, to encourage research oriented by a set of theoretical questions, and to suggest that such work might appropriately be called studies in the sociology of social problems. A fundamental point was made with regard to the ambiguous and often logically inconsistent use of "social problems" as an analytical category in sociology. Major statements on the part of the "objectivist" perspectives were reviewed and were found to typically group various social conditions (e.g., prostitution, crime) under the rubric *social problems* in an ad hoc manner. In the process the concept of social problems was rendered without theoretical precision or scope. Indeed,

> the concept *social problems* was never made to refer to a distinctive set of conditions, processes or activities. The application of the term to conditions identified as [for example] dysfunctional is simply redundant. For is anything added to the study of deviant behavior by calling it a social problem? Do we increase our understanding of crime or poverty by calling it a social problem? (pp. 38–39)

What Spector and Kitsuse proposed instead of a normative-functionalist conception of social problems was one oriented toward figuring out "what it is that people seem to know and use" (Sacks, quoted in Heritage 1984, p. 233) in discerning the objectionable amid their lives. In distancing themselves from normative formulations, Spector and Kitsuse noted that their "formulation will not offer a rival explanation for a commonly defined subject matter. We argue for a different subject matter for the sociology of social problems" (*CSP*, p. 39). In our reading, *CSP* pointed the way to an *interactionist-based* program concerned with explicating social problems as constituted by claims-making activities. Theoretical work would be concerned with elucidating the abstract features of the conventional presuppositions, interpretive practices, rhetorical devices, joint activities, and variety of forums involved in the discursive production of social problems.

The shift from the normative to the interpretive paradigm (Wilson 1971) entails sustaining the distinction between the sociologist's perspective and the member's—especially for coherently translating the theoretical statement in *CSP* to an empirical site. According to Spector and Kitsuse, the member's perspective is employed whenever *anyone* engages in *proposing or contesting* the designation of a category of putative behaviors, expressions, or processes as "offensive," about which something of a remedial nature should be done, i.e., "claims-making and responding activities" (p. 76). Now, in the normative conception, sociologists can "objectively" (and independently of members) view "social conditions" and designate them social problems—by virtue of their recognition of a disjunction between a norm-based conception of society and a state of affairs presumably antithetical to those norms and values. For these sociologists, definitional processes are marginal to the "more important" questions regarding the scope, magnitude, causes and consequences of the social problem itself. By contrast, in the constructionist perspective the sociologist observes/interprets members as perceiving subjects actively engaged in constructing social conditions (or "putative conditions") as moral objects. In this conception, definitional activities are central to the subject matter, and precedence should be given to members' interpretive practices inasmuch as social problems are possible strictly as assemblages of the member's perspective.

The conventional formulation is ironic to the extent that it attempts to display members perceiving a social problem where "in fact" there is none, or not perceiving a social problem where "in fact" there is one, as in Merton's (1974) concepts of "manifest" and "latent" social problems (cf. Pollner 1975, pp. 422–26). The constructionist perspective is ironic by virtue of bracketing the "natural attitude" that enables the analyst to discern and describe "the ways in which [members'] praxis and perception organizes and constitute a world while simultaneously masking the organizational work so as to provide for the appearance of determinate and objective or absolute entities" (Pollner 1978, p. 284), where those entities are social problems.[1] But while both analytics are ironic in their attitudes toward members' commonsense experiences and activities (albeit in different senses), this should in no way conceal the crucial difference between them. This difference rests in how the two formulations address the *warrant* members have for assuming the sensible character of their experiences and actions. Whereas conventional sociologists adopt the "expert" role in passing judgment on the "rationality," "value," "sensibleness," etc., of members' formulations of social problems or lack thereof, the constructionist examines *how* members produce determinations of warrant among themselves while flatly refusing any such privilege for him-/herself. This is not to imply that sociologists have no right to their evaluations about those they study as well as a right to consider this or that morally offensive. But we fail to see the *theoretical rationale* for employing or embedding such judgments in our analytical renditions of the member's perspective.

It is a source of endless interest that executing and maintaining a "rationality from within" stance (Garfinkel 1967, pp. 31–34) proves to be difficult for those expressing sympathy with the constructionist perspective. In our view the persistence of the so-called objective-subjective debate that dominated commentary in the mid-1980s (Woolgar and Pawluch 1985a, 1985b; Hazelrigg 1986; Schneider 1985) on the constructionist formulation is an indication of the obdurate character of this difficulty. Moreover, this focus deflected attention from the development of an empirically based theory of social problems, which was clearly the impetus for Spector and Kitsuse's formulation. More recently the theoretical significance of the objective/subjective issue has been further diffused by Best (1989), who, as a constructionist, proposes that a distinction be made between what he terms "contextual" and "strict" constructionism.[2]

This unfortunate state of affairs may reflect an absence of clear directives for theoretical development in Spector and Kitsuse's original statement. Their studied rejection of a positivist conception of social conditions, in favor of the term *putative conditions*, as well as the absence of a systematic presentation of the theoretical bases and implications of the constructionist perspective have in part contributed to these controversies. Thus Hazelrigg (1986) has criticized the constructionist formulation as "internally inconsistent" and Woolgar and Pawluch (1985a) have charged that practitioners of constructionism lapse into an objectivism at odds with their stated premises for analysis. We agree that constructionists have compromised the perspective on more than a few occasions by engaging in the "analytic" moves described by the critics. We believe, however, that an attentive reading of *CSP*, and Chapter 6 in particular, would make clear that explaining "the variability of the definitions vis-à-vis the constancy of the conditions to which they relate" (Woolgar and Pawluch 1985a, p. 215) is *not* the focus of the theory. Rather the theory directs attention to the claims-making process, *accepting as given and beginning with* the participants' descriptions of the putative conditions and their assertions about their problematic character (i.e., the definitions). From this methodological stance the research questions concern not how those definitions are produced by the sociohistorical circumstances in which they emerged, but rather how those definitions express the members' conceptions of "the problem," how they are pressed as claims, to whom, mobilizing what resources, and so forth. The constructionist conception of the claims-making process *accepts the members' constructions of putative conditions as "objects in the world,"* which thus meet the definitional requirements of social problems as subject matter for empirical investigation.

If the difficulties the field is confronting are fostered by the conceptual ambiguities in the social constructionist approach, then any act of theoretical clarification must attend to imprecisions in the language that we as sociologists use to describe, analyze, and interpret our subject matter. Especially at issue here is the ambiguous status of the concept *social problem*: Is it a technical or a vernacular term? In the constructionist formulation, the term *social problem* does double service: It is now a member's then a sociologist's concept. But when a sociologist presumes to oversee the propriety or rationality of members' usage of the term, a rigorous constructionist is obliged to consider the stance implicit in such a handling of the vernacular as a display of the sociologist's own membership. Analysis consists of reconstructing the vernacular, not downgrading it or leaving it unexplicated. Thus, the importance of the member/sociological analyst distinction rests on the constructionist's view that members provide the linguistic productions and activities (the first-order constructs in Schutz's terminology), which the sociologist can in turn subject to theoretical (as opposed to practical) scrutiny (i.e., the second-order constructs). *Social problems* points to *that class of social interactions* consisting of members' analytically paraphraseable means for formulating, describing, interpreting, and evaluating a symbolically constructed and morally charged intersubjective existence. For members, claims are "readable at a glance" (Goffman 1979), symbolic acts, and it is the sociologist's task to specify the configuration of premises, conventions, categories, and sensibilities constitutive of social problems as idiomatic productions.

If then we change our perspective and assume the gaze of members, *social problems* appears in a different light. For members, social problems do not *typically* refer to their own acts of definition and evaluation; they are not "talked into being." Rather social problems are what elicit their acts of judgment.[3] Membership is thus predicated upon what Pollner (1978) has called "mundane ontology," which entails a strict demarcation between the objects in the world, including the moral objects studied by sociologists, and persons' perceptions, beliefs, and ideas regarding those objects. What authorizes, idiomatically, the social problems process is the mundane claim that objects and their qualities have an existence independent of their apprehension. Thus, Spector and Kitsuse's proposal that we study claims "about" putative social conditions can easily be construed as a mundane directive, still grounded in an ontology where words and things are separable, that is, a correspondence theory of meaning. This view of constructionist inquiry has lent itself to research on what claims-making is "about" instead of the *conventional features of the claims-making process itself,* thus producing case studies of smoking, child abuse, wife battering, obesity, and so on. Since the members' claims are grounded in a folk version of the correspondence theory of meaning that is shared by the positivist sociologists (indeed, because members are fundamentally required to make claims *about* something), constructionist case studies of social problems are considered and critically evaluated by such sociologists as competing explanatory versions of the social conditions that the studies are "about." By entering into this dialogue, the constructionist is unwittingly drawn into assuming a stance that violates the methodological commitment to refrain from privileging or honoring certain mundane versions of the condition over others.

The recognition of the distinction between the members' *practical* project in contrast to the sociologist's *theoretical* project is fundamental in the constructionist methodological stance. The former are engaged in efforts to alter or defend some aspect of social life, and can therefore include sociologists on occasion, while the latter—insofar as s/he transforms members' practically based resources into researchable topics—is engaged in the theoretical reconstruction of the vernacular features of social problems as moral discourse. If sociologists are to be in the position of examining social problems as members' constructions, we must be willing to refrain from tacitly privileging the status of, say, scientists' versions of the condition in question and instead treat those accounts, and the sensibility they express, as items in our explications of the social problems language game (cf. Aronson 1984). Similarly, instead of incorporating interest- and value-based "explanations" in our theorizing, we should, after Mills (1940), recognize them as vernacular displays and thereby study them in their own right—for the ways in which the associations drawn by counterclaimants regarding claimants' motives can contribute to the shifting trajectories of social problems discourse. Proper consideration of the claims-making process entails attention to both how claims are licensed and acted upon as well as how they are displaced or discredited; the status of claimants' motives apparently can have something to do with both processes.

To summarize this part of our argument, Spector and Kitsuse's central distinction between putative condition and social condition may have amplified the confusion between the different layers of theoretical and mundane discourse, and seduced constructionists into making statements reflecting members' idioms instead of discerning them, thus inhibiting the development of an interpretive theory of the social problems process. Contextualist practice is both a narrow construal of the constructionist project and too bound up in a sociological discourse in which constructionists need to "score points" against the objectivists' notion that conditions can in and of themselves be harmful. We consider this practice to be fostered by the ambiguous ontological burden placed on *putative* conditions in Spector and Kitsuse's presentation. This language has been taken by constructionists to entail treating the perspective's axiom ("claims-making constitutes social problems") *as a proposition* (Woolgar and Pawluch, 1985a), thus formulating research that in one way or another focuses on social conditions. This in turn has deflected attention from the conventional features of the claims-making process that are available to participants qua participants for elaborating the social problems process. Thus, theoretical development has stalled while the perspective has been embroiled in a competitive dialogue with members' claims and those of positivist sociologists. Further, "selective relativism" or "ontological gerrymandering" (which in our reading is an act of according privileged status to apparently more respectable accounts and claims by reifying them) has generated a flat contradiction. We propose, therefore, to replace *putative condition* with the term *condition-category* as a means of eliminating the contradiction and to suggest new lines of theoretical development.

Categories, Not Conditions

Condition-categories are typifications of socially circumscribed activities and processes—the "society's" classifications of its own contents—used in practical contexts to generate meaningful descriptions and evaluations of social reality. They vary in their level of abstraction and specificity (e.g., "antismoking" in contrast to "smoke-free public spaces"), but they are the terms used by members to propose what the social problem is "about." As parts of a classification system, condition-categories are first and foremost units of language. The initial analytic topic is thus how practical accounts of these vernacular terms are situated and elaborated upon in the making of moral objects. We intend *condition-categories*, then, to highlight the symbol- and language-bound character of claims-making, as well as *how* members' facility with certain discursive strategies—including rhetorical and reasoning idioms—initiate and constitute the social problems process.

Commonsense understandings of both idiomatic competence and the function of language invite the analyst to "go native," that is, implicitly assimilate the object-subject distinction and treat the members' language of condition-categories as referents for independently documentable social conditions. But this is seductive: First, because the strict constructionist never leaves language. Whether s/he is paraphrasing members' arguments or recording their deeds, s/he is always in the realm of the textual. Protests, for example, are dramatizations of certain meanings, which make them linguistic-expressive. Lodging a complaint is an action that implies an analysis on the member's part about effective action, and thus a set of meanings. It also conveys something about him-/herself and other categories of people. In other words, the process we are studying is a language game into which actions are translated as publicly (and variously) readable expressions.

Second, "going native" can lead the analyst into the tacit use of the very vernacular resources that s/he should be assembling as data for theoretical reconstruction. In other words, it has proved difficult for constructionists to avoid making moves in the social problems language game. But, theoretically, it is unclear to us what the coding rules or even the point of the games are when analysts engage in such activities. If such activities are intended as correctives for the defective or inadequate character of members' claims-making, neither the efficacy of those correctives nor the standards by which they might be judged are evident.

The increased flexibility of *condition-categories* is important for how it alerts us to attend to the ways in which the denotations and connotations of the term become the subject of a kind of articulation contest on the part of members to establish what the social problem is "really about." In the case of the so-called abortion issue, for example, one side dramatizes abortion's status as a symbol of sexual permissiveness and murder. Legalized abortion becomes, in turn, a signifier of a more diffuse sense of moral decay. Is the social condition (or the social problem for that matter) abortion, murder, licentiousness, or moral decay? It is *semantically* ambiguous, perhaps even, as deconstructionists would say, "undecidable." It certainly cannot be said, analytically, that the social condition, putative or otherwise, is abortion as such, for to say that is to miss the subtexts and symbolic ramifications growing out of the "pro-life" group's moves in the social problems process. Similarly, the "pro-choice" side sees legalized abortion as a symbol of women's struggle to acquire "reproductive rights," which is itself a signifier of a long-fought battle to overcome men's domination of their "bodies and selves." Is the problem then *about* gender inequality, Christian intolerance, right-wing fanaticism, or anticonstitutionalism? To speak as an analyst of "the social condition of abortion" is to try arbitrarily to contain the evolution and change of meanings and subtexts as members press their claims, redefine their concerns, make alliances with some groups, collide with others, assess their political strategy, and so forth. We consider that dynamism to be the process that theorists of social problems must describe and comprehend.

The term *social conditions*, with its connotations of objective and recurrent properties, misdirects our attention, leading us to miss the central question of how there can be social problems discourse in the first place. When viewed in general terms, the social problems process resembles a kind of game whose moves are perennially subject to interpretation and reinterpretation, whose aims are subject to dispute, whose players are ever shifting, whose settings are diverse, and whose nominal topics stretch as far as the society's classification system can provide members with typifications of activities and processes. Indeed, the classification system is itself subject to transformations as new semantic distinctions and equivalences are made. Even though the process, conceived in its most general terms, is so unstable, members will nevertheless describe the social problems language game as a "controversy over the issue of X" precisely because members' participation is predicated on mundane ontology. In other words, claims-making activities reflect substantive concerns on the part of participants, but analytically we take those claims to be reflective of the interplay between their moral sensibilities and the dynamics of the process itself.

In sum, social problems discourse is open-ended, its "aboutness" being contingent upon the courses taken by members' practical theorizing on moral order, including one another's claims-making activities. These communicative activities are conceived as "language games" to indicate the sense in which our field is fundamentally concerned with understanding the constitutive ("world-making") and strategic dimensions of claimants' discursive practices in demarcating moral objects of relevance to a "public." We conceive of social problems as "idiomatic productions" to accentuate their status as members' accomplishments as well as to emphasize the sense in which scientific standards of rationality (Garfinkel 1967) cannot be used by the analyst to coherently describe the features of claims-making activities.

If pressed for a summary description of the phenomena in need of identification and theoretical reconstruction, we would name those "vernacular resources" drawn upon in claims-making activities. Vernacular resources are the conventional means by which members can realize the signifying processes called claims. Thus, they can refer to forms of talk, frames of interpretation, and contexts for articulation inasmuch as these effectively organize and circumscribe members' social problems discourse. To state the matter in still another way, vernacular resources include those rhetorical idioms, interpretive practices, and features of settings that distinguish claims-making activities as a class of phenomena while also differentiating instances of claims-making from one another.

We are thus confronted with the relationship between the general and the specific, an issue that has often remained unstated by social constructionists, yet is of central importance to the project. That is, what are the formal features of social problems theory to be about? We take the question to be basic to the enterprise, and our position is that the project of developing a theory of *social problems discourse* is a much more coherent way of proceeding with constructionism than, for example, the development of a series of discrete theories on the social construction of X, Y, and Z. To develop a theory about condition X when the ontological status of X is suspended results in "ontological gerrymandering" and "conceptual knots" (Pollner, 1978), which is to say flawed theory. It is much more exact to declare our approach to be concerned with the very discourse by which moral objects are created as objects of *address* even as the moral objects are treated by members as existing independently of their claims-making activities about them. In that sense, social constructionism studies members' distinctive ways of perceiving, describing, evaluating, and acting upon *symbolically demarcated social realities*—what we have termed condition-categories.

We believe that our conception is suited to addressing the relationship between the *specific* features of various condition-categories and their exposition in the social problems language game. This conception explicitly counters the specious objectification of the condition-category because the specificity of the "condition" is understood to be a matter of its having been situated within a network of signs, i.e., language. Nor is the social problems process itself reified, for its features are conceived to be *conventional*, not invariant. Analytically, the development of social problems is conceived to be up for grabs.

The Rhetoric of Social Problems Discourse

When constructionist theorizing blurs the basic distinction between vernacular resources and analytic constructs, it invites an indiscriminate fusion of mundane and theoretical perspectives that, among other things, leads to a retreat from the distinctive task of description posed by Spector and Kitsuse's formulation. Now, bracketing has always been a recommended policy for executing constructionist-style inquiry, and the difficulty that analysts have in sustaining that methodological attitude has provided much of the impetus for our current thinking. We wish to highlight the centrality of bracketing in our proposed clarification of the research agenda by explicitly identifying *rhetoric* as an area of study for a project that seeks to develop a theory of the vernacular constituents of social problems. *Rhetoric* brings to the fore the sense in which the task for constructionism lies less with the *referential aspects of claims* than with the constitutive techniques and processes that are entailed in claims-making as such. That is, the issues posed for us by the maxim "claims-making constitutes social problems" are clarified because rhetoric focuses our attention on the distinctive but conventional ways of speaking and reasoning that obtain whenever persons qualify as participants in social problems discourse.

To speak of the rhetoric of social problems discourse is not to limit our domain to techniques of persuasion. The concept of rhetoric is useful for providing a framework for discerning patterns in phenomena that appear "from the outside" to be incoherent and in a constant state of flux, even as participants assert their claims to be intelligible concerns about conditions. That is, it allows us to move from single social condition–centered analyses to a more comparative approach by seeking and identifying commonalities at the level of members' discursive practices.

In our view, constructionist studies of social problems discourse can profitably proceed by distinguishing four overlapping but analytically distinct rhetorical dimensions: rhetorical idioms, counterrhetorics, motifs, and claims-making styles. The last of these leads us into the study of settings. The inventory of specific idioms, styles, and so forth that we offer is composed of ideal types and thus stands to be refined, reformulated, and elaborated upon through empirical observation and further theoretical reflection.

Rhetorical idioms are definitional complexes, utilizing language that situates condition-categories in moral universes. Several operations occur in that process of signification; suffice it to say that idiomatic application of the theme to the condition-category results in its acquiring problematic status. Each rhetorical idiom calls forth or draws upon a cluster of images. The *rhetoric of loss*, for example, evokes symbols of purity and tends toward nostalgic tonalities. The *rhetoric of unreason* evokes images of manipulation and conspiracy. The *rhetoric of calamity* situates condition-categories amid narratives of widespread devastation, and so on.

The *counterrhetorics* are discursive strategies for countering characterizations made by claimants. They tend to be less synoptic or thematic:

For example, instead of arguing for ozone layer destruction, it is the claimant's description, proposed remedies, or something other than the candidate problem that is rebutted. These counterrhetorics tend not to counter the "values" conveyed in the rhetorical idioms so much as they address their current application or relevance.

Motifs refer to figures of speech operating as shorthand descriptions/evaluations of condition-categories. They are probably independent of rhetorical idioms, though certain motifs may have affinities with particular idioms. *Plague*, for example, has close and obvious affinities with the rhetoric of calamity, as does *crisis*. *Tragedy* may, on the other hand, be closely tied to the rhetoric of loss, though it is not difficult to think of applications in other formats. Thus, the relationship between idioms and motifs is one that requires empirical delineation. Our task is to explicate the presuppositions and indexical considerations that go into applications of motifs, idioms, and counterrhetorics. Instead of being disappointed or frustrated by the lack of easy correspondence between our analytic reconstructions, we should marvel at the artfulness with which claimants continuously innovate new meanings, associations, and implications, stretching the conventions underlying the coherence and intelligibility in social problems discourse.

The fourth rhetorical dimension that stands to provide material for a theory of social problems is what we term *claims-making styles*. By thinking of claims-making activities as possessing style, a shift in our attention is encouraged—from the language in which the claims are cast to the bearing and tone with which the claims are made. For example, claimants (and counterclaimants) may deliver their claims in legalistic fashion or comic fashion, in a scientific way or a theatrical way, in a journalistic ("objective") manner or an "involved citizen" (or "civic") manner. All of these modes are styles insofar as they inform the texture of and structure the reception accorded to claims. What each style entails and encourages, the way each style combines with different condition-categories, rhetorical idioms, and so forth—these become investigable topics.

Rhetorical Idioms

Claims-making activities are directed at problematizing specific condition-categories; rhetorical idioms refer to the distinctive ways in which their problematic status is elaborated. They are not, however, mainly concerned with documenting the *existence* or *magnitude* of the condition-categories. Instead, their domain is that of moral reasoning. Hence they function as moral vocabularies, providing participants with sets or clusters of themes or "sacred" symbols capable of endowing claims with significance. As we shall observe, each rhetorical idiom encourages participants to structure their claims along particular lines and not others.

Rhetorical idioms are also commonsense constructions of "moral competence" in the sense that their deployment tends to presume that auditors are obliged to acknowledge the import of the values expressed and consequently the claimant's current application of the idiom. Thus, the rhetorical idioms locate and account for the claimant's participation in the social problems language game by reference to moral competence (instead of strict self-interest). On the other hand, rhetorical idioms are useful in either enlisting another to make "sympathetic moves" in the social problems language game or at sustaining such moves by the already converted. In each case, what is distinctive about rhetorical idioms is their capacity to clarify and evoke the ethos implicit in the claim. This is especially facilitated by each idiom's characteristic set of positive and negative terms, that is, the idiom's preferred objects of praise and scorn.

There are several general issues that are delineated when social constructionism takes as one of its tasks the elucidation of claimants' applications of rhetorical idioms, moving investigation toward a general, comparative level of theoretical inquiry. Hence, the questions that are raised concern not specific conditions but the varieties of claims that the idioms are good for expressing. For example, what makes a claim "idiomatic" in the first place would appear to involve a certain kind of "readability," a usage of the language that is both symbolically coherent and morally competent. Given that premise, we can inquire as to what it is that members "know" when they hear a claim as especially edifying, moving, or insightful, on the one hand, or far out, incomprehensible, or mistaken, on the other. The utility of the rhetorical idioms derives from the discursive materials they provide to claimants to structure and lend urgency to their claims, but presumably those materials cannot be applied in merely any old way. The conventions underlying the idiomatic elaboration of condition-categories constitute one aspect of our subject matter. Artfulness consists of stretching and moving the boundaries of what can be construed as idiomatic.

What kinds of semiotic operations does a condition-category undergo as it is moved from one rhetorical idiom to another? Are some kinds of condition-categories more versatile or adaptable in this regard than are others? How might the idioms be variously combined? What are the distinctive kinds of vulnerabilities that each idiom poses for claimants and claims? What kinds of "atrocity tales" (Best 1987) do the various idioms accommodate? Does sponsorship (or disallowance) of a given claim under one rhetorical idiom entail sponsoring (or disallowing) other claims directed at other condition-categories that are drawing upon the same rhetorical idiom? What are the ways in which this is managed? To what extent is intractability in social problems discourse contingent on participants' usage of different rhetorical idioms? What vernacular resources do members have access to for countering an idiomatic claim while retaining moral standing?

The *rhetoric of loss* is not concerned with mourning the extinction of something but rather inveighing against its devaluation. One of its central images is that of humans as custodians or guardians of some unique and sacred thing or quality. It is by virtue of the loss of prestige or value accorded to the sacred object that its existence is threatened, with the concomitant implication that such negligence is deeply revealing of our character in the eyes of some future judge(s). The *present* is given an all-embracing context: Situated between an "enchanted" or quasi-divine moment in the past and a still to be realized judgment in the future, our actions are situated to seem *historical*.

This rhetoric works most idiomatically with objects (i.e., condition-categories) that can be construed to qualify as forms of perfection in some sense or other. The positive terms composing the idiom's moral vocabulary are *innocence, beauty, purity, nature, clarity, culture* (in the sense of civilization), *cleanliness,* and so forth. Negative terms would consequently locate types of contamination and imperilment culminating in devaluation: *sin, pollution, decadence, chaos,* etc.

Rhetorical idioms can cut across ideological divisions like liberal and socialist and conservative, inter alia. In the case of the rhetoric of loss, claims-making campaigns on ideologically incompatible fronts reflect idiomatically compatible rhetorics. Political conservatives may be preeminent in the antiabortion movement, for example, and political liberals may constitute the strongest supporters for strict environmental controls, but both groups of claimants are relying upon a common rhetorical format, one that posits clear-cut opposition between such terms as the priceless or irreplaceable character of life and nature respectively, and the selfish disregard for those objects by women and industry.

The concept of *protection* assumes a central position in this rhetorical idiom's remedial discourse, suggesting the sense in which it is well-suited to evoking the *heroism* of the *rescuer*. Indeed, although Operation Rescue is the name chosen by the now well-publicized antiabortion organization, it is a name that is paradigmatic of the idiom's characteristic rhetoric and could probably be applied or adjusted to "fit" other condition-categories by claimants who use the rhetoric of loss. (Think of the "save the planet" slogan of the environmentalists and the "save the schools" cry of antibusing parents.) When articulated idiomatically, the rhetoric of loss suggests a defensive posture that is heroic rather than merely "reactionary." Such an impression is assisted by the premise that the sacred objects or beings cannot save or help themselves and so must have the claimants acting on their behalf to protect their elevated symbolic positions and interests. (The rhetoric is wholly unidiomatic when the concern at issue is revealed to be for the loss of "white male privilege" rather than "great books," or the "profit motive" rather than the extinction of spotted owls or dolphins.) The rhetoric of loss elaborates features of condition-categories that can be likened to precious positions or presences that something or someone/group is threatening to either appropriate, displace, extinguish, or lower in prestige or value. The claimants' identification of the practices contributing to that devaluation generates the targets that remedial activities seek to eradicate ("legalized abortion" to counter the "devaluation of the gift of life," "clear-cutting" to counter the "despoiling of virgin forests").

Whereas the rhetoric of loss is rooted in a language of altruism and social responsibility to something other than the claimant's own interests, the *rhetoric of entitlement* emphasizes the virtue of securing for all persons equal institutional access as well as the unhampered freedom to exercise choice of self-expression. The sensibility expressed by this idiom is egalitarian and relativistic. It is egalitarian in its aversion to forms of discrimination against categories of people. Thus, its negative terms are emblematic of forms of discrimination: *intolerance, oppression, sexism, racism, ageism,* and even *speciesism.* The idiom's positive terms stem from its relativist philosophy: *lifestyle, diversity, choice, tolerance, empowerment,* and so forth. *Liberation* evokes the value of having the freedom to choose how one might realize one's life.

The concept of *expansion* is central to this idiom's remedial vocabulary (whereas *conservation* is the most apparent connotation of "protection" as it is inflected by the rhetoric of loss); claimants seek to expand the distribution or scope of a good, service, or right. The notion is that the greater the extension of *fair play, tolerance, justice, equality before the law, respect for human dignity,* etc., into greater spheres of social life, the greater the benefits for all members of the society. Claims cast in this rhetorical idiom are often phrased in terms that evoke the image of an inexorable march of history in a "progressive" direction toward the democratization of society (generating the idiom's preferred pejorative: *reactionary*). Condition-categories generated by typifications of gender-, race-, class-, and disability-based inequality are the most obvious candidates for exposition within the rhetoric of entitlement, but it can be applied to abstract concepts like privacy. Entitlement claims have also been extended to animals, trees, and cultural objects (such as films about to be "colorized") on the argument that they have their right to exist as "created."

Whereas the rhetoric of entitlement is applied most idiomatically when the condition-category can be rendered an instance of injustice or the inhibition of freedom, the *rhetoric of endangerment* is applied to condition-categories that can be expressed as threats to the health and safety of the human body. Thus, this rhetorical idiom is a relative of entitlement discourse inasmuch as the presumption is that individuals have the *right* to be safe from harm, to have good health, and to be shielded from preventable or reducible types of bodily risk. But the rhetoric of endangerment is composed of a cluster of themes and symbols distinct from those associated with the rhetoric of entitlement. Consequently, the urgency of its moral discourse is due less to issues regarding obstacles to freedom and equality than to optimal bodily function and health care.

In the rhetorical idiom of endangerment, condition-categories are problematic not because they are immoral per se, but because they pose intolerable risks to one's health or safety. This idiom's hallmark is a kind of moral minimalism: Claims that reflect or conceal "value judgments" have a decidedly negative valence because they don't possess the impersonality required to ensure that the claimant is not *really* attacking or seeking to undermine another's right to choose how to live. Claims are most idiomatic, i.e., suasive, when it is evident that medical judgment has taken precedence over moral judgment since the understanding of the body that is grounded in scientific knowledge is presumed to be both impartial and more factual, hence demonstrably superior to views generated by moral beliefs.

The rhetoric of endangerment shifts the site to which urgent action must attend. Where the rhetoric of loss evokes the image of transitory yet custodial human beings entrusted with an irreplaceable legacy, and where the rhetoric of entitlement evokes the fundamental importance of expressivity, the rhetoric of endangerment evokes the possibility that the transitory status of the person might be extended and the fear that it is being further curtailed. Such concerns recommend weighing the value of expressivity against the risks posed by expressive practices and beliefs. The issue is fundamentally instrumental: How might life be extended, and what might shorten it? Positive terms address the hope that has been evoked: *hygiene, prevention, nutritiousness, fitness,* and so on. Negative terms pinpoint the processes that warrant fear: *disease, pathology, epidemic, risk, contamination, health threat,* etc.

While claims employing the rhetoric of endangerment are most idiomatic when delivered in scientific style, language, and reasoning, or when endorsed by medical testimony, they are not immune to being answered. The counterrhetoric of the telling anecdote (q.v.) is a characteristically vernacular way of responding to endangerment claims. In addition, this idiom is circumscribed by being applied to condition-categories that can be shown to impinge on secondary parties (e.g., "bystanders," "the general population," "innocent victims"), precisely because of its bodily centered individualism: In the absence of an analysis linking a private act to a public consequence, the person who insists that the pleasures derivable from the problematic practice (for example, smoking) outweigh the extended lifespan attendant upon cessation is understood to be making a personal valuation that must finally be respected, though not necessarily admired.

Of course, "self-destructive" or "reckless" behavior may in and of itself become the problematic category, a sign of a less than total mastery of one's powers of the intellect. This type of claim draws upon another rhetorical idiom, what we call the *rhetoric of unreason*. Idiomatic usage is contingent upon a condition-category's describability in terms that highlight concerns about being taken advantage of, manipulated, "brainwashed," or transformed into a "dupe" or "fool." The spectre of subliminal messages, conspiracies, hidden forces, and the mesmerizing powers of advertising are common evocations in this rhetoric's lexicon.

The rhetoric of unreason posits an idealized relationship between the self and the state of knowing, and then locates an instance where that proper relationship is being distorted, undermined, and even destroyed. The assumption is that in the absence of the pernicious influence, the combined force of being fully informed and in complete control of one's cognitive powers would result in preferable courses of action. A wide range of claims-making activities reflects the logic of this rhetorical idiom: Rational (and equitable) administration of government is hampered under the influence of large campaign contributors; teenagers adopt the destructive habit of cigarette smoking because of the way advertisers "glamorize" it in targeted promotional campaigns; claims directed at the absence of full disclosure regarding the chemical contents in food are evoking the importance of making "informed decisions" regarding one's health. Given the logic of the idiom, "education," as a means of solving the social problem, acquires a particularly powerful resonance since the presumption is that knowledge leads to wiser action.

Certain categories of persons are understood to require greater vigilance in regard to the issues encapsulated by this kind of discourse. Those who can be said to be *trusting, naive, innocent, uneducated, uninformed, desperate,* and so forth can be "taken advantage of" as *easy prey, vulnerable* to being manipulated by persons or institutions of greater power or authority. "Children" provides a paradigmatic vernacular resource for articulating this rhetorical idiom. Playing off the understanding that they are as yet "unformed," interjecting into social problems discourse the suggestive question, What about the children? directs auditors to extrapolate the worst-case scenario: What a child would "end up like" were s/he to mature under the tutelage or influence of the pernicious agent(s).

Unlike the four rhetorical idioms we have so far discussed, the *rhetoric of calamity* is distinguished by being composed of metaphors and reasoning practices that evoke the unimaginability of utter disaster. Its way of articulating claims may be most significant when the social problems language game is especially crowded with a panoply of claims-making movements vying for attention. Claimants using this idiom will recognize the existence of other claims-making activities directed at nominally unrelated condition-categories, yet cast things into perspective by demonstrating how those other moral objects are contingent upon the existence of "their" condition-category. The one is either symptom, effect, or logically subordinate to the other. Thus, it is poverty that generates urban crime, drug abuse, poor schools, teenage pregnancies, and so on; it is the problem of the greenhouse effect that stands to create disasters of every imaginable kind; it is AIDS that threatens to create disease on an epidemic scale, an overburdened medical system, explosive insurance premiums, gay-bashing, etc.

This type of rhetoric can be conceived as a way of countering the centrifugal tendencies apparent when claims-making activities are considered across the board: It brings a variety of claimants under a kind of symbolic umbrella, hence providing the basis for coalition building. The rhetoric of calamity does not advocate a specific kind of moral system, as do the other idioms. It recognizes that moral reasoning may differ between allies, but the implication of the rhetoric of calamity is that now is not the time for sorting out ethical grounds: There will be time enough later for "mere" talk; now is the time for action. Thus, the idiomatic expression "the crisis of X" will be understood to mean that inaction on the condition will result in creating other social problems at an exponential rate, or exacerbate existing ones to the point of intractability. A claim expressed in this rhetorical idiom may lend itself to garnering high degrees of serious and prolonged attention in the public press (because of the various angles it delineates), as well as summary dismissals because of what may be seen as the hysterical or obsessive cast of mind of claimants using the calamitous imagery. Furthermore, the habit of linking several ostensibly unrelated conditions to the megacondition can be easily parodied, such as when an absurdist counterclaimant draws linkages that lack any "face validity" whatsoever, thereby alluding to the sense in which those kinds of claims are "merely" claims and nothing more.

The thematic complexes we have termed rhetorical idioms are vernacular resources, each serving as a kind of narrative kit through which is articulated a condition-category's socially problematic and justifiably treatable status. Analytically, they locate one area in which the central insight of social constructionism—that claims-making activities constitute social problems—can be investigated.

Counterrhetorical Strategies

If rhetorical idioms render claims both symbolically coherent and morally competent, then auditors are obliged, as members of the same cultural community the claimant has invoked, to either convey sympathy or else have "good reasons" for refraining from doing so. Rhetorical idioms usually posit hierarchies of value (e.g., freedom over oppression) with which it is difficult to disagree without discrediting oneself; to invert the hierarchy is to marginalize oneself as a social problems participant. Countering claims entails an artfulness that comes with being versed in the uses of certain vernacular resources, especially since counterclaimants can be told, "If you're not part of the solution, then you're part of the problem."

Before describing what we identify as the counterrhetorical strategies, we should note the service that alternative rhetorical idioms can perform in countering claims. Idioms other than the one implicit in a claim are useful in shifting the focus of discourse from the condition-category the claimant has singled out to the meaning of the claimant's claims-making itself. An example: The "war on drugs" initiated under the Reagan and Bush administrations was itself rendered problematic when civil libertarians cited the intrusiveness of such measures as drug testing in the workplace (Staudenmeier 1989). In this case the rhetoric of entitlement (viz., the right to privacy) was evoked to counter a claim arguably rooted in a rhetoric of endangerment. A similar discursive move was made by critics of antiabortion claimants, the charge being that one kind of moral belief (itself not disputed) was taking precedence over another to the point of usurpation (e.g., the blocking of entrances to abortion facilities by protestors).

Whereas the rhetorical idioms are drawn upon in amplifying and justifying one's claims while seeking to sway others to sympathetic stances, counterrhetorics block either the attempted characterization of the condition-category or the call to action, or both. These rhetorical strategies are generalized ways of speaking as morally competent counterclaimants, and thus can be articulated with reference to a variety of provisionally problematized condition-categories. The strategies fall into two classes: (1) sympathetic counterrhetorics, which accept, in part or whole, the problematic status of the condition-category, but which in effect block the request for remedial activities; and (2) unsympathetic counterrhetorics, which countenance neither the proposed characterization and evaluation nor the suggested remedies.

First the sympathetic counterrhetorical moves: *Naturalizing* is a move that accepts the assessment proposed while rejecting the call for action by making inevitable the very condition-category that claimants seek to render problematic and contingent (i.e., eradicable). The claimant may be met with the response, "Well, what did you expect? *Of course* society is violent, the world has always been, and always will be, a hostile place." If the condition-category is an instance of how the world "naturally" is, then calls for remedies are hopelessly naive. Yet the user of this gambit runs the risk of being labelled a "cynic" or "pessimist," labels that acquire negative connotations when applied to certain categories of persons in certain settings, such as politicians during reelection campaign debates.

Second, one might use the counterrhetoric of *the costs involved.* The upshot of this technique is to say that the problematic condition-category must be lived with rather than remedied through the claimant's specific measures, either because "two wrongs don't make a right," or because the claimed "benefits" do not outweigh their "costs." "Saving" the spotted owl might result in "costing" thirty thousand logging jobs; implementing civil rights legislation to eradicate racism in the workplace might involve "reverse discrimination"; pornography is the "price" of free speech. A term that often indicates the use of this counterrhetoric is *draconian measures,* a figure of social problems speech that equates the remedy with either imprudent short-sightedness or heartless punishment, or both. While the counterrhetoric of *naturalizing* is fairly unequivocal about the inevitability of our suffering the condition-category, there is some imprecision in the costs involved gambit: Adapting to a preexistent condition is implied in the first; contemplating a "trade-off" is encouraged in the second, meaning that one might well find that the costs involved are not very "costly" after all.

A third way to accept the claimants' complaint or dissatisfaction with a condition-category while withholding support for remedial action lies in *declaring impotence,* which entails registering one's moral sympathy while pointing to an impoverishment of resources at hand for dealing with the issue. In personal terms, this may mean not having enough time, energy, or authority for countering the problem in question. Or it may involve constructing a calculus of priorities: Yes, racism is a problem, but it is futile to try and do away with it until class oppression is countered. At an institutional level, budgets may be declared to be too tight to allow deployment of clean-up agents, as when a police chief, in response to demands that something be done about the problem of crime in the ghettos, contends that there simply aren't enough men and women on the force to eradicate the condition. Those who declare impotence, in either personal or institutional capacities, may be subject to charges of merely giving "lip service" to the problem and become objects of distrust. Indeed, officials may in turn become the object of claims-making activities for their very declared impotence. This occurred when missing-children advocates turned their attention to the government itself for its inept, confusing, or unresponsive styles of bureaucratic record-keeping: Thus the FBI became part of the problem of missing children (Best, 1987).

The fourth sympathetic counterrhetorical strategy we call *perspectivizing*. This form of talk is possible because the social problems process is premised on the object-subject distinction (Pollner 1978). That is, it consists of observing that the claimant's account is a "take" on a state of affairs that is distinct from the state of affairs itself: The claim is characterized as an opinion. In the locution, "You're entitled to your opinion," the counterclaimant avers the right of the claimant to participate in the social problems process while simultaneously placing a check on that participation by implying the counterclaimant need not, as a matter of opinion, subscribe to either the same view or the call for remedies. The significance of this move can vary: It may express anything from an indication of cool disinterest to an assertion of a competing definition of the condition-category that indicates the issue to be precisely that it is a matter of perspective or personal philosophy. In the case of abortion, for example, for a prochoice activist to say to a prolife demonstrator that she is merely expressing a personal preference is in effect to substantiate the former's stand that abortions should be left legalized: The latter can refrain from having an abortion if she so desires, but she does not have the authority to deny the right of the prochoice woman to an abortion, inasmuch as the personhood of the "fetus" is contingent on personal philosophy. At this point then, the strategy moves from being sympathetic to being actively hostile, from the claimant's perspective. Perspectivizing is in effect a mundane form of relativism. And claimants who proceed to insist that such a relativizing characterization reflects a lack of moral competence may open themselves up to being considered intolerant of differing opinions. (In this way, this strategy has an affinity with the rhetorical idiom of entitlement noted above.) Thus, this rhetoric is being employed whenever counterclaimants make reference to "life-style" as a legitimation of a series of activities: That the condition in question is a life-style is supposed to guarantee its propriety.

A fifth counterrhetorical style in this category we call *tactical criticism*. Tactical critics accept the characterization of the condition-category being proffered, but demur in the means claimants employ. "Yes, women are oppressed, but do those feminists have to be so militant and strident about publicizing the fact?" is an example here. Tactical critics can either imply their status as a potentially supportive group of fellow travelers, or suggest that the means claimants are employing might themselves be viewed and treated as a social problem (as when prolifers who engage in the bombing of abortion clinics are characterized by fellow travelers as a "fringe element" that is potentially dangerous, both to society and to the cause). Of all sympathetic counterrhetorical moves, this one carries the possibility of being seen as the least hostile by claimants, for the "counterclaimant" is both sympathetic with the effort to problematize *and* is willing to discuss tactics.

Then there are the *unsympathetic* counterrhetorical strategies. These oppose the condition-category's candidacy as a social problem and therefore also reject the call for remedial activities. First, *antipatterning* holds that the claim has not in fact characterized a full-scale social problem at all, but rather is focused on something akin to "isolated incidents." This was a characteristic response to charges of racial harassment on college campuses in the 1980s. Or, it might be held that "victims of magnetic radiation" were merely "unlucky" in developing cancer (Brodeur 1990). Claimants may interpret the gist of the counterclaim as suggesting that the incidence of the phenomenon has been exaggerated or its nature misunderstood. In this usage, antipatterning serves in effect as a challenge for the claimant to verify the magnitude of the condition-category, or specify the meaning of the terms being used to link instances of the condition-category into a social pattern worthy of attention. This can thus engender "hair-splitting" debates over the meaning of a key term employed by claimants ("What counts as sexual harassment?" or "How should one define racism?") or a kind of numbers game ("Are there three hundred thousand or three million homeless persons?").

In a related form, the counterrhetoric of the *telling anecdote* presumes to invalidate a claim by virtue of citing an instance, for example, a personal instance or one that the media has treated as a novel case, illustrating that the generality of the analysis offered by claimants is suspect. To a charge that "the streets are unsafe to walk at night," the anecdotal response can be, "Oh, I've been doing just that for many years with no difficulty." To the charge that smoking is a problem since it causes cancer can come the response, "My grandfather smoked two packs a day and lived to be a good eighty years and then some." The telling anecdote thus holds the claims-maker's characterization accountable to invariability instead of likelihood. Therefore, claims couched in the language of scientific generalization are particularly susceptible to the usage of this strategy.

In using the *counterrhetoric of insincerity* the counterclaimant either suggests or declares that the claimant's characterization is suspect because of a "hidden agenda" on his part: namely that he is either participating in the social problems process as a means of advancing or guaranteeing his career, or as a means of securing or gaining power, status, or wealth. The successful use of this device is premised on the notion that claims forwarded by self-interested parties are by definition or tendency more reflective of the claimants' designs than of what is "best for society." Thus, prolife men are involved in the movement to reassert masculine privilege; social workers trumpet poverty programs because it further solidifies their source of income; civil rights leaders aren't really interested in ending racism because, should they realize that goal, their political power and leadership positions would be undermined (Steele 1988), and so forth. (A variant of this rhetorical gambit emphasizes the exploitation of rank and file participants by careerist leaders.) This form of talk can have an accusatory, ad hominem tone, and it often is delivered in the shape of "sincerity tests": If prolifers really cared about children, then why don't they do something about malnutrition or children in poverty? If antivivisectionists really cared about animal rights, then why don't they wear synthetic fibers on an exclusive basis? and so forth.

A fourth unsympathetic strategy is the *counterrhetoric of hysteria*, a way of speaking commonly involved in efforts at deproblematizing condition-categories. It is unsympathetic insofar as its usage implies that the moral judgment of the claimants is not based in a "sound" assessment of the condition but is under the influence of "irrational" or "emotional" factors. Thus, the U.S. economy is not really in a recession, though the nervous perceptions of panicky stockholders might ironically induce one; the involvement of "Hollywood liberals" in efforts to "save the Amazon rain forest" is yet another demonstration of their susceptibility to "faddish causes"; Evangelical Fundamentalists are on a "crusade" against pornography because of a "suspicious" obsession with sexuality nurtured by their leaders. The counterrhetoric of hysteria characterizes the claimants as members of a social category, and then dismisses their claims as "typical" expressions of "bleeding heart liberals," "narrow-minded religious fundamentalists," "crazy environmentalists," and so forth. In other words, auditors are instructed to note that the claims display (cultlike) features of the claimants' subcultures, rather than matters of concern to the "mainstream" of society.

Whether the counterrhetorics be sympathetic or not, the format that they have in common is, "yes, but . . . . " Yet each counterrhetoric carries its own shadings of meaning, and therefore conceivably preferable and less preferable uses. Theoretical reconstruction of social problems discourse can proceed by investigating the kinds of uses the strategies are good for, and the kinds for which they fall flat. How are they adapted to different condition-categories, rhetorical idioms, settings, and claims-making styles? What do participants know when they read a counterclaim as an indication of the speaker's being morally incompetent? The matter of marginality in social problems discourse is a subject that greatly interests us; here we would just note that counterclaimants always skirt having their moral standing questioned, and thus their capacity for being participants in social problems discourse in the first place. By studying counterrhetorics we can discern how credibility is sustained by virtue of being well-versed in the vernacular.

Motifs

Motifs are recurrent thematic elements and figures of speech that encapsulate or highlight some aspect of a social problem. They are not complexes of moral discourse in the same sense as rhetorical idioms; rather, they are a kind of generic vocabulary conventionally used in claims-making, each term or phrase acquiring distinctive connotations in being situated in one kind of context instead of another. The study of motifs in social problems discourse ought to focus our attention on how morally imbued metaphors and phrases can be intelligibly applied in claims-making.

Some examples of motifs: *epidemic, menace, scourge, crisis, blight, casualties, tip of the iceberg, the war on* (drugs, poverty, crime, gangs, etc.), *abuse, hidden costs, scandal.* Some of these terms refer to kinds of moral agents, others to practices, and still others to magnitudes. What is entailed in using these terms in one's moral discourse? For example, what variety of descriptive requirements is associated with applications of a motif like *scandal*, as opposed to *crisis*?

More specifically, one set of issues involves the versatility of members' vocabularies given the constraints imposed by their vernacular origins and standards of idiomatic articulation. As an example, consider the metaphor of the *ticking time bomb.* Now, it is common to hear that phrase employed in a range of claims-making contexts, with respect to diverse condition-categories, and under the auspices of different rhetorical idioms. Urban poverty, depletion of the ozone layer, and AIDS are often spoken of as ticking time bombs, but why would it be unusual to find "abortion" spoken of or associated with that metaphor, and not, say, "the politics of abortion'? What do condition-categories have to be presumed to share such that they can be said to involve a common motif? What features are shared by those to which no such motif can be applied? What would be an innovative usage of a motif? What do such innovative applications and adaptations involve as symbolic operations? When is freshness a consideration in motif usage, as opposed to clichéd application? What mixtures of revelation and confirmation seem to be preferred by claimants?

The study of motifs also calls attention to the need for understanding their *symbolic currency,* that is, why some motifs are prized while others are considered best avoided. In fact, the *identical* motif may undergo such a transformation of value. Consider Holstein and Miller's (1990) study, which provides a reconstruction of members' "victimization practices" that we take to be illustrative of the kind of work that the study of motifs can generate. Working with the motif *victim,* they describe how it is that the victim identity is sometimes considered valuable, and other times pointedly not, because the connotations of the victim motif vary when positioned amid diverse kinds of claims.

Holstein and Miller's study offers an indication that motifs afford us an avenue for reconstructing social problems discourse without succumbing to the ontological gerrymandering that Woolgar and Pawluch addressed (1985a). Research formulated in terms of motifs readily jettisons that single-social-condition emphasis of contextual constructionism (Best 1989) in favor of another emphasis: how the terms of social problems discourse evolve and are fine-tuned, and how their symbolic implications are contained. As we see it, these constraints have more to do with the politics and poetics of description—that is, with articulation—than with the "ontology of the described" that has so dogged social constructionism. Whether studied for their "grammar" or utility, motifs offer us a way to appreciate what claimants make when they make claims.

Broadening the Subject Matter

Joseph Gusfield has observed that "the concept of 'social problems' is not something abstract and separate from social institutions," stating that the "conceptualization of situations as 'social problems' is embedded in the development of the welfare state" (1989, p. 432). His examples of how social agencies, professions, and institutions claim "ownership" of public problems (a term that Gusfield prefers to *social problems*) direct attention to processes of conflict and consensus with regard to such problems, and the language and rhetoric in which those problems are cast. Gusfield's discussion reflects a conceptual tilt in the sociology of social problems, one that neglects social problems discourse formulated in and addressed to *private realms* in favor of a state-centered model. In turn, the focus on ownership leads to assessments of claimants' "successes" or "failures" at inspiring collective redefinition or new legislation and public policies supportive of the claimants' concerns. Such an emphasis inhibits theoretical development inasmuch as it presupposes that members' discourses on social problems are most exhaustively reconstructed for their sociological weight or significance when situated within a unidimensional analytic scheme of success or failure.

In light of these implications for constructionist theorizing we would argue for a reconsideration of the kinds of activities worth attending to as claims-making, extending them beyond the legal-rational and state-centered realms. In the section that follows we would like to indicate how considerations of claimant *style* and *setting* will facilitate such a broadening of constructionism's scope, especially when we theorize our subject matter *comparatively*.

Claims-Making Styles

We introduce the concept of *claims-making styles* in order to suggest a research agenda derived from the central premise of social constructionism—the constitutive character of claims-making activities. That is, if we extend the scope of what counts as claims-making, social constructionists are poised to take inquiry in new directions.

By using the noun *style* in the context of claims-making activities, we are pointing to a neglected but investigable issue within the purview of our subject matter: how various groupings of the claimant's bearing, tenor, sensibility, and membership category can inform both a claim's general appearance and specific content as well as instruct auditors on how the claim should be interpreted. As a transitive verb, *style* refers to the act of fashioning a claim that is consistent with the conventions of claims-making styles, as when one styles, say, a scientific claim. Our task is to specify, first of all, the kinds of styles that are evident across the range of social problems discourses; second, discern the practices constitutive of the various styles; and third, comprehend the range and shadings of meaning that these genres of moral representation are capable of conveying. In other words, how is style useful? What difference does style make?

What is going on when a claimant is described or recognized as speaking in a *scientific style*? The frame of reference being invoked probably includes certain typifications: a bearing that is "disinterested;" a tone that is "sober;" and a vocabulary that is "technical" and "precise." Presumably, anecdotes should serve prefatory or illustrative purposes only, thus "humanizing" or "making accessible" the presentation, but such anecdotes should be incidental to the substance of the claims produced.

Similarly, to be "too rhetorical," "political," or "poetic" can be taken to be a liability, a departure from the hallmark of the style. The point of the style is not to fashion emotive imagery or reveal the personal stamp of its authors, but rather be anonymous, even "styleless," while diminishing uncertainty about the "properties" of condition-categories. It is quite evident that many practitioners of claims-making recognize the importance of scientific style for lending "objectivity" to their claims. Thus, examining how members communicate "scientifically" is relevant for the realization of an interactionist understanding of the social problems process. Analytically, "the scientific method" is subsumed under the concept *scientific style*, and it is not given any greater epistemological significance than any other body of practices associated with a particular kind of style. Even if some styles seem to carry the day and are more often "effective" (i.e., accorded credibility by auditors of claims), that does not detract from the importance of studying alternative or "oppositional" styles as well in view of the comparative theoretical perspective we recommend.

Since they are general ways of articulating moral stances, we take claims-making styles to be as valuable in rendering condition-categories problematic as in making the categories seem unobjectionable, harmless, or otherwise not warranting attention. Claimants and counterclaimants can both draw upon aspects of the same style even though they hold opposing views, as when scientists have disagreements over, say, recognizing the problem of "the greenhouse effect." As Aronson (1984) and others have argued, scientist's disagreements about "scientific claims" can also be the disagreements of participants in the social problems process (Spector and Kitsuse [1977] 1987). Now, the significance of an "intrastylistic" dispute can vary. In the context of scientific-styled discourse, disagreement over the applicability of the social problem epithet will be thought indicative of a failure in methodology. Insofar as the premise of this style assumes that the "facts of the case" are objective, stable, and discoverable (a premise that is also central to legalistic styles; Pollner 1987), intrastylistic disagreements focus on challenges to the methods employed to assert "the facts." On the other hand, intrastylistic disputes conducted within other "speech genres," to borrow Bakhtin's term (1986), such as what we call the civic style, can point to a different kind of significance altogether. There, intrastylistic disjunctions can be indicative of the very magnitude of the problem with which participants are contending. That is, the hallmark of civic-styled claims and claimants—"mad as hell" moral indignation—can itself be taken as a sign of the extent to which the dispute "touches a raw nerve." The presence of "citizen anger" on either side of the conflict points to the intractability of the problem itself.

Aside from concerning ourself with the symbolic interaction that is activated during intrastylistic disputes, we can obviously inquire into the trajectories social problems discourse tends to take when disputants draw upon different stylistic options. Claims-making styles embody or express a variety of ways of engaging in moral representation and understanding. The study of interstylistic discourse can attend to what happens when ways of "showing the moral" are framed by participants as being as important to what gets claimed about a condition-category as the category itself. Indeed, in the event of purportedly "subversive" subcultural styles (Hebdige 1979), such as that amalgam of speech and music known as "rapping," a style's alleged implications or politics may themselves be construed as "the issue."

In addition to the scientific style of claims-making, we would like to point to what might count as specific kinds of styles in claims-making. Such a listing is undertaken for illustrative purposes only, to suggest the range of interactional practices that we can concern ourselves with describing more precisely and exhaustively.

Under the term *comic style* we wish to include those practices by which members foreground absurdities in certain positions, highlight the hypocrisies of claimants or counterclaimants, or draw upon some measure of irony or sarcasm to point up a particular moral. Comic styles represent interesting problems of claim-readability inasmuch as the esthetic imperative of making a good joke can come into conflict with the practical goal of building a constituency. Requirements that humor not be "off-color," a "cheap shot," or a "low blow" are apparently conventionally present, even though what counts as being in "poor taste" is itself variable. Another issue is whether there are circumstances under which the comic style seems most pointed or strategic. That is, with respect to what kinds of categories does it make the most difference? Is it a style better suited to claiming or counterclaiming?

Consider how the comic style of caricature might be used to fashion a counterclaim by ad absurdum extension of claims couched in the entitlement idiom. Thus, recent efforts by gay educators in California to include recognition of the contribution of gays in high school history textbooks (as a way of "empowering" gay teens) was countered by such rhetorical questions as "Should we mention the contributions of pedophiles and prostitutes as well?" Implied in this rhetorical gambit are at least two subtexts: first, a moral equivalence between gays and pedophiles that would presumably embarrass proponents of the project, and second, the notion that history textbooks would, by the logic of entitlement, soon take on the character of a perverts' gallery and thus could not be placed in the hands of the impressionable young. This counterclaim charges those who press such entitlement claims with creating a "slippery slope" from which there would be no return—evoking the spectre of nihilism. Thus, the central concept of the entitlement idiom's remedial vocabulary—i.e., expansion—is countered in this instance by "exposing" the absurd, i.e., the unidiomatic lengths to which the rhetoric of entitlement can be taken.

The *theatrical style* encompasses those instances of claims-making that make a point of illustrating the group's moral critique in the very way in which the claim is represented. ACT-UP's various "actions," such as "die-ins," are dramatizations of the issue being contested. "Guerilla theatre" activists also seek to become living illustrations of their claim's substance, such as when an anti–Miss California Pageant demonstrator in Santa Cruz dressed up in a bathing suit consisting of pieces of meat. Theatrical styles seem to have gained wider usage in recent years, so that what might have once been, and probably still is, the preferred style of artists and other cultural workers, has filtered out to other segments of society. Thus, Operation Rescue demonstrations against abortion have featured such actions as symbolic mass funerals. The danger in this style is inscrutability, especially when the symbolic stagings carry the burden of being produced for the edification of both the claimants themselves as well as the larger public (Gamson 1989). When that occurs, we may find literary critics or social scientists brought in to "translate" for the public the allegorical or symbolic meaning embedded in the representation, or vouch for the integrity of the speech style itself, as when Henry Louis Gates, Jr. testified on behalf of rap musicians 2 Live Crew in a 1990 obscenity trial. (However, in our classification scheme, rapping is better considered a subcultural style.)

The *civic style* of claims-making entails making claims that have what we might call "the look of being unpolished." That is, the civic style's distinctive character is based in being "honest," "sincere," "upright," "unstylized." Where premeditation is clearly the rule in the theatrical style, claimants using the civic style should be readable as participating in social problems discourse out of strict moral indignation or outrage. To appear too well organized or "too slick" is to be part of an "interest group." The civic style involves trading off an ideal of the "common, decent folk," and its character is often used as the face of commonsense morality, especially in such popular culture icons as the film "Mr. Smith Goes to Washington." Ross Perot's 1992 presidential campaign exemplified the civic style: Witness his references to his supporters as "volunteers," and his denunciations of "handlers," "spin doctors," etc.

The *legalistic style* is premised on the notion that the claimant is in fact speaking on behalf of another party, a defendant or plaintiff, and that the merits of that party's case are consistent with rights and protections embodied in the law. The reason that the legalistic style is not subsumed under the theatrical style, in spite of the courtroom theatrics of attorneys, is because a legalistic-styled claim is presumably neither allegorical nor symbolic, but rather particular, specific, and analogic, with the full weight and prestige of institutional justice supporting it.

Finally, we would like to point to a category that might provide a linkage between social constructionism and cultural studies: *subcultural style*. Here we have in mind the notion that various segments of society—whether self-defined by class, race, ethnicity, gender, sexual orientation, or geographical location—tend to evolve unique or "local" (Geertz 1983) ways of commenting on the larger social world. Possible connections that might be considered: the relationship between "camp" and moral positioning; the styles of moral discourse evolved in such dialogical situations as "self-help groups," or consciousness-raising sessions; and the claims-making formats nurtured by bilingualism or the use of nonstandard English. The value of including the category of subcultural style is that it reminds us of something easily overlooked: Social problems discourse occurs in all manner of forums and among a wide range of persons. The concerns that these diverse peoples may have in commenting on and their characteristic ways of describing the symbolic order in which they are involved are not necessarily apparent if we take state- or, for that matter, media-sponsored discourse as offering us a privileged point of entry into the sociology of contemporary moralities.[4]

Settings

The issues posed by rhetorical strategies, motifs, and styles are particularly context sensitive; with that in mind, we would like to indicate the importance of *setting* for understanding the articulation of claims-making.

Studies of the settings in which claims are delivered also stand to move research onto a trans-condition-category level of analysis, since the settings we have in mind are not related exclusively to claims regarding one type of condition-category. Indeed, the variety of condition-categories that have been addressed in constructionist-style research using bureaucratic data is proof of this. The ways in which these various settings are constituted such that they can provide us with records of the claims-making process can thereby become an investigable topic. Conceiving of settings as contexts for scrutiny and representation, we can pose the following kinds of questions: How do the formal qualities of particular settings structure the ways in which claims can be formulated, delivered, and received? What kinds of rhetorical forms can be employed because of the imperatives or conventional features constituting the various locations? What are the various categories of persons populating these settings, and how do their characteristics entail accountably interacting with claims and claims-makers?

The media constitute one class of setting in which claims-making occurs, for example, and these can be further broken down into the subclasses of print, radio, television, cinema, and so forth. These can be further distinguished: Television has news programs, talk shows that address social issues, documentaries, etc., each of which has occasion to disseminate claims in presumably distinctive ways. What are the explicit or tacit rules for admissible testimony, fairness, objectivity, and so on? How does the visual component of some of these media alter the claim's sense, reception, and structure? A comparison with radio as a medium would be an instructive contrast in this regard. How are some rhetorical treatments of condition-categories made to possess greater visuality than others; in fiction versus nonfiction presentations? Are the print media able to engage in the depictions of claims in ways that are distinct from the other media? How does the size of the audience, or members' understanding of the viewership, become a consideration for the assertion of claims? What are the modes of address that are commonly employed in mass-mediated claims-making, what are the assumptions made thereby, and what are the implications of such practices for understanding social problems as a language game?

The second type of setting is *legal-political.* The obvious candidates for inclusion are courts, city council meetings, congressional hearings, electoral campaigns, policy think tanks, public interest groups, and so forth. What are the distinctive features of these contexts, and how do these structure social problems discourse? Questions regarding standing, admissible testimony, and dramaturgy might be particularly relevant issues here. This category encompasses a wide range of activities—from the tightly regulated courtroom, to the congressional hearing, to the electoral strategies of political campaigns—and thus requires that we be attuned to the distinctive sensibilities and conventional purposes obtaining in each. What needs to be kept in mind is the project of theorizing each context's particular engagement with claims-making activities.

The third setting in which social problems discourse can be readily observed is in *academia,* including academic conferences and journals. Presumably, Woolgar and Pawluch's call for constructionists to examine their own practice would be included under these auspices. Once again, the general issue here is the distinctive contribution of the setting to the way in which the social problems process proceeds. This can involve taking a sociology of knowledge approach to the various academic disciplines as they have engaged various condition-categories. How does the distinction between the humanities, sciences, and social sciences give distinctive accents to each academic division's participation in the process? What are the understandings of personhood (e.g., professional vs. laypersons) that are operative in the claims offered by each? How does "professional" status entail engaging the social problems process?

Settings may themselves be framed as moral objects, of course. The process of so viewing settings usually involves a *mundane* reflexivity about the social problems language game itself. Consider recent charges of "political correctness." They are usually setting specific: It is not the mass media or the various levels of government that are being invoked but rather the academy. Political correctness refers to a condition of communication: a "climate of opinion" that regulates what can be idiomatically claimed and counterclaimed in academic forums.

The discourse on political correctness plays off an idealization of the university as a freewheeling "marketplace of ideas," one that is being stifled by "liberal orthodoxy" and the "timidity" of professors who avoid critical discussion and examination of that orthodoxy, thus abdicating educational responsibility. The argument is that political correctness trivializes the notion of "diversity," transforming a "legitimate" concern for multiple philosophical perspectives into simple-minded representation of demographic heterogeneity. At a more concrete level, critics of political correctness hold that the kind of condition-category targeted by the politically correct (usually campus-related, such as "date rape," "racism in the humanities curriculum," and "hate speech"), and the ways in which they address them, is reflective of ideological, obscure, frivolous, or otherwise mistaken thinking. In any case, such condition-categories are held to be so ambiguous as to permit "diversity of opinion" about them, which is precisely what political correctness discourages.

Claims about political correctness ordinarily employ the comic style (q.v.). Note the series of ironic reversals that these claimants like to point out: The tolerant are intolerant; the international university is a parochial institution; "freethinkers" spout narrow-minded political dogmas; anti-racists are reverse racists; the educated do not educate; and so forth. These ironic reversals carry the tone of discovery—between subject and predicate is the adverb "really."

The study of such varied and specific settings would also enable us to understand how it is that we are able to have a record of the claims-making process. Sociologists of deviance have been sensitized to the distinctive contribution made by bureaucratic organizations to the deviant-making process (Cicourel 1968); there has not yet been a similarly concentrated focus on the importance of settings for the study of the social problems process, even though it would appear to be an elementary task in any effort to understanding claims-making as a general process.

Summary

In this paper, we hope to have demonstrated the fruitfulness of investigating vernacular resources, especially rhetorical forms, in the social problems process. In proposing the term *condition-category* to rectify the confusions that have been generated by *putative condition* we have outlined an agenda that directs our attention to research sites consistent with Spector and Kitsuse's premises that will be productive of an interpretive theory of the social problems process. In particular, the discursive practices through which the claims are constituted attune us to the richness of language and reasoning that participants are capable of tapping as a continually available resource. Our task as theorists is to note the differences in meaning and consequence that the strategic uses of vernacular forms can have for the shape of the social problems process.

In sum we believe that the study of the vernacular constituents of social problems provides us with new ways of conceiving our project—an ethnography of moral discourse—as well as indicating to us the necessity for rethinking or refining the theoretical language we employ to reconstruct those social interactions we have called "claims-making activities."

Acknowledgments

Earlier versions of this paper were presented at meetings of the Society for the Study of Social Problems in 1989 and 1990. The authors express their appreciation to Herman Gray, Melvin Pollner, Joseph Schneider, Carol Ray, Jay Gubrium, and Doug Maynard for their thoughtful responses to earlier drafts. We wish also to acknowledge Jim Holstein and Gale Miller for their substantive as well as generous editorial contributions.

Notes

1.   An illustrative aside: Constructionist irony could have led us to title this paper "In Appreciation of Social Problems."
2.   The "contextual constructionist," according to Best (1989), would seek to analytically locate the constructions of members in everyday life in the "social

and historical contexts" in which they are presumably embedded to "account" for the construction. We consider this analytic maneuver to represent just the sociology of knowledge rationale that generates the conceptual inconsistencies noted both in *CSP* and Woolgar and Pawluch (1985a). Instead, our outline reflects an interactionist conception of the social problems research agenda.

3. Obviously, the member's perspective can self-reflexively comprehend the social problems process. Such reflexivity seems to be especially encouraged during strategy sessions, when members compare notes on what modes of presentation work best with what topics before what audiences. The paradigm case is provided by political consultants employed by presidential election campaigns, since such efforts invariably embrace more than one topic, audience, and setting. The difference between member's and analyst's reflexivity is that the former's is practical while the latter's is theoretical. Indeed, there are interesting papers to be written about just this topic: how such reflexivity tends to emerge, the courses it tends to take, the limitations it must respect because of practical considerations, and the ways in which the practice of mundane reflexivity may eventuate in the departure from the member's perspective altogether in favor of a strictly theoretical reflexivity (in which the "natural attitude" is suspended).

4. Tuchman discusses the way in which consciousness raising sessions in the women's movements were not amenable to the conventional formats of news reporting. As she puts it "the reporter could not draw on narrative forms imbedded in the web of facticity to frame seemingly 'formless kind of talk' as a topic—a news story she could tell" (1978, p. 139).

References

Aronson, Naomi. 1984. "Science as a Claims-making Activity: Implications for Social Problems Research." Pp. 1–30 in *Studies in the Sociology of Social Problems*, edited by J. Schneider and J. I. Kitsuse. Norwood, NJ: Ablex.

Bakhtin, Mikhail M. 1986. *Speech Genres and Other Late Essays.* Austin: University of Texas Press.

Best, Joel 1987. "Rhetoric in Claims-Making: Constructing the Missing Children Problem." *Social Problems,* 34:101–21.

———. 1989. "Afterword: Extending the Constructionist Perspective: A Conclusion and an Introduction." Pp. 243–53 in *Images of Issues: Typifying Contemporary Social Problems*, edited by J. Best. Hawthorne, NY: Aldine de Gruyter.

Brodeur, Paul. 1990. "Annals of Radiation: Calamity on Meadows Street." *The New Yorker*, July 9.

Cicourel, Aaron. 1968. *The Social Organization of Juvenile Justice.* New York: Wiley.

Gamson, Josh. 1989. "Silence, Death, and the Invisible Enemy: AIDS Activism and Social Movement 'Newness.'" *Social Problems* 36:351–67.

Garfinkel, Harold 1967. *Studies in Ethnomethodology.* Englewood Cliffs, NJ: Prentice-Hall.

Geertz, Clifford. 1983. *Local Knowledge: Further Essays in Interpretive Anthropology.* New York: Basic Books.

Goffman, Erving. 1979. *Gender Advertisements.* New York: Harper and Row.

Gusfield, Joseph. 1989. "Constructing the Ownership of Social Problems: Fun and Profit in the Welfare State." *Social Problems* 36:431–41.

Hazelrigg, Lawrence. 1986. "Is There a Choice Between 'Constructionism' and 'Objectivism'?" *Social Problems* 33:S1–13.

Hebdige, Dick. 1979. *Subculture: The Meaning of Style*. London: Methuen.

Heritage, John. 1984. *Garfinkel and Ethnomethodology*. Cambridge: Polity.

Holstein, James A. and Gayle Miller. 1990. "Rethinking Victimization: An Interactional Approach to Victimology." *Symbolic Interaction* 13:103–22.

Merton, Robert K. 1974. "Introduction: The Sociology of Social Problems." *Contemporary Social Problems.*, 4th ed. New York: Harcourt, Brace & World.

Mills, C. Wright. 1940. "Situated Actions and Vocabularies of Motives." *American Sociological Review* 6:904–13.

Pollner, Melvin. 1975. "The Very Coinage of Your Brain: The Anatomy of Reality Disjunctures." *Philosophy of the Social Sciences* 5:411–30.

_____. 1978. "Constitutive and Mundane Versions of Labeling Theory." *Human Studies* 1:269–88.

_____. 1987. *Mundane Reason: Reality in Everyday and Sociological Discourse*. New York: Cambridge University Press.

Schneider, Joseph. 1985. "Defining the Definitional Perspective on Social Problems." *Social Problems* 32:232–34.

Spector, Malcolm and John I. Kitsuse. [1977] (1987). *Constructing Social Problems*. Hawthorne, NY: Aldine de Gruyter.

Staudenmeier, William J., Jr. 1989. "Urine Testing: The Battle for Privatized Social Control during the 1986 War on Drugs." Pp. 207–21 in *Images of Issues: Typifying Contemporary Social Problems*, edited by J. Best. Hawthorne, NY: Aldine de Gruyter.

Steele, Shelby 1988. "I'm Black, You're White, Who's Innocent?" *Harpers Magazine*, May.

Tuchman, Gaye. 1978. *Making News: A Study in the Construction of Reality*. New York: Free Press.

Wilson, Thomas. 1971. "Normative and Interpretive Paradigms in Sociology," Pp. 57–79 in *Understanding Everyday Life*, edited by J. Douglas. London: Routledge & Kegan Paul.

Woolgar, Steven and Dorothy Pawluch. 1985a. "Ontological Gerrymandering: the Anatomy of Social Problems Explanations." *Social Problems* 32:214–27.

_____. 1985b. "How Shall We Move Beyond Constructionism?" *Social Problems* 33:159–62.

3

The 1960s State as Social Problem: An Analysis of Radical Right and New Left Claims-Making Rhetorics

Carol A. B. Warren

The textual approach to social problems proposed by Ibarra and Kitsuse in this volume represents a third wave in social problems theorizing, following social pathologizing (from classical theory to the Chicago school to the 1960s) and building upon social constructionism (from the 1960s to the postmodernism of the 1980s). This paper is a textual analysis of New Left and Radical Right political rhetorics of the late 1960s, using—and critiquing—Ibarra and Kitsuse's framework.

According to Kitsuse and Spector (1973), social pathology theory took the sociologist as a technical expert, definer, and moral critic of society's problems. The social constructionist alternative to social pathology focuses on claims-making (Schneider 1985), or "the activities of groups making assertions of grievances and claims with respect to some putative conditions" (Kitsuse and Spector 1973, p. 415). The textual emphasis in Ibarra and Kitsuse moves social constructionism into the theoretically postmodern. The focus remains on claims-making, but on the rhetorics rather than the historically grounded actions of claimants: what they say over and above what and why they do. As Ibarra and Kitsuse summarize their approach:

> [T]he research questions concern not how those definitions are produced by the sociohistorical circumstances in which they emerged, but rather how those definitions express the members' conceptions of "the problem," how they are pressed as claims, to whom, mobilizing what resources, and so forth. . . . . [M]embers provide the linguistic productions and activities . . . . that the sociologist can in turn subject to theoretical . . . . scrutiny.

From a social pathology perspective, social scientists of the 1960s— typically politically liberal or quasi-radical—examined membership in Radical Right and (to a lesser extent) New Left political organizations.

Not claims-making activities or texts, but the social backgrounds and childhoods of these members were at issue. While the Radical Rightists and New Leftists themselves located pathology in the society they criticized, the sociologists and psychologists of the 1960s located pathology in the backgrounds of the political activists. The New Left to some degree and the Radical Right in its entirety were regarded as forms of pathology, whose members were drawn to these organizations by pathological pathways.

Hans Toch, for example, characterized the Radical Rightist as mentally ill and paranoid, whose affinity for a conspiracy theory of history "may be the final effort to maintain an unrealistic self-concept" (1965, pp. 56–57; for similar, although less extreme treatments, see Bell 1962; Epstein and Forster 1967; Janson and Eismann 1963). Although some New Leftists overlapped with or sympathized with sociological analysts (e.g., Flacks 1967), others (often older professors) were less willing to take New Left politics seriously. Feuer (1969), Keniston (1968), and Bettelheim (1969) trod more lightly through the terrain of pathology than Toch and the analysts of the Radical Right. Rather than full-blown paranoids or psychopaths, New Left activists were explained as acting out intergenerational conflicts with their fathers. The most extreme position was taken by Bettelheim (1969), who referred to activist leaders as "paranoid" individuals, trained by "leftist" parents to hate society and themselves.

The social constructionist perspective on social problems developed during the 1970s in the wake of the powerful and novel "labeling theory" of deviance. One of the main issues for social constructionism was a repudiation of the social pathology approach to deviance and social problems. Instead of condemning or curing the stigmatized, labeling theorists and social constructionists analyzed the process of labeling and the claims-making activities of both the stigmatized and their labelers. For all but the most toxic of groups, modern sociologists took an "appreciative" rather than condemnatory stance.

In rejecting the social pathology approach the social constructionists did not, however, deprivilege the sociological perspective itself. The classic studies of deviance and social problems in the 1960s and 1970s tended to be implicitly functionalist in approach, showing how deviant behavior marked out the boundaries of the normal, gave rise to a sense of collectivity, or focused identity. The literature on claims-making activities by social problems participants privileged the sociological, social constructionist perspective in its assumption that this approach was the only theoretically legitimate way to study social problems.

In an "appreciative" social constructionist study of the New Left, Antonio (1972) grounded his analysis of the Chicago conspiracy trials in

Garfinkel's degradation ceremony concept. Recognizing the "functional" aspects of Garfinkel's analysis, Antonio argues for a more dynamic interpretation in which the outcome of the degradation ceremony is rendered problematic:

> The defendants in the Chicago Conspiracy Trial expressed behaviour [sic] which violated the assumptive world of their audience. . . . . [T]hese behaviors were of an intentional nature designed to communicate directly a lack of respect to the court and to ultimately deny its legitimacy. The court is a sacred institution yet its ability to uphold this sanctity is sometimes limited. In most instances, ceremonial behaviors validating the court's sanctity are taken for granted and are complied with in a mechanical fashion. (p. 304)

A body of social constructionist social problems analysis of the New Left and Radical Right in the late 1960s, had one existed, would have examined the content of the categories "New Left" and "Radical Right" as they were constructed by sociologists and claims-makers who wished to frame these politics as social problems. A study within this genre, for example, might focus on the construction and location of New Left and Radical Right groups by the Federal Bureau of Investigation, by both administrators in policy setting and lower-level operatives in action.

A concern for the rhetorical dimensions of claims-making activities in social problems construction emerged in sociology with Gusfield's (1976) analysis of drinking-driver texts. In anthropology, Clifford and Marcus's important 1986 volume drew attention to issues of allegory, authority, and representation in ethnographic texts, a theme taken up by Best (1989), Richardson (1990), and others. Textuality, while remaining within the social constructionist tradition, directs attention away from the activities and toward the rhetoric of claims-making.

This paper is concerned with state actors and their policies treated textually as social problems by New Leftists and Radical Rightists. It is a historical study of a period in American culture when criticism of the state as a social problem was multivocal, coming from both right and left: the late 1960s and early 1970s. Although both Radical Right and New Left proposed a general cultural critique of modern American society, both located the source of social problems in the structures of the state—remediable by political ideology and action.

The data for this essay are books, pamphlets, and articles published in Radical Right organs such as *The Cross and the Flag* and the *John Birch Society Bulletin*, texts published by New Leftists, such as *Liberation* and *The Strawberry Statement*, and academic representations of New Left and Radical Right published during the late 1960s. The academic representations were used to set boundaries around the textual worlds that I represent as "New Left" or "Radical Right."

In their own textual self-representations, organizations and individuals labeled as Radical Right by 1960s academics (and by the 1960s media) sought to distinguish themselves not only from the state itself, but from allied organizations whom any cultural insider might "mistakenly" identify as like them. Thus, an article in the May 1969 *John Birch Society Bulletin* reports that a "far right" organization called the Property Rights Association refers to Robert Welch (leader of the John Birch Society at that time) as "a tool of the liberal establishment" (1969, pp. 15–16). The New Left, with its rhetorical focus on the self freed from social constraints, sought to disidentify with the concept of politics (and its left-right spectrum) itself. In Abbie Hoffman's words:

> Do your thing . . . .
> Be your thing.
> Practice. Rehearsals come after the Act. Act. Act. One practices by Acting. (1968, p. 6)
> Programs would make our movement sterile. (p. 80)

I drew rough boundaries around texts of the Radical Right by consulting the list of organizations suggested by Epstein and Forster (1967): the John Birch Society as the largest, the Christian Crusade (publication *The Cross and the Flag*), the "Manion Forum" (a radio program), the "Twentieth Century Reformation Hour" broadcasts of the Reverend Carl McIntire (publication *The Christian Beacon*), the radio broadcasts of H. L. Hunt, the "Dan Smoot Report" (radio), the White Citizens' Council, the Liberty Lobby, the Conservative Society of America, the Liberty Amendment Committee, and the Minutemen [see Westin (1964) and Janson and Eismann (1963) for similar classifications]. For New Left texts, I used Lipset and Altbach's (1966) classification: the Students for a Democratic Society (SDS) as the largest, the May 2 Movement established by the Marxist Progressive Labor party, the Trotskyite Young Socialist Alliance, the DuBois Clubs, the Marxist Youth Against War and Fascism, the Berkeley Free Speech Movement, the Vietnam Day Committee, and the Peace Rights Organizing Committee [see Jacobs and Landau (1966) and Skolnick (1969) for similar classifications].

According to Lipset, the metaphor of a left-center-right spectrum used by the mass media, laypersons, and some academics to analyze political rhetoric

> goes back to the days of the first French Republic when the delegates were seated, according to their political coloration, in a continuous semi-circle

from the most radical and egalitarian on the left to the most moderate and aristocratic on the right. (1963, pp. 127–28)

The metaphor of the semicircle suggests that the structural space between left and right moves toward one another, and is no farther distant than that between right and center or left and center. A textual analysis of the Radical Right and New Left in the late 1960s makes it clear that the central rhetorical project for both was the representation of the state as a social problem, both in a total sense and in each and every separate instance of state policy, action, or rhetoric. Like the sociology-of-knowledge analyses of belief systems described by Merton, New Left and Radical Right analyses of the state were directed toward "discounting the *face value* of statements, beliefs and idea systems [of the state] by re-examining them within a new context which supplies the 'real meaning'" (1962; 458). This, then, was the central project of New Left and Radical Right texts; in the body of this essay, I will examine the vernacular devices by which this project was accomplished.

According to Ibarra and Kitsuse, vernacular concepts and devices are among the linguistic resources used by sociologists or claims-makers to define and suggest causes and remedies for "the problem." Thus, for sociologists, the concept of *social problems* is a vernacular term linking what otherwise might be seen as separate spheres of social life into an analytic whole. For the sociologists and members described above, *Radical Right* and *New Left* are vernacular labels applied to ideologies and groups of people associated with these ideologies. Vernacular devices, with which this paper is concerned, are the linguistic tools by which claims-makers attempt to convince audiences of their construction of the problem.

The State as Social Problem

Ibarra and Kitsuse frame "categories, not conditions" as the constructionist, textual base of social problems analysis: the core terms "used by members to propose what the social problem is 'about'" and upon which claims-making rhetoric is constructed. For Radical Rightists and New Leftists in the 1960s, the state was the social problem, in a total and global manner; other specific categories of social problem were simply the outcome of the totally problematic character of the state.

For the Radical Right, the totally problematic character of the state encompassed not only the modern American state, but also most other nations (spatial totalizing) and what were claimed as its "roots" in European and other precursors of the American political system (temporal totalizing). This centrally problematic character of the state had two aspects: It was "communist," and it was a "conspiracy." A *John Birch Society Bulletin* claims that "The forces now at work to wreck our country and enslave our people are all elements of one gigantic, long active, deeply entrenched, extremely powerful, utterly ruthless, and incredibly ambitious international conspiracy" (March 1969, p. 4). This international conspiracy was described as being "as ancient as the human worldly race itself, having its beginnings in the first rebellion of Adam and Eve. . . . . Communism . . . . has had many names throughout the ages besides communism" (Redekop 1968, p. 59, quoting a Billy James Hargis radio program). All of history was read as a consequence of this communist conspiracy; Robert Welch, for example, claimed that "The Roman Empire . . . . started dying from the cancer of collectivism from the time Diocletian imposed on it his New Deal" (Welch 1961, p. 37).

The New Left also totalized the 1960s American state, extending this totalization across space, but not time. Berkeley New Left activists described

> the problem of Vietnam [as] the problem of the soul of America. What the State Department is doing in our name in Vietnam is tied directly to Alabama, the Dominican Republic, the state of freedom of the press in America, and the scope of our literature. (Menashe and Radosh 1967, p. 51)

While the Radical Right's core characterization of the state utilized a traditional (lay and academic) political-economic category—communism—the New Left's central image was that of "heartlessness" or "soullessness." This motif expressed the New Left's transmutation of political economy from a classification system into a physioemotional essence. The opposite of "heart" and "soul," the modern state, is soulless and heartless:

> We have come to the conclusion that our society was corrupt, vile and heinous, and that to obey any of its dictates, and any of its concepts, was to doom us eventually to a living death killing others as we died. (Kornbluth 1964, pp. 456–57)

Both the Radical Right and New Left nihilated—to use Berger and Luckmann's (1967) term—the state's legitimacy by a constantly repeated verbal characterization: *phony.* To the Radical Right, the state was phony in the sense that all of its claims, statements, proposals, and policies were a false front, much like a Potemkin village—but a Potemkin village with something, not nothing, behind it. And that something was the communist conspiracy. To the New Left, phoniness implied the repression or inhibition of a true, natural self inherent in human beings. The image here was not of a Potemkin village, but of a machinelike, soulless state consequent upon the "uptight," "hung-up" phoniness of state agents. Instead of a deliberate, motivated conspiracy, the New Left postulated institutionalized soullessness.

What is latent in the categorical rhetoric of social problem claims-making, the expansion of a category such as "abortion" into a whole constellation of moral meanings, is manifest where the social problem is the state itself. There were no ambiguities, or very few, in the Radical Right's and New Left's core analysis of what the state was "all about." The vernacular rhetorics used to describe specific social problems flowing from this totality are readable, however, as those described by Ibarra and Kitsuse. The rhetorical idioms, motifs, and stylistic conventions displayed in these texts can be used to frame Radical Right and New Left rhetorics of the 1960s; the meaning of counterrhetorics changes, however, when the social problem is the state itself.

Rhetorical Idioms of the Radical Right and New Left

Ibarra and Kitsuse define rhetorical idioms as vernacular claims for the existence, magnitude, and immorality of proposed problems. They identify the rhetoric of loss, which nostalgically laments the devaluation of something previously valued, the rhetoric of endangerment to the health and safety of the human body, the rhetoric of unreason, or concern about being made a dupe or fool, and the rhetoric of calamity, which evokes utter disaster. As Ibarra and Kitsuse note, rhetorical idioms can cut across ideological divisions in politics; and indeed the rhetorics of loss, endangerment, unreason, and calamity are identifiable in both New Left and Radical Right texts.

Claims couched in one rhetorical idiom can be challenged in another idiom, and also by the use of counterrhetorical strategies. Counterrhetorical strategies "block either the attempted characterization of the condition-category or the call to action, or both." While they are indeed "discursive strategies for countering characterizations made by claimants," they tend to be, in the context of the totalizing social problematic of the state, as "synoptic or thematic" as the rhetorical idioms. New Left and Radical Right counterrhetorics of the 1960s addressed both the values conveyed in the rhetorical idioms and "their current application."

Both Radical Right and New Left rhetorics of loss were concerned centrally with arcadia, and peripherally with devaluation. Extinction was a peripheral theme of the Radical Right, related to the bodily threats posed by the wars and pollutions of the modern state. For the Radical

Right, extinction as Armageddon was a central theme, counterpointed with utopian and arcadian imagery.

Both sets of political texts were profoundly arcadian; they harkened the reader back to specific time periods in American history that represented a golden age; for the Radical Right this was around 1913, while for the New Left it was colonial America (within the spaces of anti-slavery):

> The New Left was decidedly American in character. It sustained a nostalgia for a simpler, better, quasi-rural age where men are strong and true and life is as uncomplicated as it is sweet. . . . . 'Participatory democracy' came from the legend of the Town Meeting and the Congregationalist traditions. (Rader 1969, p. 52)

A "Tract for the Times" in the New Left review *Liberation* (1966, p. 9) proposed a return to "root traditions" as the way to achieve utopia, while Wayne Hansen said that "my heart . . . . is now still and patiently awaiting the return of the deepest and truest American values, the ones on which this country was founded" (Kornbluth, 1968, p. 296).

This arcadian rhetoric is indistinguishable from that of the Radical Right in its invocation of the loss of "simpler," "better," "sweeter," and "truer" times, and deeper values. Radical Rightist arcadians found simplicity and sweetness in a constellation of traditional, early-twentieth-century religious, domestic, and political-economic values: "And religion and education were so mixed up together when I was a boy you couldn't tell where one left off and the other began. . . . . Freeloading was a disgrace. Ice-cream was homemade. And marriage was forever" (Redekop 1968, p. 2, quoting Radical Right radio commentator Paul Harvey). Gary Allen (n.d.), a Radical Right economist, dated the decline of arcadia from 1913, with the establishment of centralized banking and the erosion of the "simple virtues" of religion, domesticity, and civic politics. Robert Montgomery set the date as 1912:

> In 1912 the old rules still applied. A young man who wanted to be independent in his old age worked hard, lived within his income, ignored the Jones family, saved money, got the capitalist system on his side . . . . kept clear of the money lender and the installment purchase. (1966, p. 66)

Both devaluation and extinction were implied in these centrally arcadian rhetorics of loss. What was devalued was, in the Radical Rightist texts, the values of 1913 and those people in whom such values were embedded, middle aged parents of what probably seemed like a very peculiar youth cohort:

Our young people are being encouraged from the earliest age, and by every means which such Communist-dominated influences as the National Education Association can devise, to look with increasing scorn on their parents; to regard themselves as smarter and wiser and more progressive than their parents; to flout all experience as something to which they are automatically superior; and gradually to acquire a feeling of open and active hostility toward not only their parents but toward all authority of every kind. (*John Birch Society Bulletin* March 1969, p. 20).

The cause of this devaluation was not any fault inherent in the youth cohort, but the communist conspiracy that had come to dominate the state's educational arm.

For the youthful radical leftists, what was devalued was themselves—young people uncorrupted by the heartless, soulless state or the capitalist values of the political economy—together with those oppressed peoples unusable by the state. Wayne Hanson described his refusal of the draft with a rhetorical evocation of colonial arcadia, and of the hopes of young, as yet incomplete political actors to bring about a second American revolution:

My brothers, how can I tell you. I walked to the Common yesterday without knowing all I would do by the end of the day. But I sat and I listened while men spoke, and there were times when I could not tell whether the voice that rose up over the crowd was Howard Zinn's voice or Ray Mungo's voice or everyone's voice united as one. I walked across the Common and to the Arlington street church and I could not tell if we were two thousand marching in Boston on October 16 or all of humanity on its slow, painful and joyful progression to the freedom which is its birthplace and its goal. I could not tell if we were the names and the bodies we are known by now or if we were Paine and Franklin, and Jefferson or Emerson, Lincoln, or Thoreau. We were all of them, all of them on our way to becoming more of them, for the knowledge that was theirs is yet for us to learn, but we are learning, the pure vision that was theirs we yet must see, but we are seeing, and the strength to manifest that vision that was theirs, must be ours—and yet we do not have it, but we will. (Kornbluth 1968, p. 297)

Extinction, in Radical Right texts, referred to the extinction of values and a way of life, something that was in process and that would culminate in Armageddon unless the Right was successful. Robert Welch described the strangling of arcadia by the communist conspiracy:

For the truth I bring you is simple, incontrovertible, and deadly. It is that, unless we can reverse forces which now seem inexorable in their movement, you have only a few more years before the country in which you live will become four separate provinces in a world-wide Communist dominion ruled by police-state methods from the Kremlin. (*John Birch Society Bulletin* March 1969, p. 6)

The John Birch journal *American Opinion* kept a yearly tally of communist control of the world and of the United States; in 1958, the year the Society was founded, the United States was considered 20 to 40 percent under communist control, while by 1963 the estimate was 50 to 70 percent (Overstreet and Overstreet 1964, p. 91). Dr. Frederick Schwartz, leader of the Christian Anti-Communist Crusade, predicted that Armageddon would occur in 1973 with the advent of an overtly communist government, financed by Richfield, Eversharp, and Technicolor (among other corporations), whose headquarters would be the Mark Hopkins hotel in San Francisco (quoted in Carpenter 1964, p. 29).

For the New Left, extinction was of the processes of life itself, both literal death in horrible and unjust wars, and metaphorical death of the human spirit, heart, and soul. The arcadian American dream was evoked as lost among the topian forces of an Armageddon that had already come to pass:

> The great American dream of "life, liberty and the pursuit of happiness" has been turned by a ruthless regime into a nightmare of death, destruction, and the pursuit of dollars. . . . . Even as we meet, the rulers of our nation are sending off more planes, bombs, guns and gases in a desperate effort to paralyze the progress of history, to terrorize and destroy those around the world who hold freedom more dear even than life when life means slavery. At home, these same rulers enforce a society of fear with police dogs, cattle prods, and prisons. (Jacobs and Landau 1966, p. 85)

In both Radical Right and New Left rhetoric of loss, the theme of Armageddon interwove with that of hope, since if Armageddon is in fact upon us, it is too late for the arcadian utopia. Hope was located, in these texts, in the organization and activities of the New Left and Radical Right, organization and activities that took specific form. In Radical Right texts, this form was evolutionary and dedicated; in the New Left, it was revolutionary and dedicated.

In the texts of the Radical Right, hope was found in steady and evolutionary change that took the form of persuasion—persuading legislators and the public to recognize the communist conspiracy:

> By 1973, at the present rate . . . . the terror and cruelty of the Communist police state will begin to replace the more subtle means by which Communist tyranny is imposed and maintained.
>
> It is the function and the ambition of the John Birch Society, with all of the allies that can be rallied on our side, to prevent this catastrophe. And

since we really mean it, we never deceive ourselves or anybody else about
our David-like structure, as opposed to the Goliath we oppose.

Our whole organization is engaged right now, therefore, in Herculean
efforts to raise the whole level of our strength in three categories: *Membership, Money, and Motivation.* (Welch 1969, p. 1)

As evoked by the words of Abbie Hoffman at the beginning of this
essay, the means to utopia for the New Left was a "psychic community"
(Jacobs and Landau 1966, p. 4) bringing individuals together in revolutionary activism—ACT—coupled with a studied withdrawal from topian American values and activities. The combination of arcadian, early
American, with modern utopian themes is expressed by Hoffman: "[We]
believe in participatory democracy . . . . only you call it 'everyone doing
his thing'" (1968, p. 89).

Thus, arcadian rhetorics of loss contain not only a lament for an ex-
tinct past, but a vision of its resurrection in future time. The present,
topia, is the essential problematic; for Ibarra and Kitsuse "the *present* is
given an all-embracing context" of loss, extinction and devaluation,
while the past and future contain the good. In this frame, the heroism of
the rescuer was evoked by both the Radical Right and the New Left: the
struggling, persuasive David against the Goliath of communism, and
the young messiah (for this was a male imagery) throwing off the chains
of death and soullessness. The Radical Right (and to some extent the
New Left) hero was, however, not so much protecting or conserving as
he was restoring arcadia, and staving off Armageddon.

The rhetoric of endangerment, evoking threats to the safety or health
of the bodily person, was absent in the Radical Right texts; the extinction
feared was of values and life-style, not of bodily persons; the pollution
lamented was of minds, not bodies or rivers. In New Left texts, the
theme of bodily endangerment was linked with that of extinction:
war—particularly the Vietnam war—and (occasionally) environmental
pollution.

The expansionary rhetoric of entitlement was used extensively in New
Left texts, not only proposing but also connecting, in Ibarra and Kitsuse's words, "institutional access [and] the unhampered freedom to
exercise choice of self-expression. The sensibility expressed by this idiom is egalitarian and relativistic." Indeed, the birth of entitlement rhetoric in its contemporary academic form (now derisively referred to as
"political correctness") has been traced to the New Left activism of the
1960s. The New Left's aim was to "attempt to achieve 'community' to
reach levels of intimacy and directness unencumbered by the conventional barriers of race, status, class, etc." (Jacobs and Landau 1966, p.

163). The rhetoric of entitlement was not found in Radical Right texts; its expansionary principle is the reverse of Radical Rightist arcadia.

The rhetoric of unreason, positing "an idealized relationship between the self and the state of knowing," "highlight[s] concerns about being taken advantage of, manipulated, 'brainwashed,' or transformed into a 'dupe' or 'fool.'" This rhetoric rarely characterized new left texts, but was centrally characteristic—paired with the rhetoric of loss—of Radical Right texts. The core conceptualization of the state as a "communist conspiracy" reflected this pairing. All social problems were a consequence of this conspiracy:

> As a consequence of this design we see all around us today carefully plotted and extensively conducted campaigns to bring about the following results . . . . narcotic drugs . . . . immoderate use of alcohol . . . . promiscuousness with regard to sexual relations . . . . sexual perversion . . . . filth and pornography . . . . crime . . . . vandalism . . . . rebellion against all authority . . . . dirty language, and obviously dirty minds . . . . rewards by welfare agencies of the production of illegitimate children . . . . treason . . . . deliberate lies by government, press, pulpit, and college. (*John Birch Society Bulletin* March 1969, p. 20)

The rhetoric of calamity, as described by Ibarra and Kitsuse, is antithetical to both Radical Right and New Left idioms of the 1960s; no calamity, within either set of texts, was seen as unconnected with "a specific kind of moral system," or could provoke counteraction without reference to ideology. Both Radical Right and New Left were totalizing systems that laid the cause of all calamities, as well as social problems, at the door of the state. Either the communist conspiracy or the military-industrial complex was responsible; thus there were no solutions short of resurrecting utopia within arcadia.

The same may be said of sympathetic counterrhetorics, those which "accept, in part or whole, the problematic status of the condition-category, but which in effect block the request for remedial activities." Since all the textual claims of the Radical Right and the New Left were centered on the problematic of the state and its overthrow, there could be no compromises: non–Radical Right and non–New Left claims about the nature of the state were not naturalized or perspectivized, the costs involved could not be too high nor tactics separated from ultimate values, and, in the context of hope and heroism, declaring impotence was out of the question. For the New Left:

> Corporatism or humanism, which? For it has come to that. Will you let your dreams be used? Will you be grudging apologists for the corporate state? Or will you try to help change it. . . . . We are dealing now with a

colossus that does not want to be changed. It will not change itself. It will not cooperate with those who want to change it. . . . . Help us change the future in the name of plain human hope. (Jacobs and Landau 1966, p. 100)

And from the Radical Right:

There is much to be done if America is to block communist domination of the world. Much of the work is up to *you* . . . . begin immediately to educate yourself; to embark on a program of action. If you delay, your motivation will pass, your concern will recede, but the danger will increase. (Stormer 1964, p. 115)

Unsympathetic counterrhetorical strategies were, however, used by both Radical Right and New Left to discredit their opponents, the state and its dupes or agents. Unsympathetic counterrhetorical strategies "oppose the condition-category's candidacy as a social problem and therefore also reject the call for remedial activities." The unsympathetic counterrhetorical strategies used by both right and left in the 1960s were not those described by Ibarra and Kitsuse, rather, these texts employed a counterrhetoric of reversal.

A counterrhetoric of reversal defines many of the same conditions as social *problems* as other political groups—war, drug use, crime, poverty, etc.—but reframes them as social *policies*. In the Radical Right variant, the state, and its purportedly problem-solving arms such as the church, the education system, and the welfare system, claimed to be working against the social problems of godlessness, illiteracy, and poverty, but were actually promoting policies to further these conditions. This exacerbation of social problems was undertaken to weaken the social fabric, and thus make it more receptive to the communist takeover. The New Left rhetoric of reversal was less conspiratorial, evoking machinery rather than human agency, but the outcome was the same: The social problems of war, pollution, and poverty were reframed as the social policies of a heartless, soulless military industrial "colossus." In the context of the 1960s Radical Right and New Left, there was is no room for a "yes but."

Motifs

As "recurrent thematic elements and figures of speech that encapsulate or highlight some aspect of a social problem," the "generic vocabulary" of motifs is likely to exhibit historical as well as linguistic patterning (history is not discussed in the Ibarra and Kitsuse essay). Motifs, as general cultural metaphors, are available for use within various rhetorical frameworks and can accommodate the various styles of claims-making discussed below. The motifs used by both Radical Right and

New Left were primarily images of the horrors of topia juxtaposed with images of arcadian/utopian promise. Interestingly, many of the central motifs used in both sets of texts were not directly related to moral agents. Motifs of magnitude—the magnitude of the problem of the state—were reflected in the use in both texts of the metaphor of colossus.

Counterpointed motifs in the rhetoric of the New Left, associated with a fusion of the spiritual, the bodily, and the elemental in nature, included dream contrasted with nightmare, vision with death or darkness, and sunlight with fog. There was a strong visual element in these texts, associated with the nonformal clothing and long hair and beards commonly adopted by young male radicals to symbolize dissension from the state. George Dennison contrasted sunlight with fog, and the utopian with the topian "man":

> [L]et me put it in terms of youth's own rebellion against the prevailing norms of individual life, for the long hair and the beards of many collegians are first a refusal to be the shorn and colorless Duplicate Man of the business world, who attests in his every gesture and by dress that no imperative—be it moral, religious, intellectual, or sexual—will interfere with his employer's demands . . . . our . . . . radical young . . . . have not knuckled under, nor will they. Their self-respect, their love for and admiration of each other, their moral courage and independent thought, their sense of a world to be gained—all this is like a burst of sunlight after the longest, longest fog. (Dennison 1969, pp. 31–33)

Motifs in the Radical Right texts counterpointed "nature" motifs evoking the conspiracy with religious ones evoking the opposition. The conspiracy was described in terms of roots, branches, forces, torrents; it had roots beyond the present space and time, and its tactics involved branching out and unleashing forces and torrents: "A torrent of obscene material is pouring into every area of this country" (Gumaer n.d., p. 9).

The religious counterpoint motif, sometimes alternated with Greek mythology, allied the Radical Right claims makers with ultimate good, spiritual force, and historical epics. David and Goliath were used to symbolize the colossus of the state and its puny—albeit ultimately successful due to "Herculean efforts"—challenger. Biblical authority was evoked to frame the communist conspiracy as a religiously predicted event:

> Isaiah: "Woe unto them that call evil good, and good evil; that put darkness for light, and light for darkness; that put bitter for sweet, and sweet for bitter!" This describes the very sweep of the colossal deception being practiced upon the American people today, and which it is our business to

expose as widely, as fully, and as clearly as we can. (*John Birch Society Bulletin* March 1969, pp. 1–2)

Claims-Making Styles

Ibarra and Kitsuse refer to scientific, comic, theatrical, civic, journalistic, legalistic, and subcultural styles of claims-making. The Radical Right claims-making of the 1960s was couched in a style that vacillated between highly metaphoric—as illustrated by the use of naturalistic motifs—and scientific or academic. In addition, the Radical Right adopted an ironicizing style signaled by particular textual conventions. The New Left worked from within a theatrical style, which coexisted ambivalently with a scientific/academic style; both the New Left and Radical Right also framed their claims within a journalistic style and a poetic style.

The elements of a scientific or academic claims-making style in Radical Right texts, invoking an implicit claim of objectivity, included the use of statistics (which seemed, and seems, to be a significant tool of all modern claims-making), references to evidence and education as the proper means by which outsiders might be persuaded of the existence of the communist conspiracy, and the invocation of expert evidence for its existence. Experts invoked ranged from approved state agents to unnamed "students": "According to the House Committee on Un-American Activities, a number of Americans have actually been trained in guerilla warfare in Red Cuba by agents of the Vietcong" (Gumaer n.d., p. 9). They invoked both "scholarship" and the kind of tentativeness of claims typical of academic (as opposed to the most florid type of Radical Right) style: "[O]ne student of the situation insists that evidence is available which leads to the speculation that more than one man was involved in the [Kennedy] assassination" (Evanson 1966, p. 31).

New Leftists used the scientific/academic style, but were self-conscious and ambivalent about it. The New Left movement was nurtured in the universities, leading to an irony: The universities were framed both as the cradle of revolution and of the theoretical tools to accomplish revolution, and as an arm of the oppressive state. The simplicity of soul, heart, and vision required of the New Left was antithetical to the kind of theoretical analysis found in academia:

> The trouble with trying to understand politics and society as they are taught in the university is that everything seems so complex, so subject to a multitude of seemingly unrelated and contradictory constructions and interpretations. It is only when one can confront it himself, only when it is reduced to its ultimate terms of what it means to the lives of individual

men, that "society" can really be known and understood. (Jacobs and
Landau 1966, p. 215)

And yet "Most of these writers are highly skilled in the latest techniques
of historical, political, and sociological analysis so characteristic of the
society they oppose" (Miller and Gilmore 1965, p. 205). Thus, part of the
textual representation of the New Left involved the self-conscious denial
of the relevance of academic political-economic categories to the achievement of arcadian utopia: New Leftists variously rejected leadership
(Lampe 1968, p. 18), theoretical abstractions (Lynd 1969, pp. 6–7), ideology (p. 8), and strategy (p. 8).

The use of words previously banned from academic or polite discourse also formed a motif for New Left rhetorical claims. The term
motherfucker centered the rejection of an academic or scientific style of
claims-making within the 1960s confrontations of New Leftists with
their professors. As Mark Rudd described this confrontation:

> 'Up against the wall, motherfucker" defines the terms. It puts the adminis-
> tration and the interests they represent on one side, leftist students and
> the interests of humanity on the other. Those undecided in the middle are
> forced to choose sides. (Avorn 1968, p. 52)

Rudd embedded the motherfucker motif within a rhetoric of entitlement, which in turn valorized the New Left as heroic and as among the
oppressed. Part of the heroism, and release from oppression, involved
the invocation of the "natural" body function language of the oppressed:
bullshit, motherfucker, fuck, and shit. The "unnatural language" of the
university and the state was counterpointed:

> We coopted the word "motherfucker" from the ghetto much as we
> adopted the struggle of blacks and other oppressed as our own. . . . . The
> obscenity, too, helped define our struggle. Finally, we could say in public
> what we had been saying among ourselves. We could use our own lan-
> guage, much more expressive than the repressive language of Grayson
> Kirk [a University administrator]. When I told a meeting of the Ad Hoc
> Faculty Group that the talks we were having with them were bullshit, I
> expressed myself thoroughly, naturally. All forms of authority, traditional
> "respect" (you show respect, obviously, by not using your own language),
> had broken down. The norms of repression and domination, maintaining
> the hierarchical structure of the classroom and the society, were swept
> aside. (Avorn 1968, p. 36)

The Radical Right situated its rhetorics of loss and endangerment
within what I call an ironicizing style. The ironicizing style seeks to
nihilate—in Berger and Luckmann's (1967) terms—the claims-making of

the communist conspiracy/state. This ironicizing style has two elements: using qualifiers such as "purported," and—something that it has in common with Ibarra and Kitsuse's style in the introduction—placing quotation marks around words and phrases that represent the state's portraits of reality. The following quotation, by Robert Welch, nihilates liberals' claims to liberality, implying their "real" status as communist "stooges":

> Then there is the phony reasons [*sic*], given by the Communists them-
> selves, and even more noisily shouted by their gullible "liberal" stooges,
> that men become Communists as a result of their own poverty and illit-
> eracy. (Welch n.d. b, p. 32)

Quotation marks also serve to nihilate the use of opponent claims-makers' use of common cultural motifs such as "rights" or "freedom," framing opponents' motifs as false claims: "The 'civil rights' movement is loaded, from top to bottom, with Communists, criminals, and self-proclaimed revolutionaries" (Rousselot n.d. p. 2).

Elements of journalistic and civic style informed these Radical Right texts; a comic style did not—the Radical Right of the 1960s was not known for purposeful humor. The civic style of evoking "common decent folk" was inherent in the Radical Right's depiction of a 1913 arcadia. The journalistic style of the "thoughtful alarmist" who uses a language balanced between colorful drama and objectivity characterized much of the Radical Right's description of the state. Colorful labeling of state actors was a common journalistic technique: reframing Democrats and Republicans as "communists," "comsymps," "stooges," and their claims as "phony." These labels transmuted the political symbols of what was conventionally understood as the center into symbols of the communist conspiracy. Photographs printed in a Radical Right newspaper *The Councilor* (1968) were described in the text as exhibiting the spatial reach of the communist conspiracy:

> The clenched fist is a communist salute, a symbol of revolutionary vio-
> lence. These pictures . . . . show 1. the correct form of the Red Salute, 2.
> Lee Harvey Oswald giving the salute in Dallas, 3. Nikita Krushchev, 4.
> Orville Freeman and Hubert Humphrey. (1968, n.p.)

The New Left also utilized the colorful labeling technique of the journalistic style, in particular the ubiquitous "pig" to describe those state agents, such as the police, perceived as actively vicious. In one particularly vehement repudiation of academic styles of claims-making, a New Left activist referred to sociologists as "surveyor pigs" (Brooks 1969, p. 14). Labels evoking machines, soullessness, and heartlessness were used to describe the more passive agents of the military-industrial complex, such as the "Duplicate Man."

The theatrical style of claims-making mixed uneasily with academic analysis in New Left texts. This style makes "a point of illustrating the group's moral critique in the very way in which the claim is represented." The New Left used both theater and the metaphors of theater to draw attention to their claims, distancing themselves self-consciously from the oppositional style, that of science and academia. Hoffman (1968) and others drew on metaphors of theater and advertising to describe New Left political activism, while also evoking arcadian precedents:

> 'Chicago was our Fort Sumter!"—an incredible historic epic for us. But each epic redefines the terms for the next confrontation. Chicago may be the last time we get our human heads beat in by pig clubs in order to radicalize the country. . . . . [T]he poetry or aesthetics of confrontation with the establishment is very important, and we have to wait for the right or poetic moment for the next national showdown. That was what was so brilliant about Chicago, because we could almost do no wrong. While we were mounting offensives on the streets, the Democrats were shitting all over the place on national television in the amphitheatre. ("Little Rubin Red Breast" 1969, pp. 10–17)

> Our actions in Chicago established a brilliant figure-ground relationship. The rhetoric of the Convention was allotted the fifty minutes of the hour, we were given the ten or less usually reserved for the commercials. *We were an advertisement for the revolution.* (Hoffman 1968, p. 58)

Both New Left and Radical Right occasionally used a poetic style of claims-making. This style sometimes involved the invocation of traditional American poetry, songs, or folktales as symbolic of the group's claims: Both the Radical Right and New Left appropriated "America the Beautiful" to their own uses. Occasionally members would compose their own poetry, songs, or folktales, in formats that ranged from the highly traditional (in the Radical Right) to an experimentalism that shaded into the theatrical style (in the New Left). Radical Right poetry used conventional rhyming, line length, punctuation, and capitalization; New Left poetry experimented with some of these elements:

> There is afoot a satan-scheme,
> A lulling, lethal one world dream.
> A plot to steal our sovereignty,
> Reduce us to nonentity. (Evanson 1966, p. 5)

> The world is coming to a head
> when dread of holding hands

puts rubber bands in people's brains
and smoky rains in babies milk
and fuchsia silk in contour sheets. (Steinbridge 1966, p. 115)

Sometimes, existing traditional poetics were combined with novel elements. From the New Left:

Ring around the Pentagon, a pocket full of pot
Four and twenty generals all begin to rot.
All the evil spirits start to tumble out
Now the war is over, we all begin to shout. (Hoffman, 1968, p. 8)

As this example indicates, the New Left sometimes attempted a comic style of claims-making, here in conjunction with poetic style. Michael Rossman refers to a moment of humor in a Vietnam protest song, but transmutes it into a serious symbol of the New Left's essence:

'Well there ain't no time to wonder why Whoopee!" (sing Country Joe and the Fish, in "Vietnam Rag"), "we're all gonna die." What strikes me is the genuineness of that raucous cry's humor and cheer, so distinctively ours (1968, p. 102).

Vietnam jokes in riddles, cartoons, songs, and the like were probably not so common as the pervasive Gulf jokes and AIDS jokes of the 1980s and 1990s, but they did exist—although generally in less serious forums than political activism; as Ibarra and Kitsuse point out, "the esthetic imperative of making a good joke can come into conflict with the practical goal of building a constituency."

Settings, Audiences, and History

Claims-making rhetorics, counterrhetorics, motifs, and styles occur at particular moments in history, in particular settings, and are directed toward particular audiences as actual or potential "builders of constituency." The issue of history is not raised by Ibarra and Kitsuse, but, by implication, the rhetoric of claims making is built upon the intersection of language, cohort, and historical event. Although the claims-making rhetorics of the 1960s Radical Right and New Left are analyzable within Ibarra and Kitsuse's 1990s framework, the texts of the John Birch Society in an era of what the media frames as the death of communism might or might not have changed; all new and old social problems may remain subsumable within the central problematic of the communist conspiracy, even perhaps the illusion of its demise.

The settings of claims-making reflect the claims-makers' real or hoped-for audiences: The media takes the message to anyone who will listen, the legal-political setting transforms it into law and policy, and the academic setting churns it into scientific evidence. To what extent the claims of the Radical Right were *reported* in the 1960s in media such as newspapers, television, radio, and magazines I don't know. What is certain is that their claims-making activities were relayed directly to interested audiences through radio programs financed by wealthy rightists, and through the written media of pamphlets, books, magazines, and journals. New Leftists also wrote pamphlets, books, magazines, and articles, often in formats and forums that joined the activist with the academic. Their activities, especially those of the most theatrical style, were heavily reported in the news media.

The audiences for Radical Right rhetoric were both potential converts and the legal-political setting; as John Stormer commented:

> A program for victory over communism cannot be achieved until Americans elect a President and a Congress with the will to win. . . . . To accomplish this, conservative Americans must make their voices heard in the political parties. (1964, p. 32)

John Birch Society members were exhorted to form citizens' pressure groups such as MOTOREDE (the Move to Restore Decency, an anti–sex education group), write letters to legislators, organize activity within "communized" institutions such as high schools, provide speaker's bureaus, circulate petitions, finance and use Radical Right media, and recruit new members by such activities as taking "educational" literature to neighbors, high schools, and libraries (*John Birch Society Bulletin* March 1969, pp. 21–25).

The revolutionary rhetoric of the New Left virtually precluded working within the existing legal-political system; one student spokesman said that the New Left had "only a dissenting ideology. We unhesitatingly express what we are against, but are less sure of what we are for" (Jacobs and Landau 1966, p. 100). The audience for their rhetoric was mainly potential converts, who could be reached either through the theatrics captured by the media (victims of race or class oppression) or through academic settings (fellow university students). Since the New Left was ambivalent about academia at best, appealing to academia by such conventional channels as publishing journal articles or making speeches "would make our movement sterile" (Hoffman 1968, p. 6).

While the New Left had an academic audience in the sense that some academics, both older and younger, became actual converts, Radical

Rightists did not. Radical Rightists were the object of academic discourse—indeed, they still are—but academia is not a conversion site for the Radical Right. Both Radical Rightists and New Leftists have been the object of innumerable contemporary and historical, sociological and psychological explanations of their belief systems, from authoritarian personality (Radical Right) to antiparental rebellion (New Left) theorizing.

It is characteristic of the New Left, but not of the Radical Right, that true believers also engaged in academic analysis, and even debunking, of their own actions and motivations. James Miller (Miller and Gilmore 1989) writes historically of the times he lived through in the 1960s, while Richard Flacks (1967), Abbie Hoffman (1968), and others engaged in contemporaneous academic analysis of their own activism. James Kunen, during the occupation of a Columbia University building, considered psychofunctional explanations of his activism: "It's possible that I'm here to be cool or to meet people . . . . or to be arrested" (1968, p. 25).

What is most interesting about Radical Right and New Left claims-making of the 1960s was that the audience for their rhetorics was the transmuted "center" of politics, and not one another. The threat of communism seemed not to inhere in self-labeled communism, nor the threat of rightism in self-labeled rightism. The power of the state, coupled with the purported content of its policies, was the danger within the rhetoric of endangerment: Claims-making without power, however antithetical ideologically, was not dangerous:

> I don't consider George Wallace the enemy. Corporate liberalism, Robert Kennedy, Harvard University—that is where the real power lies. (Hoffman 1968, p. 65)

> I am not afraid of Red China or of Tito or of any other Communist leader in the world. I am afraid of what my President, my Senators, and the Supreme Court Justices are doing to my country and want to do to me and my country. (Evanson 1966, p. 2)

The Radical Right and the New Left of the 1960s not only used the same rhetorics, they had the same enemies. These enemies were designated by the same name, liberals, and were often the same people, such as Robert Kennedy. The New Left and Radical Right described their enemies, and in locating them, located their vision of the sources of power in the 1960s state:

> The original commitment in Vietnam was made by President Truman, a mainstream liberal. It was seconded by President Eisenhower, a moderate liberal. It was intensified by the late President Kennedy, a flaming liberal. . . . . They are all liberals. (Jacobs and Landau 1966, p. 85)

Clarence Manion, a Radical Right radio commentator, was being kinder in his use of the word *unwitting* than most Radical Rightists when he commented that "communism has now taken all but complete command of mankind" with the "unwitting help of our modern liberal leadership" (quoted in Epstein and Forster 1967, p. 19).

In their attention to the political center, and in their use of general cultural motifs to make their claims, New Leftists and Radical Rightists of the 1960s shared postmodern sociologists' perspective on the relationship between power and discourse. Their rhetorical strategies indicate an awareness that interpretive systems

> restrict and bias the ways that persons (including institutional officials who apply public policies and influence other persons' lives) commonly understand social circumstances in such a way that some individuals' and groups' concerns, interests, and experiences are routinely treated as legitimate and accurate, and those of others as illegitimate and inaccurate. (Miller and Holstein 1989, p. 6).

In their discussion of the "politics of representation," Mehan and Wills note that there is a cultural "hierarchy" of representations, in which "one mode of representing the word and its elements gains primacy over others" (1988, p. 364).

But power is more than interpretive rhetoric. Not all culturally tailored rhetorics are equal—in audiences or in consequences. Differential audience responses to Radical Right and New Left, in the 1960s or the 1980s, indicate that the use of commonly valued rhetorics, such as science, statistics, democracy, freedom, and religion, do not suffice to convince the audience of political arguments. Other factors, including the content of the message, the social origins and current political involvements of claims-makers, and the nature of the relationship between claims-makers and the media, are, in addition to rhetorical strategies, important components of the relationship between audiences and claims.

Historical hindsight can inform us that both Radical Right and New Left in the 1960s had large audiences, but few consequences in terms of the groups' political-economic goals. Radical Rightism of the 1960s had a large audience, a converted audience, and a directly policy-changing audience. A 1960s listing of Radical Right organizations had more than eighteen hundred entries (Janson and Eismann 1963, p. 126), while the John Birch Society alone had over one thousand chapters (Epstein and Forster 1967, p. 197)—and these according to academic rather than insider estimators. Although large in terms of membership estimates, and reaching large potential audiences through radio programs, the more extreme the Radical Right position, the more its audience was limited to the converted. But at the same time, its impact on the political-legal setting was often great at the local level, especially in relation to issues pertaining to youth and sexuality (in the banning or censorship of sex education, books, and visual media). John Birch Society and other rightists did write en masse to local legislators and policymakers—they certainly did when I lived in Southern California in the early 1970s—and their activism affected many lives quite directly.

New Left activism, by contrast, had a vast audience, a smaller converted audience, and an indirectly policy-changing audience. The membership of the SDS, the largest New Left organization, was probably less than half that of the John Birch Society (see Skolnick 1969, p. 89). But the activities and theater of the New Left were seized upon, and publicized to the entire nation, by the print and visual news media. Some members of the cohort of young people affected by the Vietnam War, already in the process of rejecting state policies, were brought into New Left politics at the intersection of Vietnam, Abbie Hoffman, and freshman sociology courses. While not necessarily affecting local politics in the grass roots sense of the Radical Right, the New Left infused the national political arena with some of its spirit; indeed, the era of the 1960s has, in the changed topias of the 1990s, become a legendary arcadia all its own.

Claims-Making and Sociological Rhetorics

The historical, empirical application of Ibarra and Kitsuse's rhetorical theory of social problems reveals an oddly transhistorical applicability of the model, an applicability that perhaps indicts as premature the official historians' designation of the 1960s as a historical epoch. In the case of the Radical Right, in particular, contemporary applicability should perhaps not be all that surprising; the central motif of the communist conspiracy, and its roots across space and time, is amenable to encompassing as unchanged what the center frames as vast historical changes. But the analysis of past rhetorics draws attention to the need for theoretical attentiveness to historical change in settings (for example, the expansion of rightist messages from radio to TV), and in motifs and claims-making rhetorics.

As Ibarra and Kitsuse note,

[D]iscursive practices through which the claims are constituted attune us to the richness of language and reasoning that participants are capable of tapping as a continually available resource. Our task as theorists is to note the differences in meaning and consequence that the strategic uses of vernacular forms can have for the shape of the social problems process.

This general point is also applicable to social problems theory, and to sociological theory itself. A semantically based theory implies the possibility of translation into foreign tongues.

Change in sociological theory can be accomplished by changes in rhetoric; this is exactly the device I used in writing this essay. My original analysis of the Radical Right and New Left rhetorics was written as an MA thesis (Warren 1970). The data presented here were then embedded in the linguistic present, since I wrote of 1968 in 1968. The privileged conceptual language of the sociologist was not that of social problems, but of the sociology of knowledge and the politics of ideology. I derived conceptions of topia and utopia, Armageddon and arcadia, from Mannheim (1959) and Merton (1962), and the contrast between belief and disbelief systems (rhetorics and counterrhetorics) from Rokeach (1967). I wrote about the use of poetry, the distancing functions of quotation marks, and the invocation of experts and scientism, but referred to these—following Berger and Luckmann (1967)—as legitimating devices rather than claims-making rhetorics, styles, and motifs.

A key concept in postmodernist, rhetorical analysis of social problems is that of "deprivileging" the sociological perspective. In the social pathology frame, the sociological perspective is self-consciously privileged; the sociologist, as analyst, locates the "truth" of societal decay and remedy. In the social constructionist frame, the "appreciative" sociological stance conceals an implicit privileging of the sociological perspective on members' meanings, generally a microfunctionalist one. In the rhetorical frame, both explicit and implicit privileging of sociological analysis are repudiated.

However, there are fundamental epistemological similarities between pathology, constructionism, and textuality in the implicit privileging of sociological perspectives through the use of the concept *social problems*. This conceptual framing of abortion, New Left and Radical Right, or environmental pollution privileges the sociological category itself over members' claims-making categories (who may not think of abortion, say, as a "social problem," but as a sin, or a medical procedure). Claims-makers in arenas of abortion, ecology, and the like, as Ibarra and Kitsuse point out, engage in rhetorical displays that are both semantically and symbolically ambiguous. But what they cannot be assumed to be doing is classifying "their" issue, whatever it is "about," as an instance of generic "social problem."

We, as postmodern sociologists, are attuned to historical change in the social world we write about. We are less attuned, perhaps, to historical continuities in the world we write with. A textual theory of social problems directs attention not only to the claims-making rhetorics of those who oppose or propose the state's involvement in abortion, but also to the claims-making rhetorics of those who propose, and revise, sociological theorizing. To frame analyses in postmodern conceptual discourse rather than modern or classical theorizing does not, as if by magic, change either its fundamental meaning, or the fact that its meaning is fundamentally sociological.

Acknowledgment

Thanks to the following people for comments on earlier versions and drafts of this paper: C. Dale Johnson, Joann S. DeLora, Orrin Seright, Bob Antonio, Joey Sprague, David Smith, Joane Nagel, Jim Holstein, and Gale Miller.

References

Allen, Gary. No date. *The Conspiracy.* Belmont, MA: American Opinion.
Antonio, Robert. 1972. "The Processual Dimension of Degradation Ceremonies: The Chicago Conspiracy Trial: Success or Failure?" *British Journal of Sociology* 23: 287–307.
Avorn, Jerry L. 1968. *Up Against the Ivy Wall.* New York: Atheneum.
Bell, Daniel. 1962. *The End of Ideology.* New York: Collier.
———. 1964. "The Dispossessed." Pp. 1–45 in *The Radical Right,* edited by Daniel Bell. New York: Doubleday.
Bell, Daniel and Irving Kristol (eds.). 1968. *Confrontation.* New York: Basic Books.
Berger, Peter and Thomas Luckmann. 1967. *The Social Construction of Reality.* New York: Doubleday.
Best, Joel. 1989. "Afterward." Pp. 243–54 in *Images of Issues,* edited by Joel Best. Hawthorne, NY: Aldine de Gruyter.
———. 1990. *Threatened Children: Rhetoric and Concern About Child-Victims.* Chicago: University of Chicago Press.
Bettelheim, Bruno. 1969. "The Hard Core." *Vital Speeches of the Day* 35: 405–10.
Brooks, Thomas R. 1969. "Metamorphosis in S.D.S.: The New Left is Showing Its Age." *The New York Times Magazine,* pp. 14–27.
Carpenter, John. 1964. *Extremism U.S.A.* Phoenix: Associated Professional Services.
Clifford, James and George F. Marcus (eds). 1986. *Writing Culture: The Poetics and Politics of Ethnography.* Berkeley: University of California Press.
The Councilor. 1968. Volume 6, no. 1, September 12, Shreveport, LA.
Dennison, George. 1969. "Talking with the Troops." *Liberation* 12(8):31–33.
Draper, Hal. 1965. *The New Student Revolt.* New York: Grove Press.
Epstein, Benjamin and Arnold Forster. 1967. *The Radical Right.* New York: Random House.
Evans, Medford. 1966. "Daring Young Man on the Lying T.V." *American Opinion* 9(0):1–10.

Evanson, Kathleen. 1966. "Are You Aware?" *Cross and the Flag* 27(5):5.

Feuer, Lewis. 1969. *The Conflict of Generations*. New York: Basic Books.

Flacks, Richard. 1967. "The Liberated Generation: An Exploration of the Roots of Student Protests," *Journal of Social Issues* 23(3)3:52–75.

Glaser, Barney G. and Anselm L. Strauss. 1967. *The Discovery of Grounded Theory: Strategies for Qualitative Research*. Chicago: Aldine.

Glazer, Nathan. 1967. "Student Politics in a Democratic Society." *American Scholar* 36:539–48.

Gumaer, David Emerson. No date. *Sabotage*. Belmont, MA: American Opinion.

Gusfield, Joseph. 1976. "The Literary Rhetoric of Science: Comedy and Pathos in Drinking Driver Research." *American Sociological Review* 4:16–34.

Hoffman, Abbie. 1968. *Revolution for the Hell of It*. New York: Dial.

Hofstadter, Richard. 1964. "The Pseudo-Conservative Revolt," Pp. 75–95 in *The Radical Right*, edited by Daniel Bell. New York: Doubleday.

———. 1969. *The Paranoid Style in American Politics and Other Essays*. New York: Knopf.

Jacobs, Paul and Saul Landau. 1966. *The New Radicals*. New York: Random House.

Janson, Donald and Bernard Eismann. 1963. *The Far Right*. New York: McGraw-Hill.

John Birch Society Bulletin. 1969. March, John Birch Society, Belmont, MA.

———. 1969. April, John Birch Society, Belmont, MA.

———. 1969. May, John Birch Society, Belmont, MA.

———. 1969. August, John Birch Society, Belmont, MA.

Kenniston, Kenneth. 1968. *Young Radicals: Notes on Committed Youth*. New York: Harcourt, Brace and World.

Kitsuse, John I. and Malcolm Spector. 1973. "Toward a Sociology of Social Problems." *Social Problems* 20:407–19.

Kornbluth, Jessie. 1968. *Notes from the New Underground*. New York: Viking Press.

Kunen, James S. 1968. *The Strawberry Statement*. New York: Random House.

Lampe, Keith. 1968. "Young Rebels Rap." *Liberation* 13(5):18–20.

———. 1969. "Kops vs. Kids." *Liberation* 13(8):31–33.

Lipset, S. M. 1964. "Three Decades of the Radical Right: Coughlanites, McCarthyites, and Birchers." Pp. 373–446 in *The Radical Right*, edited by Daniel Bell. New York: Doubleday.

———. 1963. *Political Man*. New York: Doubleday.

Lipset, S. M. and Phillip Altbach. 1966. "Student Politics and Higher Education in the United States." *Comparative Education Review* 10:320–49.

Lipset, S. M. and Sheldon S. Wolin (eds.). 1965. *The Berkeley Student Revolt*. New York: Doubleday.

"Little Rubin Red Breast." 1969. *Liberation* 13(9):10–17.

Lynd, Staughton. 1969. "The Movement: A New Beginning." *Liberation* 14(2):6–20.

Mannheim, Karl. 1936. *Ideology and Utopia*. New York: Harcourt Brace and World.

————. 1959. *Essays in the Sociology of Knowledge*. London: Routledge and Kegan Paul.

McBirnie, Dr. No date. *Newsletter*. No publication information.

Mehan, Hugh and John Wills. 1988. "MEND: A Nurturing Voice in the Nuclear Arms Debate." *Social Problems* 35:363–83.

Menashe, Louis and Ronald Radosh. 1967. *Teach-Ins: U.S.A.* New York: Praeger.

Merton, R. K. 1962. *Social Theory and Social Structure*. Glencoe, IL: Free Press.

Miller, Gale and James A. Holstein. 1989. "On the Sociology of Social Problems." *Perspectives on Social Problems* 1:1–16.

Miller, Michael and Susan Gilmore. 1965. *Revolution at Berkeley*. New York: Dell.

Montgomery, Robert H. 1966. "From the North." *American Opinion* 9(3):65–66.

Muste, A. J. 1969. "Escalate the Protest." *Liberation* 14(2):6–7, 45.

Noebel, David. 1966. *Rhythm, Riots and Revolution*. Tulsa, OK: Christian Crusade Publications.

Overstreet, Harry and Bonaro Overstreet. 1964. *The Strange Tactics of Extremism*. New York: Norton.

Rader, Dotson. 1969. *I Ain't Marchin' Anymore*. New York: McKay.

Redekop, J. H. 1968. *The American Far Right*. Grand Rapids, MI: Eeerdmans.

Richardson, Laurel. 1990. *Writing Stategies: Reaching Diverse Audiences*. Newbury Park, CA: Sage.

Rokeach, Milton. 1967. "The Nature and Meaning of Dogmatism." Pp. 158–69 in *Current Perspectives in Social Psychology*, edited by Edwin P. Hollander and Raymond G. Hunt. New York: Oxford University Press.

Rosenstone, Robert A. 1968. *Protest from the Right*. Beverly Hills: Glencoe Press.

Rossman, Michael. 1968. "Look Ma, No Hope." *Commonweal* 88(4):101–3.

Rousselot, John H. 1968. *1789*. Belmont, MA: American Opinion.

————. No date. *The Third Color*. Belmont, MA: American Opinion.

Schneider, Joseph. 1985. "Defining the Definitional Perspective on Social Problems." *Social Problems* 32:232–34.

Sherwin, Mark. 1963. *The Extremists*. New York: St. Martin's Press.

Skolnick, Jerome. 1969. *The Politics of Protest*. New York: Ballantine.

Stark, Werner. 1958. *The Sociology of Knowledge*. Glencoe, IL: Free Press.

Steinbridge, Jane. 1966. "An Untitled Poem from Paul Jacobs and Saul Landau." Pp. 115 in *The New Radical*. New York: Random House.

Stormer, John. 1964. *None Dare Call It Treason*. Florrisant, MI: Liberty Bell Press.

Theobald, Robert (ed.). 1967. *Dialogue on Youth*. New York: Bobbs- Merrill.

Toch, Hans. 1965. *The Social Psychology of Social Movements*. New York: Bobbs-Merrill.

"Tract for the Times." 1966. *Liberation* 10(6):8–11.

Warren, Carol Anne. 1970. *An Application of the Sociology of Knowledge to the Radical Right and the New Left*. Unpublished MA thesis, Department of Sociology, San Diego State College, San Diego, California.

Welch, Robert. 1961. *The Blue Book of the John Birch Society*. Boston: Western Islands.

————. 1969. *In Plain Language*. Belmont, MA: American Opinion.

_____. No date, a. *The Truth in Time.* Belmont, MA: American Opinion.
_____. No date, b. *Why People Become Communists.* Belmont, MA: American Opinion.
Westerfield, Rex. No date, a. *Assassination.* Belmont, MA: Review of the News.
_____. No date, b. *Sour Grapes.* Belmont, MA: American Opinion.
Westin, Alan. 1964. "The John Birch Society: 'Radical Right' and 'Extreme Left' in the Context of Post World War II." Pp. 239–68 in *The Radical Right,* edited by Daniel Bell. New York: Doubleday.

Constructionist Responses

4

For a Cautious Naturalism

Jaber F. Gubrium

My reactions to Peter Ibarra and John Kitsuse's important paper come from one who is sympathetic to the point of view, and who indeed has framed much research in terms of social constructionism. Of course, like other frameworks, there are brands of constructionism and, to that extent, I have highlighted certain topics in my work and proceeded in my own fashion. I have not focused on claims-making activities—publicity—oriented to the state or public agencies, an emphasis that has come to virtually typify constructionist writing in the area. Rather, my instinct has been to consider the cultures of small worlds like support groups, psychiatric units, rehabilitation clinics, counseling centers, and nursing homes as a way of addressing the interactive and discursive features of personal realities (Gubrium 1989, 1991). Still, the analytic thrust of the research aligns with the spirit of Ibarra and Kitsuse's [originally Malcolm Spector and Kitsuse's [1977] (1987)] departure from the conventional position on social problems, one based on the understanding that social problems are accomplishments.

Ibarra and Kitsuse's paper, which is the latest formulation of this significant turn in social problems theorizing, centers my concern. As the authors make abundantly clear, to think of social problems as accomplishments implies that the problems are not objective conditions but are bound to the rhetorical claims-making activities of those who clarify, redefine, or counter the status of putatively objectionable conditions in society. The question is: Is the accent to be on how rhetoric *practically accomplishes* social problems, which Ibarra and Kitsuse repeatedly stress, or on the view that related rhetoric *is* social problems, which the authors seem to presume? In the following comments, I argue by means of a deconstruction of the paper's vocabulary that a perhaps inadvertent accent on the latter eclipses what Ibarra and Kitsuse refer to as *vernacular* constituents of moral discourse. While Ibarra and Kitsuse allege an interactionist focus and write about members and vernacular, their paper is about publicity, conniving rhetoric, and practices that are neither "members'" nor very vernacular.

The Sense of Agency

The question pinpoints the authors' sense of agency. With some telling exceptions, which I will take up later, their vocabulary reveals a world of wily, claims-making rhetoricians.

The Audience

Claims-makers do what they do with a certain aim (for all, or all those within a targeted category, to hear) and with a particular end (to convince everyone of their message). The audience is the public or publics at large, not small worlds such as households or friendship groups, nor delimited domains such as institutions or formal organizations. Whether the goal is to define a putatively objectionable condition or "condition-category" as a social problem or to defend the condition against such a status, messages are conveyed broadly, the more exhaustive the audience the better.

While Ibarra and Kitsuse do not expressly mention Ludwig Wittgenstein, they evidently have him in mind when they refer to a rather different sense of public, one referencing the social or dialogical, not uniquely private, character of discourse. Referring to the process they are studying, the authors state that it is "a language game into which actions are translated as publicly (and variously) readable expressions." To Wittgenstein, language games are not necessarily broadly public in the sense that they are governed by rules oriented to the public at large. Rather, regardless of the particular domain of application, language games are rules of speech and meaning that operate behind participants' backs, which participants' speech tacitly references and whose objects their speech realizes as they actively engage the game. In Wittgenstein's sense, language games are public because they do not uniquely belong to any one participant.

Ibarra and Kitsuse, however, privilege the public at large. As the authors note, "our field is fundamentally concerned with understanding the constitutive ('world-making') and strategic dimensions of claimants' discursive practices in demarcating moral objects of 'relevance' to a 'public.'" This public is the audience that reads newspapers and news magazines, and listens to the broadcast media. It is a decidedly media public, one whose received texts are to be studiously analyzed by the social constructionist for their reality-constituting features and by-products and not the more limited "publics" of smaller worlds. In describing the concept of "protection" as a rhetorical idiom, for example, the authors refer to Operation Rescue as "the name chosen by the now *well-publicized* antiabortion organization" (my emphasis). Later, speaking of the "rhetoric of unreason," they exemplify what they refer to as a "wide range of claims-making activity" in the following way: "teenagers adopt the destructive habit of cigarette smoking because of the way advertisers 'glamorize' it in *targeted promotional campaigns*" (my emphasis). Soon thereafter, in discussing the rhetoric of calamity, the "public press" itself comes to the fore, as in "a claim expressed in this rhetorical idiom may lend itself to garnering high degrees of *serious and prolonged attention in the public press*" (my emphasis). Even while a promotional campaign may be "targeted," the campaign is aimed at that particular, teenage public *at large*.

Targeted or not, the audiences to whom Ibarra and Kitsuse refer, and whom many constructionists study through media analysis, are a socially nebulous lot. While they may be teenagers, we are not invited to get a glimpse of the everyday worlds within which such an audience receives the rhetoric of claims-makers. Because the audience is a public at large, we are hardly apprised of the who, where, when, or how of what this alleged public does with the rhetoric of its forthcoming, shifting, or fictional social problems. The audience seems to be, well, "just there," mostly larger than life, resembling the conceptually fictive public that Herbert Blumer (1969, pp. 195–208) once railed against as an artifact of public opinion research.

I do not mean to suggest that fictive publics are not real in that they do not concretely enter into everyday experience. The conformist culture of teenage life makes what the public or "others" think weigh heavily on comportment, just as the widespread recognition of Alzheimer's disease has made older persons circumspect about forgetfulness in a way they might not have been if the disease had not become such a public issue. Rather, Ibarra and Kitsuse's agent speaks to an audience that is mainly just there to receive, internally undistinguished.

To be fair, Ibarra and Kitsuse do respond to Gusfield's observation about the almost exclusively public affairs focus of constructionists. The authors "broaden the subject matter" of social problems by arguing "for a reconsideration of the kinds of activities worth attending to as claims-making, extending them beyond the 'legal-rational' and state-centered realms." Yet audience still remains nebulous, for what broadening means in the text following this statement is an expansion of the research agenda to include diverse claims-making *styles*, variously appropriate to particular issues or appealing to particular audiences, among them the scientific (or styleless) style of persuasion, the comic, civic, journalistic, legalistic, and subcultural styles. The realms to be considered are stylistic, not the realms of interaction ostensibly promised by the "interactionist-based" program said to comprise Spector and Kitsuse's ([1977] 1987) original statement of the constructionist approach. Accordingly, we are not as much to be apprised of how, say, scientists and their audiences articulate and respond to diverse rhetorical idioms in practice, as Bruno Latour and Steve Woolgar (1979) describe for laboratory life, but rather how scientists, like other claims-makers, communicate with publics at large to specify or discount the problematic character of select social issues. For example, the disinterested, sober scientific style might be analyzed as a usage to convince the public that, indeed, *the* data do *clearly* speak for themselves in order to show that the ozone layer is being depleted and that, moral considerations notwithstanding, on *objective* grounds alone, there is reason to be alarmed.

The Rhetorician

Ibarra and Kitsuse's vocabulary conveys an agent who not only makes claims to publics at large, but does so as a complete rhetorician. The so-called objectivist concern with the object of a social problem and the conditions that bring the problem about gives way to a "different subject matter for the sociology of social problems" (Spector and Kitsuse [1977] 1987, p. 39). Analytically center stage are those who are engaged in *"proposing or contesting* the designation of a category of putative behaviors, expressions, or processes as 'offensive,' about which something of a remedial nature should be done, i.e., 'claims-making and responding activities'" (Ibarra and Kitsuse, quoting Spector and Kitsuse, [1977] 1987, p. 76).

But we do not encounter the actual claims-makers, only their claims, and counterclaims of course. Ibarra and Kitsuse's analytic categories are not behavioral, interpersonal, or situational; they are rhetorical. The categories serve to catalog very public speech, not conduct. Indeed, the speech is passive in the sense that its data are textual. As the authors note regarding the strict constructionist, who "never leaves language," "Whether s/he is paraphrasing members' arguments or recording their deeds, s/he is always in the realm of the textual." For Ibarra and Kitsuse, textuality refers to concrete texts—primarily the related contents of the print and broadcast media. The rhetorician is not an active persuader, who stands next to, over and above, or beneath his or her audience.

To the extent public texts become publicity, they affirm the presence of the agent. When there is a great deal of publicity for or against a putatively objectionable condition, Ibarra and Kitsuse's social constructionist subject is being loudly, and it is hoped clearly, heard. When there is little publicity, the social problem under contention hardly exists. When there is no publicity, the agent is analytically nonexistent, even while there may be actual proponents or opponents of the objectionable quietly, but "silently," festering somewhere, perhaps in laboratories, in households, in community interest groups, in political organizations, among other not so public forums.

This raises an important methodological issue. If the existence of the agent is bound to publicity, then the social constructionist who cannot find related data in public texts must conclude that there is no social problem under construction. The concrete social relations that produce public texts are irrelevant, since the relations only gain their significance in respect to putatively objectionable conditions when publicity textualizes and broadcasts the reality of the conditions. Thus a social problem is constructively born, and only then. Events leading up to the decision to "go public" are given short shrift. Strictly speaking, the events are analytically silent, not gatherable as constructionist facts because they are not publicized. We cannot know how a public social problem affects the everyday lives of those who suffer its objectionable conditions until their lives are broadcast.

When publicity is the criterion for the birth of agency, the hard work of nonpublicly formulating putatively objectionable conditions into problems is lost. Fleeting as it might be, publicity must be about something and requires some form of evidence of the objectionable to be available to go public about, even while the "evidence" may be socially constructed and suffused with rhetoric in its own right. Except for public hoaxes, whose facts are otherwise real enough before they are revealed and accepted as hoaxes, a reality that can be convincingly conveyed as "observable" in circumstances of everyday life is required for there to be a social problem. Discerning reality by publicity, however, suggests problems are purely rhetorical on the large scale. Even Baudrillard's (1988) simulacra represent something and thus require the practical work of generating facsimiles (without reference to an actual source).

My own constructionist experience studying and analyzing the Alzheimer's disease movement has shown that the movement's publicity is linked to related, nonpublic neurophysiological, cognitive, and behavioral facts in a complex way (Gubrium 1986). Accompanying the movement's publicity, which began in 1979, was a new reading of neurophysiological and psychological facts in "senile" materials and data. There was, and now to a lesser degree continues to be, nonpublic controversy, mainly in academic journals, about whether the facts of senility are those of extended normal aging or disease. At this level, it is unclear whether or not there is a social problem in the related, putatively objectionable conditions. [But see Hernandez (1991) and Russo, Vitaliano, and Young (1991) for controversy even at the level of what is to be considered objectionable.]

Knowingly or unknowingly, the movement has chosen to categorically separate normal aging and disease and their related facts so that it is forcefully claimed that "Alzheimer's disease is *not* normal aging!" Interestingly, the movement's success in turning public, political, and financial attention to the objectionable "disease" (not normal) facts has been accompanied by a lessening of the debate in academic texts. The point is that the hard, nonpublic side of the movement worked up what was needed for purposes of publicity, making it possible for certain scientific facts to be selectively and publicly referenced as the concrete neurophysiological and behavioral grounds of a disease. In turn, the academic controversies surrounding the facts are hardly, if ever, publicized. (My study itself remains academic and even rather esoteric at that.) This relatively unpublic activity is an important part of what Gale Miller and James Holstein (1989) generally call "social problems work."

While I have no reason to believe that the suppression of factual neurophysiological and psychological material has occurred in the Alzheimer's disease movement in order to sustain the public purity of the disease as a category separate from normal aging, limiting constructive agency to publicity does keep sociologically hidden what is publicly hidden. A good deal of what Ibarra and Kitsuse's social constructionist takes to be real as far as social problems are concerned might be the result of the less public work of concertedly or inadvertently insulating ontologically controversial material. It could very well be in the interest of the rhetorician of the putatively objectionable not to go public about such matters, that is, the difficult epistemological issues surrounding the nature of the reality that ostensibly is objectionable and that the rhetorician aims to call or not call a social problem, as the case might be. Evidence of this might be sociologically available in relatively nonpublic texts if not in the otherwise "hidden" confines of organizations linked in various ways to the putatively objectionable.

Ibarra and Kitsuse's rhetorician also is calculating. The language here is quite telling. The rhetorician not only is in the business of persuading or influencing, as a dictionary definition informs us is his or her stock in trade, but does so with guile. A social problem resembles a public chess game, with moves, gambits, and countermoves. As the authors write,

> When viewed in general terms, the social problems process resembles a kind of game whose "moves" are perennially subject to interpretation and reinterpretation, whose aims are subject to dispute, whose players are ever shifting, whose settings are diverse, and whose nominal topics

stretch as far as the society's classification system can provide members with typifications of activities and processes.

Later, in describing "naturalizing" as a counterrhetorical move, they write that "the user of this *gambit* runs the risk of being labeled a 'cynic' or 'pessimist' (my emphasis).

Yet, it is a very strange chess game because the players constantly change and so do the aims. The imagery of the game regularly gives way to a sense of cabal with plots, intrigue, and schemes as the undergirding of publicity. Curiously, the very public text or publicity that is the admittedly limited area of the strict constructionist has a hidden agent, one that is not at all public in the sense of being evident in the media, whose texts are read by both the public at large and the constructionist. This wily hidden agent is read for us in the publicity by the strict constructionist, presenting the social movement to us as a "put on" or public drama of the objectionable. There is something not so textual that, by implication, animates the word, as if to inform us that the text really has no life of its own.

The Contrasting Tone of the Vernacular

This sense of the agent and the audience contrasts with the ontological tone of other terms—vernacular, mundane, member, and practical—telling exceptions to the foregoing vocabulary. It is not that these terms cannot refer to publicity and the rhetorician engaged in ordinary and practical activities, as agents might appear if conduct were analyzed as the everyday work of constructing social problems. However, the very public texts and wily rhetoricians inhabiting Ibarra and Kitsuse's social problems world do not appear to be featured in the vernacular, even while the term is assigned special significance because it appears in the title of their paper. It is said that moral discourse has "vernacular constituents," which I take to mean native and natural. As the authors point out, "Analysis consists of reconstructing the vernacular, not downgrading it or leaving it unexplicated."

The Mundane

In the context of this vocabulary, the mundanity of social problems activity is highlighted. Following Pollner's (1978, 1987) usage, Ibarra and Kitsuse urge us to feature the construction of social problems, not the conditions presumed to generate them, not acting as if the problems were categorically distinct from their production. We are to look upon those engaged in the construction of social problems as *orienting* to the

world, specifically, orienting to its more or less objectionable aspects as
real and separate from themselves. As Ibarra and Kitsuse explain, this is

> predicated upon what Pollner (1978) has called "mundane ontology,"
> which entails a strict demarcation between the objects in the world, in-
> cluding the moral objects studied by sociologists, and persons' "percep-
> tions," "beliefs," and "ideas" regarding those objects.

The orientational, not objective, quality of the demarcation is underscored as Ibarra and Kitsuse add, "What authorizes, idiomatically, the
social problems process is the mundane *claim* that objects and their
qualities have an existence independent of their apprehension" (my
emphasis).

But in what sense can the mundane appear on the surface of the
public texts and in the purview of the public at large, which are taken to
constitute the ordinary actors and interactions of social problems formation? Are they not mere words in media? Are they not bereft of the
practical activities—interpretation, definition, perception, ad hocing,
categorizing, concrete denotation—that constitute texts and publicity?
Where is the hard reality work that generates the publicity, belying the
"moves" and "gambits" that media audiences hear or read about?

Like the public that is a thing at large, not a feature of language, and
like the agent whose ordinary psychology is inferred from beneath
cabalistic texts, the mundane in Ibarra and Kitsuse's framework is something vividly extraordinary. The strange chess game that is the construction of social problems is the work of actors without a concrete world,
who, while the authors take the actors to be oriented to reality, are
presented to us as oriented purely to publicity, to what can be put over
on anyone suggestible enough to believe public claims.

But there is a vernacular world of the real even among the actors of
this strange chess game, which Ibarra and Kitsuse's concentration on
publicity does not open to view. The real is made up of potential-
realities-for-their-more-or-less-wily-agents, among these the "angles,"
"stories," "images," "presentations," "reports," and other scenarios that
are worked up to encapsulate what is intended for publics at large (see,
for example, Altheide 1976, Tuchman 1978). The hyphenation is meant
to underscore the intentionality of the real, where practice is part and
parcel of the objects of production. Practice of the mundane is totally lost
to inspection in exclusive attention to by-products such as publicity. As
Marx noted in his reference to commodity fetishism in the economic
analysis of products, we are not apprised of the social relations of production and how relations enter into the products of labor. We cannot
escape the real (and its conditions), even while the real may be claimed
to be images.

Members

Is the public, in general or in particular, simply a nebulous mass of receptive agents? This brings us to another term—member—which Ibarra and Kitsuse use extensively. For example, they write with regard to their perspective, "If then we change our perspective and assume the gaze of *members*, 'social problems' appears in a different light" (my emphasis). The world of social problems formation is peopled by members, which one would understand to include the public. Shortly thereafter, the authors further specify membership as practical in their view, stating that the constructionist's methodological stance "transforms members' practically based resources into researchable topics."

The term *member* is borrowed from ethnomethodology (Garfinkel 1967; Heritage 1984) and it is important to stress that, like the term *vernacular*, member implies member-of-something. In ethnomethodological usage, it highlights the contextuality of the actor's orientation to everyday life. As members, actors orient to objects, events, and information in terms of the concrete business at hand they have in the world, which is a way of calling attention to its mundane quality. It is sometimes said that these objects, events, and information are "indexical," their reality-for-the-actor indicative of his or her membership in a particular context of the real, with no irony intended. Contexts might otherwise be called the "language games" in which the actor participates.

Ibarra and Kitsuse's borrowing has special implications for the connotation of the public. If those who receive and respond to claims are members, which we would presume all actors to be in the authors' framework, there can be no practical public at large, select or otherwise. In practice, there are only mundane members of this or that circumstance to whom claims are made. In the vernacular, members are to be taken as native to their worlds, which, in turn, present natural objects and borders of life, as mundanely extraordinary as those natural objects and borders might sometimes be.

My studies of the Alzheimer's disease movement can shed concrete light on how membership mediates the public reception of disease claims (Gubrium 1986, 1991). The Alzheimer's Disease and Related Disorders Association (ADRDA) has mounted an extensive media campaign to tout and inform the public about the so-called disease of the century. Diverse images and detailed depictions of both the victim's and the caregiver's (the "second victim") experiences are publicized through a variety of mediums, from television programming to educational videotapes and chapter newsletters. I have been interested in how a particular public, namely, family members and significant others, responds to the publicity, especially how organizations and circumstances mediate the interpretation of public claims about the disease and its typical care experiences.

Support groups for caregivers and local chapters of the ADRDA were observed over a three-year period in two North American cities. Some groups were closely affiliated with the ADRDA through a local chapter; others were not. Although all groups to some extent made use of ADRDA educational materials and usually were aware of ADRDA publicity, member responses to ADRDA claims and information depended on a group's culture of disease experiences. A few groups were decidedly self-help entities and could be stridently antiprofessional, at such times claiming that only laypersons with hands-on caregiving experience could know "what it's like," not the professionals. On these occasions, members tended to look upon professionally sponsored ADRDA claims with skepticism, preferring to see what was or was not disease, or disease related, in their own terms. Other support groups' memberships readily accepted information provided in educational material and encountered in the media, identifying and organizing the interpretation of their personal experiences according to the patterns and schemes presented.

It was often claimed that the caregiver goes through distinct stages in responding to the mental demise of a loved one, usually a spouse or parent. While this was very public information, the claim took on its meaning in the context of its reception. In support groups whose members were positively disposed to the educational materials and ADRDA publicity, members tended to interpret their own and others' disease experiences according to received experiential chronologies. Their individual problems and caregiving histories accorded with the personal side of the social problem the disease was claimed to be. In groups emphasizing self-help, members were more likely to scoff at any received pattern for the disease experience, especially on occasions of decidedly antiprofessional sentiment (Gubrium 1987b). Individual experiences, it was locally claimed, were too complicated to be captured by formulas. Group differences suggested that membership was more than a matter of the mundane, constructing reality on membership's own terms, including what is or is not a problem of everyday life.

For a Cautious Naturalism

If we are to attend to the process of social construction, as rhetorical as it might be, and if we are at the same time to treat the process as mundane and undertaken by members, we must attend to interactional practice. Practice provides an analytic context that tolerates simultaneously both Ibarra and Kitsuse's vocabulary of agency and their contrasting overture to the vernacular (see Bourdieu 1977, ch. 2). On the one hand, the language of rhetoric, publicity, and publics at large tends to decontextualize and deconcretize the social construction process in order to highlight its idiomatic quality, emphasizing its concertedly public discourse. On the other hand, the language of mundanity and membership concretizes and contextualizes, stressing what might be called the ordinary life worlds of publicity—the production, management, and consumption of images, slogans, and scripts. The view to practice centers on an agent whose enduring project is to resolve the seeming contradiction, displacing the contradiction from being theoretical to being a problem of everyday life.

We can think of the agent as a practitioner of everyday life (Gubrium 1988). As agent, the practitioner is located somewhere and therein is engaged in a project of meaning attuned both to the local conditions of his or her activity and the overall products of the enterprise. The conditions can be thought of as the *embeddedness* of the social construction process (Gubrium 1988; Gubrium and Holstein 1990), stressing the formal and informal organizational parameters of meaning that impinge on the agent or, putting it in reverse order, that provide the agent with interpretive resources. The agent's constructive activity is embedded in a context of interpretation. For example, whether or not the putatively objectionable condition of Alzheimer's disease home care is construed as a problem depends on the caregiver's interpretive resources. A support group whose local culture provides a well-articulated reading of disease and caregiving embeds the caregiver in a different understanding of what is going on at home than a support group that defends participants from the dubious interpretive claims of professionals. There are, of course, other layers of embeddedness, from the mediating conditions of gender (Smith 1987) to the categorical diversities of history and society (Foucault 1973), that figure in the social construction process. Yet location and embeddedness do not determine the social construction process. The practitioner of everyday life is a "bricoleur" in Levi-Strauss's (1962) sense of the term, making use of the bits and pieces of available interpretive material and rules of understanding to attach meaning to experience, as Weber (1947, p. 88) puts it. It is in the presentation, not the process of attachment that Ibarra and Kitsuse's rhetorical framework comes to the fore, providing a rich and intriguing set of categories for analysis.

The ordinary, practical quality of constructive agency requires one to methodologically tolerate the tension between culture and nature, attending to the mundane resolutions of practitioners. While on the one hand Ibarra and Kitsuse seem to catapult squarely into persuasive culture to argue their brand of social constructionism, their accompanying attraction to the language of the ordinary, on the other hand, suggests that a cautious naturalism is indicated. To put it simply, features of everyday life are treatable as natural and native, even if they are constructed. Members' projects take the things for granted as real and immutable. Thus what is understood as nature fixes culture, until it seems natural to undo or reinvent what was, as Garfinkel (1967) might put it, unnatural "all along." To conflate the vocabularies of rhetoric and the mundane as Ibarra and Kitsuse do, without a clear appropriation to interpretive practice, commits the kind of error that Norman Denzin (1970) made years ago in tying wholesale symbolic interaction to ethnomethodology (Zimmerman and Wieder 1970).

References

Altheide, David L. 1976. *Creating Reality: How TV News Distorts Events*. Beverly Hills, CA: Sage.

Baudrillard, Jean. 1988. *Selected Writings*. Edited by Mark Poster. Stanford, CA: Stanford University Press.

Blumer, Herbert. 1969. "Public Opinion and Public Opinion Polling." Pp. 195–208 in *Symbolic Interactionism*, by Herbert Blumer. Englewood Cliffs, NJ: Prentice-Hall.

Bourdieu, Pierre. 1977. *Outline of a Theory of Practice*. Cambridge: Cambridge University Press.

Denzin, Norman K. 1970. "Symbolic Interactionism and Ethnomethodology." Pp. 261–84 in *Understanding Everyday Life*, edited by Jack D. Douglas. Chicago: Aldine.

Foucault, Michel. 1973. *The Order of Things: An Archaeology of the Human Sciences*. New York: Vintage.

Garfinkel, Harold. 1967. *Studies in Ethnomethodology*. Englewood Cliffs, NJ: Prentice-Hall.

Gubrium, Jaber F. 1986. *Oldtimers and Alzheimer's: The Descriptive Organization of Senility*. Greenwich, CT: JAI Press.

———. 1987a. "Organizational Embeddedness and Family Life." Pp. 23–41 in *Aging, Health and Family*, edited by Timothy Brubaker. Newbury Park, CA: Sage.

———. 1987b. "Structuring and Destructuring the Course of Illness: The Alzheimer's Disease Experience." *Sociology of Health and Illness* 3:1–24.

———. 1988. *Analyzing Field Reality*. Newbury Park, CA: Sage.

———. 1989. "Local Cultures and Service Policy." Pp. 94–112 in *The Politics of Field Research*, edited by Jaber F. Gubrium and David Silverman. London: Sage.

———. 1991. "Recognizing and Analyzing Local Culture." Pp. 131–41 in *Experiencing Fieldwork*, edited by William B. Shaffir and Robert A. Stebbins. Newbury Park, CA: Sage.

Gubrium, Jaber F. and James A. Holstein. 1990. *What Is Family?* Mountain View, CA: Mayfield.

Heritage, John. 1984. *Garfinkel and Ethnomethodology.* Cambridge: Polity Press.

Hernandez, Gema G. 1991. "Not So Benign Neglect: Researchers Ignore Ethnicity in Defining Family Caregiver Burden and Recommending Services." *Gerontologist* 31: 271–72.

Latour, Bruno and Steve Woolgar. 1979. *Laboratory Life: The Social Construction of Scientific Facts.* Beverly Hills, CA: Sage.

Levi-Strauss, Claude. 1962. *The Savage Mind.* London: Weidenfeld and Nicholson.

Miller, Gale and James A. Holstein. 1989. "On the Sociology of Social Problems." Pp. 1–16 in *Perspectives on Social Problems*, vol. 1, edited by James A. Holstein and Gale Miller. Greenwich, CT: JAI Press.

Pollner, Melvin. 1978. "Constitutive and Mundane Versions of Labeling Theory." *Human Studies* 1:269–88.

———. 1987. *Mundane Reason.* New York: Cambridge University Press.

Russo, Joan, Peter Vitaliano, and Heather Young. 1991. "Russo and Colleagues Reply." *Gerontologist* 31:272.

Smith, Dorothy. 1987. *The Everyday World as Problematic: A Feminist Sociology.* Boston: Northeastern University Press.

Spector, Malcolm and John I. Kitsuse. [1977] 1987. *Constructing Social Problems.* Hawthorne, NY: Aldine De Gruyter.

Tuchman, Gaye. 1978. *Making News: A Study in the Construction of Reality.* New York: Free Press.

Weber, Max. 1947. *Theory of Social and Economic Organization.* New York: Free Press.

Zimmerman, Don H. and D. Lawrence Wieder. 1970. "Ethnomethodology and the Problem of Order: Comment on Denzin." Pp. 285–98 in *Understanding Everyday Life*, edited by Jack D. Douglas. Chicago: Aldine.

5

"Members Only": Reading the Constructionist Text

Joseph W. Schneider

Can't we be practical? Don't we want to "get somewhere" and don't we
have ways to do it—like by writing as social constructionists (or ethnomethodologists, or structuralists, or functionalists, or whatever)? Aren't
we members too?

No, no. Members are the ones we study. We are the analysts; the experts; the scientists. Our project—our mandate—is to divide the world
into them and us, and then to study them and explain why and how they
do what they do. You've got to get that clear or you're in for serious
personal problems. *They* don't analyze what they do—they don't think
about it the way we do; they just do it. We analyze, sociologically, what
they do and tell them (and each other) why they behave that way. That's
our game (and "it *is* played").

But what about us? What about what we do?

You don't get it, do you? Our job is to analyze *social life*, not us.

Oh. Yeah.

Authors of theory texts might be encouraged to theorize their own projects, namely, to account for how they bring themselves as sociologists
into being, textually; for how they cast objects for explanation in their
texts as quite distinct from themselves; and for how they sew together
narratives as convincing explanations of an external social world beyond, yet only brought to life in, those texts (see Turner 1991). We might,
in short, ask ourselves to seek greater insight into "what it is . . . . [we
sociologists] seem to know and use" (Sacks quoted in Heritage 1984, p.
233; quoted in Ibarra and Kitsuse, in this volume).

But there is little sympathy in sociology for this self-reflexive textual
analysis, this project that appears to turn, some would say destructively,
inward on itself rather than outward, analytically, on the world it is our
mandate as scientists to study and explain. We are urged rather to "get
on with the work," to pursue science's conventional project of building
unified theories to explain "social life." Even in texts devoted to examining the practical and done nature of "social phenomena," there is often

silence on the question of whether those very texts and their production are of, rather than separate from and above, that phenomena.[1]

While questions about writing, reflexivity, worlds, and the subject have been at the center of lively debates in philosophy, feminism, and literary criticism for some time (see Derrida 1976; Rorty 1979, 1982, 1989; Lawson 1985; Henriques et al. 1984; Davies 1990; Clough 1989, 1992; Eagleton 1983; Culler 1983; Fish 1989), such questions have been asked only rarely by sociologists about their own texts (but see Woolgar and Pawluch 1985; Pollner 1987, 1991; Woolgar 1988a, 1988b; Atkinson 1990; Seidman and Wagner 1992). These critical questions encourage us to deconstruct and reinscribe our own forms and practices of writing toward deepening insight into the oppositions and productivity—the typically unnoticed and inevitable "play"—found there; the aim being less to find contradictions, which can be found, than to examine how these oppositions—presumably part of what we "know and use"—work.

In that spirit, we can read the constructionist paper by Ibarra and Kitsuse in this volume to see how it trades on certain dualisms that it and past constructionist work also help simultaneously to undermine. Rather than only "getting on with the work," perhaps we need close readings of these and other theory texts (cf. Woolgar and Pawluch 1985, p. 225) for what more we can learn about sociological work and its relation to other ways of knowing; to seek not greater "clarity" and "consolidation," but rather more provocation and openness.

I

In their paper, Ibarra and Kitsuse reiterate themes of the programmatic constructionist statement along with its aim to critique prior work in social problems sociology and propose a distinctly different way of writing social problems theory and doing social problems research (Spector and Kitsuse 1973, [1977] 1987). The central theoretical point of the early proposals was to see social problems as a *process* of "claims-making activities" (reflecting certain strands of symbolic interactionist sociology and ethnomethodology). The central methodological point was to illustrate the kinds of diverse activities the recording of which would constitute *data* for sound *empirical* research. Theory's work was to examine "the abstract features of the conventional presuppositions, interpretive practices, rhetorical devices, joint activities, and variety of forums involved in the discursive production of 'social problems'" (Ibarra and Kitsuse, in this volume).

Toward "resolving conceptual problems" and "clarifying issues" in the pursuit of a "theory of social problems," Ibarra and Kitsuse propose that we jettison talk of "putative conditions" in the definition of social problems in preference for a more explicitly language-oriented focus signaled by the term *condition categories*. This is offered in service of eliminating the contradiction Woolgar and Pawluch (1985) called "ontological gerrymandering," wherein analysts background and then use certain realities as resources in social problems explanations while they deploy other realities (sometimes "realities") as topics for study, as constructed and requiring explanation. Ibarra and Kitsuse argue that the term *putative conditions* in the original formulation has led us to place too much emphasis on conditions, producing yet more debates over conditions, their characteristics, and causes, deflecting attention from "the conventional features of the claims-making process that are available to participants qua participants for elaborating the social problems process."

Inserting the new term, social problems become "the activities of groups making assertions of grievances and claims with respect to some [condition-categories]" (see Spector and Kitsuse 1973, p. 415). Condition-categories, according to Ibarra and Kitsuse,

> are the terms used by members to propose what the social problem is "about." . . . . The initial analytic topic is thus how practical accounts of these vernacular terms are situated and elaborated upon in the making of moral objects. We intend "condition-categories," then, to highlight the symbol- and language-bound character of claims-making, as well as *how* members' facility with certain discursive strategies—including rhetorical and reasoning idioms—initiate and constitute the social problems process.

The shift is one that makes "the social problems process" a process of discourse, a theory of which focuses on "members' distinctive ways of perceiving, describing, evaluating, and acting upon *symbolically demarcated social realities*—what we have termed condition-categories." The social problems process is conceived, after Wittgenstein (1966, 1969), as a "language game."

II

This characterization bears a certain congeniality to the textual analysis in literary theory that is called "deconstruction" (see Culler 1983), apparently sharing with it an unwavering interest in textual practices of speaking and writing as the object of analysis. Indeed, Ibarra and Kitsuse remind us: "The strict constructionist never leaves language. Whether s/he is paraphrasing members' arguments or recording their deeds, s/he is always in the realm of the textual."

But it is no small question whether constructionists have been willing to see these "paraphrasings" and especially the "recordings" of which Ibarra and Kitsuse speak as close kin to the "readings" of deconstructive criticism. Even so-called "strict"[2] constructionist texts have not demonstrated a full appreciation of Ibarra and Kitsuse's observations about texts and language. Although sometimes seen as a quite radical, even extreme break with so-called "objective" sociological conventions in the study of social problems (see Best 1989; Spector and Kitsuse [1977] 1987, pp. 52ff., 87), constructionist texts have remained unwaveringly objectivist, most notably in their deep nostalgia for scientific realism as seen in the metaphysical figure of "the social problems process" and in the presentation and display of "data" to support "empirical analysis." Indeed, it is the elucidation of this symbolic interactionist "process" that warrants the entire project, that is the "condition-category" of the analyst. "Social problems theory" is a theory of, "about," this language game that Ibarra and Kitsuse take to be played "out there."

Moreover, our commitment to scientific realism and theory warrants our criticism of past sociological work for being "ad hoc" and "unsystematic"; "topical" and "normative." We point to theoretical confusions and empirical impossibilities found in the functionalist and value-conflict formulations, and to the self-interested stance of the scientific expert. We insist that social problems are not to be found in objective conditions, as those earlier texts suggest, but rather in definitions, in claims, in typifications. So while our constructionist texts have sought to distinguish social conditions from putative conditions and, now, from "condition-categories," and then have claimed not to study conditions as things, as objects, to read our texts as repudiating the objective requires one to suppress much to the contrary in those very texts.

Surely these texts have depicted the social problems process as residing not in our own analytic categories—not "in our language"—but, rather, quite independent of those categories, in the world. To "record," using Ibarra and Kitsuse's characterization of what we do, is "to set down in writing; furnish written evidence of"; and, most telling, "to deposit an authentic official copy of" (Webster's Ninth New Collegiate Dictionary 1984, p. 984.) This, at least in our texts, becomes a scientific realist ontology; epistemology frames the question and the issue becomes one of correspondence between the object cast as independent of our language, the signified, and the signifier, our sociological "recordings." Yet it is precisely this separation that the authors' text also denies, warning that through it we have been drawn to an examination of what claims are about "instead of the *conventional features of the claims-making process itself*" (Ibarra and Kitsuse). But are these "features" of "the claims-making process itself" not cast as of the same ontological status as the "conditions" members claim about? Are we constructionists not too caught up in our own mundane ontology, even as we deny, forget, or background it in order to examine others' worlds and, finally, write "about," make scientific claims "about," them (see Pollner 1987, pp. 108ff.)?

While Ibarra and Kitsuse, if asked, probably would say, "Of course, we too operate in the world," we have failed to take this seriously in our own texts. It is the tension generated in the constructionist formulation by the juxtaposition of the repudiation of "objective conditions" on the lips of members (including so-called "objectivist" sociologists), on the one hand—characterizing them as "putative"—and the givenness of the reality we constructionists examine—"the social problems process," "participants' descriptions . . . . as objects in the world"—on the other, that provides a rich opportunity for criticism that might help us see why we have had so much trouble getting, and keeping, the argument "right" (see Schneider 1984, 1985a; Woolgar and Pawluch 1985; Kitsuse and Schneider 1989).

If the strength of the perspective is to highlight what people seem to know and use "in discerning the objectionable amid their lives," one is struck from the first sentence of *Constructing Social Problems*—"There is no adequate definition of social problems within sociology, and there is not and never has been a sociology of social problems" (Spector and Kitsuse [1977] 1987, p. 1)—to the present text by how we, in championing this view, become the most immediate example of that which we propose to study; by how the text insists, even as we deny it, that we are members whose claims, whose texts may be, must be, studied too. However, we have steadfastly resisted such a reading for our own activities. This play in our own language, against the claims we make for it, is perhaps the most promising opportunity to consider our own mundane idiom, our own language game. In our repeated characterization of members, we point to ourselves; the more so by refusing to consider our own local reality as putative.

III

"Sociologists who study their own society are, of course, also members of it" (Spector and Kitsuse [1977] 1987, p. 63). While presented early on as an obvious—an "of course"—claim, fifteen years later Ibarra and Kitsuse still claim that "sustaining the distinction between the sociologist's perspective and the member's" is central to the constructionist discourse, "especially for translating the theoretical statement in *CSP* [*Constructing Social Problems*] to an empirical site," a task that is not to be

seen as practical—that is, mundane—or moral but rather as "theoretical" (Ibarra and Kitsuse). Sociologists are members too, but in our texts
they have been *other* sociologists, not we ourselves.

"Members," both texts tell us, include

> *anyone* engage[d] in *proposing or contesting* the designation of a category of
> putative behaviors, expressions or processes as "offensive," about which
> something of a remedial nature should be done, i.e., "claims-making and
> responding activities." (Spector and Kitsuse [1977] 1987, p. 76, quoted in
> Ibarra and Kitsuse)

Members "are engaged in efforts to alter or defend some aspect of social
life" (Ibarra and Kitsuse). And, of course, members operate within a
mundane idiom:

> For members, social problems do not typically refer to their own acts of
> definition and evaluation; they are not talked into being. Rather, "social
> problems" are what elicit their acts of judgment. Membership is thus
> predicated upon what Pollner (1978) has called "mundane ontology,"
> which entails a strict demarcation between the objects in the world, in-
> cluding the moral objects studied by sociologists, and persons' "percep-
> tions," "beliefs," and "ideas" regarding those objects.

For constructionists, as Ibarra and Kitsuse reiterate, our "objects" are
(other) members' mundane idioms and activities. We take the ontological status of these objects seriously, never speaking of them as putative.
The objects of these (other) members' characterizations, however, we
analysts call putative. For the analyst, "insofar as s/he transforms members' practically based resources into researchable topics—is engaged in
the theoretical reconstruction of the vernacular features of social problems as moral discourse" (Ibarra and Kitsuse).

But in the context of scientific realism, "putative"—to be "thought"—
is always cast as a figure of doubt. Against the really real, the thought is
merely thought; the distinction clearly hierarchical. Moreover, although
we offer "putative" as evidence of our own disinterested neutrality with
regard to (other) members' realities, it serves to background our own
claims as part of science and linked to the really real, while it foregrounds (other) members' claims as topic. Our own claims to the contrary, then, we constructionists shape the moral terrain of our texts to
show what reality is to be taken "seriously"; it is the analyst's.

While Ibarra and Kitsuse note the fluid nature of "social problems" as
both "a member's then a sociologist's concept," what they might also
note is that when it is a "sociologist's concept"—that is, when it is a
technical term—it certainly is simultaneously a vernacular term. But this

is not the authors' reading. Rather, "vernacular," and "idiomatic" all too easily are invoked by us in a partial way, to refer to texts by those who are not us; to that which is outside the constructionist sociological text. We do not take our own vernacular language regarding social problems and sociology as a fine case of the very social problems activity the theory specifies.

Perhaps the most easily accepted invitation to read our constructionist texts deconstructively is found in specific discussions about "sociologists" and "scientists." From *Constructing Social Problems*, we read:

> Just as subjects studied by sociologists seldom view themselves as they are viewed by researchers, it is not surprising that sociologists do not subject their own activities to detached observation and analysis. However, their statements . . . cannot be understood as a reflection of an empirical reality external to and independent of the statements made about them. (Spector and Kitsuse [1977] 1987, pp. 66–67)

And speaking about scientific work as an object for scrutiny, these authors write:

> The commonplace view that scientific inquiry may determine the causes of a phenomenon and provide for adjudicating the validity of competing causal statements ignores the fact that such statements are the *social constructions of social scientists*. As such, they must be treated as objects to be explained, and the form and content of those constructions must be taken as problematic (pp. 64–65).

And in a critique of value-conflict arguments, Spector and Kitsuse might be read as describing their/our own work:

> The logic of the value-conflict approach would insist that when persons, professions, or organizations, press for public recognition of their theory or explanation of some condition, they cease to analyze the social problem and become part of it. . . . Sociologists have sometimes been aware of this dilemma, but their response has been to shift to an inclusive [or, one might say "exclusive" (see Pollner 1987, pp. 117–20)] point of view that defines their own role, not as one category of member among many, but rather as scientists who are laboring on behalf of society, protecting society, trying to improve society, and providing expertise to determine the most effective policy. (See Merton and Nisbet 1971: Chapter 1.) They invariably fail to consider the sociologist as an interested party to social problems definitions—as empire builders, academic entrepreneurs, lobbyists, and expert consultants. In short, they fail to subject their own activities to the kind of political analysis they would apply to all other categories of participants in the definitional process. (p. 69)

One could hardly ask for a more unmistakable encouragement to deconstruct the very text from which these lines are taken. Yet, save Woolgar and Pawluch's (1985) critique, one certainly related to the member/analyst dualism, constructionist texts have kept this issue of radical self-reflexivity in the background (see Pollner 1987, pp. 117–20).

Given our embrace of "putative," irony predictably has been something of a problem for constructionists. We have criticized the irony in the functionalist writings of Merton and Nisbet as clear evidence of value-infused membership. Ibarra and Kitsuse write:

> The conventional perspective is ironic to the extent that it attempts to display members perceiving a social problem where "in fact" there is none, or not perceiving a social problem where "in fact" there is one, as in Merton's (1974) concepts of "manifest" and "latent" social problems. (cf. Pollner 1975, pp. 422–26)

While the constructionist text does effect an ironic pose, the authors tell us it is of a different sort, distinguished in terms of how the viewpoints see "the *warrant* members have for assuming the sensible character of their experiences and actions." The constructionist "examines *how* members produce determinations of warrant among themselves while flatly refusing any such privilege for him-/herself [as analyst]" (Ibarra and Kitsuse). But what is lacking from the authors' and from past constructionist texts is precisely such an examination of our own warrant for the specification of the critique of the conventional perspective and our own new proposals. One searches in vain for a refusal of this privilege.

Moreover, various constructionist texts, including the programmatic statement, offer precisely the kind of ironic claims about other sociological conceptions of social problems that they themselves impeach, viz., *there is no* social problem if there are not people making claims; *there is* a social problem if there are claims made, even if experts and politicians and other, nonsociologist members say there is no social problem; even, indeed, in the case of "a complete hoax" (Spector and Kitsuse [1977] 1987, p. 76).

We want readers to see our position as an interpretive but not a normative one, as evidenced by Ibarra and Kitsuse's reference to the conceptualization of the "object" of inquiry. The familiar distinction is between sociologists who view the "social [objective] condition" as constituting the social problem or the object of complaint based on "their recognition of a disjunction between a norm-based conception of 'society' and a state of affairs presumably antithetical to those norms and values," and the constructionist, who "observes/interprets members as perceiving [observing/interpreting?] subjects actively engaged in constructing social conditions (or 'putative conditions') as moral objects" (Ibarra and Kitsuse). While the constructionist text seeks to direct our attention to members as other than analysts, it simultaneously undermines this distinction by its very language: Both analysts and members are shown to be interpreters, observers, and, as such, the status of their interpretive accomplishments is inevitably and always already mixed rather than separated.

Today we might be expected to read these bits of constructionist text as not just "about" the "objectivists"; or the functionalists Merton and Nisbet; or friendly critics Gusfield (1984; Schneider 1984, pp. ix–xi) and Best (1989; Kitsuse and Schneider 1989), but about our own texts as well. In the very pursuit of the constructionist point of view we have indeed "contested" past categories of interpretation and actions found in standard sociological texts claiming to be about "social problems." We have said that such texts are misreadings of what social problems are really about, offering our own view of the "distinctive subject matter" of social problems sociology as the reading of choice (see Spector and Kitsuse [1977] 1987: Chapters 1, 2; Schneider 1984, 1985a, 1985b; Kitsuse and Schneider 1989). We have been very much interested in our practical project of criticism and reformulation within the arena of our daily and mundane lives as professional sociologists. And, we have for the most part not been deeply reflective about our own texts as practical projects (cf. Pollner 1978, cited in Ibarra and Kitsuse).

One thus can read central claims of the constructionist text as encouragement for the deconstruction of that very text:

> The definitional approach, then, pursued to its logical conclusion, requires that the sociologist, as a participant in the *politics* of defining social problems, be denied the special status of one who stands outside the process as objective observer or scientist." (Spector and Kitsuse [1977] 1987, p. 70; my emphasis)

And,

> [W]e must be willing to refrain from tacitly privileging the status of, say, scientists' versions of the condition in question and instead, treat those accounts, and the sensibility they express, as items in our explications of the social problems language game. (Ibarra and Kitsuse)

Such games, as Culler (1983, pp. 130–31) says Wittgenstein says, "are played," and the point becomes to describe the moves and the kinds of agents, selves, "I's" that such games create (see also Pollner 1987, p. 143). This certainly is part of "what people know and use," what we sociologists know and use. Without this self-reflexive move we allow and affirm the very privilege for ourselves that we say we deny.[3]

IV

Pursuing such reflexivity also can bring us back to the dilemma of the "about" that Ibarra and Kitsuse note. It would be helpful, they suggest, to again specify that we are not interested in the "about" that members take seriously in their claims-making activities. This "about" suggests that "words and things [conditions] are separable" and that the nature of our job is to find a correspondence between them (Ibarra and Kitsuse). Down this road of "about" waits the swamp of conditions, which is what the authors seek to extricate us from in offering the present, alternative view. Instead of this about, we should study "the *conventional features of the claims-making process itself*." But isn't this "about" the same kind of thing as "conditions"? To study a vernacular language game is to inquire "about" some thing, some object.

Literary scholar Culler (1983, pp. 187–89) notes, in discussing Derrida's comments, after Saussure, on signifier (sometimes called the "sign") and signified (sometimes called the "object"), that we can hardly do without the notion that these two are different; the key, he says—staying very much within language—is to see that they both are signifiers (signs) in our texts, to which we have conventionally assigned quite different tasks. We cannot do without that which talk, writing, is "about." Pollner (1987, pp. 110–11), drawing on Merleau-Ponty's (1964, p. xiii) notion of "retrospective illusion," addresses the same point, noting that we always create the "abouts" that we address, conveniently forgetting our own creative work. The ever-conventional move then is to sustain this forgetting into a hierarchy that warrants privileging one mundane ontology (for instance, the social constructionist's) over another.

One move that is thus precluded is to examine the "constructionist perspective" itself as writing and ourselves as writers, as members too. By resisting or not taking seriously the notion that theory is writing, following the path taken by most analytic philosophers (Culler 1983, pp. 89–91; Rorty 1979), we remain quite in the dark about how theory is accomplished as a mundane and intimately moral task. We are made ripe for this ignorance by the assumptions of scientific realism and the member/analyst dualism in which we have been so well (res)trained. By examining more closely how we write the world we study into being, we might be able then to consider how, in so doing, we bring ourselves, simultaneously, into being; and why writing has been so important, for example, to feminists as a way to have a voice, an identity (see Smith 1988; Clough 1989; Davies 1990; DeVault 1990; but see Scott 1991). As we begin to deconstruct the distinction, in writing and speaking, between what we cast as "out there"—the object—and from where such an object can be "mastered," explained (see Latour 1988)—namely, the "in here," the subject—we might begin to appreciate the intransigence of "the objective" as perhaps the central figure in social scientific work.

Our thorough schooling in realism and what Pollner (1987) calls the "mundane idiom"—the uncritical assumption of an objective world separate from us as knowers—prevents us from considering how to understand our own membership, our own personal and political investments, in those worlds:

> Thus mundane reason is not simply an idiom founded on the assumption of an objective world. Rather, it is an idiom which is composed of a network of interrelated, mutually defining terms for specifying both subject and object: it includes all of the terms whose meaning implicates and is implicated by an objective world. Thus the mundane idiom includes not only variants for the real world such as "reality," "out there," and the "object" but the variants of the subjectivity which is deemed to stand over and against (and within) the world such as the "subject," "person" or "knower." And the idiom also includes the modalities which mediate, deflect or separate the "subject" from the "object": "perception," "experience," "consciousness," "dreaming," and "memory" [and observation] are but a few terms from the immense and ever-growing mundane idiom of subjectivity (Pollner 1987, p. 128).

If we are in fact concerned with "figuring out 'what it is that people seem to know and use'" (Sacks quoted in Heritage 1984, p. 233, quoted in Ibarra and Kitsuse), a serious pursuit of this aim—while never delivering us from the mundane—might force us out of the silence about our own status as "members" that the worlds we write and speak into being provide for. It might nudge us to consider, more explicitly than we have thus far, just what the figure of the sociologist appears to be and how that figure is inscribed in and inscribes power/knowledge.

Acknowledgments

Earlier versions of these comments were read at the 1989 annual meetings of The Society for the Study of Social Problems, Berkeley, California, and the 1991 meetings of The Society for the Study of Symbolic Interaction, Cincinnati.

Thanks to the editors for their invitation to submit this paper and to Peter Ibarra and John Kitsuse for their text.

Notes

1. Despite Garfinkel's (1967) description of conventional sociological analysis as practical activity, there have been few ethnomethodological critiques of ethno-methodological texts as similarly practical projects (for helpful exegetical texts, see Heritage 1984; Livingston 1987). Recent welcome exceptions to this silence are found in work by Pollner (1987, 1991), Woolgar (1988a, 1988b), and Ashmore (1989), in which sociological and social scientific writing is taken as both topic of and resource for self-reflexive analysis. Pollner's most recent paper calls for a deeper appreciation of the radical reflexivity central to Garfinkel's (1967) early formulation of ethnomethodology.

2. This term emerged in Best's (1989) text in an attempt to distinguish his own position, which he called "contextual," from that of Kitsuse and Schneider, editors of the series in which his book appeared. Best's position, according to Kitsuse and Schneider (1989) was a return to the sociology of knowledge posture that Woolgar and Pawluch (1985) had read as "ontological gerrymandering."

3. Culler (1983, pp. 130–31) notes, after his reading of Derrida, that this kind of pragmatist position on such games, namely, that they "are played," easily becomes a normative one if it is not subjected to routine deconstruction. The notion that the "language game" is played becomes "it is there," independent of our textualizations of it, to be studied.

References

Ashmore, Malcolm. 1989. *The Reflexive Thesis: Wrighting Sociology of Scientific Knowledge.* Chicago: University of Chicago Press.

Atkinson, Paul. 1990. *The Ethnographic Imagination: Textual Constructions of Reality.* New York: Routledge.

Best, Joel. 1989. "Afterward: Extending the Constructionist Perspective. A Conclusion and an Introduction." Pp. 243–54 in *Images of Issues,* edited by Joel Best. Hawthorne, NY: Aldine de Gruyter.

Clough, Patricia Ticineto. 1989. "Letters from Pamela: Reading Howard S. Becker's *Writing(s) for Social Scientists.*" *Symbolic Interaction* 12:159–70.

———. 1990. *The End(s) of Ethnography: From Realism to Social Criticism.* Newbury Park, CA: Sage.

Culler, Jonathan. 1983. *On Deconstruction: Theory and Criticism after Structuralism.* London: Routledge.

Davies, Bronwyn. 1990. "The Problem of Desire." *Social Problems* 37: 501–16.

Derrida, Jacques. 1976. *Of Grammatology.* Baltimore, MD: Johns Hopkins University Press.

DeVault, Marjorie L. 1990. "Talking and Listening from Women's Standpoint: Feminist Strategies for Interviewing and Analysis." *Social Problems* 37:96–116.

Eagleton, Terry. 1983. *Literary Theory.* London: Blackwell.

Fish, Stanley. 1989. *Doing What Comes Naturally: Change, Rhetoric and the Practice of Theory in Literary and Legal Studies.* Durham, NC: Duke University Press.

Garfinkel, Harold. 1967. *Studies in Ethnomethodology.* Englewood Cliffs, NJ: Prentice-Hall.

Gusfield, Joseph R. 1984. "On the Side: Practical Action and Social Constructivism in Social Problems Theory." Pp. 31–51 in *Studies in the Sociology of Social Problems,* edited by Joseph W. Schneider and John I. Kitsuse. Norwood, NJ: Ablex.

Henriques, Julian, Wendy Hollway, Cathy Urwin, Couze Venn, and Valerie Walkerdine. 1984. *Changing the Subject. Psychology, Social Regulation and Subjectivity.* London: Methuen.

Heritage, John. 1984. *Garfinkel and Ethnomethodology.* Cambridge: Polity.

Kitsuse, John I. and Joseph W. Schneider. 1989. "Preface." Pp. xi–xiii in *Images of Issues: Typifying Contemporary Social Problems,* edited by Joel Best. Hawthorne, NY: Aldine de Gruyter.

Lawson, Hilary. 1985. *Reflexivity: The Post-Modern Predicament.* LaSalle, IL: Open Court.

Livingston, Eric. 1987. *Making Sense of Ethnomethodology.* London: Routledge.

Merleau-Ponty, Maurice. 1964. *Sense and Non-Sense.* Translated by Hubert L. Dreyfus and Patricia Allen Dreyfus. Evanston, IL: Northwestern University Press.

Merton, Robert K. 1974. "Introduction: The Sociology of Social Problems." *Contemporary Social Problems,* 4th ed. New York: Harcourt, Brace, and World.

Merton, Robert K. and Robert Nisbet (eds.). 1971. *Contemporary Social Problems.* New York: Harcourt.

Pollner, Melvin. 1975. "'The Very Coinage of Your Brain': The Anatomy of Reality Disjunctures." *Philosophy of the Social Sciences* 5: 411–30.

———. 1978. "Constitutive and Mundane Versions of Labeling Theory." *Human Sciences* 31:285–304.

———. 1987. *Mundane Reason: Reality in Everyday and Sociological Discourse.* Cambridge: Cambridge University Press.

———. 1991. "Left of Ethnomethodology: The Rise and Decline of Radical Reflexivity." *American Sociological Review* 56:370–80.

Rorty, Richard. 1979. *Philosophy and the Mirror of Nature.* Princeton, NJ: Princeton University Press.

———. 1982. *Consequences of Pragmatism.* Minneapolis, MN: University of Minnesota Press.

———. 1989. *Contingency, Irony, and Solidarity.* Cambridge: Cambridge University Press.

Schneider, Joseph W. 1984. "Introduction." Pp. vii–xx in *Studies in the Sociology of Social Problems,* edited by Joseph W. Schneider and John I. Kitsuse. Norwood, NJ: Ablex.

———. 1985a. "Defining the Definitional Perspective on Social Problems." *Social Problems* 32:232–34.

———. 1985b. "Social Problems Theory: The Constructionist View." *Annual Review of Sociology* 11:209–29.

Scott, Joan W. 1991. "The Evidence of Experience." *Critical Inquiry* 17:773–97.
Seidman, Steven and David G. Wagner (eds.). 1992. *Postmodernism and Social Theory*. Cambridge, MA: Blackwell.
Smith, Paul. 1988. *Discerning the Subject*. Minneapolis, MN: University of Minnesota Press.
Spector, Malcolm and John I. Kitsuse. 1973. "Social Problems: A Reformulation." *Social Problems* 20:145–59.
———. [1977] 1987. *Constructing Social Problems*. Hawthorne, NY: Aldine de Gruyter.
Turner, Stephen. 1991. "Social Constructionism and Social Theory." *Sociological Theory* 9:22–33.
Wittgenstein, Ludwig. 1966. *Lectures and Conversations on Aesthetics, Psychology and Religious Belief*. Oxford: Blackwell.
———. 1969. *On Certainty*. Oxford: Basil Blackwell.
Woolgar, Steve. 1988a. "Reflexivity is the Ethnographer of the Text." Pp. 14–34 in *Knowledge and Reflexivity: New Frontiers in the Sociology of Knowledge*, edited by Steve Woolgar. London: Sage.
———. 1988b. *Science. The Very Idea*. New York: Tavistock.
Woolgar, Steve and Dorothy Pawluch. 1985a. "Ontological Gerrymandering: The Anatomy of Social Problems Explanations." *Social Problems* 32:214–27.

6

Revised Social Constructionism: Traditional Social Science More Than a Postmodernist Analysis

Ronald J. Troyer

In the preface to the Japanese edition of *Constructing Social Problems* (*CSP*), Spector and Kitsuse wrote, "We hope to avoid the interminable conceptual analysis and re-analysis that has deflected the so-called labeling theory of deviance from the more important task of building an empirical literature" (1987, p. 13). In spite of this lofty goal, the debate and discussion of the social constructionist approach continues. Why? How do we make sense of this?

Part of the answer lies in the difficulty associated with researchers' inability to remain true to the radical tenets of the original formulation. Old issues and habits, especially the tendency to comment on the relevance and nature of social conditions, often creep back into constructionist studies, and the result is research inconsistent with the theoretical intent. As Ibarra and Kitsuse note in this volume, perhaps some of the statements in *CSP* have encouraged this confusion; they have written an essay that clarifies these issues and identifies a research agenda for social constructionists.

I think there is an additional reason for the continuing debate. *CSP* located social problems analysis in the middle of the discussions about the nature, purpose, and consequence of the social science project. When first enunciated in the 1970s, the ideas in *CSP* provided new ways of thinking about social problems and new avenues for research. It was a theoretically radical proposal for a new subject matter; it was on the "cutting edge" in the late 1970s and early 1980s. In the mid-1980s, several friendly critics pointed to some of the "shortcomings" in the constructionist formulation and social problem analyses. The specific questions raised were related to some other intellectual developments, such as postmodernism, which questioned the very possibility of social science theory, argued that producing "knowledge" was a rhetorical act, and suggested that accounts purporting to represent the social world were inherently ethnocentric.

117

I read Ibarra and Kitsuse's essay as an attempt to clear up some of the confusion in social constructionist analyses and an effort to save the social constructionist project in light of postmodernist criticisms. The clarification effort works much better than the effort to accommodate postmodernist arguments because Ibarra and Kitsuse invoke elements of the traditional social science project.

Let me explain this interpretation by offering *my reading* of the history of social constructionism, the challenges raised by recent theoretical developments, and the nature of the present project.

CSP and the Critique

While there had been some earlier attempts at formulating social problems theoretical statements (e.g., Blumer 1971; Mauss 1975), they did not propose a complete departure from the traditional analysis of objective conditions (see Troyer 1989). Spector and Kitsuse's argument that the social problems subject matter was the *claims-making activities* of individuals or groups about putative conditions ([1977] 1987, p. 75) proposed such a radical break. This statement represented a basic ethnomethodological shift in subject matter by arguing that all assumptions about the actual existence of conditions must be suspended or bracketed.

Labeled "social constructionism," this approach attracted a number of people and was dominant in the 1980s as evidenced by papers and discussions at the annual meetings of the Society for the Study of Social Problems (SSSP). Perhaps an indicator of its influence is that Schneider was asked to write an essay on the state of the approach for the *Annual Review of Sociology* in 1985. This represented an acknowledgment that social constructionism had arrived and was recognized as legitimate in the discipline.

The publication of the Woolgar and Pawluch (1985) critique represented a major turning point.[1] This paper showed how social constructionists practiced selective relativism. Basically, the charge was that social constructionists continued to make assumptions about the nature of social conditions. Indeed, some researchers explicitly commented about the existence of social conditions or evaluated the truthfulness of claims. Other social constructionists practiced "ontological gerrymandering," an analytical move whereby conditions were assumed to be constant.

Initially, social constructionists responded by asking, How can we fix our analyses so that they are consistent and get on with our empirical work? Sessions at the annual meetings of SSSP were organized to address this question. Indeed, in one context or another, many of the contributors and editors of this volume asked this question and have discussed possible solutions since the publication of the Woolgar and Pawluch critique. Perhaps this was not the best question to ask. My current reading of the critique is that Woolgar and Pawluch showed that social constructionism, as presented in *CSP*, is impossible without ontological gerrymandering. Even those analysts who avoid the trap of explicitly attempting to ascertain the ontological status of the condition necessarily assume that the condition is constant. Without this assumption, the analysis cannot proceed.

What does this mean for social constructionism? Can it be repaired and, if so, how? The answers depend on our vision of the social science enterprise.

The Postmodernist Challenge

In searching for answers to the kinds of questions Woolgar and Pawluch (1985) and Hazelrigg (1986) raised, attention turned to rhetoric. Best published an article in *Social Problems* (1987) that used rhetorical concepts and categories to analyze the construction of a social problem. In many ways, this kind of approach was consistent with social constructionist thought. Indeed, *CSP* noted the importance of rhetoric in the claims-making process.

This type of rhetorical analysis, that is, an analysis of the types and forms of rhetoric used by social problems claims-makers, seemed to borrow and draw upon schema developed by rhetoricians. It did not incorporate the type of rhetorical analysis advocated by those interested in the "rhetoric of inquiry." These people pressed for a reflective look at the rhetorical practices of social scientists. This rhetoric of inquiry examined "how scholars communicate," seeking to "increase self-reflection in every inquiry" (Nelson, Megill, and McCloskey 1987, p. ix). It was not just the rhetoric of the subjects that was to be analyzed, but just as important, the "logics in use" of the analyst, the author, the scientist also became the focus of attention. The avowed goal of this approach to rhetoric was to sensitize practitioners of the human sciences to greater "awareness of their practices and assumptions" (Nelson et al. 1987, p. ix).

This approach to rhetoric was closely related to other intellectual movements of the 1980s. There seems to be no one general term to describe these developments, but the names most often invoked are structuralism, poststructuralism, deconstructionism, and postmodernism. These movements largely originated outside sociology in literary criticism and philosophy, and sociologists have only recently begun to think and write about the implications for the discipline. The ideas are so important, however, that the Ibarra and Kitsuse essay should also be read in the context of these movements.

Since so much has been and is being written under these banners, it will be possible to only touch upon a few points associated with post-modernism that have implications for the Ibarra and Kitsuse essay. There is no single statement of or a single spokesperson for postmodernist theory. (For useful discussions, see Bauman 1988; Brown 1990; Denzin 1990b; Kellner 1988, 1990; Lash 1986, 1988; Lemert 1990, 1991; Seidman 1991.) Since there are many voices, each with its own interpretations, it is difficult to render a precise description of this intellectual thrust. Risking oversimplification, I will suggest there are several major themes in this literature.

Among the most important is the assertion that the grand narratives of the past (Marxism, Parsonsian theory) simply do not work in the postmodern world.[2] The search for foundations has failed because the traditional social science epistemology that there is a real world out there that can be known through positivist methods is incorrect. Seidman (1991), for example, has recently applied these ideas directly to sociology with his essay, "The End of Sociological Theory."

Since society and social order, as described by conventional sociologists, are fictions created through rhetorical accomplishment, the focus shifts to language as the "central consideration in all attempts to know, act, and live" (Lemert 1990, p. 234). In the postmodernist view, lived experience can never be fully captured in language because of its inadequacies, its indirect nature. They cite Derrida to support the idea that language as "pure, meaningful communication between subjects" is un-workable (Lemert 1990, p. 236). As Denzin put it, for Derrida, "Language, in both spoken and written forms, is a constant process of deferral, delay, and transformation, wherein nothing is 'anywhere ever simply present or absent. There are only everywhere differences and traces' (Derrida 1981, p. 27)" (1990a, p. 202). Or, as Lemert quoting Hayden White (1978, p. 4) put it, "A discourse moves 'to and fro' between received encodations of experience and the clutter of phenomena which refuses incorporation into conventionalized notions of 'reality,' 'truth,' or 'possibility.' Discourse, in a word, is quintessentially a *mediative* enterprise" (Lemert 1990, p. 241, emphasis in the original). According to Brown, viewing language this way means that

> Theoretical truth is not a fixed entity discovered according to a meta-theoretical blueprint of linearity or hierarchy, but is invented within an ongoing self-reflective community in which "theorist," "social scientist,"

"agent," and "critic" become relatively interchangeable. (1990, p. 189; see also Burke 1964; Rorty 1979)

Related to the above, a third theme in postmodernist writings is reflexivity. On one level, this refers to a constant attention to the social scientist's rhetorical moves in creating the narrative. It comes close to Pollner's (1991) description of "referential reflexivity," an awareness and analysis of the analyst's own constitutive practices. It means an analysis of the social scientists' representational acts, as well as and along with an account of the subjects' practices.

Reflexivity also refers to the recognition that a "fixed and final account" (Lawson 1985, p. 7) is never possible because claims are based on language, which cannot transparently represent the world. This means that no statement can stand unchallenged. All claims or statements (including the one that "no statement can stand unchallenged") are reflexively paradoxical. Statements make assertions about reality but, in principle, there can be no certainty. This, in effect, is a denial of knowledge, a challenge to the idea that the analyst can provide closure. This does not mean closure is not to be attempted. Instead, such closure must be seen as a "tool, ... a locality from which to operate" (Lawson 1985, p. 128). The analyst understands that the tool being used is not, and never can be, a true representation of the social world. Therefore, the goal must be an endless deconstruction of these tools (Culler 1983).

From the postmodernist view, the nature of the sociological enterprise is changed. Whether it is Woolgar (1988) and his colleagues examining what happens in the laboratories of natural scientists or Atkinson (1990) looking at the conduct of ethnographies, the analysis focuses on how rhetorical strategies help create "knowledge." Social scientists (and natural scientists) are not just describing a world that exists, they are "creating it" with their rhetorical practices.

Reading Ibarra and Kitsuse

The point of the above discussion is that it spells out the interpretive framework for my reading of the Ibarra and Kitsuse essay.[3] I see the Ibarra and Kitsuse paper as an attempt to respond to criticisms of the original formulation and initial empirical studies, to provide a new agenda for social constructionist researchers, and to move to incorporate some of the ideas associated with postmodernism. They are successful with the first two, but their reformulation does not completely fit with a postmodern analysis.

The initial portion of their essay is devoted to a defense and clarification of the original statement. Here they are at their best. They respond to Woolgar and Pawluch's ontological gerrymandering criticism by suggesting that researchers have not been faithful to the original intent. Acknowledging some shortcomings in the initial statement, they restate the key ideas but *place the emphasis on language*. For example, in discussing the original intent of *CSP*, they add a new word:

> Theoretical work would be concerned with elucidating the abstract features of the conventional presuppositions, interpretive practices, rhetorical devices, joint activities, and variety of forums involved in the *discursive* production of "social problems." (emphasis added)

The delineation of interpretive practices, rhetorical devices, and discourse clearly shifts the focus to language. Indeed, this emphasis on language is found throughout the essay. The word *vernacular* is employed with reference to members' use of the term *social problem*, and they argue that "analysis consists of reconstructing the vernacular." They also comment that members provide the "linguistic productions" and describe social problems as "idiomatic productions." Further, they refer to the "social problems language game" and say that the "strict constructionist never leaves language." Indeed, the goal for social problems researchers is "the project of developing a theory of *social problems discourse*" (emphasis in the original). In a similar vein they propose the term *condition-categories* as a replacement for *putative condition* because they believe this will place more emphasis on language.

In other words, Ibarra and Kitsuse agree that selective relativism has been practiced by social constructionists. However, they do not believe that this has to be an inherent feature of constructionist analysis. They argue that the ontological gerrymandering problem can be solved by focusing on language, the rhetoric used by social problems claimsmakers. Ibarra and Kitsuse suggest this will counter social constructionists' tendency to fall back into the trap of commenting or making assumptions about social conditions.

Indeed, this emphasis on language directly counters a recent effort to explicitly move social constructionism back to an analysis of conditions. Best (1989) has proposed that a distinction be made between "contextual constructionism" and "strict constructionism." In the former, it is assumed that the sociologist knows something about the ontological status of conditions, knowledge that entitles him/her to evaluate the claims. Ibarra and Kitsuse suggest that use of the word *putative* in *CSP* may be partially responsible for this misreading of the original intent. The substitution of the term *condition category* helps clarify that any analysis of social conditions or evaluation of claims is inconsistent with their vision of the constructionist project.

This focus on social problems discourse is seen as the way to develop a general theory of the social problems process. Social constructionist work has been characterized by a series of case studies organized around what the claims are about (e.g., smoking, missing children). By focusing on types of discourse common to several condition-categories, the problems associated with case studies can be eliminated.

The last part of the Ibarra and Kitsuse essay also provides a useful procedural guide for social constructionist research. The identification and discussion of four "rhetorical dimensions" specifies an organizing framework for the analysis of the "social problems language game." These rhetorical dimensions provide guidance in trying to create order out of and in understanding claims and counterclaims across condition categories. The invitation is that these ideal types should be "refined, reformulated, and elaborated upon through empirical observation and further theoretical reflection." This discussion clearly identifies a research agenda.

The point is that, if examined from the standpoint of traditional social science, the Ibarra and Kitsuse paper succeeds. It clarifies original intent and statements, offers an interesting reformulation designed to avoid analytical problems, and provides a way to proceed. The essay, however, is less successful when "read" in terms of some of the critiques and ideas associated with postmodernism. Let me explain.

One of the major criticisms offered by postmodernists is that social scientists have spent a great deal of wasted energy developing theories that don't work. This effort to identify foundations and the essential social processes is seen as doomed to failure. For the postmodernist, social order is the product of human action. From such a postmodernist view, Ibarra and Kitsuse are to be criticized for pursuing the traditional social science goal of discovering the foundation. Ibarra and Kitsuse seem to suggest that there is a teleological force, the "social problems process," that exists out there waiting to be discovered. To be more precise, they argue that the social constructionist project is "developing a theory of *social problems discourse*" (emphasis in the original).

Postmodernists will find this goal troublesome. Ibarra and Kitsuse are not unaware of the criticism of traditional social science theory. Indeed, they say that although they advocate the development of a theory of the social problems process, they do not see this process as "*invariant*" (emphasis added). Instead, "its features are conceived to be *conventional*" (emphasis in the original). Thus, since the development of social problems is "up for grabs," Ibarra and Kitsuse suggest that the social problems process is not reified.

This formulation probably does not get around the postmodernist critique. First, the existence of a "social problems process," something out there, is hypothesized. Second, describing its features as "conventional" seems to say that these are identified through agreement (*Webster's Ninth New Collegiate Dictionary* 1986) among researchers. This places the analyst in the discovery role, that is, identifying the conventional features of the social problems process. From the postmodernist perspective, the talk would be more in terms of the analysts *constructing* the theory of the social problems process.

Postmodernists also will not be satisfied with the Ibarra and Kitsuse approach to language. It appears that they approach language from a symbolic interactionist perspective. Indeed, the subtitle of their essay is "An Interactionist Proposal for the Study of Social Problems." The symbolic interactionist view of language appears to be that spoken words are the true representation of what a person means, thinks, and experiences (Denzin 1990a, p. 202). As I read Ibarra and Kitsuse, they seem to work from this assumption. The discussion of the social problems rhetoric used seems to assume members are fully conscious that their claims-making language draws upon and carefully manipulates an existing "cluster of images." Indeed, Ibarra and Kitsuse note that "we should marvel at the artfulness with which claimants continuously innovate new meanings, associations, and implications." This attribution of creativity to social actors is commendable, but the assumption seems to be that claims-makers are able to say precisely what they mean and think.

For the postmodernist, these kinds of statements suggest a greater correspondence between meaning and intention than language permits. Derrida raised questions about the idea of language as "pure, meaningful communication between subjects" (Lemert 1990, p. 236). Language does not permit precise communication between author and audience. This means that speech cannot be read as a direct mirror to thought, intentionality, or presence. The "speaker is never fully present to himself or herself because his language never permits him to state with finality or clarity what he means" (Denzin 1990a, p. 202).

What does this mean for Ibarra and Kitsuse's formulation? It calls into question the idea that members mean or intend to precisely invoke the images Ibarra and Kitsuse's social problems analyst detects. It means members' rhetoric becomes more problematic and that analysts' recording acts are simultaneously transformative processes (see Scott 1991). Social problems researchers are not just collecting data (rhetoric), which represent a trace of intended meaning but, because of the nature of language, are transforming the meaning. In other words, collecting data and writing are not neutral actions. They represent the analyst's constitutive efforts (Pollner 1991).

This leads to another sense in which postmodernists will not find Ibarra and Kitsuse's efforts completely satisfactory. As noted above, postmodernists call for social scientists to be more reflexive. This is one of the points Schneider (in this volume) makes. In brief, Schneider notes that while Ibarra and Kitsuse call attention to the interpretive behaviors of members, they privilege the social problems analyst. Schneider and the postmodernists call for the analyst to be aware of and to note in the text one's role in shaping and interpreting the data. In other words, Schneider asks us to deconstruct the image of the unbiased, disinterested analyst producing a text that just relates the facts.[4]

Privileging the analyst is, of course, a key move in the traditional social science project. Sociologists, in this traditional view, have been trained to see things as they "really are." Indeed, the goal of conventional social science is to discover foundations of social life. In this sense, Ibarra and Kitsuse are conventional social scientists.

Perhaps the best illustration of what happens in this traditional social science project is provided in the last half of the Ibarra and Kitsuse essay. Here we have an extensive identification of rhetorical idioms, counter-rhetorics, motifs, and claims-making stylistics. Ibarra and Kitsuse claim that these provide the tools for the analyst to begin work. Another way to view these categories is that they will lead the analyst to bring preconceived notions to the research. The focus of analysis and research becomes whether or not particular cases or rhetorical activities *fit the categories*. The *categories* become the major concern. In other words, while Ibarra and Kitsuse note that constructionist researchers have often been sidetracked into an assessment of the ontological status of claims, their proposal may lead to a preoccupation with their analytic constructions (categories).

Conclusion

The initial formulation in *CSP* was radical in the context of the 1970s. Since then, attention has been directed to the partial or incomplete nature of the social constructionist project. Ibarra and Kitsuse address many of these challenges, clarify many of the issues, and reformulate the research task. This should lead to more fruitful work in terms of traditional social science. In that sense, many will find the essay attractive. Indeed, the discussion in the last half of the essay is seductive. It is easy to think of research projects to investigate specific aspects of the rhetorical dimensions Ibarra and Kitsuse identify. They nicely illustrate some of the potential with brief discussions, such as the one on "political correctness." In other words, Ibarra and Kitsuse have been successful in providing a way for normal science to proceed.

In my reading, they less satisfactorily meet some of the criticisms raised by postmodernism. Is that a "fair" basis for criticism? Whether fair or not, it is intended as a friendly criticism. Indeed, it appears that many of the ideas associated with postmodernism can be found in the original formulation of *CSP*. The postmodernist position on reflexivity seems to be a further development of comments Spector and Kitsuse originally raised. (See Spector and Kitsuse [1977] 1987, pp. 63–72.) Similarly the attention to language was clearly present in *CSP*, especially in the examples and explanatory discussions. *CSP* can still be seen as a path-breaking statement anticipating or even providing the ground for many of the points raised by postmodernists.

Ibarra and Kitsuse have come a long way, but I would like to see them go further. How might social constructionism become more of a postmodern project? The most important step might be to reconceive the nature of social problems theory. If this was done, greater attention to the playfulness of language and issues of reflexivity would follow. To illustrate, what would happen if "theory" were seen as an argument made by analysts rather than something that was "discovered'? This would have radical implications; a new set of interpretive issues would be relevant. Writing theory would be seen as "the unexamined way in which we mask and inscribe our desire to shape history" (Richardson 1991, p. 174). For example, how does the analyst's gender, race, and sexual orientation interact with the process of construction of a theory of the social problems process? What are the intellectual, social, moral, and political consequences of this theoretical construction? Adding these questions or considerations would not displace traditional social constructionist analysis, but it might make it more interesting.

Acknowledgments

The author expresses his appreciation to Joseph W. Schneider and the editors of this volume for thoughtful responses to earlier drafts.

Notes

1. Besides Woolgar and Pawluch, Hazelrigg (1986) and Pfohl (1985) also provided provocative criticisms.
2. Richard Rorty (1979) has provided probably the most often cited critique.

3. The above reading may not be what others intended. I make no claims for offering a "true representation." It is my production.

4. Pollner (1991) notes that ethnomethodology had elements of this "referential reflexivity" in early studies, but it seems to have greatly diminished in recent writings.

References

Atkinson, Paul. 1990. *The Ethnographic Imagination: Textual Constructions of Reality.* London: Routledge.

Bauman, Zygmunt. 1988. "Is There is Postmodern Sociology?" *Theory, Culture & Society* 5:217–38.

Best, Joel. 1987. "Rhetoric in Claims-Making: Constructing the Missing Children Problem." *Social Problems* 34:101–21.

———. 1989. "Afterword: Extending the Constructionist Perspective. A Conclusion and an Introduction." Pp. 243–54 in *Images of Issues: Typifying Contemporary Social Problems,* edited by Joel Best. Hawthorne, NY: Aldine de Gruyter.

Blumer, Herbert. 1971. "Social Problems as Collective Behavior." *Social Problems* 18:298–306.

Brown, Richard H. 1990. "Rhetoric, Textuality, and the Postmodern Turn in Sociological Theory." *Sociological Theory* 8:188–97.

Burke, Kenneth. 1964. *Perspectives in Incongruity.* Bloomington: Indiana University Press.

Culler, Jonathan. 1983. *On Deconstruction: Theory and Criticism after Structuralism.* London: Routledge.

Denzin, Norman K. 1990a. "Harold and Agnes: A Feminist Narrative Undoing." *Sociological Theory* 8:198–216.

———. 1990b. "The Spaces of Postmodernism: Reading Plumer on Blumer." *Symbolic Interaction* 13:145–54.

Derrida, Jacques. 1981. *Positions.* Chicago: University of Chicago Press.

Hazelrigg, Lawrence E. 1986. "Is There a Choice Between 'Constructionism' and 'Objectivism'?" *Social Problems* 33:S1–S13.

Kellner, Douglas. 1988. "Postmodernism as Social Theory: Some Challenges and Problems." *Theory, Culture & Society* 5:239–69.

———. 1990. "The Postmodern Turn: Positions, Problems, and Prospects." Pp. 255–86 in *Frontiers of Social Theory: The New Syntheses,* edited by G. Ritzer. New York: Columbia University Press.

Lash, Scott. 1986. "Postmodernity and Desire." *Theory & Society* 14:1–33.

———. 1988. "Discourse of Figure? Postmodernism as a Regime of Signification." *Theory, Culture & Society* 5:311–36.

Lawson, Hilary. 1985. *Reflexivity: The Post-Modern Predicament.* LaSalle, IL: Open Court.

Lemert, Charles C. 1990. "The Uses of French Structuralisms in Sociology." Pp. 230–54 in *Frontiers of Social Theory: The New Syntheses*, edited by G. Ritzer. New York: Columbia University Press.

_____. 1991. "The End of Ideology, Really." *Sociological Theory* 9:164–72.

Mauss, Armand. 1975. *Social Problems and Social Movements*. Philadelphia: Lippincott.

Nelson, John S., Allen Megill, and Donald N. McCloskey (eds.). 1987. *The Rhetoric of the Human Sciences*. Madison: University of Wisconsin Press.

Pfohl, Stephen. 1985. "Toward a Sociological Deconstruction of Social Problems." *Social Problems* 32:228–332.

Pollner, Melvin. 1991. "Left of Ethnomethodology: The Rise and Decline of Radical Reflexivity." *American Sociological Review* 56:370–80.

Richardson, Laurel. 1991. "Postmodern Social Theory: Representational Practices." *Sociological Theory* 9:173–79.

Rorty, Richard 1979. *Philosophy and the Mirror of Nature*. Princeton, NJ: Princeton University Press.

Schneider, Joseph W. 1985. "Social Problems Theory. The Constructionist View." *Annual Review of Sociology* 11:209–29.

Scott, Joan W. 1991. "The Evidence of Experience." *Critical Inquiry* 17:773–97.

Seidman, Steven. 1991. "The End of Sociological Theory: The Postmodern Hope." *Sociological Theory* 9:131–46.

Spector, Malcolm and John I. Kitsuse. [1977] 1987. *Constructing Social Problems*. Hawthorne, NY: Aldine De Gruyter.

_____. 1987. "Preface to the Japanese Edition: Constructing Social Problems." *SSSP Newsletter* 18:13–15.

Troyer, Ronald J. 1989. "Are Social Problems and Social Movements the Same Thing?" Pp. 41–58 in *Perspectives in Social Problems*, vol. 1 edited by James A. Holstein and Gale Miller. Greenwich, CT: JAI Press.

Webster's Ninth New Collegiate Dictionary. 1986. Springfield, MA: Mirriam-Webster.

Woolgar, Steve (ed.). 1988. *Knowledge and Reflexivity: New Frontiers in the Sociology of Knowledge*. London and Newbury Park, CA.: Sage.

Woolgar, Steve and Dorothy Pawluch. 1985. "Ontological Gerrymandering: The Anatomy of Social Problems Explanations." *Social Problems* 32:214–27.

7

But Seriously Folks: The Limitations of the Strict Constructionist Interpretation of Social Problems

Joel Best

Ibarra and Kitsuse's chapter in this volume, "Vernacular Constituents of Moral Discourse," is the most recent contribution in the distinguished career of John I. Kitsuse. For thirty years, Kitsuse's writings have influenced developments, first in the sociology of deviance, and later in studies of the social construction of social problems. In particular, three of his works became touchstones for labeling theorists and constructionists: "Societal Reaction to Deviant Behavior" (Kitsuse 1962), "A Note on the Use of Official Statistics" (Kitsuse and Cicourel 1963), and *Constructing Social Problems* (Spector and Kitsuse [1977] 1987). Citing these pieces has been almost obligatory, a convention that obscures the different ways Kitsuse's writings can be read.

Much of Kitsuse's work is subject to both strong and weak interpretations. A strong reading is radically phenomenological; it calls into question all commonsensical assumptions about deviant labels, official statistics, social problems, and the like. Kitsuse favors a strong reading; he has consistently criticized both labeling theorists and constructionists for presuming to know the objective reality of deviance or social problems (Kitsuse and Spector 1975; Spector and Kitsuse 1987; Kitsuse and Schneider 1989).

The irony is that many of those being criticized have been influenced by Kitsuse's writings. This is because weak readings of Kitsuse's work far outnumber strong readings; his considerable influence is due to interpretations of his work that Kitsuse himself rejects. Take "A Note on the Use of Official Statistics." There can be little doubt that most readers leave this essay with a sense that official statistics should be understood as products of organizational practices, and should be interpreted with caution. In this interpretation, Kitsuse and Cicourel (1963) merely criticize sociologists for treating official statistics as a straightforward reflection of objective reality. This is a weak reading, in that many analysts who cite Kitsuse and Cicourel proceed to use official statistics, albeit self-consciously, handling them with some care, so that the statistics are now seen as reflecting some combination of organizational practices and the social world. For instance, an analyst may acknowledge that procedures for census-taking cause poor blacks to be undercounted, yet presume that the census results are otherwise more or less accurate. A strong reading of Kitsuse and Cicourel leads in a very different direction: Given official statistics' inherent ambiguity, the analyst should avoid using them. Obviously, the weak reading is more popular; many sociologists want to continue (carefully) using census figures and other official statistics as (imperfect) indicators. They may be willing to toss the bathwater, but they want to hang on to the baby.[1]

I believe that Ibarra and Kitsuse's "Vernacular Constituents of Moral Discourse" should be read with these issues in mind. It offers a new reclarification of the authors' thoughts on the constructionist perspective. Like its predecessors, this paper is susceptible to both strong and weak readings, and once more, the weak reading is likely to be more popular and, in Ibarra and Kitsuse's view, less correct. My critique of Ibarra and Kitsuse requires first reviewing the emergence of what I've called strict constructionism (Best 1989) and discussing the limitations of that stance, before turning to their paper to identify what I see as the attractions of a weak reading and the limitations of a strong interpretation. On occasion, I will use the current concern over satanism to illustrate my points.

The Satanic Panic

The contemporary campaign against satanism began gaining force roughly ten years ago. By the late 1980s, warnings about the satanic menace could be found on television talks shows and the networks' prime-time offerings, and in dozens of books and countless articles in magazines and newspapers. Police officers and social workers could learn about occult or ritual crimes at professional seminars, presentations that described a huge, powerful, secret conspiracy, a blood cult centered around rituals of sexual abuse and human sacrifice. U.S. satanists were estimated at more than one million, their sacrificial victims at sixty thousand per year. Warnings about satanism linked such diverse phenomena as serial murder, missing children, multiple personality disorder, child sexual abuse, illicit drugs, heavy-metal music, and fantasy role-playing games in one great web of evil.

If accusations of a great satanic conspiracy seem unfamiliar, it may be because this volume's readers tend to get their news from Mac-Neil/Lehrer rather than Geraldo, from the prestige press rather than more popular or local media. But the general public is familiar with the blood cult story, and they are concerned: In a recent Texas poll, 63 percent of the respondents rated satanism a "very serious" problem, while another 23 percent said it was "somewhat serious." Moreover, academics have begun warning about satanism. One recent trade book about the satanic threat is written by a religious studies professor at the University of Denver (Raschke 1990); references to satanism and its victims can be found in the literature of criminology, child welfare, psychiatry, and other helping professions (e.g., Holmes 1989).

At this point, I could begin examining the "construction of the satanism problem," the nature of the "claims-makers" and their "claims," and so on. After all, the constructionist approach has become a—perhaps the—leading school of social problems theory, a perspective often used to study the emergence of newly recognized social problems such as satanism.[2] However, my purpose is not to interpret the rise of satanism, but to use satanism as a convenient example of the limitations of strict constructionism. I intend to show that strict constructionism places unreasonable constraints on sociologists who hope to understand social problems.

Consider the sorts of questions one might have after hearing about the blood cult menace. Most obviously, one might ask whether the warnings are correct. Is there a satanic conspiracy with a million—or perhaps only one hundred thousand or even ten thousand—members? Does the cult claim tens of thousands—or maybe just dozens—of victims each year? Further, one might wonder about the people issuing the warnings. Who are they, and what motives or interests lie behind their claims? And is the evidence they offer persuasive? How should we respond to statements linking hundreds of teen suicides to playing *Dungeons and Dragons*, to testimony by adult multiple-personality-disorder patients that they suffered ritual abuse during childhood, to discoveries of satanic graffiti and sites that seem to have been used for strange rituals, to reports by therapists that they've interviewed children who were victims of systematic sexual abuse at their preschools, or to typologies of occult crime offered by police officers? These are sensible questions, and they might seem particularly amenable to constructionist analysis. They are also the sorts of questions that John Kitsuse and other leading figures in constructionist theory—the strict constructionists—argue analysts ought not address. To understand why constructionist sociologists increasingly turn away from such interesting questions, we must consider the perspective's development.

The Emergence of Strict Constructionism

Statements by Herbert Blumer (1971) and John I. Kitsuse and Malcolm Spector (1973, 1975; Spector and Kitsuse 1973, [1977] 1987) laid the foundation for contemporary constructionism.[3] They sought to turn social problems—a concept that rarely figured in sociological analysis, other than as a topic for beginning undergraduate courses and textbooks—into a subject for serious study. They began by criticizing the standard definitions, which equated social problems with objective conditions:

> It is a gross mistake to assume that any kind of malignant or harmful social condition or arrangement in a society becomes automatically a social problem for that society. The pages of history are replete with instances of dire social conditions unnoticed and unattended in the societies in which they occurred. (Blumer 1971, p. 302)

The key to any condition becoming a social problem was subjective: "The existence of social problems depends on the continued existence of groups or agencies that define some condition as a problem and attempt to do something about it" (Kitsuse and Spector 1973, p. 415). Moreover, these collective definitions were what conditions labeled social problems had in common; there were no objective qualities shared by all the chapter topics in a standard social problems text.

This argument led to new, subjectivist definitions of social problems: "social problems lie in and are products of a process of collective definition" (Blumer 1971, p. 301); or "[W]e define social problems as *the activities of groups making assertions of grievances and claims with respect to some putative conditions*" (Kitsuse and Spector 1973, p. 415, emphasis in original). These definitions radically shifted the focus of the sociology of social problems away from social conditions and onto the process of collective definition or claims-making. Both Blumer and Kitsuse and Spector outlined agendas for further constructionist research, including natural history models of social problems construction (Blumer 1971; Spector and Kitsuse 1973).

In directing attention toward claims-making, the constructionist theorists often suggested that claims could be located within their social context. Their early articles featured many references to the empirical reality of social conditions. Thus, Blumer clearly assumed that sociologists could evaluate the truth of claims:

> [R]ecognition by a society of its social problems is a highly selective process, with many harmful social conditions and arrangements not even making a bid for attention and with others falling by the wayside in what is frequently a fierce competitive struggle, (Blumer 1971, p. 302)

and "knowledge of the objective makeup of social problems . . . . should be sought as a corrective for ignorance or misinformation concerning this objective makeup" (p. 305). Kitsuse and Spector made a similar point:

> [T]he relationship between "objective conditions" and the development of social problems is variable and problematic. It is an empirical question whether certain types of conditions are correlated with or associated with certain types of claims (Spector and Kitsuse 1973, p. 148; see also Kitsuse and Spector 1973, p. 414)

They also suggested that the sociological analyst can assess claims-makers' motives ["groups defining conditions as social problems then, may be kept going by interests or values, or any mixture of combination of them" (Kitsuse and Spector 1973, p. 415)]; experiences ["the experience of dissatisfaction will influence the kind of claims that a group will make" (Spector and Kitsuse 1973, p. 150)], and power [("a genuinely powerful group may not be willing to expend its resources on a certain issue" (p. 149)]. Such statements do not imply a strong reading; they suggest that constructionist analysis might locate claims within their broader social context.

In their later papers, Kitsuse and Spector began adopting a more cautious epistemological stance. They noted that "sociologists are participants in the definitional process," and warned that analysts must "achieve the distance needed to focus on the definitional process, rather than unknowingly participate in it" (Kitsuse and Spector 1975, p. 585). Attempts to incorporate both subjective definitions and objective conditions in the same analysis—"the balanced view"—inevitably sacrifice "the integrity of the definitional process" (p. 589). Therefore, analysts should forgo all statements about objective conditions:

> [W]e assert that even the existence of the condition itself is irrelevant to and outside of our analysis. . . . . If the alleged condition were a complete hoax—a fabrication—we would maintain a noncommittal stance toward it unless those to whom the claim were addressed initiated their own analysis and uncovered it as a hoax. (Spector and Kitsuse [1977] 1987, p. 76)

This led to recommendations that "certain kinds of questions . . . . be set aside," e.g., that analysts not attribute claims-making to the participants' motives or values (Spector and Kitsuse [1977] 1987, p. 96). In sum, Kitsuse and Spector increasingly advocated a strong reading, urging analysts to avoid discussing social conditions.

Objectivist Responses

Most critiques of the constructionist position ignored these epistemological concerns. These critics worried about constructionism's relativism; if social problems are equated with claims-making, then those who are too poor—or weak or alienated—to make claims may never attract the analyst's attention (Collins 1989; Eitzen 1984; Young 1989). One could, they insisted, define social problems objectively, and they suggested different bases for such definitions, including "moral imperatives and human needs that are trans-societal and trans-historical" (Eitzen 1984, p. 11), "the knowledge related values of science" (Manis 1985, p. 5), and "an overarching ethical framework" (Collins 1989, p. 90).

Most of those defending the objectivist conception of social problems did not reject constructionism. Rather, they proposed integrating the two perspectives, borrowing insights from each to develop a more complete interpretive framework. For instance, Jones, McFalls, and Gallagher (1989) present a model in which objective conditions cause subjective reactions, with visibility, expectations, and values acting as intervening variables. For constructionists, such models were founded on the very objectivist assumptions about social life and sociology that they had begun by rejecting, and the proposals had little appeal (Spector and Kitsuse 1987).

Ontological Gerrymandering

A far more influential critique came from within the subjectivist ranks.[4] Woolgar and Pawluch charged that constructionists inevitably adopt an epistemologically inconsistent position through what they call ontological gerrymandering:

> The successful social problems explanation depends on making problematic the truth status of certain states of affairs selected for analysis and explanation, while backgrounding or minimizing the possibility that the same problems apply to assumptions upon which the analysis depends. (1985a, p. 216)

Their first example was from a passage in *Constructing Social Problems* about changing definitions of marijuana in which Spector and Kitsuse remark: "The nature of marijuana remained constant" ([1977] 1987, p. 43). Woolgar and Pawluch noted: "[T]he key assertion is that the actual character of a substance (marijuana), condition, or behavior remained constant" (1985a, p. 217).[5] Even Spector and Kitsuse, authors of repeated warnings about the need to avoid assumptions about objective conditions, made such assumptions:

[P]roponents fail to live up to the programmatic relativism which they espouse in calling for a purportedly different, definitional perspective. In the course of specific, empirical case studies, the programmatic claims give way to clearly discernible lapses into realism. (Woolgar and Pawluch 1985a, p. 224)

Of course, Woolgar and Pawluch were right. I have already shown that Blumer's and Kitsuse and Spector's theoretical writings often implied—even stated—that analysts could and might want to assess objective conditions. The notion that sociologists must not presume any knowledge of those conditions did not appear until Kitsuse and Spector's later work. Moreover, as Woolgar and Pawluch charged, case studies routinely failed to attain this analytic ideal.

Strict Constructionism

"Ontological Gerrymandering" attracted a good deal of attention among constructionists. Joseph Gusfield's (1985) response (discussed below) was critical, but other prominent constructionists tried to defend the perspective while simultaneously accepting Woolgar and Pawluch's standards for evaluating research. Thus, Schneider's review article on constructionist research stated: "The criticism is justified for many [constructionist] studies" (1985b, p. 224). But, in his reply to Woolgar and Pawluch, Schneider dismissed their examples as "mistakes in applying the definitional perspective, ... instances of careless talk" and spoke of "researcher carelessness and confusion" (1985a, p. 233). Similarly, Spector and Kitsuse acknowledged the tendency for analysts to lapse:

[W]hen confronted with a "disjunction," analysts infer that the member/participants' definitions of social realities reflect "misinterpretations" of the "facts," incomplete knowledge or other inadequacies. [This] . . . . may reflect a "social scientistic" arrogance that seduces the analyst away from a study of definitions and leads to assuming a warrant to identify and to correct the definitional "errors" of member/participants. (1987, p. 14)

Still, they insisted that an internally consistent analysis—one that avoided ontological gerrymandering—was possible.

The debate over Woolgar and Pawluch's critique served to redefine and harden the strict constructionist position. Epistemological concerns, which had not figured prominently either in the perspective's initial theoretical statements or in the case studies that had appeared, now became central to both discussions about constructionist theory and evaluations of new research. Analysts were urged to avoid any contamination by objectivism, to shun all assumptions about the empirical world.

The Possibility and Price of Strict Constructionism

Calls for sociologists to stay within the analytic boundaries of strict constructionism, coupled with admissions that most—if not all—constructionist case studies fail to meet those standards, raise the question whether a strict constructionist analysis is possible, or even desirable. Here, it may help to return to the example of satanism and consider what a strict constructionist treatment of the topic might involve.

Claims about a secret, conspiratorial blood cult are untestable, since a successful conspiracy is one that cannot be proven to exist. Critics of the antisatanism movement are reduced to arguing that a conspiracy on the scale described in antisatanist claims would inevitably leave some trace. Thus, the FBI's Kenneth Lanning notes the failure to find even one victim's body:

> Not only are no bodies found, but also, more important, there is no physical evidence that a murder took place. Many of those not in law-enforcement do not understand that, while it is possible to get rid of a body, it is much more difficult to get rid of the physical evidence that a murder took place, especially a human sacrifice involving sex, blood, and mutilation. . . . . Those who accept these stories of mass human sacrifice would have us believe that the satanists and other occult practitioners are murdering more than twice as many people every year in this country as all other murderers combined. (1989, p. 20)

Strict constructionism allows us to note these claims (e.g., satanists sacrifice sixty thousand victims per year) and counterclaims (e.g., antisatanist claims are implausible), but enjoins us from assessing their relative merits. Not only must analysts not presume to know the truth about the blood cult—something that can never be known, since an absence of evidence may only show that the conspiracy works—but they must not let their analysis be affected by judgments that one set of claims presents a stronger case.

This suggests that strict constructionists will recognize no difference between claims about satanism and, say, claims about AIDS. Both, after all, emerged as subjects of claims-making during the 1980s, both are said to kill thousands of people each year (admittedly, the claimed death toll for AIDS is considerably lower). In both cases, the claims-makers have attracted critics, and the strict constructionist will find no differences between Special Agent Lanning and someone arguing that the purported AIDS crisis is a hoax.

Constructionist analysts rarely declare that they know the truth about objective conditions.[6] For example, even antisatanism's critics must concede that there *might* be a blood cult out there. But analysts are likely to make less explicit assumptions about objective conditions, assumptions that frame the research agenda. Thus, a sociologist who doubts the reality of the satanic menace is more likely to try to account for antisatanism's spread ("Who believes this stuff, and why?"), than to ask how major institutions manage to ignore the blood cult ("Why haven't the authorities done more about this?"). It may be possible to avoid overt "lapses"—outright declarations about objective reality—but implicit assumptions about objective conditions will almost inevitably guide researchers.

Contrast the sorts of questions analysts are likely to ask about satanism and AIDS. By strict constructionist standards, the journalists and sociologists who have written about the construction of AIDS have addressed a series of inappropriate topics (cf. Albert 1989; Fumento 1990; Gamson 1989; Shilts 1987). When they ask why the federal government was slow to respond to the epidemic, or why the press began focusing on the risk of transmission via heterosexual intercourse, or why activists chose to adopt unconventional forms of protest, we can detect a hidden, forbidden assumption that frames their research: People are sick with AIDS. A strict constructionist can no more assume that AIDS exists than presume that there's probably no large, satanic blood cult at work. This suggests that strict constructionist researchers must ask the same questions about each claims-making campaign, rather than focusing on the interesting aspects of a particular case. After all, how can an analyst who refuses to presume anything about a case identify its interesting features?

What can a strict constructionist say about satanism? What sorts of analysis are acceptable? Spector and Kitsuse (1973, [1977] 1987; Kitsuse and Spector 1973) suggest that it may be fruitful to explore claims-makers' interests. Thus, we might discover that Christian Evangelists are among the most prominent antisatanist claims-makers, that many of the police officers, psychiatrists, and therapists who warn about occult crimes acquire money, status, and influence through anticult activities (and make references to their own religious beliefs in their presentations), and that many adult cult survivors have lengthy histories of psychiatric problems. A standard constructionist interpretation might note that these claims-makers stand to gain converts, money, etc. through their claims-making. But don't such interpretations also violate the tenets of strict constructionism, don't they "background" assumptions about objective reality, e.g., by presuming that Evangelists want to convert others and that such conversions are in the Evangelists' interest? How can we know what is in a claims-maker's interest—or even have a concept of interest—without making assumptions about objective conditions?[7]

It becomes impossible to say where we might draw the line. Is there anything an analyst might say about the construction of a particular social problem, such as satanism or AIDS, that does not require the analyst to make assumptions about objective reality? Must the study of social problems wait until someone writes *Principia Sociologica*, identifying the minimum assumptions needed for sociological analysis? No wonder strict constructionists have begun suggesting that analysts avoid case studies. Case studies inevitably violate the guidelines for strict constructionist analysis. These theorists have painted themselves into an armchair.[8]

It is difficult to miss the irony in the strict constructionist position. Constructionist theorists have always insisted that their theory is empirically based, but strict constructionism demands that analysts avoid references to the empirical world in order to maintain the theory's epistemological integrity.

Contextual Constructionism

Even if it is not impossible to do empirical research within the constraints imposed by strict constructionism, there remains the question whether these limits are desirable. Analytic purity comes at a high price. Urging that analysts "move beyond constructivism" to explore the nature of sociological inquiry, Woolgar and Pawluch raise a set of new questions, acknowledging: "They will not contribute . . . . to our understanding of the world as we have traditionally conceived that pursuit" (1985b, p. 162). Similarly, Kitsuse and Schneider contrast strict constructionist concerns with "research on social problems where the researcher participates, with members, in the practical projects of documenting and explaining a state of affairs that they find objectionable or important and that they may want to change" (1989, p. xiii). In short, strict constructionists must forgo most sorts of sociological analysis.

Among the major figures in the constructionist camp, only Joseph Gusfield challenged the value of Woolgar and Pawluch's discussion of ontological gerrymandering:

> I am left uninstructed about the importance of the critique. If it doesn't change the value of the empirical work, is it significant? . . . . Woolgar and Pawluch illustrate too well a kind of sociology that seems to me to be a dead end. It is a preoccupation with the logic of theory as something apart from and independent of the substantive questions to which directed. (1985, p. 17)

For Gusfield, the value of the constructionist position rests in its ability to increase our knowledge of social life:

It provides us with new questions about the emergence, or decline, of phenomena and/or definitions of the phenomena. . . . . It raises questions about the nature of "facticity" that heretofore sociologists have not routinely raised. This is most useful, especially in a society heavily committed to information and comment through mass media, governmental organizations and professional agencies. (p. 17)

Gusfield's position can be characterized as contextual constructionism (Best 1989). Contextual constructionists study claims-making within its context of culture and social structure. In practice, this means that an analyst may doubt claims that satanists sacrifice sixty thousand victims annually (on the grounds that the antisatanist claims-makers are unable to offer much evidence to support their charges), while generally accepting the Centers for Disease Control's figures for the numbers of AIDS victims (on the grounds that there is some limit to the degree organizational practices are likely to distort the collection of these official statistics). Note, however, that the analyst's focus remains the construction of social problems. For constructionists, the issue is unlikely to be the precise number of satanist or AIDS victims. The analyst is more likely to be interested in the ways statistics are collected, the role they play in claims-making rhetoric, the responses they elicit from the media, officials, and the public, and so on. But contextual constructionists assume that claims-making occurs within some context: Thus, a sociologist studying satanism may marvel that estimates of human sacrifice victims are supported by so little evidence, and ask why these claims are relatively successful; while a sociologist studying AIDS may wonder why, in the face of accumulating evidence of a serious problem, it took officials and the press so long to attend to AIDS.[9]

Contextualist assumptions are—as the strict constructionists charge—detectable throughout the constructionist literature: in the theoretical writings of Blumer—and Kitsuse and Spector—and Gusfield; and in (no doubt all of the) dozens of case studies. These works assume that we will understand the empirical world better if we pay attention to the manner in which social problems emerge and, at a more basic level, they also assume that understanding the empirical world is desirable. That is, contextual constructionism is inspired by a sociological imagination.

This Way to the Egress? Ibarra and Kitsuse

Debate, then, has broken out within the constructionist camp, with a growing body of critiques, responses, and rejoinders concerning the appropriate stance for analysts. Although Spector and Kitsuse noted: "We hope to avoid the interminable conceptual analysis and re-analysis that has deflected the so-called labeling theory of deviance from the more important task of building an empirical literature" (1987, p. 13), Ibarra and Kitsuse's paper must be seen within the context of such an ongoing debate. They present a corrective, strong reading of *Constructing Social Problems*: That book was meant as a programmatic statement, and Ibarra and Kitsuse urge sociologists to get with the program.

In particular, they offer a new concept—"condition-category"—as the means for refocusing constructionist analysis. Just as *Constructing Social Problems* shifted the attention of sociologists of social problems away from social conditions and onto claims-making, Ibarra and Kitsuse propose another, albeit more subtle shift, away from claims-making activities and onto the language of claims.[10] The record shows that studying claims-making offers too many temptations for analysts to lapse into ontological gerrymandering. But concentrating on condition-categories—"the strict constructionist never leaves language"—seems to promise to circumvent this problem.

The Attractions of a Weak Reading

Ibarra and Kitsuse, then, explore claims-making as rhetoric. While this is not a new topic for constructionists (cf. Spector and Kitsuse [1977] 1987; Gusfield 1981; Best 1990)—let alone for scholars in speech and communications (e.g., Condit 1990)—their paper offers a fresh approach to the topic, with a useful catalog of rhetorical strategies, motifs, and styles. Constructionist sociologists will find these new concepts helpful.

Unfortunately, many of those who choose to apply these concepts are likely to give the paper a weak reading, to stray from the tight focus on language prescribed by Ibarra and Kitsuse.[11] To understand the attractions of a weak reading, let's imagine a sociologist studying claims about satanism. Once our analyst has collected examples of antisatanist rhetoric, new questions are likely to emerge. Like many social causes, the antisatanist movement is a loose coalition, involving a diverse set of claims-makers, including Evangelists, police officers, psychiatrists, and journalists (with an equally diverse coalition arrayed in opposition). Which claims-makers make which claims (or counterclaims)? And why did they choose those strategies? Do their rhetorical choices reflect their particular values or interests? Do those choices derive from available resources, such as claims-makers' prior experiences with successful or unsuccessful claims-making campaigns? To what degree does their rhetoric reflect contingencies of knowledge (as in the lawyers' aphorism—when the law favors your side, pound the law; when the facts favor your side, pound the facts; and when neither favors your side, pound the table)? In making their rhetorical choices, are claims-makers cynical or sincere—do they believe their own arguments? Another set of questions concerns the audiences for the claims: Who responds to which claims, and how? Why are particular audiences responsive to some claims and not others? Is there a form of feedback involved, in which claims-makers tailor their rhetoric to the anticipated responses of their audience(s)?

Obviously, this list of questions barely scratches the surface. We can imagine all sorts of seductive questions, each tempting our analyst to "leave language" and link rhetoric to social arrangements. And, of course, those who give in to temptation will then number among the fallen, the heretics who engage in ontological gerrymandering and contextual constructionism. Their numbers will grow. The next step, presumably, will be an acknowledgment that "condition-category" has failed to do the job, coupled with yet another reclarification of the strict constructionist position, built around yet another new concept.

In sum, constructionist sociologists are likely to borrow heavily from Ibarra and Kitsuse, but to use their concepts in ways other than those authors intended. The new conceptual apparatus may be popular, but it is unlikely to be proof against a weak reading.

The Limitations of a Strong Reading

Not only are analysts unlikely to restrict themselves to a strong reading of Ibarra and Kitsuse, but it isn't clear that a consistently strong reading is possible. As Woolgar and Pawluch (1985a) noted, strict constructionists are quick to spot the objectivist assumptions in others' work, but slower to acknowledge their own lapses. Consider Ibarra and Kitsuse's list of rhetorical strategies—rhetorics of loss, entitlement, endangerment, unreason, and calamity. They make no claim that theirs is an exhaustive list, as it obviously is not. Rhetorical strategies undoubtedly reflect particular cultures, social structures, and historical circumstances.[12] The language of claims does not exist independently of the social world; it is a product of—and influence on—that world. A strong reading that "never leaves language" is an illusion because language never leaves society. An analyst who ignores the social embeddedness of claims-makers' rhetoric takes that embeddedness for granted; this is another form of ontological gerrymandering.

Ibarra and Kitsuse describe their goal as "an empirically based theory of social problems," and references to the "empirical" foundation of constructionism appear throughout Kitsuse's writings. At the same time, the demands of strict constructionism push analysts away from empirical research. Ibarra and Kitsuse suggest that case studies have proven analytically troublesome:

> [O]ur position is that the project of developing a theory of *social problems discourse* is a much more coherent way of proceeding with constructionism than, for example, the development of a series of discrete theories on the social construction of X, Y, and Z. To develop a theory about condition X when the ontological status of X is suspended results in "ontological gerry-mandering' . . . . which is to say flawed theory. (emphasis in original)

Therefore, instead of studying the rhetoric of antisatanism and other campaigns to construct social problems—research that might provide an empirical foundation for a theory of social problems rhetoric—they present their own list of rhetorical strategies without explaining how it was derived. Where case studies of claims-makers' rhetoric inevitably incorporate assumptions about social conditions, an abstract typology of strategies seems to finesse the problem.

Ibarra and Kitsuse want to reclarify the nature of constructionist analysis; they seek to identify the errors in others' analyses and, through their focus on discourse, show that strict constructionist analysis is possible. Presumably they took great care in writing their paper. Yet assumptions about the social world creep into their analysis. Consider three statements from their discussion of their first rhetorical strategy—the rhetoric of loss:

> This rhetoric works most idiomatically with objects (i.e., condition-categories) that can be construed to qualify as forms of perfection. . . . .

> Rhetorical idioms can cut across ideological divisions like liberal and socialist and conservative, inter alia. . . . .

> (The rhetoric is wholly unidiomatic when the concern at issue is revealed to be for the loss of "white male privilege.")

These brief passages suggest the sorts of problems that plague Ibarra and Kitsuse's analysis. First, there are the evaluations of rhetoric as being idiomatic or unidiomatic—an undefined standard, but one that certainly seems to "privilege" the analyst. Second, consider the notion that some "objects . . . . can be construed to qualify as forms of perfection." This would seem to assume that culture/social structure somehow shapes the language of claims: if some objects can be construed as perfect, presumably others cannot be so construed—but how can analysts judge which are which? Third, there is the overt assumption that there are ideological divisions among claims-makers. And we could go on. Even in a statement denouncing unwarranted assumptions about the social world, a statement presumably crafted so as to avoid all such assumptions, we find evidence of such assumptions having been made. Even when analysts retreat from any discussion of empirical cases, epistemologically consistent strict constructionist analysis seems to be an unachievable goal. Like their strict constructionist predecessors, Ibarra and Kitsuse set a standard that they themselves cannot meet.

But Seriously Folks

During the 1980s, it became fashionable for sociologists to warn that they intended to "take [this or that] theory seriously." This phrase, like the stand-up comic's transitional "But seriously folks," often signaled that the analyst was about to make statements that ran a risk of seeming silly. Strict constructionism's problems reveal that theory can be taken too seriously.

Just as quantitative researchers continually risk sacrificing sociological substance for more elaborate research designs and more sophisticated statistics, qualitative researchers must balance substance against the demands of theoretical consistency. Analytic purity can come at a terrible cost. Constructionist theory warns against being distracted by the conditions about which claims are made, but the implications of strict constructionism push the analyst well beyond that boundary, into a contextless region where claims-making may only be examined in the abstract. The sociology of social problems began with the assumption that sociological knowledge might help people understand and improve the world; strict constructionism sells that birthright for a mess of epistemology.

Ibarra and Kitsuse characterize social problems claims-making as "a language game." This term seems well-suited for describing the claims and counterclaims in the debate over constructionist theory. For instance, Ibarra and Kitsuse attack contextual constructionism as "a narrow construal of the constructionist project." This criticism deserves inspection. The weak readings of contextual constructionists cause them to ask all manner of research questions that lead the analyst across borders closed to the strict constructionist who "never leaves language." In what sense is contextual constructionism "narrow'? Similarly, strict constructionist discourse conveys a sense of "ownership" (Gusfield 1981) of the right to define such key terms as *social problems* and *constructionism*.[13]

Perhaps the most damaging rhetorical device in Ibarra and Kitsuse's paper is the one quoted above: "the project of developing a theory of *social problems discourse* is a much more coherent way of proceeding with constructionism than, for example, the development of a series of discrete theories on the social construction of X, Y, and Z" (emphasis in original). This is simply a false dichotomy. There is another choice: following the albeit traditional model for qualitative researchers, staying close to the data, and developing grounded theories through analytic induction (cf. Glaser and Strauss 1967). Constructionist research seems well suited for this sort of analysis; the literature has grown dramatically since Schneider's (1985b) review essay identified more than fifty studies. And, of course, there is much relevant information to be found in sociological studies of social movements and deviance, and in the work of historians, political scientists, anthropologists, and so on.

The grounded theory approach—familiar to all qualitative sociologists—can, in fact, produce "an empirically based theory of social problems." It will not, to be sure, meet the strict constructionists' tests for epistemological consistency, but it just might help us understand how social problems emerge and develop. Isn't it time for constructionists to worry a little less about how we know what we know, and worry a little more about what, if anything, we do know about the construction of social problems?

Notes

1. The tendency to give Kitsuse's other key works a weak reading has been discussed elsewhere. On Kitsuse (1962), see Rains (1975). On Spector and Kitsuse ([1977] 1987), see Woolgar and Pawluch (1985a) and Best (1989).

2. Sociological analyses of the current antisatanist campaign include Forsyth and Oliver (1990); Richardson, Best, and Bromley (1991) and Victor (1989, 1990).

3. The argument that objectivist definitions of social problems had inherent flaws was not new. Spector and Kitsuse ([1977] 1987) review the early history of the objectivist-subjectivist debate.

4. Mauss's (1989) argument that constructionist research on social problems should be subsumed within the sociology of social movements is another subjectivist critique. For a response, see Troyer (1989).

5. This example seems to flirt with a classic logical fallacy—the argument from ignorance. Critics can always ask how one knows that the nature of marijuana—or oxygen, or Jupiter's orbit—has not changed. But, by traditional standards of inquiry, unless there is some reason to suspect change, a presumption of stability is reasonable.

6. To be sure, there are analysts who present a sort of "vulgar constructionism" which equates constructionist analysis with debunking claims. For instance, Forsyth and Oliver say: "Basically the constructionist argument is that there has been no significant change in the activity in question, but that activities which were not previously defined as problematic, or rates of activity which were not previously defind [sic] as problematic, have been defined as a problem" (1990, p. 285).

7. The less specific claims that constructionist analysis can help reveal the workings of racial, sexual, class, and other hierarchies seem vulnerable to the same criticism. Doesn't the analyst first need to accept the objective reality of

those hierarchies? This may explain the recent attraction of postmodernism for some strict constructionists; the conventions of postmodernist prose make it difficult to pin down what, if anything, the analyst believes to be true.

8. Fortunately, most researchers who adopt the constructionist perspective find themselves able to ignore this debate. In particular, the constructionist work that has appeared in sociology's flagship journals pays little or no attention to epistemological issues (Block and Burns 1986; Gamson and Modigliani 1989; Hilgartner and Bosk 1988).

9. Strict constructionists sometimes endorse similar topics: "A putative condition may be defined in terms that are not amenable to 'credible' or persuasive documentation; member/participants may be unable to sustain social problems activity organized on such definitions" (Spector and Kitsuse 1987, p. 14; cf. Kitsuse and Schneider 1989). They do not, unfortunately, explain how the analyst can identify what is credible or persuasive or sustainable without making assumptions about the context of claims-making.

10. Woolgar and Pawluch (1985b) argue for a more radical shift in focus. In their vision, analysts should explore the nature of sociological analysis. At this point, of course, social problems—however defined—cease being the object of study.

11. For instance, when Coltrane and Hickman (1992) compare fathers' and mothers' rhetoric in the debate over child custody and child support laws, they invoke Ibarra and Kitsuse. Yet their analysis links claims-makers' success to "economic, institutional, and ideological contexts."

12. Because a very large share of constructionist research concerns the contemporary United States, it has been easy for U.S. constructionists to take the arrangements in their society for granted. We need more comparative research, examining the construction of social problems in other societies and in other times.

13. Obviously, the same sort of rhetorical analysis can be applied to contextual constructionist statements, including this paper. A contextual constructionist might even venture beyond language to ask sociology-of-science questions about who says what, why, and so on.

References

Albert, Edward. 1989. "AIDS and the Press." Pp. 39–54 in *Images of Issues*, edited by Joel Best. Hawthorne, NY: Aldine de Gruyter.

Best, Joel. 1989. "Afterword." Pp. 243–53 in *Images of Issues*, edited by Joel Best. Hawthorne, NY: Aldine de Gruyter.

———. 1990. *Threatened Children*. Chicago: University of Chicago Press.

Block, Fred and Gene A. Burns. 1986. "Productivity as a Social Problem." *American Sociological Review* 51:767–80.

Blumer, Herbert. 1971. "Social Problems as Collective Behavior." *Social Problems* 18:298–306.

Collins, Patricia Hill. 1989. "The Social Construction of Invisibility." *Perspectives on Social Problems* 1:77–93.

Coltrane, Scott and Neal Hickman. 1992. "The Rhetoric of Rights and Needs." *Social Problems* 39:400–20.

Condit, Celeste. 1990. *Decoding Abortion Rhetoric*. Urbana: University of Illinois Press.

Eitzen, D. Stanley. 1984. "Teaching Social Problems: Implications of the Objectivist Subjectivist Debate." *SSSP Newsletter* (Fall):10–12.

Forsyth, Craig J. and Marion D. Oliver. 1990. "The Theoretical Framing of a Social Problem." *Deviant Behavior* 11:281–92.

Fumento, Michael. 1990. *The Myth of Heterosexual AIDS*. New York: Basic Books.

Gamson, Josh. 1989. "Silence, Death, and the Invisible Enemy." *Social Problems* 36:351–67.

Gamson, William and Andre Modigliani. 1989. "Media Discourse and Public Opinion on Nuclear Power." *American Journal of Sociology* 95:1–37.

Glaser, Barney G., and Anselm L. Strauss. 1967. *The Discovery of Grounded Theory*. Chicago: Aldine.

Gusfield, Joseph R. 1981. *The Culture of Public Problems*. Chicago: University of Chicago Press.

———. 1985. "Theories and Hobgoblins." *SSSP Newsletter* 17 (Fall):16–18.

Hilgartner, Stephen and Charles L. Bosk. 1988. "The Rise and Fall of Social Problems." *American Journal of Sociology* 94:53–78.

Holmes, Ronald M. 1989. *Profiling Violent Crimes*. Newbury Park, CA: Sage.

Jones, Brian J., Joseph A. McFalls, Jr., and Bernard J. Gallagher III. 1989. "Toward a Unified Model for Social Problems Theory." *Journal for the Theory of Social Behavior* 19:337–56.

Kitsuse, John I. 1962. "Societal Reaction to Deviant Behavior." *Social Problems* 9:247–56.

Kitsuse, John I., and Aaron Cicourel. 1963. "A Note on the Use of Official Statistics." *Social Problems* 11:131–39.

Kitsuse, John I. and Joseph W. Schneider. 1989. "Preface." Pp. xi–xiii in *Images of Issues*, edited by Joel Best. Hawthorne, NY: Aldine de Gruyter.

Kitsuse, John I., and Malcolm Spector. 1973. "Toward a Sociology of Social Problems." *Social Problems* 20:407–19.

———. 1975. "Social Problems and Deviance." *Social Problems* 22:584–94.

Lanning, Kenneth V. 1989. *Child Sex Rings*. Washington: National Center for Missing and Exploited Children.

Manis, Jerome G. 1985. "Defining Social Problems: Objectivism-Subjectivism Revisited." *SSSP Newsletter* 16 (Winter):5.

Mauss, Armand L. 1989. "Beyond the Illusion of Social Problems Theory." *Perspectives on Social Problems* 1:19–39.

Rains, Prudence. 1975. "Imputations of Deviance." *Social Problems* 23:1–11.

Raschke, Carl A. 1990. *Painted Black*. San Francisco: Harper & Row.

Richardson, James T., Joel Best, and David G. Bromley (eds.). 1991. *The Satanism Scare*. Hawthorne, NY: Aldine de Gruyter.

Schneider, Joseph W. 1985a. "Defining the Definitional Perspective on Social Problems." *Social Problems* 32:232–34.

———. 1985b. "Social Problems Theory." *Annual Review of Sociology* 11:209–29.

Shilts, Randy. 1987. *And the Band Played On*. New York: St. Martin's.

Spector, Malcolm and John I. Kitsuse. 1973. "Social Problems: a Re-formulation." *Social Problems* 21:145–59.

———. [1977] 1987. *Constructing Social Problems*. Hawthorne, NY: Aldine de Gruyter.

———. 1987. "Preface to the Japanese Edition: Constructing Social Problems." *SSSP Newsletter* 18 (Fall):13–15.

Troyer, Ronald J. 1989. "Are Social Problems and Social Movements the Same Thing?" *Perspectives on Social Problems* 1:41–58.

Victor, Jeffrey S. 1989. "A Rumor-Panic about a Dangerous Satanic Cult in Western New York." *New York Folklore* 15:23–49.

———. 1990. "Satanic Cult Legends as Contemporary Legend." *Western Folklore* 49:51–81.

Woolgar, Steve, and Dorothy Pawluch. 1985a. "Ontological Gerrymandering." *Social Problems* 32:214–27.

———. 1985b. "How Shall We Move Beyond Constructivism?" *Social Problems* 33:159–62.

Young T. R. 1989. "Deconstructing Constructionism." Paper presented at the annual meeting of the Society for the Study of Social Problems.

Ethnomethodological Concerns

8

Social Constructionism and Social Problems Work

James A. Holstein and Gale Miller

Since Spector and Kitsuse ([1977] 1987) offered their foundational statement on the construction of social problems, ethnomethodological contributions to the understanding of everyday reality as socially accomplished have been increasingly recognized, accepted, and even
appreciated by the sociological community (Pollner 1991). By the late
1980s, ethnomethodologically informed studies regularly appeared in
the journal *Social Problems*, some relating to Spector and Kitsuse's constructionist program, others taking alternative approaches and topics.
While Spector and Kitsuse avoided drawing explicit connections between their version of constructionism and ethnomethodology, their
approach was clearly compatible with the ethnomethodological tradition
(Troyer 1989).

In this volume, Kitsuse and his colleague Peter Ibarra cogently respond to many of the issues arising from various challenges to the
constructionist perspective, but their arguments seem most pointedly
directed to long-standing ethnomethodological concerns. While still
hesitant to openly embrace an explicitly ethnomethodological stance,
Ibarra and Kitsuse draw upon ethnomethodological resources to reiterate and underscore the radical impulse of their constructionist position.
The task of social problems theorists, they write, is to reconstruct members' ways—their vernacular discourse practices—of constituting social
problems as moral objects. The argument clarifies some possible ambiguities in earlier statements by unequivocally directing the constructionist program toward the conventional features of the social problems
"claims-making" process, focusing on the "condition-categories" that
are applied and used in practical circumstances to produce meaningful
descriptions and evaluations of social reality.

Ibarra and Kitsuse's focus on interaction and language use certainly
highlights the constitutive practices that are ethnomethodology's
concern as well. Indeed, in statements like the following, Ibarra and
Kitsuse's constructionist project sounds distinctly similar to eth-

methodological proposals (see Garfinkel 1967; Heritage 1984; Pollner 1987):

> [O]ur field is fundamentally concerned with understanding the constitutive ("world-making") and strategic dimensions of claimants' discursive practices. . . . We conceive of social problems as "idiomatic productions" to accentuate their status as members' accomplishments.

In application, however, Ibarra and Kitsuse's proposal—like Spector and Kitsuse's—emphasizes the construction of social problems categories through "large-scale" public rhetoric—"publicity," as Gubrium (in this volume) calls it. Neglected are the myriad everyday interactional matters that constitute social problems on a smaller scale. Ibarra and Kitsuse point the study of social problems in the direction of processes by which collective representations are assembled and promoted. While this is certainly vital to a sociological understanding of the phenomenon, a more ethnomethodological concern for the interpretive practices by which everyday realities are locally accomplished, managed, and sustained urges constructionism to broaden its focus to include those practices that link public interpretive structures to aspects of everyday reality, producing recognizable instances of social problems. We refer to such practices as *social problems work* (Miller and Holstein 1989, 1991; Miller 1992).

This essay outlines an approach to the study of social problems work, linking ethnomethodological concerns for constitutive practice with constructionist interests in social problems categories. It illustrates the articulation of problem categories with concrete cases, the interactional bases of the attachments, and the open-ended nature of the process. The essay concludes with some prospects for a sociology of social problems work.

Social Problems Work

Both the original constructionist statements (Kitsuse and Spector 1973, 1975; Spector and Kitsuse 1974, [1977] 1987) and Ibarra and Kitsuse's refinements tend to gloss over the interactional production of concrete instances of social problems, even as they focus on forms of vernacular usage as the constitutive source of social problems as social forms. A sociology of social problems work neither contradicts nor denigrates this project. Rather it both expands and transforms the constructionist project to address how social problems categories, once publicly established, are attached to experience in order to enact identifiable objects of social problems discourse. The approach combines ethnomethodological impulses with concerns for collective representation (Durkheim 1961) and discourse structures and gaze (Foucault 1972, 1973).

While ethnomethodologists have traditionally been interested in local practices of enactment, they have generally been reluctant to explicitly engage the challenge posed by the recurrence of patterned interpretations. Interpretation is certainly "artful" (Garfinkel 1967), but it also produces and reproduces categorizations that are recognizable as instances of the same phenomenon. Interpretive practice attaches meaning to occurrence in familiar ways. That sense of familiarity, of course, is not merely a matter of recognition; it, too, is artfully accomplished. Still, the analytic challenge for a more comprehensive constructionist approach lies in explicating the articulation of culturally recognized images with aspects of experience in ways that produce identifiable, indicatable instances of social problems that can be cited, in everyday interaction and through vernacular usage, as evidence of the problem's objective status.

Durkheim's analysis of social forms and collective representations provides a resource for linking everyday articulation practices to public interpretive structures (Gubrium 1988). For Durkheim (1961), social reality is enacted through collective representations—culturally recognized and shared categorization systems. As Douglas (1986, p. 96) notes, Durkheim considered collective representations to be "publicly standardized ideas (that) constitute social order." Durkheim pays scant attention to the constitutive processes through which a sense of order is achieved, but the basic framework is useful for understanding how meaning is accomplished. Indeed, analyzing the processes by which collective representations constitute order provides a link between Durkheimian structural concerns and phenomenological, ethnomethodological, and constructionist considerations.

Collective representations can be analyzed as interpretive structures that are constituted in a manner similar to Schutz's (1970) "schemes of interpretation"—that is, experientially acquired frameworks for organizing and making sense of everyday life. The structures are grounded in individual biography but reflect and perpetuate culturally promoted and shared understandings of and orientations to everyday experience. Social problems work involves procedures for expressing and applying these culturally shared categories to candidate circumstances. Interpretations are shaped by the interpretive structures and resources that are locally available and acceptable. For example, labeling persons "mentally ill" or "homeless" requires the availability of the categories plus the interpretive activity through which a category is articulated with a case.

In elaborating a neo-Durkheimian view, Mary Douglas (1986) suggests that human reason is organized and expressed through social structure by way of processes of "institutional thinking." Using this process as a metaphor, Douglas argues that socially organized circumstances provide models of social order through which experience is assimilated and organized. She states, for example, that "An answer is only seen to be the right one if it sustains the institutional thinking that is already in the minds of individuals as they try to decide (Douglas 1986, p. 4).

According to Douglas, institutions are organized as social conventions involving typical and routine ways of representing social reality. As she formulates them, representational conventions are similar to what Foucault (1972) analyzes as discursive formations. Contextually grounded discourses, vocabularies, and categories are part of local interpretive cultures (Gubrium 1991), resources for defining and classifying aspects of everyday life. Miller (1991), for example, shows how the local interpretive culture of a Work Incentive Program provides distinctive ways of formulating identities, problems, and solutions. Similarly, Gubrium's (1992) study of two family therapy agencies contrasts the ways the two institutions formulate what a family "really" is, citing distinctive local cultures and interpretive resources as the source of the differences.

Collective representations that emanate from social problems claims-making are merely candidate structures for making sense of objects and events. While they have been promoted as viable ways of understanding social conditions, there are myriad possible ways to define experience, so interpretive practices must articulate any particular structure with its object. Social problems designations are assigned, legitimated, and conventionalized as persons interpret and apply problem definitions in terms of the representational resources available to them. Social problems categories thus become a part of persons' and groups' ways of understanding and representing their everyday experience—locally available resources for constructing instances of social problems.

Social problems work articulates interpretive resources with concrete experience to constitute instances of social problems. Whereas the term can be used to characterize the activity of "street-level bureaucrats" whose formal job it is to formulate and apply general social problems policies to the concrete circumstances of everyday life (Lipsky 1980), we suggest that social problems work be more broadly understood to include any and all activity implicated in the recognition, identification, interpretation, and definition of conditions that are called "social problems." It is any practice contributing to the practical construction or definition of an instance of a social problem.

Accordingly, a sociology of social problems work focuses on interaction, conversational practice, and interpretive resources in the diverse settings where instances of social problems might be identified. Such practices and resources orient the way individuals and groups organize their interpretations, including the ways that they attach meaning to behavior. If we construe the outcomes of large-scale social problems claims-making as candidate "reality structures," we can analyze social problems work for the ways that these structures routinely infuse instances of everyday life with their social problems status.

Social problems work is a potential aspect of all social relationships and interactions where dissatisfaction with a putative condition might emerge. When individuals formulate the condition as a type of problem that warrants their attention or remedial concern, they engage in social problems work as an aspect of their ordinary conversation. In making claims and expressing complaints, persons portray aspects of relationships and circumstances as unsatisfactory, assign them to culturally known categories, and justify actions intended to change them. As Emerson and Messinger (1977) suggest, when third parties are consulted or when "troubleshooters" intervene to produce change, the problem becomes more concrete and public. Involvement of new participants provides new sources for additional social problems work, which may precipitate new depictions of the nature and causes of problems as well as remedies for them.

Analysis of social problems work may procede in several interrelated ways as it focuses on a constellation of phenomena and concerns. The following sections discuss three ways in which such analysis may be developed. First, the social problems work perspective can address the diverse interpretive and interactional procedures and occasions through which otherwise mundane aspects of everyday life are cast as social problems. Studies of social problems work analyze the attachment of shared cultural images and categories to aspects of experience to produce concrete instances of problems category members. A second, and related, focus is the interactional basis of the social problems work process. Instances of social problems are constructed through the often seen but unnoticed (Garfinkel 1967) practices of mundane interaction. Consequently, analysis of social problems work centers on the interactional dynamics of practical interpretation. Finally, social problems work is ongoing, situated, and contingent, a process that is never complete. Instances of social problems are constantly in the making—under construction, but provisional, so to speak. Analysis of the everyday construction work may thus consider the locally managed practices and practical circumstances that condition the articulation of social problems imageries with concrete cases.

Producing Concrete Cases

Instances of social problems are routinely produced and reproduced in everyday circumstance, through a variety of interpretive procedures.

The activity is so commonplace that it may be all but invisible. Reference to an individual as a gang member, or reports of a particular event as an instance of child abuse, for example, constitute as they describe. The dynamics of social problems work is perhaps most visible when the problem is the overt concern of a particular setting. Human service organizations are exemplary in this regard, as they routinely deal with, and constitute, persons and occurrences as problems (Holstein 1992). Indeed, social problems work may be the primary preoccupation of the human services (Miller 1992), even if it is not recognized as such.

As an illustration, consider how an instance of "mental illness" was publicly established during an involuntary commitment hearing. Mental illness is widely recognized and legitimated as a category for defining incomprehensible cognition, affect, and/or behavior—both professionally and in vernacular usage. It has been available in Western culture as a collective representation and interpretive resource for quite some time. Foucault (1965), for example, has described the historical emergence of the concepts and discourses of madness, insanity, mental illness, and related terms dating back to the Middle Ages, while more recent movements to popularize and institutionalize the mental illness metaphor have also been documented (Sarbin 1969; Sarbin and Mancuso 1970). The issue for the study of social problems work, then, is the local articulation of the collective representation with a concrete aspect of experience.

Involuntary mental hospitalization can be enforced only if the candidate patient is found to be mentally ill and dangerous to self or others in a court of law. Thus, commitment hearings are scenes for the assignment of social problems categories to actual cases. In the following extract from hearing testimony, a psychiatrist testifies regarding the mental condition of Gerald Simms, the candidate patient. The doctor accounts for a diagnosis of "chronic schizophrenia" by displaying evidence of the problem that justifies the label. The diagnostic work and testimony can thus be analyzed as an instance of social problems work— interpretive activity through which a category is formally attached to an individual:

> Mr. Simms suffers from drastic mood swings. His affect is extremely labile. One minute he'll be in tears, the next he's just fine. He fluctuates. His affect may be flattened, then elevated. One moment he'll be telling you about his cleaning business, then he'll flip out of character and cry like a brokenhearted schoolgirl over the most insignificant thing. Something that should never upset a grown man like Mr. Simms. During his periods of flattened affect, he seems to lose all interest. . . . . His passivity—he's

almost docile in a very sweet sort of way. He just smiles and lets every-thing pass. It's completely inappropriate for an adult male. (Holstein 1987, p. 145)

Note that while the psychiatrist is ostensibly describing Mr. Simms's con-dition and behavior, his description is also rhetorical. He selects aspects of a range of reportable features and advocates them as definitive charac-terizations. In the process, he constitutes Mr. Simms as a member of the problem category, interpretively attaching the definition in a fashion that is accountable to locally prevailing legal and psychiatric standards.

In addition, the psychiatrist descriptively accomplishes Mr. Simms's mental illness with reference to normal types, pointing out in the process how Mr. Simms's traits and behaviors are anomalous—that is, unmoti-vated by other circumstances that are described. Social problems work of this type routinely involves rhetorical devices that Dorothy Smith (1978) calls *contrast structures* to display problems or troubles. Contrast structures juxtapose characterizations of traits or behaviors with state-ments that supply instructions for seeing the traits or behavior as unusual or problematic (Smith 1978). Anomalies—in the case above, documents of mental illness—are accomplished by constructing relationships be-tween rules or definitions of situations and descriptions of an individual's behavior so that the former do not properly provide for the latter.

In the Simms case, for example, the described anomalies make it "evident" that the candidate patient is mentally ill. The psychiatrist explicitly contrasted descriptions of Mr. Simms's behavior with normal expectations for a person of his gender and age. Mr. Simms's emotions, for example, were portrayed as those of "a brokenhearted schoolgirl" crying over matters that should "never upset a grown man." His "pas-sivity" was "inappropriate for an adult male." Mr. Simms's age and gender were made salient and consequential to the diagnosis as stan-dards for invidious comparison. Apparent incongruities between ex-pected and encountered behaviors and traits were then noted as evi-dence that a problem existed, and the problem was identified as mental illness (Holstein 1993).

This interpretive technique is similar to the use of complementary oppositions, a practice often employed to establish persons or events as problematic (Douglas 1986; Loseke 1992; Miller 1991, 1992). Oppositional forms include distinctions between nature and culture, normal and un-usual, good and bad. The oppositions may be explicitly expressed as orientations to matters of practical concern or used as implicit back-ground assumptions justifying persons' orientations. In this way, com-plementary oppositions are linked to other oppositions and expressed as ideologies that justify and perpetuate the institutional discourses from which they are built. Oppositional forms and other contrastive structures can thus be used to attach social problems categories to concrete cases, specifying what a problem is as opposed to what it is not.

Loseke's (1989, 1992) analysis of the social construction of wife abuse in battered women's shelters further illustrates the practical interpretive work that goes into assigning individuals to a social problems category. The problem of battered women and wife beating was publicly constituted and recognized through a variety of claims-making activities culminating in the 1970s and 1980s (Studer 1984, Tierney 1982). The practical work of shelter workers, according to Loseke, is deciding and justifying which women to assign to the category. As an everyday matter, this amounted to accountably deciding which potential clients wanted and needed what the organization had to offer, and which women would become good members of the shelter community. This involved the practical articulation of client characteristics with organizational goals and resources using commonsense or folk reasoning and typification. Seeing candidate clients in terms of oppositional forms— "appropriate" or "inappropriate" clients, "battered" or "not battered" women—shelter workers produced decisions that were justified by their constructions of the women and their circumstances.

Social problems work is apparent in staff members' entries in the shelter "logbook," which offered accounts for the full range of workers organizational decisions and actions. Log entries noting admission decisions illustrate the application of the "battered woman" image. Consider the following entries:

> 8:30 P.M. Susan called. Needs shelter badly, has four children, husband searching for her. She's been battered and is frightened—requires shelter till she can relocate. Called [another worker] and we think we should pick her up. (Loseke 1992, p. 85)

> She seems like a classic battered case. Had a long session with her, she was crying and very hurt. Absolutely no self-esteem, husband treated her like a little child but she is still in love with him. . . . . She feels very helpless and lonely. (Loseke 1989, p. 184)

According to Loseke, Susan—from the first entry—was constructed as a member of the battered woman type by portraying her as frightened and in danger, a woman wanting to remain independent from an abusive partner and therefore a woman who could not be turned away. The battered woman collective representation reflexively emerged from the descriptions and served as an interpretive scheme for understanding and categorizing Susan's behavior and circumstance. The second woman was assigned to the battered woman type by noting that she was oppressed by her husband and felt helpless and isolated.

In contrast, many women were turned away from the shelter. The battered woman image was typically invoked as part of logbook accounts for their rejections:

> [hospital] called. Wanted to dump a woman on us because she had no place to go. She wasn't a battered woman, referred to [another shelter]. (Loseke 1992, p. 83)

> Crisis call from J.E., rather elusive, claims to battery. Husband has kicked her out of the house and refuses to let her return. She requested a place to sleep for 2–3 days. I do not see an immediate need here, she has mother, friends here. (Loseke 1989, p. 186)

The first of these entries glosses over the criteria used to deny admission, relying on the claim that the candidate client "wasn't a battered woman" to justify her exclusion. The second entry builds a case against the application of the battered woman label by first casting doubt on the woman's experiences, noting the woman's "claims to battery" rather than, say, simply reporting that she had been battered. Then it lists three characteristics of the candidate client that are not typically linked to the battered woman type: She lacked proper motivation for seeking shelter ("she requested a place to sleep"), she was not trapped in a violent situation ("husband has kicked her out"), and she was not socially isolated ("she has mother, friends here"). The woman was thus accountably constructed as "not battered" within the practical context and local interpretive culture of this particular shelter. As in the instances where women were taken into the shelter, social problems work attached or withheld membership in the battered woman category.

Concrete instances of social problems do not exist apart from the interpretive work that produces them. The "homeless mentally ill" (Campbell and Reeves 1989), the "chronically unemployed" (Miller 1991), "juvenile delinquents" (Emerson 1969), and myriad other everyday instances of abstract social problems are constituted through social problems work. A social constructionist approach should include an explicit focus on this work.

Interactional Bases

As an interpretive project, social problems work is interactive as well as rhetorical. Social problems designations are not unilaterally enforced, simply applied or withheld; instead they emerge from talk, interaction, and negotiation. Consider, for example, how a child is assigned to the social problem category "emotionally disturbed" in a meeting of a multidisciplinary team of mental health professionals and educators (Buckholdt and Gubrium 1985). The team has been assigned the responsibility of certifying children for ongoing care at a juvenile treatment facility. In the meeting concerning student Teddy Green, we encounter commonplace interpretive practices that select information from Teddy's case file and assemble it in a coherent pattern that documents his ostensible disturbance and membership in the problem category.

In the following excerpt, note how Dee Lerner (DL) and Dave Bachman (DB), a clinical educator and school psychologist, respectively, typify the child at several points, attempting to fill in what is lacking in Teddy's file to produce a consistent portrait of Teddy's problem. At one point Lerner and Bachman, together with Floyd Crittenden (FC), the facility's principal, focus on Teddy's home neighborhood and the family's residential origin as the relevant interpretive framework for understanding his problems. They use this to make further inferences about the nature of Teddy's disturbance. Decision-making rests on the unspoken assumptions that emotional disturbance exists in principle as an educational and behavioral deficit—a collective representation. The principal opens the meeting:

FC: We have new psychs [complete psychological reports] on Green and Jones.
DB: Good. Green first then.
      [Staffers try to locate Green's home address because it is not clear in the file where his parents reside.]
DL: When I don't know the home address, I put the local foster home down. I guess it doesn't matter as long as I'm consistent. Everyone does these [multidisciplinary team reports] differently. [Turning to Bachman] You know that, don't you? I'll put that down anyway. He's ten years old. So he's three years below grade level. Right?
DB: Uh-huh.
      [There is a five-minute pause for writing.]
DB: He's from Mayville.
FC: They moved into Morley [the local metropolitan area] on Logan Street. Have you ever seen Logan Street? It's like an alley. It's narrower than an alley.
DB: [Laughing as he reads Teddy's file] When he's in the classroom it says here that the teacher had to put him in his seat at least twice [on the average] in ten minutes of the school day.
FC: [Sarcastically] Active.
DB: That was two years ago.
DL: It says here that he's two years below grade level. But I think he's three years below. So I'll put that down.

[There is another pause for writing, then conversation resumes, first turning to Teddy's physical condition, then his behavior in the program.]

DB: [Laughing as he reads the file] It says you've decreased his running [being away from the center without permission]. He only runs to the A&P now.

FC: Yeah. You should have seen him go before.

[Teddy's running behavior is discussed and elaborated. There is much amused commentary and sarcasm over the image of Teddy's running being generated. Staffers then return to their report writing.]

DB: Millikin [one of the center's consulting psychologists] questioned the language dysfunction here. [He reads from Teddy's file.] Two or three years below average. Do you thing we should put that in?

FC: He doesn't have a speech problem, really.

DL: I think it's cultural deprivation. They seem like hill people. They live in an alley on the south side.

FC: They're from the South, and you might say that they're hill people. He doesn't have any deficiency in swearing though. You should see his home. What a mess!

DL: It's funny about emotionally disturbed children. They really know how to swear. I became an adult after I started to work with these kids . . . .

FC: The mother used to drive me crazy. She was always telling me when Teddy ran. He'd run from anxiety, frustration, and all that.

DB: Is the mother divorced?

FC: No. But whenever the mother disciplines the kids, it's always, "I'll club you."

[Crittenden's pager buzzes and he leaves. Bachman and Lerner take a ten-minute break, then resume their report writing.]

DL: [She talks as she read's Teddy's file] This is a classic, isn't it. The typical emotionally disturbed kid: nothing exceptional, just problems of one sort or another. (Buckholdt and Gubrium 1985, pp. 197–99)

As the participants sort through and highlight various aspects of information that might be relevant to the case at hand, they produce documents of what ultimately comes to be seen as a typical example of emotional disturbance. The selective description assembles the working picture of the student, providing the warrant for the categorization. Teddy's status is "worked up" as the staffers interactively consider his case, ultimately placing him in the emotionally disturbed category.

Social problems work need not be so intentional. Nor is it necessarily one-sided, with commonsense interpreters assigning or withholding others' membership in problem categories. Individuals may claim membership for themselves, as when an "unemployed" person applies for welfare assistance or a "battered woman" applies for shelter. Or they might resist, as in involuntary commitment hearings or criminal trials, for example. Documents that are used to justify category membership may even be collaboratively produced—not only in the intentional fashion described in the example directly above, but through practices unremarkable to those involved. This happens frequently in involuntary commitment hearings, for example.

As representatives of the district attorney's (DA) office argue that candidate patients are mentally ill and in need of hospitalization, they attempt to produce evidence of these charges to support their case. Psychiatric testimony, as we have seen, provides one form of documentation. Further evidence often emerges from the hearing interactions, not necessarily in terms of answers to testimony or narrative testimony, but through the conversational exchanges themselves. In the case considered below, the DA had asked fourteen prior questions, one immediately following the other, regarding where Lisa Sellers—the candidate patient—intended to live if she were released. The DA then initiated the following sequence:

1.	DA2:	How do you like summer out here, Lisa?
2.	LS:	It's OK.
3.	DA2:	How long have you lived here?
4.	LS:	Since I moved from Houston
5.		(Silence)
6.	LS:	About three years ago.
7.	DA2:	Tell me about why you came here.
8.	LS:	I just came.
9.		(Silence)
10.	LS:	You know, I wanted to see the stars, Hollywood.
11.		(Silence)
12.	DA2:	Uh huh.
13.	LS:	I didn't have no money.
14.		(Silence)
15.	LS:	I'd like to get a good place to live.
16.		(Silence five seconds)
17.	DA2:	Go on.((spoken simultaneously with onset of next utterance))
18.	LS:	There was some nice things I brought.
19.		(Silence)
20.	DA2:	Uh huh.
21.	LS:	Brought them from the rocketship.
22.	DA2:	Oh really?
23.	LS:	They was just some things I had.
24.	DA2:	From the rocketship?
25.	LS:	Right.
26.	DA2:	Were you on it?
27.	LS:	Yeah.
28.	DA2:	Tell me about this rocketship, Lisa. (Holstein 1988, p. 467)

The sequence culminates in the patient's reference to a rocketship. Later, the DA summarized the case, stating that this sort of talk—the "delusions" about the rocketship in particular—clearly indicated that Ms. Sellers was "mentally ill," unable to manage her life, and in need of hospitalization. While the talk about the rocketship was ostensibly produced by Ms. Sellers, close examination of the extract reveals the conversational work done by the DA that contributed to the final outcome.

Note how the DA encouraged extended and unfocused turns at talk by the way he managed his participation in the conversation. First, he altered the structure of the conversation from what may have come to be understood as a "normal" or "expected" sequence of questions and answers. In the fourteen exchanges immediately prior to this extract, and continuing in lines 1 through 4, the DA questioned the patient, then directly followed the patient's answers with questions, allowing no notable gaps between answers and next questions. Silence, however, followed line 4, to be terminated by the patient's elaboration. In line 7, the DA solicited further talk, but not in the form of a question. This was a very general request for the patient to provide more information, but the adequacy of a response to this type of solicit is more indeterminate than for a direct question. The DA's discretion is deeply implicated in what may come to be seen as adequately fulfilling the request, the completeness of a response depending, in part, on how the DA acknowledges it.

The DA did not respond at the first possible speaker transition point after the patient's next utterance (lines 8 and 9), and declined possible speakership or minimally filled turnspaces through line 20. The patient's mention of a rocketship finally elicited an indication of apparent interest ("Oh really?") from the DA at line 22. The DA then asked two additional questions before soliciting further talk about the rocketship. Once again this was done without asking a direct question, instead making a general request for information.

This segment of cross-examination produced an instance of hearably "crazy" or delusional talk that was ultimately cited as evidence of the *candidate patient's* mental illness. But it is clear that this testimony is an interactional achievement. The DA requested testimony from the patient, but repeatedly withheld acknowledgment of the testimony's adequacy, promoting further talk in the process. He further encouraged the patient to speak, using "Uh huh" to indicate an understanding that an extended unit of talk was in progress and was not yet complete (Schegloff 1982), and by declining possible turns at talk altogether. The patient, for her part, sustained the ongoing conversation by terminating silences that had begun to emerge at failed speaker transition points. She repeatedly elaborated responses, and eventually produced the "crazy" talk that was cited as evidence of her interactional incompetence. But, in a sense, it was her cooperation with the DA in extending the conversation—her conversational competence—that allowed for the emergence of that very talk. As an instance of social problems work, we can see both parties to the interaction engaged in the production of verbalizations that were subsequently used to document social problems claims. Perhaps inadvertently, but nonetheless actively, both parties contributed to the production of documents used to further social problems claims-making. The social problems work leading up to categorization was thoroughly interactional.

Social Problems Work as Open-Ended Process

The processes by which representations of social problems are applied are essentially open-ended. Analysis of the emergent construction of instances of social problems thus requires a natural history framework rather than an "endpoint" or retrospective point of view (see Emerson and Messinger 1977). If analysts simply focus on cases where an instance of a problem has been identified, the events and interpretive work leading up to the present-time definition take on a somewhat "determined" quality. That is, events and interpretations appear to lead logically to the outcome—the problematic status of the case at hand. This ignores the myriad contingencies that affect what happens in any candidate case where a problem category might be applied. Whereas a case might be assigned to the problem category, it is possible that it might also be defined differently—that is, as an instance of something other than a social problem. For example, Steve Howe, pitcher for the New York Yankees, was suspended from major league baseball for repeated drug abuse—labeled a chronic instance of a social problem. In an appeal of his suspension, however, his attorney argued that he should be tested and treated for "adult attention deficit disorder"—a medical condition— thus opening up the definitional possibility for just what Howe was and how he should be treated (*Sporting News*, August 8, 1992).

Processes of social problems work are ongoing, locally managed, and sensitive to practical circumstances. Analysis should therefore recognize that categorization is always uncertain, that more than a single category might be interpretively related to any candidate case, and that the designation of any particular instance is provisional, for the practical purpose at hand, and always subject to change.

Consider the complexities, for example, of the social problems work that might be involved in constructing concrete instances of "juvenile delinquency." Such interpretation first requires the availability of the collective representation or category as a constructive resource. Thus, images of both "juvenile" and "delinquency" must exist for instances of the problem to be constructed. Aries (1965) documents the emergence of the concept of childhood, the seeming prerequisite for juvenile problems, while others have outlined the emergence of the notion of a particular brand of trouble involving children—juvenile delinquency (Empey 1982; Platt 1969; Schlossman 1977). With the category available as an everyday interpretive resource, under what circumstances will it be applied?

Certainly the behavior of the youth in question is relevant. Its importance, however, is not because the youth's actions determine whether he or she is labeled as a problem. Rather, aspects of the youth that are made topical—matters of behavior, character, background, and the like—are themselves available as interpretive resources, factors that can be described, interpreted, and defined in the process of making sense of any particular person or situation. While interpretations of persons or actions may not be infinitely variable, neither are they certain to lead to any particular depiction; meaning is always mediated by interpretive process. Thus, analysis of social problems work must focus on what is interpretively *done* with aspects of experience to assign them to particular categories.

Analysis must also avoid presuppositions about what sort of instances may eventually be made into problems. Informal reactions and interpretations may place occurrences in a problem category, but they are also capable of making candidate problems into more-or-less "normal" aspects of everyday life (Lynch 1983; Pollner and McDonald-Wickler 1985), or locating them in alternative "problem" categories. The interpretive activity that differentiates "childish pranks" from "juvenile delinquency" is commonplace. As mundane as it is, and as overlooked in the study of social problems as it might be, the process by which "nothing" is made of a candidate problem is an important aspect of social problems work.

The same is true of more formally organized social problems work. Citizen complaints to the police, for example, must be organized into organizationally relevant response categories. Meehan's (1989) study of telephone requests for service suggests that the telephone conversations involve complex interpretive work to produce police categorizations of, and responses to, what are designated (and recorded in police records) as instances of juvenile delinquency and youth gang activity. Similarly, police encounters with juveniles are open-ended, deeply implicating the officers' interpretive practices in determining what will be made of the persons and circumstances they encounter (Cicourel 1968; Meehan 1986; Piliavin and Briar 1968; Sanders 1977). Indeed, studies of what has come to be known as the exercise of police "discretion" in the application of the law might be recast as studies of social problems work in the field.

Being an open-ended process, the designation of a case as an instance of a social problem does not finalize its interpretation. A police officer, for example, may categorize an instance of juvenile delinquency, but its classification is always subject to change. Screening procedures "divert" many cases referred by the police before they are adjudicated. Who is treated as a "delinquent" or who is disposed of in some other fashion—as a minor trouble that will go away on its own, or as a psychiatric or medical matter, for example—is determined through organizationally circumscribed interpretive procedures that construct and manipulate the "facts" of the case at hand in light of practical objectives and circumstances (Needleman 1981). Similarly, when cases reach juvenile courts, they are once again interpreted to see whether they coincide with the categories of "normal," "hard core or criminallike delinquent," or "disturbed" (Emerson 1969). Subsequently, court personnel employ "pitches" and "denunciations"—rhetorical maneuvers—to warrant their categorizations, once again "working up" the example of the social problem in the routine course of doing the work of the court.

The upshot of ongoing social problems work is that a case is never fully or finally constituted as juvenile delinquency. New processing venues may interpretively transform the problem from one form to another. As Emerson's (1969) study of juvenile court illustrates, court decision-making may construct either juvenile delinquents or emotionally or psychiatrically disturbed children from the same candidate cases. Probation officers may then have to convince the involved juvenile and his or her family that the categorization is proper—"in the best interest of the child"—often "cooling out" persons who have vested interests in alternative definitions in the process (Darrough 1984, 1989, 1990).

With the creation of medical definitions for troublesome childhood behavior—hyperkinesis, for example (Conrad 1975)—candidate juvenile delinquents may also be categorized as medical rather than social problems. And with the proliferation and popularization of psychiatric and "substance abuse" terminology, diverse resources are increasingly available for constructing instances of problems of various sorts. Categorization is transinstitutionalized (Warren 1981) as organizational settings provide distinctive orientations, vocabularies, and interpretive resources that condition the ways cases are defined.

Ultimately, the results of the varied interpretations and decisions may be tallied to produce statistical documents of the incidence and prevalence of juvenile problems. But these "hard data" that ostensibly indicate that the various problems do, "in fact," exist are themselves products of social problems work (Gubrium and Buckholdt 1979, Kitsuse and Cicourel 1963).

And as final as a statistical tally may make any particular interpretive project seem, social problems work is always open to revision. An instance of a problem is never permanently constituted. A case involving a client and workers of a Work Incentive Program (WIN) illustrates the way today's problem may interpretively evolve into something else (Miller 1985). The client (CL) had developed a reputation among WIN staff as a troublesome character, a man with a "bad attitude." In most respects he was considered an example of the "hard-core" unemployed, an especially salient category for WIN personnel. Considered a nearly hopeless case, the client was sent for some routine diagnostic tests at the Alternate Education Center. Much to everyone's surprise—including the client himself—the scores were much higher than anticipated. In light of the new information, previous formulations of the client's biography, attitude, and problems were revised, as was evident in the following discussion with a WIN staff member (SM):

> SM: You've got a brain. You just haven't always used it to make wise choices. I'll bet your problem in school was that you were bored.
>
> CL: Yeah, I was bored. About the ninth grade I lost all interest.
>
> SM: You didn't do the work, you acted out and you got put in the dummy group. You should have been in the gifted class or at least at the top of your group. You got in a group that didn't care and you didn't either. . . . Maybe you should think about college. You could go to [a local college]. What would you like to be, an engineer? (Miller 1985, p. 387)

The reassessment was profound. "He's really changed. He is taking control of his life. It's so easy to work with him," noted a staff member (p. 388). Relying upon the "documentary method of interpretation" (Garfinkel 1967), old "facts" were assimilated to a new pattern. Within a very short time, the client was interpretively transformed from the embodiment of a social problem into "the success story of the year" (Miller 1985, p. 388). As an open-ended process, interpretive practice reconstituted the client's identity and past, but left the possibility open for future interpretive revision.

Prospects and Implications

A sociology of social problems work considers how interpretation proceeds in the myriad everyday settings where instances of social problems might be constructed. There is no *theoretical* reason to assume that any individuals or groups, or any organized settings, are more appropriate than others as sites of social problems work. Instances of social problems may be constructed anywhere social problems rubrics might be invoked, anywhere problems become interpretive possibilities. As a practical matter, settings where problematic or troublesome behavior is routinely and specifically topicalized are the most likely to produce social problems discourse. Human service and social control settings are therefore rich in opportunities to observe the attachment of social problems representations to concrete cases.

But the work in these settings cannot be considered more "authentic" than other constructions; their enacted problems are no more objective or "real" than those assembled in alternative settings. Social problems work by human service or social control professionals might generally be accorded a practical legitimacy that encourages others to take professional interpretations more "seriously" than others' interpretations. But that legitimacy is also an ongoing social accomplishment.

Some forms of social problems work may also have more far-reaching effects than others. The mass media, for instance, not only participate in the promotion of social problems categories, but they provide widely publicized examples of the image as it is attached to experience. We see living representations of the homeless mentally ill, for example, in network television news programming that selects concrete cases and portrays them as the embodiment of the social problems image. Campbell and Reeves (1989) argue that television news publicizes the distinction between mainstream populations and those designated as problems of mental illness and homelessness, artfully manipulating visual images and verbal commentary to attach "public idioms" to selected aspects of experience in contrast to others. The dynamics of how interpretations are promoted, legitimated, and sustained, and the informal, professional, and technical practices used to interpret cases are thus important topics for analysis.

While studies of social problems work focus on interpretive practice, they also incorporate context. Not only are social problems representations organizationally produced and preferred models for interpretation, but their use is conditioned by prevailing local preferences, practices, and resources. Both image and attachment are organizationally embedded (Gubrium 1988); categories and the practices through which they are applied reflect local interpretive circumstances and culture. Contextual influence is apparent, for example, when we observe how juvenile problems are variously formulated in law enforcement, psychiatric, and medical surroundings. Each setting has its available resources, institutionalized procedures, and practical discourses for dealing with matters they routinely encounter. While the contexts neither predict nor determine individual outcomes, they provide orientations and resources that generally distinguish the interpretation process in one circumstance from that in another. Studies of social problems work therefore consider the practical contingencies and discursive and interactional structures that characterize the contexts within which the work takes place. Practice remains central, with recognition of its situated, contextualized character.

As social problems work is increasingly carried out in formal organizations that process and channel everyday life, interpretation may become increasingly "professionalized" and "institutionalized." Public bureaucracies, human service organizations, and social control agencies routinely formulate problems and their solutions, their work being organized around the rhetorical production of the troubles and problems they ostensibly address (Miller 1990, 1991). This suggests a more general issue regarding the pervasive bureaucratization and rationalization of experience. Weber (1958, 1968) referred to "formal rationality" as the organization of conduct according to calculated principles, formal rules, and institutionalized procedures. He argued that rationalized social relations adhere to generalized principles that promote the sort of predictability that facilitates bureaucratic activity. As life comes progressively under formal and official auspices, meaning is increasingly institutionalized. Interpretation is totalized as the tendencies of organizations assert themselves to overwhelm individual differences in representational practice.

From Weber's standpoint, the representation of experience is progressively "disenchanted" in that there is no room left for personalized, spontaneous thought and action (Bendix 1960). A social problems work perspective, however, reasserts the importance of practice without denying the role of context. Interpretive structure and culture cannot be as totalizing as Weber suggests because they must always be applied— situatedly, yet creatively, articulated with selected aspects of experience (Gubrium 1992). People are not mere captives or extensions of organizational thinking and discursive structures. They exercise interpretive discretion conditioned by a complex layering of interpretive resources and influences. So, whereas personnel in a particular human service agency may orient to social problems in organizationally promoted ways, they bring multiple resources and vocabularies to any interpretive occasion, encouraging diversity in the identification of problem cases. Practical interpretation, then, is almost unavoidably paradoxical: Individual practice yields spontaneity and diversity, while context and interpretive structure promote pattern.

A sociology of social problems work thus addresses both interpretive structure and practice as they jointly produce everyday instances of social problems. This dual focus on social process and representational resources reveals a new dimension to the construction of social problems.

References

Aires, Phillippe. 1965. *Centuries of Childhood. A Social History of Family Life.* New York: Vintage.

Bendix, Reinhard. 1960. *Max Weber: An Intellectual Portrait.* New York: Doubleday.

Buckholdt, David R. and Jaber F. Gubrium. 1985. *Caretakers.* Lanham, MD: University Press of America.

Campbell, Richard and Jimmie. L. Reeves. 1989. "Covering the Homeless: The Joyce Brown Story." *Critical Studies in Mass Communication* 6:21–42.

Cicourel, Aaron. 1968. *The Social Organization of Juvenile Justice.* New York: Wiley.

Conrad, Peter. 1975. "The Discovery of Hyperkinesis." *Social Problems* 23:12–21.

Darrough, William D. 1984. "In the Best Interest of the Child: Negotiating Parental Cooperation for Probation Placement." *Urban Life* 13:123–53.

_____. 1989. "In the Best Interest of the Child II: Neutralizing Resistance to Probation Placement." *Journal of Contemporary Ethnography* 18:72–88.

_____. 1990. "Neutralizing Resistance: Probation Work as Rhetoric." Pp. 163–87 in *Perspectives on Social Problems*, vol. 2, edited by G. Miller and J. Holstein. Greenwich, CT: JAI Press.

Douglas, Mary. 1986. *How Institutions Think.* Syracuse, NY: Syracuse University Press.

Durkheim, Emile. 1961. *The Elementary Forms of the Religious Life.* New York: Collier-Macmillan.

Emerson, Robert M. 1969. *Judging Delinquents.* Chicago: Aldine.

Emerson, Robert M. and Sheldon L. Messinger. 1977. "The Micro-politics of Trouble." *Social Problems* 25:121–34.

Empey, Lamar. 1982. *American Delinquency.* Homewood, IL: Dorsey.

Foucault, Michel. 1965. *Madness and Civilization.* New York: Random House.

_____. 1972. *The Archaeology of Knowledge.* New York: Pantheon.

_____. 1973. *The Birth of the Clinic.* New York: Random House.

Garfinkel, Harold. 1967. *Studies in Ethnomethodology.* Englewood Cliffs, NJ: Prentice-Hall.

Gubrium, Jaber F. 1988. *Analyzing Field Reality.* Newbury Park, CA: Sage.

_____. 1991. "Recognizing and Analyzing Local Cultures." Pp. 131–41 in *Experiencing Fieldwork*, edited by W. Shaffir and R. Stebbins. Newbury Park, CA: Sage.

_____. 1992. *Out of Control.* Newbury Park, CA: Sage.

Gubrium, Jaber F. and David R. Buckholdt. 1979. "Producing Hard Data in Human Service Institutions." *Pacific Sociological Review* 22:115–36.

Heritage, John. 1984. *Garfinkel and Ethnomethodology.* Cambridge: Polity Press.

Holstein, James A. 1987. "Producing Gender Effects on Involuntary Mental Hospitalization." *Social Problems* 34:141–55.

_____. 1988. "Court Ordered Incompetence: Conversational Organization in Involuntary Commitment Proceedings." *Social Problems* 35:801–16.

_____. 1992. "Producing People: Descriptive Practice in Human Service Work." Pp. 23–40 in *Current Research on Occupations and Professions*, vol. 7, edited by G. Miller. Greenwich, CT: JAI Press.

———. 1993. *Court-Ordered Insanity: Interpretive Practice and Involuntary Commitment.* Hawthorne, NY: Aldine de Gruyter.

Kitsuse, John I. and Aaron Cicourel. 1963. "A Note on the Use of Official Statistics." *Social Problems* 11:131–39.

Kitsuse, John. I and Malcolm Spector. 1973. "Toward a Sociology of Social Problems." *Social Problems* 20:407–19.

———. 1975. "Social Problems and Deviance: Some Parallel Issues." *Social Problems* 22:584–94.

Lipsky, Michael. 1980. *Street-Level Bureaucracy.* New York: Russell Sage Foundation.

Loseke, Donileen R. 1989. "Creating Clients: Social Problems Work in a Shelter for Battered Women." Pp. 173–94 in *Perspectives on Social Problems,* vol. 1, edited by James A. Holstein and Gale Miller. Greenwich, CT: JAI Press.

———. 1992. *The Battered Woman and Shelters.* Albany, NY: SUNY Press.

Lynch, Michael. 1983. "Accommodation Practices: Vernacular Treatments of Madness." *Social Problems* 31:152–63.

Meehan, Albert J. 1986. "Record-keeping Practices in the Policing of Juveniles." *Urban Life* 15:70–102.

———. 1989. "Assessing the 'Police-worthiness' of Citizen Complaints to the Police." Pp. 116–40 in *The Interactional Order,* edited by D. Helm, W. Anderson, A. Meehan, and A. Rawls. New York: Irvington.

Miller, Gale. 1985. "Client Attitude and Organizational Process." *Urban Life* 13:367–94.

———. 1990. "Work as Reality Maintaining Activity: Interactional Aspects of Occupational and Professional Work." Pp. 163–83 in *Current Research on Occupations and Professions,* vol. 5, edited by Helena Lopata. Greenwich, CT: JAI Press.

———. 1991. *Enforcing the Work Ethnic.* Albany, NY: SUNY Press.

———. 1992. "Human Service Practice as Social Problems Work." Pp. 3–22 in *Current Research on Occupations and Professions,* vol. 7. edited by G. Miller. Greenwich, CT: JAI Press.

Miller, Gale and James A. Holstein. 1989. "On The Sociology of Social Problems." Pp. 1–16 in *Perspectives on Social Problems,* vol. 1 edited by James A. Holstein and Gale Miller. Greenwich, CT: JAI Press.

———. 1991. "Social Problems Work in Street-Level Bureaucracies." Pp. 177–202 in *Studies in Organizational Sociology,* edited by G. Miller. Greenwich, CT: JAI Press.

Needleman, Carolyn. 1981. "Discrepant Assumptions in Empirical Research: The Case of Juvenile Court Screening." *Social Problems* 28:247–62.

Piliavin, Irving and Scott Briar. 1968. "Police Encounters with Juveniles." *American Journal of Sociology* 70:206–14.

Platt, Anthony. 1969. *The Child Savers.* Chicago: University of Chicago Press.

Pollner, Melvin. 1987. *Mundane Reason.* Cambridge: Cambridge University Press.

———. 1991. "Left of Ethnomethodology: the Rise and Decline of Radical Reflexivity." *American Sociological Review* 56:370–80.

Pollner, Melvin and Lynn McDonald-Wickler. 1985. "The Social Construction of

Unreality: A Case Study of a Family's Attribution of Competence to a Severely Retarded Child." *Family Process* 24:241–54.

Sanders, William B. 1977. *Detective Work*. New York: Free Press.

Sarbin, Theodore R. 1969. "The Scientific Status of the Mental Illness Metaphor."
Pp. 9–31 in *Changing Perspectives in Mental Illness*, edited by S. C. Plog and
R. B. Edgerton. New York: Free Press.

Sarbin, Theodore R. and James C. Mancuso. 1970. "Failure of a Moral Enterprise:
Attitudes of the Public Toward Mental Illness." *Journal of Consulting and
Clinical Psychology* 35:159–73.

Schegloff, Emanuel A. 1982. "Discourse as an Interactional Achievement: Some
Uses of 'Uh huh' and Other Things That Come Between Sentences." Pp. 71–
93 in *Georgetown University Roundtable on Language and Linguistics*, edited by
D. Tannen. Washington, DC: Georgetown University Press.

Schlossman, Steven L. 1977. *Love and the American Delinquent*. Chicago: University of Chicago Press.

Schutz, Alfred. 1970. *On Phenomenology and Social Relations*. Chicago: University
of Chicago Press.

Smith, Dorothy E. 1978. "'K is Mentally Ill': The Anatomy of a Factual Account."
Sociology 12:23–53.

Spector, Malcolm and John I. Kitsuse. 1974. "Social Problems: A Reformulation."
Social Problems 21:145–58.

———. [1977] 1987. *Constructing Social Problems*. Hawthorne, NY: Aldine de
Gruyter.

Studer, Marlena. 1984. "Wife Beating as a Social Problem: The Process of Definition." *International Journal of Women's Studies* 7:412–22.

Tierney, Kathleen. 1982. "The Battered Women Movement and the Creation of
the Wife Beating Problem." *Social Problems* 29:207–17.

Troyer, Ronald J. 1989. "Are Social Problems and Social Movements the Same
Thing?" Pp. 41–58 in *Perspectives on Social Problems*, vol. 1, edited by
J. Holstein and G. Miller. Greenwich, CT: JAI Press.

Warren, Carol A. B. 1981. "New Forms of Social Control: The Myth of Deinstitu-
tionalization." *American Behavioral Scientist* 24:724–40.

Weber, Max. 1958. *The Protestant Ethic and the Spirit of Capitalism*. New York:
Scribners.

———. 1968. *Economy and Society*. New York: Bedminster Press.

9

Social Problems and the Organization of Talk and Interaction

Courtney L. Marlaire and Douglas W. Maynard

As part of the analytic move away from an "objectivist" description of social problems,[1] current theoretical developments in the social "constructionist" position place an increased emphasis on discursive and linguistic practices. Indeed, Ibarra and Kitsuse (this volume) propose to reformulate the constructionist position by explicating the vernacular constituents of social problems "claims–making." Delineating the rhetoric of the "social problems language game," say Ibarra and Kitsuse, "allows us to move from single social condition–centered analyses to a more comparative approach by seeking and identifying commonalities at the level of members' discursive practices."

Although we applaud this interest in discursive practices, our sense of this development is that it threatens to lose a radical element of the original constructionist project, which also involves forms of language, but in relation to actual concerted activity. To make this contention first requires a selective synopsis of the Spector and Kitsuse ([1977] 1987) project and a short critique of relevant aspects of the Ibarra and Kitsuse reformulation. After the synopsis and critique, we will argue that studies of language and social interaction may preserve an overlooked aspect of the radical stance implicit in early constructionism. In the bulk of the chapter, then, we will discuss examples of work that, in our opinion, carry the radical stance forward, but not via a concern with social problems either as they are traditionally conceived or as "discursive" constructionism envisions them. That is, rather than pursuing either those problems of interest to policymakers, social scientists, and other professionals, or those problems that emerge in the discursive activities of a set of claims-makers, the various language-based approaches to social interaction that we review aim to understand how people handle problems of most immediate and local interest *to them* as they talk and act with one another in the here and now of ordinary, everyday life.

A Radical Element of Early Constructionism

There are probably many radical elements of constructionism. Surely the most fundamental contribution has been the way in which Spector and Kitsuse ([1977] 1987) critiqued the traditional social scientific preoccupation with both *defining* what a social problem is and then investigating what *caused* the problem. Their suggestion was to investigate how actors themselves define problems, determine their causes, and collectively act in political and ameliorative fashion to remedy these problems. Additionally, we think there is a perhaps overlooked radical element to the theory. Recall that Spector and Kitsuse regard "social problems as *the activities of individuals or groups making assertions of grievances and claims with respect to some putative conditions* ([1977] 1987, p. 75). Now, Ibarra and Kitsuse suggest replacing the term "putative condition" with "condition-category," which may be an improvement consistent with our interest in the *duality* of the constructionist approach. This duality abides in the way that Spector and Kitsuse's formulation simultaneously points to the *activities* of individuals or groups, *and* how parties come to experience *conditions* as problematic. While early constructionism thus directed renewed attention to activities of defining social problems, those activities contain, as an embedded element, participants' sense of encountering "objective" social problems. Put differently, the constructionist perspective brought actual social activities involving social problems to the fore, where a constituent feature of those activities is actors' experienced sense of confronting real problems of various sorts.[2]

Over the years, perhaps because of the "ambiguous ontological" status of the "putative conditions" phrase (Ibarra and Kitsuse), it seems that the enormous quantity of research from a constructionist perspective has been preoccupied with the activities and even social movements whereby social problems become part of the public sphere. At the same time, the other side of constructionism's duality, having to do with participants' original experience and sense of problems, has been latent. It is our contention that this latent side of constructionism needs increased appreciation, for it is here that something of the actuality and specificity of the sense and experience of social problems will be found. Addressing their critics while further developing the constructionist project as (radically) opposing the objectivist position, Ibarra and Kitsuse's condition-categories aim to remedy the ambiguity of "putative conditions," but in so doing, they remain tethered to an objectivist episteme, as condition-categories are typifications of social processes rather than actual activities.

When we refer to people's sense and experience of social problems, we are not pointing to the devastating psychological and physical effects of social problems, however real these may be. Rather, we are interested in the social organization of sense-making and experience as this organization is manifest in the procedures of real-time talk and interaction. Ibarra and Kitsuse's refinements of the constructionist position incorporate an appreciation of linguistic and paralinguistic practices, but their concern with rhetorics, counterrhetorics, motifs, and styles misses the distinctive *local* methods of social problem production and assessment. Since there is a body of work—much of it inspired by ethnomethodology and conversation analysis—that does investigate such practices, we do not have to create an understanding of local social organization de novo. This body of work, we believe, can resurrect the latent side of constructionism's radical impetus.

Local Order as Prehistorical

Our focus on the social organization of real-time talk and interaction has two facets. First, it is our contention that "problems" are in the first instance intersubjectively organized and constituted, and it is this "emic" (Geertz 1984) level of description that we feel is most lacking in current discussions. Objectivists, in assuming the substantial reality of social problems, and being concerned with their public effects, clearly take an "etic" (or outsiders') stance. By the same token, when constructionists (such as Ibarra and Kitsuse) work to detail problems as accomplishments of language, their use of second-order constructs (Schutz 1962) is still prominent, for talking about those who talk about poverty removes the condition from the realm of lived experience. Neither objectivists *nor* constructionists embrace the proximate sphere of actual talk and interaction, where participants' troubles and problems first become exhibited or made visible. That is, sociologists still need an inquiry into what we might call the *local emergence* of social problems.

Let us take an example of a study that fits with the Ibarra and Kitsuse reformulation of the constructionist position. Mehan and Wills (1988) describe rhetorical debates surrounding the nuclear arms race.[3] Against a historically dominant rhetoric of deterrence (justifying the arms build-up by suggesting that if enemies are capable of destroying each other, one's aggression against the other will be irrational), a group called MEND (Mothers Embracing Nuclear Disarmament) promoted a "nurturing" discourse in which they argued that mothers share a universal biological and spiritual bond cutting across national and cultural boundaries (pp. 367–69). In their efforts to affect the arms race, MEND attempted to garner ownership of various public meanings. Mehan and

Wills's analysis of the contingencies and complexities involved is masterful, and it fits nicely with Ibarra and Kitsuse's programmatic appeal.

From our position, however, Mehan and Wills are examining activities at a relatively late stage in the emergence of a social problem. What interests us as a second facet of the interaction order and local arenas is that which may or may not later be recast as where a social problem originally burgeoned. A tendency exists to view people's sometimes inchoate here-and-now activities from the standpoint of what, at a later point, those activities turn out to be, as if the here and now necessarily rather than contingently leads to its full-grown counterpart. In our view, Ibarra and Kitsuse's attention to language and discursive practices and their effort to define commonalities of rhetoric bypasses a whole realm in which troubles and problems occur in a literally *prehistoric* fashion, i.e., before that realm has been *historicized* by the idioms of public rhetoric about social problems.[4]

Mehan and Wills's study contains several autobiographical narratives where individuals recount immediate, interactive experiences in which troubles and problems are paramount to participants. An individual describes her "impromptu" visit to the Vietnam memorial in Washington, D.C.:

> This statue blew me away. Well what happened back there was that I began to cry looking at the faces of these young men thinking about Vietnam, just a gush of feelings, ran over me and entered my body. And my daughters looked at me crying and then they looked at the faces of the statue. And I could see that they were trying to figure out what it was that I was crying about. Why would mother be crying looking at these three men, these soldiers? I was struck that moment very powerfully by the realization, that I had *no explanation* for these children about what Vietnam was. Indeed I had no explanation about what war is. (1988, p. 367, emphasis in original; pauses deleted)

These and similar experiences turn out to be stimuli to social action for many of the members of MEND. Following our two concerns, we think it is incumbent on a sociology of social problems to examine the social organization of such experiences (1) *in themselves* (as local events) and (2) not just as the historicized precursors to activism; for every such experience that leads to involvement in social problems activities, there must be countless others that do not, and we must not exclude from analysis those participants' troubles and problems in immediate experience, which are not subsumed within a public debate.

In the above excerpt, for example, the autobiographer reacts to the memorial in an emotional way. Additionally, her response to her own reaction has noticeably socially organized aspects. She categorizes her companions and herself using the device "family" (Sacks 1972), which exhibits an orientation to the mother-daughter relationship as relevant to the *meaning* of her reaction (cf. Gubrium and Holstein 1990). There is an interesting sequencing to the narrative as well. The mother reports viewing the statue, emoting in a spontaneous way, and then seeing her daughters looking at her and at the statue. From this, she gathers that they are "trying to figure out" what was causing the crying, and coming to the realization of having no explanations.

Here, since we rely on the autobiographer's narrative, we cannot be sure of what the *actual* sequencing might have been. Her narrative is done under the auspices of accounting for her helping to get MEND started. Nevertheless, it points to a powerful experience that had some of its own organizational features—embodied perhaps most poignantly in the recounting of the ordered viewing, seeing, and looking of all the parties—that play into the narrative recasting. Our point is that we can know more about those features—how people organize and experience troubles and problems and do so "prehistorically" with others who are relationally important to them. We wish to assert that an analysis of the interaction order, at an inherently local level, can come close to a *members'-generated* sense of "social problems," and that such studies of talk and interaction provide a way of moving beyond the analyst's own definitional problems and second-order constructs.

The Interactional Bases of Problems

One of the first social problems perspectives to appreciate the interactive bases of deviant and troublesome behaviors was labeling theory. That is, labeling theory (Becker 1963), in suggesting that definitional processes can bring on the stabilization of deviant behavior, *appears* to deal with the nature of face-to-face confrontations wherein deviance and problems emerge, but the perspective is agnostic about the origins of this behavior or "primary deviance," and merely stresses that it may become "secondary" and sustained if others react by attaching stigmatizing categories (Lemert 1951). Thus, while it would seem important for these studies to examine speech in the context of interaction (cf. Pollner 1974, 1987; Boden 1991), such analyses are not traditional within the field (see also Gill 1991; Gill and Maynard 1992). Certainly large-scale examinations of the effect of labels on various measurable outcomes (such as arrest, prison sentences, mental hospitalizations) explicitly leave actual interaction untouched, and in so doing, gloss, misrepresent, or overlook important phenomena (Holstein 1987; Maynard 1982). Emerson and Messinger (1977)—in their analysis of the "micropolitics of trouble"—have suggested a means by which to chronicle whether some "difficulty" or "trouble" emerges publicly as "conflict" between parties or as the "deviance" of one of them, a perspective that has resulted in intriguing insights into how people manage trouble before it becomes labeled. The micropolitics framework has produced excellent and informative empirical work, but these studies depend on subjects' recollected interpretation (e.g., Cohn and Gallagher 1984; Lynch 1983; Schneider 1984) or on observation of rapid fire events (e.g. Emerson and Pollner 1978). They provide documentary understandings of how troubles are institutionally realized, but are still somewhat distanced from talk and action as they actually and originally occur, and so even Emerson and Messinger's (1977) framework invites a closer analysis of local interactional practice.

Recent microanalytic studies of talk and interaction using taped data have moved in this direction, demonstrating the social interaction of talk about "troubles" and "problems." Jefferson and Lee (1981) describe the interactional processes by which a "troubles-telling" becomes a "service encounter," and how interactional properties are managed such that members distinguish between talk that focuses on the "troubled person" and his or her experiences and talk that deals with the "problem" and its "properties" (pp. 411–21). For example, a way that troubles-telling can be abbreviated is for the recipient of such talk to offer advice before the teller has proffered a full account of the trouble. Resistance to the advice, in this context, may in part derive from the teller's reluctance to relinquish the "discourse identity" of speaker. Moving from telling troubles to hearing advice also involves a shift from emotional reciprocity to instrumental exchange. Thus to analyze the point at which a trouble becomes a problem requires careful attention to the organization of talk, including how participants manage relevant discourse identities in the transition from a "troubles-telling" to a "service encounter," and from "discussing 'trouble'" to formulating a "problem" and its remedies.

In focusing on the detail of real-time talk and interaction, we begin to see how members' private troubles and complaints are sequentially organized in particular ways in order to manage their becoming a public event. Emerson and Messinger have, as Drew and Holt note, effectively "pointed to the crucial role complaints have in the process of transforming the initially privately experienced and sustained nature of personal troubles into openly acknowledged interpersonal difficulties" (1988, p. 399). But, according to Drew and Holt, Emerson and Messinger stop short of demonstrating the specific moves that interactants deploy in managing complaints, and how these in turn specify, elaborate and thus constitute the nature of some trouble (p. 400). In this regard, complaints act as a sort of personal claim locating a "trouble," such that recipients' affiliation (or lack of it) has profound consequences for the organization of the "natural history of troubles management," and ultimately for the formulation of the complaint as a particular sort of trouble. In pursuit of an elaboration of the organization of complaints and responses to them, Drew and Holt (1988) describe instances where recipients of a complaint demonstrate some lack of alignment with the complainant. Speakers manage the failed attempt(s) to solicit sympathy in part through the use of idiomatic expressions, as in the following:

```
Ilene:    .hhh We've checked now on all the papers 'e <1
          has an' Moss'n Comp'ny said they were sent
          through the post we have had n:nothing from <2
          Moss'n Comp'ny through the post.
          (0.3) <3
Ilene:    Anyway, (.) Tha:t's th- uh you know you can't(.)
          argue ih it's like (.) uh:m
Shirley:                       Well <4
          (.)
Ilene:    banging yer head against a brick wa:ll. <5 (Drew and Holt 1988,
          pp. 402–3)
```

Note that at arrow 3 (and at the end of Ilene's subsequent utterance) the recipient of her complaint (Shirley) is provided a chance to demonstrate an agreeing or sympathetic response, but does not do so. In fact, at arrow 4 she overlaps Ilene's talk with the nonaffiliative "well." Then, at arrow 5, Ilene uses an idiom for the descriptive elaboration of her complaint. According to Drew and Holt (1988), idiomatic expressions are both figurative and robust, allowing sustainable versions of the complaint even in the absence of affiliation (as above). That is, figurative expressions are generally known and can be used (and understood) independent of the prior (and perhaps contested) detailing of a grievance. In being robust, idioms are akin to the work of Pomerantz's (1986) "extreme case formulations".[5] According to Pomerantz, such formulations are used frequently in complaints so as to mark the claim as worthy of complaint (p. 227). Drew and Holt note the presence of two such formulations in the previous example ("checked . . . . all the papers," and "we have had n:*noth*ing from Moss'n Comp'ny) at arrows 1 and 2, also noting that, "Similar to such extreme formulations, idioms may be designed to strengthen a complainant's case by portraying the egregious character of the complainable circumstances" (p. 405). Thus, close analysis suggests that both idiomatic expressions and "extreme case formulations" are interactional resources useful to interactants who anticipate (or receive) a less than sympathetic hearing of their complaints. As with "troubles," when and how complaints emerge as "problems" depends, in the first instance, on the radically local order of face-to-face interaction. This order includes systematicities whereby participants produce and respond to complaints and thereby provide for (or decline) interactional legitimacy.

The elucidation of the organization of real-time local interaction is much more than descriptive detail. We are not after a taxonomy of local practices that are solely in service to claims-making activity, for the interactional systematicity that we seek to describe undergirds all of social life. Nevertheless, consider how the careful packaging of any complainable matter is related to its production as an "official" problem (e.g., one worthy of police or other emergency intervention). An excellent example is Whalen, Zimmerman, and Whalen's (1988) analysis of a "failed" emergency call. The authors note (cf. Whalen et al. 1988, pp. 346–47) that there are two types of service encounters. Type I calls involve requesting a pizza or taxi, for instance, and require little more than the request and an address from the caller. The "need" for such a request is usually not questioned. Type II calls (i.e., emergency calls) involve establishing the validity of the request for service. If the parties to a service call are oriented to different frames (i.e., Type I vs. Type II), that can be problematic for giving or obtaining the service. Here is the opening segment of the "failed" request for help that Whalen et al. examine (here D is the department operator who answers the phone and C is the caller):

1. D: Firedepartment
2.   (0.8)
3. C: Yes. I'd like tuh have an ambulance at forty-one
4.   thirty-nine Haverford please
5.   (0.5)
6. D: What's thuh problem sir?
7. C: I: don't know, n'if I knew I wouldn't be calling
8.   you all. (Whalen et al. 1988, p. 336)

According to Whalen et al. (1988), the caller appears to assume the context of a Type I call, so that he treats the department operator's question at line 6 as inappropriate (lines 7 and 8). From the caller's point of view, it might be like being asked, when he orders a pizza, why he wants one. There are a number of other factors that fuel the developing disagreement(s) in this call and that result in the caller's failure to obtain the service, but we can see how this initial misframing helps to engender disagreement about the ground rules of the exchange that is unfolding (cf. Watson 1987). Overall, the interaction is characterized by mutual resistance and opposition, and quickly emerges as a dispute. In the end, the negotiation of "the problem" and its serviceable nature itself becomes "a problem."

In another institutional setting, Maynard (1991a, pp. 164, 190) identifies a "perspective-display" series whereby clinicians deliver diagnoses
to parents of developmentally disabled children. The following interactions are characteristic ways that some diagnoses begin, i.e., with a
query about how the parents view the child:

(1)   Dr: What do you see as his difficulty?
        Mrs. A: Mainly his um the fact that he doesn't understand everything
                 and also the fact his speech is very hard to understand . . . .

(2)   Dr: Now tell me what you feel is the problem.
        Mrs. B: Mm he's not learning.

These questions embody "problem proposals" and not merely requests
for information, so that if parents respond to clinicians by describing the
child's difficulties, they affiliate with the proposal that the child, indeed,
has a "problem," and this provides a warrant to the clinician to continue
with the delivery of the diagnosis. Such proposals, however, can be
discounted, resisted, or ignored, and if they are, clinicians work to rees-
tablish the proposal and get its acceptance before delivering the diagnosis. That a child has a problem becomes a presumed feature of the
interaction between parents and clinicians, therefore, but it is also a
methodic accomplishment that resides in discourse practices such as
those of making and accepting problem proposals in the course of delivering and receiving diagnostic news (see also Mehan, Hertweck, and
Meihls 1986). That is, parents arrive at clinics through a variety of circumstances, with a variety of concerns, and they do not always regard
their children as having "problems" or "developmental disabilities." Inspection of actual talk and interaction in the clinic shows that applying a
label such as "mental retardation" to some child depends at least partly
on *achieved* intersubjective agreement that there is a "problem" for which
the diagnosis can conceivably account.

Taken together, the studies of Jefferson and Lee (1981), Drew and Holt
(1988), Whalen et al. (1988), and Maynard (1991a) show that the shift
between experiencing "troubles" and having "problems" in a more public and official sense is a complex process. However, it is also manifestly
ordered in terms of the practices whereby a trouble or complainable
matter either remains private and locally contained or becomes public
and subject to interventions and "consolidations," such as those that
Emerson and Messinger (1977) analyze. These analyses thus address the
interactional organization and contingencies that must prefigure any
labeling process. Even when people seek professional help, it is too
simplistic to regard the labeling process as a straightforward application

of some textbook or institutionally based definition to some predefined symptoms (Emerson and Messinger 1977, p. 123). Interactional jockeying over whether a problem exists and, if so, what its nature and dimensions are, ineluctably precedes the successful use of a label (Scheff 1968; see also Gubrium, Holstein, and Buckholdt 1993). Furthermore, as Gill and Maynard (1992) show, "labeling" is not itself an actual activity of parties to a trouble or problem. Rather, it occurs as a feature of other discourse events, such as the delivery and receipt of diagnostic news.

Overall, then, when people come to service agencies with troubles, how and in what ways these emerge as one sort of problem and not another can not be fully known without examining the interactional context wherein they are constituted (Miller 1983; Holstein 1992). This examination should include an appreciation of ordinary conversation, wherein participants produce "complaints" (Drew and Holt 1988) and "troubles talk" (Jefferson and Lee 1981) according to a local organization. *That* social organization—along with the ways that complaints and troubles become problems for service, diagnosis, and the like—helps form what we call the *prehistory* of social problems. In institutional settings, as well as in conversational interaction generally, the organization of the emergence of a "problem" is then describable through the discursive practices of interactants.

Inequality, Interactional Asymmetry, and Problems

A corollary of describing the process by which some activities (and people or groups associated with them) are designated as social problems is the acknowledgment that the ability to influence (or resist) this process is unequally distributed. While we have known for some time that the identification of some behavior or phenomenon as a problem is to be understood in terms of a conflict between definitions or meanings (cf. Vold 1958) of particular groups, the consideration of what this means at the level of everyday experience of members is sparse. Early studies of group conflict tended to abstract and reify complex social processes (Manning 1975). Studies of language and language-in-use have promoted a deeper understanding of how actors, within a variety of institutional frameworks, impute deviance and even inferiority to groups (or individuals) who simply maintain their ordinary patterns of talk and interaction.

For example, while differential school success for black children was previously thought to be rooted in "cultural deprivation" (see the review and critique in Ogbu 1978; cf. Mehan 1984) that led to deficient speaking skills, research in natural settings has shown black children to be competent users (cf. Goodwin 1991) of an internally cohesive and distinct linguistic subsystem (Labov 1972a). Appreciating ways of speaking and talking as reflecting "difference" rather than "deficiency" has played an important part in the criticisms of the various school processes that result in designating children as inherently less capable of learning when they have a cultural and linguistic experience different from the white, middle-class standard appreciated by most schools and class-rooms (cf. Mehan 1991). Appreciating difference has extended beyond black/white distinctions in studies of the school experiences of Hawaiian (Au 1980), Indian (Phillips 1982), and rural children (Heath 1982). These studies regularly show that home-learned interactional and language practices may be at odds with the "cultural capital" (Bourdieu 1988) and language practices schools are organized to reward (cf. Mehan 1992). One result is that testing and assessment processes upon which school organization and placement rely cannot distinguish language (and cul-tural) differences from ability differences (cf. Marlaire and Maynard 1990).

Analyzing the relationship between cultural and linguistic diversity and school success helps explain how some behaviors and activities (and not others) become "problems" within particular contexts. Such analysis points to another phenomenon—the mechanisms by which certain groups are able to have a disproportionate impact on decisions and outcomes in institutional settings. That is, recent studies of members' language practices in institutional settings have begun to elaborate the linguistic packaging through which institutional processing of people occurs. For example, in psychiatric commitment hearings, Holstein (1988) describes ways in which conflicting claims, like "reality disjunc-tures" (Pollner 1987), must be resolved. In these hearings, strategic linguistic packaging facilitates the resolution of this "conflict." District attorneys (DAs) commonly try to promote contradictions between pa-tients' (PA) and psychiatrists' testimony in the discourse of the hearing because categories of the interactants (i.e., psychiatric expert vs. schizo-phrenic) privilege (for the judge) one resolution over another. The fol-lowing is an example of the way that DAs routinely promote such ambi-guity through queries about patients' mental status:

1. DA: Do you have any mental problems?
2. PA: No I'm OK.
3. DA: Doctor Lee's examined you and she seems to
4.   think you aren't OK. Why do you think she
5.   says you're mentally ill?
6. PA: She's lying. She's probably trying to get
7.   me. How does she know anyway? (Holstein 1988, p. 465)

The DA references expert testimony in lines 3 and 4 that renders suspect the patient's previous denial of mental problems (line 2). When the DA offers the patient a chance to resolve the conflicting versions (lines 4 and 5), the patient accuses the doctor of lying. By virtue of the institutional categories of the interactants, not only is one claim privileged (the psychiatrist's), but also the other category (mental patient) provides a "compelling" account for the disagreement as being due to the patient's delusion. "Establishing contradictions between patients' and experts' testimony, then, serves as a means by which DAs organize the appearance of patient incompetence" (p. 466).

Studies such as Holstein's (1988) begin to demonstrate that the descriptions of whether or not, and how, any participant might influence the designation of an "official" problem must attend to their discursive practices. Correspondingly, while it might be straightforwardly assumed that by virtue of particular group membership one is afforded a social identity (e.g., sex, age, ethnicity, class, occupation) (Gumperz 1982) that will have a corresponding influence on interaction, recent studies that examine various "asymmetries" in interaction demonstrate a more complex and tentative relationship between the "interaction order" (cf. Rawls 1987), institutional identities, and "externally-based patterns of domination and subordination" (Maynard 1988, p. 315). Whether or not, and how, an individual's various identities come to bear in direct interaction have been rarely demonstrated, even though analysts often presume that social and institutional arrangements thoroughly and pervasively anchor such identities and determine the course of talk and interaction that the bearers of such identities produce. However, patterns of talk and interaction between individuals of differing (institutionally or culturally defined) status, power, or authority cannot be understood as merely a reflection of their social relationships, for the interaction order has its own requirements.[6] When individuals interact, they are not consistently enacting their "master" identities (West and Zimmerman 1985), or involved in patterns of domination and subordination *because* of them. Rather, at the interactional level, displays engendering inequities (may) derive from the asymmetric use of conversational resources through which parties interact (Molotch and Boden 1985).

We can illustrate these issues by considering current discussions of male-female interaction. Early research (cf. Key 1972; Lakoff 1973, 1975) focused on a wide range of linguistic variation thought to be distinguishable along gender lines. Women were described as being more expressive in intonation, more hesitant, less forceful, while using more intensifiers and adjectives (e.g., "so," "quite"), more "empty fillers" (such as "umh" and "you know"), and more affectionate terms (such as "honey" or "sweetie"). Focusing on distinctions between men and women, these studies depicted the language of men and women as separate and distinct, with differences working to the detriment of women (Thorne, Kramarae, and Henley 1983; West and Zimmerman 1985). The notion of "genderlects" (Tannen 1990) probably exaggerates these distinctions while minimizing linguistic variability within (or across) gender categories. Ultimately, only two areas of research have consistently shown sex differences in speech: women's more "correct" speech, and greater pitch variability and intonation (e.g., Labov 1972b; McConnell-Ginet 1978).

Discrepancies in the findings of gender and language studies may derive from assumptions regarding the source of "differences" and the proper methods used to find and measure them. Some studies, assuming that distinguishing language variables are isolated "markers" of biologically differing endowments and characteristics, examined talk in nonconversational or specialized environs (West and Zimmerman 1985, pp. 109–10). For example, these studies fail to find significant differences between men and women's use of the "tag" questions ("you know?" or "don't you?") that Lakoff (1973, 1975) had originally described as characteristic of women's talk. However, Lakoff proposed that only one kind of tag question—that which asks for confirmation of an opinion—was more frequent for women than for men. The "disconfirming" subsequent studies examined tag questions as indicators independent of the speech environment and function. Evidently the tag question emerges as a gender "characteristic" only in particular contexts, and is better understood as an interactional resource for "doing gender" (West and Zimmerman 1987) than a marker of someone's biological endowment. The distinction is an important one, as the point is that gender identity can be an *accomplishment* of social interaction rather than its cause, and that the interaction order reflexively "organizes" that which is presumed to be externally determined. In this view, patterns of talk and interaction are constitutive of social relationships, rather than derived from institutional arrangements routinely assumed to be determinant.

To elaborate our argument, we wish to examine Tannen's (1990) suggestion that men tend to view "complaints" differently from women. Men see expressions of "troubles" as presenting a problem that they can solve by offering advice, whereas women, in telling their troubles, simply may be soliciting empathy (and support). According to Tannen, misunderstandings arise between men and women because of inherently different cultural meanings about "troubles," "complaints," "problems," and the discourse processes (and identities) that are (should be) appropriately deployed with them. However, as Jefferson and Lee (1981), whose work we discussed earlier, have shown, matters are more complex than this. In an extension of this work, Jefferson (1988) demonstrates that there is an intricate troubles-telling sequence, which, according to Jefferson and Lee (1981), can be "contaminated" in various ways. This contamination results in "interactional asynchrony," where coparticipants are improperly aligned. A proper alignment during the telling of troubles involves the teller being able to talk through the troubles and the hearer aligning as a recipient of this talk. As Jefferson and Lee (1981) note, this alignment can be disrupted in three ways, one of which is the "giving of advice," where the troubles recipient takes over the discourse identity of speaker and the troubles teller is thereby put in the position of listening to the advice. Usually such asynchrony culminates in at least a minor dispute, where the troubled person resists and counters the proffered advice.

The organization of troubles-telling, including various forms of asynchrony, exhibits how talk and interaction have an intrinsic local orderliness. It may be that there are conversational "styles," such that one person may tend to perform "giving advice" rather than "giving support" in the context of another who brings up a trouble, but whether such styles are due to the person's gender (or race or age) in any strong fashion remains to be demonstrated. In other words, males do not "own" giving advice as a linguistic mechanism, and there is no necessary connection between one feature of talk and an externally based social identity. Rather than assume that social structure automatically reproduces itself as an embedded, pervasive, and omnirelevant feature of people's direct interrelations, we think there is a necessity for more investigation of the order of interaction as such.

Our argument is *not* that category membership is irrelevant in face-to-face interaction. It is rather that the distinctive part that such objects might play in any real encounter is obscured by the presumption of their causal relationship to the interaction. Similar to the analytic problems resulting from what Wrong (1961) once pointed out as sociologists' overdetermined (oversocialized) view of action, sociologists of social problems struggle with a view of interaction that is analytically prefigured. It is our position that such analyses of interaction, then, do not really analyze interaction at all, for in considering interactional moves as inherently in service to (unequal) social or institutional identities whose origins reside outside any real-time interaction, and in failing to appreciate the collaborative and interactive bases of our social world, we render as analytically less visible the expressive, reflexive, and constitutive properties of members' talk. Dorothy Smith (1989) eloquently describes the process of alienation of women's experience as it is inscribed in textually mediated sociological categories. Relatedly, we see the jump to explain interaction on the bases of social structure (including gender categories) and the neglect of "gender" as participants make it experientially real, as ultimately leading toward a privileging of the analyst's knowledge.

Whether or not, and how, gender, class, race, or any other category relates to ongoing interaction then ultimately depends on members' own experience as it is displayed in the language and interaction they ongoingly produce.

Institutional Asymmetries and the Interaction Order

The existence of interactional asymmetries in various institutional contexts, like interaction patterns generally, has been linked to identities derived from institutional contexts. For example, though the explanatory gloss differs among theorists, conventional explanations of asymmetry in medical encounters assume it to be (or focus on it as) an exogenously produced phenomenon (whether in service to sociopolitical structures, professional authority, or the "voice" of medicine), and thus rarely focus on characteristics of medical encounters as indigenous, real-time accomplishments of participants (Maynard 1991b).

In making the "asymmetry" of the medical encounter prominent, the literature on doctor-patient interaction misses features of the encounter that are perhaps as prominent to the participants as the authority relation in which they are embedded. For instance, one of the major activities in the doctor-patient relationship is conveying diagnostic news. When such news is bad, that conveyance is an arduous experience for the bearer and recipient alike. Thus, Schegloff (1988) has shown (following Sacks) how the telling of bad news can be organized so that the recipient rather than the bearer of the news ends up pronouncing it. By prefacing the bad news, by giving pieces of information from which inferences can be made, and so on, the bearer alludes to the tidings, and thereby induces the recipient to guess at what they are. The bearer can then confirm what the recipient has already pronounced. This organization indicates how a problem (the delivery of bad news) might be handled through mechanisms belonging to the interaction order.

Delivering "bad" diagnostic news occurs with some regularity in particular institutional settings, where severe illness and death are recurrent topics (Clark and LaBeff 1982; Glaser and Strauss 1965; Maynard 1989; Sudnow 1967; Svarstad and Lipton 1977). We might therefore expect that participants would deploy the same interactional mechanisms for dealing with the problem. Indeed, Maynard (1991b, 1992) shows that the clueing-guessing-confirming pattern is exhibited in clinical discourse. As we discussed earlier, physicians employ a device that Maynard (1991a) has called the "perspective-display series" (PDS) and that operates in an interactionally organized manner to *coimplicate* the recipient's perspective in the presentation of a diagnosis. This series consists of three turns:

1. the clinician's query or perspective-display invitation,
2. the recipient's reply or assessment,
3. the clinician's report and assessment.

In the clinic, the PDS is the counterpart of a conversational device whereby any person, before delivering a report or assessment, can ask a recipient to display his or her own position and then can tie the report to what the recipient has said. Whether it manages a problem of understanding or of the fit between the parties' perspectives, the series seems particularly appropriate in social relational circumstances that warrant caution. As a device of the interactional order, it is adaptable to the clinical environment where clinicians must inform patients or their relatives of technical and sometimes highly charged diagnoses. By adducing a display of their recipients' knowledge or beliefs, clinicians can potentially deliver the news in a hospitable conversational environment, confirm the recipients' understanding, coimplicate their perspective in the news delivery, and thereby present diagnostic assessments in a publicly affirmative and nonconflicting manner.

In sum, Maynard (1991b) specifies the means by which sequential mechanisms deployed in everyday conversation comprise an "interactional bedrock" to the specialized clinical delivery of (bad news) diagnoses. Thus, it is shown that the interaction order, while it is demonstrably responsive to "institutional accountability frameworks" (Rawls 1989, p. 15), is also self-organizing, pervasive, and analytically distinct from these frameworks. Once again, we wish to emphasize the need to return to ordinary local contexts of social interaction for a fuller comprehension of problems that become manifest in institutional settings.

Similarly, Marlaire (1990) describes the interactions in special education assessments through which a child's learning (dis)abilities are discerned. We typically assume that professionals administering the test in part "control" the interaction through the specialized turn structures (McHoul 1978) endemic to the process. This structure, in its most basic form, consists of

1. the tester's question,
2. the child's response, followed by
3. an acknowledgment or evaluation of that response.[7]

By beginning and ending each "sequence," professionals presumably decide when a response is to be counted, right or wrong, as "an answer" that will ultimately, accountably stand for the child's ability. It turns out, however, that this basic form is routinely a collaboration between tester and test-taker that elaborates and accommodates a variety of mundane interactional matters.

Clinicians' third-turn invitations and corrections and or "repairs" (Schegloff, Jefferson, and Sacks 1977) of a child's problematic answer discursively, publicly, and seemingly unilaterally locate the child's "problems" in answering as documents of (and as caused by) some deficiency in the child. That is, through the mechanism of "repair" following a child's problematic answer to a question, efforts to interactionally locate the "problem" at the same time provide an account that publicly formulates a repertoire of acceptable-in-practice reasons for it (Marlaire 1992b; see also Marlaire and Maynard 1990). In other words, clinicians' responses to inadequate answers assign meaning to them by offering institutionally derived candidate locations for the source of the "trouble." Such third-turn responses to problematic answers thus suggest that the "problem" in answering relates to the child's difficulty in listening, in understanding the question, or eventually, in some skill targeted by the test.

At the same time, however, close analysis of the testing interactions reveals that through the sequential mechanisms that serve to correct and disambiguate any problematic answer, potential problems in the interaction order (such as the presentation of a test item) are also addressed. Thus, while clinicians' comments may publicly locate the source for a problematic answer as originating in the attentiveness, comprehension, or skills of the child, adjustments in the wording, intonation, or pacing of instructions or questions may orient to potential problems in the interaction order as well. And, while it is true that an institutionally based "context of accountability" (Rawls 1989) might frame the rhetoric that locates the source of any wrong answer as within the child, the testing process relies on routine conversational practices, such as the mechanism of conversational repair, that render *any* answer an inherently collaborative production. More than this, then, as a "competent" user of the mechanisms of repair, the child can thereby act strategically, in inviting "repair," to obtain help in formulating an answer.

For example, the following segment is taken from a subtest measuring visual-auditory learning wherein the instructions explicitly restrict the feedback that the test administrator may provide. In this part of the test, the aim is to discern the cognitive processing abilities of the child by examining, in essence, her language learning abilities. The tester has provided the "meaning" of various nonlinguistic symbols by saying the words for which they stand, and having the child repeat them. The scoreable portion of the test happens when the child is asked to "read" the symbols as they are strung together in a series of symbols that act like a kind of sentence, the sentences becoming progressively more complex as more symbols are learned. Of particular interest in this segment are the instances where the child (CH), in attempting to "read" the symbol for *the*, solicits "repair" and/or confirmation of her answer(s) in order to obtain feedback from the clinician (CL):

```
 1.  CH:   . . . . this one's a hard page.
 2.  CL:   Yeah I know you're doin' REAlly good. It's
 3.        the last one (.3) we do too.
 4.  CH:   ((the child points to the symbols on the page
 5.        as she "reads" them))
 6.        (Ih: . . . . ) tha . . . . right? Tha? (.2) Tha? (.4)
 7.        ((she moves hand to different symbol and,
 8.        whispering says . . . . ))
 9.        That was tha.
10.  CL:   Right. So what's that one.
11.  CH:   Tha is: . . . . IN
12.  CL:   Oka:ay (Marlaire 1992a, p. 67)
```

At line 6 the child's "Ih . . . . " is a hearably incomplete word that may be inviting repair, as does the slight pause after "tha." The "right" spoken with rising intonation is an open solicitation for confirmation. After the clinician does not respond, the child reformulates "tha" with rising intonation, and when this fails to get a response from the clinician, she tries the same device again. Counting the pauses, there are then seven separate "requests" for tester feedback, after which the child, appearing to have given up, moves her hand to the next symbol (lines 7 and 8). Rather than reading the next line, however, she tries (quietly, "whispering") one more time at line 9 ("That was tha") to elicit a response to her previous attempts by providing yet another confirmatory (or disconfirmatory) opportunity for the tester. At line 10, the clinician finally acknowledges the child's correct "reading" of the symbol, and the testing proceeds.

While testing instructions and professional ideology may require that testers remain "neutral" and/or "rule-governed" (Marlaire 1992a), management of the in situ contingencies that are a constituent feature of any interaction, including test-giving and test-taking, require attention to interactional details to get the test done at all (Maynard and Marlaire 1992). Thus, at line 10, perhaps responsive to an equally compelling charge to "maintain rapport," and the real need for the child's participation in order to finish the test, the clinician appears to adjust to local contingencies of the interactional membrane and provides the feedback that the child has so persistently sought. And again, details of the interaction demonstrate that we cannot adequately describe the organization of the interaction using exogenous variables. If we characterized the clinician as in "control" of the interaction because of her "authority," we might see the child's responses as "tentative" by-products of that authority. Rather, we argue that the child's tentativeness is an interactionally resourceful linguistic device.

As in the previous examples, we can not fully understand the emergent meanings of the interaction without attending to the actual unfolding of contingent events as they occur and as members contend with (respond to and organize) these events. How institutional processes contribute to the emergence of "social problems" depends on, in the first instance, the organization of interaction through which those institutional processes are assembled. While sociologists tend to characterize interactions as "institutional residues" (Rawls 1989, p. 15), studies that examine real-time talk and interaction in a variety of settings, including those within institutions, attest to the integrity of the interaction order, and to the need for its full organizational explication as a first priority in understanding institutional interaction. Like the delivery of diagnostic news, the process of assessing children's competence and defining some "problem" they have cannot be described without attending to the organization of interaction generally.

Conclusion

In sociology, Rawls (1989) has suggested that theorists usually presume one of two domains as a source of order in direct social relationships. The predominant strain in theory describes interactional productions as a function of their institutional context. Another strain of theory, articulated especially in conversation analysis and ethnomethodology (and in parts of Goffman's work), has been concerned with commitment, reciprocity, and meaning as members collaboratively achieve these interactional features according to locally organized social practices. (In this view, institutional contexts, from the standpoint of participants, provide a "framework of accountability" with which those participants must operate.) We contend that debates in the sociology of social problems partake of terms belonging to the former, or institutionally oriented, social theory. Indeed, Ibarra and Kitsuse's new rendering of constructionism does this:

> The thematic complexes we have termed rhetorical idioms are vernacular resources, each serving as a kind of narrative kit through which is articulated a condition-category's socially problematic and justifiably treatable status.

That is, if conditions only become sociologically real through a "narrative kit," then thematic complexes, rhetorical idioms, counterrhetorics, motifs, and other discursive practices derive from institutional moorings rather than the bedrock of interaction itself (cf. Maynard 1991b). This is further evident in Ibarra and Kitsuse's argument that settings are particularly important for "understanding the articulation of claims-making":

> Conceiving of settings as contexts for scrutiny and representation we can pose the following kinds of questions: How do the formal qualities of particular settings structure the ways in which claims can be formulated, delivered, and received?

In directing attention to these "formal qualities," constructionism is in danger of losing one of its original radical initiatives, which was an implicit concern for how people experience troubles and problems, in the first place, in and as a product of the achieved orderliness to their actual talk and interaction. Consequently, the analysis of social problems as locally realized members' phenomena will remain substantially undeveloped in the constructionist literature. Even in describing their own "language game," most constructionist analyses are at least one stage removed from the talk and social interaction that, in some cases, serve as the precursor to claims and activities that historicize such talk and interaction in terms of institutionally based frameworks of accountability.

So we wish to raise once again the sociological importance of examining the prehistory of social problems, of vernacular practices, of rhetorics, and the like. We have reviewed research concerned with troubles, complaints, and problems as parties to conversation exhibit, discuss, seek to solve, and request help for such difficulties in a variety of "ordinary" and "institutional" environments. This research shows that whether talk provides for the visibility of a trouble, whether a trouble becomes a problem, whether a problem gets "labeled" and obtains proper attention from professionals, all involve the contingencies of participants' organizing practices in actual talk and interaction.

We recognize that power, authority, asymmetry, and the like are features of the public emergence of social problems. We have also argued, however, that as real as these features of social structure may be, it is no easy task to sift the reproduced aspects of social structure from the talk and interaction in which it is embedded in a way that preserves the indigenous orderliness to actual, concrete settings. Indeed, preoccupation with social structure has probably magnified the way in which structural identities (gender, class, race, age, etc.) may "influence" interaction, and has precluded the study of the troubles and problems people actually experience; whether, for instance, it is the difficulties of giving and receiving bad news, or covert methods of seeking and giving unofficial and proscribed "help" during the course of an educational exam, or how to handle any of a variety of other directly experienced objects of need and distress.

Theoretical discussions of the construction of social problems, in short, need to attend to demonstrably local and orderly aspects of people's everyday experience of troubles and problems. To describe claims-making activities without attending to the prehistory of these activities necessarily ambushes efforts to avoid privileging the analysts' position in the description and analysis of social problems. In sum, if we wish to have a sociology that takes responsibility for documenting the full range of concerted action covered by the rubric of "constructing social problems," a compelling order of business is studying social organization in and as members' inherently local linguistic and interactive practices.

Notes

1. In the sociology of social problems, we can understand the pejorative nature of early descriptions of the "deviant" and "disorganized" experiences of individuals as partly attributable to the cultural myopia of analysts, who shared rural, Protestant, and upper-middle-class American values. Partly to transcend such bias, sociologists of social problems came to be preoccupied with definitional issues, either trying to devise objective categorizations of social problems (Manis 1974), or else studying the constructive (definitional) activities of those who declare something to be a problem (Kitsuse and Spector 1973, 1975; Spector and Kitsuse [1977] 1987, Chapter 5). That the constructionists have not altogether avoided problems inherent in the objectivist camp is evident in accusations that they engage in "ontological gerrymandering" (Woolgar and Pawluch 1985) or are inconsistent and vacillating with respect to the reality of social problems (Schneider 1985; Hazelrigg 1986). Our view, to anticipate the fuller argument in this chapter, is that neither objectivists nor constructionists have taken the reality of social problems seriously enough. This argument was articulated in part in an earlier paper (Maynard 1988).

2. Readers will recognize our indebtedness here to Pollner (1974, 1987).

3. This study and several others we discuss were published as part of a special issue of *Social Problems* on "Language, Interaction, and Social Problems," edited by Maynard (1988).

4. Emerson and Messenger's concept of "trouble" was meant to direct "attention not simply toward early phases of careers into deviance, but also toward non- and pre-deviant situations generally. . . . . [M]any troubles with deviant potentiality can 'come to nothing,' or come to something devoid of imputations of deviance" (1977, p. 131). Our perspective is sympathetic with this point.

5. Drew and Holt point out, though, that while extreme cases of the sort described by Pomerantz (1986) *embellish* details of a claim, idioms *summarize* those details.

6. For a recent and thorough discussion of the relation between talk and social structure, see Zimmerman and Boden (1991), and the other chapters in Boden and Zimmerman (19991).

7. Such sequences are extended forms of question/answer pairs (see Heritage 1984) and are common to other contexts, such as classrooms (Mehan 1979). See also the discussion in Marlaire and Maynard (1990).

References

Au, K. 1980. "Participation Structures in a Reading Lesson with Hawaiian Children." *Anthropology and Education Quarterly* 11:91–115.

Becker, Howard S. 1963. *Outsiders*. New York: Free Press.

Boden, Deirdre. 1991. "People Are Talking." Pp. 244–73 in *Symbolic Interaction and Cultural Studies*, edited by Howard S. Becker and Michael McCall. Chicago: University of Chicago Press.

Boden, Deirdre and Don Zimmerman (eds.). 1991. *Talk and Social Structure*. Cambridge: Polity Press.

Bourdieu, Pierre. 1988. *Language and Symbolic Power*. Cambridge: Polity Press.

Clark, Robert E. and Emily E. LaBeff. 1982. "Death Telling: Managing the Delivery of Bad News." *Journal of Health and Social Behavior* 23:366–80.

Cohn, Steven F. and James E. Gallagher. 1984. "Gay Movements and Legal Change: Some Aspects of the Dynamics of a Social Problem." *Social Problems* 32:72–86.

Drew, Paul and Elizabeth Holt. 1988. "Complainable Matters: The Use of Idiomatic Expressions in Making Complaints." *Social Problems* 35:398–417.

Emerson, Robert M. and Sheldon Messinger. 1977. "The Micro-politics of Trouble." *Social Problems* 25:121–35.

Emerson, Robert M. and Melvin Pollner. 1978. "Policies and Practices of Psychiatric Case Selection." *Sociology of Work and Occupations* 5:75–95.

Geertz, Clifford. 1984. "'From the Native's Point of View': On the Nature of Anthropological Understanding." Pp. 123–36 in *Culture Theory: Essays on Mind, Self, and Emotion*, edited by Richard Schweder and Robert Levine. Cambridge: Cambridge University Press.

Gill, Virginia Teas. 1991. "Labeling and the Delivery of Diagnostic News." Paper submitted to the American Sociological Association Graduate Student Competition.

Gill, Virginia Teas and Douglas W. Maynard. 1992. "On the Actuality of the 'Labeling' Process." Paper presented at the annual meetings of the American Sociological Association. Pittsburgh: August.

Glaser, Barney G. and Anselm L. Strauss. 1964. *Awareness of Dying*. Chicago: Aldine.

Goodwin, Marjorie H. 1991. *He-Said-She-Said: Talk and Social Organization Among Black Children*. Bloomington: Indiana University Press.

Gubrium, Jaber F. and James A. Holstein. 1990. *What Is Family?* Mountainview, CA: Mayfield.

Gubrium, Jaber, James Holstein, and David Buckholdt. 1993. *Constructing the Life Course.* Dix Hills, NY: General Hall.

Gumperz, John J. 1982. *Discourse Strategies.* Cambridge: Cambridge University Press.

Hazelrigg, Lawrence E. 1986. "Is There a Choice Between 'Constructionism' and 'Objectivism'?" *Social Problems* 33:S1–S13.

Heath, Shirley Brice. 1982. "Questions at Home and at School: A Comparative Study." Pp. 103–29 in *Doing the Ethnography of Schooling,* edited by George Spindler. New York: Holt, Rinehart & Winston.

Heritage, John. 1984. *Garfinkel and Ethnomethodology.* Cambridge: Polity Press.

Holstein, James A. 1987. "Producing Gender Effects on Involuntary Mental Hospitalizations." *Social Problems* 34:301–15.

———. 1988. "Court Ordered Incompetence: Conversational Organization in Involuntary Commitment Hearings." *Social Problems* 35:458–73.

Holstein, James A. and William G. Staples. 1992. "Producing Evaluative Knowledge." *Sociological Inquiry* 62:11–35.

Jefferson, Gail. 1988. "On the Sequential Organization of Troubles-Talk in Ordinary Conversation." *Social Problems* 35:418–41.

Jefferson, Gail and John R.E. Lee. 1981. "The Rejection of Advice: Managing the Problematic Convergence of a 'Troubles-Telling' and a 'Service Encounter'." *Journal of Pragmatics* 5:399–422.

Key, Mary R. 1972. " Linguistic Behavior of Male and Female." *Linguistics* 88:15–31.

Kitsuse, John I. and Malcolm Spector. 1973. "Toward a Sociology of Social Problems: Social Conditions, Value-Judgments, and Social Problems." *Social Problems* 20:407–19.

———. 1975. "Social Problems and Deviance: Some Parallel Issues." *Social Problems* 22:584–94.

Labov, William. 1972a. *Language in the Inner City: Studies in the Black English Vernacular.* Philadelphia: University of Pennsylvania Press.

———. 1972b. *Sociolinguistic Patterns.* Philadelphia: University of Pennsylvania Press.

Lakoff, Robin. 1973. "Language and Woman's Place." *Language in Society* 2:45–79.

———. 1975. *Language and Woman's Place.* New York: Harper and Row.

Lemert, Edwin. 1951. *Social Pathology.* New York: McGraw-Hill.

Lynch, Michael. 1983. "Accommodation Practices: Vernacular Treatments of Madness." *Social Problems* 31:152–64.

Manis, Jerome. 1974. "The Concept of Social Problems: Vox Populi and Sociological Analysis." *Social Problems* 21:305–15.

Manning, Peter K. 1975. "Deviance and Dogma." *British Journal of Criminology* 15:1–20.

Marlaire, Courtney L. 1990. "On Questions, Communication and Bias: Educational Testing as 'Invisible' Collaboration." Pp. 233–60 in *Perspectives on Social Problems,* vol. 2, edited by Gale Miller and James A. Holstein. Greenwich, CT: JAI Press.

———. 1992a. "Professional Idealizations and Clinical Realities." Pp.59–77 in

Current Research on Occupations and Professions, edited by Gale Miller. Greenwich, CT: JAI Press.

———. 1992b. "The Interaction Order and Institutional Accounts: Co-occurring Resources in Locating a Diagnosis." Paper presented at the International Institute for Ethnomethodology and Conversation Analysis. Boston: August.

Marlaire, Courtney L. and Douglas W. Maynard. 1990. "Standardized Testing as an Interactional Phenomenon." *Sociology of Education* 63:83–101.

Maynard, Douglas W. 1982. "Defendant Attributes in Plea Bargaining: Notes on the Modeling of Sentencing Decisions." *Social Problems* 29:347–60.

———. 1988. "Language, Interaction and Social Problems." *Social Problems* 35:311–34.

———. 1989. "Notes on the Delivery and Reception of Diagnostic News Regarding Mental Disabilities." Pp. 54–67 in *The Interaction Order: New Directions in Sociology,*" edited by David T. Helm, W. Timothy Anderson, Albert Jay Meehan, and Anne W. Rawls. New York: Irvington.

———. 1991a. "The Perspective Display Series and the Delivery of Diagnostic News." Pp. 164–92 in *Talk and Social Structure*, edited by Deirdre Boden and Don H. Zimmerman. Cambridge: Polity Press.

———. 1991b. "Interaction and Asymmetry in Clinical Discourse." *American Journal of Sociology* 97:265–67.

———. 1992. "On Co-Implicating Recipients in the Delivery of Diagnostic News." Pp. 351–58 in *Talk at Work: Social Interaction in Institutional Settings*, edited by Paul Drew and John Heritage. Cambridge: Cambridge University Press.

Maynard, Douglas W. and Courtney L. Marlaire. 1992. "Good Reasons for Bad Testing Performance: The Interactional Substrate of Educational Testing." *Qualitative Sociology* 15:177–202.

McConnell-Ginet, Sally. 1978. "Intonation in a Man's World." Pp. 54–68 in *Language, Gender and Society,* edited by Barrie Thorne, Cheris Kramarae, and Nancy Henley. Rowley, MA: Newbury House.

McHoul, A. 1978. "The Organization of Turns at Formal Talk in the Classroom." *Language in Society* 7:183–213.

Mehan, Hugh. 1979. *Learning Lessons.* Cambridge, MA: Harvard University Press.

———. 1984. "Language and Schooling." *Sociology of Education* 57:174–83.

———. 1991. "The School's Work of Sorting Students." In *Talk and Social Structure,* edited by Deirdre Boden and Don H. Zimmerman. Cambridge: Polity Press.

———. 1992. "Understanding Inequality in Schools: The Contribution of Interpretive Studies." *Sociology of Education* 65:1–20.

Mehan, Hugh, Alma Hertweck and J. Lee Meihls. 1986. *Handicapping the Handicapped: Decision Making in Students' Educational Careers.* Stanford: Stanford University Press.

Mehan, Hugh and John Wills. 1988. "MEND: A Nurturing Voice in the Nuclear Arms Debate." *Social Problems* 35:363–83.

Miller, Gale. 1983. "Holding Clients Accountable: The Micro-Politics of Trouble in a Work Incentive Program." *Social Problems* 31:139–51.

Molotch, Harvey L. and Deirdre Boden. 1985. "Talking Social Structure: Discourse, Domination and the Watergate Hearings." *American Sociological Review* 50:273–88.

Ogbu, John F. 1978. *Minority Education and Caste: The American System in Cross-Cultural Perspective*. New York: Academic Press.

Phillips, Susan U. 1980. "Sex Differences and Language." *Annual Review of Anthropology* 9:523–44.

———. 1982. *The Invisible Culture: Communications in Classroom and Community on the WARMSPRINGS Indian Reservation*. New York: Longman.

Pollner, Melvin. 1974. "Sociological and Common-Sense Models of the Labelling Process." Pp. 27–40 in *Ethnomethodology*, edited by Roy Turner. Baltimore: Penguin Books.

———. 1987. *Mundane Reason*. Cambridge: Cambridge University Press.

Pomerantz, Anita. 1986. "Extreme Case Formulations: A Way of Legitimating Claims." *Human Studies* 9:219–29.

Rawls, Ann. 1987. "The Interaction Order Sui Generis: Goffman's Contribution to Social Theory." *Sociological Theory* 5:136–49.

———. 1989. "An Ethnomethodological Perspective on Social Theory." Pp. 4–20. in *The Interaction Order: New Directions in the Study of Social Order*, edited by David T. Helm, W. Timothy Anderson, Albert Jay Meehan, and Anne W. Rawls. New York: Irvington.

Sacks, Harvey. 1972. "An Initial Investigation of the Usability of Conversational Data for Doing Sociology." Pp. 31–74 in *Studies in Social Interaction*, edited by David Sudnow. New York: Free Press.

Scheff, Thomas J. 1968. "Negotiating Reality: Notes on Power in the Assessment of Responsibility." *Social Problems* 16:3–17.

Schegloff, Emanuel. 1988. "On an Actual Virtual Servo-Mechanism for Guessing Bad News: A Single Case Conjecture." *Social Problems* 35: 442–57.

Schegloff, Emanuel, Gail Jefferson and Harvey Sacks. 1977. "The Preference for Self-Correction in the Organization of Repair in Conversation." *Language* 53:361–82.

Schneider, Joseph W. 1984. "Morality, Social Problems, and Everyday Life." Pp. 180–205 in *Studies in the Sociology of Social Problems*, edited by Joseph Schneider and John I. Kitsuse. Norwood, NJ: Ablex.

———. 1985. "Social Problems Theory: The Constructionist View." *Annual Review of Sociology* 11:209–29.

Schutz, Alfred. 1962. *Collected Papers I: The Problem of Social Reality*. The Hague: Martinus Nijhoff.

Smith, Dorothy E. 1989. "Sociological Theory: Methods of Writing Patriarchy." Pp. 34–64 in *Feminism and Social Theory*, edited by Ruth A. Wallace. Newbury Park, CA: Sage.

Spector, Malcolm and John I. Kitsuse. [1977] 1987. *Constructing Social Problems*. Hawthorne, NY: Aldine de Gruyter.

Sudnow, David. 1967. *Passing On: The Social Organization of Dying*. Englewood Cliffs, NJ: Prentice-Hall.

Svarstad, Bonnie L. and Helene L. Lipton. 1977. "Informing Parents About

Mental Retardation: A Study of Professional Communication and Parental Acceptance." *Social Science and Medicine* 11:645–751.

Tannen, Deborah. 1990. *You Just Don't Understand: Women and Men in Conversation.* New York: Ballantine Books.

Thorne, Barrie, Cheris Kramarae, and Nancy Henley. 1983a. "Language, Gender and Society: Opening a Second Decade of Research." Pp. 7–24 in *Language, Gender and Society,* edited by Barrie Thorne, Cheris Kramarae, and Nancy Henley. Rowley, MA: Newbury House.

Vold, George B. 1958. *Theoretical Criminology.* Oxford: Oxford University Press.

Watson, D. R. 1987. "Doing the Organization's Work: An Examination of the Operation of a Crisis Intervention Center." Pp.91–120 in *Discourse and Institutional Authority,* edited by Sue Fischer and Alexandra Todd. Norwood, NJ: Ablex.

West, Candace and Don H. Zimmerman. 1985. "Gender, Language, and Discourse." Pp. 103–24 in *Handbook of Discourse Analysis,* vol. 4, edited by Teun A. Van Dijk. London: Academic Press.

———. 1987. "Doing Gender." *Gender and Society* 1:125–51.

Whalen, Jack, Don H. Zimmerman and Marilyn Whalen. 1988. "When Words Fail: A Single Case Analysis." *Social Problems* 35:335–62.

Woolgar, Steve and Dorothy Pawluch. 1985. "Ontological Gerrymandering: The Anatomy of Social Problems Explanations." *Social Problems* 32:224–27.

Wrong, Dennis. 1961. "The Oversocialized Conception of Man in Modern Sociology." *American Sociological Review* 26:183–93.

Zimmerman, Donald H. and Deirdre Boden. 1991. "Structure in Action." Pp. 3–21 in *Talk and Social Structure,* edited by Deirdre Boden and Don H. Zimmerman. Cambridge: Polity Press.

10

The Reflexivity of Constructionism and the Construction of Reflexivity

Melvin Pollner

Constructing Social Problems (*CSP*; Spector and Kitsuse [1977] 1987) advanced one of the more radical and reflexive programs of its time. In lieu of the traditional focus on the "objective conditions" comprising social problems (as defined by the sociologist), *CSP* recommended focusing entirely on the definitional or claims-making processes through which "social problems" were constituted as such. *CSP*'s reflexive sensibility was evident in its critique of sociologists' failure to apply the "practiced skepticism" they apply to the claims of other groups to their "own causal analyses or explanations of social phenomena" (p. 64). The privilege given social science accounts in the analyses of social problems, argued Spector and Kitsuse, "ignores the fact that such statements are the *social constructions of social scientists*" (p. 65, italics in original). As these and other statements suggest, *CSP*'s constructionism was a reflexively attuned radical departure from the "objectivist" position.

Evolving reflexive concerns in sociology and other disciplines, however, seemed to outflank constructionism. Specifically, Woolgar and Pawluch (1985) argued that *CSP* and constructionism generally were guilty of "ontological gerrymandering." Despite programmatic ambitions to abandon a focus on objective conditions in favor of a claims-making approach, constructionism, it was alleged, imported objectivist assumptions into the definition of the phenomenon. Moreover, though prepared to view the claims of others in constructionist terms, constructionists exempted their own formulations from consideration as "social" or constructionist achievements. Thus, constructionism became vulnerable to both objectivist and reflexive critiques: The former bemoaned the intrusion of relativism, while the latter decried the vestiges of objectivism.

The reflexive critique is especially insidious in that regardless of how constructionism responds it is unlikely to produce a satisfying resolution. From a reflexive point of view, constructionist claims about the discursive or rhetorical construction of, say, social problems are themselves discursive constructions as, indeed, are determinations of their truth or falsity as, indeed, are the very concepts that initiate and suffuse constructionist inquiry—such as truth, falsity, and constructionism itself. In applying the principles of constructionism to those very principles and their products, constructionism leads itself to analytic paralysis or infinite regress. Alternatively, if constructionism circumvents the paradoxes of reflexivity by exempting itself from reflexive review, it exposes itself to the criticism that it fails to provide a complete account of social life: Constructionist explanations have not been accounted for. Thus, constructionism is in a double- or even triple-bind: Whether it opts for or against the reflexive turn, the program is liable to charges of inconsistency, incompleteness, or both.[1]

How then does constructivism respond? In this paper, I explore the emendation of constructionism by Ibarra and Kitsuse (in this volume) in response to the critique by Woolgar and Pawluch. The emended constructivist position completely purges objectivism from the formulation of the *topic* of constructivist inquiry but retains objectivism at the level of *analysis*. Although emended constructionism remains reflexively outflanked at the analytic level, Ibarra and Kitsuse suggest that reflexive approaches might be outflanked sociologically. Specifically, they suggest studying the conditions that promote or inhibit the emergence of reflexivity. The dialectic between a reflexive sociology and the sociology of reflexivity comprises, I argue, a growth plate of the sociological imagination.

Objectivist, Topical, and Analytic Constructionism

The term *constructionism* encompasses divergent understandings of the constructive process and the nature and consequences of reflexivity (Woolgar 1983; Woolgar and Ashmore 1988). Mundane (Pollner 1978) or *objectivist* forms of constructionism presuppose a determinate and analytically specifiable objective order, which actors are conceived to differentially perceive, make claims about, or define. In its objectivist expression, constructionism is concerned with the "subjective," "cognitive," or "interpretive" cognates of the objective realm. These processes are themselves incorporated into the objectivist order comprising the focus of objectivist studies. Thus, objectivist constructionism recognizes that social problems are variously "defined" by different groups and that the construction of such definitions falls within the purview of a comprehensive sociology of social problems. Merton (1968) himself acknowledges this form of constructionism in his specification of the scope of the sociology of social problems:

> [F]ull or substantial consensus in a complex, differentiated society exists for only a limited number of values, interests, and derived standards for conduct. We must therefore be prepared to find that the same social conditions and behaviors will be defined by some as a social problem and by others as an agreeable and fitting state of affairs. (p. 786)

For objectivist constructionism, radical reflexivity rarely arises as an issue and appears as anathema, absurd, or pointless when it does. Thus, if it must choose among the varieties of incompleteness and inconsistency, objectivism's preference is to be "incomplete" by exempting its own suppositions and practices from reflexive inquiry.[2]

Constitutive forms of constructionism (Pollner 1978; Woolgar 1988) suspend the distinction between definitional, interpretive, or representational practices on the one hand and the referent of those practices on the other. Constitutive forms, however, vary in their scope. *Topical* constructionism suspends objectivist assumptions in the formulation of the phenomenon or *topic* of inquiry. In crafting the object of its investigations, topical constructionism suspends objectivist assumptions by attending to social reality as inextricably entwined with and constituted through discourse and practice.[3] Objectivist distinctions—between the "objectively determined" and merely labeled, defined, or perceived— are themselves included in the topical field. These distinctions are of interest not as analytic resources for framing and shaping the topic but insofar and in the ways they are presupposed, oriented to, and enacted by the community.

Although advancing a comprehensive constructionist conception of the phenomenon, topical constructionism is objectivist at the level of analysis. At the level of analysis, members' constructionist practices— presuppositions, rhetoric, discourse—are conceived as determinate realities that can be represented veridically by the analyst. Thus, although members are construed as *constituting* reality, analysts are conceived as *discovering* reality. For topical constructionism, reflexive considerations are important in specifying the nature of the phenomenon, especially in identifying importation of objectivist conceptions in the specification of the phenomenon. At the analytical level, however, topical constructionism allies itself with the objectivist project and thus convulses at the prospect of radical reflexivity.

Analytical constructionism brings analysts' as well as members' practices under the purview of the constructionist mandate. Constructionism is no longer confined to the specification of the topic of constructionist studies: It is understood to characterize the studies and their methods as well. Thus, the objects, arguments, accounts, findings, presuppositions, texts, and so forth of the analytic community—including the conceptual infrastructure (Gasché 1986) of the community developing analytical constructionism—are understood as constituting and constituted processes and products.

In its consummate forms, analytical constructionism merges with poststructural critiques (cf. Rosenau 1992). Precisely because the radicalization of constructionism moves beyond the infrastructure of the classical or objectivist tradition, reflexivity or deconstruction is cultivated and encouraged by poststructural perspectives. In contrast to objectivist incomprehension and intolerance of the ambiguities induced by radical questioning, the poststructural preference is for constructionism to pursue the reflexive initiative and thus to reveal (and revel in) the indeterminacies, undecidables, and equivocalities in the constructions of both members and analysts.[4] The preference undermines the possibility of the project of coherent and comprehensive knowledge of a determinate social reality. For radical poststructuralism, however, it is precisely that project that needs be deconstructed. Thus, what seems epistemological suicide from the objectivist perspective is the promise of a kind of insight and enlightenment for analytical constructivism: In turn what seems to be naivete and entrapment from the latter point of view is the guarantee of the possibility of knowledge from the former.

CSP as Topical Constructionism

Woolgar and Pawluch (1985) hold that CSP among other constructionist programs retains and indeed requires objectivist assumptions regarding the independence of the conditions described or labeled as social problems from the labeling work itself. CSP contains statements that can be read as situated within an ontological space that presupposes an analytically specifiable determinate order, which members may label, perceive, define, or claim to be a "social problem." Spector and Kitsuse, for example, distinguish between the traditional concern with the "objective conditions" and CSP's intention to study "the definitions of them as social problems" (p. 5). "This distinction," the authors argue, "is central to our reformulation of the sociology of social problems" (p. 5). Framed in this fashion, constructionism is situated within objectivist conceptual space and its quintessential distinction between the objective and the subjective.

CSP's objectivism might also be found in the very formulation of the phenomenon as "claims-making." The logical grammar of "claim" presupposes an objective realm about which claims are made. Correlatively, despite their care in invoking the term, Spector and Kitsuse's "putative condition" may be read as oblique reference to an independent and objective reality. Even the encouragement to "set aside the issue of the objective basis of alleged conditions, even to the extent of remaining indifferent to their existence" (p. 78) could be adduced in support of an objectivist interpretation. The objectivist reading would note that *CSP* established the significance of claims by allowing for, but setting aside the relevance of, an objective condition about which claims were being made. Finally, the illustration cited by Woolgar and Pawluch (1985) in which Spector and Kitsuse distinguish between the constancy of marijuana use and varying definitions of marijuana as an addictive substance again suggests the typical objectivist distinction between objective conditions on the one hand and subjective interpretations on the other.

Although selected aspects of *CSP* allow for an objectivist reading, the context and trajectory of the argument indicate that *CSP* is striving to be a coherent topical constructionism (cf. Schneider 1985). Ibarra and Kitsuse's emendations crystallize *CSP* as topical (rather than objectivist) constructionism. For emended *CSP*, objectivist distinctions and discourse are themselves understood as features of the language games through which social problems are constructed as such. In replacing the concept of "putative condition" with "condition-category" they underscore that the term is *not* an oblique reference to objective reality advanced by an omniscient analyst, but a recognition that such references are deployed in the forums of social problems discourse:

> Condition-categories are typifications of socially circumscribed activities and processes—the "society's" classifications of its own contents—used in practical contexts to generate meaningful descriptions and evaluations of social reality. They vary in their level of abstraction and specificity . . . . but they are the terms used by members to propose what the social problem is "about."

Consequently, the analyst of *CSP* persuasion is no longer tempted—if s/he was previously—to divide social problems into objective conditions on the one side and claims about those conditions on the other. Indeed, such a division is part of the phenomenon: The existence (or absence) of a real condition, the specification of its nature and occurrence, and whether it is a social problem are all aspects of the claims-making process studied by the constructionist. The formulating, accounting, and claiming—including the portrayals of the conditions that such discursive practices will be said and heard to be "about"—comprise the phenomena of the construction of social problems.

These emendations remove earlier ambiguities, such as they were, and consolidate *CSP* as topical constructivism. The analyst of claims-making does not invoke a definition of objective reality against which the accuracy of members' definitions are gauged or by reference to which members' responses are conceptualized as definitions or interpretations. Thus, members' constructions are neither right or wrong nor true or false save in the sense that such determinations arise in the claims-making process. The practices and discourse (especially the latter) that occur wherever and whenever social problems are direct or indirect topics are the focus of a constructionist sociology of social problems. Of course, neither the original statement nor the emendation satisfies either objectivists or analytic constructionists.

Anticipating Objectivist and Reflexive Responses

From an objectivist point of view, the crystallization of the *CSP* program into consistent topical constructionism represents an intolerable break with objectivist ontological space. Before the emendation, the ambiguity of the term allowed *putative conditions* to be read as an acknowledgment of the real or objective processes referenced by social problem talk. After Ibarra and Kitsuse, however, there isn't even a "putative" condition. From an objectivist position, emended *CSP* lapses into idealism, as though psychology suddenly claimed that the laws of nature were the experience of the laws of nature and hence physics was no longer necessary. Thus, precisely to the extent that Ibarra and Kitsuse disambiguate the earlier statement by obviating analytic reference to an objective order, they preempt reconciliation with objectivist constructionism. Merton's remarks on the "acid of extreme relativism" (1968, p. 787) might well be the harbinger of critiques yet to come:

> Sociologists need not and do not limit the scope of social problems to those expressly defined by the people they are studying and trying to understand. Fortunately they have an alternative to the doctrine that nothing is either a social problem or a social asset but thinking makes it so. They need not become separated from good sense by imprisoning themselves in the set of logically impregnable premises that only those situations constitute social problems which are so defined by the people involved in them. For social problems are not only subjective states of mind; they are also, and equally, objective states of affairs. (p. 788)

Although analytic constructivism might take issue with Ibarra and Kitsuse's effort to purge objectivism from the topicalizing of constructivist processes, the major objection to emended *CSP* would echo the objection to the original statement: Social constructionism exempts its own practices and determinations from consideration in constructionist terms. As Woolgar and Pawluch argued, selective relativism occurs in the development of constructionism's phenomenon *and* in the development of constructionist analysis:

> Frequently, it is said of certain aspects of social life that things "could have been different." However, the ensuing explanation is not itself subject to this dictate; the analyst's construction of the "explanation" of this state of affairs is emphatically *not* to be regarded as socially contingent, as a result of current conventions, and as lacking logical necessity. In short, explanatory work has to seem distinctively "asocial." The selective application of relativism is thus crucial both in construing phenomena as "social" (for the purposes of establishing a topic for sociological investigation) and in denying the social character of sociologists' own practices. (1985, p.224)

To be sure, both the original and emended statements enunciate a broad and sweeping reflexivity: The sites of social problems discourse encompass the classrooms, conferences, and professional journals—which include, of course, papers such as Woolgar and Pawluch's and this one. Although the program encompasses virtually every aspect of social problems discourse, one aspect is exempted: the practices constituting claims-making, rhetorical moves, and the forums of vernacular discourse as analytically accessible phenomena. The entities, processes, and practices of topical constructionism are conceived as objects independent of the discursive, rhetorical, and enactive work through which their features are represented. In claiming for its objects and inquiries an exemption from the tenets of the constructionist program, topical constructionism remains reflexively incomplete at the analytic level.

Thus, at the end of the day, the double-bind has intensified. For objectivists, the emended *CSP* program is now even more relativistic and subjective—having severed itself from any relation to the objective order. For analytic constructionists, the revised *CSP* remains excessively objectivist in its presumption of an objective field of claims-making processes and practices and, correlatively, the refusal to reckon the work and assumptions of topical constructionism as a focus of study. Thus, Woolgar and Pawluch would not be deterred from their quest:

> [W]e search for forms of argument which go beyond the current impasse between proponents of objectivism and of relativism. Is it possible to establish a form of discourse which is free from the tension engendered by espousals of relativism within the conventions of an objectivist form of presentation? What would an argument free from ontological gerrymandering look like? (1985, p. 224)

These are significant questions. Although there may be forms of argument and analysis free of the tension between objectivism and relativism and that avoid the conventions of objectivism, I would suggest that it is unlikely that they will have significant influence within the social sciences. Objectivism is so insinuated in the infrastructure of disciplinary discourse and its institutional context that the successful emergence of new forms of analysis would require new forms of life. In the absence of such a transformation, constructionist analyses—or sociology generally—may chronically find itself in a quandary.

Reflexive Constructionism and the Construction of Reflexivity

Ibarra and Kitsuse refrain from throwing the constructionist into the reflexive vortex, but they are not cowed by the charge of limited reflexivity. Indeed, in a provocative footnote, they suggest that reflexivity might be examined empirically:

> The difference between member's and analyst's reflexivity is that the former's is practical while the latter's is theoretical. Indeed, there are interesting papers to be written about just this topic: how such reflexivity tends to emerge, the courses it tends to take, the limitations it must respect because of practical considerations, and the ways in which the practice of mundane reflexivity may eventuate in the departure from the member's perspective altogether in favor of a strictly theoretical reflexivity (in which the "natural attitude" is suspended).[5]

Although the sociology of reflexivity intimated by Ibarra and Kitsuse cannot resolve the binds we have discussed, it suggests that while reflexivity may illuminate sociological argument and inquiry, the latter may illuminate reflexivity. Specifically, inquiry into the social construction of reflexivity and the contexts that permit or inhibit its emergence may speak to the prospects of the alternative forms of argument sought by Woolgar and Pawluch. The sociology of reflexivity, if I am not mistaken, will attest to the difficulty of developing alternatives to "the conventions of an objectivist form of presentation." At the very least, it marshals a variety of materials suggesting that the conventions of objectivism are deeply rooted in the embodiment of sociological inquirers and their discursive and institutional contexts.

Elias's ([1939] 1982) study of the "civilizing process" suggests, for example, that the Western sense of self is entwined with objectivism. As Elias has argued, the notion and experience of the self as an encapsulated entity distinct from an objective external reality develops over a long-term process of increasing normative restraints on spontaneous affective behavior. These constraints are internalized and experienced viscerally as separating "self" from "reality." The normative constraints, argues Elias, are products of macrohistorical processes pertaining to the pacification of territory and are incorporated into our musculature as much as they are internalized in our minds. The objectivist metaparadigm is resistant to a radical critique because it is the infrastructure of our embodiment and common sense and, indeed, of our very conceptual resources for formulating and probing the parameters of objectivism.

If inquirers qua members are already constrained from radical questioning by virtue of their embodiment, they are also constrained qua participants in disciplinary discourse. Sociology is premised upon objectivism and assumes a determinate and independent domain of social facts. Insofar as these suppositions are suspended or made problematic, idiomatic concerns such as truth and falsity and eventually the infrastructure of disciplined discourse erode. The intelligibility of concepts such as *reality, truth,* and *representation* are cognate with objectivism and the unsettling of any term reverberates throughout the idiom.[6] From the point of view of objectivism, reflexive efforts to move beyond the objectivist idiom are absurd or unintelligible and given objectivist criteria for determining such matters, the charge is not without substance.

Although discursive challenges and experiments may be tolerated at the margins of the human sciences, it is not likely that objectivism will be abandoned at the core. Peters (1990) argues that the postmodern quest for new discursive styles that recognize the essentially rhetorical nature of all discourse underestimates the connection between "positivist" discursive style, the academy, and the image of self that undergirds the civic life of liberal democracy:

> [T]he ways in which academics write is [*sic*] not detached from the ways in which politicians decide or accountants figure; academic institutions, despite the misleading image of the ivory tower, are constituted together with other institutions. The transformation of one awaits the transformation of all. If a rhetorical consciousness is to prevail in academia, we need for a start, theories and practices of meaningful public discourse and public life. After all, it is mainly academics who think that the king is naked and his empire in tatters: in state and society, in the military and industry, in journalism and public talk, positivism—its characteristic attitudes, ambitions, tropes—remains one of the biggest things going. Positivism (again taken loosely as a name for a complex of attitudes about science, truth, talk, and professionalism) remains embarrassingly impervious to our critiques and continues to sustain the institutions that give us our status as professionals. It will not go away just because we stop talking in its style. "Facts" will continue to have paramount persuasive power and objectivity will continue to back up our professional claims to authority when we

speak in public. As long as public culture remains as it is, academics will be filmed in front of their book cases (a classic trope of expertise) and queried for their expert opinions, however, severely they criticize the positivism/expertise/social science complex in their writings. (pp. 225–26)

There is nothing intrinsically problematic about incessant reflexivity or the regresses and abysses by which it is supposedly accompanied. They are constituted as unacceptable, intolerable, or unintelligible within forms of life that place a premium on positivist discourse as the basis for subsequent action and inference. These demands are more intense for inquirers who are responsible to objectivist ontology as the grounds for deciding the significance and intelligibility of a claim (cf. Spector and Kitsuse [1977] 1987). Because they are closer to public policy issues, sociologists of social problems are more intensely subject to questions derived from objectivist ontology and therefore required to say something about "out there"—be it the objective conditions comprising social problems or the social construction of social problems. In fateful dialogues presupposing the conventions of objectivism, reflexive discourse is unlikely to be sought or understood.

The embodied, disciplinary, and institutional constraints on new forms of discourse ought not be overstated. It would be presumptuous to suggest that the forms of argument sought by Woolgar and Pawluch are unattainable. The consummate expression of reflexive inquiry, however, seems to require a transformation of deep, diffuse, and entwined forms of embodiment, discourse, and institutions. Short of that transformation, radically reflexive efforts *within* the social sciences are likely to have limited success and those that do succeed are likely to be limited in their radicalism (cf. Hilbert 1990).

The bleak prospects for a fully realized reflexive sociology do not entail abandoning efforts to move beyond the conventions of objectivism. On the contrary, it is through such efforts that a view is gained, however dim, of the profile of the forms of embodiment, discourse, and institutions suffusing contemporary projects and practices. While sociology teaches reflexive inquiry that it is a socially constituted (or denied) possibility, reflexivity teaches sociology (and constructionism) about the equivocality and contingency of its own discourse, practices, and accounts.

Conclusion

Three points emerge from a consideration of Ibarra and Kitsuse's emendation of *CSP*. First, emended *CSP* crystallizes the topic of constructionist investigations in consistent constructionist terms. Thus, *CSP* is not vulnerable to Woolgar and Pawluch's charge of ontological gerrymandering in terms of the definition of the phenomenon. In exempting constructionist initiatives and practices from reflexive consideration, however, emended *CSP* is vulnerable to a reflexive critique (as is virtually any form of inquiry that purports to be about the world; Pollner 1987). Second, a sociology of reflexivity or an ethnography of argument—that is, the study of how forms of argumentation, representation, explanation, and demonstration are variously open or closed to radical questioning—is a powerful and productive response to the reflexive critique. Reflexive concerns need not always outflank sociological inquiry: Sociology can hold reflexivity responsible to understanding how reflexive questioning is a socially constructed achievement. Although there is an unresolvable tension between reflexivity and sociology, the dialogue between these contrary movements harnesses the deconstructive energy of reflexivity to the sociological imagination. Third, conjectures regarding the sociology of reflexivity indicate limitations to a fully realized reflexive sociology. Insofar as the conventions of objectivism are the infrastructure of the bodies, discourse, disciplines, and institutions within which reflexivity is pursued, it is unlikely that radical reflexivity can be conceptualized let alone implemented within the academy.[7] The Sisyphean efforts to overcome these conventions, however, are the very resources for revealing their presence and potency.

Notes

1. The concept of the double-bind emerged from the Palo Alto school's (Bateson, Jackson, Haley, and Weakland 1956) efforts to explain the ostensibly unintelligible communications of diagnosed schizophrenics. The double-bind referred to situations structured such that regardless of what the individual said or did, s/he would anticipate or experience some form of loss or punishment. The apparent unintelligibility of schizophrenic communication, it was hypothesized, is an adroit effort to respond to these insidious circumstances by making communication highly ambiguous. Thus, for example, the individual might comment about the immediate circumstances and then in the next (or same) utterance negate it or use abstract metaphors without any indication that they are metaphors. In these and other ways (cf. Haley 1959), individuals who took themselves to be in double-binds might make a move and simultaneously retract it, cancel it, or make it unintelligible. The parallels between double-binds and the plight of deconstructionists, radical constructionists, and reflexive sociologists warrants attention.
2. Modernism attends to itself within the framework of its own suppositions. Thus, objectivist thought tames or "disciplines" reflexivity by permitting

a reflection whose loyalty to (enlightened or postpositivist) objectivist thought is assured. Thus, within modernism, reflexivity is transformed into a self-reflection regarding the adequacy of its own practices to provide an accurate rendering of reality.

3. For topical constructionists, members' activities are not subjective or interpretive in the sense these terms are used in modernist constructionism, where they imply a response to an already given order of objects, facts, stimuli, etc. Rather, these terms connote a constitutive process in which the domain is "realized."

4. The double-bind predicament may characterize any discipline or perspective pretending to a general or total explanation. Thus, a physics that does not explain its own findings and foundations in physical terms is incomplete: A physics that does explain its findings and foundations is inconsistent. Recognition of these issues may require marginality in relation to what passes for normal science within the discipline. Constructionism strives for a marginality and thus encounters ontological and epistemological issues to which more settled or central perspectives are indifferent and oblivious but whose resolution reverberates to the core.

5. The proposal resonates with CSP's discussion of the circumstances inhibiting appreciation of a labeling or definitionalist stance with regard to social problems. Spector and Kitsuse ([1977] 1987, pp. 63–72) described how sociologists are diverted from a definitionalist approach by virtue of their perspective as ordinary members and as members of a profession, department, and discipline competing with others to provide an account of social problems. The extension of the sociology of knowledge perspective also complements Woolgar and Pawluch's (1985) "ethnography of argument," which adopts a "distanced" or "anthropologically strange" view of activities such as reasoning, explaining, persuading and understanding" (p. 214). A significant difference, however, is that the ethnography of argument (Woolgar 1988) seems to focus on the internal structure of textual arguments and analyses: A *sociology* of argument, by contrast, examines the text in context, i.e., the social context that sustains particular forms of argumentation and analysis. The difference is akin to focusing on language games in contrast to language games as shaped by the forms of life from which they emerge and within which they function.

From this broader perspective, features apparently endemic to certain forms of argumentation and explanation (e.g., "ontological gerrymandering") may prove to reflect processes within the form of life. Thus, to use a crude example, the evasions and deferrals of reflexivity (Watson 1987) may not derive from inherent limitations in argumentation per se but the relations between explainers and those who are responding to, using or paying for those explanations. They might be unwilling or uninterested in being permanently unsettled by ceaseless reflexivity. Yet Woolgar, whose studies, regardless of rubric, are central to the reflexive examination of sociology and the sociological examination of reflexivity, increasingly recognizes something outside the text. Woolgar writes that "the ethnography of the text must develop an understanding of the text as just one element in a reader-text community" (1988, p. 32).

6. Innumerable practices presuppose and promote objectivist discourse. Lynch's (1991) discussion of the "prejudice of the page," for example, suggests how the page constrains and conditions efforts that would try to go beyond the conventions of "sensible pictures" of reality (p. 18).

7. Mulkay (1988, pp. 213–23) offers a provocative conjecture on what the

world might be like if "serious" or objectivist discourse was displaced from its privileged position.

References

Bateson, Gregory, Don D. Jackson, Jay Haley, and John Weakland. 1956. "Toward a Theory of Schizophrenia." *Behavioral Science* 1:251–64.
Elias, Norbert. (1939) 1982. *The Civilizing Process.* Translated by Edmund Jephcott. Oxford: Blackwell.
Gasché, Rodolphe. 1986. *The Tain of the Mirror: Derrida and the Philosophy of Reflection.* Cambridge, MA: Harvard University Press.
Haley, Jay. 1959. "An Interactional Description of Schizophrenia." *Psychiatry* 321–32.
Hilbert, Richard A. 1990. "The Efficacy of Performance Science: Comment on McCall and Becker." *Social Problems* 37:117–32.
Lynch, Michael. 1991. "Pictures of Nothing? Visual Construals in Social Theory." *Sociological Theory* 9:1–21.
Merton, Robert K. 1968. "Epilogue: Social Problems and Sociological Theory." Pp. 775–823 in *Contemporary Social Problems,* edited by Robert K. Merton and Robert Nisbet. New York: Harcourt Brace Jovanovich.
Mulkay, Michael. 1988. *On Humour.* Cambridge: Polity Press.
Peters, John Durham. 1990. "Rhetoric's Revival, Positivism's Persistence: Social Science, Clear Communication, and Public Space." *Sociological Theory* 8:224–31.
Pollner, Melvin. 1974. "Sociological and Common Sense Models of the Labeling Process." Pp. 27–40 in *Ethnomethodology,* edited by Roy Turner. Middlesex, England: Penguin.
———. 1978. "Constitutive and Mundane Versions of Labeling Theory." *Human Studies* 1:285–304.
———. 1987. *Mundane Reason: Reality in Everyday and Sociological Discourse.* Cambridge: Cambridge University Press.
Rosenau, Pauline Marie. 1992. *Post-Modernism and the Social Sciences.* Princeton, NJ: Princeton University Press.
Schneider, Joseph W. 1985. "Defining the Definitional Perspective on Social Problems." *Social Problems* 32:232–34.
Spector, Malcolm and John I. Kitsuse. [1977] 1987. *Constructing Social Problems.* Hawthorne, NY: Aldine de Gruyter.
Watson, G. 1987. "Make Me Reflexive, But Not Yet: Strategies for Managing Essential Reflexivity in Ethnographic Discourse." *Journal of Anthropological Research* 43:29–41.
Woolgar, Steve. 1983. "Irony in the Study of Science." Pp. 239–66 in *Science Observed: Perspectives on the Social Study of Science,* edited by Karin D. Knorr-Cetina and Michael Mulkay. London: Sage.
———. 1988. "Reflexivity Is the Ethnographer of the Text." Pp. 14–34 in *Knowledge and Reflexivity: New Frontiers and the Sociology of Knowledge,* edited by Steve Woolgar. Cambridge: Cambridge University Press.

Woolgar, Steve and Malcolm Ashmore. 1988. "The Next Step: an Introduction to the Reflexive Project." Pp. 1–13 in *Knowledge and Reflexivity: New Frontiers and the Sociology of Knowledge,* edited by Steve Woolgar. Cambridge: Cambridge University Press.

Woolgar, Steve and Dorothy Pawluch. 1985. "Ontological Gerrymandering: The Anatomy of Social Problems Explanations." *Social Problems* 32:214–27.

11

Do We Need a General Theory of Social Problems?

David Bogen and Michael Lynch

> We are unable to clearly circumscribe the concepts we use; not because
> we don't know their real definition, but because there is no real "defini-
> tion" to them. To suppose that there must be would be like supposing that
> whenever children play with a ball they play a game according to strict
> rules.
>
> —Ludwig Wittgenstein *The Blue and Brown Books*

Constructionism (or as it is sometimes called *constructivism*) has become
a highly visible and influential perspective for studying social problems.
This development is hardly unique to social problems research. Versions
of constructionism have also become prominent in the philosophy of
science, the sociology of knowledge, legal studies, literary criticism,
history, and archaeology. We are told that there is even a small but
robust group of constructionist accountants.[1] Although it has been
around for some time, constructionism is commonly promoted as a
"new" and "radical" perspective, which contrasts to the "conventional"
epistemology supposedly held by researchers who presume the reality
of the objects or events they study and who seek methodically to establish the referential adequacy of the texts, material residues, and symbolic manipulations through which they try to secure factual claims. The
outlines of a distinctive sociological variant of constructionism were established in Berger and Luckmann's (1966) influential treatment of *The
Social Construction of Reality,* which combined Weberian and Schutzian initiatives in a theory of how social institutions are constituted through an
historical process of ritualization and objectification. In the field of social
problems research, constructionists also draw upon the "labeling theory" of deviance that was popular in the late 1960s and early 1970s.
Ethnomethodology (Garfinkel 1967) gained a foothold in sociology at
about the same time, and as far as many sociologists were concerned
Garfinkel and his colleagues delivered what amounted to an abstruse
version of constructivism. There are definite parallels between the two

approaches: Both emphasize the role of constitutive practices in the formation and maintenance of social order; both develop upon phenomenological initiatives; and both stress the necessity to investigate how the "objects" and "facts" proper to the field of sociology are practical and discursive accomplishments. Many avowed constructionists draw upon ethnomethodological research, and many ethnomethodologists embrace constructionist themes and arguments. Despite such thematic continuities and literary mergers, however, we shall aim in this paper to emphasize the deep differences between constructionism and ethnomethodology.

Discussing differences within a common set of commitments is always dangerous, because it can give rise to the sorts of internecine squabbles that divide communities of scholars and empower their common opponents. While recognizing this, we nevertheless see a point to writing an "internal" critique of some entrenched constructionist tendencies. The point is to clarify differences and resolve equivocalities that are too easily glossed over by citing the literature or repeating familiar slogans. The very term *construction* takes on an equivocal sense in constructionist usage. Ordinarily, *construction* refers to a deliberate process of manufacturing or manipulating an object in accordance with a plan of action, but when used as a theoretical term in philosophy, literary theory, or sociology it describes actions that are performed "unwittingly" or "tacitly," without any overt recognition (and in some cases a denial) that construction is actually taking place.[2] A favored way to set up the general relevance of construction in descriptions of social actions is by treating the actor's vernacular understanding as a naive version of philosophical realism, which differs fundamentally from the constructionist researcher's own analytic vantage point. This distinction enables the researcher to gain leverage for a coherent theoretical position that apparently stands outside the naive "natural theories" held by the ordinary members whose actions are investigated. In this paper, we shall draw upon ethnomethodology and Wittgenstein's later philosophy to question whether it makes sense to consider the member's constitutive relation to social problems as though it was based in a coherent philosophy or theory, and by the same token we shall question the need for a general constructionist theory to guide social problems research.

Our task would be easier if we could simply play ethnomethodology off against constructionism, but since the tendencies we are ascribing to constructionism are no less prevalent in some well-regarded versions of ethnomethodology (Heritage 1984; Hilbert 1990; Pollner 1991), we are faced with having to build the scaffolding for our arguments as we go along. The version of ethnomethodology we advocate resonates with Garfinkel's (1991) and Garfinkel and Sacks's (1970) arguments, but in some respects it is an endangered form of the art, whose survival requires a systematic dismantling of some of the analytic tendencies that have become established in the literature. In this paper, rather than launching into such a project we shall lay out our arguments in a particularized way by focusing on a specific exemplar. Ibarra and Kitsuse's paper in this volume offers a convenient target for our purposes, as it happens to be an excellent example of a constructionist study that draws extensively upon a programmatic distinction between everyday discourse and professional analysis. Our critique begins by questioning whether or not Ibarra and Kitsuse's general theory of the construction of social problems provides a necessary or relevant basis for studies of particular "social problems language games," and in the course of arguing that such games are intelligible and investigable in their own right, and without need for such a theory, we shall have occasion to critically reexamine the fundamental distinction between vernacular and analytic understandings.

The Social Problems Language Game

Ibarra and Kitsuse begin their paper by reviewing the major theoretical points of Spector and Kitsuse's *Constructing Social Problems* (*CSP*; [1977] 1987). In that work, they argue, "A fundamental point was made with regard to the ambiguous and often logically inconsistent use of *social problems* as an analytical category in sociology." According to them, one of the central findings of *CSP* was that mainstream approaches to social problems research "typically group[ed] various social conditions (e.g., prostitution, crime) under the rubric *social problems* in an ad hoc manner. In the process, the concept of social problems was rendered without theoretical precision or scope."

On this account, the principal task for a theory of social problems is to improve upon the imprecise and theoretically impoverished conceptual apparatus that has (until now) served social problems research in a merely tacit and ad hoc way. The objection Ibarra and Kitsuse raise to the standing traditions in social problems research is therefore *not* that researchers have *wrongly* theorized the concept of social problems, but rather that they have *under*theorized it; that they have merely *used* a concept of social problems without having given it a clear and unambiguous definition. This is a crucial matter, they argue, because by taking the definition of "social problems" for granted, conventional social problems researchers have adopted commonsense definitions of the phenomena they investigate.

The central aim of the theoretical introduction to Ibarra and Kitsuse's paper seems to be to articulate a blind spot generic to the conduct of social problems research; a meta-analytic puzzle that requires for its solution precisely those theoretical remedies the authors recommend. Hence, the purpose served by identifying defects in conventional studies of social problems is to disclose a space within which theory in general, and their theory in particular, can be seen to be doing some legitimate work.

Creating a space for theory's work is, we shall argue, a canonical move in the language game Ibarra and Kitsuse are playing. We shall call this game "the social problems language game." By that we mean the collection of practices, textual or otherwise, involved in constituting the literary object "social problems per se" as an intelligible, interesting, relevant topic for sociological research. We offer this definition of the social problems language game as a viable, radical alternative to the use Ibarra and Kitsuse make of that terminology. In this way, we mean to distinguish what they are doing from lines of social problems inquiry that remain fundamentally indifferent to the perspective they recommend.

At one point in their argument, Ibarra and Kitsuse note that CSP's central distinction between putative condition and social condition may have amplified the confusion between the different layers of theoretical and mundane discourse, and seduced constructionists into making statements reflecting members' idioms instead of discerning them, thus inhibiting the development of an interpretive theory of the social problems process. While it seems correct to say that the differences between "the different layers of theoretical and mundane discourse" are at times difficult to decipher, and that this tends to inhibit the development of general theory, the confusion Ibarra and Kitsuse mention only arises on the assumption that separate "layers" must be distinguished in the first place. This confusion arises because one of the principal requirements of a general interpretive theory is the identification of a discrete, isolable, stable—i.e., *researchable*—subject matter. Thus, one of the first things a general theory of social problems needs to do is to provide grounds for drawing a *principled* distinction between sociological and commonsense knowledge of social problems.[3] Only in this way can "members' commonsense knowledge of social problems" emerge as a phenomenon free and clear of the work of sociological analysis.

For Ibarra and Kitsuse, the social problems language game is a coherent organization of the claims-making activities comprising the vernacular or idiomatic resources through which members of the society at large initiate, define, promote, and regulate "the social problems process." As such, they conceive the social problems language game as a "members' phenomenon," where what is meant by this is that members of the society at large engage in the game, independent of professional social scientists' interests in and orientations to social problems.[4] One advantage of this conception of "the social problems language game" is that it neatly distinguishes between professional analyses of social problems and the subject matter of those analyses, namely, "the configuration of premises, conventions, categories, and sensibilities constitutive of 'social problems' as idiomatic productions."

As noted above, we are treating "the social problems language game" as a set of constructive-analytic practices for making a literary-theoretical object of "social problems per se."[5] There is a sense in which our recharacterization of that game may seem unduly restrictive, and even precious. Where Ibarra and Kitsuse recommend the social problems language game as a substantive phenomenon of interest for a large corpus of constructivist investigations, readers may conclude that we identify it as a (mere) construct of Ibarra and Kitsuse's text. Where Ibarra and Kitsuse introduce the social problems language game as a broad way of speaking about members' definitional work in varieties of real-worldly settings, we attribute its nominal coherence to the definitional work accomplished in Ibarra and Kitsuse's text. Where Ibarra and Kitsuse want to investigate the rhetorical practices through which members accomplish the social problems language game, we refuse to separate the existence of that game from Ibarra and Kitsuse's rhetorical practices. Consequently, many readers may be inclined to accuse us of making an ironic substitution of a dry and scholastic subject matter for a lively and significant real-worldly phenomenon. Moreover, they may be inclined to pursue the regress one step further by problematizing our definitional work and our rhetorical construction of Ibarra and Kitsuse's text. Such a regress, however, is precisely what we intend to warn against.

Far from accusing Ibarra and Kitsuse of having made an epistemic blunder, we commend their paper as an outstanding exemplar of the constructivist approach. If their conception of the social problems language game is nothing more than a theoretical invention, it is also nothing *less*. That is to say, it is a seriously intended, seriously used conception that animates a large and lively body of contemporary scholarship, and it figures deeply in the terms of reference, modes of argument, and citational preferences of that literature. Ibarra and Kitsuse formulate their theory of social problems with exemplary clarity and courage, and by so doing they bring a common discursive tendency to a head.[6] When we criticize that tendency, we do not mean to imply that constructivist research generally is worthless, nor do we mean to detract from the instructive quality of Ibarra and Kitsuse's discussion of narrative frames in public controversies over health risks, environmental hazards, abortion, and other issues. Indeed, one of the most striking things about

Ibarra and Kitsuse's paper is that the analysis is extremely convincing even though the theory upon which it (presumably) is based is not.

Hence, the point of interrogating their text is not only to question their particular conception of the social problems language game, but more importantly to raise the question of whether social problems research needs a general theory at all. We want to ask, What *use* is a general theory for studies of the various social problems? In trying to provide an answer to this question we need first to consider what the relationship is between theoretical statements and the subject matter they presume to be about, and second, what place (if any) theorizing has within persons' displayed mastery of social practices.

Membership Has Its Privileges

In his essay, "Dennis Martinez and the Uses of Theory," Stanley Fish (1989, p. 372) describes an interview between Dennis Martinez, who at the time was a pitcher for the Baltimore Orioles, and Ira Berkow, a local sports writer.[7] Berkow had apparently wandered into the Orioles' locker room just prior to the start of a game with the Yankees and noticed Martinez talking to his manager, Earl Weaver. Thinking that there might be a story in it, Berkow approaches Martinez and asks him what he and Weaver had been talking about. Martinez turns to Berkow and says, "He said, 'throw strikes and keep them off the bases,' and I said, 'O.K.'" As Fish continues:

> This is already brilliant enough, both as an account of what transpires between fully situated members of a community and as a wonderfully deadpan rebuke to the outsider who assumes the posture of an analyst. But Martinez is not content to leave the rebuke implicit, and in the second stage he drives the lesson home with a precision that Wittgenstein might envy: "What else could I say? What else could he say?" (p. 372)

The point Fish makes with this story concerns a fundamental difference he sees between the *doing* of some activity or practice, on the one hand, and what he terms "the practice of discoursing on practice" (p. 377) on the other. Having established a use of this distinction in baseball, Fish goes on to discuss its relevance to legal disputation and scientific research. In the latter case he applies the distinction to a discrepancy between the way a team of industrial researchers collaboratively come up with a novel solution to an engineering problem versus the way they "theoretically" account for their innovation after the fact.[8] This discrepancy is well established in constructivist studies of natural science, where it is often pointed out that what scientists actually do in their laboratories differs in many respects from how they report upon their methods and findings in published articles (Latour and Woolgar 1979; Knorr-Cetina 1981), but Fish encourages a nonstandard conclusion about the discrepancy. Rather than suggesting that "fully situated members" (whether they be industrial engineers or baseball players) produce *deficient* accounts of their methods, he questions the whole point of assuming an analytic stance toward members' practical actions.[9] Although sports writers and sociologists certainly have rights to describe and analyze the practices of ball players, natural scientists, police officers, and social workers, just as members of those professions have rights to develop formal accounts of their practices, Fish refuses to accord a *special epistemic status* to formal analytic accounts, over and against members' ad hoc uses of expressions and actions. In his view, formal accounts do not necessarily consolidate a dispersed array of partial and deficient, lower-level accounts within a more comprehensive framework of understanding. Instead, formal accounts are produced and justified *as further versions* that have their own rhetorical and practical uses. This cuts to the quick of a fundamental distinction that Ibarra and Kitsuse repeatedly stress, namely "the distinction between the sociologist's perspective and the member's." Like Fish, Ibarra and Kitsuse distinguish the practical circumstances of everyday discourse and action from the adoption of an analytic or theoretical posture. But, unlike Fish, they propose that something *in general* is missing from "mundane" accounts, something that theoretical analysis can supply. In this, they align with the very sort of analytic enterprise that gets squelched for soliciting an account of the "what else" Martinez and Weaver might have said in their reportedly banal conversation.

So how could Fish, with a touch of irony, speak of Martinez's riposte to Berkow as displaying "a precision that Wittgenstein might envy?" Weaver's recommendation to "throw strikes and keep them off the bases," hardly counts as an interesting, original, or exacting formulation of a pitcher's actual practices, so the "precision" of Martinez's utterance must lie elsewhere. And indeed, the point of the story is that the sense and adequacy of Martinez's utterance has nothing to do with describing, explaining, or analyzing the game, but has instead to do with the fact that persons who have no need to describe the general practice of playing baseball nevertheless have things to say to others of their kind.[10] The *intelligibility* of "throw strikes and keep them off the bases" consists in its use as a maxim or reminder—a kind of litany—to be rehearsed *for* the game and recalled *in* the course of game-specific situations. The precision of Martinez's rebuke consists in his use of Weaver's words to exploit a kind of natural equivocality intrinsic to the baseball cliché: namely, that although overhearers may take it to be nothing more than a trite restatement of the obvious, for players engrossed in the game it is not only about all they can say, it is also enough.

To imagine a need to describe the skills and situations of the game comprehensively—i.e., in other than an occasional or ad hoc way—is to demand something extraordinary. This demand is far from extraordinary to those of us who work in the academy, and in the present context it has a dignified history that can be traced back to a legacy from transcendental philosophy that has become entrenched in constructivist sociology.

Distinguishing Topics from Resources

Like many before them, Ibarra and Kitsuse utilize a series of visual metaphors to distinguish the member's "perspective" on social problems from that of the analyst. When acting as agents in the social problems language game, members "perceive" through a "viewpoint" that projects a particular objective definition on one or another social problem. In the familiar language of art criticism, members see the trompe l'oeil composition *as* a realistic portrait or pastoral scene, while ignoring the artful arrangement of brush strokes and the conventions of linear perspective that establish, rely upon, and systematically hide the relational context of the realistic illusion (Gombrich 1960). The analyst steps outside the frame of the naturalistic illusion in order to disclose the artful practices and conventions that "the gaze of members" ecstatically ignores.[11]

This perspectivist picture has a certain classical pertinence, though it becomes far less apt when applied to nonrepresentational modes of art or speech, and it stretches the imagination rather painfully to treat "the members' orientation to social problems" as though it could be like gazing at a visual field from a fixed standpoint. Ibarra and Kitsuse articulate a kind of moral translation of this perspectival picture: Lines of sight become moral commitments, and a focal theme becomes an *idée fixe*. In order to get a glimpse of the invisible grid that locks the member's gaze in place, the analyst must withdraw from the conventional commitments that articulate the relation between field and standpoint. Ibarra and Kitsuse acknowledge that the analyst's task is by no means easy, and that it requires a severe methodological discipline in order to resist the "seductive" tendency of "going native": "In other words, it has proved difficult for constructionists to avoid 'making moves' in the social problems language game." The key, as they elaborate it, is to place vernacular or "folk" versions of social problems into a state of suspended animation in order to maintain a "basic distinction between vernacular resources and analytic constructs."

The distinction between vernacular resources and analytic topics is a long-standing theme in ethnomethodology and phenomenological sociology. In an early statement, Sacks proposed that in order to emerge as a science, sociology "must free itself not from philosophy but from the common-sense perspective."[12] This, he added, distinguishes its historical task from that of the natural sciences:

> Its predecessors are not such as Galileo had to deal with, but persons concerned with practical problems, like maintaining peace or reducing crime. The "discovery" of the common-sense world is important as the discovery of the problem only, and not as the discovery of a sociological resource. (Sacks 1963, pp. 10–11)

For Ibarra and Kitsuse, however, there is little difference between the commonsense perspective and a particular philosophy that stands in the way of a constructivist theory. According to their distinction between member and analyst, the vernacular or commonsense perspective is placed on one side of a dialectic, while constructivist analysis is placed on the other. Common sense is characterized as a coherent epistemological orientation; a dim version of positivism or naive realism. This treatment of common sense as a coherent, although naive, variant of a philosophical position is a well-established maneuver in constructivist and ethnomethodological theorizing. Pollner (1987), for instance, speaks of "positivistic common sense," and Holstein and Miller characterize an "everyday life" orientation to "a reality that is objectively 'out there,' existing apart from the acts of observation and description through which it is known" (1990, p. 104). This imputation of a coherent philosophical view to the ordinary member is similar to the tendency in sociology of scientific knowledge to attribute a positivistic or realist orientation to the practicing scientist as well as the philosopher of science (Pickering 1984, pp. 3ff.).

According to Ibarra and Kitsuse, members are practical rather than analytic or theoretical, and yet the member's perspective consists in a philosophically coherent, "mundane ontology" dominated by a demarcation between words and things. Essential to this ontology is the "mundane claim" that objects and their qualities have an existence independent of their apprehension. Members' conceptions of social problems are "grounded in a folk version of the correspondence theory of meaning." In short, members—a category that now includes most social problems researchers—are made out to be "philosophical dopes," whose commonsense reasoning is captivated by a folk ontology that *to them*, but not to the analyst, is indistinguishable from the world itself.

At this point it might be well worth asking what leads members to be so persuaded by *that* particular ontology, but to paraphrase Garfinkel (1967, p. 68) we are led instead to ask, "What are analysts *doing* when they make members out to be philosophical dopes?" When construed as a philosophical dope, the member becomes an agent who takes for granted a "mundane world" that the analyst recasts as the product of taken for granted "social" practices.[13] This construal not only creates endless work for analysts (a central task for any theory), it also sets up a familiar move in the ubiquitous realist/constructivist debate. Once the member is made out in the image of a realist philosopher, constructivist researchers can accuse their professional colleagues who express realist or objectivist tendencies of taking for granted an unanalyzed member's sense of the objective facticity of social structure. Their very espousal of objectivism thus affiliates such researchers with the commonsense knowledge they despise! The constructivist analyst then shows that this sense of objective facticity is interactively constructed and retained: It is a reality that is "talked into being" (Heritage 1984, p. 290) or constituted through "mundane reason" (Pollner 1987). *Analysis* undermines the claim that members, whether lay actors or sociologists who tacitly adopt members' presuppositions, are reporting about an objective reality. Consequently, within constructionist arguments, social, rhetorical, and interactional agencies—i.e., constructive practices and ethnomethods—occupy the grammatical role of presuppositions in a classic idealist rebuttal to philosophical realism.

The injunction to treat commonsense reasoning, natural language categories, and vernacular intuitions as topics and not analytic resources for sociological investigation has been stated so often in the ethnomethodological canon it has become something of a central dogma (Garfinkel and Sacks 1970; Zimmerman and Pollner 1970; Heritage 1984; Schegloff 1987; Hilbert 1990). When presented to readers who presume that sociology ought not to be contaminated by its subject matter it is an effective rhetorical device, but when taken literally—as Ibarra and Kitsuse seem to take it—it implies that an analyst can somehow stand outside the commonsense world when investigating its constitutive organization. Somehow, it would seem, the analyst must conduct an activity that is not itself practical, vernacular, conventional, mundane, or informed by intuitive categories. Although they do not make a major point of it, Ibarra and Kitsuse apparently call upon a Husserlian solution to this problem of transcending the mundane perspective of members when they propose "bracketing of the 'natural attitude.'"[14] For our purposes, it is worth reconsidering the consequences of such a classic phenomenological solution for a constructivist theory of social problems.

A Multiplicity of Attitudes

In his essay "The Problem of Rationality in the Social World," Schutz characterized the "attitude of scientific theorizing" as being remote from the world of everyday practical relations:

> This [everyday] world is not the theatre of his [the scientific theorist's] activities, but the object of his contemplation on which he looks with detached equanimity. As a scientist (not as a human being dealing with science) the observer is essentially solitary. He has no companion, and we can say that he has placed himself outside the social world with its manifold relations and its system of interests. Everyone, to become a social scientist, must make up his mind to put somebody else instead of himself as the center of the world, namely, the observed person. But with the shift in the central point, the whole system has been transformed, and, if I may use this metaphor, all the equations proved as valid in the former system now have to be expressed in terms of the new one. If the social system in question had reached an ideal perfection, it would be possible to establish a universal transformation formula such as Einstein has succeeded in establishing for translating propositions in terms of the Newtonian System of Mechanics into those of the theory of Relativity.
>
> The first and fundamental consequence of this shift in the point of view is that the scientist replaces the human beings he observes as actors on the social stage by puppets created by himself and manipulated by himself. What I call "puppets" corresponds to the technical term "ideal types" which Weber has introduced into social science. (1964, p. 81)

Accordingly, the scientist performs a kind of transcendental reduction of the everyday natural attitude in order to construct a simulacrum of the actor's practical orientation. In contrast to Garfinkel's (1967, pp. 68ff.) later discussion of the "cultural dope" of classic social theory, Schutz explicitly ascribed legitimacy to the ideal-typical puppet's construction. Although the puppet incorporates only and entirely what the social theorist puts into it, Schutz does not repudiate the project of constructing "personal ideal types," but he demands that any such type be checked against the "mind of the individual actor" described by it.[15]

By invoking a version of the Schutzian opposition between "the natural attitude" and the "attitude of scientific theorizing,"[16] Ibarra and Kitsuse put themselves in an awkward position with respect to other constructivist studies. Numerous studies on the social construction of

scientific knowledge have rejected the image of the scientist as a cogitat-
ing ego withdrawn from the myriad embodied skills, social interactions,
and practical interests in the everyday life-world.[17] The scientist now
appears to be more of a *bricoleur*. But this characterization itself poses
problems for constructivist analysis.

The image of the *bricoleur*—a kind of jack-of-all-trades and handy-
man—is owed to Lévi-Strauss (1966), who contrasts the *bricoleur's* im-
provisory use of the array of tools ready to hand with the engineer's
explicitly planned and rationally articulated choice of means to a specific
end. In his essay, "Structure, Sign, and Play in the Human Sciences,"
Derrida expounds upon the internal relation between *bricolage* and the
figure of the engineer in Lévi-Strauss's work.

> If one calls *bricolage* the necessity of borrowing one's concepts from the text
> of a heritage which is more or less coherent or ruined, it must be said that
> every discourse is *bricoleur*. The engineer, whom Lévi-Strauss opposes to
> the *bricoleur*, should be the one to construct the totality of his language,
> syntax, and lexicon. In this sense the engineer is a myth. A subject who
> supposedly would be the absolute origin of his own discourse and sup-
> posedly would construct it "out of nothing," "out of whole cloth," would
> be the creator of the verb, the verb itself. The notion of the engineer who
> supposedly breaks with all forms of *bricolage* is therefore a theological idea;
> and since Lévi-Strauss tells us elsewhere that *bricolage* is mythopoetic, the
> odds are that the engineer is a myth produced by the *bricoleur*. As soon as
> we cease to believe in such an engineer and in a discourse which breaks
> with the received historical discourse, and as soon as we admit that every
> finite discourse is bound by a certain *bricolage* and that the engineer and
> scientist are also species of *bricoleurs*, then the very idea of *bricolage* is
> menaced and the difference in which it took on its meaning breaks down.
> (1972, p. 285)

On Derrida's account, the Lévi-Straussian engineer who dwells in an
idealized world of rational choice is an absurdity, and so would be the
Schutzian scientist who theorizes with an "attitude" divorced from the
everyday world. The use of these figures as ideal-typical constructs—
viz., as methodological heroes, and even straw men—is accompanied
by a principled acceptance of a performative contradiction: "conserving
all these old concepts within the domain of empirical discovery while
here and there denouncing their limits, treating them as tools which can
still be used" (Derrida 1972, p. 284). An entire edifice of contrastive
terms—engineer/*bricoleur*, scientist/practical reasoner, and in the present case, analyst/member—becomes "menaced" by the effervescence
of the initial term in each of these pairs into a "mythopoetic" counterpart
of the other. All we are left with are *bricoleurs*, practical reasoners, and

ordinary members who occasionally, contingently, and opportunistically conjure up various mythic creatures: gods, heroes, rational actors, scientists, engineers, social theorists, and analysts.

As soon as they deny the possibility of transcending the natural attitude, along with its vernacular accounts and ordinary linguistic categories, aspiring analysts might seem doomed to succumb to the "seductions" of membership. To paraphrase Dennis Martinez, "What else could they do?" In line with Derrida's suggestion, however, the very coherence of the natural attitude is itself "menaced" by the absence of a contrastive category (the attitude of scientific theorizing), and hence there is no longer any reason to impute a coherent philosophical standpoint to something so inclusive. It makes just as much sense to suppose that the natural attitude includes every imaginable scientific, philosophical, and mundane "attitude." This, in turn, would mean that the natural attitude comprises a multiplicity of attitudes, none of which constitutes a standpoint from which to view the entire array.

A Plurality of Language Games

We began this essay by proposing a conception of the social problems language game that would open up a radical alternative to the program of constructive analysis proposed by Ibarra and Kitsuse. We argued that the phenomenon they theorize—viz., "social problems per se"— appears in and only in the conduct of "the social problems language game." We argued further that even (and perhaps especially) the claim that the "social problems process," the "social problems language game," or "social problems per se" exist independently of the work of constructive analysis is itself a move in the social problems language game.

Lest we be read as having reached a purely negative conclusion regarding the prospects of Ibarra and Kitsuse's program of research we wish to reiterate that we are quite untroubled by the kind of analysis they pursue, that we find it informative and rewarding, and that it is only for this reason that we have been caused to wonder what the connection between their study and their theory might be.

Clearly there are differences between the program that Ibarra and Kitsuse are recommending and the methods of research toward which we incline, and it has been our argument that many of those differences can be brought to light by examining their use of "the social problems language game." Such differences arise whenever parties to a discourse are operating with understandings of a concept that are so different that the difference itself needs to be thematized. For our part, the issue that spells the difference is not that we disagree about how properly to conceive "the social problems language game," rather, it is that we disagree about the relevance of such disputes to the conduct of social problems research. This point can perhaps be made clearer by considering how the concept of language games arises as a topic of concern for the social sciences in the first place.

Wittgenstein's concept of language games (if indeed it is a concept) is subject to innumerable interpretations, but one thing that is especially clear is the *plurality* of different examples he gives of them. At one point in the *Philosophical Investigations* he writes that "the term 'language-game' is meant to bring into prominence the fact that the *speaking* of language is part of an activity, or of a form of life." He then lists the following examples of language games:

> Giving orders, and obeying them—
> Describing the appearance of an object, or giving its measurements—
> Constructing an object from a description (a drawing)—
> Reporting an event—
> Speculating about an event—
> Forming and testing a hypothesis—
> Presenting the results of an experiment in tables and diagrams—
> Making up a story; and reading it—
> Play-acting—
> Singing catches—
> Guessing riddles—
> Making a joke; telling it—
> Solving a problem in practical arithmetic—
> Translating from one language into another—
> Asking, thanking, cursing, greeting, praying. (Wittgenstein 1958b, §23)

These various language games do not seem to form a unitary cognitive system. Although Wittgenstein never wrote of "social problems" language games, we can imagine that were he to do so he would not write of *the* social problems language game at all, nor would he describe "it" as a coherent metaphysical picture. More likely, he would list an array of social problems language games or, more precisely, a plurality of language games affiliated with specific orders of activity that are in turn associated with the various substantive topics included in lay and professional discussions of social problems. Since "crime and the criminal justice process" has an unquestioned place in contemporary discussions of social problems, consider the following list of language games associated with that topic:

Arresting a suspect and reading him his rights—
Cross-examining a witness in a trial—
Plea bargaining—
Selecting a jury—
Jury deliberations—
Doing "count" in a maximum security prison—
Generating a picture of an assailant from a victim's description—
Cooling out the mark in a con game—
Interviewing victims of a burglary—
Examining a corpse for evidences of "foul play"—
Passing contraband at a prison visitation facility—
Tap codes among inmates—
Receiving emergency calls and dispatching police—

Many of these language games have been investigated in detail by ethnomethodologists and constructivist sociologists (Garfinkel 1967; Sudnow 1965; Bittner 1967; Cicourel 1968; Wieder 1974; Maynard 1984; Brannigan and Lynch 1987; Goffman 1952; Atkinson and Drew 1979; Pomerantz 1987; Whalen and Zimmerman 1987; Meehan 1989).[18] Note, however, that these language games are constituents of various substantive actions and institutions associated with a *presumptive* condition-category of social problem. The status of crime as a social problem for the most part is not thematic to the various language games in criminal justice institutions, nor is it thematized in studies of those particular language games. It would be unusual to find, for instance, adversaries in a criminal trial debating about whether or not "common assault" is a "social problem." They would more likely argue about whether or not a particular defendant committed the assault in question, whether his "joining a fight" in fact constituted "an assault," or whether, having been convicted, the assailant remains a "menace to society."

When in the later part of their article Ibarra and Kitsuse outline the properties of the social problems language game, it is not clear that they bring into relief a *general* set of properties that covers the range of language games that social problems researchers typically investigate. Instead, they seem to be thinking of some language games and not others. The various rhetorical claims and counterclaims Ibarra and Kitsuse describe *do* have a recognizable place in the way many public controversies are prosecuted. Some of the things that come to mind are the language used in junk mail sent to potential contributors to single-issue causes; the arguments and counterarguments used in dialogues between callers and radio talk show hosts; slogans shouted at protest marches and pasted on bumper stickers; journalistic summaries of arguments on both sides of a public controversy; or the arguments used in a class action suit in which the plaintiff charges a company with having created a public hazard by releasing industrial wastes into a local river.[19] Ibarra and Kitsuse's paper sketches a set of rubrics that may assist researchers to develop and deepen their understandings of an array of such controversies. But even in these cases, the slogans and terms of debate are circumscribed by sets of considerations that are conceptually distinct from a definition of *the* social problems language game in general. By analogy, one can say that players in a game of chess are "playing a board game," and it may even be possible to develop an abstract conception of what it is that all board games typically have in common, but it would be odd to say that a particular move in chess was a move in *the* board game.[20]

The important feature of the social problems language game for Ibarra and Kitsuse is that the condition-categories featured in an interchange of slogans and arguments are *relativized* by reference to a chronic standoff between the disputants' positions. Where antiabortionists define the condition category of "abortion" as "murder," advocates of legalized abortion argue that it should remain a matter of "right" and "free choice"; where opponents of smoking emphasize the harmful effects and social costs of "secondhand smoke," advocates argue that smoking should remain a matter of "right" and a "free choice." In classic sociology of knowledge fashion, Ibarra and Kitsuse treat the interplay of positions in these public disputes as an opportunity to distance their analysis from the substantive claims identified with the contending positions. Such contentious situations are as though tailor-made for a program of analysis that distinguishes the formal properties of the partisan "claims" from assumptions about their truth and moral virtuousness.

Although many such controversies and disputes can be analyzed in the way Ibarra and Kitsuse recommend, not all social problems language games necessarily take the form of opposing arguments by different sides. From the short list of crime and criminal justice language games listed above, we can see that all sorts of routines, arguments, and modes of symmetrical and asymmetrical exchange have a constitutive role in their production. If the language games associated with crime and criminal justice are diverse and difficult to group under a covering definition or a coherent set of narrative frames, the difficulties get much worse when we consider the full range of topics commonly represented in social problems literatures.

Concluding Discussion

Ibarra and Kitsuse are bothered by the "heterotopias" (Foucault 1970, p. xviii) of vernacular categories that researchers adopt when they study diverse social problems. As a solution, they propose a general interactionist theory as a remedy for the "ambiguous and often logically inconsistent use of 'social problems.'" The problem as they see it is that researchers too often presume the relevance of particular social problems to their studies, without *defining* how the discursive organization of, for example, "plea bargaining" or "passing contraband" is related to social problems, generally speaking. We have argued that to stipulate such a relation as a criterion for social problems research buys little in the way of either theoretical clarity or analytical advance. Although it is sometimes helpful to have in hand a definition of social problems, to us it would seem unduly restrictive to limit the agenda for social problems research to the study of those language games where the status of a given condition-category as a social problem is called into question, and we do not figure that Ibarra and Kitsuse would want to impose such definitional limits on what counts as a bona fide topic for social problems research.

Ibarra and Kitsuse say that constructivists should bracket particular condition-categories, because analysts should not trade upon vernacular conceptions of "abortion," "child abuse," or "hazardous pollutants". Note, however, that when they give examples they do not carry this bracketing to absurd extremes. They do not bracket everything having to do with the ontological status of the social problems they examine. Following their policies we would be careful to say that some groups *claim* or *define* abortion as [murder] while others define it as a morally legitimate [choice], and we would not say that abortion *really is* "an act of murder" or that it *really is* "a legitimate choice." To follow Ibarra and Kitsuse's policies in this case would neither be impossible nor senseless, since the intelligibility of the bracketing is *internal* to the substantive dispute being investigated (the vernacular terms of the dispute themselves establish *just* what is problematic about "abortion"), but it would be absurd to generalize the analytic procedure in an attempt to transcend an entire "members' ontology." Notice, for instance, that Ibarra and Kitsuse do not suggest that we should refer to abortion clinics as [abortion] clinics (or as abortion [clinics]), as though to suggest that what *abortion* or *clinic* denotes in such a context should be bracketed for the sake of analysis. Disputes about abortion clinics do not problematize the matter of whether or not abortions actually occur, or whether or not there actually exist facilities called abortion clinics . Even the most radical antiabortionist saboteurs give little thought to such ontological concerns when they stage their protests or plant their bombs.[21] Consequently, in order to have anything specific to say about the abortion controversy, social problems researchers must trade upon vernacular concepts of clinic and abortion. The lesson from Dennis Martinez and Wittgenstein is that *this is not a problem* (and therefore it is not a problem to be remedied by a theory), since it is their vernacular concepts that enable members and analysts alike to problematize what they see fit to debate about, explicate, or relativize in accordance with some language game.

This returns us to the question we asked earlier: What use is a general theory for studies of the various social problems? From what we can see it is of very little use, either for investigators who study particular language games associated with conventionally recognized types of social problem, *or* for Ibarra and Kitsuse when they begin to explicate some of the narrative tropes that come into play in various public disputes. Although we applaud their having begun a study of an array of language games specific to a variety of social movements and public controversies, we see no reason to believe that their study, however promising and insightful, will yield a *comprehensive framework* for investigating the myriad language games that in one way or another constitute the familiar themes and settings associated with the various vernacular categories of social problem.

From what we have said thus far, readers may be inclined to ask, "So what are you trying to do? What would you suggest as an alternative?"[22] One thing we are *not* aiming to do is to offer an alternative theory to supplant the one proposed by Ibarra and Kitsuse. Despite the fact that we have focused our critique on their theory, we would not want readers to conclude that their theory is inadequate compared to another actual or possible theory of the social problems process. Instead, we have questioned their initial conception of the field of social problems—and of social action more generally—that sets up a need for a general theory. We have suggested some reasons for doubting whether a general social problems process subsumes the various language games associated with the public manifestation and practical management of members' social problems. Although we recognize that what counts as a social problem is a "members' phenomenon," which therefore can change with different social and historical conditions of membership, we see little reason to believe that a general theory of how members rhetorically constitute social problems would fare any better than an objective definition of the social problems themselves.

It might seem at this point that we are advocating a hyperrelativistic perspective that disavows any possibility of investigating substantive social problems. Such a position would be far from what we are in fact advocating. It would be a fundamental mistake to suppose that because social problems are vernacular, rhetorical, or indexical phenomena, researchers should first devise a stricter and more demanding conception of the field before they can hope to investigate those phenomena. To suppose this would be to forget that students of social problems are masters of the vernacular (that is, they are members) before they begin their studies, and that the many ordinary and more specialized discursive practices pertinent to the transgressions, institutionalized routines, disputes, and negotiations that make social problems accountable are *finely ordered*. Although a vernacular concept is far from an epistemological guarantee, and there may be no invariant definition of social problems or of the discursive practices associated with their production and recognition, this should not deter researchers from taking up the task of explicating the way those practices are ordered (Sharrock and Anderson 1991, p. 52). The fact that social problems may always be bound to temporal and practical circumstances does not make them unreal, nor does it justify an invariant attitude of skepticism toward them. So far from arguing in favor of a remote epistemological attitude toward the field of social problems research, we would rather encourage further research about the discursive practices through which social problems manifest in specific social and historical circumstances. As mentioned earlier in this paper, numerous studies of this sort are in hand, and while they may not provide readers with a coherent and noncontentious perspective on a general social problems process, they do provide occasional glimpses into the unfathomably complex fields of practical action in which social problems arise.

Notes

1.   This information comes in a personal communication from Richard Harper, of Rank Xerox, Ltd., Cambridge EuroPARK. According to Harper, these accountants adopt a version of deconstructionism, which for present purposes can be treated hand in glove with constructionism.

2.   See Fish (1989, p. 226) for a discussion of this "equivocation."

3.   By principled, here we mean a distinction that must be seen to identify nonarbitrary qualities of the members' phenomenon under study, as distinct from the contingent products of a methodological interest that ignores or overrides the system of relevancies interior to the production of the phenomenon. This is a particular way of attending to the "postulate of adequacy" that Schutz develops from Weber:

> Each term used in a scientific system referring to human action must be so constructed that a human act performed within the life-world by an individual actor in the way indicated by the typical construction would be reasonable and understandable for the actor himself, as well as for his fellow men. (1964, p. 85)

Note, however, that this postulate retains a strong element of methodological individualism (the reference to the "individual actor") that does not operate when "actor" is transformed into "member" (see note 4).

4.   In ethnomethodology, the term *member* refers not to a person but to "mastery of natural language" (Garfinkel and Sacks 1970, p. 342). Ibarra and Kitsuse apparently use the term in the more familiar sense of *member of a society or group*, although they do associate members with particular rhetorical practices.

5.   Garfinkel and Sacks (1970, pp. 339–40) use the term *constructive analysis* to cover a "remedial program of practical sociological reasoning" that aims to accomplish "a thoroughgoing distinction between objective and indexical expressions." Among the specific research objectives and tasks listed under this "remedial program" are

> the elaboration and defense of unified sociological theory, model building, cost-benefit analysis, the use of natural metaphors to collect wider settings under the experience of a locally known setting, the use of laboratory arrangements as experimental schemes of inference, schematic reporting and statistical evaluations of frequency, reproducibility, or effectiveness of natural language practices and of various social arrangements that entail their use, and so on. (p. 340)

Although Ibarra and Kitsuse align with ethnomethodology's program and obviously oppose "objectivistic" modes of research, their effort to build a general theory of "the social problems language game" that remedies the "ambiguous" and "ad hoc" uses of the concept in the research literature is a prime example of the constructive analytic enterprise.
6.   Ibarra and Kitsuse's paper also displays a kind of groundless optimism with regard to the future prospects of the theory and its consequences for the actual conduct of research that is a characteristic (perhaps essential) feature of "programmatic" theorizing. This faith in theory's power to redefine our ordinary concepts is a variant of what Fish (1989, p. 322) has dubbed "theory hope," or "the hope that our claims to knowledge can be 'justified on the basis of some objective method of assessing such claims' rather than on the basis of the individual beliefs that have been derived from the accidents of education and experience."
7.   The interview took place in 1985. Dennis Martinez is now a veteran pitcher for the Montreal Expos, had outstanding 1991 and 1992 seasons, and pitched a perfect game on July 28, 1991. As Jim Holstein (personal communication) put it: "Something must be working for Martinez—Weaver's litany, a rejuvenated fastball, his newfound sobriety—that surely wasn't doing the trick in 1985."
8.   Fish (1989, pp. 374ff.) draws this example from Schön (1979).
9.   Compare, for instance, Aronson (1984, pp. 7ff.), who argues that the disjuncture between science methods and scientists' descriptions of their methods should make us skeptical of the facticity of science findings. Notice, however, that this skepticism arises only once we suppose that *descriptions* of science methods ought to map directly onto those methods in situ—i.e., that there ought to be some direct correspondence between the two—rather than that science methods and scientists' descriptions of those methods are, practically speaking, designed simply to do different kinds of work. It is perhaps for this reason, and not because they are interested in veiling their actual practices (although they sometimes are), that scientists' reports cannot possibly meet the criteria of correspondence implicit in Aronson's treatment of their factual claims.
10.   This is related to the argument about formulations made by Garfinkel and Sacks (1970). By "formulating" they mean giving a verbal account that says "in-so-many-words-what-we-are-doing" (p. 351). Like the more familiar varieties of scribes and pundits, social scientists have an occupational interest in formulating what various other members of the society are doing when they engage in their activities. For instance, when conducting interviews they demand explicit verbal accounts that stand as indicators of attitudes, practical skills, and bodies of knowledge. Often such inquirers get disappointing results when they ask for

explicit accounts from practitioners, but they are able to fall back on some well-established techniques for clarifying, coding, elaborating, and enriching partial, cryptic, and even hostile answers. Consequently, it can often seem that ordinary usage is inherently partial, schematic, unreflective, ambiguous, or otherwise faulty until an accompanying formulation can draw out its meaning and clarify its sense. This, according to Garfinkel and Sacks, places an undue burden upon formulating. For them, the intelligibility of ordinary usage does not depend upon an accompanying formulation to clarify it:

> [I]nsofar as formulations are recommended to be definitive of "meaningful talk," something is amiss because "meaningful talk" cannot have that sense. This is to say either that talk is not meaningful unless we construct a language which is subject to such procedures, or that *that* could not be what "meaningful talk" is, or "meaningful actions" either. (p. 359)

In the case at hand, an expression like "throw strikes and keep them off the bases," is a disappointing cliché when what is wanted is an elaborate formulation of how a wise old manager instructs a nervous pitcher prior to a big game. But, in line with Garfinkel and Sacks's argument, to hear it *only* as a description answerable to an outsider's inquiry would be to miss its role in the game.

11. For an instructive essay on the limitations of visual metaphors in sociological and psychological theory, see Coulter and Parsons (1991).

12. Although it is not of concern to us here, Sacks expresses a puzzling view of the relationship between natural science and "the common-sense perspective." Bacon's protoexperimental program was set off against the "idyls" of common sense, and while it is well documented that Galileo and other seventeenth-century heroes struggled against theological orthodoxy, they did not at the time propose to free their inquiries from philosophy. For a discussion of related considerations see Lynch and Bogen (forthcoming).

13. Pollner's (1987) account of the epistemic limitations of "mundane reason" has made this move virtually paradigmatic for constructivist social science. See Bogen (1990) for a critical discussion of Pollner's notion of the "mundane world."

14. Although Ibarra and Kitsuse cite Pollner (1975, 1978) as proximate authority, it should be evident from the expression "bracketing the 'natural attitude'" that they are indebted to Husserl and Schutz. Husserl (1970) proposed the "transcendental reduction" as a method through which the solitary theorist reflectively withdraws from active engagement in the life-world in order to thematize the pre-predicative "acts" through which a cognizing subject apprehends real-worldly objects and their categorical relations. Schutz elaborated upon Husserl's analysis of the life-world, and he revised transcendental phenomenology in order to make it more suitable for social scientific investigations. Like many others, Schutz (1966) found Husserl's concept of the "transcendental ego" to be an inadequate starting point for investigating the intersubjective structures of the life-world, and he attempted critically to integrate Husserlian phenomenology with established theoretical traditions in sociology. For Schutz, "the attitude of scientific theorizing" offered a perspective—analogous to that of Husserl's transcendental ego—for viewing "the natural attitude" of daily life as though from outside its sphere of operations.

15. Schutz raises the question, "But why form personal ideal types at all?" (1964, p. 84), but then goes on to formulate a postulate of subjective interpretation that regulates the analytic construction by reference to "what happens in the mind of an individual actor whose act has led to the phenomenon in ques-

tion" (p. 85).The only alternative Schutz considers is to simply collect empirical facts, and he argues that one cannot do this without taking account of subjective categories.

16.   Ibarra and Kitsuse make only brief mention of Schutz. Nevertheless, we read their article to be indebted to the conceptual distinction between the attitude of sociological theorizing and the "natural attitude" of everyday life (or, as they sometimes put it, the contrasting "perspectives" of the member and the sociological theorist), which is a familiar tenet of much constructivist and ethnomethodological writing, and which was given extensive and original development in Schutz's seminal writings.

17.   See Lynch (1988) for a critical discussion of Schutz's cognitivist views on natural science. A more charitable clarification of Schutz's distinction between the theoretical and everyday attitudes is given by Sharrock and Anderson (1991).

18.   This is but a small sample of a much larger group of studies relevant to various "language games" associated with discursive activities and institutions that presuppose the "problematic" character of condition-categories like mental illness, poverty, and contagious disease. See the extensive bibliography of ethnomethodological studies by Fehr, Stetson, and Mizukawa (1990), for other examples. Many of these studies employ variants of the programmatic distinction between analysis and vernacular orientation that is so central to Ibarra and Kitsuse's theory, and they are therefore not exempt from the critique of the member/analyst distinction we are giving in this paper. The point of mentioning these studies here is to argue that the diverse "language games" they investigate do not readily fall under the rubric of a general "social problems process."

19.   In note 3, Ibarra and Kitsuse mention a "paradigm case" where members "self-reflexively comprehend the social problems process." This is where political consultants advise presidential election campaigns on strategies for topicalizing "social problems" for different audiences. In our terms, such strategy sessions are no more or less "reflexive" than are any other natural language activity, nor do they provide a "window" on a general social problems process that remains obscure within less "self-reflexive" uses of language. See Czyzewski (forthcoming) for a criticism of the conflation of ethnomethodological "reflexivity" with a cognitive concept of "self-reflection."

20.   Wittgenstein (1958b, §2) makes a related point: "It is as if someone were to say: *A game consists in moving objects about on a surface according to certain rules* . . . . —and we replied: You seem to be thinking of board games, but there are others. You can make your definition correct by expressly restricting it to those games."

21.   'Ontological gerrymandering" (Woolgar and Pawluch 1985) is not the issue here. *Gerrymandering* suggests a kind of arbitrary or unwarranted definitional project, while the controversy in this case establishes what it is about abortion that is problematic; and not *everything* about abortion is arbitrary as far as participants or analysts are concerned. Woolgar and Pawluch's argument has "devastating" effects only for readers who continue to suppose that social problems researchers should not trade upon *any* vernacular characterizations of the phenomena they study. We are suggesting that there is a world of difference between locally and accountably "problematic" vernacular characterizations versus those that are used and accepted as a matter of course for the sake of some argument.

22.   We are indebted to Jim Holstein for raising these questions about an earlier draft.

References

Aronson, Naomi. 1984. "Science as a Claims-Making Activity: Implications for Social Problems Research." Pp. 1–30 in *Studies in the Sociology of Social Problems*, edited by J. W. Schneider and J. I. Kitsuse. Norwood, NJ: Ablex.

Atkinson, J. Maxwell and Paul Drew. 1979. *Order in Court: The Organisation of Verbal Interaction in Judicial Settings*. London: Macmillan.

Berger, Peter and Thomas Luckmann. 1966. *The Social Construction of Reality*. New York: Anchor Books.

Bittner, Egon. 1967. "Police Discretion in Emergency Apprehension of Mentally Ill Persons." *Social Problems* 14:278–92.

Bogen, David. 1990. "Beyond the Limits of Mundane Reason." *Human Studies* 13:405–16.

Brannigan, Augustine and Michael Lynch. 1987. "On Bearing False Witness: Perjury and Credibility as Interactional Accomplishments." *Journal of Contemporary Ethnography* 16:115–46.

Cicourel, Aaron V. 1968. *The Social Organization of Juvenile Justice*. New York: Wiley.

Coulter, Jeff and E. D. Parsons. 1991. "The Praxiology of Perception: Visual Orientations and Practical Action." *Inquiry* 33:251–72.

Czyzewski, Marek. Forthcoming. "Reflexivity of Actors vs. Reflexivity of Accounts." *Theory, Culture, and Society*.

Derrida, Jacques. 1972. "Structure, Sign and Play in the Discourse of the Human Sciences." Pp. 242–72 in *The Structuralist Controversy: The Languages of Criticism and the Sciences of Man*, edited by R. Macksey and E. Donato. Baltimore, MD: Johns Hopkins University Press.

Fehr, B. J., Jeff Stetson, and Yoshifumi Mizukawa. 1990. "A Bibliography for Ethnomethodology." Pp. 473–559 in *Ethnomethodological Sociology*, edited by J. Coulter. London: Edward Elgar.

Fish, Stanley. 1989. *Doing What Comes Naturally: Change, Rhetoric, and the Practice of Theory in Literary and Legal Studies*. Durham, NC: Duke University Press.

Foucault, Michel. 1970. *The Order of Things*. Translated by Alan Sheridan. New York: Pantheon.

Garfinkel, Harold. 1967. *Studies in Ethnomethodology*. Englewood Cliffs, NJ: Prentice Hall.

————. 1991. "Respecification: Evidence for Locally Produced, Naturally Accountable Phenomena of Order*, Logic, Reason, Meaning, Method, etc. in and as of the Essential Haecceity of Immortal Ordinary Society, (1)—An Announcement of Studies." Pp. 10–19 in *Ethnomethodology and the Human Sciences*, edited by G. Button. Cambridge: Cambridge University Press.

Garfinkel, Harold and Harvey Sacks. 1970. "On Formal Structures of Practical Actions." Pp. 337–66 in *Theoretical Sociology: Perspectives and Development*, edited by J. C. McKinney and E. A. Tiryakian. New York: Appleton-Century Crofts.

Goffman, Erving. 1952. "On Cooling the Mark Out: Some Aspects of Adaptation to Failure." *Psychiatry* 15:451–63.

Gombrich E. H. 1960. *Art and Illusion: A Study in the Psychology of Pictorial Representation.* Princeton, NJ: Princeton University Press.

Heritage, John. 1984. *Garfinkel and Ethnomethodology.* Oxford: Polity Press.

Hilbert, Richard. 1990. "Ethnomethodology and the Micro-Macro Order." *American Sociological Review* 55:798–808.

Holstein, James and Gale Miller. 1990. "Rethinking Victimization: An Interactional Approach to Victimology." *Symbolic Interaction* 13:103–22.

Husserl, Edmund. 1970. *The Crisis of European Sciences and Transcendental Philosophy.* Translated by David Carr. Evanston, IL: Northwestern University Press.

Knorr-Cetina, Karin. 1981. *The Manufacture of Knowledge: An Essay in the Constructivist and Contextual Nature of Science.* Oxford: Pergamon.

Latour, Bruno and Steve Woolgar. 1979. *Laboratory Life: The Social Construction of Scientific Facts.* London: Sage.

Lévi-Strauss, Claude. 1966. *The Savage Mind.* Chicago: University of Chicago Press.

Lynch, Michael. 1988. "Alfred Schutz and the Sociology of Science." Pp. 71–100 in *Worldly Phenomenology: The Influence of Alfred Schutz on Human Science,* edited by L. Embree. Washington, DC: Center for Advanced Research in Phenomenology and University Press of America.

Lynch, Michael and David Bogen. Forthcoming. "Harvey Sacks's Primitive Natural Science." *Theory, Culture, and Society.*

Maynard, Douglas W. 1984. *Inside Plea Bargaining: The Language of Negotiation.* New York: Plenum Press.

Meehan, Albert J. 1989. "Assessing the 'Police Worthiness' of Citizen's Complaints to the Police: Accountability and the Negotiation of 'Facts'." Pp. 116–40 in *The Interactional Order: New Directions in the Study of Social Order,* edited by D. T. Helm, W. T. Anderson, A. J. Meehan, and A. W. Rawls. New York: Irvington.

Pickering, Andrew. 1984. *Constructing Quarks: A Sociological History of Particle Physics.* Chicago: University of Chicago Press.

Pollner, Melvin. 1975. "'The Very Coinage of Your Brain': The Anatomy of Reality Disjunctures." *Philosophy of the Social Sciences* 5:411–30.

————. 1978. "Constitutive and Mundane Versions of Labelling Theory." *Human Studies* 1:269–88.

————. 1987. *Mundane Reason: Reality in Everyday and Sociological Discourse.* Cambridge: Cambridge University Press.

————. 1991. "Left of Ethnomethodology." *American Sociological Review* 56:370–80.

Pomerantz, Anita M. 1987. "Descriptions in Legal Settings." Pp. 226–43 in *Talk and Social Organization,* edited by G. Button and J. R. E. Lee. Clevedon, UK: Multilingual Matters.

Sacks, Harvey. 1963. "Sociological Description." *Berkeley Journal of Sociology* 8:1–16.

Schegloff, Emanuel A. 1987. "Between Micro and Macro: Contexts and Other Connections." Pp. 207–34 in *The Micro-Macro Link,* edited by J. Alexander,

B. Giesen, R. Münch, and N. Smelser. Berkeley: University of California Press.

Schön, Donald. 1979. "Generative Metaphor: A Perspective on Problem-Setting in Social Policy." Pp. 254–83 in *Metaphor and Thought*, edited by A. Ortony. New York: Cambridge University Press.

Schutz, Alfred. 1964. "The Problem of Rationality in the Social World." Pp. 64–90 in *Collected Papers II*, by A. Schutz. The Hague: Martinus Nijhoff.

———. 1966. "The Problem of Transcendental Intersubjectivity in Husserl." Pp. 51–83 in *Collected Papers III*, by Alfred Schutz. The Hague: Martinus Nijhoff.

Sharrock, Wes and Bob Anderson. 1991. "Epistemology: Professional Scepticism." Pp. 51–76 in *Ethnomethodology and the Human Sciences*, edited by G. Button. Cambridge: Cambridge University Press.

Spector, Malcolm and John Kitsuse. [1977] 1987. *Constructing Social Problems.* Hawthorne, NY: Aldine de Gruyter.

Sudnow, David. 1965. "Normal Crimes: Sociological Features of the Penal Code in a Public Defender's Office." *Social Problems* 12:255–76.

Whalen, Marilyn R. and Don H. Zimmerman. 1987. "Sequential and Institutional Contexts in Calls for Help." *Social Psychology Quarterly* 50:172–85.

Wieder, D. Lawrence. 1974. *Language and Social Reality: The Case of Telling the Convict Code.* The Hague: Mouton.

Wittgenstein, Ludwig. 1958a. *The Blue and Brown Books.* Oxford: Basil Blackwell.

———. 1958b. *Philosophical Investigations*, translated by G. E. M. Anscombe. Oxford: Basil Blackwell.

Woolgar, Steve, and Dorothy Pawluch. 1985. "Ontological Gerrymandering: The Anatomy of Social Problems Explanations." *Social Problem* 32:214–27.

Zimmerman, Don H. and Melvin Pollner. 1970. "The Everyday World As a Phenomenon." Pp. 80–103 in *Understanding Everyday Life: Toward the Reconstruction of Sociological Knowledge*, edited by J. D. Douglas. Chicago: Aldine.

Conclusion

12

Reconstituting the Constructionist Program

James A. Holstein and Gale Miller

The constructionist approach to social problems initially emerged as a challenge to the dominant sociological paradigms in social problems theory. While the original debates between realists and constructionists flourished for over a decade, the constructionist program—most often exemplified by Spector and Kitsuse's *Constructing Social Problems* ([1977] 1987)—has increasingly been challenged on different fronts. Although the realist-constructionist debates persist, they have recently been pushed aside by new concerns raised from *within* the constructionist camp.

In the wake of Woolgar and Pawluch's (1985) provocative critique, many in the constructionist movement have begun to rethink, refine, and reconstitute the theoretical and empirical program. Part I of this volume represents a range of constructionist responses to the recent internal challenges, raising and attempting to answer a variety of questions regarding the theoretical integrity and empirical scope of the approach. This essay summarizes and assesses some of the major arguments that have emerged. As we consider the controversies, we hope to specify some of the major issues that must be confronted and propose some directions for further change and development of the constructionist program.

The essays in Part I suggest three sets of issues that point out new directions for social problems. The first and perhaps most compelling set of issues is concerned with reflexivity and social problems analysis, focusing on the extent to which this is a concern, problem, resource, or topic for the study of social problems. Accusations of ontological gerrymandering remain at the heart of the discussion. A second set of issues revolves around the role of interactional interpretive practice in social problems construction. Finally, some commentators have raised questions about the usefulness of a general theory of social problems. We consider these issues in the following sections.

Constructionism, Ontological Gerrymandering, and Reflexivity

Woolgar and Pawluch (1985) provoked a flurry of responses when they accused constructionists of ontological gerrymandering in the analysis of social problems. One way their critique may be read is as a commentary on the selective relativism invoked by constructionists in presenting and arguing their analyses. At this level, the critique centers on the rhetorical strategies employed by analysts that compromise theoretical consistency by invoking realist assumptions about the phenomenon under consideration. On a deeper level, however, Woolgar and Pawluch suggest that constructionist analysis and writing is itself is a constructive activity, little different from other versions of social problems claims-making that constructionists study. This implies the need to analyze constructionist analysis itself, as well as the essentially reflexive character of social reality more generally.

Ibarra and Kitsuse directly address the ontological gerrymandering critique in their refinement of Spector and Kitsuse's ([1977] 1987) original programmatic statement. Their emendation calls for a theory of social problems *discourse*. By emphasizing that members' rhetorical constructions of putative conditions are the focus for constructionist analysis, Ibarra and Kitsuse attempt to prevent the separation of social problems into objective conditions on one hand and claims about those conditions on the other. Their recommendation to study the use of "condition-categories" further discourages reference to objective conditions, underscoring instead the importance of explicating how people *use* commonsense categories and practical reasoning to construct social problems.

As Pollner (in this volume) suggests, Ibarra and Kitsuse have elaborated a "topical" constructionism, minimizing objectivist assumptions and focusing on the constitutive practices through which social reality is accomplished. Best (1989, in this volume) would call it a "strict constructionist" approach. While Ibarra and Kitsuse's proposal is a careful refocusing of Spector and Kitsuse's original program, it remains fundamentally objectivist in that it makes members' reality-constructing practices—assumptions, discourses, and acts of interpretation and representations—objects for analysis.

This appears to be an unavoidable feature of all analysis—including those done from the topical or strict constructionist perspectives. Where realist analysis objectifies social structures and conditions, constructionism, ethnomethodology, and related enterprises objectify interpretive practice. Reality-constituting social process is descriptively organized by constructionist analysis, making it visible and coherent through textual representation. As Woolgar and Pawluch (1985) imply, this is more an inevitable aspect of analysis—a "pervasive feature of all attempts to explain social phenomena" (p. 224)—than a correctable theoretical inconsistency.

While Ibarra and Kitsuse seem satisfied with their reformulation, others are troubled by ignored or unresolved issues relating to reflexivity. Schneider (in this volume), for example, is uncomfortable with constructionists' reluctance to acknowledge that their analyses "objectify" and "construct" aspects of reality while they privilege their constructionist epistemology over all others. He argues that constructionists must become more "self-reflexive," examining the "language games" through which they produce renditions of social problems processes. The practical implication is to examine constructionist analytic practices, treating constructionist analysts as members "in the world," engaged in language games that compete to structure reality.

This, of course, echoes Woolgar and Pawluch's call for an "ethnography of argument." Schneider's objective is to better understand the sociologist's role in the construction of reality and the inscription of power/knowledge. Woolgar and Pawluch take the argument one step farther, suggesting that studying writing practices might lead to new forms of discourse that are free from the tensions engendered by claims of relativism that are embedded in the analytic conventions of objectivism.

While most constructionists seek to eliminate the tensions associated with reflexive inquiry, Pollner (1991, in this volume) embraces them. The reflexive critique, he acknowledges, is a threat to the theoretical underpinnings of constructionism:

> [C]onstructionist claims about the discursive or rhetorical construction of, say, social problems are themselves discursive constructions as, indeed, are determinations of their truth or falsity as, indeed, are the very concepts that initiate and suffuse constructionist inquiry—such as truth, falsity, and constructionism itself. In applying the principles of constructionism to those very principles and their products, constructionism leads itself to analytic paralysis or infinite regress. (in this volume)

While this is a rather daunting prospect, Pollner argues that reflexivity itself provides a worthy topic for examination. More specific to the constructionist debate, he recommends inquiry into the social construction of reflexivity and the contexts that permit or inhibit its emergence. The sociology of reflexivity, he suggests, will make visible the deep foundations of objectivism and point out impediments to developing alternatives to the conventions of objectivist analysis and presentation.

The constructionist camp, however, is not universally responsive to the reflexive critique. Best (1989, in this volume), for example, is clearly impatient with sociologists' persistent concerns for "how we know what we know" as well as recent questions raised regarding sociology's claims to "special knowledge" of the empirical world. He argues that the "strict constructionist" approach embodied in Ibarra and Kitsuse's paper neither resolves the problem of reflexivity nor advances sociological understanding. All constructionist analysis makes *some* assumptions about objective reality, even though they are generally unacknowledged or "backgrounded." Best implies that since analysis inevitably violates strict constructionist principles, the strict constructionist has nowhere to go sociologically, except into an "armchair." He fears that the cost of "analytic purity" is too high; for him, strict constructionism means forgoing most traditional sociological pursuits, including empirical studies. Instead, he recommends a "contextual constructionism" that balances substantive description of the empirical world against the demands of theoretical consistency. Faced with hard choices between the two objectives, Best sacrifices analytic purity for sociological knowledge that might help people understand and improve the world.

While this seems a reasonable choice, it might also be argued that theoretically compromised analysis cannot render a useful picture of the empirical world. Moreover, taken to its "realist" extreme, contextual constructionism (or "objectivist" constructionism, in Pollner's terms) can result in what is little more than partisan "debunking" of subjectively objectionable claims. While it is difficult to specify how many "realist" assumptions may be allowed to sneak in the "back door" of constructionist analysis before theoretical compromise is fatal, it is equally hard to justify the unexplicated use of assumptions about objective conditions to support evaluative assessments of claims-making. Once involved in such an enterprise, the analyst openly becomes a commonsense claimsmaker as well, and the questions about the theoretical grounding of constructionism arise once more. One might be tempted, then, to ask contextual constructionists when they are going to "get serious" about their theoretical groundings.

Faced with slim prospects of resolving the controversy over theoretical consistency and the need for reflexive awareness, it might be more profitable to abandon the quest for a singular resolution in favor of a more pluralist—and self-aware—constructionist program. This does not imply some grand triangulation aimed at producing a comprehensive, multiperspectival explication of social problems. Nor would it necessarily require a rapprochement between countervailing positions. Rather, the family of constructionist orientations provides a diverse set of agendas emphasizing various aspects of constructionism that do not necessarily need to be reconciled for the practical purpose at hand. A wide range of objectives can be pursued through social constructionism, and while they may not all make compatible assumptions or respond to the same theoretical impulses, their coexistence may be justified by their collective utility. Indeed, a pluralistic constructionist program might tolerate analytic differences as sources of productive tension, growth plates of sociological imagination, to borrow Pollner's (in this volume) phrase.

Papers in this volume articulate at least three sets of objectives and orientations to constructionism, corresponding roughly to Pollner's *objectivist, topical,* and *analytic* constructionism. Each makes distinctive assumptions in service of different practical and analytic goals. Objectivist or contextual constructionism aims to describe claims-making in order to inform social action—to understand and improve the world (Best, in this volume). From this point of view, the desire to evaluate and act upon aspects of the life world justifies the judicious importation of realist assumptions. Practical utility is the warrant for theoretical compromise. The peril to constructionism intensifies as the reliance on realist assumptions turns compromise into theoretical surrender, once again relinquishing the study of social problems to the functionalists, Marxists, and fellow positivists.

Topical or strict constructionism minimizes realist incursions to promote disinterested analytic clarity. Interpretive practice is foregrounded, while the substance of the social problems process under consideration is virtually unimportant. Explicating interpretive aspects of the life world, not changing it, is the paramount goal. But topical analysis remains in and of the world, an objectivist enterprise that constitutes social problems in terms of social process. As such, it must acknowledge its own availability as a topic for constructionist analysis. Moreover, as Troyer (in this volume) implies, while refinements of the strict constructionist program—like Ibarra and Kitsuse's—may clarify and advance an empirical research agenda, they do not extend the enterprise into the postmodern, for better or worse.

Forms of analytic constructionism might exploit the tensions in the inconsistencies between and within the alternative expressions of constructionism. They might pursue deeper understandings of reflexivity, deconstructing even constructionist depictions of the life world. Attempting to understand the very possibility of constructionism (as well as objectivism, positivism, and other epistemologies) becomes the goal, but at the cost of moving to the very periphery of modern intelligibility. As Pollner (in this volume) suggests, much of what this approach has to offer will be unappreciated—even rejected—by practical and intellectual communities thoroughly embedded in and indebted to objectivist discursive styles. Making no pretense at practical utility, its value may be purely academic, at least for the time being.

In a life world shaped by the conventions of objectivism, the less radical versions of constructionism will be more understandable and applicable to issues of social change and social policy. To secure this grounding in the life world, however, they will sacrifice theoretical consistency and theory- building potential (Troyer 1992). The more reflexive enactments of constructionism seem to have less to offer modern society in any practical sense. Still, ethnographies of argument and reflexive studies of the production of social scientific findings may yield insights into both the process by which knowledge is created and transmitted, and into more generic interpretive, representational, and rhetorical practices. As Best implies, however, sociologists studying sociology for the sake of knowing "how we do what we do" is a relatively limited enterprise. To confine sociological activity to this topic hints of professional conceit. Reflexive inquiry is merely one of several directions in which the constructionist program might advance. Those suggesting this as an agenda should be encouraged to follow up their commentaries with concrete, reflexive studies and substantive proposals for alternative forms of analysis and communication.

Interactional Practice and the Construction of Social Problems

The constructionist program might also expand to more fully engage the range of interactional interpretive practices involved in the construction of social problems. *Constructing Social Problems* and Ibarra and Kitsuse's emendation focus on social problems claims-making, but their approach addresses only a limited range of activities that might be subsumed by the social problems process. As Gubrium (in this volume) notes, the emphasis is almost exclusively on "publicity"—large-scale, consciously manipulative public rhetoric. Despite its seeming affinity with ethnomethodological concerns for social accomplishment, the approach articulated by Spector and Kitsuse and Ibarra and Kitsuse only implicitly suggests that other forms of claims-making—interpretive and representational matters at the microinteractional level—might also be important topics for constructionist studies of social problems.

Spector and Kitsuse, and now Ibarra and Kitsuse, seem guarded or uncertain regarding their appreciation of and indebtedness to ethnomethodology and its concern for locally managed constitutive practice. While *Constructing Social Problems* has been characterized as ethnomethodologically informed (Troyer 1989), the authors did not reference the ethnomethodological literature. Ibarra and Kitsuse are more explicit in their use of ethnomethodological insights, yet they subtitle their paper "An Interactionist Proposal for the Study of Social Problems," once again obscuring what might otherwise be seen as an abiding concern for constitutive practice. In any case, the result is a call for a theory of social problems *discourse,* yet scant mention is made of the need to study mundane talk and interaction as part of the social problems process.

In their own ways, several of the authors in Part I of this volume suggest that the constructionist agenda for the study of social problems must broaden to include everyday interactional interpretive practices. Gubrium, for example, calls for the study of ordinary, practical, constructive activities that are embedded in local interpretive contexts and cultures. Similarly, Bogen and Lynch's interest in rich, detailed descriptions of unique ensembles of discursive routines and embodied praxis leads them to recommend research about the specific interactional and discursive practices through which social problems emerge in specific social and historical circumstances.

Marlaire and Maynard call further attention to the close connection between social problems and the organization of real-time talk and interaction. Their focus is on the proximate interactional sphere where troubles and problems are first made visible. Social problems analysis, they argue, should deal with how people organize and experience troubles and problems "prehistorically"—that is, before the problems have been historicized by the social problems idioms of public rhetoric.

The notion of social problems work (Holstein and Miller, in this volume; Miller and Holstein 1989) highlights another interactional aspect of the social problems process. Social problems work is the interpretive activity through which social problems categories, once publicly established, are attached to experience in order to produce identifiable objects of social problems discourse. The process involves the articulation of culturally recognized images—Ibarra and Kitsuse's rhetorical idioms and vernacular resources, for example—with aspects of experience to produce identifiable, indicatable instances of social problems. Social problems categories (condition-categories, in Ibarra and Kitsuse's terms) are merely candidate structures for making sense of objects and events. While they have been promoted as viable ways of understanding aspects of the life world, there are myriad possible ways to define experience. Interpretive practice attaches category to experience, employing available representational resources.

Social problems work, then, interactionally constitutes instances of social problems. A constructionist approach to social problems and social problems work focuses on interaction, conversational practice, and interpretive resources, complementing and extending the other calls for greater attention to interaction. It also links analytic concern for local accomplishment with more structural or cultural concerns—Durkheim's interest in collective representation (1961) and Foucault's concern for discourse and gaze (1972, 1973), for example. Adding an explicit emphasis on the locally managed, interactional production of social problems to the long-standing interest in publicity and social problems rhetoric would enrich and diversify the study of social problems construction.

What Use Is a General Theory of Social Problems?

While the essays in Part I all endorse a constructionist approach to social problems, Bogen and Lynch raise a sympathetic, yet pointed question. What use, they ask (rhetorically), is a general theory of social problems? Their answer is "very little." Bogen and Lynch reject the assumption that a general theory of social problems—any theory, constructionist or realist—is warranted. Casting the issue within an ethnomethodological and Wittgensteinian framework, they argue that the term *social problems* is a gloss for the myriad concrete activities or language games through which aspects of the life world are produced. The actual processes though which social problems are constructed involve such mundane activities as asking and answering questions, reporting findings, making recommendations, and giving advice and speeches. The activities are constituted by such observable aspects of the life world as enrolling clients in social service programs, deliberating on and delivering verdicts or sentences in criminal trials, and diagnosing illness. There can be no general theory of social problems, Bogen and Lynch contend, because of the plurality of language games that may be involved in what is analytically construed as a social problem. None of these explicitly raises the issue of whether the activity in question is a social problem. Thus, "social problem," is not a member's categorization device. Perhaps more importantly, the multiplicity of language games cannot be coherently assimilated under a single rubric of *the* social problems language game. The diverse language games are not parts of a coherent phenomenal field about which generalizations can be made.

Clearly, many of the activities that constructionists analyze as part of the social problems process are not described in the same fashion by participants in the settings under consideration. For example, human service professionals often describe their everyday work as mediating disputes, giving tests, and orienting clients to agency programs. And, as Bogen and Lynch point out, participants in criminal justice system activities can conduct their business without ever considering whether crime or substance abuse is a social problem. Everyday life is organized within so many language games that a constructionist theory of social problems games would be inadequate for comprehensive description.

Nevertheless, there are many situations in which members do use—or, perhaps more accurately, trade on—the concept of social problems. It is a culturally shared orientation to locally and situationally assembled constellations of practical issues. While members may disagree about some conditions that others describe as social problems, they recognize the concept as a label for circumstances that are deplorable and about which something must be done. To insist that the concept is only analytically useful when members explicitly employ it invites us to ignore the rubric as a general orientation and interpretive resource.

If, as Bogen and Lynch imply, the category "social problems" is mainly an analyst's theoretic construction, does that negate its usefulness? To be sure, constructionist depictions of social problems constitute the objects of their analysis through their analysis. There appears to be no alternative. Even ethnomethodological analyses of phenomena like work or science constitute those activities as work or science as they produce their analyses. Like social problems, these rubrics gloss the diverse and concrete language games within which the phenomena are made visible and recognizable as those things the analyst makes them out to be.

To reorganize the field of social problems analysis as the study of the myriad language games that constitute the diverse phenomena—homelessness, poverty, mental illness, and so forth—of social problems studies does not solve the problem. Each language game is a gloss for the diverse, concrete, situated moves made in accomplishing the interpretive activity at hand. Such glosses are necessary "fictions" that make everyday, as well as constructionist, discourse possible.

While no comprehensive framework is on the horizon for explicating the myriad language games and diverse interpretive practices that are called social problems, the category "social problems"—construed in terms of interpretive practice—appears to be a useful analytic device. Perhaps the social constructionist approach to social problems is better cast as a constellation of kindred orientations rather than a general theory. In any case, a broadly construed constructionist program promises to be both a useful way of organizing and referencing related phenomena and a source of ongoing theoretical engagement, contention, and growth.

* * * * *

Having considered critiques emanating from within the constructionist camp, we have indicated some promising directions for the future of social problems analysis. We now turn in a new direction, toward issues raised from outside the constructionist perspective. Part II of this volume considers critical, poststructural, and representational challenges to the constructionist orientation to social problems.

References

Best, Joel. 1989. *Images of Issues.* Hawthorne, NY: Aldine de Gruyter.

Durkheim, Emile. 1961. *The Elementary Forms of the Religious Life.* New York: Collier-Macmillan.

Foucault, Michel. 1972. *The Archaeology of Knowledge.* New York: Pantheon.

————. 1973. *The Birth of the Clinic.* New York: Random House.

Miller, Gale and James A. Holstein. 1989. "On the Sociology of Social Problems." Pp. 1–18 in *Perspectives on Social Problems*, Vol. 1, edited by J. Holstein and G. Miller. Greenwich, CT: JAI Press.

Pollner, Melvin. 1991. "Left of Ethnomethodology: The Rise and Decline Of Radical Reflexivity." *American Sociological Review* 56:370–80.

Spector, Malcolm and John I. Kitsuse. [1977] 1987. *Constructing Social Problems.* Hawthorne, NY: Aldine de Gruyter.

Troyer, Ronald J. 1989. "Are Social Problems and Social Movements the Same Thing?" Pp. 41–58 in *Perspectives on Social Problems*, Vol. 1 edited by J. Holstein and G. Miller. Greenwich, CT: JAI Press.

————. 1992. "Some Consequences of Contextual Constructionism." *Social Problems* 39:35–37.

Woolgar, Steve and Dorothy Pawluch. 1985. "Ontological Gerrymandering: The Anatomy of Social Problems Explanations." *Social Problems* 32:214–27.

PART II

New Challenges to Social Constructionism

13

New Challenges to Social Constructionism: Alternative Perspectives on Social Problems Theory

Gale Miller

While several points of contention persist, contemporary challenges to social constructionism differ in several respects from those offered by structural functionalists and Marxist sociologists. Some of the differences are related to the elaboration of diverse feminist perspectives since the publication of *Constructing Social Problems* (Spector and Kitsuse [1977] 1987), while others relate to movements within Marxism and other international intellectual communities concerned with social critique and change. This essay outlines several important theoretical challenges that may be loosely categorized as social criticism and poststructuralism. Indeed, the categories are not mutually exclusive because many recent critics of social constructionism often blend aspects of social criticism and poststructuralism.

Such blending is evident in many of the essays found in this section, particularly those concerned with the ways in which social constructionists represent social life. The essay offers an intellectual context for the subsequent chapters by discussing the major assumptions and concerns of social criticism and poststructuralism, and their implications for social problems theory. First, it discusses five contemporary challenges to social constructionism that raise questions about the approach while maintaining an appreciation for at least some aspects of the perspective. Subsequent sections consider how the challenges are embedded in and articulated through general critical and poststructuralist theories, and some of the implications of recent developments in the analysis of scientific writing for social problems theory.

Contemporary Challenges to Social Constructionism

Whereas previous challenges to social constructionism tended to disallow any possibility that social problems are social constructions, many contemporary critics acknowledge that social problems are at least partly constructed. For example, many critical-feminist theorists and other social critics treat public understandings of and orientations to everyday life as social constructions, but they also emphasize how the understandings and orientations are constructed within gendered and/or capitalist social institutions and relationships. Thus, contemporary criticisms are not organized as outright rejections of the constructionist perspective, but as attempts to relocate social constructionists' concerns and studies within perspectives that the critics argue are more comprehensive.

A second set of challengers emphasize the realist and elitist assumptions of social constructionism. They argue that while social constructionists state that social problems conditions only exist as claims-making activities, social constructionists' analyses actually treat social problems conditions and claims as observable and objective (Hazelrigg 1985; Pfohl 1985). Recent critics also accuse social constructionists of being elitists who wish to produce a "pure" theory of social problems that is uncontaminated by any moral and political assumptions and concerns (Rafter 1992). They add that social constructionists' pursuit of such a theory is impossible and, in pursuing it, social constructionists gloss over the values underlying and political implications of their perspective.

A third challenge involves the ways in which social interests are related to social problems claims-making. While contemporary critics of social constructionism state that political, economic, and other social interests are aspects of social problems claims-making movements, they also argue that persons' knowledge about social reality and their social problems claims are related to conditions that are largely unrecognized by them. From their perspective, social problems claims-making involves assumptions, desires, and concerns that are so fundamental that claims-makers and others are unlikely to recognize the conditions as anything other than facts. So viewed, the conditions are not matters for conscious reflection, public debate, or social constructionist analysis.

For example, feminist theory assumes that persons' gender status shapes their experiences and understandings of social reality. Not only is gender a master status, but women and men orient to social relationships and practical issues in different ways. The differences are related to their positions within social relationships and institutions, including the ways in which they are socialized as children, expectations associated with their adult roles, and practical opportunities made available to them. Thus, differences in female and male orientations to practical issues (including their definitions of social problems) may not be reduced to simple differences of political and economic interest. The differences are also related to the unrecognized ways in which modern social existence is gendered.

A fourth challenge involves the political and economic contexts (or structures) within which social problems claims-making occurs. Critics of social constructionism state that while diverse orientations to and understandings of social problems are likely to emerge in industrialized and urbanized societies, the knowledge and practical concerns of only a few groups are likely to be expressed in the social problems claims-making movements that receive mass media and public attention. An important difference in the life circumstances of politically marginal groups and others (particularly groups associated with such major public institutions as government, medicine, law, and education) is the greater availability of the mass media to the latter.

For example, Fishman (1980) analyzes how the organization of news reporters' work within "beats" ensures that reporters will regularly encounter government officials and other politically organized groups who may use the interactions to make social problems claims. Members of the news media depend on such groups to provide reporters with information that may be printed or broadcast as news. Thus, news reporters and commentators are likely to describe politically organized groups' social problems claims as matters for serious public concern and discussion while ignoring claims that are not so well organized or publicly available. As Tuchman (1978) states, an important indicator that the feminist movement was gaining political influence was the news media's reorientation to its message as a call for equal opportunity. Previous stories treated feminist claims-making as little more than bra burning.

Finally, recent critics of social constructionism challenge the usual ways in which social problems texts are written. The challenges are expressed as critiques of typical writing practices and as experiments with new writing forms. The forms include combining information about authors' biographies with their analyses of social reality, organizing sociological texts as personal narratives written or spoken by nonsociologists, and presenting "sociological data" as poetry. Such experiments are partly intended to reformulate the central question of the sociology of knowledge, What is the relationship between social structure and knowledge? Social critics, poststructuralists, and others reformulate the question by directing attention to themselves as creators of social realities. As Richardson states,

> How *should* we write our research? *Who* is our audience? The rhetorical, ethical, and methodological issues implicit in the question are neither few nor trivial. Rather, the question reflects a central contemporary realization:

all knowledge is socially constructed. Writing is not simply a true representation of an objective reality, out there, waiting to be seen. Instead through literary and rhetorical structures, writing creates a particular view of reality. (1990, p. 9)

Thus, alternative writing forms may be seen as one way in which social problems theorists accept responsibility for the social realities that they create through writing.

Social Criticism and Social Problems Theory

I use the term *social criticism* to characterize a wide array of theoretical perspectives that include various types of Marxian analysis (such as Agger 1989; Edwards, Reich, and Weisskopf 1978; Piven and Cloward 1971), perspectives that blend aspects of Marxian theory with other perspectives (such as Schwalbe 1986; Smith 1987, 1990; Willis 1977), and non-Marxian analyses of oppression and dominance (such as Adam 1978; Collins 1986, 1989; Levesque-Lopman 1988). Despite their diversity, social critics share two major concerns that justify their classification within the same theoretical category.

First, social critics use their analyses of social problems to encourage, justify, and/or facilitate social change. Social criticism involves taking the side of disadvantaged groups, and pointing the way to a more just and equal society. Put in Marxian terms, critical theories of social problems are intended to foster radical praxis (radical consciousness and action) through which oppressive social structures will be changed. Smith (1987) makes a similar point in arguing that it is insufficient for sociologists to strive for gender-neutral research and theories. Rather, they should develop perspectives and pursue projects that are *for* women. For strict constructionists, social critics' analyses are themselves claims-making activities because they involve treating putative social conditions as instances of real social problems.

Social critics agree that they are claims-makers, and portray their claims-making activities as responses to the inequalities, injustices, and suffering that are observable in society. They argue that a major purpose of social problems theory should be to point out, analyze, and take political stands on how to change conditions that are social problems. They state that the subject matter of social problems theory is so infused with moral and political issues that a theory that tries to be value neutral runs the risk of being irrelevant. Indeed, many social critics argue that social constructionists' focus on others' definitions of social problems helps to perpetuate existing oppressive social systems.

One way in which social constructionists perpetuate social problems is by refusing to take a stand on what is "really" a social problem. As Collins states,

> Focusing on claims-making activities without using some "objective" criteria to determine which problems merit investigation can easily lead to failing to see a range of important social problems where the activism of legitimate claimants has been effectively suppressed. One potential contribution of objectivist approaches is that they can provide an overarching framework cognizant of these unequal power relations and thus may recognize social problems of groups whose claims-making activities have been suppressed. (1989, p. 87)

The second major concern shared by social critics is their focus on the ways in which concrete social problems are reflections of and are caused by the social organization of society. Specifically, most social critics analyze social problems as reflections or results of capitalism and/or patriarchy. Critical studies of capitalism emphasize how such social problems as poverty, sexism, and racial hatred are embedded in and products of contemporary economic, political, and cultural structures. For example, many social critics analyze poverty as an inevitable product of capitalist economic structures that unequally reward workers for their contributions, political structures that are unresponsive to poor, unorganized, and powerless citizens, and ideological structures that justify and perpetuate existing inequalities.

Critical studies of patriarchy focus on the social organization of male dominance, and the consequences of patriarchy for women (Walby 1990). Patriarchy is partly organized as gender-based divisions of labor within families and occupational settings. Both divisions of labor involve explicit and implicit understandings of men's and women's "proper" roles and work activities. For example, women's traditional work in families has included taking major responsibility for caring for the children, and being their families' primary meal preparers, house cleaners, and launderers. Similar divisions of labor are evident in occupational settings and labor markets outside households. For example, female-dominated jobs frequently involve tending children or other types of caregiving, cooking, and/or cleaning. Such jobs often involve few opportunities for intellectual development, little power, low pay, and unique emotional stresses that are often unrecognized.

Critical social problems analysis involves taking a skeptical stance toward others' definitions of their troubles and social problems. Social critics state that their skepticism is justified because people frequently do not think of their own and others' troubles as related to larger social structures and processes. Rather, most people describe social problems as private troubles that are often caused by "bad" people, including troubled persons' own improper attitudes and actions. As Mills, a major critical social problems theorist, states,

> In so far as an economy is so arranged that slumps occur, the problem of unemployment becomes incapable of personal solution. In so far as war is inherent in the nation-state system and in the uneven industrialization of the world, the ordinary individual in his restricted milieu will be powerless—with or without psychiatric aid—to solve the troubles this system or lack of system imposes upon him. In so far as the family as an institution turns women into darling little slaves and men into their chief providers and unweaned dependents, the problem of a satisfactory marriage remains incapable of purely private solution. In so far as the over-developed megalopolis and the overdeveloped automobile are built-in features of the overdeveloped society, the issues of urban living will not be solved by personal integrity and private wealth. (1959, p. 10)

Levesque-Lopman (1988) makes a similar point in her critical-feminist assessment of phenomenological sociology, a perspective that shares strict constructionism's uncritical concern for the ways in which social realities are socially constructed. She states that while it is clear that women and men rhetorically construct social realities (such as definitions of social problems conditions), to focus only on their reality-creating activities is to ignore the social contexts within which the activities occur. Levesque-Lopman analyzes the contexts as practical constraints on actors' abilities to define realities in positive ways and effectively act in their social worlds. Thus, a critical-feminist phenomenology of social problems involves getting beyond others' assumptions and claims about social problems by analyzing the ways in which social problems definitions are "affected by the social forces and social systems in the societies in which we live" (1988, p. 153).

Social Problems as Real and Invisible Conditions

Social critics' concern for analyzing persons' troubles as caused by capitalist and patriarchal structures involves treating some social conditions as real social problems. So analyzed, social problems are neither putative conditions nor claims, but observable features of everyday life. All observers do not see them, however. Rather, social critics emphasize that many of the most important social problems in capitalist-patriarchal societies are invisible to most citizens, policymakers, and social scientists because most observers interpret everyday life in ideologically biased ways. While persons' ideological biases are partly related to their obvious self-interests, social critics argue that an equally important factor is the social organization of knowledge in society.

The latter concern is central to Marx and Engels's ([1852] 1977) approach to the sociology of knowledge. For them, the dominant ideas of society are based on and perpetuate the interests, concerns, and assumptions of powerful groups. This is so because one aspect of social dominance is control over the institutions and processes through which knowledge is produced and disseminated. Such institutions include news, entertainment, and other private organizations engaged in information production and dissemination, but also universities and other organizations that are presumably organized to seek unbiased, scientific truths. Further, because capitalist society is organized as opposed social classes, Marx and Engels analyze the dominant ideas and biases of capitalism as those of the ruling class, i.e., the bourgeoisie. Patriarchy may be similarly analyzed as a form of society that is dominated by masculine ideas, orientations, and biases.

An example of how ideas are related to dominant social interests is instrumental reasoning, an orientation to knowledge and action that is pervasive in contemporary Western institutions. It emphasizes the efficient and effective achievement of observable goals over such other values as morality or tradition, and involves conceptualizing human beings as abstract objects who must be organized and managed (Weber 1978). From an instrumental standpoint, increasing worker outputs, increasing profits, and/or cutting costs matter more than the conditions under which workers work, uses to which the profits are put, and/or human consequences of cost cutting. For social critics, then, instrumental reasoning is central to the operation of capitalism (Habermas 1975; Horkheimer and Adorno 1972), and is a masculine way of knowing and relating to everyday life (Code 1991; Ferguson 1984; Sacks 1988).

Another focus of critical studies involves the ways in which members of subordinate groups accept and use dominant ideas to explain their circumstances. The explanations often involve blaming themselves and other subordinate groups for their plight. For example, working-class whites sometimes explain their economic problems as caused by unfair competition from ethnic minorities who are similarly or more disadvantaged, and women sometimes explain their occupational segregation as an accommodation to their gender-based natural abilities and orientations. From a Marxian standpoint, such explanations are expressions of false consciousness that justify existing inequalities and institutional practices. Ryan (1971) makes a similar point in analyzing such explanations as ways of blaming the victims of inequality for their plight. They are "validated" and the cycle (or self-fulfilling prophecy) of blaming the victim is completed with poor, powerless, and outcast groups' failure to improve their circumstances taken as proof of their inferiority (Adam 1978).

Thus, one way in which social problems are made socially invisible involves the conventional explanations available to ordinary persons and policymakers in interpreting social reality. The explanations treat social problems as natural conditions or otherwise not warranting public concern and intervention. Real social problems are also made invisible and/or distorted by the official languages used by policymakers and social problems analysts in describing governmental responses to social conditions. Such languages often justify responses that involve "fixing" people, diverting attention, for example, from the ways in which poverty and unemployment are perpetuated by unfair economic structures, or in which violence against women is related to culturally approved orientations to masculinity and femininity.

In sum, while some contemporary social critics argue that Marx and Engels' ([1852] 1977) analysis overstates the hegemony of one dominant ideology in capitalist-patriarchal society (Abercrombie 1980), their analyses still take account of (often extend and elaborate on) basic Marxian themes and concerns about knowledge and ideology. For example, Smith (1990) analyzes psychiatric knowledge as largely a class- and gender-based ideology. As such, it is organized as a reasoning process for *not* knowing. Smith explains that what is systematically left out of psychiatric reasoning is an adequate recognition and understanding of the practical experiences, needs, concerns, and knowledge of women and others who are powerless within the psychiatric profession. Thus, psychiatric definitions of social problems mystify, rather than reveal, the true nature and causes of the distress felt by women and other subordinate groups.

Smith and other social critics counter such ideologies and the invisibility of many "real" social problems by analyzing how social class, gender, race, and age are partly epistemological statuses. That is, they are alternative ways of knowing (Belenky, Clinchy, Goldberger, and Tarule 1986; Collins 1990; Fonow and Cook 1991). Their analyses emphasize how persons' and groups' social positions involve knowledge and orientations that may be different from—even opposed to—those held by persons and groups occupying different social positions (Davies 1982; Gilligan 1982).

Social critics also achieve their theoretical ends by critiquing conventional forms of knowledge. Of special importance are their critiques of so-called scientific forms of knowledge, which are often described as offering objective knowledge that accurately describes and applies to all social classes, genders, and racial and age groups. One such form of *not knowing* is conventional social scientific research and analyses of social problems.

Social Problems Research and Theory as Ideology

Contemporary social science is one aspect of a general trend in capitalist-patriarchal society that emphasizes the usefulness of instrumental reasoning in understanding and managing everyday life. It is concerned with predicting and controlling human behavior and thereby homogenizing human experiences and options. It denies the ways in which individuals and groups are shaped by their unique histories and social positions. Further, as Smith (1990, p. 14) states, when social problems researchers and theorists cooperate with institutional officials, they "participate in ruling." One way in which they do so is by studying the "management" questions asked by institutional leaders, and using research techniques that treat people as objects.

For social critics, such studies perpetuate dominant institutional practices and reasoning by affirming institutional elites' assumptions about social reality and human nature, and providing them with information that they may use to maintain institutional control. The studies are also mystifications because in portraying their analyses as objective and value-neutral accounts of the facts, analysts hide the political assumptions and commitments of their research from themselves and others. As Horkheimer states, "The scholar and his science are incorporated into the apparatus of society; his achievements are a factor in the conservation and continuous renewal of the existing state of affairs, no matter what fine names he gives to what he does" (1972, p. 196).

One way in which social critics counter such tendencies is by emphasizing the political concerns and assumptions underlying their own work. They also critique the objectivist claims and other value commitments of conventional social scientists by showing how they relate to the social scientists' positions in society. The critiques emphasize conventional social scientists' commitments to mainstream institutions, and membership in dominant racial, gender, and social class groups. Social critics' concerns and critiques are related to their interest in developing a self-aware, reflexive sociology, which Gouldner analyzes as a radical approach to knowledge,

> because it would recognize that knowledge of the world cannot be advanced apart from the sociologist's knowledge of himself and his position in the social world, or apart from his efforts to change these. Radical,

because it seeks to transform as well as to know the alien world outside the sociologist as well the alien world inside of him. Radical, because it would accept the fact that the roots of sociology pass through the sociologist as a total man, and that the question he must confront, therefore, is not merely how to *work* but how to *live*. (1970, p. 489)

Finally, social critics emphasize the relationship between the lived experiences of members of marginalized groups and the routine practices of social institutions that shape and restrict their lives (Susser 1982; Valentine 1978; Westkott 1990). One research strategy used to study lived experience is institutional ethnography (Smith 1987). It involves describing the everyday work that marginalized individuals and groups do to manage and sustain their lives and relationships, and linking the descriptions to the—often invisible—institutional structures and processes that shape their lives.

Two examples of institutional ethnography are Griffith and Smith's (1990) and Smith and Griffith's (1990) studies of how women's family work (such as mothering and coordinating the activities of family members) is shaped by and sustains extrafamilial institutional schedules and practices, such as those associated with employment and school. They analyze how teachers depend on mothers to monitor and help manage their students' educational activities in the home, and the practical problems faced by poor and working-class mothers in fulfilling this expectation while also holding jobs. Through such studies, critical theorists make visible the mundane (but essential) work that marginalized groups do to sustain social institutions.

A related research strategy and methodology focuses on the narratives that marginalized groups and individuals tell about themselves and their lives in interviews or personal documents, such as letters and diaries. Narratives are significant for social critics because they emphasize the subjective aspects of everyday life, offer insight into the ways in which marginalized individuals' and groups' lived experiences are shaped by institutional assumptions and practices, and point to the ways in which members of marginalized groups deal with the practical circumstances of their lives (Mishler 1986; Personal Narratives Group 1989). Thus, narratives are useful for countering social scientific analyses that treat members of marginalized groups as anonymous and homogeneous, and as victims who are without the resources needed to properly manage their lives.

Through these research strategies, social critics seek to build an alternative social scientific literature that makes presently "invisible" social problems visible, and takes account of the unique interests, needs, and experiences of marginalized groups. Their research strategies are also intended to foster the emancipation of oppressed groups and the development of just societies.

Social Criticism and Social Justice

Social critics' interests in using sociological knowledge to foster social change are varied, ranging from "applied" sociologists' efforts to reform institutions from within to radical sociologists' calls for fundamental transformations in culture and social structures. Within this diversity, however, are two important themes that cut across most forms of social criticism and distinguish it from the poststructuralist perspectives discussed in the next section. The themes are social critics' faith in human reason as a resource for understanding and changing society, and their tendency to construct "totalizing" theories of society. The latter reduce social reality and sociological explanation to one, or a few, foundational structures and processes, such as Marx's analysis of all societies as based on modes of production.

Social critics' faith in human reason is related to their interest in using critical knowledge to foster social change. They assume that reasoned argument and analysis are central to the creation of new forms of social consciousness and organization. For social critics, analysis and social change are related because social structures persist to the extent that individuals and groups act in ideologically and institutionally prescribed ways. Reasoned critiques of oppressive ideologies and practices offer insight into existing social conditions, and encourage others to imagine alternative cultural and institutional forms. For example, social critics' critiques are partly organized to show that the seemingly rational beliefs and practices that dominate contemporary institutions are really irrational, and that the creation of a rational society requires fundamental social change (Habermas 1970a, 1970b, 1970c).

A second major theme in social criticism involves the tendency to construct totalizing theories of society and social problems. It is related to analysts' interest in framing social problems as the products of capitalism, patriarchy, or similar social forms. Such theories often include far-reaching explanations of history, culture, and social relations (Kellner 1989). They also emphasize how aspects of everyday life that others treat as disconnected are related to each other and to foundational social structures and processes. For social critics, effective social changes must alter such structures and processes. The hope that they offer to their audiences is that such changes can be made through rational analyses of the past and present, and collective actions that are informed by the analyses.

Poststructuralism and Social Problems Theory

Poststructuralists differ from social critics in their concern for the ways in which "nonrational" factors influence social scientists' analyses and treatment of contemporary Western societies as made up of diverse and loosely connected institutional domains, which may function and change without greatly affecting or being affected by other institutions. They also differ in their orientations to reflexivity. Many poststructuralists argue that it is insufficient for social scientists to be aware of the ways in which their ideas are related to their social positions. They state that social theorists should also write in ways that acknowledge that their texts are social constructions of reality.

Although they are often used interchangeably, I use the terms *poststructuralism* and *postmodernism* to highlight related, but different aspects of recent social, cultural, and philosophical trends. I use the term poststructuralism as a general rubric for discussing a number of recent trends in European (particularly French) social thought. The trends are partly responses and alternatives to structuralism, a perspective that is associated with intellectual developments in France in the 1960s (Caws 1988; Pettit 1975). I use the term *postmodernism* to highlight the emergence of new social and cultural forms that blend and mystify previous (modernist) forms and distinctions. Postmodernist blendings are not intended to produce new unities. Rather, postmodernists emphasize how the diverse and distinctive aspects of their work are loosely associated.

For example, postmodern architects design buildings that include shapes, textures, and surfaces that are associated with very different architectural styles and eras. Depending on observers' standpoints, the buildings convey a variety of messages, and reflect the diversity, complexity, and lack of coherence of their urban settings. A source of insight and inspiration for some postmodern architects is the Las Vegas Strip. As Venturi, Scott-Brown, and Izenour state,

> The emerging order of the Strip is a complex order. It is not the easy, rigid order of the urban renewal project or the fashionable 'total design' of the megastructure . . . . the order of the Strip includes; it *includes* at all levels. . . . . It is not an order dominated by the expert and made easy for the eye. The moving eye in the moving body must work to pick out and interpret a variety of changing, juxtaposed orders. (1977, pp. 135–36)

Themes evident in postmodern architecture are also aspects of postmodern developments in such art forms as literature, film, television, and music. Postmodernist artists also counter the abstract and rationalized unities of modernism with cultural forms that celebrate diversity, difference, eclecticism, irony, and superficiality. Such cultural forms offer no certainties to their audiences; rather, they express the interplay between ambivalence and joy, uncertainty and opportunities, and seeming contradictions of contemporary life. Like the Las Vegas Strip, postmodern society is a world of unending, mass-produced images that have no necessary relationship to one another or everyday life.

In part, then, poststructuralist perspectives apply and extend themes found in postmodern architecture and art to issues that have traditionally been associated with philosophy and the social sciences.

Structuralism and Poststructuralism

French structuralism is generally built from Saussure's (1959) semiological approach to language as a system of rules that determine the meanings of statements, objects, and events. One way in which Lévi-Strauss (1963, 1966) and other structuralists have extended Saussure's perspective is by analyzing the universal (but hidden) aspects of human thought, language, and culture, treating the surface appearances of diversity within and across cultures (such as myth and everyday speech) as determined by underlying and unified linguistic, cognitive, and/or cultural systems.

For Lévi-Strauss, an important aspect of the systems that underlie surface appearances is binary (or complementary) oppositions. Such oppositions include distinctions between us and them, right and wrong, men and women, and inside and outside (Needham 1973). The oppositions are binary because they involve two elements, and are complementary because understanding one element necessarily involves understanding its opposite. For example, the concept of "good" makes no sense without the concept of "bad," and, as Boon (1982) states, part of portraying something as "good" involves portraying it as "not bad."

Lévi-Strauss analyzes complementary oppositions as the building blocks that individuals and groups use to construct meanings. They are fundamental aspects of culturally shared classificatory systems (such as kinship) and myths, as well as shared understandings of such diverse activities as proper table manners and writing (Lévi-Strauss 1968; Sahlins 1976; Schwartz 1981). Lévi-Strauss considers complementary oppositions to be aspects of universal and unconscious mental structures. He states that persons' use of complementary oppositions to categorize and create meanings reflects the natural functioning of the brain and unconscious (Lévi-Strauss 1963). In so linking mental activity with culture, Lévi-Strauss constructs a unified and universal theory of culture and nature, and justifies scientific studies intended to discover their fundamental structures and laws.

Poststructuralist theorists challenge structuralists' efforts to be objective, discover scientific truths, and interest in developing comprehensive and unified analyses of culture and social life. One challenge emphasizes the literary aspects of scientific work, and the inevitability of interpretation in all human understanding, including science. This underscores the importance of language (or discourse) in shaping what we know and how we know it. As Foucault (1973) states, knowledge is produced through "gazes," which are inextricably linked to the discourses available to us for seeing social realities. Thus, there are no absolute or objective truths for poststructuralists, only the local and partisan truths of individual and collective interpreters of social life.

The assumption is central to poststructuralists' orientation to description and analysis—including scientific and philosophical analyses—as political activities. For example, Foucault (1977a) analyzes knowledge as power and uses his historical studies to describe the politics of truth. He states that truths are organized as discourses and knowledge codes for constructing worlds within which we live, and our place in them. They are practical aspects of everyday life that have implications for our orientations to and actions within settings. As Arney and Bergen state about medical discourse (truth),

> It is more than just a set of facts known by physicians and embodied in a professional, specialized, inaccessible language. The medical discourse is a set of rules that enables facts to become facts for both physicians and patients. It is a set of rules that covers not only what is important to doctors but also what patients can speak about as important. Knowledge is power precisely because the knowledge embedded in the medical discourse supplies rules by which patients ascertain when they are speaking true about the self and when they are speaking about things that are imaginary. Knowledge tells the person what is important and not fanciful about his or her experience of illness and patienthood. . . . . Invoking knowledge about what is important to the person is the activity of power. (1984, p. 5)

For Foucault (1977b), domination emerges when some truths become hegemonic within their social domains, such as the medical discourse analyzed by Arney and Bergen. The practical impact of such a development is that alternative truths are silenced and, eventually, may become unthinkable. Further, because the silenced truths are those associated with the experiences of marginalized groups and individuals, one effect of institutionalizing a truth is to further marginalize and silence such groups and individuals. Two ways in which poststructuralist perspectives have been applied and developed, then, are by analyzing the ways in which dominant discourses silence others, and helping marginalized groups and individuals to develop and express their own "local" truths.

Poststructuralists also differ from structuralists in their orientations to binary oppositions. Poststructuralists treat the oppositions as ideological divisions and use their analyses to undermine them. Binary oppositions are ideological because they are ways of understanding that treat good-bad, truth-falsehood, man-woman, sane-insane and other such cultural distinctions as mutually exclusive categories and aspects of everyday life. Derrida (1981) suggests that binary oppositions involve rigid boundaries, and therefore mystify the ways in which seemingly opposed elements are interrelated. He undermines binary oppositions by "deconstructing" them, a process that involves questioning their boundaries and showing how they are interrelated (Leitch 1983).

It is important not to overstate the differences between structuralism and poststructuralism, however. My caution is partly related to the difficulty that commentators have in agreeing on how to categorize some theorists as structuralists or poststructuralists. An important example is Lacan's (1977) reformulation of Freud's approach to the unconscious and psychoanalysis, which includes structuralist and poststructuralist themes. Specifically, Lacan analyzes the unconscious as structured like language (it is related to underlying syntactic patterns), and constantly in process. He states that the language of the unconscious is a language of desire (Freud's id), and involves diverse binary oppositions. Thus, the unconscious is not a thing, nor is it separate from culture and language.

My reluctance to analyze poststructuralism as a complete rejection of structuralism is also related to the social organization of French intellectual life, which may be analyzed as a long-standing conversation about philosophy, politics, art, and everyday life. As with new positions emerging within other conversations, French poststructuralism is built from assumptions, concerns, and debates of previous discussions. Thus, I treat poststructuralism as a multifaceted (perhaps contradictory) intellectual movement that both extends (by reconsidering and transforming its concerns and assumptions) and rejects aspects of structuralism.

Poststructuralist Writing

Poststructuralist texts are both provocative and evocative. They provoke others by describing and analyzing postmodern society, culture, and selves in new and challenging ways. They sometimes do so by inverting commonsense understandings of social reality, including taken-for-granted complementary oppositions. For example, poststructuralists reject the Western assumption that individuals exist prior to, and independent from, society. The assumption is central to Western cultural understandings of and orientations to individualism. It under-lies economic theories that analyze consumers as calculating actors who make decisions based on their rational self-interests. Poststructuralists invert such understandings by emphasizing how individuals' seemingly unique and autonomous decisions and actions are shaped by language, culture, and institutions.

Poststructuralists also analyze our desire to understand as inseparable from our concerns about our own existence. Barthes (1975, p. 63) ex-tends this theme in arguing that reading is best understood in psycho-analytic terms. He states, for example, that fetishistic reading involves dividing the text into disconnected units (such as quotations and figures of speech), obsessive reading (such as that done by linguists) focuses on the metalanguages of the text, and paranoid reading emphasizes the argumentative complexities and gamelike qualities of the text. Poststruc-turalists' writing practices highlight and affirm poststructuralists' inter-est in writing at the "edge of," but not outside culture (Barthes 1975).

For example, Derrida's (1976, 1978) approach to deconstruction is a critique of the taken-for-granted logocentrism of Western culture, which assumes that meaning is available to speakers in the present and, conse-quently, that their representations of social reality are adequate and stable. Derrida counters the assumption by analyzing meaning as a sup-plement to texts, because it is a re-presentation, which sometimes adds to the texts and other times replaces aspects of them. Meaning shifts, is unstable, and is never finally resolved. Derrida also acknowledges, how-ever, that he and other deconstructionists can never write outside the cultures that they critique. Thus, deconstructive criticism does not promise cultural and political emancipation to readers, as social criticism does.

In sum, the provocative aspects of poststructuralists' writings chal-lenge readers to rethink their assumptions about and understandings of social reality. Frequently intermingled with such intellectual appeals are the evocative aspects of poststructuralist writing, which involve appeals to readers' imaginations and desires. Indeed, poststructuralists' evoca-tive moves may be understood as inversions of two commonsense as-sumptions: that "serious" writing (such as science and philosophy) is different from "nonserious" writing like fiction and poetry, and that "serious" writing and reading are unrelated to other pleasures of every-day life.

The first assumption is basic to our expectations about, and orienta-tions to, reading and writing. That is, we expect "nonserious" writing to be pleasurable and even playful, and "serious" writing to be straightforward, factual, and perhaps ponderous. The assumption glosses over the ways in which "serious" writing involves metaphor, irony, and other "fictional" writing practices. It also glosses over the ways in which scientific and other "factual" writings are organized as partisan arguments and stories intended to persuade readers (Brown 1987). Poststructuralists partly counter typical assumptions about "serious" writing by writing about serious matters in unconventional ways. For example, they use puns and unconventional spellings to highlight the ambiguities and multiple meanings that are associated with their own and others' claims (Derrida 1987).

Such writing practices are intended to simultaneously evoke playful responses from readers and encourage them to develop new understandings of what philosophy and cultural analysis might entail. The writing practices also point to the reflexivity of poststructuralists' texts; that is, how the texts are rhetorical constructions that advocate for partisan truths and assign identities (Lawson 1985). For example, writers may rhetorically construct worlds within which they exist as aloof observers and experts, narrators of others' stories, or active participants in their stories' ongoing action. Nietzsche—a major philosophical influence on many poststructuralists—analyzes such constructions as the will to truth. As the name implies, it is a desire or compulsion, and not a simple product of human reason:

> One should not understand this compulsion to construct concepts, species, forms, purposes, laws . . . . as if they enabled us to fix the *real world*; but as a compulsion to arrange a world for ourselves in which our existence is made possible. . . . . The world seems logical to us because we have made it logical. ([1901] 1968, p. 282)

Poststructuralists' evocative writing moves are also challenges to the commonsense assumption that "serious" writing is unrelated to the mundane pleasures of everyday life. We partly distinguish philosophical, scientific, and other "serious" writing from such pleasures by treating "serious" writing as impartial, objective, and privileged. Poststructuralists challenge the distinction by treating the mundane pleasures of everyday life as equal to those associated with the privileged texts of philosophers and human scientists. Two ways in which privileged and mundane texts may be equalized is through deconstructive criticism, and reflexive writing practices that point to the partiality and constructedness of "serious" writers' stories.

Poststructuralists also equalize privileged and mundane texts by discussing the desires and concerns associated with their "serious" writings. The discussions might be analyzed as "confessional tales" (Van

Maanen 1988), because they locate the writer as a partisan and feeling subject within the text. One way in which poststructuralists do so is by offering evocative vignettes that remind themselves and readers that the text is a story (one of many that might be told), and describing how they are participants in the stories (Kondo 1990; Stewart 1989; Tylor 1986). A related procedure involves interspersing information about the writer's biography, feelings, concerns, and desires within the "serious" text.

Poststructuralism and Social Problems Theory

Looked at one way, poststructuralism is a form of social construction-ism because poststructuralists emphasize the ways in which meanings are discursively constructed and organized, matters of political conten-tion that may shift and change. Indeed, the social constructionist aspects of poststructuralism are a major concern for social critics who object to what they sometimes describe as its excessive relativism and nihilism (Habermas 1981). For example, some critical-feminist theorists argue that poststructuralists deny the universality of gender by emphasizing the diverse and situated nature of meaning (Bordo 1990). They also object to poststructuralists' skepticism about the possible emancipation of women (Hekman 1990), and denial that any theory should be privi-leged over others (Hartsock 1983, 1990).

But to only focus on the similarities between social constructionism and poststructuralism is to gloss over major differences, two of which are important for analyzing current debates in social problems theory. First, poststructuralists challenge social constructionists' orientation to analyzing claims-making processes. Social constructionists' analyses in-volve taking a detached attitude toward others' claims-making activities, and focusing on the general processes through which social problems are constructed. Social constructionists' writings seldom locate writers within their texts. Poststructuralists partly challenge the social construc-tionist project by questioning the desirability of general theories (meta-narratives) of social life (Lyotard 1984), the objectivism of social con-structionist analyses and writing, and the possibility of detaching the analyst from the issue under analysis.

The poststructuralist alternative involves developing a variety of theo-ries or narratives about social problems. The narratives highlight the variety of local and partisan truths that may be told about everyday life, and how such truths are connected to the practical circumstances of persons' lives. Such stories highlight the diversity of postmodern society and give voices to silenced individuals and groups. Writing stories by and about marginalized groups is also part of "local determinism" (Lyotard 1984). It begins with the recognition of the heterogeneity of language games (knowledge and interests) in postmodern society: "The second step is the principle that any consensus on the rules defining a game and the moves playable within it *must* be local, in other words, agreed on by its present players and subject to eventual cancellation" (p. 66).

Poststructuralists also point to resistance strategies used by marginalized individuals and groups to manage the institutionalized and hegemonic discourses (metanarratives) that suppress them (Foucault 1972; Lyotard 1984). For example, Ong (1987) analyzes the resistance strategies of women factory workers in Malaysia, describing how the workers are periodically seized by spirits, during which they sometimes destroy factory equipment. While some factory managers treat the episodes as evidence of the women's psychological problems, Ong treats them as part of the women's localized efforts to deal with their material and subjective positions in the factory and, more generally, within capitalism. Ong argues that spirit possession and other activities that were taken by others as irrational were "the unconscious beginnings of an idiom of protest against labor discipline and male control in the modern industrial situation" (1987, p. 207).

Second, some poststructuralists challenge social constructionists by incorporating aspects of Freudian theory within their analyses (Barthes 1975; Lacan 1977). For example, they use aspects of Freudian theory to challenge and counter the "overly rational" explanations of social constructionists who assume that claims-makers are rational actors. While social constructionists do not analyze claims-makers as acting from absolute free will, they do emphasize the ways in which claims-makers self-consciously assess, select, and use rhetorical and other political tactics to achieve their ends.

Poststructuralists emphasize how seemingly rational aspects of everyday life are filled with conscious and unconscious desires and pleasures. It is one way in which poststructuralists undermine the culturally shared opposition between rational (or calculated) and nonrational (pleasure-seeking) behaviors. When they analyze social problems claims-making, poststructuralists focus on the desires and pleasures associated with constructing others as social problems, and the related pleasures of observing and dominating persons so constructed. In so doing, poststructuralists merge aspects of Freudian theory with Foucault's analyses of language, knowledge, and dominance, Barthes's approach to reading texts, and Derrida's deconstructive criticism.

For example, Pfohl and Gordon (1985) use a videotext to analyze how criminology emerged as a pleasure-seeking process that required that some persons be treated as normal and others as dangerous. The process was related to the rise of correctional and other institutions within which "dangerous" others are observed and contained. Such institutions allow criminologists the pleasures of "documenting" the differentness of "dangerous" others, and justifying criminological theories of normality and dangerousness. Indeed, Pfohl and Gordon compare the pleasures of criminology with those described by the Marquis de Sade (1964) as aspects of sadism. One such pleasure is the control of others.

Writing Social Problems Texts

A major difference between current and past debates in social problems theory is the recent recognition that sociological texts about social problems are themselves representations of everyday life. Social problems texts do not mirror an external social reality; rather, they construct social realities (Bazerman and Paradis 1990; Clifford and Marcus 1986; Hazelrigg 1986; Nelson, Megill, and McCloskey 1987; Simons 1989). They are partial and partisan formulations of issues and experiences (Brown 1990; DeVault 1990; Krieger 1983; Marcus and Fischer 1986), and stories that involve themes or plots (Brown 1977; Jacobson 1991; McCloskey 1990; Van Maanen 1988).

The stories written by social problems theorists may be analyzed as rhetorics writers use to persuade readers that their positions are credible (if not the only correct understanding of the issues at hand). Social problems theorists' writing "choices" are not simple matters of individual preference and imagination, however. They are influenced by audience considerations and, more generally, cultural orientations to and expectations about proper writing and argumentation.

In sum, current debates about the textual representation of social problems focus on the ways in which social problems are, and might be, textually constructed. The debates require that social problems theorists reflect on and justify the choices that they make in writing texts, including the types of audiences that they wish to reach and images of social reality that they wish to convey. In debating such issues, social problems theorists often blend aspects of strict and contextual constructionism, social criticism, and poststructuralism. While such blendings sometimes result in new theoretical insights and developments, they also point to the practical difficulties faced by theorists who wish to construct radically reflexive texts while advocating for social change.

Social problems theorists have responded to questions raised about their writing practices in two major ways. The first response involves treating social problems texts as partisan accounts, and developing arguments that advance writers' political and theoretical interests. Contextual constructionists, social critics, and some poststructuralists orient to writing social problems texts in this way. For example, Brown (1987, 1989) analyzes social science as a civic discourse that may be used to reconstruct public issues in ways that allow others to see and discuss matters that are now invisible. Seidman offers a similar argument in his declaration of the end of modernist sociological theory, and defense of a postmodernism that favors "deconstructing false closure, prying open present and future social possibilities, detecting fluidity and porousness in forms of life where hegemonic discourses posit closure and a frozen order" (1991, p. 131).

An important feature of such writing is that it takes the form of conventional social problems argumentation, including writing conventions that cast the writers' claims as descriptions of objective, real, and external social conditions. Such writing also frequently turns on the complementary oppositions emphasized by structuralists, the most obvious being the modernist-postmodernist distinction that is essential to writers' definitions and analyses of postmodernism. The texts may be further analyzed as examples of how social scientists engage in social problems claims-making.

While such an analysis of their writings is unproblematic for social critics who describe their studies as efforts to transform social consciousness and foster social change, it is a vexing problem for poststructuralists, who state that they wish to get beyond the assumptions, oppositions, and writing practices of modernist social science. The problem is not fully remedied by writers' brief indications that they recognize that they are telling stories. Thus, to the extent that poststructuralists rely on conventional social problems argumentation, their writings can be read as extensions and updatings of aspects of social criticism.

The second response to issues raised about social problems writing practices emphasizes the reflexivity of texts. Reflexive writing involves authors turning back on themselves and their texts by using writing conventions that highlight how they are constructing and interpreting the objects of their analysis. I have already discussed several such alternative writing practices used by poststructuralists, including their use of videotexts, "fictional" writing devices, and biographical information to tell their stories. Another reflexive writing practice involves organizing texts as conversations between writers, writers and editors, or writers and readers (Ashmore 1989; Mulkay 1989; Woolgar 1988). The latter conversationalists question writers about their claims, assumptions, and writing practices.

Organization of Part II

The essays that follow address the issues raised in this chapter. They extend and elaborate on major critical and poststructuralist themes, and apply the perspectives to the analysis of social problems. While they are sympathetic to aspects of constructionism, the essays challenge many of the central assumptions and claims of the perspective. First, we consider three critical challenges to constructionism. Agger's essay emphasizes how constructionism is shaped by the conservative political and organizational context of American sociology. He argues that an adequate social problems theory would analyze how social problems are the products of capitalism.

Gordon's and Smith's essays are critical-feminist challenges to constructionism. Gordon emphasizes the objectivist aspects of constructionism, and political interests associated with it. She argues for an approach that blends aspects of poststructuralism with critical feminism. The approach involves taking political stands on public issues, and developing new ways of representing social conditions. Smith's essay applies aspects of her approach to textually mediated discourse to adult illiteracy. She uses interviews with business managers to analyze how social problems definitions are shaped by public discourses that reflect and perpetuate managerial interests.

The second section involves poststructuralist challenges. Leslie Miller challenges constructionists to reconsider their focus on public claims-making. She uses aspects of feminist theory and Foucauldian discourse studies to analyze how social problems discourses marginalize women and silence potential claims-makers. Miller stresses that social problems discourses are embedded in power relations, and all talk is claims-making. Michalowski focuses on deconstructionist themes in constructionism and poststructuralism. He distinguishes between Ibarra and Kitsuse's rhetorical deconstruction, and recently emergent ritual deconstructionist perspectives. He argues that the latter perspectives offer a broader theoretical framework for analyzing social problems and encouraging social change. Pfohl's and Orr's essays also argue for and are examples of the ritual deconstructionist approach to social problems.

The third section focuses on the representation of social problems. The essays draw from both critical and poststructuralist perspectives. Hazelrigg criticizes Ibarra and Kitsuse's objectivist assumptions, and argues for an approach that dispenses with the concept of objective reality. Brown offers a rhetorical approach to social problems and civic discourses that emphasizes how public discussions of and responses to social issues are shaped by interpretive conventions that are invisible to most citizens. He calls for a sociology of social problems that analyzes the ideologies embedded in conventional rhetorics, and offers alternatives to them. Richardson also argues for the expansion of social problems discourse by experimenting with new writing forms, such as poetry. She states that scientific prose is a conventional rhetoric that restricts theorists' efforts to see and represent social problems.

References

Abercrombie, Nicholas. 1980. *The Dominant Ideology Thesis.* Boston: Allen and Unwin.

Adam, Barry D. 1978. *The Survival of Domination.* New York: Elsevier.

Agger, Ben. 1989. *Fast Capitalism.* Urbana: University of Illinois Press.

Arney, William Ray and Bernard J. Bergen. 1984. *Medicine and the Management of Living.* Chicago: University of Chicago Press.

Ashmore, Malcolm. 1989. *The Reflexive Thesis.* Chicago: University of Chicago Press.

Barthes, Roland. 1975. *The Pleasure of the Text.* New York: Hill and Wang.

Bazerman, Charles and James Paradis. 1991. *Textual Dynamics of the Professions.* Madison: University of Wisconsin Press.

Belenky, Mary Field, Blythe McVicker Clinchy, Nancy Rule Goldberger, and Jill Mattuck Tarule. 1986. *Women's Ways of Knowing.* New York: Basic Books.

Boon, James A. 1982. *Other Tribes, Other Scribes.* Cambridge: Cambridge University Press.

Bordo, Susan. 1990. "Feminism, Postmodernism, and Gender Skepticism." Pp. 133–56 in *Feminism/Postmodernism,* edited by Linda J. Nicholson. New York: Routledge.

Brown, Richard Harvey. 1977. *A Poetic for Sociology.* Cambridge: Cambridge University Press.

_____. 1987. *Society as Text.* Chicago: University of Chicago Press.

_____. 1989. *Social Science as Civic Discourse.* Chicago: University of Chicago Press.

_____. 1990. "Rhetoric, Textuality and the Postmodern Turn in Sociological Theory." *Sociological Theory* 8: 188–97.

Caws, Peter. 1988. *Structuralism.* New Jersey: Humanities Press International.

Clifford, James and George E. Marcus. 1986. *Writing Culture.* Berkeley: University of California Press.

Code, Lorraine. 1991. *What Can She Know?* Ithaca, NY: Cornell University Press.

Collins, Patricia Hill. 1986. "Learning from the Outsider Within." *Social Problems* 33:14–32.

_____. 1989. "The Social Construction of Invisibility." Pp. 77–93 in *Perspectives on Social Problems,* Vol. 1, edited by James A. Holstein and Gale Miller. Greenwich, CT: JAI Press.

_____. 1990. *Black Feminist Thought.* Boston: Unwin Hyman.

Davies, Bronwyn. 1982. *Life in the Classroom and Playground.* London: Routledge and Kegan Paul.

Derrida, Jacques. 1976. *Of Grammatology.* Baltimore: Johns Hopkins University Press.

_____. 1978. *Writing and Difference.* London: Routledge and Kegan Paul.

_____. 1981. *Positions.* Chicago: University of Chicago Press.

_____. 1987. *The Post Card.* Chicago: University of Chicago Press.

DeVault, Marjorie L. 1990. "Talking and Listening from Women's Standpoint." *Social Problems* 37:96–116.

Edwards, Richard C., Michael Reich, and Thomas E. Weisskopf (eds.). 1978. *The Capitalist System*. Englewood Cliffs, NJ: Prentice-Hall.

Ferguson, Kathy E. 1984. *The Feminist Case Against Bureaucracy*. Philadelphia: Temple University Press.

Fishman, Mark. 1980. *Manufacturing the News*. Austin: University of Texas Press.

Fonow, Mary Margaret and Judith A. Cook. 1991. "Back to the Future." Pp. 1–15 in *Beyond Methodology*, edited by Mary Margaret Fonow and Judith A. Cook. Bloomington, IN: Indiana University Press.

Foucault, Michel. 1972. *Power/Knowledge*. New York: Pantheon.

———. 1973. *The Birth of the Clinic*. New York: Pantheon.

———. 1977a. *Discipline and Punish*. New York: Pantheon.

———. 1977b. "Nietzsche, Genealogy, History." Pp. 139–64 in *Michel Foucault: Language, Counter-Memory, Practice*, edited by D. F. Bouchard. New York: Cornell University Press.

Gilligan, Carol. 1982. *In a Different Voice*. Cambridge, MA: Harvard University Press.

Gouldner, Alvin W. 1970. *The Coming Crises of Western Sociology*. New York: Equinox.

Griffith, Alison I. and Dorothy E. Smith. 1990. "What Did You Do in School Today." Pp. 3–24 in *Perspectives on Social Problems*, Vol. 2, edited by Gale Miller and James A. Holstein. Greenwich, CT: JAI Press.

Habermas, Jurgen. 1970a. "On Systematically Distorted Communication." *Inquiry* 13:205–18.

———. 1970b. "Towards a Theory of Communicative Competence." *Inquiry* 13:360–75.

———. 1970c. *Toward a Rational Society*. Boston: Beacon.

———. 1975. *Legitimation Crisis*. Translated by Thomas McCarthy. Boston: Beacon Press.

———. 1981. "Modernity Versus Postmodernity." *New German Critique* 22:3–14.

Hartsock, Nancy. 1983. *Money, Sex, and Power*. New York: Longman.

———. 1990. "Foucault on Power." Pp. 157–77 in *Feminism/Postmodernism*, edited by Linda J. Nicholson. New York: Routledge.

Hazelrigg, Lawrence E. 1985. "Were It Not for Words." *Social Problems* 32:234–37.

———. 1986. "Is There a Choice Between 'Constructionism and' 'Objectivism'?" *Social Problems* 33:1–13.

Hekman, Susan. 1990. *Gender and Knowledge*. Boston: Northeastern University Press.

Horkheimer, Max. 1972. *Critical Theory*. New York: Seabury.

Horkheimer, Max and Theodor Adorno. 1972. *Dialectic of Enlightenment*. New York: Herder and Herder.

Jacobson, David. 1991. *Reading Ethnography*. Albany, NY: SUNY Press.

Kellner, Douglas. 1989. *Critical Theory, Marxism and Modernity*. Baltimore: Johns Hopkins University Press.

Kondo, Dorinne K. 1990. *Crafting Selves*. Chicago: University of Chicago Press.

Krieger, Susan. 1983. *The Mirror Dance*. Philadelphia: Temple University Press.

Lacan, Jacques. 1977. *Ecrits*. London: Tavistock.

Lawson, Hilary. 1985. *Reflexivity*. La Salle, IL: Open Court.

Leitch, Vincent B. 1983. *Deconstructive Criticism*. New York: Columbia University Press.

Levesque-Lopman, Louise. 1988. *Claiming Reality*. Totowa, NJ: Rowman & Littlefield.

Lévi-Strauss, Claude. 1963. *Structural Anthropology*. New York: Basic Books.

———. 1966. *The Savage Mind*. Chicago: University of Chicago Press.

———. 1968. *The Raw and the Cooked*. New York: Harper and Row.

Lyotard, Jean-Francois. 1984. *The Postmodern Condition*. Minneapolis: University of Minnesota Press.

Marcus, George and Michael M. J. Fischer. 1986. *Anthropology as Cultural Critique*. Chicago: University of Chicago Press.

Marquis de Sade. 1964. *Justine*. New York: Harper and Row.

Marx, Karl and Frederick Engels. [1852] 1977. The German Ideology. New York: International Publishers.

McCloskey, Donald. N. 1990. *If You're So Smart*. Chicago: University of Chicago Press.

Mills, C. Wright. 1959. *The Sociological Imagination*. Oxford: Oxford University Press.

Mishler, Elliot G. 1986. *Research Interviewing*. Cambridge, MA: Harvard University Press.

Mulkay, Michael. 1989. *The Word and the World*. London: George Allen & Unwin.

Needham, Rodney. 1973. *Right and Left*. Chicago: University of Chicago Press.

Nelson, John S., Allan Megill, and Donald N. McCloskey. 1987. *The Rhetoric of the Human Sciences*. Madison: University of Wisconsin Press.

Nietzsche, Friedrich. [1901] 1968. *The Will to Power*. Translated by Walter Kauffmann and J. R. Hollingdale. New York: Vintage Books.

Ong, Aihwa. 1987. *Spirits of Resistance and Capitalist Discipline*. Albany, NY: SUNY Press.

Personal Narratives Group. 1989. *Interpreting Women's Lives*. Bloomington: Indiana University Press.

Pettit, Philip. 1975. *The Concept of Structuralism*. Berkeley: University of California Press.

Pfohl, Stephen. 1985. "Toward a Sociological Deconstruction of Social Problems." *Social Problems* 32:228–31.

Pfohl, Stephen and Avery Gordon. 1985. *Criminological Displacements*, videotext. Boston: Parasite Cafe Productions.

Piven, Frances Fox and Richard A. Cloward. 1971. *Regulating the Poor*. New York: Random House.

Rafter, Nicole H. 1992. "Some Consequences of Strict Constructionism." *Social Problems* 39:38–39.

Richardson, Laurel. 1990. *Writing Strategies*. Newbury Park, CA: Sage.

Ryan, Michael. 1971. *Blaming the Victim*. New York: Free Press.

Sacks, Karen Brodkin. 1988. *Caring by the Hour*. Urbana: University of Illinois Press.

Sahlins, Marshall. 1976. *Culture and Practical Reasoning*. Chicago: University of Chicago Press.

Saussure, Ferdinand de. 1959. *Course on General Linguistics*. New York: McGraw-Hill.

Schwalbe, Michael L. 1986. *The Psychosocial Consequences of Natural and Alienated Labor*. Albany: SUNY Press.

Schwartz, Barry. 1981. *Veritical Classification*. Chicago: University of Chicago Press.

Seidman, Steven. 1991. "The End of Sociological Theory." *Sociological Theory* 9:131–46.

Simons, Herbert W. 1989. *Rhetoric and the Human Sciences*. London: Sage.

Smith, Dorothy E. 1987. *The Everyday World as Problematic*. Boston: Northeastern University Press.

———. 1990. *The Conceptual Practices of Power*. Boston: Northeastern University Press.

Smith, Dorothy E. and Griffith, Alison I. 1990. " Coordinating the Uncoordinated." Pp. 25–44 in *Perspectives on Social Problems*, Vol. 2, edited by Gale Miller and James A. Holstein. Greenwich, CT: JAI Press.

Spector, Malcolm and John I. Kitsuse. [1977] 1987. Constructing Social Problems. Hawthorne, NY: Aldine de Gruyter.

Stewart, John O. 1989. *Drinkers, Drummers and Decent Folk*. Albany, NY: SUNY Press.

Susser, Ida. 1982. *Norman Street*. Oxford: Oxford University Press.

Tuchman, Gaye. 1978. *Making News*. New York: Free Press.

Tylor, Stephen A. 1986. "Post-Modern Ethnography." Pp. 122–40 in *Writing Culture*, edited by James Clifford and George E. Marcus. Berkeley: University of California Press.

Valentine, Bettylou. 1978. *Hustling and Other Hard Work*. New York: Free Press.

Van Maanen, John. 1988. *Tales of the Field*. Chicago: University of Chicago Press.

Venturi, Robert, Denise Scott-Brown, and Steven Izenour. 1977. *Learning from Las Vegas*. Cambridge, MA: MIT Press.

Walby, Sylvia. 1990. *Theorizing Patriarchy*. Oxford: Basil Blackwell.

Weber, Max. 1978. *Economy and Society*. Edited by Guenther Roth and Claus Wittich. Translated by Epraim Fischoff, Hans Gerth, A. M. Henderson, Ferdinand Kolegar, C. Wright Mills, Talcott Parsons, Max Rheinstein, Guenther Roth, Edward Shils, and Claus Wittich. Berkeley: University of California Press.

Westkott, Marcia. 1990. "Feminist Criticism and the Social Sciences." Pp. 58–68 in *Feminist Research Methods*, edited by Joyce McCarl Nielsen. Boulder, CO: Westview Press.

Willis, Paul. 1977. *Learning to Labor*. New York: Columbia University Press.

Woolgar, Steve (ed.) 1988. *Knowledge and Reflexivity*. London: Sage.

Critical Challenges

14

The Problem with Social Problems: From Social Constructionism to Critical Theory

Ben Agger

The occasion of a retrospection on Spector and Kitsuse's ([1977] 1987) *Constructing Social Problems* (also see Ibarra and Kitsuse, in this volume) offers a welcome opportunity to reflect on social problems analysis in general and on its social constructionist branch in particular. My reflections are informed by a whole host of developments in German critical theory and French cultural theory, including postmodernism and post-structuralism. In interesting ways, German critical theory and French cultural theory offer their own versions of social problems analysis as well as social constructionism. But in crucial ways they diverge from American social problems constructionism (e.g., Spector and Kitsuse [1977] 1987), notably in their overall perspectives on knowledge and power. Although I am not a social constructionist, I am sympathetic enough with some of its main themes to offer what I hope is an informed (if unsparing) immanent critique of social problems social constructionism as well as social problems analysis generally.

The Subtext of Social Problems

First, before I get into social constructionism, let me address what one might call the political subtext of all social problems analysis, especially as developed in the distinctively American sociological tradition (via the Chicago school, Merton, deviance theory, labeling theory, and finally social constructionism). Social constructionism in this regard is no different from other brands of social problems analysis. In my conclusion, I will return to these larger concerns. The very fact that American sociologists meet annually under the rubric of the Society for the Study of Social Problems (SSSP) is symptomatic of social problems analysis's role within American sociology as both separate from the main discipline and yet somehow connected to it. The SSSP's annual meetings are held just before the annual meetings of the American Sociological Association (ASA), always in the same city but never in the same hotel! Although sociologists attend both meetings, there is no official connection between their staging or schedules.

This reflects the fact that social problems analysis is central enough in American sociology to command a separate national association, annual meeting, and journal, but not so central as to be mainstreamed into the ASA itself. Virtually every American sociologist would agree that social problems exist—although they would disagree over the list of these problems and possibly (as I do here) over the definition of a social problem in the first place. In this sense, social problems analysis has always belonged to U.S. sociology (e.g., the Chicago school of urban sociology). But in some sense social problems sociology remains on the periphery of the main discipline, especially today when technique and quantification reign as never before. American sociology's positivism trenchantly bifurcates the study of facts and the advocacy of values, in this simply repeating the tired protocol of early-twentieth-century logical positivism (which has long since been abandoned in the natural sciences).

A casual perusal of the *American Sociological Review* (*ASR*) reveals virtually no engagement with social problems analysis, even though many of the articles treat issues of inequality that could well be problematized. For the most part, social problems analysis subsists on the fringes of the discipline and in the classroom. (Almost every department of sociology in this country offers undergraduate, if not graduate, courses on social problems.) The simultaneous institutionalization and marginalization of American social problems analysis at once imply that there are such things as "social problems" but that social problems analysis should be relegated to specialty journals and specialty conferences. Of course, critical sociologists of one kind or another reject these assumptions out of hand, as I develop here.

From my critical perspective, the very subtext of social problems analysis conveys two inappropriate messages: First, it implies that every society will contain social problems, disqualifying precisely the utopianism that makes Marxism so attractive. One of the versions of this eternalization of social problems takes place in so-called conflict theory, a Weberianized version of Marxism that drops out altogether Marx's stress on the possibility of struggle and social change. Conflict theorists target social problems as if they are at once remediable and here to stay. Second, the discourse of social problems analysis as a separate specialist vocabulary suggests that concern with inequality and exploitation should take place somehow outside the disciplinary mainstream. The professionalization of social problems analysis can, of course, be explained in terms of the very sociology of organization first offered by Weber: People interested in social problems analysis recognized early on that it was necessary to specialize their discourse in staking out a certain territorial claim. Without classes, a conference, journal, and specialist rhetoric, it is thought, social problems analysis will not have a very long shelf life among other competing subdisciplinary brands.

These are problematic assumptions from the point of view of the paradigm of all social problems analysis—Marxism. I have already noted how Marx suggested that we can create a society without social conflict/social problems; he called this communism. As well, Marxists argue that the professionalization and concomitant specialization of social problems analysis assure that mainstream sociology will neglect the discussion of social problems. For Marx, Marxism was to be a thoroughgoing engagement with all manner of social problems of capitalism (and now, feminists would correctly add, of patriarchy). Indeed, *for Marx capitalism was the central social problem*—the source of all others. Although that view needs to be modified in light of the subsequent evolution of market capitalism into state-managed, racist, sexist, and imperialist forms, I believe that it is largely correct.

Thus, I contend here that the discourse of American social problems analysis blunts the sharp edge of social criticism, reducing it to a piecemeal problem-by-problem policy analysis conducted in essentially positivist terms. Interestingly, various postmodern theorists (e.g., Lyotard 1984) also militate against the totalizing, all-encompassing aims of Marxism, an issue to which I return later. The postmodernization of American sociology (e.g., Brown 1987) converges with the dominant approach to social problems analysis where it rejects the Marxist approach to "grand narratives" of world history in favor of the small stories told by local groups and individuals. Social problems analysis, especially in its postmodern versions, is thoroughly pluralist and liberal in this sense. It rejects totalizing analyses as well as radical solutions.

Deconstructing Social Constructionism

Social constructionism (e.g., Spector and Kitsuse [1977] 1987; Berger and Luckmann 1967) is a special version of social problems analysis that shares its metaphysical view of social problems. Heavily influenced by European developments in phenomenology, social constructionism arose as a reaction to the dominant Parsonsian structural functionalism of the 1950s. Alfred Schutz (1967) helped translate Husserlian assumptions about the relationships among subjectivity, intersubjectivity, and society into a workable research agenda for empirical sociology, a project that was carried forward by Berger and Luckmann (1967) and Garfinkel (1967). Indeed, social constructionism is inseparable from Garfinkel's ethnomethodology, which deploys Husserlian and Schutzian insights methodologically.

Essentially, social phenomenology, of which both ethnomethodology and social constructionism could be seen as allies, challenged structural functionalism, which seemed to efface the role of voluntary action in social explanation. Drawing on Husserl's notion that knowledge is constituted intentionally and not simply reflected on mind's blank slate, social phenomenologists like Schutz argued that the person has a much more "constitutional" role in the social world, engaging in all sorts of personal and interpersonal projects that actively shape, as well as reproduce, the social world. Husserl's own phenomenology draws on a long tradition of German idealism, which stood opposed to mechanistic materialist explanations of the world, stressing the active roles of imagination and action in history.

Where Parsonian-era structural functionalists, following Durkheim (1950), argue that society can be conceptualized as an impinging social fact external to the person, social phenomenologists argue that society is both intersubjective and objective. People through the interactive creation of meaning give shape to society, which in turn acquires an objectivity somehow independent of them. At least, this is the balance struck by Schutz and later reinforced by Berger and Luckmann in their (1967) influential Americanization of Schutzian themes, *The Social Construction of Reality*, probably the first genuine statement of what later came to be called social constructionism. No simple idealism, this version of sociology stresses the mutuality of subjective and intersubjective motivation, on the one hand, and objective social institutions, on the other. Similar to Marx's notion that history influences human beings but that human beings can change history, the social phenomenological mutuality of meaning and social structure has been highly influential in reducing the hegemony of a mechanistic structural functionalism.

Structural functionalism also came under attack in a parallel way from pragmatist-influenced symbolic interactionists, who drew their antimechanism not from Schutz but from George Herbert Mead. Indeed, social constructionism has both phenomenological and interactionist articulations, with interactionism being the dominant mode of social constructionist social problems analysis in American sociology. Blumer's (1969) and Becker's (1963) versions of symbolic interactionism parallel Garfinkel's ethnomethodology in important ways, although their philosophical inflections are somewhat different. It is no accident that so-called social constructionism in social problems analysis (Spector and Kitsuse [1977] 1987; Schneider 1985) is paralleled by a symbolic-interactionist version of social problems analysis (see Ibarra and Kitsuse, in this volume), which in turn is increasingly fertilized by some of the same postmodernist influences I mentioned above (e.g., see Denzin 1986). All of these versions of sociology have in common the assumption that *human beings actively create and interpret social reality,* which is conceptualized as a moving structure of interpenetrating, dialectical forces subject to transformation.

It is easy to see how this assumption is remarkably similar to Marx's own dialectical materialism. The radical implications of the notion that people create society just as they are created by society are obvious, especially in the Marxist version. The important difference between social constructionism and Marxism becomes clear where social constructionism is translated into a version of social problems analysis that, as I have argued, is inherently inimical to the totalizing Marxist agenda. Although social constructionism has radicalizing potential, especially in the notion that society is not an external reality standing over against the individual, this potential is severely blunted where social constructionism is harnessed to the essentially liberal project of social problems analysis and thus safely integrated into (and marginalized from) the mainstream discipline of American sociology. I believe that the phenomenological version of social constructionism (e.g., Piccone 1971; Paci 1972) is potentially more radical than the interactionist version (e.g., Ibarra and Kitsuse) as I develop below.

This is not to say that social constructionism in its best sense is simply a version of dialectical materialism. There are important differences. Few in the phenomenological tradition have explicitly linked Marxism to phenomenology (exceptions include Piccone 1971; Paci 1972; O'Neill 1972). Even fewer self-identified social constructionists are Marxists either in their political program or substantive social theory. Indeed, their identity as social constructionists is highlighted by differentiation from both structural functionalists and Marxists, who are regarded as a combined, even self-same, opponent. Of course, it is easy to make this case where one conflates economic-reductionist versions of Marxisms with all possible Marxisms—a conflation effectively disqualified by the long history of Western Marxism (Lukacs, Korsch, the Frankfurt school, etc.).

Unfortunately, we rarely find social constructionist versions of social problems analyses in their best sense. Such versions border on Western Marxism and socialist feminism in their dialectical approaches to the societal subject-object problem. But Spector and Kitsuse in their original ([1977] 1987) statement of a social constructionist perspective on social problems slide toward idealism, as we can clearly see in the programmatic Ibarra and Kitsuse retrospection on Spector and Kitsuse's book. (Indeed, I regard Ibarra and Kitsuse's self-proclaimed interactionism to

regress significantly behind Schutz, Berger and Luckmann in their obliv-
iousness to the dialectic between agency and structure). Spector and
Kitsuse's very definition of social problems is tellingly idealist:

> [W]e define social problems as *the activities of individuals or groups making*
> *assertions of grievances and claims with respect to some putative conditions* . . . .
> *The central problem for a theory of social problems is to account for the emergence,*
> *nature, and maintenance of claims-making and responding activities.* (Spector
> and Kitsuse [1977] 1987, pp. 76–77, emphasis in original).

In other words, *for social problems to exist, people must identify them as such.*
But a Marxist and feminist would argue that some of the most intractable
social problems are precisely those which remain invisible, ill-articu-
lated, unchallenged. The force of hegemonic ideology or false consciousness is powerful enough that dominant groups keep these potentially
problematized issues concealed, chalking them up to virtual forces of
social nature. Although undeniably the claims-making process is important to understand (e.g., through media, grass roots groups, established
political institutions), it in no way exhausts the universe of social problems. Indeed, one might well argue that the most disabling social problems are those which remain outside the universe of consciousness and
discourse altogether.

This was Marx's very notion of ideology—belief systems that portray
exploitation as naturelike, hence unavoidable. His *Capital* argues that
economic exploitation (a social problem) is mystified under capitalism,
especially by bourgeois economic theorists who depict the marketplace
as rational and necessary. Instead, Marx carefully unpacks exploitation
from the mystified (or commodity-fetishized) relationships that appear
to be naturelike but are, in fact, outcomes of a determinate social history.
Marx considers the role played by ideology in preventing problems from
being problematized, hence reproducing them. As a dialectician, he
addressed the interplay between ideological belief systems and social
institutions, recognizing that claims-making activity, in Spector and Kitsuse's sense, is inherently politically, indeed pivotally so. But unlike
them he refuses to view claims-making as an inevitable or necessary
process in the objectification of social problems. There can well be problems that are perceived and discussed as products of unalterable social
nature—particularly, capitalism.

Social constructionist versions of social problems analysis tend, with
Spector and Kitsuse, to concentrate exclusively on claims-making activity, missing the defused dialectic between subjective and intersubjective
process, on the one hand, and institutional realities, on the other. A
materialist account of the problematization process regards claims-

making as important, to be sure. But it views claims-making as a variable and not a constant—i.e., sometimes claims get made whereas other times they are suppressed. According to the Frankfurt school theorists, *domination* is the social condition under which people lose the ability almost entirely to distinguish between the present and the possibility of a different future. Under these conditions, so-called social problems are products and processes of the *suppression* of claims-making activities.

The signal contribution of the Frankfurt school theorists to the revivification of Marxism lies in their reformulation of Marx's concept of ideology. Where Marx stated or implied that ideology was a straightforward process of deception that could be addressed counterfactually, Adorno, Horkheimer, Marcuse, and later Habermas regard ideology as an interstitial process of the falsification of all experience and language. Marcuse's (1964) emblematic statement of the Frankfurt school's theory of ideology, *One-Dimensional Man*, spells this out succinctly. What Marcuse calls the "universe of discourse" has been rendered one dimensional. That is, people do not possess the categories of understanding or expression through which to process critically what is happening to them. Instead, in late capitalism domination is "introjected," internalized so deeply in thought, gesture, and speech that it is virtually impervious to deconstruction.

In this context of what Adorno (1973) called "total administration," the social constructionist notion that people can and do make effective claims about social problems is untenable. Instead, people are lulled into acquiescence and adaptation, notably through sociological and economic lawmaking that depicts late capitalism as an immutable modernity. The Frankfurt theory of domination has been fortified by more recent developments in interpretive theory, including the more sharply political tendencies in deconstruction, postmodernism, and feminist theory (see Ryan 1982; Agger 1990, 1991a, 1991b). Taken together, these more recent developments in French cultural theory further enrich the Frankfurt school's revision of Marx's theory of ideology, showing (e.g., Baudrillard 1983) that ideology is a "simulation" encoded in the micropractices of late-capitalist everyday life—as such, virtually impossible to detect and thus rebut. I have developed a notion of "fast capitalism" (Agger 1989a) as a way of understanding what I have called the dispersal of ideology from texts into the sense and sentience of everyday life itself, further extending the Frankfurt school's revision of original Marxism.

Let me be specific about the contributions of postmodernism, deconstruction, and feminism to a critical theory of social problems. Postmodernism stresses the discursive nature of ideology, showing the ways in which false consciousness is promulgated through the various cultural products and practices dominating the quotidian today (e.g., televi-

sion, advertising). Derridean deconstruction offers interpretive strategies with which to decode these powerfully hegemonizing discourses,
demonstrating their contradictions and omissions. Feminism addresses
the vital link between production and reproduction, the social and the
personal, enabling us better to understand the link between structure
and agency or what Habermas (1984, 1987) calls system and lifeworld.
For its part, social constructionism in its strongest sense overlaps with
each of these perspectives, especially in its phenomenological version.
For example, Foucault's (1977) claim that the discourse of criminology
creates the category of the criminal, and hence leads to a whole system
of incarceration, is highly reminiscent of social constructionist themes.
Although the attempt to synthesize these diverse traditions risks becoming alphabet soup, I would argue that the most relevant version of
critical theory incorporates these discursive, culture-critical, and sexual-
political insights in order to understand the heterogeneous nature of
domination in everyday life today.

It is simply impossible in fast capitalism to retain Spector and Kitsuse's
definition of social problems. Ideology is at once too intensive and extensive for that. But neither must we embrace Adorno's dismal metaphor of society as a concentration camp. There are avenues of resistance
and revolt, as even Marcuse acknowledged in *One-Dimensional Man*.
People do problematize their social situations and struggle to create
better ones. Yet this problematization is not the rule but the exception in
totally administered society. And even where problematization does occur, it is usually false: Most people simply do not have the theoretical
resources with which to understand the world in all of its complexly
interrelated totality. Although it is tempting to wish that people could
address and mobilize around their grievances—indeed, that is the very
promise of Marx's theory-practice merger—social constructionism errs
empirically where it assumes that people do see clearly and then get
their voices heard.

One wonders why people like Spector and Kitsuse define social problems so narrowly, even assuming that we find the discourse of social
problems useful at all (as I do not). Granted, the problematization process is worthy of serious investigation. But so are the processes by which
problematization is either blocked or distorted, a topic ignored by social
constructionists of Spector and Kitsuse's ilk. One might simply suggest
that social constructionism's essentially idealist response to structural
functionalism's and orthodox Marxism's mechanism is borne of good
intentions: Social constructionists want to believe that agency matters,
or should matter, even if particular agents do not have much impact at
this historical moment, especially in capitalist societies. For Spector and
Kitsuse, though, these issues become inextricably tangled: From the

ontological assumption that people at some deep level are authors of their own history, one derives empirical claims about the effective agency of people and groups in the here and now, to which social problems analysis is devoted. This is of course the traditional problem with idealism: Is and Ought are conflated.

I would go as far as to say that a social constructionist perspective on social problems is oxymoronic in the sense that social constructionism emphasizes agency whereas social problems analysis, both functionalist and Marxist, stresses the absence of agency [with the important difference being that Marxists want to restore agency while functionalists like Parsons (1951) ontologize people's subordination to the social]. Latter-day social constructionists like Spector and Kitsuse emphasize the absence of structural constraints on action, even if Schutz (1967) clearly noted the dialectic between personal subjects and institutional objects. It is decidedly strange that social constructionists even tackled social problems theory given their disposition to ignore precisely the institutions—domination—that cause social problems in the first place.

Ibarra and Kitsuse retreat from the agency emphasis of Schutzian social constructionists in their interactionist program of social problems analysis, which drops Schutz's dialectic of subject and object. Ibarra and Kitsuse's interactionism has no avowed transformative intent—the timeworn stance of positivism, reproduced in conservative versions of Husserlian phenomenology as well as mainstream interactionism. Ibarra and Kitsuse dispense with even the vestiges of an institutional approach to social problems, which for them becomes an abstract exercise in taxonomizing analytical categories and not a real engagement with empirical social reality. They reduce social problems to quotidian interpretive practices involved in their weak notion of "vernacular." If Spector and Kitsuse's book contains few references to the world, Ibarra and Kitsuse's piece reads like sheer metaphysics.

The Future of Social Problems

Having raised questions about social problems analysis in general and social constructionist approaches to social problems in particular, let me turn to the future of social problems analysis in American sociology. My comments extend far beyond the future of the SSSP and its journal, far beyond so-called social problems theory and its social constructionist variant, whether phenomenological or interactionist. I believe that all of these institutions and discourses are fatally flawed by both their ontology of social problems and their self-marginalizing disciplinary discourse. Furthermore, as I develop in my concluding section, below, the whole discipline of American sociology (including American sociological theory) needs to be reformulated so thoroughly that we would not even recognize it by comparison to present disciplinary practices and institutions. In other words, what is wrong with social problems analysis is wrong with the whole discipline. I realize that these sentiments are unpopular, especially at a time when American sociologists are fighting a rearguard action against academic administrators who question the legitimacy of sociology, which they view as an exotic animal from the 1960s that is increasingly expensive to feed and house. I am not advocating the abolition of sociology departments, only of what passes for standard American sociology, including its social problems wing.

It is galling that the critical, eye-opening promise of social problems analysis is disciplined and banalized. Where "society"—i.e., domination—is the problem, we need to analyze social structures of domination carefully in order to understand how to change them. But social problems analysis has become so professionalized, methodologized, and marginalized that these concerns about the theory-practice linkage have been virtually eliminated from social problems discourse, which is dominated by social constructionists like Spector, Kitsuse, and Ibarra.

Absent from this conglomeration is the rigorous structural analysis originally exemplified by Marx in *Capital*. Of course, American sociology has never understood Marx, domesticating him into a conflict theorist, hence purging his political radicalism with a stiff dose of a Parsonsianized Weber. Even to utter these thoughts is laughable at a time when the so-called "end of communism" is celebrated far and wide, including in American sociology. But the putative end of communism has nothing to do with Marxism—the Western-Marxist Marx of alienation theory, reification, commodity fetishism, ideology critique. The postmodernization of social problems theory, currently in vogue, repeats the tired 1950s critique of Marxism leveled by Daniel Bell (1960). Marx is denounced yet again, this time from within the cozy confines of social problems sociology. Marxism is dismissed as antiquated and authoritarian; in its place subject-centered sociologies are proposed (of which social constructionism is a prominent one).

Meanwhile the mainstream discipline maintains its devotion to what are vaguely called issues of policy by protecting its social problems rump. This continues the legacy of the earlier Chicago school, which expressed a concern with the detritus of emerging American capitalism, while recognizing that social problems are now to be ameliorated by the state. Tellingly, the literature on social problems does little to challenge our dominant assumptions about the inevitability of so-called social problems and about how the state (through "policy") is responsible for reducing the human cost of these problems. At a time when mainstream sociology has become virtually a mathematics discipline, this pretense to policy relevance, if ultimately inadequate, is crucial lest sociology lose all touch with its reformist auspices in the classical sociologies of Durkheim and Weber, who also were concerned to reduce the human costs of modernity.

Social problems analysis as a latter-day statist strategy arose not in order to ameliorate human suffering at all but as a way of redressing the systemic disturbances caused by urbanization, unemployment, poverty, discrimination, and environmental degradation. The structural-functional view of social problems has always been statist. That is, social problems were relevant to the extent to which they impeded progress (whatever that was supposed to mean). It is a serious misrepresentation to portray most students of social problems as radicals when, in fact, they are mostly liberals and even conservatives—concerned with protecting the system by protecting individuals against the exuberant growth of the system. This is easily seen in the array of papers published in *Social Problems* and presented at the SSSP's annual meeting. Most papers are in fact narrowly formulaic exercises in sociological analysis; few are even vaguely political. Indeed, the journal *Social Problems* has become a mini-*ASR*, valorizing scientistic scholarship as well as political dispassion. SSSP leaders have defended this as the necessary cost of subdisciplinary legitimation, a dubious argument at best. Where *Social Problems* used to be controlled by radicals, today it is a pale version of every other regional and specialty journal in American sociology questing for a higher prestige ranking among mainstream journals. For that matter, the SSSP annual meetings are so unexciting (and so artificially fractured from the ASA annual meetings) that attendance has dropped off precipitously, causing consternation among SSSP's leadership.

I would argue emphatically that SSSP declines in direct proportion to its integration into the mainstream discipline—its emulation of disciplinary methods and substance. Of course, for it to be more politically and theoretically emboldened would risk the very legitimacy among mainstream sociologists deemed valuable today. But without a decidedly more political identity within American sociology, the social problems rump will have no reason for being. This is perfectly alright to those of us who have been skeptical about "social problems" as well as disciplinary sociology from the beginning. We have always known that social problems are not discrete disconnected episodes in the social process but structurally integrated features of what Marx originally called "contradictions." We on the left view social problems not as episodic upsurges of systemic irrationality or excess but as integral features of a disorganized, irrational capitalism, sexism, and racism (see Offe 1985). As Marx brilliantly understood, capitalism is *defined by* its contradictions between social production and private consumption—contradictions that doom capitalism to swing turbulently from crisis to crisis.

Indeed, social problems analysis is designed to reduce the intensity of these crises, somehow managing these cycles of boom and bust. Although the rhetoric of liberal statism since Durkheim and Weber has maintained that social engineering can make the world a better place to live, this is to be a decidedly capitalist world in which most of the world's billions face the desperation of survival. And survival is in no way guaranteed under capitalism. On this view, then, social problems are not episodic but endemic to the system. Even to identify singular social problems is folly when, in fact, social problems are structurally grounded in the social system's axial principles of private productive property, male supremacy, racism, and the domination of nature. Radical students of social problems will argue with some conviction that to characterize capitalism, sexism, racism, and the domination of nature as "problems" is valuable in the sense that it deconstructs the functionalist mythology of benign equilibrium. True—as far as it goes. *But inevitably the discourse of social problems destructures, disconnects, and pathologizes social problems in ways that defy structural analysis and critique of the kind originally intended by Marx.* This is not to say that Marx is literally adequate today; of course, he is not. But we need to recognize that social problems analysis and social problems theory are, at best, pale imitations of critical social theory, especially at a time when "social problems" have become a highly professionalized mini-industry within (and necessarily apart from) the main enterprise of technical sociology.

What social problems analysis most visibly lacks is *theory*, a way of making connections among discrete social problems (which, once theorized, no longer appear to be discrete). The SSSP has established a section called social problems theory, but this is little more than a dumping ground for macroconcerns of all sorts (which are typically neglected by most ground-level social problems empiricists, of whom there are many, at least judging by what regularly appears in *Social Problems*). Indeed, I would argue that social problems theory is social theory itself, notably critical theory, which complexly theorizes the totality comprising the seeming singular "problems" to which individual chapters are devoted in those omnibus undergraduate social problems textbooks. Social problems theory in its own terms cannot theorize the totality because "problems" by their very nature are viewed as episodic—acid rain, child abuse, AIDS, ... the list is endless. At its best, social problems analysis ought to be a deep political economy and demography of issues no longer framed singularly from the vantage point of a serializing sociology that destructures the totality in order to keep it hidden.

I am lamenting, then, the absence of both political and theoretical radicalism in American social problems analysis today. The postmodernization of social problems analysis does not in itself indicate either type of radicalism but only an acquaintance with another recondite rhetoric. In fact, as I have argued, the postmodernization of social problems analysis deradicalizes social problems analysis by disqualifying what Lyotard (1984) calls the grand narratives told by Marxists in their Archimedean hubris. These totalizing accounts of the social world are rejected by most postmodernists and feminists for their putative conceptual, hence political, imperialism. Marxism is rejected (by postmodernists) as modernist and (by feminists) as male supremacist, both of which are largely true. Yes, as I (1990, 1991a, 1991b, 1993) and others (e.g., Fraser 1989; Best and Kellner 1991) have shown, there can be a postmodern feminist critical theory attentive to the modernist dialectic of enlightenment as well as to Marxism's historic male supremacy. The possibility of this synthesis of French cultural theory, feminism, and German critical theory depends on a radicalizing reading of postmodernism and feminism, which, in other articulations, stand opposed to the totalizing project of Marxist critical theory. This synthesis requires bold theoretical risk-taking and not the rejection of the totalizing project of theory. By in effect rejecting theory, social problems analysts condemn themselves to political irrelevance.

Of course, to be concerned with the political fate of social problems analysis is hopelessly old-fashioned! At a time when both the right (Bell) and left (Lyotard) proclaim politics dead, the posture of politicization provokes hilarity among the world-weary, who increasingly converge from both ends of the ideological polarity toward a postmodern center. But one must risk hilarity as well as apostasy when the chips are down: We must resist the forces of depoliticization now more than ever, recognizing that the pretense to be apolitical is the most political stance of all, as Horkheimer and Adorno (1972) argued in *Dialectic of Enlightenment*. For sociologists of social problems to clamor for their own professional legitimacy is self-defeating; professionalization inevitably amounts to neutralization, especially in the byzantine bureaucracy of academic life today.

This is very much the problem confronting feminists in the academy. Should issues of gender be concentrated around a single pivot, like women's studies programs, or should the study of gender march through every discipline? In the first case, women's studies programs invite their own ghettoization. In the second case, gender studies dispersed through the disciplines risk their own harmless diffusion and integration. Once we assume that the study of social problems must be integral to the sociological project, which should be shamelessly social change oriented, do we ghettoize social problems analysis across the city in its own convention hotel, with its own patois and professional hierarchy? Or do we integrate social problems analysis into every part of the discipline, hence changing the discipline significantly? As with the study of gender, I prefer the latter strategy, if only because it is less easy to ignore. The professionalization and specialization of social problems analysis as a subdiscipline in its own right have reproduced the professionalism and specialism of the discipline at large; the SSSP could as well be the ASA, albeit somewhat less high-powered in a technical, methodological sense.

It is hard to defend the disciplinary project of sociology that does not make social problems analysis central. As I noted earlier, the roots of sociology in Comte, Durkheim, and Weber were directly in social problems analysis, to use a latter-day turn of phrase. The founders were all concerned to ameliorate the disruptions and grievances of nascent capitalism through technocratic fine-tuning, precisely the role laid out for sociologists by Comte. Only in the post-1950s era of American sociology, when sociology became a highly technical discipline, did the concern with social amelioration give way to LOGIT and LISREL. But for a person with my political orientation it is not enough simply to return sociology to the problematizing orientation of the founders. Like Merton much later, these founders (see Institute for Social Research 1972) conceptualized social problems in functionalist terms as dysfunctions blocking the smooth evolution of capitalism. In an earlier book (McDaniel and Agger 1982) I contrasted this functionalist evolutionism with Marxist approaches to social problems. For Marxists, of course, social problems are deeply imbedded at the volcanic core of capitalism, which is necessarily prone to irrupt periodically in world-threatening ways.

Thus, to deprofessionalize social problems analysis is only worth doing if social problems are construed broadly as deep problems of modernity (capitalism, sexism, racism, etc.). A concern with "policy," to use the contemporary reformist parlance, simply reformulates the classical sociological program of functionalist evolutionism in statist terms. Critical theory's version of social problems analysis (e.g., see Forester 1985 and Agger 1991a for examples of such a program) would both drop the discourse of "social problems" as discrete events or phenomena and eschew subdisciplinary specialization. Indeed, a critical theory of social problems would be a supradisciplinary project, as Kellner (1989) has forcefully argued. It is far too late to pretend that disciplinary specialization somehow enlightens or emancipates. As I elaborate below, disciplinary object domains and methods are too intermingled for us even to retain the notion that sociology is worth preserving as a distinctive discipline (see Agger 1989c for this argument at much greater length).

In saying these things, I realize that I am working against the grain. But there is no getting around the fact that academic institutionalization and discursive specialization have been obfuscating. My agenda is Luddite only when seem from the vantage of disciplinary identity and territoriality. Newcomers to sociology would probably find it strange indeed that we have segregated social problems analysis into a hotel across town, from which people conduct essentially the same business with the same rhetoric as at the main hotel. I am not simply saying that we should all stay at the same hotel or find a new one. Perhaps—to pursue this metaphor one more step—we should not even hold our annual meetings at an expensive downtown hotel but instead, as in Canada, hold them at a college campus, where social science disciplines conduct their annual meetings back to back, thus allowing for ample interdisciplinary commingling as well as cheap rooms for graduate students. In other words, there is nothing inviolable about the way we have set up our discipline or pursue it discursively (e.g., see Brodkey 1987; Klein 1990; Richardson 1990). Social problems analysis can and should be seriously reformulated within the wholesale reformulation of the discipline. Only thus will we arrive at what Habermas calls a genuine interdisciplinary materialism, necessary to comprehend the complexly interrelated social totality.

Is Sociology the Problem?

I have suggested some rather far-reaching problems with social problems analysis as it is presently practiced in American sociology. Let me look beyond that discussion toward the future of sociology itself. Sociology as a discipline exists in large measure to exact discipline, Foucault's term for what the Frankfurt school, following Lukacs and Weber, called domination. Sociology seeks to reproduce the existing order by provoking conformity with its postulated social laws—the market economy, patriarchy, racism, and the domination of nature. This is not to say that the average *ASR* article endorses such evils, but rather that our essentially positivist discipline (positivist in the sense of being committed to a presuppositionlessly representational view of knowledge) wittingly or unwittingly reinforces a passive everyday life. I am not saying that sociology is a central or even particularly significant social and political force today. But the thousands of students educated every year in introductory sociology courses ingest powerful lessons about the intractability of the contemporary social world, lessons that are by-products of Comte, Durkheim, and Weber's timeworn search for social laws.

It is no wonder that social problems sociology reflects the overall
positivism of the discipline at large, assuming that social problems are
endemic features of organized social life and thus disqualifying utopian
political projects and radical social movements. I am saying that this
notion that sociology qua science reflects a world that can be understood
lawfully and representationally is deeply conservative. Although few
methodologists or theorists teach positivism as an explicit epistemological doctrine, the whole methodologized discourse of mainstream sociology (including the type of work published in Social Problems as well as
ASR) reflects and hence reproduces the notion that sociology stands
outside the world and can adequately approximate its reflection.

American sociology has become virtually a science discipline. The lav-
ish figural displays dominating journal articles and technical monographs
enhance sociology's science aura (see Agger 1989b). They discursively
produce positivist textual outcomes, hence contributing to an overall
political culture in which people both accept and reproduce their lot
as seeming fate—the characteristic of the quotidian in fast capitalism.
Traditional texts enjoying an old-fashioned distance from reality fade
into the dusty archives that are being increasingly reduced to microfiche
and indexed on computer systems. People rarely interact with books,
thus failing to be stimulated, angered, mobilized by them. Texts (see
Agger 1990) are commodified to an unprecedented extent, negating the
possibility of critique, which as ever relies on a certain distance from
things. In the case of science, distance is reduced to near nothingness by
the elaborate discursive rituals of journal science, notably including the
pyrotechnic use of figure and gesture, which increasingly become the
main text of sociology. These methodological rituals are supposed to
bring us into the presence of the world, reflecting the world on the
science page, hence earning a certain indubitability for science—what
the methodologists dryly call validity.

I, too, am concerned with validity, but much more in the classical
Greek, Hegelian, and Marxist senses of the unfolding of Reason. Science
eschews these pursuits as the follies of metaphysicians and poets. The
new characteristic of positivism today is that it has shifted from the
explicit program of the Vienna circle to an inchoate set of literary rituals
(e.g., the elaborate use of figure and number in science texts) that are
very difficult to deconstruct as concealed arguments for a certain state of
affairs—the present social order. This is an even farther cry from Comte's positivist program, which has been entombed in sociology's museum of founding ideas. Positivism today is proclaimed dead because it is
still very much alive in a new form—science writing. Horkheimer and
Adorno (1972) made the case in Dialectic of Enlightenment that positivism
is the new ideology, an argument that I fertilize with concepts from

literary and cultural theory, enabling me to read science itself as a decisive social text.

In this sense, social problems sociology, to the extent to which it affiliates itself to the disciplinary project (and almost all of it does), is secret positivism, reinforcing discipline by writing under the aegis of discipline. Social problems people will protest loudly that social problems sociology wants to make the world a better place. Although true, that caveat misses the point: By participating in the deceptively positivist language game of mainstream methodologized sociology, social problems sociologists only add value to the disciplining project of disciplinary sociology. In my book *Socio(onto)logy: A Disciplinary Reading* (1989c) I indict mainstream positivist sociology as a modal discourse of discipline, reinforcing domination through its representation of a representable social world. Although sociology is not all ideology, it is powerfully ideological in its representational stance to the social world, a posture assumed by nearly every social problems analyst that I have read.

To be sure, *Social Problems* and the SSSP proceedings are slightly more likely to embrace postmodernists, feminists, and critical theorists than are *ASR* and the ASA convention. I was invited to give a talk on postmodernism at the 1990 SSSP meetings, attended by a meager handful of postmodern converts. As Marcuse (1964) carefully noted, one-dimensional society is not seamless; there are cracks and fissures if one looks closely enough. That is the possibility of all radical social change. But just because social problems sports a few more weirdos than mainstream sociology means very little when one considers the remarkable discursive and organizational similarities between the two groups. Indeed, I can count on two hands the number of American sociologists I know who seriously interrogate their disciplinary identity for the political reasons I have outlined above. Sure, lip service is being paid to discourse, rhetoric, vernacular, culture, gender, race, and the other code words of the day. But these words quickly degenerate into slogans that fail to do our thinking for us. They change nothing when repeated liturgically, as almost always they are.

I have little idea "what" to do about all this. American sociology, including its social problems wing, will continue to write, publish, teach, and confer in the usual ways. It is facile to suggest that disgruntled sociologists decamp to the Modern Language Association (MLA) annual meeting, where postpositivist discourse is certainly better entrenched. English and comparative literature possess their own insularity, notably an aversion to totalizing social theory. Perhaps the real action will be found in cultural studies, especially on its more politicized flanks (e.g., Birmingham school, cinefeminism, the Frankfurt studies of mass culture). I have attempted an elaboration of cultural studies as critical social theory (Agger 1992), pursuing many of the themes outlined here. But already cultural studies has become cultic, with its own journals, conferences, and superstars, reproducing discipline in its own small way by becoming a discipline.

To assume that we can "solve" the "problem" addressed in this paper is part and parcel of what is wrong with social problems sociology. Americans assume that things can be fixed with more of something and less of something else. Although it is embarrassing to call for enlightenment, critique, and reason, these are the slogans that I would invoke when confronted by the disciplinary monoliths that have come to dominate the American academy. The fact that they mean different things to different people is precisely "the problem" that preoccupies the critical theory of society.

References

Adorno, T. 1973. *Negative Dialectics*. New York: Seabury Press.

Agger, B. 1989a. *Fast Capitalism: A Critical Theory of Significance*. Urbana: University of Illinois Press.

————. 1989b. *Reading Science: A Literary, Political and Sociological Analysis*. Dix Hills, NY: General Hall.

————. 1989c. *Socio(onto)logy: A Disciplinary Reading*. Urbana: University of Illinois Press.

————. 1990. *The Decline of Discourse: Reading, Writing and Resistance in Postmodern Capitalism*. London/New York: Falmer Press.

————. 1991a. *A Critical Theory of Public Life: Knowledge, Discourse and Politics in an Age of Decline*. London/New York: Falmer Press.

————. 1991b. *The Discourse of Domination: From the Frankfurt School to Postmodernism*. Evanston, IL: Northwestern University Press.

————. 1992. *Cultural Studies as Critical Theory*. London/New York: Falmer Press.

————. 1993. *Gender, Discourse and Power: Toward a Feminist Postmodern Critical Theory*. Forthcoming.

Baudrillard, J. 1983. *Simulations*. New York: Semiotext(e).

Becker, H. 1963. *The Outsiders: Studies in the Sociology of Deviance*. Glencoe, IL: Free Press.

Bell, D. 1960. *The End of Ideology*. Glencoe, IL: Free Press.

Berger, P. and T. Luckmann. 1967. *The Social Construction of Reality*. Garden City, NY: Doubleday.

Best, S. and D. Kellner. 1991. *Postmodern Theory*. London: Macmillan.

Blumer, H. 1969. *Symbolic Interactionism: Perspectives and Method*. Englewood Cliffs, NJ: Prentice-Hall.

Brodkey, L. 1987. *Academic Writing as Social Practice*. Philadelphia: Temple University Press.

Brown, R. 1987. *Society as Text*. Chicago: University of Chicago Press.

Denzin, N. 1986. "Postmodern Social Theory." *Sociological Theory* 4:194–204.

Durkheim, E. 1950. *The Rules of Sociological Method*. Glencoe, IL: Free Press.

Forester, J. Ed. 1985. *Critical Theory and Public Life*. Cambridge, MA: MIT Press.

Foucault, M. 1977. *Discipline and Punish*. New York: Pantheon.

Fraser, N. 1989. *Unruly Practices: Power, Discourse and Gender in Contemporary Social Theory*. Minneapolis: University of Minnesota Press.

Garfinkel, H. 1967. *Studies in Ethnomethodology*. Englewood Cliffs, NJ: Prentice-Hall.

Habermas, J. 1984. *The Theory of Communicative Action*, Vol. 1. Boston: Beacon Press.

———. 1987. *The Theory of Communicative Action*. Vol. 2, Boston: Beacon Press.

Horkheimer, M. and T. W. Adorno. 1972. *Dialectic of Enlightenment*. New York: Herder and Herder.

Institute for Social Research. 1972. *Aspects of Sociology*. Boston: Beacon.

Kellner, D. 1989. *Critical Theory, Marxism and Modernity*. Baltimore: Johns Hopkins University Press.

Klein, J. 1990. *Interdisciplinarity: History, Theory and Practice*. Detroit: Wayne State University Press.

Lyotard, J.-F. 1984. *The Postmodern Condition: A Report on Knowledge*. Minneapolis: University of Minnesota Press.

Marcuse, H. 1964. *One-Dimensional Man*. Boston: Beacon Press.

McDaniel, S. A. and B. Agger. 1982. *Social Problems through Conflict and Order*. Toronto: Addison-Wesley.

Offe, C. 1985. *Disorganized Capitalism*. Cambridge, MA: MIT Press.

O'Neill, J. 1972. *Sociology as a Skin Trade*. New York: Harper and Row.

Paci, E. 1972. *The Function of the Sciences and the Meaning of Man*. Evanston, IL: Northwestern University Press.

Parsons, T. 1951. *The Social System*. Glencoe, IL: Free Press.

Piccone, P. 1971. "Phenomenological Marxism." *Telos* 9:3–31.

Richardson, L. 1990. *Writing Strategies: Reaching Diverse Audiences*. Newbury Park, CA: Sage.

Ryan, M. 1982. *Marxism and Deconstruction*. Baltimore: Johns Hopkins University Press.

Schneider, J. W. 1985. "Social Problems Theory: The Constructionist View." Pp. 209–29 in *Annual Review of Sociology*, Vol. 11, edited by R. H. Turner and J. F. Short. Palo Alto, CA: Annual Reviews.

Schutz, A. 1967. *Phenomenology of the Social World*. Evanston, IL: Northwestern University Press.

Spector, M. and J. I. Kitsuse. [1977] 1987. *Constructing Social Problems*. Hawthorne, NY: Aldine de Gruyter.

15

Twenty-Two Theses on Social Constructionism: A Feminist Response to Ibarra and Kitsuse's "Proposal for the Study of Social Problems"

Avery F. Gordon

I

Present and absent at the same time, for feminism, marginality is not only a question of borderlines and frames, but a function of how we are accounted for in the economy of source and authority, which cites knowledge into being real, useful, and authoritative. Nagging, repetitive complaining constrains feminists to repetitively assert the ground zero of our positions, often preventing us from getting anywhere else. "What woman writer wants to say . . . that men still aren't reading feminist work?; that women are being 'left out again'" (Morris 1988, p. 11)? What woman wants to be accused of being vulgar for being so assertively repetitive?[1]

II

Being angry about having to begin again and again by saying that gender and race are, among other things, epistemological categories that affect what we know, how we know it, and what we do with what we know when that is only the first step to saying anything specific can make you crazy and make you start having imaginary conversations with your interlocutors. You imagine yourself shouting: ghosts in the house, skeletons in the closet, unseen forces broadcasting, large white men in uniform with guns, invisible hands across the globe, polar bears in the zoo (Williams 1991, p. 202–15), contracts and property and markets and profits and the color line . . . . while they quietly write it all down preparing to report to someone else (somewhat) like you how "members" of your group make claims. Not ones to pass judgment in public, you imagine that any interaction with them would end in a white line of typologies and abstractions in which you would probably look like a nice specimen of a more or less sympathetic hysterical counterclaimant. You know you are not acting like any hysterical claimant, but like a hysterical woman, and are momentarily grateful if they don't call you that in public. This kind of conversation is unhealthy and professionally immodest, so you materialize a different kind of imaginary conversation.

III

In the 1990s, social constructionism may very well turn out to be neo-objectivism. Rather than extending constructivist questions of narrative structuring, fictive composition, and historical provisionality of claims to knowledge, neo-objectivism treats the powerful discursive field in which social reality and social problems are constructed and deconstructed as a transparent object available to the independent, but professionally employed, sociologist. Neo-objectivism understands how the "real" is a fiction (or creative construction) that is experienced as true, but it does not recognize that constructionists and the people they study are subject to the multiple determinations and sites of power in which narratives of and about social problems are produced and disseminated.

Ibarra and Kitsuse critique and dismiss the "normative" constructionists' claim to independently and objectively describe and analyze the reality of constructed social problems in favor of independently and objectively describing how "members" discourse social problems. They argue that discourse is and can be separated from what they call social conditions; they also argue that discourse *analysis* is and can be separated from an analysis of social conditions. Ibarra and Kitsuse do not believe that normative constructionists can be objective in the analysis of social conditions (partially because there are no strictly objective social conditions, and partially because these constructionists tend to recognize and acknowledge a social problem when something troubles them and/or society), but they do believe that constructionists can be objective in the analysis of discourse.

According to Ibarra and Kitsuse, normative constructionists believe they "can 'objectively' (and independently of members) view 'social conditions' and designate them social problems." This is a problematic position, which they propose to correct.

In contrast to normative constructionists, Ibarra and Kitsuse argue that there are *effectively* no analyzable social problems apart from what is produced by interpretive intersubjective discourse. Social problems "points to *that class of social interactions* consisting of members' analytically paraphrasable means for formulating, describing, interpreting, and evaluating a symbolically constructed and morally charged intersubjective existence." It is through discourse or rhetorical idioms that "members as perceiving subjects [are] actively engaged in constructing social conditions (or 'putative conditions') as moral objects." Normative constructionists marginalize discourse, or what Ibarra and Kitsuse call "definitional processes," in favor of "the 'more important' questions regarding the scope, magnitude, causes, and consequences of the social problem itself."

Although Ibarra and Kitsuse argue that neither they nor Spector and Kitsuse ([1977] 1987), "offer a rival explanation for a commonly defined subject matter," one of their primary concerns is that the "concept of social problems [is] without theoretical precision or scope." The definition of social problems and the interactionist program they propose amount to no less than an argument for what should count as a social problem:

> We argue for a different subject matter for the sociology of social problems . . . . [where] definitional activities are central to the subject matter, and precedence should be given to members' interpretive practices *inasmuch as social problems are possible strictly as assemblages of the member's perspective.* (emphasis added)

Such an argument can be viewed as an accounting procedure whereby designations or definitions constitute credits and debits. Everything hinges on what remains their unarticulated calculation of how much and in what way "social problems are possible strictly as assemblages of the member's perspective." "Inasmuch" is what Ibarra and Kitsuse bracket, or put under erasure. Consequently, as I argue below, the traces of this missing calculation come back to haunt their model persistently.

Normative constructionists marginalize discourse, according to Ibarra and Kitsuse, because they think a social problem exists when they can ecognize a "disjunction between a norm-based conception of 'society' and a state of affairs presumably antithetical to these norms and values." Because normative constructionists can only recognize a social problem when they perceive a troubling contradiction, they tend to be invested in and make judgments about what people think and do; some of them also make judgments about what's wrong with society and how those wrongs might be improved. Ibarra and Kitsuse do not see any "*theoret-*

ical rationale for employing or embedding such judgments in our analytical renditions of the member's perspective," although they do believe that "sociologists have . . . . [a] 'right' to their evaluations about those they study as well as a right to consider this or that morally offensive." This distinction between theory and politics is key to Ibarra and Kitsuse's model. Politics, or evaluative analysis, is private; it is what the constructionist can do after work, so to speak. It has no place in the actual production of knowledge, or "analytical renditions," which must be dependent on a mode of production (or a methodology) that insists on its neutrality or indifference to politics, critical judgment, or standpoint.

Ibarra and Kitsuse suggest that members distinguish between "a norm-based conception of 'society' and a state of affairs presumably antithetical to these norms and values" in the discursive construction of moral objects or social problems that are objectively real (to them). Constructionists, however, should know that there are no objective social conditions or social problems, only "putative" ones produced within an interactive language game. Thus, constructionists cannot "objectively" view constructed social conditions. For Ibarra and Kitsuse, imputing objectivity to constructions is a form of ontological gerrymandering; ontological gerrymandering produces a logical paradox wherein claims made about one so-called reality (the social problem) are not equally made about another (the account of the social problem). Ibarra and Kitsuse suggest the avoidance of ontological gerrymandering can be accomplished by objective description and classification of intersubjective discourse into various rhetorical idioms.

Because discourse or definitional process is the only thing constructionists can count on in a socially constructed world; because constructionists should avoid making judgments about the nature and resolution of social problems, or more precisely, moral objects; because constructionists should avoid critical analysis that challenges members' perspectives; and because description appears to be the only methodology available to the sociologist that eschews critique, evaluation, and "'making moves' in the social problems . . . game," Ibarra and Kitsuse's version of social constructionism is actually a form of neo-objectivism. Neo-objectivism involves conceiving social conditions as discursively produced or constructed while at the same time objectifying discourse by treating it as an object available for independent empirical scrutiny. It would be more accurate to say that Ibarra and Kitsuse's proposal substitutes discourse or definitional processes for the normative constructionist's social conditions. Where the normative constructionist can claim to determine whether a social problem is objectively a problem or not, Ibarra and Kitsuse can claim to objectively render the discursive. The discursive can be rendered objectively because in Ibarra and Kitsuse's model it exists independently of those forces that unite the constructionist and his or her object of analysis. The issue here is not objectification in the existentialist sense: All representations, including scientific and feminist ones, objectify (or turn into objects for analysis) complex and heterogeneous processes and relations. Objectification in this sense is an inevitable feature of social life. The question is rather "Why would we want to retreat into the transparency of the discursive when the central thrust of Ibarra and Kitsuse's theoretical project is to question the transparency of "social conditions"?

IV

Neo-objectivism, unlike objectivism, grants the discursive a determining role in the making of empirical realities. It claims that social reality does not exist objectively apart from the discourse that describes it. However, neo-objectivism, like objectivism, claims it can objectively render the discursive. In Ibarra and Kitsuse's version, this claim is made possible by two moves. First, the discursive is decontextualized from the social relations with which it reciprocally interacts. Second, and similarly, the constructionist is decontextualized by his or her presumed neutrality and separation from the site where social problems are constructed—the "member's" epistemological and practical world.[2]

Ibarra and Kitsuse's proposal promotes a topical and subject-centered view of social problems by focusing on how people "dynamically" and interactively engage in and constructively produce what counts as a social problem for them. Their model draws attention to some of the micrological processes by which everyday life seems to proceed insofar as it reminds those constructionists wedded to a strictly macrological approach that forces, conditions, contexts, sociohistorical circumstances are, conceptually speaking, structures that are often invisible in and of themselves, even if their effects are brutally material. Ibarra and Kitsuse, in my opinion, rightly foreground the meaningful nature of agent's activities and their focus on "rationality from within" is an important counterposition to models of false consciousness that unnecessarily assume a corrective stance. As an aside, it is worth noting, however, that characteristic of the social problems tradition are researchers *who view themselves and are viewed* as members of a "social problems" community. Being an interested insider may help explain the presumption of these researchers to correct, to "tell the truth". As members, they do conceive of themselves as having the right and the responsibility to tell what they believe to be true as part of their contribution to resolving the problem in question. Indeed, professional knowledge workers are often asked to contribute their expertise precisely because it is so valued (or over-valued) in the public claims-making arena. Within the community itself, members' claims are often tested against what counts as a persuasively rhetorical and affective position. In this sense members' claims-making is always "propositions" tested against the prevailing understanding of operative social conditions. In this context, "correction" is neither the only option available nor does it carry the same punitive force that outsider corrections might. Debate and strategizing generally will not proceed without an elaboration of the "standards by which [correctives are] judged [to be] evident."

Ibarra and Kitsuse's proposal encourages the social problem re-searcher to respectfully investigate what matters to people and they believe that what matters, sociologically speaking, is what people say.[3] Not only are these sayings "artful," but they also represent, for Ibarra and Kitsuse, "different [and legitimate] kinds of knowledge." As they expand the intelligence community by including "*anyone* [who] engages in *proposing or contesting* the designation of a category of putative behav-iors, expressions, or processes as offensive," so too do they hope to "refrain from tacitly privileging the status of . . . . scientists' versions."

But these proposals and contestations are themselves part of a power-laden world that articulates itself and its divisions in both what is said and what is not. By delimiting the social problems field to what certain unmarked members (which is a rather weak operationalization of the social group) say, Ibarra and Kitsuse have no way of contextualizing or explaining how this talk and its rhetorical forms are produced, or what its meanings signify in the social accounts ledger. Their phenomenologi-cal/ethnomethodological orientation prevents them from recognizing that "cognitive [or rhetorical] structures which social agents implement in their practical knowledge of the social world are internalized, 'embod-ied' social structures" (Bourdieu, cited in Chartier 1988, p. 44). Such representational structures, as discourse, however are never simply the result of external or crude material determinations: They become the constituent features of social reality (p. 44). As Clifford Geertz suggests, to deny hierarchical structuration "risks seeing the social domain dis-solve into the meanings that are given it by social agents through their theoretical or practical knowledge of it" (Chartier 1988, p. 48). It seems banal to add that this is true for the researcher him- or herself. So that although Ibarra and Kitsuse seem to define the field of social problems so as to deauthorize the cultural capital of professional expertise that ostensibly possesses the power to know when a problem really exists or not, the very definition and delimitation of the site of the construction of social problems produces the opposite result.

The epistemology embedded in Ibarra and Kitsuse's proposal presumes that discourse is *not* in the world and "objectively" so—*not* part of the relations of power that produce and constrain discourse, *and* discursively enable and limit social conditions. For example, in criticizing the "ad hoc manner" in which "social conditions" are "typically group[ed] . . . . under the rubric 'social problems,'" Ibarra and Kitsuse ask the following question: "For is anything added to the study of deviant behavior by *calling* it a social problem? Do we increase our understanding of crime or poverty by *calling* it a social problem?" (emphasis added). I would argue that much is gained, including the very possibility that sociology could distinguish itself from psychology and transcendental philosophy. What is gained is a recognition that individuals are not "bad" or "good" except in relation to a historical normalization process that helps to explain why certain behaviors are commonsensically, legally, rhetorically, and psychically known and often experienced as deviations from a presumed norm. To identify so-called deviant behaviors as social problems points our attention to an investigation of the norms themselves and to our collective responsibility for maintaining and reproducing them; to an analysis of who systematically embodies the normal and who does not; to an analysis of the historical and social embeddedness and constructedness of normality and discourse; and finally, to a refusal to assume as inevitable the taken-for-granted, in other words, to an analysis of alternatives that could structure the possibility of changing norms and behaviors.

Ultimately, Ibarra and Kitsuse separate discourse and power to differentiate member and analyst. Differentiation provides the distance (the gap) necessary for the researcher to experience that he is ultimately *not* enmeshed in this same power/knowledge world, not also stuck in language and in institutions or settings that produce the very conditions of possibility for what he will see or will *not see*.[4] What gives the constructionist this special privilege of transcendence that the "member" does not have? Policing the borders between subjects and objects, between the constructionist and her objects/subjects of analysis, Ibarra and Kitsuse protect the constructionist from the "mundane," from precisely the (epistemological, if not practical) impossibility of distinguishing between a condition and a construction. If the mundane is where social problems are produced and thus where their articulation can be discovered, protection from the mundane turns out to mean protection from the social problems arena itself.

One way in which the constructionist's transcendence is secured is through his belief that he can objectively and neutrally, as if separate from the very construction process, render talk, "the meanings that are given by social agents," as the real social problems process. This claim reflects a fear that constructionists might confuse themselves with the people they study, and a fear that they might "'make moves' in the social problems language game." In order to prevent such a "fusion" and to keep constructionists out of the social problems arena as players, two key distinctions are made by Ibarra and Kitsuse, which enforce the presumption that neutrality is both possible and disinterested.

First, according to Ibarra and Kitsuse, "members" speak in vernacular; sociologists in "analytical constructs." Vernacular is the raw material; analytical constructs, or theory, what the constructionist uses to process the data. Vernacular is not considered theoretical in the sense that it represents the world to its speakers, representing at the same time a web of intertextual assumptions, values, beliefs, and theories that are available for analysis based on these same theories or based on alternative ones. Neither is vernacular viewed as being a sophisticated textual/ritual production comprised of all kinds of analytical constructs also available for analysis whether or not the speaker can tell you what they are. For Ibarra and Kitsuse, there is a "basic distinction between vernacular resources and analytical constructs," a distinction between those who possess theory and those who do not. They are adamant that the "fusion of mundane and theoretical perspectives" is an illegitimate boundary crossing. Maintaining the distance necessary for treating others as available for objective description is impossible if members are theorists and sociologists are vernacularists in essentially the same ways. Ibarra and Kitsuse at once privilege theory by making it the distinctive mark of the professional and at the same time withhold it from the very people who are seemingly the center-stage subjects of social problems discourse.

Second, in the possession of the constructionist is a theory that enables him or her to see the distinction between mundane epistemology and professional epistemology. This distinction is at the heart of the paradox that Ibarra and Kitsuse's model confronts: While "members" believe that they "'objectively' view 'social conditions' [which they] designate . . . . social problems—by virtue of their recognition of a disjunction between a norm-based conception of society and a state of affairs presumably antithetical to those norms and values," constructionists know that objective social conditions are really just constructions ("putative conditions"), which other people experience as real and true. Implicit in this distinction is the imputation that constructionists (and professional knowledge workers in general) are different than the people they study: We know something fundamental about the nature of social reality that they don't. Ibarra and Kitsuse's researcher *"accepts the members' constructions of putative conditions as 'objects in the world'"* because while the constructionist may be smarter than the member about how things really are, describing people's mundane epistemology (or mistakes) is a legitimate job that meets the criteria for nonevaluative description of independent claims.

Another way to put this point would be to offer a different conception of "acceptance" than what I take to be essentially a form of consumption. To accept another's constructions as objective (as having the force of an acknowledged reality) could mean treating what people think as worthy of debate, argumentation, and critique. It could mean respecting others enough to engage with them on the merits, implications, and even weaknesses of their position. It could mean treating all claims, including our own, as partial and provisional, but subject to both critical scrutiny and reciprocal exchange. It could mean acknowledging and acting on the understanding that "others" have a strategy toward us. It is in this spirit that I ask of Ibarra and Kitsuse to answer more adequately the question: what is wrong with critique?

V

Neo-objectivism implies a managerial ethos. It involves assumptions that justify not simply an insight, but an *oversight* that escapes the limitation of standpoint, the contradictions of the mundane, and the "properties of the relations of ruling" (Smith 1990) that are articulated and imprinted in and through discourse. Neo-objectivism has to manage the implications of its epistemological insights and it does so by managerialism.

Constructionism, as an epistemological characterization of the fabricated nature of social reality, or social problems, tells us little about those constructions if it cannot account for why some and not others predominate; if it cannot link origin and social implication. When the analyst is presumed not only to be a socially dislocated (and therefore disinterested) observer, but also exempt from the very construction process itself, a kind of critical paralysis sets in that transforms the epistemological insight into a crisis of professional authorization: What can I say that's true? In Ibarra and Kitsuse's model, screening the borders between competing authorities (member and analyst) leads to a crisis situation in which the constructionist is empowered and disempowered simultaneously. On the one hand, the constructionist has so much power that even the slightest acknowledgment of our inevitable desires, investments, structural interests, cathexes, judgments, moral evaluations, or critical theories—the whole apparatus of our mode of production—can contaminate the very social problems process itself. On the other hand, we are so powerless to offer potent, albeit partial and provisional, statements about the nature and consequences of social problems themselves that we must refrain from even broaching that which appears irretrievable as object(ive).

The resolution of this crisis is managerialism. Separate from the messy world of production, as a manager I can at least supervise my own uncertainties and the myriad constructions within my domain. Ibarra and Kitsuse's researcher becomes a manager or an administrator of other people's discourses and worlds because insight is only ever a function of oversight. Objectivity, as it takes the form of nonevaluative descriptive knowledge, is based on a particular kind of corporation, or incorporation: an agency cut off from the very mode of production that makes oversight a seemingly neutral project. Ibarra and Kitsuse's researcher is ultimately responsible only to this corporate agency, which amounts to a set of bureaucratic operating procedures that always seem to come from somewhere else. The manager is not a producer: He is only ever the living alibi for the invisibility of the mode of production.

As an analytics, managerialism can be humane. And Ibarra and Kitsuse's analyst is a human relations manager. At the heart of their social problems world, ordinary people are hurting or wanting in relation to problems that feel morally or politically meaningful to them. Nonevaluative description and classification of how people are talking about that which is problematic for them could be thought to be a benign, yet responsibly indifferent response. But it is nonetheless the response of the manager, and not the critic whose obligation is precisely to transform the oversight authority of the professional into insights that not only can show what discourse is or means to individuals or groups, but can also analyze the complicated conditions that inform such discourse. These analyses involve the researcher willy-nilly in the construction of social problems.

VI

Hiding inevitable judgments and values about the nature of social problems behind neutral description; excising any discussion of the power field in which discourse occurs and to which it contributes; leaving both researcher and "member" unmarked by these very power relations; foregrounding language and discourse but eviscerating them of their material constitution and effectivity; and positing a free market where there is power and unequal access to resources, reality construction, and truth-making (see theses 12–15) do not help to foster a critical sociological research agenda for investigating, evoking, and analyzing the complex conditions and realities of that which is (and is not) socially problematic.

The project for studying social problems Ibarra and Kitsuse propose, not only for themselves, but for all of us who could claim an interest in social problems, represents a quiet and polite assault on feminist and other explicitly "interested" social and cultural studies. It is a model for building a research machine that forecloses new technologies for investigating important questions of power, which could displace the binary and limiting oppositions between discourse and social relations of power, between agents/subjects and institutional structures, and between the researcher and their subject/object of investigation.[5] In the context of current neoconservative critiques of interested scholarship in the university, their model promotes a technocratic intellectual ethos where the researcher/scholar eschews not only intervention (in the traditional activist sense), but also eschews acknowledgment (and therefore debate) of her or his partial (but "objectively" meaningful) positions for a moderate, managerial description of problems that primarily occur elsewhere. In the context of increased social immiseration and public crisis, their model effectively abandons the intellectual's responsibility for the knowledge she or he produces.

VII

There is a stronger thesis. The production of neutral, objective knowledge unmarked by the complex condition of its production is impossible. The promotion of such a project is a social and intellectual problem. It is a problem because it ignores the social relations of power and pleasure that inform and structure our work—the knowledge we produce. It is a problem because it enforces the banishment of critique, of politics, of the necessity of justifying our claims and arguing their merits. It is not a matter of separating knowledge from politics by making knowledge public and politics private: by entitling the researcher to an opinion or a judgment that is a civic right, but not an analytically salient condition. Nor is it a matter of arguing that neutral knowledge, once produced, can be used for political purposes. Claims to neutral knowledge are political precisely because they claim to be outside the world that made them. Only those privileged *to experience themselves* unconstrained by world-making forces could be assured they have no standpoint that matters, that is a material constituent of knowledge. Authority and the signs of social location are masked only when they are so totally disavowed. The professional authority of the knowledge worker, and especially the sociologist, rests on the always elusive possibility of objectivism, of being able to transform what is only ever critical distance into the real. One way to manage the impossibility of neutrality is through pluralism. This is essentially Ibarra and Kitsuse's method. A different form of managing this problem, a problem that goes to the heart of the seriously problematic and complicated nature of our work, that is, constructing accounts of already constructed and deconstructed worlds, is through politics or ethics. As Patricia Hill Collins (1989) suggests, analytical adequacy can only result from ethical theorizing. Such ethical theorizing is neither individualistic, nor situated in a "relativistic framework" of equally competing ethics (p. 89). Ethical theorizing is situated, minimally, within the "unequal power relations among constructionists": one aspect of its job is managing the relationship between the determination of that which is socially problematic and the source of prevailing ethics (p. 90).

VIII

Social constructionism, broadly speaking, has been an important feminist theory and methodology for denaturalizing social and so-called personal problems. The feminist project is driven by critique and a desire to transform the social relations of power that construct and deconstruct the world and its inhabitants in particular ways. Giving notice to the nonnatural, nonessential, and fundamentally social nature of arrangements, institutions, bodies, knowledges, desires, and so on, has allowed feminists to make visible how we and things are engendered, in the multiple sense of that term. Visibility, however, is a complicated phenomenon entirely bound up with the available and dominant technologies of representation and the social and "personal" forms invisibility takes. *Visibility is a complex system of permission and prohibition, of presence and absence, punctuated alternately by apparitions and hysterical blindness* (Kipnis 1988, p. 158).

IX

It has therefore been important for feminists to try to evocatively describe how *specific* people, who may or may not experience themselves as members of groups, express their concerns. (Indeed, we may very well want to know how their multiple locations and identities collide and coalesce.) But it is equally important for us to critically analyze those expressions as themselves symptomatic of the "constraints" that Ibarra and Kitsuse say have to do with "politics and poetics." Constraints are understood here as both prohibitive and productive, as both constraining and enabling, as both "outside" and "inside" us. We tend to ask questions like: Where does the language that people speak and the ideas that are conveyed by that language come from? What if language speaks us just as often as we speak it? What if language is anything but simply the words it speaks? What if "analytically para-phras[ing]" is a complicated process of translation, involving the re-searcher in rituals of writing and storytelling? If words and things and passions and pains and pleasures and injuries and investments and in-differences come partially and unevenly in relation to what Ibarra and Kitsuse call "condition-categories," isn't it important to investigate those conditions? For example, in their discussion of the rhetorical idiom of endangerment, Ibarra and Kitsuse argue that

> claims are most idiomatic, i.e., suasive, when it is evident that medical judgment has taken precedence over moral judgement since the under-standing of the body that is grounded in scientific knowledge is presumed to be both impartial and more factual, hence demonstrably superior to views generated by moral beliefs.

If this presumption is a condition-category itself, isn't it important to know who presumes this, why, since when, and to what effect?

X

Just what exactly is a social problem? What do we call that which is not a social problem? What are social problems that have not gained public currency? Investigating the constraints and conditions in which some things become socially problematic and others do not helps to explain not only what is, but what can be. Sociologically oriented feminists write histories of the present because they are invested in the future and because they are full of passion for arguing about differences and for the difference a feminist vision of social justice entails. A history of the present, which could be considered the sociologist's special province, is always a project looking toward the future. To write a history of the present requires stretching toward the horizon of what can't been seen with ordinary clarity yet. And to stretch toward and beyond a horizon requires a particular kind of perception where what's transparent and what's in the shadows put each other into crisis. As an ethnographic project, the desire to inscribe the present within the past tense points to the rhetorical and experiential form ideological interpellation takes— "we have *already* understood"—and to the challenge of imagining be-yond the limits of what is already *understandable* in a given social time and space.

XI

With all due respect to Ibarra and Kitsuse, some of us already understand that we are in an "articulation contest . . . . to establish what the social problem is 'really about.'" We already understand that many claims seem "readable at a glance," even if some claims never get a look, and even if some claims are barely audible stutters while others consist of deafening sounds. We already understand that the social problems process (which is hardly just a "language game") involves "interpretation and reinterpretation," disputing aims, shifting players, diverse settings, and unstable claims. And we also understand that a seemingly epistemologically fragile reality feels solid, real, and about life and death issues. What we don't understand as well, and what Ibarra and Kitsuse's proposal is less helpful in explaining, is why certain groups of people historically and systematically have the power to "win" in this process. Do they simply possess a surfeit of appropriate rhetorical strategies?

XII

Asking the "why" question is antidescriptive and maybe even anti-American.

Ibarra and Kitsuse take as a theoretical given what could be construed as a major social problem and symptomatically evade the exclusionary logic of both linguistic and sociopolitical economies. What their model assumes is that there are many different interests and "moral objects" that contest one another in a kind of social problems marketplace. Since there is no discussion of unequal access to the resources of *rhetorical* contestation (and remember they are not concerned with the problems themselves, however they are conceived and by whom, only with the claims process) Ibarra and Kitsuse seem to suggest that this is a free market, constrained only by the (seemingly outer space) limits of "society's classification system." The social researcher enters this pluralistic marketplace only to describe the rhetorics, counterrhetorics, motifs, and settings that constitute the market. The constructionist should not pass judgment on people who are making moral judgments, or be or get involved in the claims-making process. The constructionist needs to be especially careful not to confuse "mundane" and "theoretical" perspectives.

What Ibarra and Kitsuse take as given—a chaotic, mediated, and mediatized political arena that has become the site of a proliferation of claims about interests and morality—is a social problem ripe for socio-logical investigation. Why does political discourse take place in moral and rhetorical terms (see Brown 1991)? Is this true of American political discourse historically? Is there something different about "now" that might tell us why we should be especially concerned with style, sur-faces, forms, and rhetorics (see Pfohl, in this volume)? To treat a political problem as a phenomenological truth is to enact a symptomatic detour around just those issues of power the descriptive accuracy aggressively renders explicit.

Equally important is Ibarra and Kitsuse's argument that researchers' de-scriptions of equally competing positions and languages do not involve them in taking a position, or in making a judgment, or in excluding some other, or other story. The perspective Ibarra and Kitsuse promote recog-nizes that "some styles seem to carry the day" and that "studying alterna-tive or 'oppositional' styles" is important for a "comparative" view of the marketplace. But they do not view *their* comparative perspective as a position. Within American society, this is a position. We call it liberal pluralism. Liberalism presumes that everyone has an equal opportuni-ty of speaking, of being heard, of acquiring resources for mobilization; that the "best man"/position wins by virtue of some invisible hand that guides the competition to a provisional close. In the technocratic ver-sion of liberal theory, to be an interested citizen at work involves what C. Wright Mills called "simply understanding." Mills also thought that "simply understanding" was a peculiarly professional middle-class form of assumed powerlessness through self-censorship (Mills [1944] 1979, pp. 292–304). What's wrong with critique?

XIII

Even to simply analyze "verbal transactions" within a "linguistic mar-ket" must involve an analysis of the market itself:

> The linguistic market can no more be a "free" one than any other market, for verbal agents do not characteristically enter it from positions of equal advantage or conduct their transactions on an equal footing. On the con-trary, not only can and will that market, like any other, be rigged by those with the power and interest to do so, but, no less significantly, it always interacts with *other* economies, including social and political ones. Individ-ual verbal transactions are always constrained, therefore, by the nature of the social and political relationships that *otherwise* obtain between the par-ties involved, including their nonsymmetrical obligations to and claims upon one another by virtue of their nonequivalent roles in those relation-

ships, as well as by relations *within* the transaction itself. (Herrnstein
Smith 1988, p. 108)

Herrnstein Smith's argument suggests that the missing "rationale" for
judgment in Ibarra and Kitsuse's vision is available in the inevitability of
the "constraints" and "nonsymmetrical obligations . . . . and claims" on
and within "verbal transactions." If the linguistic market is not "free,"
but "rigged," only an analysis of those riggings will explain what has
been transacted and why. If the linguistic market is never on its own, but
always interacting with other economies, isolating it will only foster
continued unequal market relations, or, communicative utopia. Only a
critique of the taken-for-granted freedom and independence of markets
or economies enables the possibility of conceiving social exchange as
other than the exchange of unequal positions masquerading as freedom.

XIV

The markings, however faint, of gender, race, and class are the
signposts to rigged markets.
   This reminds me of a real estate developer I met recently. A passionate
man whose belief in the free enterprise system was bold and compas-
sionate, his discourse about the shopping mall he was building was
without doubt a moral one. Equally committed to private profit and
public good, he gave a rousing speech one evening on the merits and
ethical preferability of the market logic of American democracy. Any
group, large or small, powerful or powerless, can enter the lobbying
arena and win their solution to their articulated claims, he said. While I
was deciding whether it was polite to dissent from my host's opinions,
his wife, herself in the real estate business (albeit not a developer),
simply asked: Why don't you tell them how much you had to pay to get
in to see your congressional representative? This question did not phase
him in the least. His unflappable response speaks to the accuracy of one
way of interpreting the *absence* of an analysis of "rigged" markets in
Ibarra and Kitsuse's model: The problem of unequal access to sites of
power and to powerful "members" of public decision-making bodies is
not a social problem for this man or his fellow compatriots in the Devel-
opers Association. Where Ibarra and Kitsuse err is to imply that there is
simply another side or two that frame a debate or a social problems
discourse about development, or democracy, or public housing, or commodity capitalism, or the political economy of husbands and wives, or
. . . . More than just sides in a rhetorical contest, these positions consti-

tute the materiality of discourse. What is unequally exchanged are the worlds that make discourse.

When social problems are disassociated from systematic structures of power, all that is left are strongly held moral goods and bads, absolute choices in the supermarket of publicly acceptable and commonsensically secured problems. As a researcher, as a feminist, as any number of names that might sign my concern with rigged markets, one social problem here is that all the rational and irrational arguments the three of us listening could muster did not shake the moral utopianism (Baudrillard 1988, pp. 75–105) that alibis for the exercise of American power both at home and abroad. This is a problem some people (and I count myself among them) want to do something about. We do have a public and a professional interest in the outcome of this man's talk, his shopping center, and how his economic power within his family licenses and does not license his wife to speak and act.

XV

One of the most significant contributions of feminist theory and practice has been to address the implications of rigged markets by showing how the so-called public and private are fully imbricated with one another, forming an unstable hierarchy in which both terms of the opposition continually subvert one another (Williams 1991; Pateman 1989). Some feminist scholars have tried to resist making the professional equivalent to the private and in turn setting the public world of interested citizenship against the seemingly uninterested citizenship of the private (or even public) university.

Later in the conversation, "the developer's wife" argued strongly that she did not consider herself represented either by her congressman or senator, or by various lobbying groups. Why? She didn't know to what group she belonged. She was economically invested in the ability of the Developer's Association to articulate and win their claims; her everyday existence hinged on her husband being a winner. For twenty years, she was a single mother raising two children as a secretary, then as a real estate agent. This marriage had changed her class position and she was acutely aware of the fragility of her recent upward mobility. Yet she was in no way morally invested in that kind of development, and indeed spoke eloquently of wanting an alternative to competitive capitalism for herself and her children. This was a personal and a social problem for her, which she expressed as the problem of not knowing where she belonged exactly; unable to become a member of an antidevelopment group, for example, she had no "real" access to belonging somewhere public. The complexity of this woman's situation is not part of the existing public discourse, except when "it" becomes a sign of public apathy, counted up in opinion polls that market Americans to themselves. She, and the many others like her, principally affect the terms of social problems discourse by their invisibility and silence.

XVI

Visibility is a complex system of permission and prohibition, of presence and absence, punctuated alternately by apparitions and hysterical blindness (Kipnis 1988, p. 158).

How would Ibarra and Kitsuse find her? She is not a member of a group whose talk or writing constitute public claims and counterclaims. What methodology would they employ to find this woman's talk and the larger discourse that it silently haunts? Ibarra and Kitsuse leave several serious methodological questions unattended: What motivates their research, such that they would even know to look for this woman, or anyone "missing"? How will the social history of missing persons impact who gets counted as a member and influence what group membership is named as salient? How would they distinguish between oral texts and written texts? Can they find the traces of the unwritten and unspoken? Will they count or account for those forces that make her rhetoric available or unavailable to herself and others, including us?

XVII

Hysterical blindness to apparitions and to the complex systems of permissions and prohibitions can be a symptom of the loss of the legitimating function of the empirical couple: I see/I know.

What would Ibarra and Kitsuse's constructionist do with her, if they found her? What would they think they knew when they were finished investigating her claims? An analysis of her talk in her living room would indeed demonstrate that her claims are made in more or less the language that is available to her from newspapers, television, magazines, books, neighbors, friends, family members, and so on. In that specific setting, these languages also repeated themselves sometimes in the kind of rhetorical idioms Ibarra and Kitsuse describe. But the overwhelming issue of importance *to her* was precisely what Ibarra and Kitsuse describe as constitutive of the social problems process itself, yet what also deauthorizes "the normative conception" of social constructionism: that a "disjunction between a norm-based conception of 'society' and a state of affairs . . . . antithetical to those norms and values" forms the moral objectivity around which a social problem is felt and articulated to be true.

This woman confounds the split between definitional processes and social conditions that structures the entire logic of Ibarra and Kitsuse's model. For her, "definitional processes" were neither "marginal" to, nor autonomous from, the "'important' questions regarding the scope, magnitude, causes, and consequences of the social problem itself." The definitional processes were part and parcel of a specifically gendered, raced, and classed social problem requiring analysis; they were already constructed social conditions bearing the weight of an object. Only a gender-, race-, and class-conscious epistemology would enable Ibarra and Kitsuse to recognize that only *certain* "members [of society] . . . . do not *typically* refer to their own acts of definition and evaluation." Only a gender-, race-, and class-conscious epistemology would enable Ibarra and Kitsuse to recognize that for certain members of society "objects and their qualities [*do not*] have an existence independent of their apprehension." Only a gender-, race-, and class-conscious epistemology would enable Ibarra and Kitsuse to acknowledge that only certain members of society have the right to separate words and things as if the mundane were their unquestioned prerogative. *Noninterpretive devices, extrinsic sources, and intuitive means of reading may be the only ways to include the reality of the unwritten, unnamed, nontext of race [and gender]* (Williams 1991, p. 117).

XVIII

Socially constructed worlds, problems, and persons are haunted by the shadows and ghosts of these constructions. This is a social problem. An *account* of socially constructed worlds, problems, and persons is also haunted by the shadows and ghosts of its constructions. This is a related social problem. A concern with that which shadows or haunts what is already constructed can guide an effort to participate in the reinvention of a sociological tradition of social problems research by exploring the disciplinary consequences of developing new methods for analyzing visible and invisible forms of social injury and pleasure. The theory of the ghostly haunt (Gordon 1990), which looks to locate the ways in which complicated relations of power symptomatically announce themselves in the signs of the gaps between what is said and what is not, and between what is marked and what is not, may help to address the question of how to write descriptively evocative and analytically critical stories about various forms of systematically gendered and racialized injury and identity within a rapidly changing social field.

This project differs radically from Ibarra and Kitsuse's, not because it claims that some things are real and others are constructed. Like Ibarra and Kitsuse's, it sees the social world and its inhabitants as socially constructed even when it feels like it is not. It differs from Ibarra and Kitsuse's proposal in the assumptions and questions that provisionally guide its work and that contingently secure its claims. One of these assumptions is that power and knowledge are intricately and intimately imbricated with one another. One of its questions has been to ask how treating the ghost or the ghostly haunt as a case could help understand how marginality and invisibility are figured and lived. One of its methods has been to attempt to develop a methodology that can foreground the memories of the conditions under which the facts and the real story are produced. Can the social problems tradition cohabit with the project of writing ghost stories? I hope so. Because to write stories concerning exclusions and invisibilities is to write ghost stories. To write ghost stories implies that ghosts are "real," that is to say, that they produce material effects. To impute a certain kind of empiricity to ghosts implies that, from certain subject positions, the relations of visibility and invisibility, or appearance and disappearance, involve a constant negotiation of what can be seen and what's in the shadows.

XIX

A different language and a different frame are needed than those Ibarra and Kitsuse offer to even begin the work of "reconceptualizing from 'objective truth' to rhetorical event" in such a way as to "foster a more nuanced sense of . . . . social responsibility" (Williams 1991, p. 11) for our accounts and for the social problems with which we are engaged.

XX

Over the past ten to twenty years, there has been a veritable assault on traditional ways of conceptualizing and writing about the social world and the individuals and cultural artifacts that inhabit this world. Whether conceived as the loss of the West's great metanarratives of legitimation, or as a series of signposts announcing the arrival of significant reconfigurations of our dominant social and theoretical frames— i.e., postindustrialism, postcolonialism, post-Marxism, poststructuralism, and even postfeminism—many scholars across various disciplinary fields are now grappling with the epistemological, social, and political crises that have increasingly come to characterize the post-1945 period. These claims and challenges to traditional notions of the individual (or the human subject), meaning, truth, language, writing, desire, difference, power, and experience more recently have been placed within a larger context known as postmodernism. This larger condition or context situates what is often construed as strictly philosophical or epistemological questions within a decidedly sociological terrain or field.

While there is considerable debate about the specific features and contours of what could be called a mode of production (cf. Jameson 1991), and considerable debate over whether *post*modernism is a very good name for signing the significant, but heterogeneous, changes to which the name refers, nonetheless "postmodernist culture is a real medium in which we all live to some extent, no matter how unevenly its effects are lived and felt across the jagged spectrum of color, sex, class, region, and nationality" (Ross 1988, p. viii). At the core of the postmodern field or scene is a crisis in representation involving a breakdown in the modern epistemological regime and a loosening of standard disciplinary boundaries.

For example, although the origin and development of sociology as a unique discipline is historically related to the field of literature, and although sociology in the broadest sense is concerned with the production and interpretation of stories or narratives of social and cultural life, literature (story/fiction) and social science (fact) remain theoretically and institutionally distinct enterprises. Indeed, the dominant disciplinary methods and theoretical assumptions of sociology constantly struggle against the fictive, which could be said to mark its constitutive horizon of error. The authority of sociology as a discipline rests on its ability to distinguish a fact from a fiction and to eliminate the fiction, the error. Now, however, the distinction between fact and fiction and the attendant faith in the reality effect of social science discourse has been put into question. This development has resulted in a paradigm shift: Writing, analysis, and investigation—whether of social or cultural texts—are no longer entirely viewed as a "scientific" project, but as a cultural practice that organizes particular rituals of storytelling, at the center of which is a historically situated investigating subject. If sociology and its analysis of social problems may itself be viewed as a historically and institutionally specific form of cultural and literary production, then we may need to develop models for sociological analysis that could operate under this guiding assumption.

Such an epistemological and social rupture, rather than leading away from an analysis of social relations of power, leads directly to a different agenda for asking how power operates, an agenda that attempts to connect these newer questions of representation and subjectivity to more established sociological and feminist questions of power. For feminism, as for other critical discourses and movements that arose out of a modern episteme, the challenge to our faith in the socially (and politically) effective distinction between ideology and truth, between reality and fiction (or myth) is simultaneously exciting, frightening, necessary, and uncertain. For almost two centuries a critical tradition has been built that privileges truth, the transparency of language, a centered and unified subject, and the primacy of given experience and reality. Now, as the twentieth century draws to a close, this critical tradition finds itself faced with a series of problematics to which it must respond.

Questions of what is real and how that reality is produced are crucial if we want to write about exclusions and invisibilities, a major social problem. Questions of what the "I" is and is becoming are crucial if we want to ground our work in autoethnographic experiences, if social problems and pleasures travel in and through people who are never quite themselves. Science fiction scenarios are happening now and toward a future within very powerful institutions. These scenarios are about how power will be deployed and received. As feminists, we are already concerned with understanding and challenging the disciplinary technologies that affect us, write themselves on and through our bodies, and also fracture those bodies powerfully, but differentially. And, finally, questions of how language operates are crucial if we are committed to producing a counterdiscourse, if we intend to speak and write, that is, ritually enact our various resistances toward social transformation.[6]

Although sociology historically has been concerned with the relationship between power and knowledge, its analysis of the problematic nature of social relations of power is far more developed than its analysis of the social problem of knowledge and forms of representation. New interdisciplinary approaches to the study of power, politics, and people, especially interdisciplinary feminist and race-conscious scholarship, have criticized sociology's reliance on positivistic empirical methods, especially its claim to objectively describe experience, its assumptions about the nature of individuals, and its lack of concern with issues of how it represents its findings and itself. On the one hand, questions of narrative structuring, fictive composition, and historical provisionality of claims to knowledge direct sociology and a sociologically oriented feminism to the ways in which our stories can be understood as fictions of the real. To challenge the hegemony of facticity as it has been understood in our discipline—to challenge the assumption that sociology can provide a transparent window to view a taken-for-granted reality—is to begin to understand how the real itself and its ethnographic or sociological representations are also fictions, albeit powerful ones, that we do not experience as fictional, but as true. At the same time, sophisticated understandings of representation and of how the social world is discursively constructed and deconstructed need to engage the traditional province of sociological inquiry: namely, the multiple determinations and sites of power in which narratives of and about our social problems are produced and disseminated.

XXI

I propose socio*graphy* as one model for social problems research. Sociography is a project for refiguring ethnographic authenticity as the ground for claims of political or professional effectivity, and a project for trying to understand why constructionist-but-realist (or empirically descriptive) representations of social problems have been so popular, and, yet often seem so ineffective a mode of writing about certain forms of social injury and certain social problems. Sociography wants to show how and in what ways socially constructed worlds, problems, and persons are haunted by the shadows and ghosts of these constructions. Sociography also wants to show how and in what ways accounts of socially constructed worlds, problems, and persons are also haunted by the shadows and ghosts of their constructions. In short, sociography attempts to foreground as real and operative just those twists and turns, forgettings and rememberings, and ghostly haunts that a normal social scientific account attempts to minimize. It also seeks to draw attention to a whole realm of experiences and social practices that can barely be approached without a theory and a methodology attentive to what is elusive, fantastic, contingent, and often inarticulate.

XXII

A different language is needed than the one Ibarra and Kitsuse offer to even begin the work of writing a text that would have something to say about *smeared print, ghost images* (DeLillo 1985, p. 326). A different language is needed to have something more than I can say here and now about a real estate developer's wife in northern California who is anything but idiosyncratically herself. A different language is needed to have something more than I can say here about a problem with which I leave you.

Acknowledgments

I am particularly grateful to Christopher Newfield, whose insights have been invaluable and who generously provided me with his time and attention. I would also like to acknowledge the extensive and helpful feedback I received from Jim Holstein and Gale Miller. Although Holstein and I continue to disagree on the separability of methodology and politics, his careful analysis of my essay reflects a valuable and productive ethics of critique.

Notes

1. I refer here to Daniel Bell's 1960 essay, "Vulgar Sociology. On C. Wright Mills and the 'Letter to the New Left'" (Bell 1980, pp. 138–43). In the context of a critique of Mills's letter, Bell identifies five characteristic features of his overall work that lead him to conclude that Mills is a proponent of vulgar sociology, if not a vulgar sociologist: (1) an "explosive, detonative" style, which makes it "hard to know when Mills is talking to himself, anticipating questions and answering them by exhortation, and when he is addressing the reader" (p. 138); (2) a politics of style that is "discourteous . . . . impatient" and emotional (p. 142). For Bell, the politics of style is an objectionable style of politics: "Mills, basically, is an American anarcho-syndicalist, a 'Wobbly'" (p. 142); (3) a "conceptual apparatus" lacking concepts with "fairly sharp boundaries so one knows what is included or excluded by the term" (p. 139); (4) a tendency to assert and reassert points, or "catchphrases" (p. 142), foregrounding "strateg[ies] of rhetoric" rather than "argument" (p. 140); and (5) a "failure to confront moral issues other than through the 'judgement of history'" (p. 143). It is precisely something like "history" that enables the contemporary reader of Bell's essay to be struck by the repetition or reemergence of these same discursive terms (politics and style) in current debates about the university and its scholarly mission. This is unfortunately not the place for an extended commentary on Bell's essay, which is, among other things, a very interesting example of the rhetorical claims-making process.

2. Dorothy Smith's (1990) critique of objectivity in the social sciences would be a different but complementary analysis to the one I make below. What is significant about Smith's analysis here is how she conceives of standpoint (which is not an individual subjectivized experience) as precisely that which can undo the bonds that tie objectivity to relations of ruling. For readers interested in a more phenomenologically based social constructionism that incorporates strong conceptualizations of power, I recommend the important work by Smith (1990) and Collins (1989).

3. Ibarra and Kitsuse return us to the dialectics of structure and agency in which "agents" and "structures," as distinct entities, battle it out for casual and/or analytic primacy. The agents win in Ibarra and Kitsuse's model, although they are synthetically encoded, if not within language structures, then within words and rhetorics. Nineteenth-century notions of both the individual and society repeat themselves here not only as metatheoretical questions, but as political ones: the self-contained, self-centered, individual protects his freedom

against the overbearing collectivity known as society. Committed, at least in principle, to equality within a democratic community, American individualism has historically been tortured by equating freedom with lack of social and personal restraint. The social ties that bind form an ambivalent site of attraction and repulsion that marks not only modernist sociological notions of the individual and society, but also the very possibility of conceiving equality, democracy, and freedom in different terms. I see these same ambivalences and torsions in Ibarra and Kitsuse's analysis and discuss them below.

4.   Academia, for instance, is one of three "settings" Ibarra and Kitsuse acknowledge and briefly discuss at the end of their essay. They raise a number of important questions and issues, including the call for "constructionists to examine their own practice." However, they provide no answer to nor analysis of how the various questions they ask affect their own practice. Indeed, nothing that I can see in the essay takes into consideration precisely the kind of regulatory "climate of opinion" that Ibarra and Kitsuse attribute to settings. Ibarra and Kitsuse's sociologist seems always to remain in a world of discourse without limiting or enabling power.

5.   I read Ibarra and Kitsuse's project as literally a business proposition. They seem to be building a research machine that can (1) function smoothly (i.e., not be disrupted by epistemological and political crises); (2) provide jobs (i.e., can produce research problems subject to empirical investigation for students and others); (3) distinguish between research and development (theory) and manufacturing (empirically based typologies); and (4) produce a consumable and useful (it is, after all, useful to know how folks talk about social problems) line of products that could garner state funds (the Bush administration could be served, for example, by an "impartial" analysis of the rhetorics of affirmative action), or acquire private consultation contracts (just as family mediation centers might profit from the kind of classificatory scheme proposed). Conversations with Beth Schneider about building for science and the distribution of research shops by gender helped me to elaborate this point.

6.   Leaving aside sociologists for the moment, many feminists are "against postmodernism" and against any coalition between feminism and postmodernism. To assert that feminists are *in* postmodernity often meets with denials and refusals. As Wendy Brown argues,

> feminists who array themselves "against postmodernism' . . . . rare[ly] acknowledge . . . . a distinction between postmodern conditions and theory, between epoch and politics. . . . . The conflation of such elements by those steeped in materialist analysis and practiced at attending to fine gradations of modernist feminisms speaks a stubborn determination to vanquish evidence of historical developments which its antagonists blame on thinking—the latter often portrayed as dangerously relativist, irresponsible, unpolitical, or unfeminist. (Brown 1991, p. 65)

But Brown also suggests that "to speak of postmodernity as specific configurations and representations of social, economic, and political life is not (yet) to take a political position on it or within it nor even to adopt . . . . a particular 'sensibility'" (1991, pp. 64–65). To conceive of postmodernity as a social formation is also just the first step in doing the work of specifying how, for example, the simultaneous concentration and fragmentation of capital is specifically gendered and raced, and what new social problems arise in such a context. The spirit possession that Aihwa Ong (1987), for example, analyzes in her recent study of

Malaysian factory women working in export process zones is impossible to understand without radically reconceiving the social time and space in which it occur.

References

Baudrillard, Jean 1988. *America.* Translated by Chris Turner. New York: Verso Books.

Bell, Daniel 1980. *The Winding Passage. Essays and Sociological Journeys 1960–1980.* Cambridge: ABT Books.

Brown, Wendy 1991. "Feminist Hesitations, Postmodern Exposures." *differences* 3:63–84.

Chartier, Roger 1988. *Cultural History. Between Practices and Representations.* Translated by Lydia G. Cochrane. Ithaca, NY: Cornell University Press.

Collins, Patricia Hill 1989. "The Social Construction of Invisibility: Black Women's Poverty in Social Problems Discourse." Pp. 77–93 in *Perspectives on Social Problems,* Vol. 1, edited by James A. Holstein and Gale Miller. Greenwich, CT: JAI Press.

DeLillo, Don 1985. *White Noise.* New York: Viking Books.

Gordon, Avery. 1990. "Feminism, Writing, and Ghosts." *Social Problems* 37:485–500.

Herrnstein Smith, Barbara 1988. *Contingencies of Value: Alternative Perspectives for Critical Theory.* Cambridge, MA: Harvard University Press.

Jameson, Frederic 1991. *Postmodernism, or, The Cultural Logic of Late Capitalism.* Durham, NC: Duke University Press.

Kipnis, Laura 1988. "Feminism: The Political Conscience of Postmodernism?" Pp. 149–66 in *Universal Abandon? The Politics of Postmodernism,* edited by Andrew Ross. Minneapolis: University of Minnesota Press.

Mills, C. Wright [1944] 1979. "The Social Role of the Intellectual." Pp. 292–304 in *Power, Politics and People. The Collected Essays of C. Wright Mills.* Edited by Irving Louis Horowitz. New York: Oxford University Press.

Morris, Meaghan 1988. *The Pirate's Fiancée: Feminism, Reading, Postmodernism.* New York: Verso Books.

Ong, Aihwa 1987. *Spirits of Resistance and Capitalist Discipline: Factory Women in Malaysia.* Albany: SUNY Press.

Pateman, Carole 1989. *The Disorder of Women.* Stanford: Stanford University Press.

Ross, Andrew 1988. "Introduction." Pp. vii–xviii in *Universal Abandon? The Politics of Postmodernism,* edited by Andrew Ross. Minneapolis: University of Minnesota Press.

Smith, Dorothy 1990. *The Conceptual Practices of Power: A Feminist Sociology of Knowledge.* Boston: Northeastern University Press.

Spector, M and John Kitsuse [1977] 1987. *Constructing Social Problems.* New York: Aldine.

Williams, Patricia J. 1991. *The Alchemy of Race and Rights.* Cambridge, MA: Harvard University Press.

16

"Literacy" and Business: "Social Problems" as Social Organization

Dorothy E. Smith

This paper explores "social problems" as a distinctive organizing process operating in the social relations of public text-mediated discourse. It draws on research designed as part of a study of skills training in the plastic processing industry. As part of a series of interviews with managers of plastics processing companies, George Smith, my research associate, and I interviewed the manager of a small fiberglass manufacturing company who complained of problems of the educational level and literacy of workers available to his company on the local labor market. Problems of "literacy" and adult educational insufficiency had already been established in the public text-mediated discourse. Their business content had been specified. They had been given currency in business discourse. Talk in the interview was ordered with reference to the public definition of an issue shared by respondent and interviewers. Here in practice was the operation of a social problem as an ordering or organizational process. The intersection of a particular local historical site in which we ourselves were involved, with interpretive and ordering practices originating in public text-mediated discourse, called for analysis in terms of social problems. Yet features of the situation resisted the traditional objectification associated with that analysis.

George Herbert Mead (1932) describes how social objects are brought into existence in the concerted practices of a group. The concerting of sociological research and theoretical activity on the boundaries of discourse and policy has produced social problems as a distinct object, a constituent of sociology's phenomenal domain. Sociological discourse itself accomplishes the textual presence of social problems. Originating in concerns shared by sociologists with reformers and progressives, it has been reconstructed in new contexts of sociological theory and method, as well as changing historical contexts. Labeling theory inserted a critical reflexivity into the discussion of this object while preserving the original boundaries. Functionalism shifted the theoretical ground, attempting to incorporate the determination of social problems into functional relations. Social constructionism calls for inquiry into the actual socially organized practices accomplishing the phenomenon. Peter Ibarra and John Kitsuse's proposals in this volume build on this discursive base, going beyond constructionist conceptions in calling for the exploration of the constitution of social problems in members' language practices. They propose that social problems be investigated as members' practical theorizing, their claims-making activities, and the vernacular resources on which they rely: "[C]laimants' discursive practices in demarcating moral objects" constitute social problems as objects.

As social problems are embedded in discourse as an object they become more than "a distinct subject matter" (Troyer 1992). Each new theoretical design reproduces and reconstitutes it as a discursive object.[1] Though, as Spector and Kitsuse ([1977] 1987) show, the term *social problem* is imprecise, it is the focus of sociological debate, theory, teaching, and other discursive practices. Its disciplinary status is taken for granted; there are courses in social problems; a society for studying them; a journal named for them; books and articles written about them; a series such as this, which introduces new approaches to them. An external subject-object relation is created. The object is constituted, within discourse, as having a determinate character independent of particular individual members of the discourse.

In relating the discursive object to "the world," the shape of the discursive object is laid over society like a sewing pattern. The phenomena to be addressed by sociological inquiry are cut out accordingly. The contours of a determinate entity are imposed.[2] Even the social constructionist procedure, which avoids the reification common to earlier sociological versions of "social problems" by exploring the activities that accomplish them, adopts the object-status established in discourse. A social problem is constituted as a discrete entity by determinate types of activities. The sophistication of advances introduced by Spector and Kitsuse ([1977] 1987) and by Ibarra and Kitsuse's insistence on activities in language preserves this procrustean bed.

Because social constructionism is oriented to people's actual activities, it has created a rich and important body of research. Yet observing the contours of social problems as an entity constituted by those activities detaches those activities from the social relations and processes in which they were embedded. Typically, accounts of social problems have reference to state and state agencies, institutions, and the transformation of local and particular problems into issues of general public concern.[3] They have reference to an interplay, a recursively coordinated interchange, between a generalized schematization of a problem within public text-mediated discourse (media, professional discourse—including sociology, legislative pronouncements, and so forth), state and institutional activity—and the sometimes multiple, localized particularities of the everyday that are thereby coordinated with and within this complex of social relations. This interplay, however, is not made part of the social problems problematic.

The approach I want to recommend proposes to investigate social organization and relations. While it takes for granted that sociologists have identified some determinate process, it does not assume that social problems exist as entities with which definite activities can be identified. In other work (Smith 1987, 1990a, 1990b) I've emphasized the dialectic between the localized and particular sites of people's ongoing activities and the text-mediated, generalized and extralocal organization of what I call *the relations of ruling*. The latter term locates that complex of bureaucratic, administrative, managerial, and professional organization, and the professional, academic, cultural, and related discourses that together represent a specialization and differentiation of the functions of governing, regulating, organizing, and controlling contemporary society.[4] These are characteristically objectified forms generalized across multiple local sites.

Social problems, I suggest, may be considered as a device or mechanism operating in what Habermas (1989) has called the "public sphere," the contemporary form of which is public text-mediated discourse, a coordinating complex of the relations of ruling. In public text-mediated discourse I include the media, the professional discourse that generates research, concepts, arguments, facts, authorized judgments, and so on, legislative debates, the reports and pronouncements of government agencies, commissions of inquiry—all those forms of text-mediated communication that are part of a public process. Public text-mediated discourse constitutes a system or, perhaps better, a field, of social relations within the relations of ruling. It has determinate forms of social organization. Social problems are, I suggest, one of these.

The investigation of social problems does indeed explore these "devices" as phenomena within this discursive field of relations. I take it that Ibarra and Kitsuse's recommendation to explore the "vernacular resources includ[ing] those rhetorical idioms, interpretive practices, and features of settings that distinguish claims-making activities as a class of phenomena while also differentiating instances of claims-making from one another" is essentially an exploration within public text-mediated discourse. And indeed much of the substance of social problems research has this focus (for example, Gusfield 1966; Lemert 1970; Rafter 1992). I suggest that text-mediated discourse and organization are central to the processes identified as social problems. Every formulation of social problems discussed by Spector and Kitsuse ([1977] 1987) in their comprehensive and exemplary treatment of the topic relies on this: Concepts such as legitimation (Blumer, cited by Spector and Kitsuse [1977] 1987, p. 139), the notion that social research may be a constituent of the development of a social problem (Bossard, cited by Spector and Kitsuse [1977] 1987, p. 138), the transformation of private troubles into public issues (p. 143), presuppose these relations. The press and media are referred to (p. 145) but are not explored as a medium integral to the social organization of a social problem. Nicole Rafter's (1992) study is focused on interplay within the relations of public text-mediated discourse—the definition of categories used, the emergence of poverty as a policy dilemma (p. 20), the effects of a popular treatise on the understanding of pauperism (p. 21), and the incorporation of new categories, concepts, and codes into institutional practices—yet these relations and their organization are not a topic. They are presences integral to any account of social problems as phenomena, yet they are incidental to investigatory and analytic strategies governed by the concept.

My view is that social problems, as sociologists have addressed them, are a form of social organization of and in public text-mediated discourse. It is a distinctive device, entering into the organization of local actualities, and bringing them into conceptually ordered relations hooked to a political process. Particular, locally experienced problems arising in determinate social relational contexts are translated into standardized and generalized forms within public text-mediated discourse.[5] The generalized or *societal* character of a social problem is discursively accomplished. Further, the generalized status of a problem within public discourse does more than transform the status of the original problem, it also "collects" and mobilizes other local difficulties that fit and can be interpreted as instances of it. There is a characteristic cycle here, I suggest, that sociologists have recognized and explored using the social problems frame.

Texts mediate both the contemporary organization of the economy as well as the discourses constituting the public sphere.[6] Textually mediated forms of organization have therefore a distinctive character and capacity that are quite unlike those of organizational forms built on locality, territory, and particularized relations.[7] A distinctive feature of such organization is the capacity of printed texts to produce the same set of words in multiple sites at once or at different times. This is essential to the reproduction of large-scale managed or administered organization as the same from one day to the next; it is essential to the reproduction of the "same" organizational forms in work sites separated from one another in time and space.[8] Similarly, public text-mediated discourse creates an interpretive coordination of multiple local and particular sites. In this paper, I explore the relevance of this understanding of the text-mediated character of public discourse in contemporary society for social problems. The manager of the fiberglass manufacturing company that George Smith and I visited had introduced a new managerial regime; problems arose with workers that he identified as problems of their "mentality"; he sought to recruit others, but found those he could recruit equally problematic; he complained about the educational system. Problems of workers' educational insufficiencies, and specifically problems of literacy, had been and were being discussed widely in the media at that time. Reports, briefs, and so forth were being produced and discussed. Such formulations of problems of literacy as a generalized societal problem within public text-mediated discourse organized the interview as a dialogue, how the manager talked about his difficulties, how we understood him. It also organized our postinterview review of the interview. Until we took up a careful analysis of the transcribed interview (and of other materials), our own discussions were informally and unselfconsciously organized by the schemata of work force literacy and educational insufficiency. The concept of literacy as a component of public text-mediated discourse organized relevant parts of our local dialogue (the interview), coordinating it with debates in news media and professional educational discourse. Here, I suggest, is the social problems device at work. My interest is in exploring it as local organizer of a particular setting of talk and in how it connects up a local setting of particular problems to problems posited as of societal significance at the level of public text-mediated discourse.

This paper addresses three topics substantively: (1) the constitution of adult illiteracy as a societal problem in public text-mediated discourse in which business has specific interests; (2) the social relations within which the manager's locally experienced difficulties emerged; (3) the organizing effects of the public conception of problems of literacy and educational insufficiency in the discussion of the manager's local difficulties.

Literacy Defined as a Societal Problem

Literacy has been a topic for educators for some time. It has also been a concern of grass roots organization focused on popular education. It became a topic of more general concern in Canada in the context of public discussion, carried on in the media and in professional and academic discourse about the changing relation of Canada to the world economy, the exigencies imposed on industry by intensified competition, and the changing work force requirements of new technologies.

Richard Darville (n.d.) identifies an article written by Peter Calamai and published by Southam News in 1987 as "enter[ing] the literacy issue into the governing process" in Canada. Among other materials, Calamai's article relied on statistics showing high levels of illiteracy in the Canadian adult population. Following this, issues of literacy were widely discussed in feature articles, in the business pages and business newspapers, and in many other sites; studies were being done estimating the rates of illiteracy in the Canadian population. People commented critically in letters to the newspapers about the state of the Canadian educational system, and so forth. Thus a problem was given formulated presence *as a problem* in public text-mediated discourse; it was defined as a *generalized* problem for the society at large rather than an issue relevant only to specific interests.

Literacy or illiteracy appears to name and identify definite phenomena, but in fact it can be specified in many ways. As it became identified as a problem in public text-mediated discourse, a space was created in which different interests competed to define its content and hence, presumably, hoped to influence government policy and budgetary allocations. Popular educational focus on literacy as essential to full citizenship and to empowerment defines the issue quite differently than business concerns with types of skills needed in new managerial and technological contexts. The concept of literacy as a problem was specified in the ongoing debate.

Business intervention related the problem of literacy to debates on the future direction of national economy. A Canadian Business Task Force on Literacy was set up and a report prepared for it by a firm of consultants.[9] The scant research basis of the report suggests that its ideological function was more significant than its informational. Issues of literacy were related to technology represented as an originator of change, and global competition imposing increased productivity as a national imperative. Both new technology and the new global economic order link business interests in a trained work force to national interests. Radically new managerial strategies began to be called for; the new technologies cutting costs, and particularly labor costs, are represented as essential to an effective response to competition. The supply of labor adequately trained to respond to a restructured industrial base is seen as inadequate. The formulation of the problem of literacy identifies within public text-mediated discourse such specific business interests as matters of national concern.

The business formulation provides a framework for the interpretation of local managerial problems as instances or expressions of the societal or national problem. This ideological function is not just conceptual. Consider the formulation of a social problem as a paradigm for local interpretive practices. Local practitioners of a social problems discourse make local applications, deploying the circularity of the "documentary method of interpretation" (Garfinkel 1967). Harold Garfinkel proposes that we participate in the social organization of the everyday world through interpretive procedures that treat what is present to us as indices or documents of underlying patterns. Garfinkel conceives of the relation between documents and underlying pattern as open-ended and reciprocally determined—each next document adds to the pattern that interprets it. The ideological form of this circle is somewhat different. It fixes both underlying interpretive pattern and its documents. An ideological circle locks together the interpretive schemata (here the concept of "literacy" as a social problem) and textually given exemplars of documents or indices. Hence the importance of the ideological function of providing generalized instances and specifications of the "problem." Just what problems of literacy might look like in industrial context and just what literacy might mean are specified in the task force report. For example:

> The new technologies are having an impact on the types of skills people require. Some of the tasks which workers have traditionally undertaken are now being taken over by technology. Almost all industries are introducing computer based technologies which require a level of comprehension and ability over and above previous requirements. (Canadian Business Task Force on Literacy 1988, p. 11)

Literacy is given substance. New technologies require workers with the ability to *read* specifications, instructions, etc., enter them into a computer, and evaluate the resulting product:

> The individual on the shop floor must be more literate than he was in the past. He must be able to read instructions, diagnose problems, input numbers and read from operating manuals. He must be able to communicate problems with his fellow workers and use analytical thinking to arrive at solutions. (p. 12).

Literacy here is specified as more than, say, being able to read a newspaper or the instructions on a cake mix package. Reference is made to "reading efficiency, blueprint reading, business writing, effective communications, and so on" (p. 14), and:

> With an ever more complex business environment, new communications needs are constantly emerging. For example, there is a demand for sales personnel with a sophisticated understanding of technical products. Some engineers are now required for these types of jobs. Often there may be a demand for these individuals to be comfortable with selling concepts, or

understanding complex problems which a client may have. Clearly, these
require sophisticated communications skills. (p. 14.)

Texts such as the report of the Canadian Business Task Force on Literacy, in addition to newspaper articles, features in the business sections
of newspapers, and so forth, provide for managers such as the one we
interviewed schemata of interpretation through which problems embedded in the course of managerial projects pursued under particular local
conditions are subsumed under categories of public text-mediated discourse. They are hooked into an arena of public and national concern as
relevant to state intervention. The managerial literature represents a
need for workers capable of participating in the new managerial order;
workers must become part of the process, not just producing to a standard or quota set by a foreman or supervisor; a redesigned worker is
called for, capable of operating as a constituent of such an integrated
managerial organization of production. But the training or education of
workers prepared to function in these new relations does not lie within
the managerial jurisdiction—at least as it is defined by management.
Somehow responsibility for such functions must be transferred to government and hence must be defined as a problem at the societal level.
The managerial problem is repositioned within public text-mediated discourse. There it is redefined not as a special interest, but as a matter of
general public concern. Here the phenomena identified by Ibarra and
Kitsuse kick in. The rhetoric of social problems seeks to mobilize public
pressure on government to act; a claim, at least by implication, on the
expenditure of public monies is made.

Generating the Problem: The Managerial Project

In formulating a problem at the societal level, its dimensions are described in ways that justify societal concern. Problems of literacy and
educational insufficiency are defined by business in relation to issues of
the international competitiveness of Canadian business. But, of course,
here the construction of the problem of adult literacy within public text-
mediated discourse justifies translating the special interests of business
into issues of national concern. But this doesn't necessarily tell us much
about the local contexts within which actual problems emerge or how
local problems come to be "organized" as instances or expressions of the
generalized public formulation. Actual problems are embedded socially
and are located and appear *as problems* in the context of socially organized courses of action. In this, local problems and the social relations in
which they arise become hooked interpretively into public discourse.

In this section the emergence of a problem in the context of a managerial project is described. The managerial problems arise at the intersection of the economic relations of market, competition, costs of capital investment, and so forth, with the actual process of production in a given plant. Management is the active work of coordinating the latter to operate effectively in the economic environments organized by the former. The fiberglass manufacturing company that George Smith and I visited had formerly been owner-managed but had recently been sold to a large corporation. Our interest in the company arose because it had participated in a government-funded scheme to assist companies to develop internal skills training programs. In the course of our interview, the manager of the company described problems he was experiencing with his workers and the local labor market that he interpreted as problems of competence in reading and writing and of general educational level. His difficulties did not originate in technological change; there was no changed technology. Rather the difficulties that came, in the context of our interview, to be interpreted in this way were constituted as such by the introduction of a radically new managerial regime following the previously owner-managed company's purchase by a large-scale corporation.

The original owner-managed organization, as it was made visible to us in the contrasts drawn by the present manager between the old and new regimes, did not have a distinct text-based managerial system. The owner-manager was active on the shop floor. The company's production was oriented toward manufacturing products for particular customers rather than for a generalized market. Quality, sales, and standards of productivity appeared to have been determined primarily by a relatively stable localized market environment. Customers were expected to be satisfied with the product as the production process produced it and when it was produced. It seems not in fact to have been a fully developed capitalist enterprise. Growth was not an objective. Presumably the company paid its bills, paid its workers, paid its taxes, paid its accountants, and then what was left over from its receipts was the profit that paid the equivalent of a wage to the owner-manager. More particularly, the organization of the labor and production process wasn't "managed," i.e., it wasn't organized to articulate to the textual control of the rate of return on investment.

The purchase of the company by a large transnational corporation lodged it in quite different economic relations and subjected its production processes to quite different managerial organization. It was now embedded in the generalized problems of regulating the rate of return on investment in a particular plant in relation to the dynamics of financial capital in the markets for credit, stocks, and other forms taken by capital in those relations where money appears purely in its text-mediated forms. Its production and sales had to be coordinated with how its parent company participated in economic relations at a wholly different level than those it had been active in before. The new manager was in process of radically restructuring the system of management. He was intensely concerned with how to organize production and market products so as to optimize the rate of return on investment. He projected production and marketing strategies that would introduce or establish the company in markets organized extralocally in which its products would have to compete with others.

He was working with the identical machinery and the same workers. The difficulties that were organized in our discussion with him as problems of the literacy and educational background of workers had not, apparently, existed under the previous managerial regime. Rather the difficulties arose in the course of introducing new managerial practices into the company. These were intended to subordinate the production process to the kinds of growth (of profit and capacity to produce profit) objectives envisaged by the new manager as representative of the corporation that is now its owner. In contrast to the largely word-of-mouth management of the previous owner-manager, these new managerial practices were an impersonal *text-based* system of coordination. They would articulate the point of production to the overall process of accumulation given textual form as assets, returns on investment, and so forth. Rather than meeting costs and earning an income for its owner, the company now had to aim at growth—in sales, increased production and productivity, and increasing profitability. Production had to be redesigned to enable the *textual* appraisal and regulation of constituent sequences in terms of their contribution to the rate of return on the parent corporation's investment in the company. The routine textually mediated practices organizing this relation *are* management in its contemporary practice.[10] Here's how its manager describes the new managerial strategies:

What we've done with the parent company is we've put me in place as the manager; we've hired a production manager who is a "hands-on" production manager; we have an accountant. So we are trying to put in place a structure to bring this to an intermediate size company. At the moment I think we are doing reasonably well. Our sales are up about 60 percent from the previous year. We are still getting that million dollar a year plus. That is the level we are at now. And we have to move to the next level. We've got to get to a two million dollar company to give us the momentum to justify the people who are required to do the job. You know, engineering skills—if the customer wants to make a new mold that's sophisticated or has properties that we don't normally work with, then we have to go an outside consultant.

Rational accounting procedures are needed to appraise the position of the company in relation to its growth objectives. Reaching growth objectives will enable the company to pay for the additional kinds of expertise enabling it to grow further. The manager contrasted the previous "system" of management with what he was attempting to introduce:

Manager: The philosophy of the previous foreman—let's call him a foreman—was everybody had to be a general-purpose practitioner, or so to speak, to do all jobs at any time. The problem with that is that, no, you didn't become proficient at any one function. So now under our new program . . . although it's not perfect, it's not 100 percent that way—you always have to be a little flexible—but now what we have tried to do is just have no interruptions in a certain department. We try and keep those people there working consistently. So they have a routine. And I think maybe it's . . . . maybe you or I can deal with interruptions and be more flexible and get back to your task at hand if you have an interruption or ten interruptions, in the meantime we don't lose track of the main thought or main focus. Whereas it seems—maybe it's the mentality or the intellect of the people we are dealing with in a plant environment—if you have a routine they seem to fit into it and they like the routine. And it's more efficient that way too. But if you get interruptions in that routine, then to start up again . . . .

DS: The "interruptions" would be that they would be called away to do something else?

Manager: That's right . . . . and many times with the knowledge they have, if they were called away they wouldn't say, "I can't come right now because I have to wait until this cures another ten minutes and do the trimming." They would just go. Now they would come back a half an hour later. It's cured. Now they've got a half an hour to do something that should have taken one minute, before. Because now it is cured and they have to cut it and saw it and shape it.

The fixing of the worker's job as part of a systematization of the division of work involves a textual order. The job is given a job description. The latter writes boundaries, what is and what is not part of a worker's job. A position is created; coordination with others is via how his/her work is textually defined vis-à-vis others, rather than by calls on him/her to give a hand, to shift over to another task, or the like. The systematic treatment of workers' time is also integral to this system. This is more than the introduction of quotas and some form of piece rates. It requires the careful planning and organization of the process of production itself so that workers' time will not be wasted, for example, by having to wait for the transfer of a product in process from one stage to another, to repeat a process, or to repair a botched piece of work. The manager we interviewed used the phrase "touching it [a completed product] again" as a recurrent problem that he was trying to avoid. "Touching it again" meant having to run a finished product through part of a process again or repairing it because of flaws in the production process. The phrase refers implicitly to a textual system of management that enables examination of a production process for sites from which inessential time can be pared away.

The problem of literacy formulates for the manager of this entrepreneurial firm problems arising in the relations to which his company is now connected and in which it is active. It was formerly owner-manager operated; workers had been employed for some time; they had settled into patterns of work that were learned in part from the original owner and in part through experience; they were paid on an hourly basis and not in relation to individual productivity. The new system of management was designed to regulate costs at the point of production in relation to the overall profitability and growth capacity of the company. It involved giving workers written job descriptions specifying the tasks for which they were responsible, tying them to specific tasks to develop proficiency—devices that enabled management to appraise the relationship between different phases or parts of the production process and wage costs as well as to give the worker a direct interest in improved productivity. It involved changing the system of remuneration so that it recorded and gave an incentive for productivity, and organizing the shop into departments assigned quotas, a move seen as an incentive system, but also building in a method for accounting for costs and productivity in different units or parts of the process, thus refining cost controls. All these moves added up to an increasingly refined system of text-based control over the temporal organization of production.

The Locally Discovered "Incompetence" of Workers

In introducing these text-based systems of management, the manager ran into problems with the workers. He sees the workers currently employed as the major barrier to the kinds of growth objectives framed for the company. He says that "with the staff that I had, I really could not take this company from where it was to where we want to go with it." His problems with staff are identified as problems of their lack of training. The workers had been in the plant

Quite a few years. Some many years, and others between, let's say, three, four, five, six years. That kind of thing. And they came, primarily, off the street, fitted into a shop situation with no one with formal fiberglass training. It was someone [the previous owner-manager] who had acquired practical skills on the job [who was] now training people to acquire these skills.

He continues, making the relation between their lack of formal training and their inability to articulate work process to a managed organization of production:

But in our case, in my view, we were at the bottom of the barrel. These guys were off the street. They had been trained by people that really didn't have a broad range of knowledge in this application. They made do! And it was just by trial and error they got through this. So many of the things that they were doing were very inefficient and uncoordinated. So from our point of view we had to train them in the basics of fiberglass processing.
   We had to start doing training anyway. We started that program and then we realized that the fellows we had in the plant really couldn't absorb the training that we had to give them.

This passage contrasts an exclusively experientially based knowledge learned on an ad hoc basis from someone who has evolved production practice by trial and error, with a "broad range of knowledge," i.e., a knowledge mediated by texts, in which an individual has been formally trained. More than that, workers are required who can operate in a textually governed environment, who are able to go back and forth between their experiential knowledge of the job and a knowledge of how to interpret and control the production process in relation to standards, specifications, organization, and so forth, vested in texts, and in terms of a knowledge learned from diagrams and formal explanation of the actual workings of the machine being operated.
   . The manager represents his problem as the absence of an adequately trained and literate labor force. However in an earlier context he had described his difficulty in obtaining appropriately qualified workers in terms of the supply of labor at a price compatible with his entrepreneurial objectives for the company. Rates of unemployment at that time in Ontario were very low and the company was situated in a relatively small community near a large corporation able to pay significantly higher rates of pay:

I understand between twelve and fourteen dollars is their [large corporation's] base wage per hour. Now, if they weren't here we could probably pay six to seven to eight dollars an hour—which has been the norm. And

now you just can't get reasonable people . . . . [T]hey're not even really
literate.

Thus a big problem for management was not an absolute unavailability
of people with the appropriate educational level to participate in the
new production environment but their unavailability at a cost compatible with sustaining a rapid increase in the rate of return on investment.
The manager's problems in securing a labor force appropriate to his new
managerial strategies were generated in the particular social relations of
capital in which his company was now embedded.

In the interview, the manager insisted that the workers already in the
plant could not be trained; they would not respond to training programs; they would get it right for a while and then lapse back into old
ways. So they were fired and other workers were sought. The issue of
literacy was pulled into play as it was indexed in interviews with pro-
spective workers by, for example, some having difficulties filling out job
applications (note that written job applications were unlikely to have
been part of the previous managerial regime):

> When we first started advertising, we would say, "Fiberglass experience
> required." Well we would get two or three people coming in. And then we
> said, "Will train." So we got quite a few more people but these people
> could hardly fill out their applications. I mean, they were grade seven to
> eight type people and . . . . ah . . . . well, even in the initial interview—in
> five minutes—you know . . . . they just didn't give you confidence in
> them to do a job. The odd one would. And we were fooled many times.
> We hired someone and got them in the plant, and they were so confused.
> [chuckle] I mean it's really disheartening to see people coming through our
> system, generally . . . .

Ability to read and write competently is an indicator for the manager
of the trainable worker—in the context of the new text-based managerial
regime he is introducing. Indicators of literacy are interpreted as indicators of ability to learn the kind of job required of workers under the new
managerial regime. His difficulties might have been related simply to
competition from the larger, better-paying company in the same city; he
might have called his induction procedures into question; he did not ask
why the "off-the-street" recruitment procedures of the displaced owner-
manager seem to have worked; he did not question his managerial strategies and ask whether they might be modified to adapt the new productive organization to the labor actually available; he did not broach the
possibility of paying wages at a rate competitive with the larger local
firm. Instead he ascribes the difficulties generated in this context to
generalized problems of "our" system of education: "Our schools are

just not doing the job we want . . . . we can't just take people off the street like they used to, we've got to have people we can train."

It isn't possible to establish with precision whether or how the schema of the societal problem enters into the interview talk, including how the interviewers heard the talk and our later discussions. The organizing logic, however, is the same: New systems of management encounter a work force that exhibits educational insufficiencies, particularly in the area of reading and writing; these problems are not interpreted as generated by the new managerial system, but are external to it; they are problems of an educational system that is doing an inadequate job. "Our" and "we" of the first sentence in the last quotation do not longer refer to the company, but are spoken as what might be described as the "societal we," locating a generalized subject external to the particular local context. Our later discussions of the interview as researchers were also organized by the public text-mediated formulations of the social problem of literacy. As we discussed the interview and its implications for skills training in our verbal review immediately after the interview, we reflected on how the manager's account of the labor force problems he was encountering indicated issues the kind we later discovered to have been identified by the Canadian Business Task Force on Literacy Report. It was only on further reflection and in the light of other thinking we were doing on ideology and on the recursive organizing functions of concepts that our attention was drawn to how our own participation in the interview as well as how our later discussions were ordered by a "problems" schema established in public text-mediated discourse.[11]

Discussion

This account has investigated the embedded character of difficulties formulated under the rubric of literacy as a social problem. The company's work force had been stable under the previous regime. The new regime, introducing a strongly text-based system of management geared to regulating production and sales to maximize the rate of return on investment, actually creates new problems, both in relation to the established work force and in seeking replacements.

The new problems aren't seen as generated by new management. The new managerial regime is part of a text-based and technically highly developed system of management. It establishes its own interpretive paradigms. These can be located in how the manager talks about his problems with his work force. The established work force had "no formal fiberglass training"; they were "off the street," had learned by trial and error; they were unable to absorb the training provided; there is a problem with their "mentality" (as compared with "ours," the members of the interview) and hence they need to be controlled by routines if they are to work efficiently; new employees in the plant are "confused." In the interview, it is the manager's standpoint in the managerial system that generates and defines the workers' incompetence.

This standpoint is relocated in a larger societal arena as it is defined according to the logic of social problems. As organizer of local practices, a "social problem" provides something like a device for converting particular interests and perspectives to objective status; a one-sided view is translated into a generalized state of affairs. So the standpoint in management organizing the manager's account of his difficulties with workers is transposed. The problems are lifted out of the managerial context; the relations constituting the perceived incompetence of workers disappear from view; the incompetence is objectified as its context drops away. Workers' incompetence is a product of the system the manager calls "ours." The managerial standpoint is translated and carried forward into the generalized standpoint of public text-mediated discourse.

The viewpoint and concerns of the workers in the plant do not get a look-in here. Nor do the workers in the local community. This company had had a long-standing stable presence in the community and had had previously, according to the manager we talked to, a relatively stable work force. People had worked there for quite a while and learned ways of doing from the previous owner-manager. The company thus had roots in the local community. While from the standpoint of the manager, he was hiring people "off the street" (a phrase we encountered more than once) in a market he assumed to be individuated, we might imagine him to be hiring into a fairly well developed local gossip network in which his reputation and that of his managerial regime had already been traveling. Had the workers employed in the plant had an opportunity to speak back it is likely they'd have had to begin with talk about the manager and production manager as individuals. They would not have had a standpoint in an institutionalized and generalizing system to formulate their problems with management in the same mode as the mode of public text-mediated discourse. They were not union members; they did not command the formulations of class. And in any case, they were not consulted nor were their perspectives recognized in their absence as views that would need to be expressed to "get the whole picture." We can see the shadows moving behind the screen, but we do not hear from them. Similar problems attended the early days of the women's movement and it was the function of consciousness-raising groups to create a generalizing language and constitute a standpoint in relation to which local experiences could be accorded a generalized power.

All this, of course, is entirely speculative; indeed it's an effect of the social organizational logic of social problems that it is so. [12] I introduce this speculation here in order to fill out and give substance to the collapse of alternative perspectives into the objectified standpoint that is characteristic of "social problems" as a social organizational device. Operating within the framework provided by the public text-mediated formulation of the social problem of "literacy," we, the interviewers, did not catch ourselves in this conceptual conspiracy until our later reflections.

We should distinguish here between differences in perspective arising in experience from competing interpretations or claims to interpret social problems. The latter are formulated in an objectified mode and as expressions of general societal values. Of course, diverging definitions and interpretations of a social problem are explicitly attended to in the literature. It is the very stuff of Joseph Gusfield's (1966) functionalist study of the temperance and prohibition movements in nineteenth-century United States. In the social constructionist context, it becomes a systematic analytic tool in Spector and Kitsuse's ([1977] 1987) and Ibarra and Kitsuse's development of the concept of "claims-making." But competing claims are already transposed into objectified form; they are already in the mode of public text-mediated discourse; they are activities within the relations of ruling [vividly exemplified in Spector and Kitsuse's ([1977] 1987, pp. 97–125]) fascinating account of "social problems in the American Psychiatric Association"].

An effect of not returning to local experiences embedded in determinate social relations is, for me, exemplified by Gusfield's (1966) study of the temperance movement in the United States. The analysis is organized around differences in religious viewpoints between Catholics and Protestants. But it neglects as a topic the distinctive interests of women, the connections between the women's suffrage movement and the temperance movement, the issues of marital property (men's legally enforced right to spend their wives' property, and their wives' and children's earnings),and of the emergence of the saloon and the interests of mothers in the moral preservation of their sons. In part, of course, this blindness can be attributed to the general gender blindness of the sociology of the time the work was produced. But if his investigation had been called on to explore the locally occurring experiences that mobilized people, and women in particular, around issues of temperance, or how the formulations of temperance and of prohibition interpreted, named, and generalized locally experienced problems in the context of more than local relations, at least some of these issues for women must have come into view.

"Social problems" as a device play a distinctive part in processes articulating the expression of local experience to public text-mediated discourse, and creating standardized interpretive practices applying across multiple local settings. We have also seen how this device may function to create connections across different "sectors" of the complex of text-mediated relations that make up what I've called elsewhere the relations of ruling. Investigation and analysis are incomplete without extending investigation to what is governed by this device and how the device operates. I have suggested a cyclical organization in which originally localized and specific problems are translated into the generalized forms of public text-mediated discourse. The latter then become the interpreters, and organizers, of localized problems. This small study has examined only one phase of the cycle, but it exhibits some of the social organizational properties of the device. We saw how the device generalizes and accords societal value to a localized problem, selectively authorizes those whose voices it will make heard in defining it, and standardizes procedures for determining what kinds of local difficulties and problems may be included. In so doing the particular perspectives of the "participants" in the localized problem, here managers and workers, are transposed into a single, objectified, and generalized standpoint at the level of public discourse. Thus only one of the perspectives generated by the social relations within which the problem arises is publicly accorded societal value. Hence to explore "social problems" as a device of public text-mediated discourse organizing locally experienced problems is to explore the allocation and appropriation of "voice" and power in the contemporary life of democratic society.

Acknowledgments

This paper was originally presented at the J. S. Woodsworth Conference, Institute for the Humanities, Simon Fraser University, April 1988. I am in general indebted to Richard Darville for discussions that led to the interpretation of *literacy* that I've used here. The research on which the paper is based was supported in part by the Ontario Ministry of Education (via its "transfer grant" to OISE) and in part by Social Sciences and Humanities Research Council Grant #484-87-0057. The final rewriting was done while I was Visiting Scholar at the Center for the Study of Women in Society at the University of Oregon.

Notes

1.   Malcolm Spector and John Kitsuse's ([1977] 1987) *Constructing Social Problems* provides an exemplary critical account.
2.   This, of course, is precisely the strategy that Robert Park identified as the peculiarly sociological move: "[A]s soon as historians begin to emphasize the typical and representative, rather than the unique character of events, history ceases to be history and becomes sociology" (Park 1955, p. 194).
3.   See, for example, Spector and Kitsuse's summation of the natural history of social problems as a series of stages ([1977] 1987, p. 142).

4. The notion of relations of ruling transposes "idealist" conceptions of rationality into a complex of actual relations, practices, organization, and so forth that can be subjected to investigation as such (Smith 1990b).

5. The notion of "social problems" as transforming private troubles into public issues (Spector and Kitsuse [1977] 1987, p. 143) recognizes but does not problematize this operation.

6. See some of the recent examinations of accounting and managerial practices as text-mediated discourse or social relations (Cassin 1986; Yates 1989; Montagna 1990; Devitt 1991; McCoy 1991). Albert Sloan's autobiographical account of the early-twentieth-century reorganization of General Motors stresses the significance of innovative accounting practices (Sloan 1964). Recent studies challenging the positivist ontology of accounting also sustains this interpretation, and certainly journalistic accounts of the working environment of business make its textual character patently visible (see, for example, Burrough and Helyar 1991; and Pizzo, Fricker, and Muolo 1991).

7. Weber does not address the distinction between traditional and rational-legal forms of authority in these terms (although he does recognize files and records as an important constituent of the latter). Nonetheless his distinction breaks along the same line of fault.

8. More extended treatments of the distinctive properties of this social form can be found in my (1990b) essay on "Textually Mediated Social Organization," and in David Olson (1977).

9. I am very much indebted to Betty Ann Lloyd for informing me about this report and for getting a copy for me at very short notice.

10. Cassin (1986). The focus is that system of textual coordination known as management that articulates labor and production process to capital accumulation. At one end is the legally regulated and mandated process of evaluating the assets, profits, and losses of a corporation as information guaranteed by publicly mandated accountants, and available to the "owners" of a corporation, its shareholders, internal revenue departments, and so forth. At the other, the appraisal and control, stage by stage, of the rate of return on investment achieved at each phase of the production process in different departments and divisions. Rate of return on investment introduces a powerful temporal component to the evaluation of the production process. Rates of return on investment are estimated in relation to a continuous time series, in contrast to earlier procedures in which profits were established for a definite lump of time, ordinarily a year, or some fraction of a year, by deducting overall costs from overall sales.

11. George Smith has made an important but as yet unpublished theoretical contribution in this area.

12. Our research project was focused on managerial training initiatives in relation to a particular government program, and exploring workers' experience and perspective was not part of it.

References

Burrough, Bryan and Helyar, John. 1991. *Barbarians at the Gate: The Fall of RJR Nabisco*. New York: Harper.

Canadian Business Task Force on Literacy. 1988. *Measuring the Costs of Illiteracy in Canada*. Toronto: Canadian Business Task Force on Literacy.

Cassin, Marguerite. 1986. Presentation on the documentary construction of management, Meeting of the Social Organization of Knowledge Proseminar, Toronto, Ontario Institute for Studies in Education.

Darville, Richard. No date. "Framing Il/literacy in the Media." Center for Policy Studies in Education, University of British Columbia, Vancouver.

Devitt, Amy J. 1991. "Intertextuality in Tax Accounting: Generic, Referential, and Functional." Pp. 336–57 in *Textual Dynamics of the Professions: Historical and Contemporary Studies of Writing in Professional Communities*, edited by Charles Bazerman and James Paradis. Madison: University of Wisconsin Press.

Garfinkel, Harold. 1967. *Studies in Ethnomethodology.* Englewood Cliffs, NJ: Prentice-Hall.

Gusfield, Joseph. 1966. *Symbolic Crusade: Status Politics and the American Temperance Movement.* Urbana: University of Illinois Press.

Habermas, Jurgen. 1989. *The Structural Transformation of the Public Sphere: An Inquiry into a Category of Bourgeois Society.* Cambridge, MA: MIT Press.

Lemert, Edwin. 1970. *Social Action and Legal Change: Revolution within the Juvenile Court.* Chicago: Aldine.

McCoy, Liza. 1991. "Accounting as Interorganizational Organization." Paper presented at the meetings of the Society for the Study of Social Problems, Cincinnati.

Mead, George Herbert. 1932. *Mind, Self and Society—From the Standpoint of a Social Behaviorist.* Chicago: University of Chicago Press.

Montagna, Paul. 1990. "Accounting rationality and financial legitimation." Pp. 227–60 in *Structures of Capital: The Social Organization of the Economy*, edited by Sharon Zukin and Paul DiMaggio. Cambridge: Cambridge University Press.

Olson, David. 1977. "From Utterance to Text: The Bias of Language in Speech and Writing." *Harvard Educational Review* 6(3):47.

Park, Robert E. 1955. *Society: The Collected Papers of Robert Park*, Vol. 3. Glencoe, IL: Free Press.

Pizzo, Stephen, Mary, Fricker, and Paul Muolo. 1991. *Inside Job: The Looting of America's Savings & Loans.* New York: Harper.

Rafter. Nicole A. 1992. "Claims-Making and Socio-Cultural Context in the First U.S. Eugenics Campaign." *Social Problems* 39(1):17–34.

Sloan, Albert. 1964. *My Years with General Motors.* New York: Doubleday.

Smith, Dorothy E. 1987. *The Everyday World as Problematic: A Feminist Sociology.* Boston: Northeastern University Press.

———. 1990a. *The Conceptual Practices of Power: A Feminist Sociology of Knowledge.* Boston: Northeastern University Press.

———. 1990b. *Texts, Facts and Femininity: Exploring the Relations of Ruling.* London: Routledge.

Spector, Malcolm and John I. Kitsuse. [1977] 1987. *Constructing Social Problems.* Hawthorne, NY: Aldine de Gruyter.

Troyer, Ronald J. 1992. "Some Consequences of Contextual Constructionism." *Social Problem* 39(1):35–37.

Yates, JoAnne. 1989. *Control through Communication: The Rise of System in American Management.* Baltimore: Johns Hopkins University Press.

Poststructuralist Challenges

17

Claims-Making from the Underside: Marginalization and Social Problems Analysis

Leslie J. Miller

I. Introduction

In the course of their discussion of social problems analysis in this volume, Ibarra and Kitsuse state: "The matter of marginality . . . . is a subject that greatly interests us." They are not alone. The existence of communities whose typical ways of knowing and talking about the world have been discredited, or marginalized, is a matter of increasing interest to scholars within the social problems field as well as outside it. My purpose in what follows is to sift the larger theoretical discussion of marginality for what it has to say to analysts of social problems.

Most sociologists first encountered the issue of marginalization in its epistemological form: What counts as a (legitimate) way of knowing the world? Anchored in the recognition that knowledge was always knowledge from somewhere,[1] this formulation of the question made it plain that *some* ways of knowing (e.g., professional medicine, science) had put to rout *other* ways (e.g., commonsense, the "voice of experience"), which, if they survived at all, had retained little credibility as "prejudice," "ignorance," and "myth."[2] For the analyst of social problems, the question of marginalization takes the form, What counts as a (legitimate) way of talking problems? The question acts as a reminder of the perspectivality of dominant ways of making claims, and suggests that some ways of raising concerns will be less successful than others. But while the social problems literature reveals little systematic discussion of marginalized social problems talk, it has shown a growing recognition that problems can be talked up in a number of ways.[3]

Several developments in the field have come together to broaden our sense of what counts as social problems talk. The first is a heightened

awareness of the highly organized yet heterogeneous character of everyday life, especially the "seen but unnoticed" sphere of women and the
family, which has worked to expand the study of claims-making activities beyond its initial focus on what goes on in professional people-
processing institutions. Although the centrality of "public problems" to
the field is still advocated by some, most sociologists see the merit in
extending the study of social problems talk to what Featherstone calls
"the life left behind" (Featherstone 1992, p. 160). Sometimes framed as
the study of "troubles," this research has demonstrated how people
struggle to achieve an account of what's objectionable in their lives long
before (or at the same time as) their accounts are reformulated by professional claims-makers and official discourses (e.g., Jefferson and Lee
1981; Emerson and Messenger 1977; Smith 1987).[4]

The second factor is our richer understanding of language and the
way it works. Many sociologists now take it as axiomatic that the world
is unavailable to us except in language, i.e., in the ways we have to think
and speak about it. This means that language is not simply an aspect of
social life (a kind of behavior) but the basis of it. Definitional matters
have long been seen as important in social problems research (notably in
labeling theory) and more recently a different body of scholarship has
demonstrated, through a wide array of substantive studies, that "the
order of things" is created, sustained, and resisted discursively (e.g.,
Davies 1989; Gubrium and Holstein 1990; Holstein 1987; G. Miller 1991;
L. Miller 1990, 1991; Smith 1987). These studies are a pointed reminder
to analysts of social problems that realities are negotiated in talk.[5]

The implication of these developments for social problems theorists is
that different communities of speakers will have different ways of making claims, and some of these ways will be less visible than others, as
Ibarra and Kitsuse recognize. But the analysis of marginalization as a
process in the social problems literature is thin.[6] One reason is that the
classic early studies of marginal or deviant subcultures, while documenting insider knowledge and insider jargon, tended to emphasize the
legitimate, autonomous social orders these communities displayed,
rather than their marginality per se or the impact this had on their
characteristic ways of raising problems. In general, these ethnographies
showed that subcultural communities were hidden from the perspective
of dominant groups, without showing how that invisibility was imposed, sustained, recognized, and resisted. Inspired by the conviction
that the social world of the hobo or the hustler was separate but equal,
this generation of researchers emphasized cultural difference, rather
than domination and resistance. As a result, the features of marginalized worlds (and discourses) were not systematically connected to
power—as if these worlds "just happened" to be obscure.

A second reason is the blind spot toward large-scale discourse that has handicapped the ethnomethodological contribution to social problems analysis in the 1970s and 1980s. Ethnomethodologists and conversation analysts have consistently maintained their fealty to the interaction order. While studies have been able to show how social order is achieved in routine interaction, and even how members accomplish domination and subordination in their talk—I am thinking here especially of work on gender and communication—they are unable to account for the fact that different ways of talking (including ways of talking problems) carry different degrees of authority, for these considerations would take them beyond the interactional setting into the historical conditions surrounding the emergence of large-scale hegemonic discourses (such as the institutional discourses of professional medicine, or the commonsense discourses of masculinity and femininity that rose to prominence in the nineteenth century). Ethnomethodological inattention to the insights of scholars like Foucault and Gramsci is based largely on the principled rejection of what they take to be top-down, totalizing discourses, which turn actors into cultural or linguistic dopes. But this view is misguided,[7] and has weakened their ability to öffer an adequate treatment of power and marginality. These issues will be taken up elsewhere in the paper.

Finally, social problems theorists have been interested in the question, What counts as a claim? mainly as a way of defining and widening the scope of the field. In effect, the question has been treated as a (theorist's) limit, rather than a (member's) exclusionary practice to be studied. I return to this argument in a later section; for now, the point is that the study of marginalization, as a practice that silences some styles of claims-making, itself remains a marginal issue in the social problems literature.

By contrast, the discussion of marginality *outside* the social problems field is well developed, and it is a discussion that places power at the forefront. A broad scan of the contemporary theoretical scene reveals a growing interest in what we might call, in social problems parlance, "claims-making from the underside." Some sociological perspectives, notably poststructuralism and postmodernism, take their point of departure from Foucault's (1979) recommendation that we amplify the "voice of the other" by "entertain[ing] the claims to attention of local, discontinuous, disqualified, illegitimate knowledges" (Foucault, in Coles 1991, p. 110) in order to recover some sense of the power struggles that have silenced them. In social psychology we find the well-known studies of Gilligan (1982), and Belenky, Clinchy, Goldberger, and Tarule (1986), which attribute distinctive styles of moral discourse to women, ones that have been trivialized and in other ways discredited by a privileged masculine form of reasoning. In linguistics, anthropology, and sociology

there is a steadily evolving literature exploring the display and reproduction of dominant and subordinate status in talk (e.g., Lakoff 1990;
Thorne, Kramarae, and Henley 1983), a literature that puts power at the
forefront despite the aforementioned problems that accompany much
conversation analysis. Also well known are feminist analyses of "wom-
en's ailments," such as anorexia and "hysteria" in the last century,
which reformulate these conditions as women's ways of raising problems through the distinctively feminine language of body (e.g., Bordo
1989). And the current boom in cultural studies (see, for example,
Grossberg, Nelson, and Treichler 1992) is tied to a new interest in how
"the people" evade or resist dominant ideologies through their participation in popular pleasures. As Ibarra and Kitsuse observe, the theme of
"resistance from below" runs through British studies of popular culture,
where (for example) the idea that members of youth subcultures make
claims through "fashion statements" is by now a familiar one.

What is of interest to us in these diverse studies is their commitment
to read the activities of these groups as marginalized, i.e., depoliticized
ways of raising problems. As well, they share an assumption that the
form of these activities is related in some way to the specific conditions
of oppression experienced by each group. In every case, the effect of the
analysis is to *reinstate these inaudible speakers as claimants,* thereby re-
politicizing their talk. This is done in the belief that the ways problems
are raised, including the ways they are ignored or trivialized, are members' achievements, which can and should be studied. In what follows I
shall suggest that the social problems theorist can learn much about
marginalization from these other perspectives. The salient research
questions are two: (1) How have some ways of talking problems (making
claims) emerged as privileged or normative, as others have been
eclipsed or silenced? (2) What do these processes reveal about power
and how it operates?[8]

II. The Poststructuralist Vision: All Talk Makes a Claim

For an adequate understanding of marginalization as process, there is
no better place to turn than to the approaches that place marginalization
at the top of their theoretical agendas. I refer here to poststructuralism
and to some variants of feminist theorizing. While these perspectives are
not in agreement in all respects,[9] they do come together around their
common interest in "subjugated knowledges"—ways of saying and
knowing that have been silenced or discredited by dominant discourses
and practices. In what follows I want to explore several of their insights,
in order to indicate what should interest social problems theorists in

them, and how they make a difference to the social problems research agenda.

At the heart of the poststructuralist vision is a reconceptualization of *power*. Formerly understood as "owned" by elite groups (classes) and individuals (kings), power in a contemporary milieu is understood to exist in a host of microsites all across the social landscape as the struggle over meaning. Following the later Foucault, poststructuralists argue that if power "resides" anywhere, it is in the dominant discourses of the day. Thus power is displaced from the activities of politicians and interest groups to language, that is, to the routine encounters between those who artfully represent and reproduce the era's dominant discourses and those whose accounts of the world have been marginalized or silenced by them.

It is important to see that the Foucauldian reconceptualization of power does not work to destroy politics, but rather to politicize all talk. Because power is located at the level of saying and knowing, it infuses all, not just some, aspects of social life. "All talk is a text" means that all talk promotes a preferred account of the world, one that necessarily disqualifies other accounts. In short, *all* talk makes a claim—though not all ways of making claims will be equally valued.

The implications of this relentlessly politicized vision of social life could not be more radical for the constructionist approach to social problems. Its most important result is to undermine the very basis of social problems study as the analysis of a distinct class of phenomena, by undermining (or deconstructing) the empirical distinction between activities that make claims and those which do not. By recommending that we read all talk as a text, poststructuralism has taken the very feature of *social problems* talk that makes it special, according to the social problems theorist—its rhetorical or claims-making character—and has installed it as the characteristic feature of *all* talk.

I commented earlier on the gradual trend within the social problems literature to widen the net of what constitutes claims-making; perhaps social problems theorists too would in time arrive at the conclusion that all talk makes a claim. At present, however, the trend moves forward in empirical, piecemeal fashion, so that first one area of social life, then another, is "discovered" to harbor claims-making activities, or social problems talk. There remain, by implication, some kinds of talk that *don't* make claims (for example, see Ibarra and Kitsuse).

The position that social problems theorists and researchers are edging up to—"Read *all* talk as a claim"—is asserted as a matter of theoretical election by poststructuralists and some schools of feminist thought. I remarked earlier that these approaches stand out for their willingness to take marginality seriously, and it is important to note here that it is precisely *the view from the margins* (what some feminists have called an "oppositional consciousness" and the "standpoint of the other") that reads claims-making (the contesting of meaning) as *the* important feature of interaction/talk. Moreover, their insights suggest that it is only from the standpoint of the powerful (from the perspective of dominant discourses) that "some" people *do not* appear to be engaged in claims-making (or to be taking moral stances), and that "some" social worlds *do not* appear to harbor "recognizable" social problems talk.

The point, of course, is Recognizable to whom? The value of the view from the margins is precisely its recognition that the "absence" of social problems talk in some situations is an achieved invisibility or marginalization—in short, a discursive accomplishment whose structure and workings can be studied. If people are always and everywhere raising matters of concern to themselves, then we can ask in what sites and with what discursive resources can talk's readability as claims-making be suppressed? Moreover, when all talk is read as making a claim, then the salient theoretical distinction is no longer between talk that makes a claim and talk that doesn't, but between the kinds of claims-making styles that are "readable at a glance," and those whose claims-making status is "unrecognized" or discredited.

It is against the background of a radically politicized landscape of meaning struggles that we can evaluate recent efforts to delimit and describe the field of social problems study. The perspective we have developed out of poststructuralist insights indicates that Ibarra and Kitsuse, for example, do not go far enough when they suggest broadening "the scope of what counts as claims-making," or when they observe how "social problems discourse occurs in all manner of forums and among a wide range of persons," for these comments continue to assume that we live in a world divided into two kinds of talk (talk that makes claims and talk that doesn't) and that even though the dividing line may be shifting, social problems analysts should accept it unproblematically and let it define the boundaries of the field.

By contrast, poststructuralism implies that what counts as a claim (or an instance of social problems talk) must be a topic of inquiry, rather than a limit to be assumed; "who qualifies" as a participant in social problems discourse is a matter negotiated among members and thus a differentiating practice to be studied, not an empirical fact or property that identifies a distinct "class of phenomena." The poststructuralist insight forces us to reexamine the markers (some) communities use to identify claims and claimants, according to Ibarra and Kitsuse, and it suggests that such markers mark only those kinds of claims-making activities that achieve visibility within the terms of some dominant discourse or system of meaning. If the kinds of rhetorical figures described by these authors (loss, crisis, etc.) are the conventional ways of making claims visible as claims, then how are marginalized claims-making activities marked? What are the vernacular features of claims-making *from the underside?*

The example that follows is meant to raise some of these issues. Unlike the kinds of conversations ordinarily analyzed by social problems theorists, this exchange is not noticeably rhetorical. I will argue that this outcome is *itself* an achieved appearance: just as there are discursive practices or strategies that politicize talk, thereby putting problems *on* the agenda, so there are strategies that depoliticize talk and keep them *off.* We shall want to examine how the depoliticization (or marginalization) of some kinds of talk is achieved, and how it is resisted (if it is). In this case, I shall be suggesting that the political character of the conversation is recessed or made invisible through a collaboration that works to deny the status of claimant to one of the speakers.

III. Depoliticizing Others' Claims: An Example

The exchange analyzed below is drawn from a British study of dual-earner households and focuses on women's decisions to return to (paid) work after the birth of their first child (Brannen and Moss 1987). The authors are interested in the persistence of the "male breadwinner ideology" and accordingly, in the ways that wives' contribution to the household economy through their wages is defined. The ideology in question says, in part, that husbands are the primary earners while women's earnings "help out," i.e., are secondary to their husbands'. The study included women who, before they left the labor force, had earned both less and more than their husbands. In this transcribed conversation, the interviewer talks with a Mr. and Mrs. Dunn, whose wages are "roughly similar":

Interviewer:	How important is the money you earn to the household/family budget?
Alice Dunn:	Oh! It helps. I don't think—well, yes it would matter if I didn't work, wouldn't it, Michael? I can't say it wouldn't. I think it's quite necessary.
Interviewer:	You see it that way?
Mr. Dunn:	(interjecting) Her money does buy the extra bits and pieces.
Alice Dunn:	(answering the interviewer's question) I do and I don't. I suppose if we really put our minds to it I wouldn't have to work, would I Michael? We could manage if we wanted to if we didn't have all the little bits.

Interviewer:	Do you see your money as for extras or for the basic essentials?
Alice Dunn:	(starts to do sums out loud) . . . . Well, I suppose I *was* thinking of it for basic living. If I was thinking of it *now* I suppose we could manage. I was thinking of it—
Mr. Dunn:	(interjecting) We were without it for ten months!
Alice Dunn:	(continuing) In my mind I was thinking we probably couldn't manage without it. I was sort of thinking about it I suppose— looking at your wage—I suppose we would have been really pushed wouldn't we? But I suppose I can't say that now. I suppose it's for luxuries and going on holidays and things—
Mr. Dunn:	(interjecting) We don't spend a great deal. We don't smoke and we don't drink. We only have a car and a certain other person.
Alice Dunn:	(with an air of finality) Yes, I suppose it is for luxuries! (Brannen and Moss 1987, p. 89)

In their discussion, the authors make a number of insightful comments regarding the way that the meaning of Mrs. Dunn's financial contribution is negotiated in the course of this and other conversations. They note Mrs. Dunn's initial tendency to define her wages as important, and how by the end of the excerpt, they have been firmly redefined as secondary (expendable, "for luxuries"), thus reaffirming the husband's role as primary breadwinner in accordance with the gendered division of labor prescribed by the dominant ideology. Their interest is largely in the substance of the talk.

Our interest, by contrast, is in this exchange as a site of (suppressed or marginalized) claims-making activity—in particular, in the discursive practices that succeed in keeping the issue raised by Mrs. Dunn (how to evaluate her contribution) off the conversational agenda. We should note at the outset that although poststructuralists and feminists alike would read this conversation as a site of claims-making activities, the passage displays none of the vernacular markers of social problems talk generally identified by social problems researchers. The conversation does not take place in an institutional setting (a courtroom, a doctor's office) nor is there present a professional claims-maker whose business it is to enforce a privileged version of "the problem" (e.g., as in Darrough 1990). Neither does husband or wife attempt to compare their family economy to the "family in the large"—a sign, for authors like Gubrium and Holstein (1990, pp. 61–70), that speakers agree *that* they have a problem, even as they disagree on its particular type. There is no "troubles-telling" of the sort that either Emerson and Messenger, or Jefferson and Lee describe; there is not even a discernible "problem proposal" (Maynard 1988, p. 319) that can be honored (or not) by one of the parties. And finally, though we hear indignation from the husband, we do not hear the sound of moral stances being taken as Ibarra and Kitsuse describe them: Nowhere does Mr. Dunn employ a "rhetoric of loss," for example, to inveigh against the demise of the good old-fashioned family; there are no "crisis motifs" apparent (see Ibarra and Kitsuse). In short, this stretch of talk does not look like social problems talk, for there are none of the "distinctive but conventional ways of speaking and reasoning that obtain whenever persons qualify as participants in social problems discourse" (Ibarra and Kitsuse) and it is probable that on these grounds, Ibarra and Kitsuse, among others, would disqualify it as a site of claims-making.

In contrast, the mandate of poststructuralism as I have developed it here invites us to read this exchange as any other, that is, as a *political* encounter centered in rhetoric and negotiation. It invites us, in other words, to challenge this disqualification by reading the talk as a marginalization, not an absence, of claims-making. In this case we shall want to examine how such marginalization is achieved, and how it is resisted (if it is).

To say that the conversation remains finally apolitical is to say that Mrs. Dunn is never able to seriously contest her husband's account of the familial division of labor. In particular, she is unable to formulate her resistance in a way that obliges Mr. Dunn to read it as a claim; as a result, "an intersubjective agreement that there is a 'problem' is never achieved" (Maynard 1988, p. 319). What might have shaped up as a dispute (claim, counterclaim) becomes in short order a descriptive collaboration, in which Mrs. Dunn is repositioned not as a claimant, but as an incompetent describer who tries to "get it right" over the course of the conversation ("Well, I suppose I *was* thinking of it . . . . If I was thinking of it *now*," etc.)—that is, one whose first description of herself as a equal contributor ("I think it's [her wage] quite necessary") is revealed as incorrect and then replaced by a more accurate one ("Yes, I suppose it is for luxuries!"). At the moment she is successfully constructed as an incompetent describer, her status as a claimant—one who raises a problem—is defused.

The politicizing of this exchange—the road not taken—might have occurred in several ways. Mrs. Dunn might have contested her husband's account by presenting herself as the victim of male oppression (one whose husband refuses to give her her due) and in response, Mr. Dunn might have come on as the champion of old-fashioned family values, both forms of rhetoric that work to up the moral ante of the talk (see Ibarra and Kitsuse). Or the interviewer, instead of retaining a neutral role, might have intervened in a therapeutic mode, and begun to engage the couple in the sort of categorizing work described by Gubrium and Holstein—say, by suggesting that the "Dunns' problem" around Mrs. Dunn's earnings was probably of *this* sort, rather than *that*.

But none of these scenarios occurs; the conventional account of the familial division of labor (as articulated by Mr. Dunn) never surfaces as a bone of contention. Because Mrs. Dunn is unable to halt the reformulation of her status from potential counterclaimant to "poor describer"— and indeed collaborates in it—her initial challenge to the dominant framework of meaning is rapidly absorbed back into it. As the producer of mere comments and incompetent descriptions, not claims (speech that must be heeded), Mrs. Dunn is herself effectively depoliticized, so that what she has to say is read as making no difference to the order of things.

The discursive subordination of Mrs. Dunn as a claimant is accomplished, of course, in the interactional situation. Here we are on the terrain of the conversation analyst, who would point out how Mr. Dunn's talk displays many of the features associated with the dominant "masculine" style: He interrupts Mrs. Dunn three times, a turn-taking violation disproportionately practiced by the more powerful speaker; he asserts his views in direct fashion, while his wife ruminates, equivocates, and couches her views as opinions: "I do and I don't," "I was thinking" (five times), "I suppose" (eight times). Furthermore, only Mrs. Dunn personalizes her utterances by using her husband's name (twice), and she employs three tag-questions ("Wouldn't it Michael?"), both features of subordinate talk oriented to producing the speaker as "poor wee me" (Zwarun, in Mackie 1991, p. 188).

But for the poststructuralist, marginalization is not adequately explained by referring to these kinds of linguistic practices and techniques alone. In addition, speakers are empowered by their ability to access and strategically deploy the dominant discourses of the day (as any speaker who has exploited the prestigious rhetoric of scientific sociology will readily acknowledge). This point represents a shift away from the interactional setting to the cultural repertoire of discourses that speakers invoke as resources for their interactional encounters. And while such discourses are employed in the interaction setting, it is important to remember that they are *collective* representations of reality—that is to say, they are social, not individual, facts. Mr. Dunn's disempowerment of his wife, then, is not simply a matter of the linguistic methods he employs (interruption, and so on), it is also a matter of his ability to invoke a dominant discourse (here, of the patriarchal family), which validates his account of the familial division of labor and empowers him as a speaker in crucial ways.

These considerations shed some light on the question of what it means to produce a readable or intelligible claim. A useful contribution is provided by the British researchers, whose theoretical interest in marginalized subjects requires them to "take women's accounts seriously" (Brannen and Moss 1987, p. 12)—in our terms, to read their utterances as claims, albeit failed ones. The researchers also note that silence and ambiguity are frequently the responses of women who are asked about their own contribution to the family economy. By instructing us to read these "muted responses" as interesting findings in themselves rather than as methodological obstacles (i.e., as unsuccessful claims rather than coding problems) the authors restore the talk's political character. Moreover, they imply that silence, contradiction, and so on are, we might say, the conventional vernacular markers of marginalized claims, or claims-making "from the underside."[10] Here we have the idea that the claims-making styles of subordinate groups will display distinctive, describable features, for those who are able to see and hear them. I return to this point in Section IV.

The British researchers then turn to why these "muted responses" fail as claims. They observe: "What is striking about these [women's] accounts is the absence of a clearly and confidently articulated set of codes" with which to talk about their concerns (in this case their economic contribution to the household). Here they suggest an important insight into the discursive basis of claims-making: For a comment to be heard as a claim, it must be able to draw on "a clearly and confidently articulated code" with which to talk about X. Thus the features of individual utterances (silence, ambiguity), as well as their fate (whether they will be intelligible as claims or not), are explicitly tied to the availability of discourses or "codes" at the macrolevel. This means that a claim is not just a comment: to make a claim is to be heard to be articulating an already available conventional discourse or account of the world, and to be marshalling it as a position or stance.[11] A claim relies on an authoritative discourse to give it moral and political force *as* a claim. By contrast, talk that is grounded in fragmented or marginalized discourses (or ones unavailable to the community of speakers) cannot be formulated as a recognizable stance or position, and is read as idiosyncratic or personal comment, having no political force.[12]

In the case at hand, Mr. Dunn is able to draw on the dominant discourse of the domestic patriarchal family. A large nexus of taken-for-granted beliefs about marriage, gender, and child-rearing enshrined as commonsense, its most salient feature for our purposes here is a set of paired assumptions concerning what husbands do (primary breadwinning; "helping out" at home) and what wives do (primary mother-work; "helping out" economically). Borrowing Schutz's insight, we may say that such dominant discourses are typifications that furnish the individual with categories for the ordering of reality. Such categories are shared, public formulations, and it is Mr. Dunn's ability to draw on them that gives his talk readability as a claim. For example, we the readers, the interviewer, and both Dunns are able to hear Mr. Dunn's comment "We were without it [his wife's income] for ten months" as the claim (or partisan position) "I support this family" because "everybody knows" that if they did without her income, it must have been expendable.

By contrast, an alternative discourse that might ground Mrs. Dunn's resistance as a counterclaim is not available, at least for her, as a resource upon which to draw: Her world provides no social rhetoric of equality or of women's rights—no *other way* of describing her economic role outside the dominant category of one who "helps out." In the absence of an alternative formulation, her talk is not heard as a position or stance, and is readily silenced or defused as incompetence. In sum, it is the availability of an alternative discourse (e.g., of equality) in a community's cultural repertoire—as well as the speaker's ability to marshall it in talk—that differentiates the fully articulated claim from the sound of inchoate resistance (silence, ambiguity). Insofar as Mrs. Dunn's concerns are excluded by the dominant discourse, her plight is like that of other marginalized speakers. Describing the problems of the oppressed, the novelist Gabriel Garcia Marquez has stated: "[O]ur crucial problem has been a lack of conventional means to render our lives believable. This, my friends, is the crux of our solitude" (Marquez, in Hartsock 1990, p. 25). The "means" the oppressed lack is language, not dollars or armies, and Marquez's point is that exclusionary practices are discursive at root.

There are several important implications to be drawn from this example. The first has to do with the way we understand power. Under the auspices of a poststructuralist, feminist reading of this conversation, we have asked how the denial of one of the speakers as a claimant—as the poser of a problem—is achieved. We are now in a position to see that it is the power of the dominant discourse (here, of the domestic patriarchal family)—not the interactional power of Mr. Dunn—that undermines her talk as a claim. Mrs. Dunn's ability to construct her talk as a (counter)claim (to problematize the received account as voiced by her husband) is very much constrained by the terms of the dominant discourse (the "code"), which hegemonically limits her way of knowing and speaking about her work to the categories available within the existing framework (mother-work and secondary earning). The capacity of powerful dominant discourses to ward off or preclude challenges to their fundamental assumptions or categories, and to conceal their exclusionary practices, is a favorite theme of Foucault's: In our example this power is displayed in the fact that Mrs. Dunn's resistance to the dominant discourse never attains the status of challenge, and is rapidly absorbed back into the dominant framework of meaning.[13]

The first point, then, is that the exercise of power in this situation is not adequately depicted as an oppressive interaction between a dominant husband and a resistant, yet finally subordinate wife; nor can Mrs. Dunn's prospects for raising a successful problem-proposal around the contribution of her work, or for renegotiating its meaning, be assessed by considering the *interactional* order alone. Instead, we have here a more complex collaboration between the speakers and the dominant discourse upon which they draw to make sense of the world ("what everybody knows" about family life). This discourse not only limits what kinds of claims can be made substantively—what kinds of moral stances can be taken—but also *whether* counterclaims and claimants are likely to emerge at all. Power is indeed at work in this situation, but, as Holstein has noted in connection with gender, it is not adequately conceptualized as a variable that predetermines talk (Holstein 1987). Instead, power is a matter of discourses, and it is exercised by speakers who deploy them as conversational resources to argue for preferred versions of social reality (or indeed to prevent a struggle over meaning from ever emerging). This point follows directly from Foucault's insistence that power is located first in the dominant discourses of the day, and only secondly in those who artfully use them.

The second point to note in connection with this example is the extraordinary hegemonic power of *commonsense* discourses—descriptions of reality that "go without saying." Like other discourses, they provide members with preferred ways to know and talk about the world. What sets everyday or commonsense discourses apart from others, however, is their extraordinary power to eclipse competing accounts of reality, and it has not escaped feminist scholars that some discourses, notably those of the domestic family and biological discourses of sexual difference, lie at the heart of Western culture and are perceived, accordingly, as unchallengeable, natural orders. Their unusual moral authority lies precisely in the fact that they are taken by "everyone" to be beyond dispute: As the way the world (allegedly) goes round, and ought to go round, they are accepted as objective truths outside human intervention. In contrast to professional discourses, they are more thoroughly naturalized. That is, they marginalize *other* ways of knowing and saying more completely.[14]

Professional discourses, however, make claims about the world that tend to be both less inclusive of social life and also more arguable. Thus, for example, Gale Miller notes how in exchanges between unemployed clients and staff members in a government work incentive program, clients will often be able to counter the staff member's descriptions of "the problem" "by pointing to aspects of everyday life that are deemphasized and left out of [bureaucratic discourse]" (1991, p. 10). By contrast, the difficulty Mrs. Dunn has in countering the dominant discourse of family invoked by her husband is precisely the problem she (and any other member) has in imagining and describing the world in ways outside the conventional channels. This outcome is not a personal failure of Mrs. Dunn's, but rather a testimony to the comparatively greater hegemonic power of the commonsense discourse of family to silence difference. Unlike the clients in the WIN program that Miller describes, Mrs. Dunn is never able to articulate "what has been left out" of the received framework to the point of raising a counterclaim. In short, to say that commonsense discourses have greater hegemonic power than professional ones is to say that they exclude "what they leave out" more effectively.

Two consequences follow from the fact that commonsense accounts of the world are so securely installed as "natural" orders: (1) Members, like Mrs. Dunn, will find resisting or challenging them (i.e., voicing an alternative discourse) more difficult, and (2) social problems theorists will be less likely to see routine everyday conversations, such as the Dunns', as sites of social problems talk, for it is precisely at these sites that the political character of the encounter, as a struggle between claimants, is most thoroughly concealed. Here is where the poststructuralist research agenda parts company from that of the social problems theorist: For while the latter, taking the apolitical character of the talk at face value, would likely find such sites of no interest (i.e., not sites of claims-making), the poststructuralist, by contrast, will home in on them as sites where the power of dominant discourses to silence resistance and to mask the achieved character of this outcome is greatest, because it is the most perfectly hidden.

The division of interaction into political and apolitical types, which most social problems theorists appear to take for granted, is no doubt at the heart of their tendency to focus on institutional claims-making activities or on well-marked encounters between partisan interest groups in the public sphere, for it is these kinds of encounters (e.g., between ordinary citizens and parole officers, or between pro– and anti–gay rights groups) that are most easily readable as claims-making activities. But for the poststructuralist, these are only the most obvious sites of conversational politics. By focusing only or primarily on meaning struggles in these sites, the theorist risks leaving intact "the regions where the logic of exclusion disguises its operations more completely" (Kamuf 1990, p. 106).[15]

As I argued earlier, the force of the poststructuralist perspective as I have developed it here is to challenge this division. Social problems theorists appear to treat it as a natural feature of the world, rather than as an achievement whose workings they must analyze. While this perspective allows them to mark off for themselves a distinct field of study (with a mandate to study social problems talk, rather than *all* talk) it also means that they will miss (i.e., read as not political) a whole range of interaction whose political character as an exchange of claims is marginalized (rendered invisible, denied, concealed). Moreover, it blinds them to an important insight about discursive power: Power is exercised not only in the reality struggles between claims-makers, but also in sites where these struggles have been silenced.

If, as the poststructuralist argues, *all* talk involves struggles over meaning, then instead of a division between political and nonpolitical talk, we must posit a continuum, at one end of which are claims-making activities that are easily readable as such, and at the other, those which are marginalized (primarily because the status of claimant is refused or concealed). Moreover, *where* a given exchange will fall on this continuum is not a natural feature of talk, but an achievement that will depend on members' artful use of discursive resources and strategies. This view recognizes that the hegemonic power of particular discourses and speakers to exclude or silence counterclaims (competing accounts of the world) will vary, and that a speaker's ability to voice alternative accounts in given situations—to resist or contest dominant meanings—will range from the confident articulation of partisan positions and counterpositions (over abortion, nuclear power, and so on) to the inchoate styles of resistance such as that of Mrs. Dunn, in whose comments a claim is barely audible. But whether resistance emerges as a fully developed counterclaim or is marginalized to the point of inaudibility, the poststructuralist perspective will read speakers as on all occasions *negotiating* what the order of things is, and how it should be.

This is the bottom-line assumption that gives poststructuralism the edge over other perspectives when it comes to theorizing marginality. It is the source of its appeal for feminists as well. In this connection then, it may be useful to briefly compare poststructuralist and ethnomethodological perspectives in order to assess their relative contributions to the analysis of marginalization. As I have emphasized, ethnomethodologists must broaden their conception of members' methods and resources to include large-scale discourses that influence the ways interaction is accomplished, but do not have their origin there—and they must do so in a way that does not reduce speakers to the puppets of these macrolevel forces.[16] An exclusive focus on the "interaction order" as conversation analysts understand this term (that is, on turn-taking, and other features stemming from the Sacks-Schegloff corpus) will never tell us, for example, why a chat about finances between working-class women at the laundromat is discredited as "gossip," while the same matters taken up in the legislature are valorized as "debate," whatever *other* linguistic similarities these two exchanges display. Nor will broadening their analysis to include these social facts require the ethnomethodologist to step outside the realm of members' knowledge, for members are demonstrably aware of these differences and orient to them in their own talk. Members (tacitly) recognize these social facts as important components of marginality;[17] so then should conversation analysts. In contrast, the appeal of poststructuralism for feminists lies partly in its willingness to recognize how dominant discourses (or "ideologies") have been able, historically and at present, to depoliticize whole styles of saying and knowing, and whole communities of speakers.

Beyond this, there is a second difference. As I noted in Section I, an important strength of the ethnomethodological approach is its commitment to agency, that is, to a strong version of members as artful reality constructors. Each interaction is understood as the opportunity for the situational accomplishment of the phenomenon at hand; the Dunns, for example, are seen as jointly accomplishing dominance and subordination in the course of their talk. Thus, it is important to reiterate that from this perspective, the features of the exchange (violations of turn-taking order, and so on) are not understood as a *result* of differential power (or gender), but rather as an instance of power *enacted*. If power is understood as the ability to have one's position heard, then Mr. Dunn interactionally achieves this, while Mrs. Dunn does not.[18]

This way of understanding the issue brings into relief an important difference between ethnomethodological and poststructural assumptions about the nature of action. For where the conversation analyst sees Mrs. Dunn as actively accomplishing her subordination, the poststructuralist would see her as actively (albeit ineffectively) resisting or contesting it. By declaring that *all* interaction is essentially about struggles over meaning, the poststructuralist transforms the documents of Mrs. Dunn's subordination (her silences, her tag-questions) into evidence of her resistance. In short, ethnomethodology formulates actors as *constructors of order*; the poststructuralist reads them as *constructors of power and resistance*.

This is a difference at the level of theoretical assumptions, not an empirical matter. And in the move from order-constructor to contester, the poststructuralist gives the concept of action/speech a political spin that amounts to a more proactive conception of agency than is possible under the ethnomethodological agenda. For the poststructuralist, talk is not just work (in the ethnomethodological sense of an achievement), it is adversarial work. Whether it succeeds or fails in its claim, talk promotes its version of the world against some other: Every apparently settled order conceals a reality struggle. The appeal of this position for members of marginalized groups is obvious, and the poststructuralist's radically politicized assumptions about the nature of action has made it an important drawing card for feminist scholars and activists. As Nancy Fraser remarks in her assessment of the utility of the poststructuralist approach for feminism, "even under conditions of subordination . . . . conflict and contestation are an important part of the story" (Fraser 1992, p. 54).

IV. Claims-Making from the Underside

I have suggested to this point that the poststructuralist's relentless politicizing of interaction opens up new areas of interest for the sociologists of social problems, by drawing their attention to those conversational sites and practices that recess the political character of talk. Our analysis of the Dunns' conversation is meant to highlight the discursive strategies Mr. Dunn employs that work to depoliticize the conversation by, in effect, depoliticizing his wife (i.e., by "refusing" to formulate her talk as a counterclaim to the dominant framework of meaning).

The silencing of potential claims-making activities or problem proposals as "just talk"—talk that makes no difference—is a fate that may befall not only subordinate individuals, like Mrs. Dunn, but also whole groups, whose typical ways of raising concerns come to be discredited or excluded by dominant or privileged claims-making styles. Consider, for example, *gossip*, originally a term referring to a child's male "godsib," now used to refer to the idle chatter of "old women" (Rysman 1977). Insights from feminist thought would invite us to consider gossip as, perhaps, a "women's way" of talking, a historically marginalized way of discussing problems now denied (i.e., "unrecognizable") as a claims-making style at all.

One of our concerns as theorists will be in how the marginalization of certain claims-making styles has been achieved,[19] and the example of gossip reminds us that their present status has a social history that can be traced. The marginalization of styles and speakers is not a creation of interactants in the course of their talk, except concretely. Instead, it is the outcome of historical processes that, in the case of gossip, saw male discourses of rationality and generality in the public sphere become the privileged standard of serious political exchange, against which the female, home-centered, personal, and anecdotal exchange would come to be discredited as "nothing but gossip," i.e., no "real" contest of viewpoints, no "real" expression of moral stances, no "real" negotiation of troubles—only idle chatter about who beats who in the neighborhood, who cannot make ends meet and why, and so on. From the standpoint of the dominant discourse of public-sphere discussion and argument then, *gossip* is a term which silences a local, anecdotal, and feminine style of claims-making by denying its character as "real" social problems talk. Its history, we suspect, is intimately bound into the major event of the early modern era—the cultural separation of the world of male, paid work (the public sphere) from the female world of family and unpaid work (the private sphere), and the inferior status that was ascribed to the latter.[20]

We take it that it is just this kind of moral discourse that Ibarra and Kitsuse mean to alert us to, when they discuss claims-making styles we may overlook if we take state- and media-sponsored styles as the standard (see Ibarra and Kitsuse on "subcultural style" and on "rapping"). *Our* point however—the poststructuralist point—is that it is not enough to note that these are "unique" or "local" ways of commenting on the world; we must recognize in addition that their distinctive features are the products of a marginalizing or discrediting process.[21] Gossip, I have argued, (like "black English") is not a neutral term describing a simply local way of talking problems; it is a term for *inadequate* talk. The term *gossip* is thus an expression of power, and it is applied as a way of discrediting one style of claims-making from the perspective of another, historically privileged one. And as a *style,* it is marked by that history of discredit. This is only to say that an inventory of claims-making styles will be no more than an inventory unless we examine the relationship between style and power. Some ways of making claims are more authoritative than other ways, and an important strategy for retaining privilege will be to deny other styles (such as gossip) the status of claims-making activities at all.

V. Underdog Skills: Managing the Readability of Claims

The relationship between style and power becomes clearer when we see how historically marginalized styles can be adopted by subordinate groups as *strategies* of influence. Such groups may use "underdog" styles (e.g., rapping) to press their claims, whatever the topic, and this may include masking (suppressing, concealing) their readability *as* claims in the first place, since overt claims-making talk (framed as loss, crisis, etc., as Ibarra and Kitsuse point out) is conventionally identifiable by all as a contest of viewpoints (that is, as *political*) and thus inevitably brings the struggle for power into the open. Accordingly, underdogs may use particular styles to raise a concern while recessing its contentious appearance—perhaps, by *avoiding* the very rhetorics Ibarra and Kitsuse describe. Damning with faint praise, for example, or kidding might be theorized as a style of claims-making used by subordinate speakers (wives, children, employees, colonized peoples) when pressing a claim with a superior group. Like rapping or gossip, these are styles that can artfully be used by speakers when they wish to make a claim without overtly appearing to do so; in such cases "the peace is kept" precisely because the matter of a problem (e.g., "Whitey's oppression of ghetto youth") never surfaces in an unambiguous or accusatory way.[22]

This does not mean that claims-making is absent, from the theorist's point of view, but only that people know that overt, "readable-at-a-glance" social problems talk is recognizably contentious, that it involves moral positions and the conflict of viewpoints, and that knowing this, people raise problems *as problems* only when they feel they can afford to. I am suggesting here that underdogs are skilled in playing—in managing—the readability of their claims. Recessing the political character of one's talk by making it appear, ambiguously, as kidding or only music (that is, as harmless) can be a protective strategy of use to individuals and groups who speak from a position of structural inequality in the system. Part of the difference between an established civil rights organization and a rap group is that one can afford to take a partisan position on matters of concern and be seen to do so, while the other, more vulnerable, may expediently adopt a style not so unambiguously readable as a claim. Thus underdogs are always able to depoliticize their talk by playing off the possibility that it is really something else ("only music").[23] The artfulness of underdog styles, then, cannot be fully appreciated until this strategy is recognized as a feature of their marginalized position (or history); and the artful manipulation of talk's ambiguity—now you see a claim, now you don't—is part of the appearance-work that marginalized speakers are skilled in.

In the foregoing I have begun to consider the ways historically/culturally marginalized styles of claims-making may be strategically taken up by individuals in microsettings. I have suggested that some groups have learned to exploit a marginalized claims-making style—in effect, a legacy of subordination—by turning it into a strategy for achieving specific conversational ends. Thus the strategic use of different claims-making styles, from "just gossip" or kidding, to the openly accusatory styles favored by protest movements, is also a careful manipulation of talk's degree of politicality. The artful use of such styles displays a concerted orientation to the political consequences of framing a claim in this way, rather than that.

The main point, then, is that claims-making styles are systematically related to power; to ignore this is to reduce the artful, concerted manipulation of the political tenor of talk to accident or incompetence. The political status of talk (whether it is or it isn't a claim) is not a natural feature of the world, but a discursive accomplishment; by using strategies that are available to them in the cultural repertoire, speakers are able to endow their talk with a political character, to mask that character, or to deny it in the talk of others. In this way, some talk is *produced* as "social problems talk" and some is not.

The concept of underdog skills—power from the underside—has received some attention in other theoretical quarters and is of real importance to social problems theorists. Almost a decade ago the sociologist Jean Lipman-Blumen introduced the term "micromanipulation" to describe the techniques of power used by subordinate groups to survive, and to exert influence, "in a world fashioned by the dominant group's definitions, rules, rewards and punishments" (Lipman-Blumen 1984, p. 30). According to Lipman-Blumen, members of low-power groups (notably women and children) spend many years "learning the underside of power relationships, including the techniques of micromanipulation," while members of dominant groups (here, adult males) are able, in general, to assert their demands directly ("macromanipulation"). While Lipman-Blumen's discussion of micromanipulation does not focus exclusively on discursive strategies, students of social problems will find much of interest in her brief discussion:

> Restricted to micromanipulation, women, as well as other powerless groups, become well versed in interpreting the unspoken intentions, even the body language, of the powerful. They learn to anticipate their governors' behaviour, to evoke as well as smother pleasure, anger, joy and bafflement in their rulers, to charm, to outsmart, even to dangle the powerful over the abyss of desire and anguish. By the various interpersonal strategies of micromanipulation, women have learned to sway and change, circumvent, and subvert the decisions of the powerful to which they seemingly have agreed. They know when to observe the rules the dominant group has created. Women have also mastered how to "obey without obeying" those rules they find overly repressive. When necessary they cooperate with men to maintain the mirage of male control. (p. 30)

Micromanipulation, then, is the way of the fox, not the lion (p. 31). Some of these techniques might include playing the fool (thus creating the appearance of acquiescence or unseriousness, e.g., the "dumb blonde," the Uncle Tom) and strategies of withholding (of love, sex, or conversation; the "silent treatment"). In a similar vein Haraway observes that the knowledges of the dominated are "'savvy to modes of denial' including repression, forgetting, and disappearing" (Haraway, in Hartsock 1990, p. 30). For our purposes, the key to all such strategies is the way actors learn to manipulate the political appearance of their practices; underdogs are especially attentive to talk's politicality because they *have* to be. Like rap musicians who can depoliticize their comments on the world by framing them as "only music," the underdogs Lipman-Blumen discusses have learned to use micromanipulative techniques to raise problems that contest the dominant order of things without overtly appearing to do so.

Related insights into the workings of power from the underside can be found in the work of such very different writers as the French philosopher de Certeau, who differentiates between "tactics" and "strategies" much as Lipman-Blumen does between micro- and macromanipulation (de Certeau 1984; esp. Ch. III), and the American historian Robert Darnton, whose reading of French peasant folk-tales (e.g., Tom Thumb/Le Petit Poucet) emphasizes the hero's survival by the use of his wits—"the only defence," says Darnton, "of the 'little people' against the rapacity of the big" (1984, p. 42).[24]

In calling these strategies, these authors all make the assumption that power, no matter how unequally distributed, is always a negotiation—a two-way street—but that the negotiating styles of under- and topdogs are likely to be different. In short, they all imply that the ways claims are shaped (their styles) will be related to the power distribution in the community, though not in mechanical ways. Unlike Ibarra and Kitsuse, for example, who mention such styles (e.g., the comic approach) but do not see them as the ways power or the lack of it can be inflected, the feminist scholars, de Certeau, Darnton, and others are very clear that certain describable ways of raising matters of concern are not merely "subcultural" styles but *subordinate* ones (see Houston and Kramarae 1991 and Troemel-Ploetz 1991). A tactic, says de Certeau," is determined by the absence [sic] of power just as a strategy is organized by the postulation of power," and likens the use of tactics to the art of the Sophists who, according to Aristotle, adopted "procedures . . . . which perverted the order of truth" (1984, p. 38).

Once again it is important to remember that in labeling these styles "subordinate," I do not argue that members of subordinate groups will everywhere and always talk like this. Maynard is quite right to conclude that this is *not* the way power and speech are related (1988, p. 317). Although some feminist scholars seem to hold that literary style, for example, will "reflect" the oppositional consciousness of their oppressed authors in a direct way, there is no simple correspondence between talk and consciousness, knowledge, or social conditions. Underdog strategies are learned and deployed by underdog groups, but they may also be used by topdogs who find themselves in underdog situations (e.g., males working for female bosses) as well as by topdogs in topdog situations who may resort to underdog styles to soften the blow when dealing with subordinates (as, for example, when the boss raises an employee's problem of poor work habits with a joke, instead of making the claim in a more direct confrontational way). In principle, these styles are available in the cultural repertoire to all competent members as part of their tacit knowledge (that is, as resources not topics); whether they are deployed and by whom is an empirical matter. We readily acknowledge the importance of the ethnomethodological insistence on the artfulness of members, as any theorist must who adopts the concept of "strategy."[25] Nevertheless, such strategies are born out of hierarchical systems; they bear the marks of power and members orient to that fact in their use.[26]

VI. Conclusions

In this paper I have taken Ibarra and Kitsuse's recent programmatic statement on social problems analysis as an occasion to consider the phenomenon of marginalized social problems talk. In the final section I want to summarize the major contribution the poststructuralist perspective makes to a constructionist sociology of social problems. It has to do with power.

Poststructuralism's most important contribution is to invite systematic consideration of marginalized (or invisible) claims-making activities, an area to which sociologists of social problems have given little sustained attention. Instead they have focused on talk that is "readable at a glance" as social problems talk. Despite their recognition of gray areas, marginal cases, and so on, most social problems theorists agree in practice that social problems talk, as claims-making activity, is identifiable as a distinct class of activity and it is this they should study. Here they hold that whether a remark is a claim or not can be decided by appealing to *members' decisions* on the matter (much as Spector and Kitsuse do when they decide that the disruptive student's eccentric diatribe on the post office in Eastern religions class is not a claim; Spector and Kitsuse [1977] 1987, pp. 80–81). The sociologist says, in effect: Members didn't grant it status as a claim, so we have no interest in it; if they had, it would have been another story. Like many other social problems theorists, Spector and Kitsuse treat the "fact" that this was not a claim as a feature of the natural order—it is or it isn't—rather than as a members' achievement to be analyzed. But in taking this tack, they have adopted a members' gloss as their own. As a result, they close themselves off from a systematic look at claims-making styles in their less visible forms.[27]

By contrast, the later Foucault and the poststructuralists have put marginalized ways of saying and knowing in the spotlight. By raising the issue of marginalized claims-making styles, poststructuralism makes it possible for the social problems theorist to draw on a diverse body of work in feminist literary theory, cultural studies, and elsewhere, which all display an interest in power from the underside. Some scholars argue that oppressed groups are structurally restricted to marginalized discursive styles and are fated never to be heard; others suggest that "underdog" styles become part of the cultural lore, to be used by both dominant and subordinate groups, but always in the (tacit) knowledge that their use carries a legacy of discredit.[28] Both lines of thought are fruitful directions for the sociologists of social problems to pursue.

Above all, the poststructuralist approach emphasizes (discursive) power, and serves as a reminder to the social problems theorist that speakers are attentive to the political consequences of their different claims-making styles. The difference this point makes to the analysis of claims-making can be readily seen if we consider Ibarra and Kitsuse's brief discussion of the comic style. According to these authors, "comic styles represent interesting problems of claim-readability inasmuch as the esthetic imperative of making a good joke can come into conflict with the practical goal of building a constituency." Here the writers make reference to the fact that a claim in the comic style, if it is good comedy, runs the risk of being read as no claim at all ("just a joke"). In short, comedy mutes the political appearance of a claim. For Ibarra and Kitsuse, this "problem" is treated as something interesting, but incidental—an unintended consequence, as it were, of the use of the comic style. I have argued instead that this "problem" (i.e., the utterance's ambiguity) is an important feature of the member's discursive strategy, and that underdogs in particular (children, employees, wives—like the King's fool) will be drawn to such equivocal or muted ways of voicing their concerns as protective strategies. Furthermore, studies in other fields of scholarship suggest that this is only one in a large repertoire of underdog strategies for use in the conversational politics of everyday life. At the macrolevel, the relevant research question is: Which claims-making styles have been privileged, which marginalized? And at the microlevel: How are they used as strategies (in what situations, and by whom)? Questions like these can form the foundation of a politics of social problems talk.

In sum, the view from the margins tells us that apparently settled accounts of the world are never entirely settled, that dominant discourses are always being contested, whether as clearly visible confrontations between claimants and counterclaimants, or as "depoliticized" encounters between claimants whose status as claimants has been defused. In either case, exclusion is a member's (discursive) practice, and thus a legitimate object of study, i.e., one that does not require the theorist to rewrite or "correct" the member's agenda. From its inception the field of social problems study has made an important place for questions of power and injustice. We should not like to see these concerns abandoned. Poststructuralist insights into marginalization show us one way to bring power back in.

Acknowledgments

The author gratefully acknowledges the editors' valuable comments and suggestions on an earlier draft of this paper.

Notes

1.   See Haraway's (1988) discussion of "situated knowledges." A widely known study of marginalized knowledges from a feminist perspective is *Women's Ways of Knowing* (Belenky et al. 1986). For a thorough review of the issue of "epistemic standpoints" (and the standpoint of science), see Harding (1986, esp. Chs. 6 and 7).

2.   The most widespread example of marginalization within conventional sociology is the persistent debunking of commonsense knowledge and terminology in favor of the allegedly more precise and accurate concepts and terms of professional social science. Comparisons between commonsense and sociological discourse are a perennial feature of introductory textbooks, usually in an attempt to entice novice students into a greater interest in how the world "really" is.

3.   It is important to remember that I am speaking here of the marginalization or "invisibility" of *ways of talking*, not social conditions (or "unconstructed problems").

4.   Although Smith's work de-emphasizes the independence of members' mundane formulations, and highlights instead the degree to which their accounts of troubles or problems (e.g., the accounts of mothers) are colonized almost from the start by official state-sponsored categories (Smith 1987).

5.   Maynard (1988) provides a good summary of the implications of new language studies for social problems analysis, but inexplicably omits any discussion of Foucault.

6.   Exceptions are Pfohl and Gordon's (1986) deconstructionist reading of the history of social science discourse in deviance and criminology, and the work of Dorothy Smith and Alison Griffith on school children, in Smith (1987).

7.   See in this connection Fraser's (1992) discussion of French discourse theories.

8.   These questions are much the same as those identified by Joan W. Scott as salient for feminist theory; I have adapted her formulation to a social problems context (Scott 1990, p. 135).

9.   For an example of feminist criticism that rejects Foucault but is very much interested in marginalization, see Hartsock (1990). And for a consideration of why feminists should reject structuralism for poststructuralism, see Fraser (1992).

10.   See in this connection Etter-Lewis's discussion of omission, euphemism, and indirect speech ("keeping quiet"), and other related papers in this special issue entitled *Women Speaking from Silence* (1991, p. 434).

11. Here we are suggesting that discourses offer a way of hearing "mere comments" as claims. Thus, for example, prolifers will claim, "Abortion is [a case of] murder." Similarly, the complaints of native peoples are elevated to claims once they are hitched to recognizable discourses of "distinct societies," or "guardians of the Earth."

12. This consideration suggests a different take on the theme of "private troubles and public problems," which crops up frequently in the feminist literature. Feminists usually argue that getting women's private troubles recognized as public problems is a matter of recognizing that they are shared concerns (thus addressing the issue of isolation), and of successfully placing them on a *political* agenda. The discursive reformulation of the issue implied here is that a (private, personal) utterance becomes a readable claim (a public problem) when it becomes empowered by an authoritative discourse.

13. In this connection see Coles's discussion of the normalizing of Hercule Barbin's difference, and Foucault's remark that this is the "first form of subjection" characteristic of Western thought (in Coles 1991, pp. 102–3.

14. For an analysis of the resilience of one such commonsense discourse, the social rhetoric of the harmonious family, see L. Miller (1990).

15. In this passage Kamuf is, in fact, berating some feminist scholars (not social problems theorists) for restricting their analysis of women's exclusion to institutional power; nevertheless, the argument as a whole is relevant to the field of social problems studies.

16. Here again, the work of Dorothy Smith and Alison Griffith on mothers and the school system is exemplary.

17. As studies of members' creative "code switching" show. See Houston and Kramerae (1991, pp. 395–96) for a brief discussion of this phenomenon.

18. This point I owe to Jim Holstein.

19. Unlike some feminist scholars, my primary concern here is not to resuscitate marginalized styles in order to argue that they should be revalued. The immediate goal is to understand the *process* of marginalization, and second, to analyze members' artful *use* of historically marginalized claims-making styles.

20. This conjecture is supported by the fact that social control in the pre-modern world is largely informal, and that gossip, which threatens the individual's good reputation, is an important social curb in a small world. For a discussion of the feminization and demise of informal strategies of social control, see L. Miller (1987).

21. See in this connection Hartsock's discussion of the characteristic features of fiction produced by writers who are members of marginal groups (Hartsock 1990). For a discussion of the tendency to read the political out of the analysis by treating discursive styles as "different" (rather than super/subordinate), see Troemel-Ploetz (1991).

22. On this reading, the wives interviewed by Brannen and Moss use silence, contradiction, and so forth as strategies of influence over their (structurally more powerful) husbands while minimizing the risk of open conflict. However, Mrs. Dunn's strategy, in this exchange at least, does not seem to shift the status quo in any way. For an elaboration of this idea, see the discussion of micromanipulation (below).

23. This is of course a risky strategy, since it can also be used by members of powerful groups to *dismiss* the claims of subordinates (as Mr. Dunn does to his wife). Hebdige's (1979) well-known study of the ways entrenched interests neutralize the resistance of youth subcultures shows how real this risk is.

24. Darnton's essay offers a number of other suggestive insights into power from the underside, including the idea that the "view from below" can detect "no discernible morality" in the dominant system (feudalism, in Darnton's context), and that underdog strategies, such as those of Le Petit Poucet or Jack-and-the-Beanstalk, represent holding strategies or orientations to the system, rather than resistance to it. Danton also argues a cultural thesis on the French character: specifically, that the French are still trying to "outwit the system" rather than to change it, that this characteristic orientation to the world sets them apart from the Germans and the British, and that it is reflected in distinctive French versions of these widespread folk-tales. Another case study of peasant strategies of power from the underside—this time from within the social problems literature—is found in Brown 1987.

25. There are other theoretical perspectives (e.g., rational-choice theory) that occasionally employ the concept of "strategy." However, they are usually interested in locating predictors of action, and so violate the ethnomethodological insight we want to retain (and without which the notion of strategy is emptied of value), that is, that strategies are always *situated* accomplishments, which will require us to consult interaction. Writers like Darnton and de Certeau preserve a sense of situated accomplishment, in the notion of "wits"; presumably, one can only live by one's wits if one is finely attuned to the shifting demands of the situation. But these theorists ascribe "wits" disproportionately to underdogs, on the assumption that underdogs have few other power resources at their disposal. This sets them apart from ethnomethodologists, for whom "wits" (artfulness) is an essential feature of all members, regardless of their position in the social hierarchy. In general, I would argue that the affinities between the now popular concept of strategy and the older ethnomethodological concept of artfulness invite a more systematic look, and that some approaches that employ the concept of strategy (e.g., social historians of women and the family; see Anderson 1980, Ch. 4) owe a debt to ethnomethodological insights that they fail to recognize.

26. I use the term *orient* deliberately here, to indicate that members will use underdog styles (humor, gossip, and so forth) without *conscious* awareness of their status as marginalized. Nevertheless, this social fact is part of their tacit knowledge; if a comment is described as "just gossip," "everyone knows" that this label acts to discredit it as something to be taken seriously.

27. This is partly rectified in Ibarra and Kitsuse's later formulation (this volume), wherein they take up the question of different claims-making styles.

28. It is important to remember that a "legacy of discredit" is not inherent in a style of claims-making; it is entirely likely that some styles will shed their marginal status over time, much as the subcultural symbols of resistance Hebdige describes (e.g., punk fashions) lose their legacy of discredit as they are taken up—commercialized and sanitized—by the mainstream (Hebdige 1979).

References

Andersen, Michael. 1980. *Approaches to the History of the Western Family, 1500–1914*. London: Macmillan.

Belenky, Mary Field, Blythe McVicker Clinchy, Nancy Rule Goldberger, and Jill Mattuck Tarule. 1986. *Women's Ways of Knowing: The Development of Self, Voice and Mind*. New York: Basic Books.

Bordo, Susan R. 1989. "The Body and the Reproduction of Femininity: A Feminist Appropriation of Foucault." Pp. 13–33 in *Gender/Body/Knowledge: Feminist Reconstructions of Being and Knowing*, edited by Alison M. Jaggar and Susan R. Bordo. New Brunswick and London: Rutgers University Press.

Brannen, Julia and Peter Moss. 1987. "Dual Earner Households: Women's Financial Contribution After the Birth of the First Child." Pp. 75–95 in *Give and Take in Families: Studies in Resource Distribution*, edited by Julia Brannen and Gail Wilson. London: Allen and Unwin.

Brown, Julie V. 1987. "Peasant Survival Strategies in Late Imperial Russia: The Social Uses of the Mental Hospital." *Social Problems* 34:311–29.

Coles, Romand. 1991. "Foucault's Dialogical Artistic Ethos." *Theory, Culture and Society* 8:99–120.

Darnton, Robert. 1984. "Peasants Tell Tales: The Meaning of Mother Goose." Pp. 9–72 in *The Great Cat Massacre and Other Episodes in French Cultural History*. New York: Basic Books.

Darrough, William D. 1990. "Neutralizing Resistance: Probation Work as Rhetoric." Pp. 163–87 in *Perspectives on Social Problems*, Vol. 2, edited by G. Miller and J. A. Holstein. Greenwich, CT: JAI Press.

Davies, Bronwyn. 1989. *Frogs and Snails and Feminist Tales: Preschool Children and Gender*. Sydney: Allen and Unwin.

de Certeau, Michel. 1984. *The Practice of Everyday Life*. Berkeley and Los Angeles: University of California Press.

Emerson, Robert M. and Sheldon L. Messinger. 1977. "The Micro-Politics of Trouble." *Social Problems* 25:121–35.

Etter-Lewis, Gwendolyn. 1991. "Standing Up and Speaking Out: African American Women's Narrative Legacy." *Discourse and Society* 2:425–37. (Special issue entitled Women Speaking from Silence.)

Featherstone, Mike. 1992. "The Heroic Life and Everyday Life." *Theory, Culture and Society* 9:159–82.

Foucault, Michel. 1979. *Discipline and Punish: The Birth of the Prison*. New York: Vintage.

Fraser, Nancy. 1992. "The Uses and Abuses of French Discourse Theories for Feminist Politics." *Theory, Culture and Society* 9:51–71.

Gilligan, Carol. 1982. *In A Different Voice*. Cambridge, MA: Harvard University Press.

Griffith, Alison I. and Dorothy E. Smith. 1991. "What Did You Do in School Today?" Pp. 3–24 in *Perspectives on Social Problems*, Vol. 2, edited by G. Miller and J. A. Holstein, Greenwich, CT: JAI Press.

Grossberg, Lawrence, Cary Nelson, and Paula Treichler (eds.). 1992. *Cultural Studies*. New York and London: Routledge, Chapman and Hall.

Gubrium, Jaber F. and James A. Holstein. 1990. *What Is Family?* Mountainview, CA: Mayfield.

Haraway, Donna. 1988. "Situated Knowledges: The Science Question in Feminism and the Privilege of Partial Perspective." *Feminist Studies* 14:575–99.

Harding, Sandra. 1986. *The Science Question in Feminism*. Ithaca and London: Cornell University Press.

Hartsock, Nancy. 1990. "Postmodernism and Political Change: Issues for Feminist Theory." *Cultural Critique* 13:15–33.

Hebdige, Dick. 1979. *Subculture: The Meaning of Style*. London and New York: Methuen.
Holstein, James A. 1987. "Producing Gender Effects on Involuntary Mental Hospitalization." *Social Problems* 34:141–55.
Houston, Marsha and Cheris Kramarae (eds.). 1991. *Women Speaking from Silence.* (Special issue of *Discourse and Society*, Vol. 2.)
Jefferson, Gail and John R. E. Lee. 1981. "The Rejection of Advice: Managing the Problematic Convergence of 'Troubles-Telling' and a 'Service Encounter'." *Journal of Pragmatics* 5:399–422.
Kamuf, Peggy. 1990. "Replacing Feminist Criticism." Pp. 105–11 in *Conflicts in Feminism*, edited by Marianne Hirsch and Evelyn Fox Keller. New York and London: Routledge.
Lakoff, Robin Tolmach. 1990. *Talking Power: The Politics of Language*. New York: Basic Books.
Lipman-Blumen, Jean. 1984. *Gender Roles and Power*. Englewood Cliffs, NJ: Prentice-Hall.
Mackie, Marlene. 1991. *Gender Relations in Canada*. Toronto and Vancouver: Butterworths.
Maynard, Douglas W. 1988. "Language, Interaction and Social Problems." *Social Problems* 35:311–34.
Miller, Gale. 1991. *Enforcing the Work Ethic*. Albany, NY: SUNY Press.
Miller, Leslie J. 1987. "Uneasy Alliance: Women as Agents of Social Control." *Canadian Journal of Sociology* 12:345–61.
———. 1990. "Family Violence and the Rhetoric of Harmony." *British Journal of Sociology* 41:263–88.
Pfohl, Stephen and Avery Gordon. 1986. "Criminological Displacements: A Sociological Deconstruction." *Social Problems* 33:94–113.
Rysman, Alexander. 1977. "How the 'Gossip' Became a Woman." *Journal of Communication* 27:176–80.
Scott, Joan W. 1990. "Deconstructing Equality-Versus-Difference: Or, the Uses of Poststructuralist Theory for Feminism." Pp. 134–48 in *Conflicts in Feminism*, edited by Marianne Hirsch and Evelyn Fox Keller. New York and London: Routledge.
Smith, Dorothy E. 1987. *The Everyday World as Problematic: A Feminist Sociology.* Toronto: University of Toronto Press.
Spector, Malcolm and John I. Kitsuse. [1977] 1987. *Constructing Social Problems*. Hawthorne, NY: Aldine de Gruyter.
Thorne, Barrie, Cheris Kramarae, and Nancy Henley (eds.). 1983. *Language, Gender and Society*. Cambridge, MA: Newbury House.
Troemel-Ploetz, Senta. 1991. "Selling the Apolitical." Review of Tannen, Deborah, *You Just Don't Understand. Discourse and Society* 2:489–502.

18

(De)Construction, Postmodernism, and Social Problems: Facts, Fictions, and Fantasies at the "End of History"

Raymond J. Michalowski

Prologue: Two Sociologists and a Lamp

As I threaded my way through the moving steel tangle of I-95 between Rich-mond and Washington D.C. the voice on the car radio spoke about Brazilian cinema, about its patterns and its meaning. The political history of Brazil, it said, was inscribed in the ebb and flow of realism in Brazilian film-making. Periods of relative political openness, the spirit in my dashboard told me, were characterized by "realist" portrayals of the political and economic contradictions of a country that had both the world's fifth largest GNP and the world's largest single slum—the infamous favela *of Rio de Janeiro. During repressive periods of military rule filmmakers retreated into the allegorical and the metaphorical. These nonrealist representations, the voice told me, pursued the same political agendas as their more realist counterparts; however, under repressive regimes filmmakers obscured their real intent from the (apparently) limited artistic com-prehension of the culture police behind the smokescreen of "magical realism." It was a tale of language, of its selective construction, and of the purposefulness with which ritually resistant expressive practices alter their linguistic and bodily manifestations in response to changes in the shape of hegemonic power.*

The radio's gentle voice tunneled through my mind, coming to rest in a postmodern chamber inhabited by surrealistic shadows. Radio words, floating, detached, gradually entwined themselves like bitterroot vine, or perhaps a lover, around images of social horrors that rolled forward like fog and offered themselves as magical realist tales for sociologists of social problems in the so-called post-modern world. These images had been carved on the retina of my imagination by Criminological Displacements *(Pfohl and Gordon 1985), a videotext about the METAphorical construction of modernist control system.*

I stitched my way between the exiting Saab Turbo and the entering Ford Taurus while my mind reeled (real/ed?) backwards to a night somewhere in early

ReagANOMIA. We sat on the upstairs porch while an anemic floor lamp struggled to keep the dark of a moonless summer night just beyond the table where we sat. We talked of sadism, of the sadism inherent in a DOMINANT ideology, and of a sociology where CONTROL was elevated to the level of theory. Then he began to read.

A penumbra of weak light cast by a lone bulb behind his head illuminated close-cropped hair. I rewrote (rewrite?) the scene. We were in a B-grade movie about World War II, at the part where the Aryan authority figure interrogates a darker person. Then I wrote (write?) us back into that moment of our present-becoming-the-past to be (re)rewritten as part of this tale.

Words wove images of the pleasures of pain in intimacy, of the intimacy of pleasure in pain. The words were epistolary in form and, on that porch, on that night, disturbing in content. It was my first encounter with the flirtation between postmodernist imagery and the rationalist boundaries of sociology. Haunted specters mocked the ordered limits of my historical-materialist ideology and cast sideways, menacing glances at my social-activist self-image. I was frightened.

The spaces in this reading, with their awful invitation to an Alice's Wonderland of horrific collages, would later inform Criminological Displacements, the remembered videotext that had been called forth by words of Brazilian cinema. But we did not know that then.

Introduction

My contribution to this volume is a (sometimes) autobiographical and (always haltingly) reflexive inquiry into the implications for the study of social problems of what I will term *ritual (de)construction*.[1] In the process I will examine the relationship between ritual (de)construction and other forms of "social constructionism" in social problems inquiry, as well as consider the implications of ritual (de)construction for more openly interventionist approaches to social problems.

Social constructionism, broadly understood, is an approach to the study of social problems that problematizes the definition of social problems, and takes as its central task the analysis of the sociolinguistic and other representational rituals whereby such definitions are produced and either succeed or fail in becoming part of the hegemonic understanding of what constitutes "social problems" at concrete moments in history.[2] For social constructionists, social problems reside not in some set of objectively knowable conditions external to the beholder, but rather in the reCOGNITION of those conditions as problematic. As formulated by Specter and Kitsuse, the task of social constructionism is to analyze "claims making," i.e., the activities of individuals or groups *"making assertions of grievances and claims with respect to some putative conditions"* ([1977] 1987, p. 75). Constructionists are centrally concerned with what social problems activists, the so-called members, say and do about what they perceive to be problematic conditions. The conditions themselves serve only as the stimulus for claims-making and, indeed, need not even exist "in the world" so long as they exist in the mind of the claims-makers (Aronson 1984).

The search for a general theory that would bind the disparate topics that normally fall under the heading of "social problems" into a coherent field of study provided much of the impetus behind social constructionism. The birth of social constructionism was less the product of a search for a theory about human problems than it was the product of efforts to develop a metaframework for the sociological study of those problems. Social constructionism is not simply a "slightly different perspective" on the same topics studied by objectivist approaches to social problems research. As Best (1989, p. xviii) observes, constructionism's focus on claims-making activities constitutes an entirely different topic from that studied by those concerned with either establishing the "objective" nature of social problems by measuring, counting, or classifying phenomena assumed to be "objective' in character, or by those animated primarily by a desire to ameliorate these "objective" social problems.

By focusing its analyses on claims-making rather than the putative problematic conditions themselves, social constructionist analyses often *appear* to be relatively neutral in political and moral terms in comparison to positivist forms of social problems inquiry, which concern themselves more with the behavioral world represented by the conditions claims-makers claim are problematic than with the linguistic world of the claims themselves. This appearance of neutrality results from social constructionism's refusal to grant ontological priority to "objective reality." Once the purpose of inquiry becomes (exclusively) the analysis of representational moves made by moral entrepreneurs, rather than the supposed conditions toward which these "moves" are directed, there remains little basis, and even less reason, to inquire (or perhaps even be concerned) about the "actual" lived experiences of those who are the "victims" of the putative social problems. As a topic of sociological inquiry, participants' thoughts and words about their (or someone else's) injuries are never as compelling a call to social action as inquiries that assume the injuries spoken about are "real." Within a truly constructionist framework there are no "actual" lived-lives, or "victims" of social problems, only *claims about* lived lives and victims.[3] While the efforts of claims-makers can be evaluated strategically (i.e., did they or did they not advance the goals of the claims-makers), under the theoretical rubrics of mainstream social constructionism little can or should be said about whether or not any real, embodied human beings experienced any improvement or deterioration in their (subjectively) very real lives. There is an irony in all of this insofar as constructionism's critique of "objective reality" is, on the one hand, a fundamental challenge to hegemonic power structures (including science), and yet, on the other, it leads to less direct involvement in attempting to ameliorate the conditions generated by those structures of power than approaches that rely on what are often considered to be more conservative, positivist frameworks. These latter, by treating the problems as "real," can generate a substantially more stirring call to action and social change. Objectivist approaches to social problems research, while frequently marching under the hegemony-reinforcing banner of positivist science, are often more unapologetically committed to social change than their constructionist counterparts because constructionism's radical implications are submerged beneath its theoretically informed incapacity to become part of the process of social struggles dedicated to improving the conditions of human lives.

Two Modes of Deconstruction

Social constructionism has never been a unified or monochromatic theoretical movement. Early versions of symbolic interactionism as developed by Mead (1965) and expanded by Blumer (1969) foregrounded the Gordian subject-object within sociology, giving rise to labeling/societal-reaction approaches, and to ethnomethodology, both of which bear a close kinship and share key metatheoretical assumptions with social constructionism. More recently, the currents of symbolic interactionism within social constructionist versions of social problems have been joined by another wide-flowing theoretical stream—*deconstruction*. This stream has two main arteries, and each has produced its own form of deconstructionism both beyond and within sociology.

One branch of deconstruction is heavily informed by the structural linguistics of Saussure (1959; Culler 1976) and the semiotic philosophy of Derrida (1967), and it has had its greatest influence both epistemologically and methodologically in the arena of literary criticism (e.g., Barthes 1967, 1977; Jameson 1972). Thus, I term this framework *literary deconstruction*, although its influence extends well beyond literature. The other deconstruction is more closely aligned with the poststructuralist work of Foucault (1970, 1977, 1980) and with the surrealist inheritors of the Durkheimian tradition such as Bataille (1985) and Bakhtin (1968).[4] I term this latter version *social deconstruction* because its ultimate reference is not literary texts but ongoing social rituals undertaken by human bodies located in historical contexts.

The distinction between literary deconstruction and social deconstruction is curiously and reminiscently Cartesian. Literary deconstruction is rooted in efforts to analyze literal *texts*, that is, to decipher written texts as they appear, above all else, in literary documents (White 1984). Within this mode of analysis, writing—the consummate product of the rational/creative mind—is privileged in comparison to what social analysts call *behavior* (Lynch, Lynch, and Milovanovic 1990, p. 14). Other forms of representation such as speech and rituals of the body play very little role within the concerns of literary deconstruction.

Social deconstruction, by contrast, folds itself around a concern for actual bodies, a concern that is largely absent in the more literary versions of deconstruction. This focus on the body reflects the influence of writers such as Foucault and Bakhtin. Foucault (1977), perhaps more than any contemporary social analyst, sought to detail the body as the site where power is actually and finally inscribed through rites of control—control of appearance, of movement, of pleasure, of odor, of shape, of consumption—expressed in speech and action as well as in written forms. Bakhtin's (1968) study of carnivalesque rituals of release, and particularly the release of the body in both speech and action, on the other hand, details the inscription of the power of hierarchy and authority on the body from a different direction by examining, not how control is exerted, but how it is periodically and ritually transgressed. The rituals of carnival "celebrated temporary liberation from the prevailing truth, from the established order: it marked the suspension of all hierarchical rank, privileges, norms and prohibition" (p. 10). This attention, within social deconstruction, to the meaning of rituals of power (re)visited on the body stands in distinct contrast to literary deconstruction's focus on formally written texts. Social deconstruction accepts the corporeality of the social world and seeks to reveal the way in which embodied humans become the site for the exercise of *meaningful* rituals of power. Literary deconstruction, by contrast, focuses on texts as the self-contained, abstract products of absent minds whose very existence, let alone *whose* corporeality, is nearly irrelevant.

Another distinction between literary deconstruction and social deconstruction is their views regarding the stability and commensurability of meaning. Literary deconstruction, theoretically informed by Derrida (1967), rejects the notion that the meaning of any text can be determined through appeals to some external system of validation. The apparent stability of meaning provided by syntax and grammar, is only that, an appearance. Textual meaning, within this framework, can be neither transhistorical nor historical. Rather, it only al(l)ways resides in the *de-*

coding of a text by the specific, individual "readers" of that text fixed in their own subjective space. Every text has as many potential meanings as there are decoders/readers, making it al(l)ways impossible to discern either the "True" meaning intended by the author, or the "actual" meaning given to it by any reader other than oneself. Within this framework the ability to "know and discover Truth is restricted by the boundaries and structure of language [and by the] inherent split between communicators (interlocutors) and audiences, or between the authors of texts and the readers/consumers of texts" (Lynch et al. 1990, p. 3). Taken to its ultimate conclusion (which few of its practitioners do) literary deconstruction implies that all seemingly social rituals are little more than radical solipsism misunderstood as shared reality. More narrowly used, literary deconstruction suggests that, given the lack of any possible external validation of the meaning of the text, texts can only be deconstructed *relative to themselves,* and that the purpose of deconstructive discourse is an (al(l)ways faulty) exchange of interpretations among "readers." For the literary deconstructionist, texts are nonrepresentational, or as Gertrude Stein said of Hollywood, "There is no there, there" (cited in Niven, 1975, p. 13).

When insights of literary deconstruction are transported into the realm of *sociological analysis,* the literary text is replaced by a social/behavioral text, by society understood as a "text" to be "read" by social analysts. In keeping with the literary deconstructionist concern with the construction and interpretation of meaning *within* texts rather than with what texts refer to (because there can be no knowable external referent) social analysts in this tradition approach the meaning of behavior and rituals as self-contained. Fiske captures this translation of literary deconstruction's image of nonrepresentational texts into social analyses when he says, "the process of making and communicating meanings is representative *even though the meanings made by it are not*" (1985, p. 2, my emphasis). Rituals may have meaning that can be shared by their participants, but that meaning refers to nothing beyond the ritual itself. There is *only* there, there.

The focus on individuals as active decoders/meaning-makers that is characteristic of social analysis in the literary deconstructionist mode directs attention away from, and in some cases even denies the possibility of, hegemony. The image of centers of power able to "fix" or "bind" sliding signifiers to broadly understood meanings in the pursuit of specific, sectoral interests is radically diminished by the placement of meaning-making in the hands of the "readers" rather than "writers."[5] Social analysis informed by literary deconstruction represents a radical return of the subject to social inquiry. It stands as an aggressive rejection of structuralism, and suggests that rumors about the "death of the subject" are highly exaggerated. In doing this, however, literary deconstruction, at least when taken to its more radical conclusions, problematizes the very existence of *culture*. Can there be collective rituals that bind individuals within a shared meaning system if the construction of meaning is a subjective and individual enterprise?

By comparison, social deconstruction approaches society less as an analog to the literary text and more as an integrated patterning of ritual performances. Its concern is less with how meanings are made in and out of written texts, than with the ways in which representational rituals visited on human bodies ultimately construct a "commonsense that certain ways of doing things are acceptable, or even valued, while others must be resisted, prohibited, or confined within socially constituted limits" (Pfohl, in this volume). Throughout analyses influenced by social deconstruction there are rumors of power. Society is more than an accumulation of private, subjective meanings. Meanings are bound to historical conditions. Specific and powerful representational practices are born and die with historical epochs. It is the task of social deconstruction to tell contemporary and historical *social* texts "what they [do] not know" (Gordon 1990, p. 40), that is, to read them by the light of something other than "common sense."

From Literary and Social Deconstruction to Rhetorical and Ritual (De)Constructions

The implications of both literary deconstruction and social deconstruction have found their way into the study of social problems, producing what I term rhetorical deconstruction and ritual deconstruction. In what follows I will consider an example of each of these contemporary approaches to social problems analysis. The work of Ibarra and Kitsuse, appearing in this volume, is an example of literary deconstruction reformulated as rhetorical (de)construction. The previously mentioned videotext *Criminological Displacements*, by contrast, is an example of the social deconstructive strategy of tempting social texts to reveal not so much their HIStory nor their HERstory but a newSTORY.[6] While I will comment on both forms of (de)construction within social problems, I will be primarily concerned with ritual (de)construction as used in the videotext *Criminological Displacements* because this form of (de)construction represents the more significant departure from the established logocentric modes of social constructionism, and thus poses a more fundamental challenge to the constructionist framework.

Parenthetically, I want to explain my use of the term *sociological (de)construction*. This is not just an attempt to be clever. Rather, it is done to foreground what I think is a telling distinction between the terms *social construction* and *deconstruction* as they refer to frameworks for the study of social problems. The term *social construction* directs attention to what is done *by those being studied,* i.e., how the written-about proceed to construct social problems. As a way of naming a method for studying social problems, the term *social construction* places the author of the sociological tale being told in the background. *Deconstruction,* on the other hand, foregrounds what is done *by those doing the studying,* i.e., how those telling the sociological tale set about tempting social texts to yield up new meanings. In both cases, however, the process is one of dissecting communicative acts and (re)constructing them in a way that presumably reveals the deeper and (often) hidden meaning of those communications. From this view, both the social construction of Spector and Kitsuse ([1977] 1987) and the rhetorical analyses of Ibarra and Kitsuse are no less forms of (de)construction than those approaches that actually claim "deconstruction" as their name. All social constructionist texts can be considered (de)construction insofar as they dismember social texts as part of the process of telling new sociological tales.

Rhetorical (De)Construction

Ibarra and Kitsuse propose that the social constructionist model for the study of social problems can be advanced by developing a "theory of the vernacular constituents of social problems." The goal of this theory is to erect a more impermeable barrier between "vernacular resources and analytic constructs" so as to avoid the "indiscriminate fusion of mundane and theoretical perspectives." Doing so, they suggest will help overcome the "difficulty that analysts have in sustaining [the] methodological attitude" of social constructionism. This attitude is the ability to bracket "the members' *practical* project" as distinct from "the sociologist's *theoretical* project" (emphasis in original).

This approach is derivative of literary deconstruction in several ways. First, it is clearly concerned with the analysis of verbal texts more than with social behaviors as bodily rituals. While more oriented toward the analysis of *speech* than conventional forms of literary deconstruction, it is nevertheless primarily concerned with revealing the linguistic coordinates of social problems construction.

Like literary deconstruction, the rhetorical (de)construction of Ibarra and Kitsuse also seeks to operate on the text being analyzed largely from *within the text.* On this point they say, "*Rhetoric* brings to the fore the sense in which the task for constructionism lies less with the *referential aspects of claims* than with the constitutive techniques and processes that are entailed in claims-making as such" (emphasis in original). Whether or not there is a there, there, is simply not the question.

Another similarity between rhetorical (de)construction and literary deconstruction is that while linguistic acts are viewed as the essential constituent of social "reality," the authors give relatively little reflexive attention to *their own* linguistic constructions as also being rhetorical moves, perhaps not in the construction of social problems themselves, but in the construction of the way sociologists construct social problems.

As a mode of presentation Ibarra and Kitsuse's "Vernacular Constituents of Moral Discourse" is, like most sociology, linguistically conventional and logocentric. Their goal is to develop a convincing, rational argument through a highly crafted, formally written text. I will not review the specific arguments of Ibarra and Kitsuse since they can easily be (re)read by anyone holding this book. In the following discussions of ritual (de)construction, however, Ibarra and Kitsuse's rhetorical approach will serve as a comparison and foil to help reveal the implication of the former's more erocentric approach to the study of social problems.

Ritual (De)Construction

In November 1985, at the American Criminological Association meeting in San Diego, Parasite Cafe Productions, represented by Stephen Pfohl and Avery Gordon, screened *Criminological Displacements* for the first time to a generally (and genuinely) puzzled academic audience. The text of the video was later published as "Criminological Displacements: A Sociological Deconstruction" (Pfohl and Gordon 1986).

The selection of a video vehicle for *Criminological Displacements* approaches the contemporary social world as one where the camcorder's ability to construct holistic visual images is seen as mightier than the linearity of the written word. By challenging the logocentricity of canonical social science practices, Pfohl and Gordon imply that the study of social problems in a postmodern world is better served by postmodernist modes of expression than the literal and literary ones characteristic of the modernist epoch.

Criminological Displacements reveals its roots in the corporal focus of social deconstruction by making its central theme the insistence that social scientists recognize their pleasures (EROS), not only in contributing to the control of so-called deviants, but in transforming them from "fleshy human animals" (Pfohl 1990, p. 424) into two-dimensional, written-about characters (LOGOS):

> The pleasure of criminology is to displace the Other's unfixed pleasure into the pain of a certain victim and to master her, to keep an eye on her, to induce her to confess herself the proper subject of the law. (Pfohl and Gordon 1986, p. 597)

This demand that the EROS of social science be returned to the conscious life of social scientists is consistent with the concern of social deconstructionist themes that emphasize the sensate quality of human experience (Kroker and Cook 1986).

The central vehicle for accomplishing this return of the repressed erotic quality of life is through a visual collage of the cultural imagery of control. This collage is not a random disordering of the symbolic real. It is a reordering of it. As both theory and method the (de)construction of *Criminological Displacements* attempts to foreground symbolic linkages and connections that are normally submerged beneath the weight of ordinary perception. This is done by deroutinizing and estranging the taken-for-granted symbolic rituals. In its constant mixture of image, word, and sound it epitomizes Jameson's suggestion that the postmodernist challenge is to develop a practice capable of imploding the domination of the "year-by-year experience of cultural and informational messages, of successive events, of urgent priorities" by revealing "the secret affinities between those apparently autonomous and unrelated domains, and . . . the rhythms and hidden sequences of things we normally remember only in isolation and one by one" (1989, p. 33). By taking us through a series of images that interweave pictures of sadistic rituals, the words of de Sade, the cacophonic sounds of industrial society, and the intellectual pronouncements of the intelligentsia of crime and deviance studies, *Criminological Displacements* disorders time and juxtaposes realities to achieve just such an implosion.

Doubts

His words wove images of the pleasures of pain in intimacy, of the intimacy of pleasure in pain. The words were epistolary in form and, on that porch, on that night, disturbing in content. With their lexical inversions and fractured brutal imagery the words were disturbing, as they were intended to be. On this particular night they challenged the order of my historical materialist rationality—just as some years later Criminological Displacements *was to disturb many of its viewers in San Diego.*

A different day. It is humid. My clothes cling. I am in a room in an eighteenth-century castle in old Havana, now a museum. The floor is littered. A carved wood and leather throne squats over a flat of thick green Coca-Cola bottles. A bust of FDR on the floor, half on its side, stares in dumb amazement at the throne and the Coke bottles that loom above. A large bronze American eagle tilts at an improbable angle threatening to collapse into the head of FDR. Disordered symbols of U.S. majesty are everywhere. I am in the museum of the city of Havana, looking at a Cuban display of images of U.S. imperialism at the moment of the 1959 revolutionary victory—deconstruction as museology.

And now I imagine the balls and wombs of tens of thousands of humans denied a proper burial by the bulldozers of international CAPITAL as they turn to desiccated leather beneath the arid sands of Kuwait and Iraq. Another triumph of imperialism. Shall we now "deconstruct" this horror? Shall we produce surrealistic video images of smart bombs and the dumb dead? Or perhaps we should inquire into the rhetorical devices used to justify or oppose this slaughter. And if we apply our intellect and cleverness to this task will it change the probabilities of sanguinary yellow-ribbonism in the future? And if not, is there a point to all this impotent commentary?

Why am I writing like this? Is it because it permits me to say things forbidden by the official language of establishment sociology? Or simply because it is pleasurable? And if so, what is the source of my PLEASURE? Is it the pleasure of self-indulgent autobiography? Or is it the pleasure of straining the (con)straining barriers of official sociology? (Perhaps it would be amusing to submit this to the ASR.) Or is it just to set aside my own guilt as I sit here, alive and privileged in my snug apartment looking beyond my CRT at the ragged gray sky spitting snow on the mountains of northern Arizona?

How/Do Ritual (De)Constructionist Images Work (?)

The reordering of familiar images is central to ritual (de)constructionist practices. This desire to estrange popular images rose from the ashes of earlier theses regarding the existence of a "dominant ideology" (Abercrombie, Hill, and Turner 1980). For the latter half of the twentieth century, the central problematic for most Western Marxists, that is, those not living in (formerly) Marxist-Leninist states, has been the failure of working classes in the core capitalist nations of the North to replace the presumably repressive forces of capitalism with a socialist alternative (Jay 1975).

The initial, unsatisfactory, left-elitist answer to this question was posed in terms of "false consciousness." This conception was reformulated as hegemonic consciousness by Gramsci ([1935] 1971), later by Althusser (1971) as a necessary imagined reality, and still later by Poulantzas (1975) as the consciousness of lived experience. In each case these theorists were attempting to reconstruct the so-called masses, not as mystified victims of capital's control of the apparatus and administration of communication and culture, but rather, as coproducers of the ideological frames they inhabit. It was Foucault (1980), however, who most effectively suggested that power, the power to shape the images that shape the consciousness of life is not a *thing*.

Power, within a Foucaldian framework, is not fixed and located, but rather a force that is circulated within the society, with images a primary vehicle for this circulation. The image of the man behind bars, whether in serious drama, cartoons, public service advertisements, or any other form, is the (re)presentation of the state's carceral power over bodies. As this image circulates through the myriad channels of everyday life, it becomes ratified as we (re)produce in us, through our consumption and use of the image, our own assent to the normalcy of a power that is authorized to control the bodies of those it names deviant. Naming this power that names and controls is a central problematic for ritual (de)constructionist practices, and *Criminological Displacements* follows this path.

To some extent the disturbance frequently felt by first-time viewers of (de)constructionist productions such as *Criminological Displacements* is achieved by a simple theatrical device. This device consists of first instigating internal emotional contradictions in the viewer, and then, in violation of Aristotelian rules of catharsis, refusing to resolve them, leaving the contradiction with/in the subject (Fiske, 1985). But toward what purposes do these (de)constructions of the communicative rituals (in)scribed on bodies as well as in words disturb? Are they mere theatrical tricks designed to reveal the creative genius of the avant-garde? Or do these disturbances work in more significant ways? The question Hazelrigg (1986) posed of social constructionist practices can also be asked of ritual (de)constructionist practices. What work do they do? What, if anything, can these practices add to the study of social problems?

The first bit of work ritual (de)constructionist images do is to challenge the notion of a world of (ultimately) transparent facticity. This assumption historically has served, not just sociological positivism, but also those versions of social constructionism that assume an "ironic" posture by either seeking to debunk claims-makers' claims, or recording the absence of claims-making that, according to the sociologist as claims-maker, is presumably warranted. Although Ibarra and Kitsuse make a similar observation, their work is different from that of ritual (de)construction. When Ibarra and Kitsuse criticize debunking and claims-making practices in the study of social problems they are concerned with the possibility that students of social problems are "unwittingly drawn into assuming a stance that violates the methodological commitment to refrain from privileging or honoring certain mundane versions of the condition over others." The failure of analysts to remain neutral (objective?) with respect to some "versions of the condition over others" is the central flaw of "ironic" forms of constructionism according to Ibarra and Kitsuse. The epistemological bedrock of their plea for a rhetorical (de)construction that requires a nonevaluative stance toward all claims and claimants, however, remains the possibility of an ontological separation between claims-makers' words and sociologists' interpretations of those words. In this sense Ibarra and Kitsuse offer a modernist version of (de)constructionism—modernist in that their approach retains modernism's epistemological commitment to the possibility of a categorical distinction between knower and known, i.e., to a separation of reason and desire.

By contrast, postmodernist analysts such as Baudrillard (1983), Gordon (1990), Kroker, Kroker, and Cook (1990), Orr (1990), Pfohl and Gordon (1986), and Pfohl (1990) see the putative analytic neutrality of modernist science as an illusion. It is canonical wisdom among postmodernists that the desiring body and the reasoning mind are inseparable, and that the belief in an ontological division between fact and value that informs all versions of positivism is not only undesirable, it is unattainable. Contrary to modernist conceptions of knowledge, postmodern analysts take an openly valued stance toward the conditions of modern consciousness and modern life. When Kroker et al. write that "Panic is the environmental mood of postmodern culture" (1990, p. 443), or when Baudrillard (1983) suggests that images of reality have replaced the real as the central human experience in the late twentieth century, they are not engaged in dispassionate analysis. Rather, they are unapologetically engaged in what Ibarra and Kitsuse would consider to be claims-making rhetoric.

The stance of many postmodern analysts of the contemporary social scene is an activist one based on what Ibarra and Kitsuse would classify as a "rhetoric of endangerment." This approach is not, however, activist in the same sense as more established liberal and radical traditions in sociology. Ritual (de)construction does not rely on an assemblage of facts to prove claims or disprove other claims-makers. It is, instead, an assemblage of images aimed at disordering the appearance of reality enjoyed by more hegemonic images, including those characteristic of modernist social science. It is these popular images that serve as the basis for widely experienced communicative rituals that ritual (de)construction in social problems takes as its central problematic (Pfohl, 1990).

Much traditional social constructionism, including that of Ibarra and Kitsuse, also appears to challenge positivism through its acceptance of a highly relativistic stance toward the subjective meaning of social reality. It does this, however, while presuming the givenness of the representational system through which it constructs these challenges to positivism's assumption of a fixed social world (Hazelrigg 1986). In contrast, sociological (de)construction disorders that representational system, and in doing so, attempts to arrive, not at answers, but at disturbing questions, by demonstrating the fragility of the socially real.

Deconstruction, in all of its postmodern forms, has become the target of critics who wonder out loud about the emperor's clothes. The (apparent) willingness of postmodern deconstructionists to abandon structural analyses of political-economic processes for the study of cultural images has generated considerable criticism from the more traditional academic left (Jameson 1989, p. 32). Brian Palmer (1990), for instance, suggests that the sometimes brutal and always fractured images of postmodernist productions are the work of people who have simply succumbed to the charms of language and discourse, and who are doing nothing more than reveling in the creative thrills of deconstructive imagery.

Palmer goes on to claim that poststructuralism rose to prominence as a response by a generation of professional, university-based intellectuals who found themselves increasingly marginalized in the face of an emergent conservative political hegemony in the late 1970s and early 1980s. From this vantage point, postmodern deconstructionism with its non-vernacular language and confounding imagery, begins to appear as a Northamerican analog to Brazilian film during times of repression.

These nonrealist representations pursued the same political agendas as their more realist counterparts, the disembodied voice nestled in my dashboard told me, but now filmmakers obscured their real intent from the (apparently) limited artistic comprehension of the culture police behind the smoke screen of "magical realism."

As a theoretical movement, deconstruction does have some of the signs of a retreat of academic radicals behind strategic barriers of a language comprehensible only to the initiated, just as Brazilian film periodically reconstitutes itself as metaphor in order to hide from the prying eyes of the generals. This would appear particularly to be the case to those who privilege the political-economic, institutional realm as the central theater for social change. In the eyes of its left-materialist critics, by reducing all life to language, and in doing so retreating from concrete political action in the realms and on the terrain of institutionally organized power, postmodernist forms of deconstruction are little more than creative self-indulgence.

Many practitioners and defenders of postmodern forms of deconstruction, however, argue that its theory and method, its critics notwithstanding, are deeply political. They hold that it represents an attempt to construct a new politics, not only of discourse, but of life, by fracturing the current hegemonic discourse of power (Williams 1977). It can serve, its supporters suggest, as the theoretical replacement for an economistic historical materialism whose contradictions have become increasingly evident in the face of challenges from the feminist movement, the struggle for black power, the battle against normative heterosexuality, and most recently, the apparent repudiation of the concrete political practice of socialism in Eastern European countries that had embraced historical materialism as their operations manual (Caplow 1990).

I will not try to adjudicate between these claims and counterclaims about postmodern forms of deconstruction here. They are offered primarily to contextualize the subsequent discussion within the theoretical tensions that exist between modernist and postmodernist social theory. What I will do is to examine the implications of *Criminological Displacements* as a prototypical example of ritual (de)construction in sociology, and by extension (hopefully) provide a critique of the wider project of deconstruction as it bears on the study of social problems.

Beyond the Subject-Object Question

In many respects ritual (de)construction of the type represented in *Criminological Displacements* attempts to reach beyond the debate between "objectivism" (including Marxian historical materialism) and "constructionism," by presenting the claim that the human experience is fundamentally that of socially constructing a localized objective world (Jameson 1981). This socially constructed objectivity resides in the (implied?) existence of systems of power and dominance that, while logically prior to their (re)interpretation and (re)construction by social subjects, only continue to exist by virtue of this constitutive (re)interpretation. Within this framework, the facticity of power resides in fluid systems of representation rather than in the more substantial, and more easily triangulated, organizations, institutions, and ideologies that populate the writings of both Marxian and non-Marxian social science. What is retained, in comparison to more literary forms of deconstruction, however, is the assumption that human actions are constrained by socially constituted forms of power, and that some people experience constraints that are more destructive of body, mind, and soul than do others.

The metatheory underlying ritual (de)construction recognizes history as neither a teleology nor an ontology, but apprehends its effects as socially reconstituted realities that can be found in the language, the ideology, and the ritually communicative behaviors of a society's members. It further proposes that sociologists, as the producers of cultural texts, are either complicit in (re)presenting (and thus (re)producing) these worlds of power and dominance, or they are partisans in their (de)construction and (hopefully) their ultimate destruction.

The kind of postmodernist critique found in *Criminological Displacements* rejects the central canon of SCIENCE. Archimedes supposedly said, "Give me a lever and a place to stand, and I will move the world." Since the "Enlightenment" the idea of science has offered itself as just such a point outside history where human agents can firmly stand while applying the lever of scientific practice to move the world. The rise of science and its struggle to replace religion as the hegemon in the Euro-Anglo West was a struggle over which mode of thought would dominate social life. There was no debate over whether a place to stand outside history existed, only over where it could be found. Scientific socialism, as a concrete political practice, for its part, was a further elaboration of the idea of science, only now politically reconstituted as a system in the service of the masses rather than as a tool of the class enemy (Sahlins 1977).

The world that has fashionably come to be termed "postmodern" is precisely one wherein the modernist project, that is, the belief in and the pursuit of the endless expansion of human potential through the application of technorational systems to industry, economics, and politics, has foundered on the shoals of its own contradictions (Habermas 1973). One consequence of this foundering is the emergence of various "postmodernist" forms of intellectual practice, including deconstruction. In addition to the rise of deconstruction in literary criticism, art, and the social sciences, there are other signs of the decline of the hegemony of modernism. The spread of religious fundamentalism, and the increase in the many forms of speaking and acting that privilege religious authority are other expressions of the modernist project's weakening grasp and wheezing gasp as the center of cultural authority (Fitzgerald 1990).

Social constructionist theories of social problems were themselves a harbinger of a decline in the modernist project in the sociology because they challenged the canon of an (ultimately) transparent social reality. By privileging "claims" rather than "conditions," social constructionism questioned the central assumption on which a putatively empirical social science rested. The apparent reduction of the world to consciousness within social constructionist theories, however, as Ibarra and Kitsuse note, left no ground on which to stand except the informed consciousness of the social scientist. This consciousness, in turn, relegated the subjectivity of participants in social problems struggles to a transparent otherness. In doing so, these versions of constructionism threatened a dissolution of the sociological project into a pluralism of private intuitions. By denying the possibility of the Archimedean point, but offering no alternative stance, constructionist theories of social problems tendered a quiet resignation from the active struggle to change the world.

Ibarra and Kitsuse attempt to redeem constructionism from the disorder of pluralist intuitions by posing a new Archimedean point—the dispassion of rhetorical deconstruction. The project of unveiling the rhetorical devices of claims-makers offers a set of questions that they hope students of social problems can agree upon as appropriate and meaningful. That is, they propose a new paradigm for social problems analysis. Once social problems analysts agree that the tools of rhetorical analysis themselves stand outside history and are independent of the world being analyzed, the Archimedean point threatened by more intuitive forms of constructionism will be restored. Ritual (de)construction, like earlier forms of social construction in the study of social problems, can also be read as a radical denial of the possibility that there is a concrete world that can be known, critiqued, and consciously altered by social actors. I would argue, however, that this critique misapprehends the project, if not sometimes the practice, of ritual (de)construction.

The Crisis of Modernity

The developed world (and probably the rest of the world along with it) contemporarily faces a three-way struggle for cultural authority among premodern ways of knowing (religion/magic), modernist ways of knowing (science/technology), and postmodern ways of knowing (deconstruction/surrealism). The more nearly hegemonic grasp of modernist science on the cultural core is under threat from both its pre- and postmodern antitheses. Like a large vessel upon the rocks, the modernist project with its reliance on positivist science remains for many— probably for the vast majority of those in the developed West—the most solid and certain life support system in sight. The complex intractability of invested lives means that relatively few are ready to abandon modernism in search of new shores in the lifeboats of religion or so-called "postmodern" practices, whether these be detailed analyses of rhetoric or surrealist collages of language and video images. But the ship *has* foundered, and those aboard *are* in panic. There is no long-term future aboard, although one can continue living in the relative comfort of one's cabin, hoping that the generators continue to function, the food supply holds out, and the water rises not too swiftly during one's own lifetime.

The central theoretical problem for postmodern intellectuals posed by the erosion of the modernist belief in science concerns the relationship between conscious subjects and that accumulation of their actions we call history. Until the latter half of the twentieth century both Marxian and non-Marxian social science approached history as the more-or-less deliberate project of conscious actors. The certainty of this belief, however, was openly challenged by the French structuralists in the 1960s.

The French anthropologist Claude Levi-Strauss (1966), in particular, challenged the positivist view of history as a potentially transparent facticity by arguing that any attempt to understand history as the project of conscious subjects ignores the role of the linguistic and cultural systems within which human actions take place. These systems exist prior to, and independently of, individual actors and serve to constitute the subjectivity of these actors. By extension, the conscious project of those who set about to understand "history" would likewise be, according to Levi-Strauss's view, the unrecognized (unconscious?) product of the cultural system that authored the subjectivity of the historian. According to Levi-Strauss, historical forms are either incommensurable, making "history" impossible altogether, or they are selectively interpreted through the cultural project of the present. This latter makes the construction of *a* history possible, but it necessarily involves imposing a spurious continuity upon discrete historical moments, swallowing up the specificity of those periods and their cultural forms in a kind of "intellectual cannibalism" (Benton 1984, p. 13). This structuralist episteme painted social science into a corner. If all "rational" discourse about the human past and the human present was the unrecognized expression of anterior mental patternings embedded in the linguistic structures of the culture, then the entire project of constructing a social science of human knowledge was self-deluding.

Under the tutelage of structuralism, human subjects became not the makers of meaning, but the prisoners of meaning. Freeing the human subject from this theoretical prison is the animating force of what have come to be called "poststructuralist" theories. Both Althusser and Poulantzas, though structuralists, struggled, largely unsuccessfully, to find a way beyond the narrowing implications of French sociolinguistics that would recognize both the powerful structuring forces of existing cultural systems and the human potential to function as meaning-maker (Carib 1984). The bulk of their work, however, predates the profound effect of feminism on social theory in the late 1970s and 1980s, and suffers for it.

Feminist theoretical practice moved the project of understanding the process of obtaining a gendered identity to center stage. In pursuing this project many feminists sought a reconciliation of Marx and Freud, a reconciliation many felt they found in the works of the French psychoanalyst Jacques Lacan (1972). For Lacan, the process of obtaining a gendered identity is experienced through the categories of structural linguistics as steps in the process of subjection to the authority of one's culture, experienced as symbolic order. Within Lacan's reformulation of Freud, the resolution of the oedipal phase requires that the individual submit to the rules of the symbolic order as a condition of the communicability and satisfaction of desire. A necessary component of this submission, however, is that the original form of the desire must be repressed. It must be excluded in its original form from the conscious life and speech of the subject, and (re)constituted through socially acceptable speech acts (Gallop 1982).

At first glance this does not seem to be much of an improvement over the narrow corridors of linguistic action allowed by the structuralists. Lacan himself says that "language and its structure exist prior to the moment at which each individual at a certain point in his (*sic*) mental development makes his entry into it" (1972, p. 289). Yet there is an important difference. For Freudians, such as Lacan, repressed desire continues to exist. It has a life independent of the permissions granted by the culture, and for this reason it can be discovered, albeit in a (re)interpreted form, by the careful deconstruction of the conscious speech and unconscious expressions (dreams, Freudian slips, etc.) of the subject. Desire that is repressed can be recovered to the conscious mind, and the symbolic expressions of that desire can be (re)interpreted in light of this new awareness. In other words, the subject can be made to yield up the repressed desire to the scrutiny of the conscious mind, to the scrutiny of the world.

The deconstructive devices used in *Criminological Displacements* reflect the general framework of Lacan's view of why the conscious life of individuals is not a sufficient explanant of human behavior. The video-text relocates Lacan's insights from the realm of the psychoanalytic to the realm of the socioanalytic by pursuing the return to consciousness of a (re)interpretation of social science's repressed desire. Through this imagery, it attempts to overwhelm the ever-present cultural white noise that is the source of the repression—a white noise that at its center envelops a silence in which the voice that is repressed speaks but cannot be heard. *"Your comfort is my silence . . . . the hardest thing was simply to speak"* (Pfohl and Gordon 1985). Through collage and the surrealist methods of postmodernist deconstruction, the videotext attempts to sur-round the viewer with a mirror image of the dominant cultural white noise.

On-screen a woman is subject to her own gaze in the mirror. This image is accompanied by a voice-over chanting the once-innocuous-sounding words by Sting, "Every breath you take/Every move you make/Every bond you break/I'll be watching you" (Pfohl and Gordon 1985). Love in the postmodern world is (re)presented to us as surveil-lance. Familiar images are offered with an alternative and more ominous cast.

By operating at the same frequency, but from a different origin, the images of *Criminological Displacements* struggle to cancel out the image waves emanating from more privileged sectors of the culture, shattering their organization into disorder, forcing them to reveal the pleasures of their discourse, and creating a new silence within which the repressed desire of social science can be heard.

The idea that deconstructionist methods pursue the return of the re-pressed should not be confused with the idea that it is serving as a voice

for the oppressed, even though the oppressed in the form of the gendered "she" of nonnormative behavior in *Criminological Displacements*
serves as a central on-screen and voice-over image. Acting as a voice for
the oppressed, speaking on their behalf, transforming one's context and
syntax so as to mimic the voices of those without public voices in the
contemporary constructions of public power—the poor, the nonwhite,
the nonmale, the nonheterosexual—is the exercise of the race, class, and
gender privilege enjoyed by the majority of intellectuals in the developed West. It is often altruistic in intent, but it nevertheless remains
privileged and paternalistic in practice. This form of speaking on behalf
of the "other" is not the intention of *Criminological Displacements*.

Rather than serving as a voice for the oppressed, the videotext attempts to give voice to that which is repressed within the psyche of
social scientists. It suggests that these analytic examiners are driven by a
repressed desire, a desire that can only seek its pleasure in the repression of the Other—the "she" of the video. Students of social problems,
particularly those who study deviance and crime, are challenged to
question whether those they seek to classify, count, and control represent what they repress in themselves and thus hate in "the Other"
precisely because these Others enjoy what they cannot, and which in
their repression, they would deny to all Others.

Social scientists as privileged intellectual practitioners in a world dominated less by what Habermas (1973, p. 108) terms "power of the better
argument" than by historically sedimented and structurally established
institutions of money and political power, have no substantially greater
power to control their lives than do the majority of their contemporaries.
Many of the significant aspects of their lives, like those of most people in
contemporary industrial societies (and others as well) appear to be hos-
tage to forces beyond their control. The work of social scientists in
counting, classifying, and potentially controlling the deviant, the criminal, the poor, the uneducated, the unemployed, and a myriad of other
socially weak populations, however, provides the illusion of power. For
those who practice this science appropriately and skillfully, it can even
occasionally afford them access to the decision-makers who do wield
institutional power. Articles in "major" journals and positions in "prestigious" universities, eventually a seat on a policymaking board, or a
state-level—or better yet—a federal-level commission, are all the possible rewards of appropriate practice of establishment sociology. Admission to this elite club simply requires turning the suffering of actual
people into abstractions, charts, coefficients, Bs, and betas. This is the
displacement that *Criminological Displacements* brings into focus through
its (de)construction of the images of order.

Toward a Beginning: A Conclusion

But what of ritual (de)construction's challenge to the normal ordering of images and its attempt to return the repressed? What does it serve? What work does it do? Herein lies the central problem of (de)constructionist endeavors such as *Criminological Displacements* for any approach to the study of social problems that is actively concerned with amelioration. While it intimates a theory of history, *Criminological Displacements* appears to lack a theory of history of its own. It fails to provide a coherent explanation as to why things occur. This is not accident or oversight. Rather, as Pfohl argues in this volume, the very attempt to construct such a theory would be yet (an)other expression of intellectual and, in his (or my) case, "white male" privilege. Instead *Criminological Displacements* devotes the core of its energy to (re)organizing our awareness of how things appear. Its language and imagery struggle to challenge the dominant order of interpretation in sociology. This is good. But what disturbs *me* is that it does not offer a political practice for this liberation other than the politics of its own speaking.

I am not making some distinction between practice and discourse that views the adjective *political* as appropriately belonging only to the former and not to the latter. Discourse is practice, and all practices are political. The question is not whether the discourse of ritual (de)constructionism is political, but rather whether it is either sufficiently or appropriately political.

Ritual (de)constructionist practices such as *Criminological Displacements* represent a useful first stage in the (re)construction of a political practice of human liberation. I say they are a first stage because they serve as a revealing critique of the power of hegemonic discourse and imagery by laying open that discourse and forcing it to speak what it would hide, what it does not know about itself. It offers the potentiality of a far more powerful critique than does (de)construction in either its established forms, a la Spector and Kitsuse ([1977] 1987), or in the rhetorical (de)construction of Ibarra and Kitsuse. The former tends to obscure its political implications from both reader and researcher alike by masking the subject-object question. The latter appears to pursue a dispassionate social problems theory of rhetoric that precludes the pursuit of social change from inside the theory. Ibarra and Kitsuse do not object to sociologists participating in value-laden political actions. They do, however, see these as distinct, i.e., outside, the practice of the "theoretical reconstruction of the vernacular features of the social problems process."

The ritual (de)construction of *Criminological Displacements* offers a method to reveal the power of hegemonic discourse and imagery, but it too remains a circumscribed form of political practice. Something more remains to be done. Those (and I count myself among them) who are concerned for the development of an activist alternative for social problems research must still engage the world of institutional power. The world of ritualized power that burdens the bodies of women, people of color, the struggling peoples of the (now misnamed) Third World will not vanish like some frightened shade if we merely call it by its proper name. We must still act politically with our bodies as well as our minds in solidarity with those who are the victims of institutional power, and with those who seek a transformation that will lessen the pain, the exploitation, and the shattering of human bodies that passes for laudable progress at the *fin-de-millennium*. This requires the development of theory and research adequate to identifying and responding to both the politicoeconomic as well as the sociocultural sources of social injury, and to foregrounding the linkages between these forces.

A new politics of discourse may be necessary, but it is not sufficient for this task. A new politics of discourse as represented in the practices of ritual (de)construction may be valuable for exposing the taken-for-granted sadism of much of the academic study of social problems. In doing so it may stimulate some of the practitioners of these arts to examine the relationship between their work and extant systems of cultural domination. Its reliance on a language and syntax that is relatively inaccessible at the popular level, however, limits its utility for efforts aimed at political transformation. Passwords and code phrases have always been part of clandestine and/or elite groups. These groups, however, do not become part of popular movements until they utilize a language and a syntax comprehensible to the people with whom they are supposedly in solidarity.

I am not suggesting that activist approaches to social problems must be forever wedded to the vernacular of the past, but as a practical, political strategy, neither can that language be abandoned altogether. Nor am I suggesting that the academicians of social problems can or should serve as the leaders and "saviors" of those whose bodies are the bearers of the greatest weight of international capital. What I am suggesting is that the world of institutionalized power that required some people to sleep on the streets of Washington, D.C., while it simultaneously enabled sociologists to meet amid the glitter, the pastiche, and the technopromise of a postmodern hotel with automatically flushing toilets in that same city, must be engaged institutionally, by organized political practice. Doing so requires taking the insights of ritual (de)construction beyond its intellectual confines, and transforming them into a language that can contribute to the efforts of those outside the academy engaged in a struggle for social change.

Acknowledgments

I want to thank Avery Gordon and James Livingston for helpful critiques of an earlier draft of this paper, and Avery Gordon and Stephen Pfohl for sharing their respective contributions to this volume with me.

Notes

1. My contribution to this volume is the bastard child of speaking and writing. Much of the text presented here was initially part of a critical verbal performance in connection with a screening of *Criminological Displacements* at the 1990 Society for the Study of Social Problems meeting. I later revised the text for inclusion in this volume as a broader meditation on sociological (de)construction. This broader meditation, in turn, was stimulated by reading Ibarra and Kitsuse's contribution to this volume, and by reflecting on the implications of (de)constructionist assumptions on the objectivist social activism that has animated much of my own past (and probably future) work.

2. By the term *social problems* I mean any state of human affairs or set of human conditions that are (1) recognized as caused by human social behavior, (2) perceived as controllable through organized social actions, and (3) are, consequently, the focus of collective efforts aimed at the recognition and/or amelioration of these affairs or conditions.

3. This is not to say that those working (more or less) within the constructionist model always adhere strictly to its most radically subjectivist implications.

4. For a detailed discussion of this particular tradition within contemporary deconstructive analyses, see Stephen Pfohl, "Revenge of the Parasites: feeding off the ruins of sociological (de)construction," in this volume.

5. It is important to note that not all literary deconstructionists follow the path of radical denial of power centers. Barthes (1977), in particular, with his distinction between "writerly" and "readerly" texts suggests that the openness of texts to alternative interpretations is variable. He suggests that certain texts, i.e., "readerly" ones, are constructed so as to avoid inviting alternative readings. This leaves open the possibility of hegemonic texts in a number of areas of social life.

6. Much has been made of the fact that the apparent prefix of the word *history* is HIS. This is a strategically useful ritual in the struggle to reveal the gendered nature of what we have treated as *history*. *History* is derived from the Greek word *istoria*. In Greek *istoria* has two possible meanings. An *istoria* can be either a true tale of the past, or simply a story. Thus, from a deconstructionist perspective, perhaps it is equally significant that we attend to his(STORY) as well as HISstory. Even if we had a HERstory, it would still be herSTORY.

400   Raymond J. Michalowski

References

Abercrombie, Nicholas, Stephen Hill, and Bryan Turner. 1980. *The Dominant Ideology Thesis.* Boston: Allen and Unwin.

Althusser, Louis. 1971. "Ideology and Ideological State Apparatuses." In *Lenin and Philosophy and Other Essays.* New York: Monthly Review Press.

Aronson, Naomi. 1984. "Science as a Claims-making Activity: Implications for Social Problems Research." Pp. 1–30 in *Studies in the Sociology of Social Problems,* edited by J. Schneider and J. Kitsuse. Norwood, NJ: Ablex.

Bakhtin, M. 1968. *Rabelais and His World.* Cambridge, MA: MIT Press.

Barthes, Roland. 1967. *Elements of Semiology.* London: Jonathan Cape.

———. 1977. *Image-Music-Text.* London: Fontana.

Bataille, Georges. 1985. *Visions of Excess: Selected Writings, 1927–1939.* Translated by A. Stoekl. Minneapolis: University of Minnesota Press.

Baudrillard, Jean. 1983. *Simulations.* New York: Semiotext(e).

———. 1988. *America.* New York: Verso.

Benton, Ted. 1984. *The Rise and Fall of Structural Marxism.* New York: St. Martins Press.

Best, Joel. 1989. *Images of Issues.* Hawthorne, NY: Aldine de Gruyter.

Blumer, Herbert. 1969. "Public Opinion and Public Opinion Polling." Pp. 195–208 in *Symbolic Interactionism,* by Herbert Blumer. Englewood Cliffs, NJ: Prentice-Hall.

Caplow, Jane. 1990. "The Purpose Is to Change It." Review of Descent into Discourse by Brian Palmer. *Nation* (August 13–20):173–75.

Carib, Ian. 1984. *Modern Social Theory.* New York: St. Martin's Press.

Culler, James. 1976. *Saussure.* London: Fontana.

Derrida, Jacques. 1967. *On Grammatology.* Translated by Gaytri Spivak. Baltimore: Johns Hopkins University Press.

Fiske, John. 1985. *Television Culture.* New York: Methuen.

Fitzgerald, Francis. 1990. "Jim and Tammy." *New Yorker* (April 23):45–72.

Foucault, Michel. 1970. *The Order of Things: An Archeology of the Human Sciences.* Translated by Alan Sheridan. New York: Vintage Books.

———. 1977. *Discipline and Punish.* New York: Pantheon.

———. 1980. *Power/Knowledge: Selected Interviews and Other Writings 1972–1979.* New York: Pantheon.

Gallop, Jane. 1982. *The Daughter's Seduction.* Ithaca, NY: Cornell University Press.

Gordon, Avery. 1990. "Feminism, Writing, and Ghosts." *Social Problems* 37(4):485–500.

Gramsci, Antonio. [1935] 1971. *Selections from the Prison Notebooks.* London: Lawrence and Wishart.

Habermas, Jurgen. 1973. *Legitimation Crisis.* Boston: Little, Brown.

Hazelrigg, Lawrence. 1986. "Is There a Choice Between 'Constructionism' and 'Positivism'?" *Social Problems* 33(6):S1–S13.

Jameson, Fredric. 1972. *The Prison-House of Language.* Princeton, NJ: Princeton University Press.

———. 1981. *The Political Unconscious: Narrative as a Socially Symbolic Act.* Ithaca, NY: Cornell University Press.

———. 1989. "Marxism and Postmodernism." *New Left Review* 176(July/August):31–45.

Jay, Martin. 1975. *Marxism and Totality.* Berkeley: University of California Press.

Kroker, Arthur and David Cook. 1986. *The Post-Modern Scene: Excremental Culture and HyperAesthetics.* Montreal: New World Perspectives.

Kroker, Arthur, Marilouise Kroker, and David Cook. 1990. "PANIC USA: Hypermodernism as America's Postmodernism." *Social Problems* 37(4):443–60.

Lacan, Jacques. 1972. "The Insistence of the Letter in the Unconscious." Pp. 287–323 in *The Structuralists,* edited by Richard DeGeorge and Fernande DeGeorge. New York: Doubleday.

Levi-Strauss, Claude. 1966. *The Savage Mind.* Chicago: University of Chicago Press.

Lynch, Michael, Richard Lynch, and Dragan Milovanovic. 1990. "Deconstruction and Radical Criminology: An Analysis of Post-Modernism and Its Possible Uses in Criminology." Unpublished paper presented at the Academy of Criminal Justice Sciences, Denver.

Mead, George Herbert. 1965. *Mind, Self, and Society.* Chicago: University of Chicago Press.

Niven, David. 1975. *Bring on the Empty Horses.* New York: Putnam.

Orr, Jackie. 1990. "Theory on the Market: Panic, Incorporating." *Social Problems* 37(4):460–84.

Palmer, Brian. 1990. *Descent into Discourse: The Reification of Language and the Writing of Social History.* Philadelphia: Temple University Press.

Pfohl, Stephen. 1990. "Welcome to the Parasite Cafe: Post-Modernity as a Social Problem." *Social Problems* 37(4):421–42.

Pfohl, Stephen and Avery Gordon. 1985. *Criminological Displacements,* videotext. Boston: Parasite Cafe Productions.

———. 1986. "Criminological Displacements: A Sociological Deconstruction." *Social Problems* 33(6):S94–S113.

Poulantzas, Nicos. 1975. *Classes in Contemporary Capitalism.* London: New Left Books.

Sahlins, Marshall. 1977. *Culture and Practical Reason.* Chicago: University of Chicago Press.

Saussure, Fredinand de. 1959. *Course in General Linguistics.* New York: Philosophical Library.

Spector, Malcolm and John I. Kitsuse [1977] 1987. *Constructing Social Problems.* Hawthorne, NY: Aldine de Gruyter.

White, James Boyd. 1984. *When Words Lose Their Meaning: Constitutions and Reconstitutions of Language, Character, and Community.* Chicago: University of Chicago Press.

Williams, Raymond. 1977. *Marxism and Discourse.* New York: Oxford University Press.

19

Revenge of the Parasites
feeding off the ruins of sociological (de)construction

Stephen Pfohl

A blank white virus cut through the back of her mind. Her stomach
tightened. In theory, what was happening seemed, at once, terroristic and
absorbant of all HIStorical perspective. As s/he labored to partially remember the shifting material "origins" of the story in which s/he found herself
entangled, s/he turned upon the staging of the tale whose god-awful
silence fed the development of "strict social constructionism" and fell
between the lines like an ill-scripted character in a play whose author(s)
escaped memory, but not entirely. The next thing you know she was
hearing strange sounds and uncanny voices, like the dial tone of a mis-
placed echo or the acidic reminders of thought-for-food resisting digestion.
S/he spun to the left, staggered stepped but not denied an appetite for
revenge. Thereafter her methods became more laughable.
                    —Black Madonna Durkheim, *A Constructivist Genealogy*
                                                    of Missing Memories

It is the summer of 1991 and amidst a flurry of fading yellow ribbons I'm
trying to *collage* together a sociological story about the critical possibilities and limitations of social constructionism. By employing collage
writing strategies I sometimes feel as if I'm inviting a dialogue between
constructionism, as a sociological perspective, and *constructivism*, as a
militant "art form" committed to blurring the distinction between critical
research and performative remembrance and to the political denaturaliz-
ation of seemingly real social facts by such strategies as synchronic juxtaposition, montage, and noticeably open-ended assemblage demanding
active audience engagement and participatory rewritings.

To my left are questions concerning how an academically employed
whitemale U.S. sociologist might begin (again and again) to critically
respond to the challenge posed both by constructionism and by the
voices of those marginalized by the parasitic construction of contemporary hierarchies of power. To my right is television and a fiber-optics of
evidence suggesting that a politically effective construction of social

problems is today being managed by men with their eyes/"I"s on the screen and fingers on the trigger. Perhaps as many as 150,000 Iraqi bodies LIE outside the dominant construction of our collective HIStorical memories, while within one U.S. inner city neighborhood after another the countless lives of others are racially and economically managed as if the unfortunate outgrowth of youth-gang-led drug wars, rather than the publicly unnamed institutionalization of dense and high-speed forms of general economic parasitism and the sacrificial devaluation of some bodies to the profit of others.

How to best critically re-member the HIStorical and material "origins" of social movements powerful enough to construct a collective recognition of something as problematic and in need of control, change, or reform? This question haunts constructionist perspectives on social problems. I am here writing of *restrictive economic movements* of people, ideas, linguistic classifications, communicative resources, transferential emotions, bodily sensations, and moral tones. How do such movements construct a commonsense that certain ways of doing things are acceptable, or even valued, while others must be resisted, prohibited, or confined within socially constituted limits?

Social movements capable of labeling situated social actions as generalizable social problems emerge out of and feed back upon boundary-setting social rites, sacrificing certain possibilities while appearing to almost naturalize others. Like representational parasites eating off a vast material landscape of imaginary possibilities, social movements that effectively construct a sense of things as problematic repeatedly enact a compulsive reduction of social action to the hierarchically charged languages of common sense and taken-for-granted hegemony. The theoretical description or conceptual arrest of such powerful social movements LIES at the core of constructionist perspectives on social problems. By emphasizing the interactional, HIStorically specific, and political-geographic contingency of all social problems, constructionist perspectives double back upon the sacrificial violence of artful moral claims-making, exposing these, *like the claims of constructionists themselves*, as no-thing but the mobilizing effects of powerful representational practices that authorize certain modes of social action, just as they condemn, silence, marginalize, or exile others.

Critical uses of constructionism recognize themselves as making claims about the problematic character of claims-making social movements that are not essentially different than the politically charged epistemic labors of those they study. Although some constructionist theorists have called for a "nonevaluative stance" with regard to the "validity" of social actor's artful claims (Ibarra and Kitsuse, in this volume), more radically reflexive enactments of this perspective recognize even their own "truthful" depictions of others as "social science fictions" that are, at best, partial, socially situated, and evaluatively charged (mis)recognitions, allied in the provisional and contradictory service of certain narrative constructions (of objectivity) in opposition to others.[1] Such critical reflexivity requires a doubled analytic movement. This involves the tension-filled and contradictory recognition that both the "objective" claims-making of others and the claims we make concerning others' activities are forever being (re)constructed in the transferential space of a given sociological story. This is HIStory. This is sacrifice.

A reflexive enactment of a constructionist framework demands a critical recognition of this transferential space as the material locus of the only knowledge we are given. This recognition not only partially decenters the "objective" character of problematic social conditions, relocating the "objectivity" of social problems as a constitutive feature of the interpretive labor of those who (powerfully) claim knowledge of these conditions. It also manifestly decenters the "subjectivity" of the analyst within a scene of situated knowledge in which one's "truthful" recognition of *what's going on* is itself recognized as being socially moved by a shifting play of dramatic scenes and the invisible (but material) screens by which all knowledge is itself sacrificially evocationed.[2] This doubled decentering moves radical constructionism toward a form of sociological deconstruction—a rigorous, if laughable, commitment to the partial and interventionist character of all objective truths, including the truths of constructionism itself.

The Truth of Constructionism: The HIStorical "Origins" of This Story

A message illuminates the screen, that partially cuts my flesh from what remains pulsating. Its color is pink, light green and violent. This message in-forms me that somebody is knocking at the door of what might yet be critically re-membered. Somebody or somebodies. This message comes with a byte.

I open the door that is myself to this (im)possible situation. I hope against hope, not simply to access what's been forgotten but to exceed the almost instant binary framed oscillations that occasion my most compulsive repetitions and power. Looping densely modulated wavelengths speed across the surface of what's becoming time going nowhere. Literally. The message reads:

OPEN THE DOOR GIVE YOURSELF AWAY
HOT FIERY FLOWING
AS FOR LAUGHING MATTERS CONJURED

I feel that it's really useless (w)riting this way, so let me tell you I was truly scared. And fascinated. Both materially and in the imaginary realm. It was a physical thing with me. Not metaphysical but bodily. Transference without tran-

scendence. Displacement without sublation or its opposite. Difference without iden-
tity. A desire that's full of wholes. "And the compromise is this. What is recorded as
a mnemic image is not the relevant experience itself—in this respect the resistance
gets its way; what is recorded is another psychical element closely associated with
the objectionable one—and in this respect the first principle shows its strength, the
principle which endeavors to fix important impressions by establishing reproducible
mnemic images. The result of the conflict is therefore that, instead of the mnemic
image which would have been justified by the original event, another is produced
from the former one. And since the elements of the experience which aroused
objection [or the feeling of contra-diction] were precisely the important ones, the
substituted memory will necessarily lack those important elements " (Freud [1899]
1986: 307). SCREEN TO SCREEN. DESIRE TO DESIRE. LACK TO LACK.
    When I open the door a figure appears whose past is in my future. It is the Black
Madonna Durkheim and I know it in an instant. MAMA DADA MAMA DADA
DADA MAMA DADA. I flash dead pan(icked) to black and she says, "If you want,
I'll be your host. Pack up your possessions and let's dance."
    Don't ask me to explain what "I take" to be the Black Madonna's desires for me to
accompany her on the constructivist adventure I'm enacting. Although I was aware
of research by Cheryl Gilkes suggesting that Black women's decisions to become
community activists were often in response to the needs of their own children,
believe me, I was never under the delusion that the Black Madonna had mistaken
me for one of her own (Gilkes 1982a, 1982b, 1983; Collins 1990). And yet when she
spoke of her own contradictory longings she made herself partially reflexive in
relation to me and others. I am (w)riting here of something quite material: difficult
attempts to enact a reflexive method of knowing that's never innocent of power. She
did this in her (w)riting by drawing pictures on, or dancing with, or singing from
within what appeared as both a syntax and vocabulary of motives. This language of
such constructions defies the simple male-minded or narcissistic pleasures of
love/hate or guilt. She would confess as much, and then laugh at confessing
nothing. It was difficult methodologically to perform this way to re-fuse clear
distinctions between what's real and what's constructed, without forgetting the
difference. And although she sometimes sought the accompaniment of others, she
failed a lot and said so often or most often as (k)not.
    Occasionally she attempted to re-screen herself in plain view. In this, the Black
Madonna gave strategic if complicit notice to the local circuits of power in which
she found a contradictory charge. At the same time, she labored to display connec-
tions at multiple electric levels and in masked interfacings with the semi-conductive
flows of a transnationally abstracted CAPITAL violence. This violence is routinely
inscribed within the ritually constructed force-fields or body language of the sex-
gender, race and class-coded currents of CAPITAL in the USA TODAY.
    Currents of Power. Currents of Knowledge. To be honest with you, I didn't
understand every word she spoke. But neither did I feel the loss. She appeared
urgently concerned with matters of great importance and I felt it unnecessary to
master her every nuance. Better, perhaps, that I myself risk being conjured out from
within the dominating networks in which I have been HIStorically engendered.
Better that I allow myself to be transferred into a space of potential dialogue and

social change. In any event, this was my embodied frame of mind when I heard her say a second time, "Pack up your possessions and let's dance." This was less a command than a compelling invitation.

Being profoundly affected by the Black Madonna's words, and being equally bored by the predominantly whitemale culture of social science in which I found myself (w)riting, I said yes. Almost immediately. Not immediately, but almost immediately. Huge chunks of time broke like picture puzzles and flew rebus-coded across the space between us.

She told me that I had no business following her and broke into laughter. I tried to act as cool as possible. I tried to pretend that I was rough and ready. I explained that I was without illusions and that I understood the difficulties of the choreography that LIE before us. One particularly nasty chunk of time smashed itself against the side of my face. I fell to my knees blood streaming from a gash above my left eye/I.

The Black Madonna Durkheim laughed now more deeply, saying, "This is (k)not a very good beginning, is it? Things seem bad. Maybe you should reconsider." Then she spoke fresh and bluntly. She indicated that (in all probability) what LIES ahead would be different for each of us. Significantly different. As different as the HIStorically material differences in which we found ourselves called out in relations that were not one. It was (k)not that she had no desires for some (im)possible future convergence. It was simply that our journeys would and must be constructed differently. She told me that she'd secretly prepared some (w)ritings and that, although these (w)ritings were (k)not originally intended for my eyes/I, I was challenged to try to try to read myself out through the body of the words she was offering into somethings other. If I dared. I was both terrified and fascinated. I realized that to accept the Black Madonna's traverse offer would entail much more than my coming (along for the (w)rite cowboy). And much less as well. It's (k)not simply that I'd stop coming, it's also that I'd be asked to give away my most favorite (order) of things, and to partially lose what I'd taken for granted as the pale-faced single male and metropolitan privileges of CAPITAL(ized) self-possession. This would involve much more than coming (along for the (w)rite cowboy). And much less.

She handed me a text that included her (w)riting. As I read this text, I discovered my body slipping beyond the always only fragile state of what's been metaphorically called (out to be) the ego. I was slipping beyond what's positive (or positivistic). I felt stage struck dumb and awkward. At the same time I was taken by the sensation of being screen-tested beyond my wildest dreams. Annihilated and yet spinning out from within. Words appeared to lose meaning and yet retain significance. Or was it the reverse? Matters drifted with a vengeance. Suddenly things had become expensive. Excessively expensive. And within the inflation of the moment I sought the Black Madonna's recognition of my economic plight down-loading. Should I come or should I go? "What do you think?" I asked (k)not knowing.

I gazed in what I mistook to be her direction and tried to listen as best I might when she answered. "You have no business taking chances with other people's fortunes." She spoke carefully. "But to spend your own chances wheeling fortunes—that's (an)other matter. It demands, or countermands, that you actively give yourself over to transferences that will carry you beyond the borders of what you've always daydreamed as socially constructed. There, on the other sides of what's safe and self-securing, you might be asked to help defuse or re(de)fuse the time bomb of what's been HIStorically marked as normal or normative. There you might be called upon to joyously sacrifice your own white lighted desires for constructive mastery over me, my kind, and others. This will not be easy. Nor is this a task demanding heroism. Too many heroes have already always produced the HIStorical condition in which we find ourselves—this (k)nightmare. Should you be confused about this matter, let me re-mind you that the blood of many has and continues to be spent (sociologically) simply for you to have poetic inklings about such sublime impossibilities.

Listen Yankee! Whether or (k)not you decide to take leave of your commonsenses is of little importance to "we" others who are (k)not culturally constructed as if one. But maybe, if you do, when things become noticeably worse for everybody who refuses to become anybody, then . . . . just maybe then . . . . you can be of some minor help to those of us who are always already HIStorically insignificant.[3] No more closed-circuited white male revolutionaries! No more saviors! No more pimps! We've enough of those already. But some other form of parasite? Perhaps? Maybe in time you'll discover and re-mask yourself in a form that's more power-reflexive. But that's an expensive proposition and (k)not One that will make you feel complete. But as I said before, if you want I'll be your host. Pack up your possessions and let's dance."

And so I decided to follow the traces of this Black Madonna and the stories that she's (w)riting. (K)not without a certain nausea and self doubt. Nor without passion. For of this I was certain: "**To a greater or lesser extent, everyone depends on stories . . . . to discover the manifold truth of life. Only such stories, read sometimes in a trance, have the power to confront a person with [her or] his fate**" *(Bataille 1978, p. 153).*

And so I threw a few black T-shirts, bikini cut underwear, books, boots, condoms, eyeliner, pens, paper, and what (k)nots into my traveling bag and set off in re-search of parts unknown and/or what's missing from our collectively constructed HIStorical memories. This re-search seems perverse. As we approached the cross-roads of the words that follow I asked the Black Madonna Durkheim to speak of what LIES before us. She tossed her head in laughter, casting echoes into the (k)night. Thereafter she spoke complexly in a language I find impossible to describe. This much I understood, if ambivalently. We were traveling under the influence of a strange and power-reflexive method. We were traveling under the influence of sociological deconstruction.

From Social Construction to Sociological Deconstruction

Among the rights which man claims for himself, he forgets that of being stupid; he is necessarily stupid, but without the right to be so, and so sees himself forced to dissimulate. I would get angry at myself for wanting to hide.

—Georges Bataille, *Inner Experience*

I graduated with a B.A. in sociology from the Catholic University of America in Washington, D.C., in 1971. That being twenty years ago, there are many things I don't remember, and many others I now remember differently. The same applies to my experiences in Columbus, Ohio, where I completed a Ph.D. in sociology at The Ohio State University and worked for a time as a researcher for the Ohio Division of Mental Health, and more recently at Boston College, where, except for a one-year Post-Doc at Yale and a sabbatical, I have taught since 1977. Today, in the space in of this (w)riting, I have learned different ways of remembering things—such as how to partially embody myself in relations of more vulnerable reciprocity with others and how to better resist those who would (k)not take no for answer. For better and for worse. This is fate. I believe that I may also be more in rhythm with the queer erotics of the humananimal stupidity I share like a laughable curse with others. But shortly after the Gulf War (or, is it more accurate to say "after the U.S. led destruction of much of Iraq"?), when the Black Madonna asked me to UNFREELY ASSOCIATE to what I remember most about my years in college, the following experiences came to mind:

a. Walking seven blocks from one black ghetto church basement to another during the midst of a 1968 riot by citizens of the District Columbia following the assassination of Martin Luther King. The streets were filled with angry and impoverished African-Americans in resistance to every WHITE thing this nation stood for and thousands of gas-masked soldiers, firing tear gas and occasional bullets, and guarding the banks with armored vehicles of war. I was a well-meaning white volunteer carrying food. Fires were being set everywhere. Much that was burnt down, a mere ten blocks from the White House, has never been rebuilt.

b. Trying to work through issues in phenomenological sociology and texts such as Peter Berger and Thomas Luckmann's *The Social Construction of Reality* (1967), in order to understand how so many of us "Americans" are able go about our everyday lives with virtually no memory of the sacrificial costs we routinely impose upon others. At the time I found more theoretical resources for elaborating questions such as this in the philosophy department than within sociology per se. In graduate school, where I was introduced to the sociological study of both Marx and anarchism, economic questions concerning the ritual structuring of everyday experience already paved the way.

c. Coming to suspect—through a variety of pleasurable and painful personal experiences, theoretical meditation, popular cultural rituals (including seeing large numbers of movies, masturbating to mass mediated pornography, and feeling physically charged by various forms of white rock and African American music), reading books, and by endless talk with women friends and other men, including lovers—that the "normative" erotic repetition of "compulsive heterosexuality" was both stupid and extremely violent. This was something I would later learn (and unlearn) much more about, but in college the suspicions were already there.

d. Talking late into the night with Sam Williams, a fellow student and militant black activist about our different HIStorical positionings and about how to begin (again and again) to effectively counter the racism by which others lives were tattooed in relation.

e. The day (I believe it was during the so-called Tet Offensive) that I recognized that I was no longer simply against the U.S. involvement in Viet Nam, but that I was actually rooting for Viet Nam, with all its contradictions, to rid itself of my own nation's imperial violence. This was a shocking awareness. I am sure that it was influenced by reading as much as I could about Viet Nam and (w)riting a HIStory term paper on events leading up to war, especially the Eisenhower administration's efforts to shore up Western defenses against "movements for national liberation" in IndoChina following the overthrow of French colonial rule in 1954.

f. Being tear-gased to the point of temporary blindness and uncontrolled vomiting, and then being assaulted by waves of police attacking antiwar demonstrators.

g. Being asked to "please refrain from speaking in social theory class," having come to the verbal defense of a feminist student, who had taken issue with a professor's characterization of Durkheimian sociology ("Unlike you and your radical friends Ms. Rada Rada") as scientifically detached from politics. And the grade I would later "receive."

h. Sleeping for a couple of hours in a student-occupied office at the university, having spent most of the night helping organize an upcoming antiwar rally. Then at dawn being greeted by the shocking red sight of a spray-painted sign on the side of the National Shrine of the Immaculate Conception reading PIGS 4/ STUDENTS 0. That was when I first learned of the killing of students at Kent State. When word came soon afterward of more blood spilt at Jackson State University many of us glimpsed (if only briefly) what many of the nation's poorest citizens are forced to fear most everyday—the power of state bullets to silence HIStory. In Mexico City the memories were more sacrificial yet.

i. Loving to read and write and have serious conversations with others; and in this process learn about such matters as government-orchestrated attacks upon leading members of the Black Panther Party, efforts to undermine the viability of the American Indian Movement, the wretched conditions of most American prisons, the routinization of physical and cultural violence against gay men and lesbians (particularly after "Stonewall"), and U.S. corporate-state complicity in the genocidal disappearance of peasant populations in Guatemala. Although it was several years before I would read Foucault, you might say that I was learning (and unlearning) a HIStory of my present.

j. Being vocationally positioned to work my way out from within a radical theological critique of Western Christian categories and "Trinitarian" logic into the space of a critical sociology.

k. Receiving my draft notice, but knowing that it was no longer conscientiously possible for me to militaristically serve U.S. imperial interests.

In graduate school, in symbolic interaction with questions raised by Marxism and anarchism, my phenomenological concerns with the social structuring of everyday consciousness led me to experiment with politicalized forms of both "societal reaction theory" and "ethnomethodology." While societal reaction theory (when most radical) argues that what appears as "real" or "factual" is in actuality nothing but the cultural, political, and material effects of a human struggle for the organization of power in (and as) HIStory, critical ethnomethodology attends to the subtle power of interactional rituals in shaping perception and taken-for-granted experience. The influence of a societal reaction perspective is most evident in my 1977 study of the role of bureaucratic and professional power informing the "discovery" of child abuse (Pfohl 1977). Ethnomethodological concerns, on the other hand, guided my ethnographic work on the social construction of diagnostic classifications, including the prediction of dangerousness, by psychiatric professionals at a maximum security hospital for "the criminally insane" (Pfohl 1978).

In both studies, I observed how the ritual organization of power guided the "professional vision" of influential agents of social control. In both the "discovery" of child abuse and the labeling of psychiatric patients, clinicians produce "expert" accounts of deviance that deflect attention from the contradictory character of existing structures of (unequal) power. This was not to suggest that control agents intend their work as a perpetuation of hierarchy. Indeed, my ethnographic contact with social actors (such as those) I was studying convinced me that most were well trained and well meaning. How do people with such "good" intentions produce such "bad" effects? How are control agents' conscious experiences "professionally abstracted" from the ritual scenes and consequences of their own labor? Questions such as these have led my (past) work to be labeled as "an exemplar" of what is today commonly referred to as a "social constructionist" paradigm (Woolgar and Pawluch 1985).

According to Donna Haraway the "temptations" of a "social constructionist" framework LIE in its contention that "*all* . . . . knowledge claims, most certainly and especially scientific ones" are to be "theorized as power moves, not moves towards truth" (1991, p. 184). While sympathetic to this "temptation," Haraway voices reservations about a perspective that seemingly offers no "objectively" defendable or "ethically scientific" position from which to critique power's multiple HIStorical abuses. For Haraway, radical constructionism represents "a terrifying view of the relationship of body and language for those of us who would still like to talk about reality with more confidence than we allow the Christian right's discussion of the Second Coming" (p. 184). In a different vein, Steve Woolgar and Dorothy Pawluch criticize "constructionism" for its unreflexive deployment of "ontological gerrymandering," a rhetorical device that is said to cast doubt on the "reality claims" of those being studied, while "backgrounding" or partially disguising the "fact" that constructionist accounts are no less artificial than those they HIStorically circumscribe (Woolgar and Pawluch 1985). Yet, rather than condemning constructionists for such practices, Woolgar and Pawluch speculate that ontological gerrymandering may itself be a constitutive feature of all "successful" sociological explanation. Because of the importance of both critiques, and because the text you are reading represents a move from "constructionism" toward what might be better characterized as "sociological deconstruction," I will briefly respond to both Woolgar and Pawluch's and Haraway's positions.

Pointing to instances of "selective relativism," Woolgar and Pawluch charge constructionists with "foreshadowing" a "realist" view of social conditions. While not an inaccurate characterization of some constructionist texts, this is a limited reading of the more radical possibilities of this perspective. If constructionism foreshadows anything it is a "surrealist" view of social conditions. By this I mean that those "things" which appear as social facts are *paradoxically* no-thing but the fictive effects of the powerful structuring practices by which "we" repeatedly embody ourselves in HIStory. This is a loaded sentence. In the 1920s and 1930s, surrealism represented a convergent movement of radical artists, writers, social theorists, and political activists seeking to partially disrupt and structurally transform what they collectively perceived (and represented in (w)riting) as the white Eurocentric and militaristic organization of modern CAPITALIst consciousness. Condemning "the positivist idealism" and "commodification" of Western thought and action, surrealists experimented with such alternative research methods as automatic writing, sensory derangement, poetic collage, dream narration, social applications of psychoanalysis, new ways of engaging in political conversation, and the collective construction of art, literature, and social criticism aimed at turning inside out a society they believed to be both repressive of themselves and oppressive to others.

Although commonly misunderstood as a "modern art movement,"

surrealism, like its predecessor Dada, is better recognized as a radical conjuncture of theoretically informed social criticism and artistic activism.[4] Understanding reality as itself "composed of signifying elements" (Lash 1990, p. 181) rather than timeless substantial forms (something appealing, perhaps, to the post-Catholic epistemology of many surrealists, and endearing them to the more poetic, not to say "mystical," of their Jewish and African-Caribbean political allies) surrealists sought to construct new linguistic practices by which to reflexively explode existing cultural artifice and open the imagination to new and revolutionary social possibilities. Furthermore, radically dissident forms of surrealism, such as that woven around the figure of Georges Bataille, infected the ethnographic methods of French sociologists and anthropologists. Many of those attracted to this strange countercultural virus found it related to radical readings of the late Jewish sociological (w)ritings of Emile Durkheim and those of his nephew, Marcel Mauss. For surrealist ethnographers, as later for dissident French psychoanalysts, this resulted in new theories about the HIStorical character of what was bodily lacking in modern Western culture. In some it also elicited a desire to (deconstructively) turn the eye/"I" of social science *stupidly* back upon its own construction. In this, dissident surrealist (w)ritings called for *general economic* sacrifices that would laughingly burn through the blind homogeneity of modern reason. Bataille, who advocated the dangerous gift of such stupidity, called not simply for an abandonment of scientific reason but to use science against science in order to "keep science from blindly emptying the universe of human content. . . . . [T]o use it to limit its own movements and to situate beyond its own limits what it will never attain" (1985, p. 81).

Reading the material exigencies of "objective" social conditions from a "surrealist" viewpoint, radical constructionism takes leave of a world of fixed facts in order to examine ritual practices that situate us in a world of moving artifacts. This is to recognize that there is "really" nothing here but the transferential effects of being positioned within the rites of a powerful domesticating drama. Comte, a founding figure of modern sociology, had dreamed of a positivist paradise where factual truths would end both religious superstition and metaphysical speculation—a (Newtonian) social physics of sort. For surrealists, social matters were more quantum in their ritual mechanics. Comte's positivism was read as thought frightened of its own ghostly shadows (Picon 1977). While some surrealists, such as Andre Breton, appeared influenced by the synthetic (intellectual) force of Hegelian dialectics, the most radical (of the white men at least, for there were certainly "others" that fell under the sign of surrealism) passed through Alexander Kojeve's critical reading of Hegel into an artistic imagination that was more Nietzschean in its affirmative play of difference. Nevertheless, in one way or another, surrealists sought to reverse the dreams of positivism in both science and everyday life.

To live within the repressive shadows of Western culture was for surrealists to live within the confines of a terrible imperial prison. Who are the guards and who and what is being guarded against? These were questions that surrealists addressed both to the dominant institutions of their society and to each other. For the surrealist Antonin Artaud, life within modern bourgeois society was likened to the putrid stench of civilized rot. This was life amidst a mass of sleepwalkers and the living dead, a world haunted by its unrecognizable doubles. Artaud served for a time as the coordinator of the Surrealist Research Bureau in Paris. He also attempted to construct a form of theatre that would double back upon the shadowy confines of its own culture, and with "gestures, sounds, words, screams, light, [and] darkness" rename and redirect the play of such shadows from within. "To break through language in order to touch life," this according to Artaud was a research method that "leads to the rejection of the usual limits of man and man's powers, and infinitely extends the frontiers of what is called reality" (1958, p. 13). Maybe some of you will "discover" (ab)uses of such a method embodied within the very text you are reading.

The ritual physicality of Artaud's doubled theatre was meant to both remind and heal its participants of what was repressed by the unnoticed doublings of modern social dramas. The radical German dramaturgy of Bertolt Brecht, although employing different theatrical strategies, was aimed at related ends. Brecht's methods of estrangement or distantiation aimed at breaking with the unreflexive identifications fostered by everyday forms of (political) theater. In this Brecht hoped to defamiliarize his audiences with what otherwise might appear "natural." Brecht also formulated what he called a *productivist esthetics* to give dramatic notice to the artifice of even his own *epic theatre*. In both Artaud's and Brecht's dramaturgical methods LIE reflexive strategies that supplement those of radical constructionism (Lunn 1982). Together, these *power-reflexive* methods of (theatrical) research embody truthful spaces of "objectivity" without covering over the recognition that these too are spaces of ritual artifice. This doubled reflexivity makes such methods more "objective" than traditional forms of modern theatrical and social science representation.

By placing surrealism and the methods of Artaud and Brecht in the service of constructionism, I am trying not so much to defend previous constructionist theses as to suggest directions for the perspective's continued movement. Woolgar and Pawluch are correct in observing numerous theoretical, methodological, and empirical inconsistencies in various examples of constructionism. With this I am in not disagreement. My concern is with what is excluded by such criticism—the possibility of more radically reflexive versions of constructionism, versions more attuned to thorny epistemological problems, versions that approach a *social deconstructionist perspective*.

In their critique of constructionism, and of my study of the "discovery" of child abuse in particular, Woolgar and Pawluch point to passages in my 1977 text that seem to indicate that, while I claim that "child abuse" is a HIStorically specific construct, in reality I believed this phenomenon "really" exists independent of its label. How stupid of me! According to Woolgar and Pawluch, I betray constructionism by believing "abuse not only existed but could be differentiated from the more general problem of poverty." Moreover, in discussing my contention that powerful structural forces enabled "pediatric radiologists" to see "beyond previous barriers" and name what had been "invisible" to other medical professionals,

> [T]he use of such words as barriers, impediments, deterrents and constraints, reaffirms that Pfohl's article is an account not of the creation of a label but of the slow removal of one barrier after another until the parental abuse of children was finally revealed for what it was. (Woolgar and Pawluch 1985, p. 221)

I read my 1977 (w)riting differently than Woolgar and Pawluch. In part, this may be because my "original" article contained few clues as to my own epistemological commitments. No surrealist jammings, Artaudian breakdowns, or Brechtian distance. For failing to sufficiently foreground my positions I take responsibility and now attempt to set the record straight, or at least re(w)rite the straight record. There were several reasons for not having done this previously, the most obvious is that my thinking is today both more complex and more acknowledgedly in contradiction. This is no small admission. In 1977 I was immersed in the relativist language of phenomenological sociology. But to what is such language relative? At the time I was, as I am now, struggling to connect interpretive practice to matters of HIStorically circumscribed power. (W)riting on "child abuse" was part of that struggle. Whether in describing "factors" associated with the medical labeling of "abusers," or in discussing "barriers" to previous "recognition" of "abuse," I never understood my claims "as if" these were in any way independent of my own social positioning as an actor in the theatre of HIStory. I am here (w)riting of what really matters or materializes as "objective fact." This, I believe, distinguishes my use (or abuse?) of the constructionist perspective from that ascribed to me by Woolgar and Pawluch. They see my discussion of "documentary evidence" about the beating of children prior to what was medically labeled as "abuse" as evidence of "assumptions about the unchanging (objective) character of underlying conditions." In actuality, I had chosen the word *documentary* as a play upon the ethnomethodological term, *documentary interpretation*, a reference to the "constructionist" character of that which only always appears to exist below a given conjuncture of social "surfaces" and immediate "interactional effects" (Garfinkel 1967). My intent, although implicit, was to suggest what Woolgar and Pawluch make explicit—that HIStorical evidence of all sorts is itself a social construction, including the very words I am now economically permitted to place before your eyes/"I"s.

My point was not that there was really something, which today "we" call "child abuse," and that certain "barriers" prevented it from being seen before around 1960. I was trying to tell a story, not about the transituational reality of such things as "barriers," but about the "objectivizing" (constructionist) effects of a shifting web of powerful ritual practices. Such practices once inhibited and later invited a reading of children's broken bones and bodies as matters of parental pathology. The difference, if subtle, is theoretically and politically important. The aim of my (w)riting was not *constructive*—to uncover the "true" story of child abuse and to show how this truth was obscured by HIStory. My aim was *deconstructive*—to noticeably displace the truth of a dominant story about the humanitarian progress of medicine into a "truthful fiction" of power operating in even the most unsuspected of places. In part, this was to open a space of HIStorical inquiry concerning why child "abuse" continues to be read "as if" it were a parental "sickness" rather than the violent offspring of white CAPITAList patriarchy. In retrospect, I reread my 1977 work as related to Michel Foucault's claim that critical forms of HIStory enact a HIStory of the present (1977a, p. 31). This, as Avery Gordon points out, "requires a particular kind of perception where what's transparent and what's in the shadows put each other in crisis" (1990a, p. 15).

What is the relation between this "particular kind of perception" and what social science has long called "objectivity'? In commenting on the "desire of deconstruction" to show a "text what it does not know," Gayatri Spivak remarks that, "as she deconstructs, all protestations to the contrary, the critic necessarily assumes that she at least, for the time being, means what she says. . . . . In other words, the critic provisionally forgets that her own text is necessarily self-deconstructed" (1974, p. lxxvii). This adds a new wrinkle to constructionism's critique of all claims to objectivity. Is Spivak's deconstructive position more objective because it (repeatedly) foregrounds its own provisional forgettings, without disavowing the (strategic) necessity for such forgetfulness? Provisional forgetfulness weaves itself throughout all constructionist projects. This was certainly the case with my study of "child abuse." In constructing a "believable" sociological narrative I metaphorically condensed an analysis of ongoing ritual practices into a discussion of "factors" and "forces." In this way I "objectively" froze an indeterminate conjuncture of powerful relations into terms implying a constancy of "things"—barriers, impediments, obstacles to seeing, and the like. Woolgar and Pawluch arrest my (theatrical) play of theory. They seize my provisional freezing of frames as evidence that (temporary) backgrounding is a constitutive feature of explanatory work in general. Here Woolgar and Pawluch appear in agreement with Spivak when she describes the critic who by necessity "provisionally forgets" the socially constructed nature of her own "mastery."

But what if the provisionality of forgetting were to become a reflexive feature of theorizing itself? Today, a continuing dialogue with feminist, multicultural, and critical poststructuralist perspectives allows me to imagine other aspects of power than those envisioned by constructionism alone. In attempting to reflexively situate myself in relation to questions raised by these convergent critical frameworks I am challenged to both theorize and act upon the sex/gender and racially troubling assumption that my own truthful positioning in power-charged fields of knowledge is limited by the contradictory ways in which I repeatedly participate in reproducing both complicity and resistance to blind white spaces of compulsive heterosexist hierarchy. These are binary structured spaces of great homogeneity; white-washed and homo(geneous)sexual spaces; spaces that compellingly vocation particular conjunctures of moral and bodily knowledge, but not others. These spaces envelop everyday experience like a second skin or second nature, or like a ritual mix of physical and psychic geographies that call me out to enact certain performances, while closeting others. Not that I am determined to answer!

Rituals that performatively mask the sacrificial privileges of straight-shooting-white-phallic-male-fantasized standpoints construct densely hierarchical spaces of material and imaginary power; moral and economic spaces; spaces of defensive fears and alluring fascinations; spaces suppressive of not only mutual vulnerability between men and women but also between those ritually classified as *beings of essentially the same gender and beings of essentially different races*. Indeed, as critical gay and lesbian theorists observe (from a variety of heterogeneous standpoints denied legitimacy by dominant modern social-sexual constructions), such hegemonic ritual spaces are suppressive of almost any but the most militaristic-competitive-angry-anxious-jealous-possessive-criminal-erotic intimacies between men; and suppressive, as well, of intimate relations between women, whom homo(geneously)sexualized men attempt (with varying degrees of success) to exchange as if mirrored screenings of their own power; filtering, repressing, denying the possibility of reciprocal vulnerability to each other; sacrificially giving the would-be captured bodies of women to each other as substitutes for the more laughable vulnerabilities of men's own bodily fluid(itie)s (Butler 1990; Sedgwick 1990; Dollimore 1991; Fuss 1991). And no less terrifying are rituals suppressive of color (de)codings other than those violently filtered by spaces of compulsive blind whiteness. These commodified spaces are so performatively thorough and so magnetic in their racism that they may appear false-faced and transparent to almost everybody but those (of us) most attracted by their repulsive caucasian white circlings.

A partially reflexive recognition of our active, if different, (dis)positionings within such performative rituals of power leads to significantly more complex ways of seeing, smelling, touching, tasting, and hearing the social world in which we live. But is this also more objective? Without denying the situated and power-infused character of all knowledge, a recognition that links constructionism to feminism and other critical viewpoints, Haraway asks:

> [H]ow to have simultaneously an account of radical historical contingency for all knowledge claims and knowing subjects, a critical practice for recognizing our own "semiotic technologies" for making meanings, and a nononsense commitment to faithful accounts of a "real" world, one that can be partially shared and friendly to earth-wide projects of finite freedom, adequate material abundance, modest meaning in suffering, and limited happiness. (1991, p. 187)

Haraway refuses to oppose radical versions of constructionism and what she calls "feminist critical empiricism" (a sense of the "embodied objectivity" that LIES within women's different but related experiences of being "marked" by patriarchal power). I read this as a strategic move away from all pure "doctrines" of scientific thought—be these realist or constructionist. In Avery Gordon's terms, this is to open a critical space where what is shadowy and what may seem transparent put each other in crisis. By explicitly foregrounding (1) the situatedness of all claims to "objective" knowledge, (2) the strategic need to make claims to "objectivity" (if only to defend those marginalized against the sacrificial claims of "the center"), and (3) the recognition that to make anything present is to (at least partially) make somethings else absent (women's knowledge, for instance, in a world of information governed by men), both feminism and poststructuralism here put a spin on *constructionism* that moves it toward *deconstructionism*. In this sense,

> objectivity turns out to be about particular and specific embodiment, and definitely not about . . . . false vision promising transcendence of all limits and responsibilities. The moral is simple: only partial perspective promises objective vision. This is an objective vision that initiates, rather than closes off, the problem of responsibility for the generativity of all . . . . [epistemological] practices. (Haraway 1991, p. 191)

Mid-Speech, Mid-Way—A Place without Signs in Florida

I'd like to inform you that my theoretical concerns with constructionism originate in a viciously labored field in northern Florida during the summer of 1971. I arrived in this field, social research instruments in hand, to record stories of health services (or the lack of health services) given to migrant farm workers along the east coast of the United States. I was a fledgling sociologist and part of a team. The migrant workers, whose health constituted the object of our research, flowed northward each summer, a nearly invisible stream of structurally exploited labor. I was whitemale, well intentioned, and willing. Most seasonal east coast farm workers were African-American, virtually propertyless and re-signed. For some, I was the first white person with whom they had ever exchanged words. In Vietnam and Cambodia and Laos, the U.S. military, which included some of my childhood friends, was attempting to bomb a peasant population to its knees. And this, so that the people of Southeast Asia might experience the same democratic freedoms enjoyed by U.S. migrant farm workers—the freedom of being indebted to a "crew leader," who often as (k)not ensured the paid appearance of workers as commodities with armed guards, terroristic threats, and the routinized alcoholization of entire subaltern populations. The freedom of being bused from one dilapidated rural shed to another. The freedom of sweating in toxic fields picking chemically poisoned produce for a nation of overweight and cancer-infested consumers. The freedom of sometimes having your only pair of shoes taken away at night, just in case you had second thoughts. The freedom of being interviewed by me and other researchers. Degrees of freedom, I believe its called in the manuals of statistical sociology. These are HIStorically material aspects of U.S. democracy.

I'd like to inform you that this represents the "origin" of my concerns with constructionism. I'd like to tell you that this text begins one afternoon in a field in northern Florida, in a place known locally as "Mid-way," a signless place located halfway between one white populated town and another. And to let you know how I was affected sociologically by interviewing a white Florida farmer about the "health status" of workers whose "services" he obtained by paying a crew leader (or labor contractor) one dollar a head per day per worker and twenty-five cents a bushel picked. In listening to the farmer's words, I was struck by theoretically complex and personally troubling questions concerning the ritual social construction of binding images of economic, sexual, and racial power. These questions haunt my present writing.

"The health of the workers?" responded the farmer. "Oh, you mean the Darkies. Yeah, well they're just fine. I mean they're different from you and me. Maybe they do a bit too much drinking and sometimes get to fightin' amongst themselves. And maybe for you or me that'd be a problem. But not for them. That's the way they like. A huh the way they like it. That's just the way they are. Its in their nature. Its in their blood."

The farmer answered each of my questions without shame. And without the appearance of contradiction. He had all the information. All the facts. And so did the U.S. governmental agency to whom our research team submitted its findings. With our words the government too had all the information; a clear documentation of the problems, the lack of services, the lack of alternatives. And through the government all U.S. citizens were also given access to this information. In theory. Each of us must only exercise our right to information to be given the facts about this or virtually any contemporary social problem. Information about the discriminatory racial, gendered, and class-specific characteristics of urban violence. Information about the role of Oliver North, Jr., George Bush, and other loyal U.S. men in facilitating the smooth passage of cocaine into this country's inner cities in exchange for illegal funds to support the contra-terrorists in Nicaragua. Information about the genetic violence being caused by the corporate pollution of the earth from which we as a people take flight into space.

I'd like to inform you that in a seemingly contradictionless field of information in northern Florida, I began a power-reflexive process of re(w)riting that today brings these words before you. This is (k)not exactly true. Nevertheless, a doubled remembrance of this field might prove helpful in partially situating the sociological dance this text enacts. So, should you be tempted to imagine that the words you are reading are nothing but abstract plays of rhetoric, ontological gerrymandering, and the like, I implore to remember the sacrificial social construction of this awful place. For it is indeed from a space near Mid-way that these words come repeatedly. This is a space begotten in contradiction and mid-speech, a space thick and slowing reeling against the smooth and telematic surface of contemporary information systems. I am (k)not joking.

"Hush," cautioned the Black Madonna Durkheim. "There are certain constructivist secrets that are (im)possible to give away. At least (k)not unilaterally. And certainly (k)not for profit. Secrets that truly matter. Secrets of HIStory or hers. Its possible to dance with such secrets, or to dialogue with the field of forces they set (theoretically) in motion, but (k)not to give them away. That's impossible. These secrets are more seductive than that. Secrets such as these demand fortitude. Otherwise they stick to your throat and wrap themselves around your stomach so fearfully that you'll be begging for release. No, try as you may, secrets such as these are impossible to forget. These deconstructive secrets keep coming back. They return to haunt you with a sense of what's already always excluded, repressed, shut out, or shit away. Such are the secrets of re-membering some stories while remarking upon the unlawful passage or exile of some (unspeakable) others. Try as you may to cover the traces, such terrible secrets recur again and again. These secrets (dis)position everything, overflowing with what you yourself had always assumed

was lacking. Secrets such as these are literally too much. They involve doubled exposure of what feigns to be singular or self identified."
    Laughter followed in the wake of the Black Madonna's words. I listened, attempting to remember her every sentence and dance step. Nevertheless I remain uncertain about what it was she was trying to say. What was the meaning of her strange and elusive word-plays? I figured that they must have something to do with what "we" modern white men have always said to be missing. And about what "we" have promised would fill in the (w)holes. I sensed also that when she spoke of dance she was referring to some form of radically reflexive method of re(w)riting a HIStory of "our" present. Perhaps she meant to evoke an (im)possible image of some form of dialogical epistemology—a deconstructive choreography of social movements that is at once graceful and decentered, and seductive if provisionally a-functional.
    The Black Madonna's words were hardly heroic and (k)not prescriptive in the least. Yet, in listening, I felt myself carried beyond the boundaries of social constructionism as previously defined. This fateful epistemic dance again recalled images of Mid-way, Florida, and its field of black-bodied migrant laborers. Only this time I re-membered these images differently. And so I fell from the clarity of strict constructionist discourse into the indeterminate laughter of another form of HIStory, or hers. The Black Madonna recognized this deconstructive metamorphosis, and said: "Now tell me, what exactly do you mean in using the term (dis)autobiographical method?"

Doubling Social Science: A Power-Reflexive Re-Membering

[This] whole effort consists in materializing the pleasure of the text, in making the text the object of pleasure like others. . . . . The important thing is to equalize the field of pleasure, to abolish the false opposition of practical life and contemplative life. . . . . What we are seeking to establish in various ways is a theory of the materialist subject.

—Roland Barthes, *The Pleasure of the Text*

Given the importance of sacrificial ritual activity in the (re)production of biographical, HIStorical, and even geographical constructions of social problems, it may prove helpful to meditate briefly upon the (dis)autobiographical strategies guiding the text you are reading. How to mirror back upon the embodied social relations that partially constitute the manner in which I am able to re-member the construction of certain aspects of social problems, while forgetting others? Please bear with me. Unlike the bodies of those most victimized by contemporary constructions of power, these questions will not disappear. At least not until a major social changes alter *the order of things* in which I find myself (w)riting.

What methods most shape my reading (and re(w)riting) of social constructionism? If reflexive of the situated confines of my own partial knowings, such methods must entail a *doubling back* upon social scenes that today bring these words before you. Materially and in the imaginary realm. Such doublings are neither easy to read nor re(w)rite. They operate upon and within me (and you too, if in different ways) as signs constituting the perceptual frameworks and narrative conditions by which "we" both recognize and misrecognize ourselves as situated actors within HIStory. Such doubling gives *form* to what I routinely take for granted or consider as if natural. Indeed, as Michael Ryan suggests,

> We exist and have being or content as social entities in the [doubled] forms of behavior we practice, the modes of interaction we engage in, the formal patterns of speech and communication we under take, the styles of work we assume, and so forth. (1989, p. 5)

At the same time, such doublings may operate as thickly filtered screens separating *what is* from *what might be (or might have been)* different. IF this screening operation is (ideologically) effective "I" may not even notice that the doubles that envelope me are, in actuality, no-thing but the powerful effects of sacrificially filtered framings. This is what makes the world of doubles (in which I am (w)riting to you) neither easy to read nor re(w)rite. Please bare with me.

Methodologically this text may be read as an effort to deconstruct the dominance of a positivist aesthetics in the (w)riting of contemporary social science. Encouraged by the convergent efforts of a variety of feminist and poststructuralist critics, I am here laboring to resituate sociological texts as themselves bound to HIStorically specific forms of literary production. I have also been inspired by Roland Barthes's attempts to retrace material pleasures effected by various styles of epistemological engagement. Within the lawful confines of "normal" social science, these ordinarily involve the masterful pleasures of either "objectively" operationalizing or "subjectively" de(in)scribing the "facts" of the researched Other. What pleasures are these and how do they operate?

To ask this question is to begin to re(w)rite the methods of "normal" social science. It is also to come to partial terms with the hierarchical pleasures "we" modern men have traditionally discovered in our efforts to master what we have named as "nature." In an earlier text by Avery Gordon and myself (1986), we argued that the pleasures of modern social science are recognizable under the signs of *sadism, surveillance,* and *the production of a "normalized" observer* to the disciplinary exclusion of others. Modern social science was described as *sadistic* because, like the cold, calculating, and dispassionate protagonists of Sade's pornography, persons dominating the scene of social science inquiry have recurrently found pleasure in producing a transcendent or metaphysical distance between themselves and those they predictively study. This "positivism" penetrates the unruly orifices of the "natural" social world, plugging up the (w)holes and reducing as much variance as possible. This mode of social science was characterized as *surveillance* because the eyes/"I"s of the positivist must remain fixed upon *his* object lest *she* escape the master's gaze and return to a space of noticeable social contradiction. When this happens the paranoid borders of positivism become leaky, as anxious objects consigned to "the other side" begin to show through, displaying aspects of the dramaturgical bondage by which our "normal" identities as seemingly neutral observers are constructed. As Max Horkheimer and Theodor Adorno point out, positivist reason "comprises the idea of a free, human social life in which men organize themselves as the universal subject," but only within "the court of judgement of calculation, which adjusts the world for the ends of self-preservation and recognizes no function other than the preparation of the object from mere sensory material in order to make it the material of subjugation" (1972, pp. 83–84).

Sadism, surveillance, and the production of the "normalized" (whitemale) subject in a discourse that exiles or consumptively incorporates difference—these are the dominant pleasures of positivist social science.[5] This is a harsh image. If we contemporary social scientists rarely recognize ourselves in such descriptions, perhaps it is because the "disciplinary" confines within which most of us work help insulate us from grasping the sacrifices (of others) that makes positivism (structurally) possible. Under the sign of positivist logic, "Being is apprehended under the aspect of manufacture and administration. Everything—even the human individual, not to speak of the animal—is converted into the repeatable, replaceable process into a mere example" (Horkheimer and Adorno 1972, p. 84).

Under positivism the model comes first. But where does the model come from? What is unexamined (or unexaminable) under the sign of positivism are the everyday rituals of power and knowledge that sacrificially constitute the very social experiences that positivists seek to explain. Positivist rituals conjure a screen that separates the cultured researcher from the HIStorically material scene in which one's own epistemological framework is processually filtered. In this way positivism rigorously reflects what's already premodeled. At the same time, it is compulsively unreflexive about the powerful social structuring of its own perceptual apparatus. Here LIES a blind spot at the center of positivism's

dazzling promise of enlightenment, a hole around which its whole pre-
dictive quest for reliable measurement and lawful explanation converge. A
hole before (or at the blind center of) one's eyes/"I"s. A hole that remains
taboo, a hole that must be (w)holly covered over for positivism to work its
magic. An immaterial (w)hole that substitutes a universal or "extra-local
standpoint" for the fleshy HIStorical contradictions out of which the
positivist screen itself is erected (Smith 1987). For positivists, "the conceptual apparatus determines the sense, even before perception occurs . . . .
images are pre-censored according to the norm . . . . which will later
govern their apprehension" (Horkheimer and Adorno 1972, p. 84).

   In the (de)construction that constitutes this text, I am trying to double-
cross or write against the grain of the dominant positivist social science
pleasures. I am here laboring to "partially" resist the temptation to forget that my own representations of these matters LIE truthfully in the
sacrificial epistemological rituals by which any "successful" act of theorizing covers over the fictive narrational structures by which it identifies
(with) a story of the facts. As such, in the construction of this text I am
struggling to deny myself a place of empirical privilege outside the social
scene in which I am dramatically called out or interpellated in HIStory.
This literary refusal, if doubly incorporated into the imagination of social
science, has troubling implications for both the style and content of
ordinary social science literature. As Julia Kristeva re-marks: "Literary
practice remains the missing link in the socio-communicative . . . . fabric of the so-called human sciences. . . . . [Moreover] the insertion of
this practice into the social science corpus necessitates a modification of
the very notion of pleasure" (1975, pp. 59, 61).

   I read Kristeva's words as a challenge to us social scientists to double
back upon the HIStorical scenery of our own modes of literary production. One response to such a challenge takes the form of what might be
called *power-reflexive methods of sociological (dis)closure*. This demands that
"we" partially display (and thereby evict or give notice to) the boundary
work by which the social worlds we inhabit are being sacrificially constructed. This is to actively *derealize* the always only apparently "natural"
settings of our own (w)ritings. This is also to recognize (and thereby
reframe) our artful complicity in the reconstruction of such settings. It is
also to re(w)rite our HIStorical relations to other people, things, and
ourselves as no-thing but powerfully constructed doubles of the contradictory material and imaginary positionings by which we are situated in
relation to others.

   To take seriously the rigorously advanced claim to the situated character of all knowledge is not to deny the "objectivity" of intellectual truths,
but to demand of "objectivity" that it reflexively locate the (always only)
provisional adequacy of its own partial positionings within the world it

studies. This is no simple task—theoretically or personally. Theoretically it demands that "we" dialogically resituate the objects of our inquiry within the economic, cultural-linguistic, and sexual frame-workings in which they partially speak to us (just as we speak about and to them). To do so we must become acutely sensitive to the subtle ritual technologies by which "our" knowledges are differentially embodied. For those of us trained within the predominantly whitemale and heterosexist confines of Western educational institutions, this may entail a contagious *double-crossing* out from within the specialized boundaries of the *disciplines* into which we have been socialized. Those of us disciplined by sociology, for instance, may have to open ourselves to questions and methods falling between the force-fields of philosophy, literature, linguistics, HIStory, economics, women's studies, psychoanalysis, the iconic or performing arts, and even theoretical physics. And to knowledge derived from cultures traditionally designated as outside or south of what's West. And vice versa.

A *power-reflexive* method demands an impure, if rigorous, commingling of multiple forms of inquiry. Perhaps, only by risking what Jacques Attali describes as the rigors of "theoretical indiscipline" might we today put into practice such *epistemological double-crossings* (1985, p. 5). For most of us this will involve as much *unlearning* as learning, a process involving both the dangers and pleasures of speaking (or (w)riting) out of place. Or, as Edward Said suggests, "to generalize exactly at those points where generalizations seem impossible" (1983, p. 157).

More uneasy yet may be the personal discomforts engendered by attempts to double back upon, and thereby institutionally displace, the hierarchical forms in which Western knowledge has been traditionally prepackaged. Such discomforts are a likely effect of any serious challenge to the reproduction of existing social power. While most discomforting to those privileged by an existing order of power, such a strategy of reflexive doublings may be experienced as both anxiety producing *and* pleasurable for those regularly sacrificed to the reproduction of power. In this, one (who is not One) might encounter the more fluid material and imaginary pleasures of being both a heterogeneous and contradictory subject.

> This is an uncertain pleasure of an uncertain subject: a subject who knows we are interpellated—that we respond to the hailing of our names. But this subject recognizes the provisionality of centering, the uncertainty of that seemingly certain anchorage, only produced by the rituals of taking the world within us. This is the uncertain pleasure of the subject whose truth is always inscribed in the power to know, to entrap in a name. (Pfohl and Gordon 1986, p. S109)

Toward a (Dis)Autobiographical Method

In an earlier meditation upon the methods of *a power-reflexive social science* I suggested that the critical researcher must ask her- or himself three questions (Pfohl 1985b). How does my biographical positioning within contemporary scenes of power affect the truths I am capable of recognizing? How do my observations about a site-specific scene of social inquiry connect to the ritual organization of power relations in society as a (w)hole? And, once having examined a particular conjuncture of biographical and structural relations, what have I learned about power that may contribute to struggles for social justice? To attempt to (re)make such connections between biographical experience and power is to recognize that power is an omnipresent feature of all social relations. As Michel Foucault (1982) suggests, power is that which gives social relations their transformative force. It is that charged aspect of relations that ritually affects other relations, setting into place and continually replacing the fields of force in which we humans find ourselves embodied with and over against others. While omnipresent, power is nevertheless differently structured in different social times and spaces. Thus, while it is possible (and perhaps even critically necessary) to imagine relatively equalitarian or reciprocal forms of power in which the exchange of forceful effects is mutually enabling (if not the same or in any way homogeneous), such forms are far from the reality of power as it plays itself out violently within our hierarchical present. As such, *power-reflexive methods* ask not simply that we (as researchers) cross paths with considerations of *power in general*, but that we risk strategies of inquiry that permit us to increasingly double-cross our way out from within the HIStorical and material confines of the economic, racial, and sexual hierarchies that shape the *specific modes of power* in which so many of us are presently positioned.

The questions I list above emerge out of my attempts to teach university students to write critically about our own participation in the social construction of boundaries between what is acceptable and what is viewed as socially problematic. In my teaching about such matters I have encouraged my students not just to think critically but to (w)rite critically, as well. I have urged them to deploy writing as a social technology for reflexively doubling back upon ritualized scenes of power that we might otherwise take for grant. The hope here is that by developing power-reflexive writing practices we might better construct connections between the immediacy of autobiographical experience and HIStorical spaces within which experience might be re-membered relationally. The political importance of such a doubled writing practice, or what I call *(dis)autobiographical analysis,* is articulated in the collective "memory-work" of Frigga Haug and her German feminist co-authors when they state:

> Writing is [or can be] a transgression of boundaries, an exploration of new territory. It involves making public the events of our lives, wriggling free of the constraints of purely private and individual experiences. From a state of modest insignificance we enter a space in which we can take ourselves seriously. As an alternative to accepting everyday events mindlessly, we recalled them in writing. (1987, p. 36)

This lesson or gift or curse I offer to you as well. In reading or (re)writing (dis)autobiographically

> you will be faced with the creative task of how to weave autobiography with HIStory, how to write of/in your body as both *yours* and (k)not yours, as both an individual body with borders you can *really* feel, and as ritual body really (k)notted and entangled with other stories not of your own making. This is no simple task. Remember, however, you are not being asked to create the FULL STORY, COMPLETE TRUTH, or FINAL AC-COUNTING of your tale [but] to play seriously with your own memories using the critical techniques of power-reflexive storytelling to create, hopefully, a different story than the one you've written before. So *remember* . . . . and, failing that, ... *invent* a creative critical social [science] fiction that might raise questions as well as answer them. (Orr 1989, p. 2)

'Other Weapons" for (K)not Knowing

> It was only after I had completely conceded my defeat as an artist—my inability to master the material in the image of my own intention—that I became aware of the ambiguous consequences of my failure, for in effect, the reasons for and the nature of my defeat contained, simultaneously, the reasons for and the nature of the victorious forces as well. I have come to believe that if HIStory were recorded by the vanquished rather than by the victors, it would illuminate the real, rather than theoretical, means to power; for it is the defeated who know best which of the opposing tactics were irresistible. The Russian peasant has another way of saying this: "He who wears the shoe knows where it pinches"
> —Maya Deren, *Divine Horsemen: The Living Gods of Haiti*

The opening words of Luisa Valenzuela's *Other Weapons* read:

> She doesn't find it the least bit surprising that she has no memory, that she feels completely devoid of recollections. She may not even realize that

she's living in an absolute void. She is quite concerned about something else, about her capacity to find the right word for each thing and receive a cup of tea when she says I want (and that "I want" also disconcerts her, that act of willing) when she says I want a cup of tea. (1985, p. 105)

Valenzuela invites her readers to follow the ritual journey of a woman protagonist as she gradually, and not without considerable anguish, recovers her memories of being bodily positioned as an object of (secret) exchanges between men in a game of war. Retracing her sacrificial positioning as an object constructed among other objects, as a woman-object positioned among men's (secret) words, concepts, photographs, names, plants, mirrors, windows, colleagues, wells, whips, peepholes, keys, and voices, "she" comes to a revelation about the HIStorical geography of her memory-loss. This "discovery" is both reflexively situated and objective. It also hastens the ending of her imprisonment.

> She looks at herself, first out of obligation and then out of pleasure, and then she sees herself up there in the mirror . . . . , cast on the bed, upside down and far away. She looks at herself from the tips of her toes where he is now tracing a map . . . . ; she looks at herself and, without acknowledging it altogether, travels up her own legs, her pubis, her navel, the surprisingly heavy breasts, a long neck and that face of hers which suddenly reminds her of the plant—living, but somehow artificial—and, unwittingly, she closes her eyes. (Valenzuela 1985, p. 114)

In (w)riting within (and about) the warring contours of socially constructed problems and in attempting to respond to the embodied memories (and forgettings) of others, I too *want* to be performing an analysis that is both reflexively situated and objective. But as U.S. white man with CAPITAL credentials and an academic job, my positioning in the HIStory of memories is markedly different than Valenzuela's woman protagonist. There are, moreover, some very good reasons for suspecting that the situated materiality of her constructed memories may be more "objective" than mine. At least until I doubly dance back upon my relation to her, unlearning many of the blind rituals that (dis)position me as one of power's privileged sons.

> Open your eyes, he commands, watching her watch herself in the mirror. . . . . Open your eyes, spit it out, tell me who sent you, who gave the order, and she shouts such an intense, deep *NO* that her answer is silent in the space they're in and he doesn't hear it, a *NO* that seems to shatter the mirror . . . . , that multiplies and maims and destroys his image, almost like a bullet shot although he doesn't perceive it and both his image and the mirror stay there, intact, impervious, and she, exhaling the air she'd

kept in, whispers . . . . his real name, for the first time. But he doesn't
hear that either, as distant as he is from so much trauma. (Valenzuela 1985,
pp. 114–15)

In saying NO she accesses a space (of forbidden knowledge) that situates her reality constructions within a contradictory and *excessive awareness* of how power works (unequally) between them. But "distant as he
is from so much trauma" he doesn't hear. In this, she comes to knowledge painfully and from a position that his militaristic (or phallic) defenses protect him from recognizing. In this she is more objective. This
is not to suggest that the oppressed are ever entirely clear-sighted about
the dynamics of power to which those most privileged are blinded. All
forms of knowledge are partially mediated. It is, however, to acknowledge that, as Gloria Anzaldua (1987), Nancy Harstock (1981), Dorothy
Smith (1987), Donna Haraway, and others argue, "there is good reason
to believe vision is [objectively] better from below the brilliant space
platforms of the powerful" (Haraway 1991, pp. 190–91). Why? Because
in the process of reflexively saying no to hierarchy, the oppressed are
able to partially make use of traumas imposed upon or triggered within
their bodies as these bear (or bare) witness to the "objective" play of
parasitic power itself. This may be difficult for even the most well meaning of us more privileged by power to recognize. Perhaps we need first
to publicly unlearn certain of our most militaristically guarded secrets.
Only after making such (self) sacrifices might we actually become more
"objective" and, thus, better able to assist others in overturning the
social construction of hierarchical forms. Otherwise, all good intentions
aside, those of us in positions of (epistemological) privilege may remain
more part of the problem than part of its solution. This is why I feel
compelled (as a critical whitemale sociologist) to enact what I call (dis)au-
tobiographical methods. Paradoxically, this partial enactment of what
Avery Gordon labels *a sociographical project* may give you (as readers)
more access to certain aspects of myself that are conjured by this (w)rit-
ing than I, stupid as I am, may initially realize. Please read this as both a
warning and invitation to dialogue:

> As a sociographical project . . . . [this text] insists on being read as writing,
> as "literature." One of the key lessons of deconstruction is that both the
> writer and the text perform moves and tell stories of which they are un-
> aware. An important part of the deconstructive project of reading is pre-
> cisely to tell the text what it does not know. This is your job. Because the
> conscious intentions and desires of the writer form a kind of interference
> pattern within which a writing and a reading occur, I am perhaps the least
> qualified person to unscramble the codes that are used and which the text
> itself produces. (Gordon 1990a p. 40)

Toward such modest ends, the text you are reading stupidly mixes
social-psychoanalysis with collage (w)riting, deconstructive ethnography, and a genealogical approach to HIStory. Collage techniques are
employed because they *visibly double* (and thus give reflexive notice to)
the already cut up and repasted frameworkings of ultramodernity. This
is (k)not to merely simulate a random access–like pastiche of free-
floating and contextless commodity hook-ups (Jameson 1984). By intersecting collage strategies with methods attentive to specific cultural rituals, scenes of psychic over-determination and the shifting HIStorical
configurations of power, I am trying to (de)construct a reading environment that disinforms as much as it gives knowledge. Hopefully this will
offer an experience closer to the uncertainties of *dialogical research* than
the more masterful pleasures of dialectical analysis.

According to surrealist Max Ernst, collage involves "the coupling of
. . . . realities, irreconcilable in appearance upon a plane which apparently doesn't suit them" (cited in Clifford 1988, p. 117). Consider, for
instance, the coupling of social science with a form of (w)riting more
typically associated with poetry or avant-garde prose, or the mixing of a
language that noticeably demands real social change with a mode of
artistic investigation intent upon derealizing, and thus giving notice, to
the demand structures of all language.[6] Consider, for instance, this text:
"The orientation . . . . that I invoke cannot be neatly defined" (Clifford
1988, p. 118). Indeed, the promise of collage is to mess up or tear gaps in
an otherwise neat, enchanting, and seemingly seamless social ordering
of perception. Like the photomontages constructed by Hannah Hoch,
John Heartfield, and other Berlin Dadaists, its aim is to conjure "a chaotic, explosive image, a provocative dismembering of reality" (Ades 1976,
pp. 12–13). In this way collage critically interrogates material relations
between a putative "original" object and the copies for which it allegedly
poses as a model.

Collage (w)riting strategies take as their

> problem—and opportunity—the fragmentation and juxtaposition of cul-
> tural values. From this disenchanted viewpoint stable orders of collective
> meaning appear to be constructed, artificial, and indeed often ideological
> or repressive. The sort of normality or commonsense that can amass em-
> pires in fits of absent-mindedness or wander routinely into world wars is
> seen [or re-visioned by collage work] as a contested reality to be subverted,
> parodied, and transgressed. (Clifford 1988, p. 118)

If collage (w)riting works it may facilitate an (un)working of the often
taken for granted world of our everyday lives. It may quite literally serve
to denaturalize the existence of certain things; or to re-make our sensations of things contingent upon the material and imaginary practices by
which they have been not so "originally" constructed.

That is why my subject is not the truth of being but the social being of truth, not whether facts are real but what the politics of their interpretation and representation are. With Walter Benjamin my aim is to release what he noted as the enormous energy of history that lies bonded in the "once upon a time" of classical historical narrative. The HIStory that showed things "as they really were," he pointed out, was the strongest narcotic of our century. And of course it still is. (Taussig 1987, pp. xiii–xiv)

Within this collage, ethnography is intersected with social-psycho-analysis because when crossing into and out of each other these strategies may assist decentering the (working) identities of those of us trained as Western social scientists. For as Michel Foucault notes,

In relation to the human sciences; psychoanalysis and ethnology or rather "counter sciences," which does not mean that they are less "rational" or "objective" than others, but that they flow in the opposite direction, that they had them back to their epistemological basis, and that they ceaselessly "unmake" that very man who is creating and recreating his positivity in the human sciences. (1970, p. 379)

To double back upon and thus partially remake that very man who is me! By engaging deconstructively with ethnography and sociologically with psychoanalysis I hope to better reflex upon the embodied scenes of ritual transference in which my own claims to truth are reflexively situated. This double-crossing of strategies raises "difficulties in the register of method," which, as Georges Bataille suggests, provide partial access to spaces of both the cultural and psychic "unconscious" (1988b, p. 115). But even this is never innocent of my desire that you will recognize me in these words and respond transferentially to the cursed gift they offer.

To play off social-psychoanalysis in relation to ethnography is to (de)constructively open spaces between my (w)riting and your eyes/"I"'s. Within such spaces perhaps we might better learn (and unlearn) things about what binds us together within a *transferential* field charged by the *repetitious drive* of conscious and *unconscious* social power. For better and for worse. In this way, those concerned with the critical potential of constructionism might more materially engender a dialogue with "others" seeking to "objectively" subvert sacrifices demanded by the repro-duction of white CAPITAList patriarchy. Indeed, a critical convergence of ethnographic and social-psychoanalytic strategies is already a feature of what Avery Gordon refers to as "the theoretical/political interventions of . . . . a feminist poststructuralism" (1990b, p. 488). For Gordon, a feminist engagement with these always "less than adequate" methods may assist in "grappling with issues related to the narrative structuring, fictive composition, and historical provisionality of [gendered] claims to knowledge'(p. 488). Gordon's sociological use of psychoanalysis gives notice to the ghostly haunt of powerful forces rendered "invisible" by their incorporation within the mundane scenery of everyday social life. By detouring ethnography through psychoanalysis, she articulates a provisional method whereby feminist researchers might strategically attend to "the material rituals of the production of knowledge, those vectors of power—institutional, social, personal, sexual—which call us out to desire to know" (p. 490). In this way, Gordon's work raises critical questions concerning the gendered field of constructionist research itself. A related perspective is offered by Jacqueline Rose, who states:

> [T]he importance of psychoanalysis is precisely the way that it throws into crisis the dichotomy on which the appeal to the reality of the event . . . . clearly rests. Perhaps for women it is of particular importance that we find a language which allows us to recognize our part in intolerable structures—but in a way which renders us neither the pure victims nor the sole agents of our distress. (1987, p. 14)

An interaction between psychoanalysis and HIStorically informed ethnography is also an element of deconstructive scholarship aimed at dislodging the psychic materiality of racial and economic exploitation. This is particularly evident in the (w)ritings of Gayatri Spivak (1987), Trinh T. Minh-Ha (1989), Homi K. Bhabha (1989), and Michael Taussig (1987). In a related manner, Simon Watney (1989) crosses these perspectives in interrogating "popular cultural" fears of gay men and alternative sexualities that LIE behind (and within) discourses controlling the public (image) management of the AIDS epidemic. To further the (dis)auto-biographical collage between these several (de)constructionist methods, each may subsequently be resituated at a cross-roads with what Foucault depicts as a genealogical method. Genealogy attempts to displace master narratives of (continuous) world HIStory by emphasizing the somewhat *laughable* impurity of discrete and localized conjunctures of power and knowledge. This attracts attention to both the institutional and counterinstitutional practices by which powerful forms of knowledge are constructed, deconstructed, and reconstructed.

When most radically deployed, Foucault's methods challenges us to risk the materiality of our own (in)significance before (re)producing the ideality of (partial) meanings. Foucault's methods honor "archaic" demands for (deconstructive) descent prior to the (constructive) promise of theoretical emergence. This is a "secret" of *genealogical* HIStory. To know what I mean perhaps some of you must risk descending (out of) yourselves. This is (k)not uniform advice. As Foucault was all too painfully aware, somebodies are unfortunately quite low in the (w)hole already. Beginning from the position of descent is (k)not the only one way to enact a genealogical method. There is (k)not any predetermined place of "origin" in this dance. This dance is spiral. For those already condemned to HIStory's margins a better first movement might involve preparing for the emergence of collective forms of social resistance. But for those of us already somewhat privileged, in one way or anOther, initial descent may prove a radical mandate. Either way, this dance is (k)not linear. Waxing waning waxing, emerging descending emerging, or the re-verse—it is an alternating rhythmic movement that is demanded, (k)not the cut and dry econometrics of a linear sequence.

Of the genealogical method, Foucault (w)rites It "is gray, meticulous and patiently documentary. It operates on a field of entangled and confused parchments, on documents that have been scratched over and recopied many times"—like our bodies (1977b, p. 139). Foucault recommends that the genealogist attend to the singularity of "unpromising" events falling outside, or at the margins of, HIStory's "monotonous [sacrificial] finality," and that s/he be sensitive to patterns of "recurrence," while also examining possibilities that are denied material realization. In this, the genealogist may come to recognize that what poses as the true "origin" of any event is nothing but a "fleeting articulation" of power and knowledge. "Truth is [thus] undoubtably that sort of error that cannot be refuted because it was hardened into an unalterable form in the long baking process of history" (pp. 143–44). Rather than trying to uncover some original truth, genealogy constructively realizes "that there is 'something altogether different' behind things: not a timeless and essential secret, but the secret that they have no essence or that their essence was fabricated in a piecemeal fashions [like a collage] from alien forms" (p. 142).

This is a self-implicating discovery. It suggests that one is forever (re)constructing rather than simply revealing "origins." This prompts Foucault to embrace a methodological strategy that literally laughs at the solemnities of (always fictive) "origins." This is a DOUBLE STRATEGY involving an interplay of "descent" and "emergence." In using the term *descent*, Foucault asks that we follow Nietzsche (and Dionysos), (k)not back in time to restore an alleged unbroken linear continuity (filling in the wholes, stopping the gaps) but the opposite—to make holes in what might, otherwise, appear seemless and totalizing. This is (k)not the appropriation of a stable, solid, or continuous set of "facts," but "an unstable assemblage of faults, fissures, and heterogeneous layers." This challenges the powerful facticity of taken-for-grant social constructions. As such, "descent is not the erecting of foundations: on the contrary, it disturbs what was previously considered immobile; it fragments what was thought unified; it shows the heterogeneity of what was imagined consistent with itself" (p. 147).

As a strategy of dislodging the masked character of artificial constructions, descent involves a bodily retracing of previous descents. This makes reflexive demands both on the body of the researcher and on "one's" object of inquiry. Accordingly:

> Descent attaches itself to the body. It inscribes itself in the nervous system, in temperament, in the digestive apparatus; it appears in faulty respiration, in improper diets, in the debilitated and prostrate body of those whose ancestors committed errors. Fathers have only to mistake effects for causes, believe in the reality of an "afterlife," or maintain the value of eternal truths, and the bodies of their children will suffer. (p. 147)

If the epistemic effect of these words appears radically (de)constructive of relations of power, Foucault's comments about emergence are no less so. Having descended into a bodily recognition of the artifactual vectors of truth's power, emergence marks the constructivist entry of new forces. It "is their eruption, the leap from the wings to center stage" (p. 148). But this is also a sacrificial leap. It pushes other things aside from memory, just as it asserts its own (always provisional) claims to truth's power. In this way, emergence suggests a social form of "palimpsest," a dancing overlay of images, whereby one "text" can only be read through the screenings of others. This, I believe, is strategically related to Jacques Derrida's (de)constructive iteration of *differance* (1982)—a perpetual play of delays and exclusions. According to Foucault, this is space

> of confrontation but not as a closed field offering the spectacle of a struggle among equals. Rather . . . . it is a "non-place," a place of pure distance, which indicates that the adversaries do not belong to a common space. . . . . In a sense, only a single drama is ever staged in this "non-place" the endlessly repeated play of dominations. (Foucault 1977b, pp. 148–49)

In this, genealogy reflexively implicates the researcher in a ritual social movement in and out of particular social forms. For the modern researcher, positioned as if eagle-eyed above the object of "one's" analysis, Foucault's method may appear savagely incestuous. It unlawfully conjoins the bodies of investigating subjects with the objects of our own research. Moreover:

> This relationship of domination is no more a "relationship" than the place where it occurs is a place; and precisely for this reason, it is fixed, throughout its history, in rituals, in meticulous procedures that impose rights and obligations. It establishes marks of its power and engraves memories on things and even within bodies. It makes itself accountable for debts and gives rise to the universe of rules, which is by no means designed to temper violence, but rather satisfy it. (p. 150)

Closing Words That Open

Throughout the collage that constitutes this text, I find myself (ab)using ethnography and social-psychoanalysis at the cross-roads of collage (w)riting and a genealogical method. This is not so much to recover a story of lost HIStorical origins as to re-story the HIStorical covers that keep us (as desiring subjects) at a loss. Nor is it to search nostalgically to recapture an always already missing past. Such is nobody's HIStory—a murderous HIStory of simulations of self-evidency. In resistance to the pleasures of such self-evidency, this writing attempts to provisionally re-member the transferential relations which practically and politically link constructionist theorists to those whose social constructions we study. In urging a critical social movement from constructionist theory to a deconstructionist sociological practice I am here stupidly seeking words to articulate a desire for a different narrational practice: an imminent re(w)riting or theatrical re-staging of epistemological rituals permitting a more reflexive sociological imagination of the HIStory (or HERstory) of our present. Having double-crossed these several methods within the discursive confines of this essay, I now find myself yearning to partially reopen spaces "the other side" of the socially constructed scenes of power and knowledge in which so many of us today find our memories data-banked and militaristically reprocessed. As such, the body of this writing I offer recoils with the awareness that nearly everywhere there's sacrifice. Like a snake feeding upon the tale/tail that sustains "her," these parasitic pages are no exception. Believe me, this awareness is no simple gift—such poison.

Notes

1. While sympathetic to Ibarra and Kitsuse's reformulation of constructionism in terms of the rhetorical character of claims-making acts of language, I feel it important to recognize that all effective rhetoric, my own included, reductively channels some material possibilities into the ideational confines of "others." This is politics. It accomplishes more than "reconstructing" members' "vernacular expressions." It reconstructs the vernacular from the point of view of a subject who is "constructively" enmeshed within a contradictory network of evaluatively charged desires and fears, memories and forgettings. As respectful of members' linguistic productions as an analyst may be, by simply recognizing members as "figures" differentiated from an "otherwise" unproblematic or unnoticed social background s/he is (for better and/or worse) reducing somebody else's lived bodily experience to a ideally "downgraded" categorization. In this sense, as Jacques Lacan so aptly observed, all recognition involves misrecognition. This leaves *partially unexplained* the reality of other's actions as they appear phenomenologically within the shifting scene of constructionist theorizing itself.

Something terrifying from the dreamy vantage-point of "pure" and totalistic scientific explanation, the gaping (w)hole between the subject and object of knowledge is, nevertheless, a hopeful place for perhaps remobilizing a reflexive embodiment of knowledge as a transferential act that occurs between "us" and "others." I am here writing of a partial and provisional knowledge, whose full mastery "stupidly" escapes all but those who would willfully pave over spaces of moving indeterminacy in concrete, or worse yet, in the plastic of fiber-optic fill-ins. A reflexive recognition of the contradictory embodiment of such perspectival knowledge, the forever nonoriginal "origin" of a sociological deconstruction, seems (to me) glossed over by Ibarra and Kitsuse. The conventional presuppositions and rhetorical devices they catalog, like bits and pieces of truthful but contextless information, appear "ideally" to float free of the problematic desire of the analyst as a (social) subject seduced or driven by the promise of powerful knowledge. Who speaks within the (political) space authorized by strict constructionists' allegedly "nonevaluative" writings? And who is condemned to silence?

2. This decentering of subjectivity moves critical constructionism beyond the conceptual boundaries of various phenomenological sociologies. While phenomenology is rooted in descriptions of the interpretive dynamics of consciousness experience, critical constructionism (in the poststructuralist manner in which I am here presenting it) addresses itself, as well, to the ritual dynamics of powerful cultural and linguistic processes that sacrificially (dis)position subjective experience in *intersubjective* and, thereby, never fully conscious ways. The difference is (I believe) theoretically and politically important. Poststructuralist thought begins with an acknowledgment of a debt to phenomenology for its depiction of the dynamic realities of everyday social life as interpretive constructions. But what limits, filters, or screens the social orchestration of such constructions? In asking such postphenomenological questions, critical constructionism decenters the manifest truth of experiential consciousness into shifting networks of bodily and imaginary power, as these both limit and make possible certain experiential awarenesses, while excluding others.

3. Indeed, as Hal Foster points out, drawing upon the (w)ritings of Gilles Deleuze and Felix Guattari

> [T]he minor (which is precisely *not* a value judgment) is an intensive, often vernacular use of language or form which disrupts its official or institutional functions. . . . . Unlike other discourses or styles in major (bourgeois) culture, the minor has no "desire to fill a major language function, to offer [its] services as the language of the state, the official tongue. Yet, by the same token, it has no romance of the marginal." . . . . Indeed, in the minor "there are only collective arrangements of utterance." (Examples of the minor might include Black gospel, reggae, surrealist Latin American fiction.) This is a "death of the author" that is perhaps new to us: a post-industrial experience based less on the dispersal of subjectivity than on the articulation of collectivity, one that does not heed the normative categories of major culture. (1985, p. 177)

4. This is not to suggest that, after World War II and even before, important tendencies within surrealism did not betray its political radicality by the seductive aestheticization of its art. This critique is made nowhere stronger that by members of the Situationist International who, between 1957 and 1971, strug-

gled to advance the radical potential of an art (against art) in the service of social revolution. See, for instance, Guy Debord (1977). At the same time, there is evidence of the continued radicalism of some surrealists well into the 1960s. This is documented by Helena Lewis, *The Politics of Surrealism* (1988), and Franklin Rosemont (1978). For an excellent study that situates surrealism within the "interwar" years in France see Sidra Stich, *Anxious Visions: Surrealist Art* (1990). For analysis of the role of women in relation to surrealism, see Whitney Chadwick (1985) and Mary Ann Caws, Rudolf Kuenzli, and Gwen Raaberg (1991).

5. For an elaboration see Stephen Pfohl and Avery Gordon, "Criminological Displacements" (1986). A video cassette version of this text is also available in VHS format. For a copy send $10.00 (U.S. currency) to Parasite Cafe Productions, c/o Stephen Pfohl, Boston College, Department of Sociology, Chestnut Hill, MA 02167.

6. My own immersion in collage methods dates back to my collaboration with Joseph LaMantia in the design and production of photomontages included in my book *Images of Deviance and Social Control: A Sociological HIStory* (1985a). Shortly thereafter I began to work with collage and montage as aspects in the sociological construction of analytic texts. The influence of Kathy Acker's critical (w)ritings were, at that point, enormous, as were the works of Berlin Dadaist Hannah Hoch and John Heartfield. For a mix of visual, auditory, and analytic college work see the videotext I produced in collaboration with Avery Gordon (1986).

References

Ades, Dawn. 1976. *Photomontage*. London: Thames and Hudson.

Anzaldua, Gloria. 1987. *Borderlands/La Frontera*. San Francisco: Spinsters/Aunt Lute.

Artaud, Antonin. 1958. *The Theater and Its Double*. Translated by Mary Caroline Richards. New York: Grove Press.

Attali, Jacques. 1985. *Noise: The Political Economy of Music*. Translated by Brian Massumi. Minneapolis: University of Minnesota Press.

Barthes, Roland. 1975. *The Pleasure of the Text*. Translated by Richard Miller. New York: Hill and Wang.

Bataille, Georges. 1978. *Blue of Noon*. Translated by Harry Mathews. New York: Urizen Books.

———. 1985. *Visions of Excess: Selected Writings, 1927–1939*. Translated by Allan Stoekl. Minneapolis: University of Minnesota Press.

———. 1988a. *Inner Experience*. Translated by Leslie Anne Boldt. Albany: State University of New York Press.

———. 1988. "Attraction and Repulsion II." Pp. 113–24 in *The College of Sociology, 1937–39*, edited by Denis Hollier. Minneapolis: University of Minnesota Press.

Bhabha, Homi K. 1989. "Remembering Fanon: Self, Psyche, and the Colonial Condition." Pp. 131–50 in *Remaking History*, edited by Barbara Kruger and Phil Mariani. Port Townsend, WA: Bay Press.

Butler, Judith. 1990. *Gender Trouble: Feminism and the Subversion of Identity.* New York: Routledge.

Caws, Mary Ann, Rudolf Kuenzli, and Gwen Raaberg (eds.). 1991. *Surrealism and Women.* Cambridge, MA: MIT Press.

Chadwick, Whitney. 1985. *Women and Surrealism.* Boston: Little, Brown.

Clifford, James. 1988. "On Ethnographic Surrealism." Pp. 117–51 in *The Predicament of Culture: Twentieth-Century Ethnography, Literature and Art.* Cambridge, MA: Harvard University Press.

Collins, Patricia Hill. 1990. "Black Women and Motherhood" Pp. 115–37 in *Black Feminist Thought: Knowledge, Consciousness, and the Politics of Empowerment.* Boston: Unwin and Hyman.

Debord, Guy. 1977. *Society of the Spectacle.* Detroit: Black and Red Press.

Deren, Maya. 1953. *Divine Horsemen: The Living Gods of Haiti.* New Paltz, NY: McPherson.

Derrida, Jacques. 1982. *Margins of Philosophy.* Translated by Alan Bass. Chicago: University of Chicago Press.

Dollimore, Jonathan. 1991. *Sexual Dissidence: Augustine to Wilde, Freud to Foucault.* New York: Oxford.

Durkheim, B. Madonna. 1991. *A Constructivist Genealogy of Missing Memories.* Boston: Parasite Cafe.

Foster, Hal. 1985. *Recodings: Art, Spectacle, Cultural Politics.* Port Townsend, WA: Bay Press.

Foucault, Michel. 1970. *The Order of Things: An Archeology of the Human Sciences.* Translated by Alan Sheridan. New York: Vintage Books.Foucault, Michel. 1977a. Discipline and Punish: The Birth of the Prison. Translated by Alan Sheridan. New York: Vintage Books.

———. 1977b. "Nietzsche, Genealogy and History." Pp. 139–64 in *Language, Counter-Memory, Practice,* edited by D. F. Bouchard. Ithaca, NY: Cornell University Press.

———. 1982. "The Subject and Power." Pp. 208–26 in *Michel Foucault: Beyond Structuralism and Hermeneutics,* edited by Hubert L. Dreyfus and Paul Rabinow. Chicago: University of Chicago Press.

Freud, Sigmund. [1899] 1986. "Screen Memories." In *The Standard Edition of the Complete Works of Sigmund Freud,* Vol. III. Translated by James Strachey. London: Hogarth Press.

Fuss, Diana (ed.). 1991. *Inside/Out: Lesbian Theories, Gay Theories.* New York: Routledge.

Garfinkel, Harold. 1967. *Studies in Ethnomethodology.* Englewood Cliffs, NJ: Prentice Hall.

Gilkes, Cheryl Townsend. 1982a. "'Holding Back the Ocean with a Broom': Black Women and Community Work." Pp. 217–32 in *The Black Woman,* edited by La Fraces Rodger-Rose. Beverly Hills, CA: Sage.

———. 1982b. "Successful Rebellious Professionals: The Black Woman's Professional Identity and Community Commitment." *Psychological Quarterly* 6:289–311.

———. 1983. "Going Up for the Oppressed: The Career Mobility of Black Women Community Workers." *Journal of Social Issues* 39:115–39.

Gordon, Avery. 1990a. "Ghostly Memories: Feminist Rituals of Writing the Social Text." Ph.D. dissertation, Boston College, Chestnut Hill, MA.

———. 1990b. "Feminism, Writing, Ghosts." *Social Problems* 37:485–500.

Haraway, Donna J. 1991 "Situated Knowledges." Pp. 185–201 in *Simians, Cyborgs and Women: The Reinvention of Nature*. New York: Routledge.

Harstock, Nancy. 1981. "The Feminist Standpoint: Developing the ground for a Specifically Feminist Historical Materialism." Pp. 283–310 in *Discovering Reality: Feminist Perspectives on Epistemology, Metaphysics, Methodology, and Philosophy of Science*, edited by Sandra Harding and Merill Hintikka. Dordrecht: Reidel.

Haug, Frigga, et al. 1987. *Female Sexualization: A Collective Work of Memory*. Translated by Erica Carter. London: Verso Books.

Horkheimer, Max and Theodor Adorno. 1972. *Dialectic of Enlightenment*. Translated by John Cumming. New York: Seabury Press.

Jameson, Fredric. 1984. "Postmodernism, or the Cultural Logic of Late Capitalism." *New Left Review* 146:53–92.

Kristeva, Julia. 1975. *Desire in Language: A Semiotic Approach in Literature and Art*. Edited by Leon S. Roudiez. Translated by Richard Miller. New York: Hill and Wang.

Lash, Scott. 1990. *Sociology of Postmodernism*. New York: Routledge.

Lewis, Helena. 1988. *The Politics of Surrealism*. New York: Paragon House.

Lunn, Eugene. 1982. *Marxism and Modernism: A Historical Study of Lukacs, Brecht, Benjamin and Adorno*. Berkeley: University of California Press.

Orr, Jackie. 1989. "Autobiographical Essay: Assignment #1." Course syllabus for *Technologies of Control*. Chestnut Hill, MA: Boston College.

Pfohl, Stephen. 1977. "The 'Discovery' of Child Abuse." *Social Problems* 24:310–23.

———. 1978. *Predicting Dangerousness: The Social Construction of Psychiatric Reality*. Lexington, MA: D.C. Heath.

———. 1985a. *Images of Deviance and Social Control: A Sociological HIStory*. New York: McGraw-Hill.

———. 1985b "Toward a Sociological Deconstruction of Social Problems." *Social Problems* 32:228–32.

Pfohl, Stephen and Avery Gordon. 1986. "Criminological Displacements: A Sociological Deconstruction." *Social Problems* 33:S94–S113.

Picon, Gaetan. 1977. *Surrealists and Surrealism*. New York: Rizzoli.

Rose, Jacqueline. 1987. *Sexuality in the Field of Vision*. London: Verso.

Rosemont, Franklin. 1978. "Introduction" to Andre Breton, *What Is Surrealism? Selected Writings*. New York: Monad Press.

Ryan, Michael. 1989. *Politics and Culture: Working Hypotheses for a Post-Revolutionary Society*. Baltimore: Johns Hopkins University Press,

Said, Edward. 1983. "Opponents, Audiences, Constituencies and Community." Pp. 134–59 in *The Anti-Aesthetic: Essays on Postmodern Culture*, edited by Hal Foster. Port Townsend, Washington: Bay Press.

Sedgwick, Eve Kosofsky. 1990. *Epistemology of the Closet.* Berkeley: University of California Press.

Smith, Dorothy. 1987. *The Everyday World as Problematic: A Feminist Sociology.* Boston: Northeastern University Press.

Spivak, Gayatri Chakravorty. 1974. "Translator's Introduction" to Jacques Derrida, *Of Grammatology.* Baltimore: Johns Hopkins University Press.

――――. 1987. *In Other Worlds: Essays in Cultural Politics.* New York: Methuen.

Stich, Sidra. 1990. *Anxious Visions: Surrealist Art.* New York: Abbeville Press.

Taussig, Michael. 1987. *Shamanism, Colonialism and the Wild Man: A Study in Terror and Healing.* Chicago: University of Chicago Press.

Trinh T. Minh-Ha. 1989. *Woman, Native, Other: Writing Postcoloniality and Feminism.* Bloomington: Indiana University Press.

Valenzuela, Luisa. 1985. *Other Weapons.* Translated by Deborah Bonner. Hanover, NH: Ediciones del Norte.

Watney, Simon. 1989. *Policing Desire: Pornography, AIDS and the Media.* Minneapolis: University of Minnesota Press.

Woolgar, Steve and Dorothy Pawluch. 1985. "Ontological Gerrymandering: the Anatomy of Social Problems Explanations." *Social Problems* 32:214–27.

20

Panic Diary: (re)constructing a partial politics and poetics of dis-ease

Jackie Orr

I. Openings: History Dis-Membered

[At the beginning of the nineteenth century], the clinician's gaze becomes the functional equivalent of fire in chemical combustion, it is through it that the essential purity of phenomena can emerge. . . . . [T]he clinical gaze is a gaze that burns things to their furthest truth.

—Michel Foucault, *The Birth of the Clinic*

It is time to write *The Death of the Clinic*. The Clinic's methods required bodies and works; we have texts and surfaces. Our dominations don't work by medicalization and normalization anymore; they work by networking, communications redesign, stress management. . . . . Foucault's *Birth of the Clinic* . . . . name[s] a form of power at its moment of implosion.

—Donna Haraway, "A Manifesto for Cyborgs"

A Red Eye

I'm a sick woman who studies history. Michel Foucault studied history and became a sick man but a year or so before he died of AIDS he said, "Don't cry for me if I die."[1] I don't. I read late into the night 'til my eyes grow red and I dream. Don't cry for me if I'm diseased. "I assert, to begin with, that 'disease' does not exist. . . . . What does exist is not disease but practices," I read in the work of François Delaporte (1986, p. 6), colleague of Michel Foucault and historian of the 1832 cholera epidemic in Paris. It is the practices of nineteenth century medical clinicians, crystallized in the new truths of the "clinical gaze," that Foucault studies in *The Birth of the Clinic: An Archaeology of Medical Perception* (1975). A history of the present, this dreamtime of plagued and panicked scenes, might begin there.

A Peeling Tongue

The Birth of the Clinic opens with the figure of a woman-hysteric, somewhere in the mid-eighteenth century, soaking in cool baths ten to twelve hours a day for almost a year. Foucault cites her physician's description of the treatment's effects: Layers of internal tissue peeled from her uterus and intestines "like damp parchment" and were observed passing out of her body through the urine and rectum (1975, p. ix). Over time, her tongue, esophagus, and arterial trachea also peeled; entire pieces of these organs were shed during the treatment. Juxtaposed with this text is another medical description of a brain lesion, written by a doctor less than one hundred years later. Precise, meticulous, the description performs a "constant visibility" that now even reigns over knowledge of internal organs. Between these two small samplings of doctors' words, Foucault will elaborate worlds of significant difference. Tracing a "mutation in discourse" that marks a shift from the fantastic imaginary of eighteenth-century classical medicine to nineteenth-century modern clinical practices of positivist vision and pathological anatomy, Foucault recounts the emergence of modern medicine's clinical gaze, which constructs, out of the clinical theatre of illness and pain, new configurations of medical truth. A whole body of knowledge fuses in the charged discursive field where doctor and patient meet, a new and perverse anatomy of encounter where the doctor focuses a listening eye upon the color, the shape, the exact intonation and rhythm of chatter now pouring from the mouth of disease.

The truths made visible by this clinical gaze, truths that bend back upon the sick body in new forms of diagnosis and treatment, are not for Foucault a sign of medical knowledge progressing toward objective, positive science. Rather, the truths are themselves cultural signs chronically produced out of a specific language and practice, out of a discourse itself implicated in particular forms of human experience and historical force. Here is a labyrinth of historical details difficult to know not only because of its complexity but because the moments of greatest importance are just those in which the labyrinth changes shape, reconstructing the borders of "the fundamental spatialization and verbalization of the pathological," changing what and where the eye can see or speak and where it simply stops in white silence, its epistemological limit (Foucault 1975, p. xi). The nineteenth-century doctor mapping disease onto the organs of the body, charting the essential course of disease as it is revealed through repetitions now observable within the architecture of the hospital clinic, is working within a social geography where truth and error not only change their content but also, and most significantly, change their form. What comes to count as a medical truth, and what will serve as the silent, invisible, and necessary support for such an accounting, is for Foucault the formative event shaped at the intersections of medical and social history. The story he tells points to the objects and truths of modern medicine as constructions grounded in a reorganization of the modern subject of knowledge, in practices of language effecting a rationalized order of words and things, and, finally, in a historical convergence of medical and social space that awards doctors new powers in defining and managing the diseased, as well as the healthy and "normal" bodies of national populations.

As in several later works, Foucault assigns in this study a central importance to the individualization of the modern subject of knowledge. The individual-ized subject is portrayed as an emergent form of human experience radically reconstituting the possible relations between power and knowledge. The individual subject of medical science (*The Birth of the Clinic*, [1963] 1975), of the law (*Discipline and Punish*, 1977), and of desire (*History of Sexuality*, Vol. 1, 1978) stands as the condition of possibility and the historical effect of the modern "human sciences," which take man [*sic*] as their object of investigation, control, and self-reflection. In search of the historical construction of modern disease and medical truth, Foucault finds a (re)construction of relations of knowing:

> New objects were to present themselves to the medical gaze in the sense that, and at the same time as, the knowing subject reorganizes himself, changes himself and begins to function in a new way. . . . . [A]t this level there was no distinction to be made between theory and experience. (1975, p. 90)

Foucault reads in the coded knowledge of disease a resonant, relational shift in the organization of human experience. Modern medical constructions of the diseased body involve the simultaneous, mutually implicated restructuring of the subject-who-knows, both bodies reformed through discursive, historically specific changes in technologies of speaking, of seeing, of saying what's seen.

Indeed, the construction of the individual subject of medical knowledge is profoundly fused with the new perceptual reach of a medical language rationalized and deployed within the positivist practices of the clinic. Positive medicine both produces and founds itself upon its powerful claims to an unmediated truth told by a "language of things," which alone can authorize a knowledge of the individual (p. xiv). The central fantasy animating clinical medicine's pursuit of positive knowledge is the peculiar compulsion for a fully transparent and rational language, a mythic desire for "a pure Gaze that would be pure language: a speaking eye." This "speaking eye" would define the clinic's scientific methods and norms, and perfectly describe an immediate communication between vision and knowledge, the eye and its object, with language as the transparent medium through which the eye "would be the servant of things and the master of truth" (pp. 114–15).

For Foucault, the modern clinical gaze, its foundation in individualized experience, and its transmission through the rationalization of language, is produced within a nineteenth-century convergence of medical and social space administered by the nation-state and organized in part by the new political demand to understand and control epidemics. At the juncture of this demand for the medical control of sickness and the policed supervision of the healthy, the practice of doctors becomes enmeshed with the positive, productive politics of defining and maintaining the "normal." The medical clinic is the space in which this medical/political authority becomes institutionalized. And so "from the moment that sickness, which had come to seek a cure, was turned into a spectacle," the clinical gaze was simultaneously sanctioned by the virtuous pursuit of public health and disease prevention (p. 85).

The richness of Foucault's analysis in *The Birth of the Clinic* is condensed in his later work into the notion of a pervasive "bio-power" linking the productive powers of political control to the management of the life, health, and diseases of individuals and entire populations. To "put life in order," to manage both the social body of national populations and the bodies of individual subjects, becomes the function of complex mechanisms operating at various levels of medical discourse, economic organization, and political control (pp. 139–40). By historicizing the modern subject as the effect of productive techniques of modern political management, Foucault's concept of bio-power enables a different, frightening analysis of where contemporary political struggles may be located—within the individual-ized body:

> Maybe the target nowadays is not to discover what we are, but to refuse what we are. We have to imagine and build up what we could be to get rid of this kind of political "double bind"; which is the simultaneous individualization and totalization of modern power structures. . . . . We have to promote new forms of subjectivity through refusal of this kind of individuality which has been imposed on us for several centuries. (1982, p. 216)

The body, then, is refused as the site of a liberatory politics of a "true" self or "essential" subjectivity presumed to lie beneath the social structurings of power. Rather, even in its deepest sensibilities, the body remains a surface open to the inscriptions of a power that does not so much repress the individual as produce her. The freedom Foucault points to is not a liberation of the subject, but of the *terms of political struggle*, a "liberation of the act of questioning" what we have come, historically, to embody (p. 386), a questioning that may in turn provoke the liberty to imagine how we might be embodied differently.

A Liberated Mouth of Disease

Can sick women study history? Do sick women make history? Are sick women in (a) social movement? Historically speaking, can becoming a woman make you sick? Is a sick woman a social construction? If so, how can she ever find a cure?

How would bodies constructed as the subject-ed effects of modern bio-power discover strategies to resist or (re)construct these effects? How would differences of gender, class, culture, race, sexuality, or nationality play out in theatres of resistance and social transformation?

Is disease structured like a language? If so, what does it want to say?

Can language be structured like disease? If so, can it become contagious?

An Other Ear

The power and limitations of Foucault's insights have become an important subject of contemporary feminist theory and research. The encounter of feminism and Foucault finds some feminists cautiously recognizing Foucault's work as a useful and disturbing supplement to feminist concerns. The encounter is *cautious* because feminist readings of Foucault critically notice the absence of women as historical subjects and of gender as a discursive category in most of his writings. The engagement is *useful* because Foucault demonstrates a compelling literacy toward the body as an inscription of historical traces, situating his genealogical methods "within the articulation of the body and history" where a heterogeneous play of power "inscribes itself in the nervous system, in temperament, in the digestive apparatus" (1984a, pp. 82–83). Together feminism and Foucault focus attention on the operations of power at the level of bodies and the everyday "micro-politics" of dominations, foregrounding the radical contingency and constructed-ness of socially (en)gendered experiences of identity, sexuality, or subjectivity.

Finally, a feminist engagement with Foucault is *disturbing* because his insistence on the historical specificity of forms of human knowledge and experience forces feminist attention to the difficult, necessary, and provocative contradiction where some of us presently find our bodies, our selves: the contradiction between an acknowledgment of the social constructed-ness of the category "women," and the strategic, historical use of that construct as a ground for feminist practice and knowledge-production. Foucault, together with some feminists, moves social theory toward the *de*constructive openings or "immanent critique" of all claims to authentic experience and authoritative truth (Martin 1988, p. 15). Biddy Martin cites the consequences of Foucault's deconstruction of the "self-evident" or "apparently natural" as social artifacts of the workings of power:

> All categories of the natural or the normal . . . . are exposed as social constructs rather than distinctions given at the level of the body or individual psyche, categories that have been produced discursively and which function as mutually determining oppositions to normalize and to discipline. (1988, p. 10)

This deconstructive challenge to the practice of establishing feminist politics on the authenticity of "women's experience" or "women's bodies" foregrounds questions about how these categories may operate as authoritative, normalizing constructions within feminist discourse.

The ambivalence with which some women respond to these questions is deepened by a history of conflicts within feminist movements over what the category "women" represents, and who produces, and controls "our" representations. Women of different colors, classes, nationalities, sexual practices or cultures recognize (sometimes with and often without an alliance with deconstructive methods) that the "women" politically organized and publicly represented within activist or academic feminist struggles compose a quite specific social group: mostly white, well-educated, middle-class, "First World," and heterosexual. The "subject" of feminism promoted by these "women" is often a "parody of the masculine subject of consciousness," an individualized, unified, autonomous, "self-making" subject who unreflexively reproduces a form of consciousness that is historically male, white, privileged, and Western (Alarcon 1990, p. 357). The centering of gender as *the* significant, single category for a feminist analysis is criticized as an effect of the particular social positioning of the women who authorize and control most feminist discourse, i.e., privileged white women whose "experience" of gender is *not* shared with women marked differently within complex, simultaneous histories of gender, race, class, cultural, or heterosexual power (Alarcon 1990; Moraga and Anzuldua 1981; hooks 1981; Sandoval 1990).

The demand for an articulated politics of difference within feminist practices, combined with the critical questions opened by a deconstruction of "women" as a socially constructed, culturally specific representation, signals a moment of potent trouble within feminist theories and politics. Possibly the trouble can lead to more radical understandings—that both use and abuse Foucault's insights—of how "our" bodies come to be elaborately (en)gendered through specific, and different, historical practices. The significance of these differences for a convergent, critical politics is only beginning to be constructed (hooks 1990; Anzuldua 1990; Collins 1990; Mohanty, Russo, and Torres 1991; Trinh Minh-ha 1989). The meeting of feminism and Foucault can be counted, then, as a cautiously productive one, generating alliances, troubles, questions, and potentials for pursuing insights into the historical construction of different social bodies and experiences, of difference itself. For those of us practicing the peculiar politics of dis-ease and its constructions, the encounter encourages a serious consideration and careful questioning of the radical constructionist claim that "disease does not exist." In Foucault's work, the modern clinical gaze that names disease involves the specificity of historical conditions, political conjunctures, and a thick weave of discursive power relations in the construction of its "speaking eye," which in turn makes visible the classifiable contours of disease. While not disagreeing about the power of medical practices to configure the diseased body, some feminists have also examined *the specificity of disease* as materially, historically, politically embedded or embodied in a whole wide world of powerful relations that constitute its particular cultural forms (Bordo 1988; Ong 1987; Showalter 1985; Davis 1990; Cixous and Clément 1986).

The discourses of feminism have turned a listening ear and a careful gaze upon the dis-eases of some women's bodies to find there not only the produced effects of medical discourse, but possibly also the signs of resistance to the social relations in which dis-eased matters find their shape. This is not a romantic reenvisioning of the resistive potential of a symptomatic language of protest that speaks most often as individualized suffering. This is a materialist feminist claim for the sick body as a possible imaginative, productive site of an effective symbolics of social disturbance. The effectivity of the symbolics of sickness is neither universal nor without contradictions. Important, even fatal, differences abound between types of dis-ease and how, where, and to what effect they occur within social bodies. But the truth of some dis-eases as forms of resistance to an uninhabitable social situation has yet to be fully written. The "language of organs," speaking symptomatically and symbolically, is rarely heard as a social expression of protest and refusal (Scheper-Hughes and Lock 1991, p. 410). The significant social fact that dis-ease is not a consciously willed resistance may itself be a materially informed response to fields of social power that do not always operate at the level of conscious discourse or intention, which also may be entangled in mythic, imaginary structurings of social relations.

While the effectiveness of some dis-ease as resistance cannot claim to produce widespread, systematic social change, it may well produce curious, significant, and local questionings within the intimate circles of sickness. The relations between family, friends, lovers, or workers must find some response to the unsettling of routines, the demand for care, or the threat of contagion variously enacted by the sick body. This is not to suggest that all, even most, practices within the social relations of sickness promote a successful or recognizable subversion. (Indeed, a sick body may contradictorily produce the disruption of a "pathological" form even as this very form can produce a medical demand to be normalized, returned, or readjusted to individual health.) But it is my suggestion that certain forms of dis-ease, and especially those categorized as "mental dis-orders," might be (re)constructed by a feminist gaze attentive to the complex possibilities of resistance within intricate fields of power. Power that works, as Foucault indicates, at multiple levels of our everyday lives, microphysics and tactics of power that don't fully comprehend each other or reveal themselves whole to the critical eye searching for total systems of structural or superstructural dominations.

While Foucault's work does not emphasize the historical production of resistance to power's operations, his analysis has encouraged some feminists to retheorize how subject-ed bodies might resist most effectively. With both power and resistance working in multiple, de-centered social locations,

> a very different form of political organization and struggle suggests itself . . . . local struggles that undermine institutional power where it reveals itself . . . . as it operates in homes, schools, prisons, therapists' offices, and factories, wherever the work of normalization is carried on. (Martin 1988, pp. 9–10)

Understanding some outbreaks of dis-ease as local resistances to a social order of things that the body cannot inhabit without dis-order may raise valuable questions about some bodies' potential for intelligently (if not consciously or politically) producing an other, more inhabitable world. If, as Foucault imagines in The Birth of the Clinic, the dis-eased body comes to be heard and constructed as a truthful language by the clinical gaze, then can other truths—partial, constructed—emerge that would understand some dis-eases as a social response that arises within a cultural order of things, and also from a resistive, elusive "somewhere else'? If a different ear meets the chattering mouth of dis-ease, what different stories might be heard?

A Devilish Hand

Her story goes like this (Ong 1988):[2]

In the early 1970s in Malaysia, large numbers of young Malay women from rural villages begin to enter urban schools and factories set up by transnational corporations. The migration is initiated by the government's introduction of a New Economic Policy targeted at a massive restructuring of the nation's political economy. The policy is partly a response to widespread race riots in the late 1960s, which pressed an angry, spontaneous demand for the redistribution of power among Malaysia's multiethnic society (p. 29).

Many young Malay women find jobs in the "free trade zones," where U.S. and Japanese transnationals, "freed" from most labor and tax laws, hire female workers as cheap factory laborers. Commonly, the factories produce computer chips and other parts for a burgeoning microelectronics industry.

The shop floors become the scene of a strange spectacle. The women workers experience collective forms of what they call spirit possession (pp. 29–30), named in public discourse as "epidemic hysteria," "hysterical seizures," or "trance states." The episodes sometimes begin with the vision of a black apparition, often sighted in "liminal" places such as the toilets or locker rooms. Dark visions also commonly materialize inside the microscope, which some workers must stare into for hours at a time. The possession, in which women scream threats—"I will kill you!" "Let me go!"—and violently fight off the spirits trying to possess them (and the restraining hold of male managers and foremen), can be contagious and transform into a collective seizure of dozens of women sobbing, shouting, and struggling powerfully against all efforts to constrain them. In 1978, at a U.S. factory in Sungai Way, some 120 workers were involved in a "large-scale incident" while performing assembly work with microscopes. The factory was shut down for three days (pp. 29–34).

The women workers come from villages where local folk traditions embrace a history of spirit practices and beliefs. Guardians of moral and social boundaries, these spirits inhabit the borders of amoral spaces, protecting against human transgressions. Before the changes forced by industrialization and urbanization, spirit possession was most commonly experienced at critical passages (childbirth, divorce, or widowhood) in the lives of rural, married Malay women. Within folk traditions increasingly influenced by Islamic beliefs, the possessions are explained by women's "spiritual frailty, polluted bodies, and erotic natures," which make them more susceptible to moral transgressions and invasion by spirits (pp. 30–31).

Women possessed by spirits in the space of the transnational factory are managed by the discourse of a "cosmopolitan medical model." Constructing the disturbance as disease, this medical model prescribes sedatives (Valium) and isolation for the afflicted women. Other workers are sometimes forbidden to look at the possessed women out of concern that visibility spreads contagion. The troubled woman worker is converted into a patient and her problem, individualized and medicalized, is treated with pharmaceuticals, behavioral intervention, and, in some cases, removal from her job. Other workers' fears of becoming possessed encourage self-discipline and censorship of sympathy, intensifying the normalizing effects of "corporate and self-control" in the workplace (pp. 35–37).

This medical model of disease forecloses attention to the radical shifts in social relations brought about by the local effects of a transnationally organized economy. Excluded from this medical discourse is the possibility that the Malay women workers' possession speaks a disturbing challenge to reorganize social relations within the moral space of the factory. The medicalization of spirit possession in Malay factory workers makes it difficult to hear, or contagiously pass on, this story:

> [T]he spirit imagery speaks of danger and violation as young Malay women intrude into hitherto forbidden spirit or male domains. . . . . [T]heir employment as production workers places them directly in the control of male strangers who monitor their every move. These social relations, brought about in the process of industrial capitalism, are experienced as a moral disorder in which workers are alienated from their bodies, the products of their work, their own culture. The spirit idiom is therefore a language of protest against these changing social circumstances.
>
> In Malaysia, medicine has become part of hegemonic discourse, constructing a "modern" outlook by clearing away the nightmarish visions of Malay workers. *However, as a technique of both concealment and control, it operates in a more sinister way than native beliefs in demons.* Malay factory women may gradually become dispossessed of spirits and their own culture, but they remain profoundly dis-eased in the "brave new workplace." (pp. 38, 40, emphasis added)

A Panicked Heart

In the spring of 1986 in New York City, I worked in front of a computer screen for ten dollars per hour, processing words and organizing the electromagnetic possibility of transmitting coded manuscripts through the telephone wires to a typesetter whose computerized equipment could read the electromagnetic signals and produce a text designed according to the coded specifications. It was my job to design and input the codes: *italics*. **bold**. CAPS. underline. I worked for a small feminist publishing firm with an all-female staff. We produced feminist fictions and nonfictions.

I get the computer publishing job 'cause in July, 1985 I fly to Nairobi, Kenya, on a Boeing 747 **with money I make waiting tables at night and being a temporary secretary during the day** to join 10,000 or so other women

who're all coming to Kenya for the End of the Decade for Women that
the United Nations gives us in 1975 five years before Ronald Reagan'll be
U.S. president and ten years before he'll send Maureen his daughter to
join the many, many other female relatives of men who're running national governments and choosing all their female relatives to be official
delegates to the 1985 U.N. conference at the End of the Decade for
Women which starts twelve days after 10,000 or so women unofficially
gather with a measured political hope and hardly any male relatives in
power to do politics some and celebrate the End of Our Decade and
organize workshops like the one where I met the feminist publisher
**while listening to two women from Denmark and a woman from Tan-
zania talk about how dumb and useless a lot of U.S.-European development programs in Africa are 'cause these development experts'll ride
out to villages to teach the men who're pretty thin and don't talk much
how to be better farmers and after the development experts are gone
nothing changes in the village 'cause women're the ones doing most all
the farm work** who went to dinner with me at a cheap Indian restaurant
in Nairobi where she asks me to work for her feminist publishing house
for a few weeks inputting on a Digital DecMate II the names of all these
really great women from around the world so there'll be one big
computerized international mailing list and I say yes of course *and end up
working there for a year 'cause none of the women in the office really know how to
work the computers out of a little bit being afraid of them I think* **I am not
afraid.**
ONE SPRING NIGHT IN 1986 IN NEW YORK CITY AS I WAS TURNING
OVER TO SLEEP I SUDDENLY BECAME AFRAID I WAS ABOUT TO DIE. I
STARTED SHAKING AND MY HEART BEAT SO FAST IN MY CHEST I WAS
SURE IT WOULD JUST STOP. I GOT HOT THEN COLD. THIS LASTED UNTIL
ABOUT 5 A.M. WHEN I DRANK A GIN AND TONIC AND CRIED FOR SOME
TIME BEFORE I FINALLY FELL ASLEEP. THE NEXT DAY AT WORK I GOT
TERRIFIED AGAIN WHILE SITTING IN FRONT OF THE COMPUTER. THEN
WHEN EATING AT A RESTAURANT. THEN AT THE MOVIES. THEN WHILE
WALKING DOWN THE STREET. MY WHOLE LIFE WAS A STRUNG-
TOGETHER BUNCH OF ATTACKS OF TOTAL TERROR I DIDN'T KNOW
WHAT TO DO.
*I went to a doctor. She checked me over and decided I was ok and should
probably take a vacation. I couldn't afford to take a vacation.*
I went to a psychiatrist. She listened to me for awhile and decided I
probably had panic disorder so she wrote me a prescription for this
drug called Xanax, which I thought was pretty nice of her 'cause I could
afford to take the drug but I couldn't afford to see a psychiatrist again. I
started taking the Xanax.
In the fall of 1986 I entered graduate school to study how to understand and resist the effects of transnational corporations in the lives

of women worldwide. I had a small scholarship and panic disorder. At first, my sickness and my studies didn't make any sense together at all.

A Sick and Sociological Mind

If Foucault's insights are at least partially true—that the truth of disease is constructed by the discourse of medical knowledge itself constituted by specific cultural, economic, and political practices—then a sociological study of sickness might take from his work several cues. First, sociological accounts of disease must be historical. If disease and medicine are constructed as "identities" within power-invested discursive fields, these are historical fields that can and do change form. Historical forms make a difference. Next, the discursive production or construction of disease (or just about any object of human knowledge) is always already implicated in forms of social experience and human subjectivity, which are both revealed by and produced as medical knowledge. "To know" an object is always also "to experience" a social position. In modern society, this positioning is powerfully allied with forms of individual-ized consciousness that are no less social for producing an experience of the individual self. Sociologists are, of course, their selves subject to these forms of experience. So when we study disease we're also studying our selves even though we may not be sick. If we are sick, most of this is already pretty clear.

If the insights of some feminists are at least partially true, then a few considerations follow. When studying disease as a social thing we should remember that while disease may be constituted through the discourse of medicine, it is almost always also some "thing" outside its citing by a clinical gaze. This "thingness" of disease is not its natural or biological features but its particular relations to the scene in which it materializes as a form, a cultural, economic, symbolic, and gendered scene that includes but is never restricted to the site of medical practices. Next, it should be remembered that some diseases, while shaped by contemporary social relations, may also be imaginary, material forms of resistance to those relations. Women in this society have a lot to resist. Finally, everybody and certainly every sociologist should know that some things that come to be medicalized or individualized as disease, especially "mental" diseases or disorders, are potentially quite other social forms—of moral protest, of imaginary and physical escape from uninhabitable social relations, of a nonconscious, not self-controlled attempt to initiate a profoundly social movement, a symbolic and material response to a profoundly social dis-ease.

Her Cyborg Lips

The contemporary scene in which disease and medical discourse meet, its specific historical contours of power and subjectivity, is the concern of several recent voices in critical social thought. The work of Donna Haraway in particular offers a compelling geography of the new dangers and forms of domination, as well as possible political and creative responses to the present history in which we find ourselves embodied. A feminist theorist and historian of science, Haraway accelerates with a vengeance Foucault's analysis of modern bio-power, suggesting that post–World War II cultures have indeed crossed a horizon Foucault did not see to successfully engineer more excessive and total(izing), if sometimes less visibly violent, forms of bio-manipulation. As a social researcher and somewhat panicked, I want to take seriously the suggestion that the human body, its desires and dis-eases, is increasingly constructed by new techno-social forms of subjectivity, by unprecedented plays of postmodern power.

If as Haraway writes, "*The Birth of the Clinic* . . . . name[s] a form of power at its moment of implosion," her work suggests it is the power of implosion itself that is defamiliarizing modern "objects" of human knowledge and reconfiguring current operations of social power (1985, p. 69). The implosive collapse and blurring of boundaries that previously defined the differences between human and animal, organism and machine, and physical and nonphysical matters is a techno-social fact of enormous significance (Haraway 1981, 1985). This deconstruction of boundaries indexes the implosive features of contemporary Western epistemology, or practices of knowing. The epistemological ground for disciplinary identities and empirical methodologies in the modern social and physical sciences—that is, the possibility of knowing the difference between social/science facts and social/science fictions, a difference charged with maintaining unpolluted borders between "truth" and "error"—is thrown into radical confusion by the rapid, seemingly irreversible mutations wrought by the multiplication of new technologies mediating an ever wider range of human activities: from the researchings of social science, to the processing of food, or to the making of stealthy wars or healthy babies. Located at a de-centered and unfamiliar ground zero, the subject-of-knowledge, including the social scientist, experiences the deconstruction of the familiar boundaries of the "human object" itself. Here, in this epistemological and historical rupture, Haraway situates the emergence of a new form of human subjectivity: the *cyborg* (a science fiction shorthand for *cyb*ernetic *org*anism).

The cyborg's appearance as an unsettling figure of both social fact and science fiction marks for Haraway a critical shift in how contemporary power and knowledge operate, and an urgent moment of political imagination and intervention. In a world where the boundaries and historical dualism between social categories of woman/man, nature/culture, machine/organism, or self/other have been not so much transgressed as cannibalized, each category can now be "techno-digested" in the deconstructive and re-constructive methods of biologists, software designers, military strategists, and transnational capitalists (Haraway 1985, p. 82). Haraway's analysis presents a disturbing challenge to those who would rely on unambiguous differences between these categories for their political frame of reference. For feminists faced with Haraway's claim that gender is a mutable social/science fiction being de- and reconstructed through new techno-social structures of power, embracing the contradictory dangers and possibilities of the cyborg-subject is a risky business. But Haraway urges the task:

> Cyborg gender is a local possibility taking a global vengeance. Race, gender, and capital require a cyborg theory of wholes and parts. There is no drive in cyborgs to produce total theory, but there is an intimate experience of boundaries, their construction and deconstruction. There is a myth system waiting to become a political language. (p. 100)

"A Manifesto for Cyborgs: Science, Technology and Socialist Feminism in the 1980s" is Haraway's attempt to (re)construct a political language rooted in the partial facts and potent fictions of cyborg imagery. Holding out the possibility of cyborgs collectively resisting and restructuring current forms of social power and experience, Haraway at the same time locates the materialization of the cyborg-subject in a history of post–World War II scientific, sociological, and military "advances" aimed at the technological engineering of evermore accurate control strategies for a systemswide coordination of human, animal, and machine parts. Emergent humanimachine mutations are constructed and increasingly controlled by "scary new networks" of information flow, communications exchange, and socio-bio-techno-logical engineering (p. 80). These mutations are partially conceived and modeled after the military's mythic C^3I, the strategic deployment of command-control-communication-intelligence theory during World War II: "Communications technologies and biotechnologies are the crucial tools recrafting our bodies. These tools embody and enforce new social relations for women worldwide" (pp. 82–83). Within the circuits of these new social networks, "real" human bodies are materially, mythically (re)constructed through the instruments and imagery of science and technology.

The social relations inscribed on cyborg-bodies may also be read in the imaginary and material (re)constructions of everyday life. Communications technologies promote an unprecedented militarization of the daily, private peactimes of cyborgs at work and at play:

> The new communications technologies . . . . facilitated the mushrooming of a permanent high-tech military establishment at the cultural and economic expense of most people, but especially of women. Technologies like video games and highly miniaturized television seem crucial to production of modern forms of "private life." The culture of video games is heavily oriented to individual competition and extraterrestrial warfare. High-tech, gendered imaginations are produced here, imaginations that can contemplate destruction of the planet and a sci-fi escape from its consequences. More than our imaginations is militarized. (p. 88)

Published six years before the real-time TV miniseries war titled "Desert Storm," Haraway's analysis is an unsettling premonition of the video game violence that played out with fatal seriousness in the U.S.-led war against Iraq. The centralized, satellized control of all flows of information and imagery was readily accepted by many (cyborg?) U.S. subjects; the MEDIAted *absence* of informed accounts of the effects of U.S. violence was displaced by the repetitive video *presence* of "high-tech" images of the accuracy of U.S. violence, reproduced in the screened living rooms of millions of TV viewers. The cyborg, it seems, has blood on her hands—even if her relation to the screened censorship of violent social relations is one of very, very remote control.

Many of Haraway's concerns resonate with efforts within sociology to stake out the methodological and substantive significance of some social thing called the 'postmodern.' Viewing the postmodern not only as a theoretical style or intellectual position but as a powerful social formation in which we are deeply, if differently, involved, some recent social theorists suggest, with Haraway, the need for a profound rethinking of how contemporary social reality and social subjects are constructed. The MEDIAted technologies engineering these new constructions, while abstract in their electro-magnetic-bio-chemical-pharmaceutical-digital-compact forms, are nonetheless producing quite concrete, material changes. Sociologist Avery Gordon explains:

> [I]f the dominant social relations of reality construction no longer operate "realistically," but televisually; if what we experience as everyday reality is thoroughly bound up with the most fantastic of images, then even a commitment to describing social reality requires new and complicated signings, and a recognition that as subjects we are involved in screening ourselves across and through a range of technologies or mediums, literally channels of communication. (1990, p. 58)

The radical, techno-logical (re)constructions of social matters and symbolic meanings produced through evermore omnipresent channels of communication present, for sociologists, a challenge to (re)construct an adequate approach to how postmodern forms of power work in, or work over, social bodies. Stephen Pfohl rewrites a story of human bodies as material hosts to the compulsive parasitism of disembodied, effective, and affective waves of information: "Here people play host to electronic memories of fears and attractions that have no substance independent of the simulative restructuring of experience within the vacant . . . . data banks of an advancing transnational corporate economy"; the subjective social effects of such electrifying play are nothing less than an abstract *and* embodied cybernetics of social relations in which "the consumer of signs [is drawn] into an apparently almost infinite network of productive informational effects and instantaneous electro-magnetic feedbacks" (1990, p. 424). Feeding back and forth between command-control-communications systems and subjects of postmodern power. Wildly signing the effects of nothing but televisual images magnetically networked through social subjects/screens. A cyborg sociology—partially by, for, and against cyborgs—suspects that new techno-social-science relations in the postmodern might reconfigure the very channels through which power, and our knowledge of it, flow.

A Brain Mis-Firing

Live on screen, a young white girl in braids and braces sits on the couch next to her mother. She doesn't know what neural networking activity is, really, but in front of the camera she calmly tells the talk show host and today's home TV viewing audience about her first attack of panic. The sudden terror, a pounding heart, sweaty palms, shortness of breath—the same dramatic symptoms her mother experienced in her twelve-year battle with panic disorder. The camera swings to a gray-suited man seated in a swivel chair. Dr. Gerry Rosenbaum, Psychopharmacology Unit Chief at Massachusetts General Hospital (MGH) in Boston, where clinical research on panic has been conducted since the late 1970s, describes panic disorder as a biochemically based disease, explaining how genetic vulnerability to the problem can be passed through the family. Before the commercial, the talk show host assures home viewers who believe they might suffer from this disabling disorder that they are not alone. For more information, viewers may phone the number (highlighted on the screen) of the Anxiety Research Unit at MGH. Studio audience applause. A quick shot of a young girl in braids and braces, smiling. The phone number flashes again. Break to commercial.

WITH MCI'S SPECIAL TOTAL TELEPHONIC PACKAGE YOU GET SOMETHING OTHER COMPANIES ONLY DREAM OF GIVING.

COMMAND
CONTROL
COMMUNICATIONS.
IT'S YOUR CHOICE. CALL NOW AND GET ONE MONTH FREE.

Over three hundred people, over two thirds of them women, phone the Anxiety Research Unit within two weeks of the airing of an episode on panic disorder on a regional TV talk show. From among the pool of panicked callers, screened by a twelve-item questionnaire administered over the phone, a handful of subjects with appropriate profiles are chosen to participate in MGH's clinical research program on panic disorder. MGH runs the largest U.S. clinical study on the cause and treatment of panic. The study is privately sponsored by Upjohn Co., a transnational company that manufactures Xanax, a popular antianxiety drug. A recently discovered "disorder," panic reportedly affects about 5 percent of the American population at any one time, the vast majority of them women (Sheehan 1986, p. 11).

She doesn't know what neural networking activity is, really. But she knows what it's like to experience sudden attacks of terror when she's crossing the street, turning over to sleep, eating in a restaurant, shopping in the mall, watching TV. She knows what it's like to receive a panicky relay of screened information, to phone the Anxiety Research Unit and respond to a voice across the electric wires. . . . . On a scale of one to ten: How severe was your most recent attack? Yes or no: Any thoughts of suicide? Never, sometimes, frequently, a lot of the time: Fear that something is wrong with your mind?

She knows what it's like to become a voluntary participant in a clinical research program and hear the young doctor tell her that a panic attack is like "a brain misfiring." His words offer a short-circuited re-call of the overtly militaristic models of neural activity used a hundred years ago by Sigmund Freud to chart the "defence systems" and "contact-barriers" of the not-yet-central nervous system. An explosive geography now displaced within the conceptual-technological fallout of. two world wars by the contemporary "nonviolent" language of the "communications" model. This new model of neural activity evokes a seemingly neutral and nonaggressive landscape of neuro-transmission to ground the elusive materiality of just how the human nervous systems functions. The central activity of the system becomes the relay and reception of biochemical information. In this model, disorders of the central nervous system are represented as the transmission and reception of irregular or deviant information. In the 1984 Upjohn Co. corporate annual report, the story goes like this:

> Information passed along a nerve cell's axon is assimilated by the . . . .
> receiving cell through synaptic connections. Neurotransmitters (chemi-

cals) . . . . diffuse across this space [the synapse] and bind to receptors on
the receiving cell, and the message has been delivered. Contemporary
neuropharmacology seeks to modify aberrant messages that occur in certain disease states. (Upjohn 1985, p. 21)

She feels her brain mis-fire. Dry-throated thoughts race anxious
through her brain enflamed. Messages. . . . . delivered. She doesn't
know exactly what neural networking is but she knows she's deeply
entangled.

A Central(izing) Nervous System

The networking of local effects—social, political-economic, imaginary,
subjective—through technologically MEDIAted channels of evermore
effective and universal communications, threatens to outdate previous
understandings of the epistemology and politics of resistance. If indeed
the postmodern scene ushers in new and unfamiliar relations between
human embodiment and "high" technology, between social facts and
fictions, and procedures for knowing the difference, then modern historical precedents for resisting the dominations of racial, gender, and class
hierarchies and other forms of socially sanctioned violence may face this
situation: a social scene in which practices of local, specific resistance to a
hegemonic order of things can be almost immediately fed back into formal
channels of NORMALizing communications (Pfohl 1990). Resistive social
movements, whether political organizations or less conscious or self-
consciously political forms of dis-ease, protest, or cultural difference, may
be recoded or networked into instrumental or simply entertaining channels of information.

Haraway develops the notion of an "informatics of domination" to
conceptualize those features of postmodern power that, built upon
familiar dynamics of gender, race, cultural, or class differences, are
now (re)constructing those differences through new capacities for socially controlling human bodies and human productions of meaning.
The universal(izing) geography of MASS COMMUNICATIONS charts
an ambitious course: to absorb or recode heterogeneous resistances
to its detailed, planetary restructurings of social relations and social
meanings.

Communication sciences and modern biologies are constructed by a common move—the translation of the world into a problem of coding, *a search
for a common language in which all resistance to instrumental control disappears*
and all heterogeneity can be submitted to disassembly, reassembly, investment and exchange. (Haraway 1985, p. 83, emphasis added)

The consequences of an "informatics of domination" for the restructuring of social relations can be seen as much in the sufferings of a "new worldwide working class," especially women workers who feel the daily, local effects of increasingly mobile and global movements of capital, as in the ecstatic pleasures of human imaginations mediated, miniaturized, digitalized, and militarized through everyday techno-social interactions with TV and video—cheap, accessible microelectronic pleasures made materially possible by new international divisions of labor and wealth (pp. 84–85).

To contest these global recodings, which are in no way "outside" our bodies, to resist the flattening of cultural, sexual, symbolic differences that circulate in excess of normal(ized) social relations, becomes a struggle for other sites of social power, meaning, or practices that do not make claim to TOTAL solutions or COMPLETE interpretations of culturally specific and complex human conditions. But the specificity of a postmodern or cyborg condition may demand a panicky recognition that the risk of such TOTAL, FINAL, COMPLETE, and INDIFFERENT solutions is, for the first time in history, technologically possible and actively pursued through universal(izing) codes of power and knowledge previously only abstractly imagined. The global reach of such structured INDIFFERENCES—indifference to moral and historical claims for self-determination or cultural autonomy, indifference to the disassembly of unionized work forces in Detroit and the almost instantaneous reassembly of a nonunionized, dis-located and cheaper work force in the "free" trade zones of Mexico or Malaysia, indifference to the deeply gendered and racialized distributions of poverty, hunger, illiteracy, mortality, sickness, and silence among populations within and outside a world that names itself "First"—is a frightening social fact. Such indifferent facts are built in part upon the fictive powers of this "First World" to mass communicate transnational promises of improved "standards" of living, of increased access to commodified versions of play and medicalized versions of health, of televisually MEDIAted pleasures of participating in "free" markets, "free" elections, and the "free" world. Resisting the materialization of these fictions as global facts may require new (dis)orderings—not universal, not fully wor(l)ded—of epistemological and political response.

To understand contemporary constructions of disease, and particularly the appearance of some thing called "panic disorder" in late-1970s U.S.A., requires then a shift in perspective and a willingness to consider the dangerous intimacies between disorders inscribed at the level of individual bodies, and re-orderings written in the language of transnational encodings. Panic disorder, first named as a mental disorder in the 1980 revision of the *Diagnostic and Statistical Manual of Mental Disorders*

(DSM-III), seems to fit with uncanny and anxiety-provoking precision just the type of social dis-ease predictably produced by the (re)construction of cyborg-subjects. Within a social system that rewires the boundaries between human/machine or animate/inanimate, between the mortal contingencies of bodies that birth and die and the electromagnetic spectacles of instantaneous universality broadcast live-via-satellite, the floating attacks of terror that invade a panic-disordered body may be making quite contemporary claims about the physical, psychical situation of individual bodies operating as the nodal points of universal(izing) communications, technology transfers, and economic neuro-transmissions within this system.

> Our best machines are made of sunshine, they are all light and clean because they are nothing but signals, electromagnetic waves, a section of spectrum. . . . . The diseases evoked by these clean machines are "no more" than the minuscule coding changes of an antigen in the immune system, "no more" than the experience of stress. (Haraway 1985, pp. 70–71)

No more than the invisible, internalized studio of panic, of stress condensed and recomposed into a silent, filmic attack of terror. No more than the absence of wild gesticulating, outside the anatomy of a scream or a seizure or a visible display of suffering, without a dramatic faint from consciousness, followed by a fall. "Like the fade-out to white at the end of a movie," as a woman friend once described her panic attacks.

Panic, theorized in an earlier sociological literature as a form of contagious, nonrational crowd behavior in response to an apparent life-threatening situation (McDougall 1920; LaPiere 1938; Strauss 1944; Schultz 1964), materializes today as an individual, fragmenting "disorder" triggered by nothing more dangerous than shopping at the mall, watching TV, turning over to sleep, walking down the street. With little discursive possibility of noticing the specific features of panic disorder as a collective, gendered, and highly contemporary response to new forms of techno-social power, panic disorder circulates as a medicalized and biochemical problem within the social body. The "fact" that a remarkable majority of panicked bodies are female escapes notice or, if noticed, escapes analysis, in the proliferating popular and medical/psychiatric literature.

Other readers of panic may see in the dramatic gendering of the disease the effects of some women's accelerated participation, as both workers and consumers, in a global economy structured by fantastically mobile, abstract, speculative, and powerful technologies of (dis)embodiment (Orr 1990). Panic may be viewed as a dis-ordered but articulate response to "the actual situation of women . . . . their integration/exploitation into a world system of production/reproduction and communication," a world system that reproduces new forms of domition as fast as it (re)constructs new desires and dis-ease (Haraway 1985, p. 82). Within this scene some women's bodies may be particularly well-positioned to speak in an "episode" of panic—in a form coinsized, materially detailed and concrete enough to feel in the frantic pulsing of a heart or the bounded attack of ten or fifteen minutes—a vernacular and embodied language telling wor(l)ds of terror, confusing and re-fusing familiar boundaries of human experience. Between life and death. Between panic that circulates in the headlines of the "outside" world and panic that comes inside, invasive, live-wired, and electric into an "individually" nervous system, evermore centrally networked.

If panic disorder can be (re)constructed as a culturally specific disease, a symptomatic response to gendered, violent shifts in the organization of social structures and subjects, the dominant story of panic circulates within a quite different discourse of medical control and pharmaceutical treatment. The production of panic disorder within the intersecting fields of psychiatry, medicine, clinical research, transnational capital, and popular culture is closely regulated by what may be most accurately termed a corporate techno-medical discourse. Within this ordering of words and things, panic is diagnosed and treated as a biochemical disorder, possibly passed via genetic codes in the family, and most successfully treated with pharmaceutical drugs (Sheehan 1982, 1986; Klein 1981, 1984; Taylor et al. 1986; Liebowitz et al. 1986; NIMH 1989; Ballenger et al. 1988). The corporate manufacturers of these drugs are deeply involved in the discursive production and clinical investigation of panic. At Massachusetts General Hospital in Boston, one of the earliest and largest centers for research on panic, two long-term clinical studies of panic disorder were privately, entirely sponsored by Upjohn Co., the transnational chemical and pharmaceutical company that manufactures Xanax. Introduced into U.S. markets in 1981, a year after the discursive "discovery" of panic disorder, Xanax has quickly become the most popularly prescribed drug for the treatment of anxiety and panic (Upjohn 1982). Information gathered through Upjohn-sponsored clinical research was used by Upjohn to petition for and win an FDA-approved indication for Xanax in cases of anxiety disorder (Klerman 1988). The FDA indication gives Xanax a significant edge in the extremely profitable and growing market for antianxiety drugs.

Upjohn's sponsorship of the Worldwide Panic Project launched in 1982 (and later renamed the Cross-National Collaborative Panic Study), one of the largest international clinical research studies ever conducted, is an ominous exemplar of the corporate techno-medical discourse driving a universal codification and standardization of psychiatric diagnostic categories and treatment techniques. The project, designed to "discover" panic disorder as a homogeneous experience across cultural and national borders, promotes transnationally a biochemical model of mental disorder, and panic disorder in particular. The universalization of psychiatric classifications strategically enables transnational corporate access to globalized, and highly lucrative, markets for pharmaceuticals. Panicked bodies operate within this discourse as a secure (because they're panicked) site of pharmaceutical "desires" and corporate profits, feeding back into the universalizing tendencies of a hegemonic model of medicine already aggressively promoted by a transnational drug industry whose profit margins (18–20 percent) are second only to the oil industry. Circulating as decontextualized pieces of computerized information, the backgrounds, stories, symptoms, and differences of the research subjects in the Worldwide Panic Project—over two thousand people in fifteen countries (Upjohn 1985)—are coded into digestible, instrumental data for the trained clinical eye of medical statisticians, corporately employed physicians, neurologists, biologists, and pharmacologists.

Appropriately, then, panic disorder may be viewed as an acute, even perfect, example of the homogenizing effects of what sociologist John O'Neill (1989) calls "globalizing panics." Analyzing the practices and panic surrounding AIDS discourse, O'Neill suggests the universalizing consequences of MEDIAted panics that spread across the technosurfaces of image and information systems, only to speed up the unification of those surfaces into one (new?) world order:

> The globalizing panics that confirm the world order rely heavily upon the media and television, newspapers, magazines, films and documentaries to specularize the incorporation of all societies in a single global system destined to overcome all internal division, if not to expand into an intergalactic empire. (p. 79)

Panic disorder as a globalizing panic within corporate techno-medical systems of information, classification, and pharmaceutical treatment represents the frightening potential of a world health system that is always "only the promissory side of a world disease system" (p. 84). Worldwide health and disease systems, operating through global transmission routes of diagnosis and treatment, promote the profitable (for some) erasure of cultural, national, and ethnic differences in naming and curing disease.

Is it really time, then, to write *The Death of the Clinic* as Haraway has called for? Or rather, to sit down at a computer(ized) terminal and input, with a panicked and partial sensibility, *The Incorporation of the Clinic*? Incorporated into transnational and global phrasings of power and knowledge, "techno-digested" into consumable bytes of human suffering, contemporary clinical corporate-medical technologies of, by, and for cyborgs aim at the disassembly of deviant, panicked signals of (mis)communication and their pharmaceutical reassembly into something more normal, more rhythmically attuned to a globalizing relay and reception of standardized information. "Our dominations don't work by medicalization and normalization anymore; they work by networking, communications redesign, stress management" (Haraway 1985, p. 69). But what if some forms of domination do both, working through global networks of medicalized knowledge, redesigning more effective communications with and within the NORMALized subject of pharmaceutically controlled panic? Through these postmodern networkings of power, disease is relayed as useful feedback information emitted by a cybernetic social body. Such dis-eased information allows a medical and militarized intelligence to locate the specific routes of pathologies and develop the corporate techno-medical technologies to engineer more centralized, site-specific controls, to communicate a more pharmaceutically tuned normalization. This is a paranoid and panicked suggestion. This is a postwar vision of "magic bullets" (an early name for pharmaceutical pills) become "smart bombs"—surgical strikes aimed at the command-control-communications centers of some very nervous systems, some wildly panicked bodies.

A Clinical Eye, Incorporated

In 1983, Scribner, Inc., published *The Anxiety Disease* by David Sheehan, M.D. Sheehan, an early "pioneer" in the study of panic disorder and anxiety, was founding director of the largest U.S. clinical study on panic disorder conducted at Massachusetts General Hospital. In the opening acknowledgments, Sheehan thanks his "valuable mentor" Jim Coleman, director of the Worldwide Panic Project, and his several colleagues at the Upjohn Co.: "These men have set an example of how industry can forge a constructive, responsible alliance with academic medicine" (1986, p. xi). *The Anxiety Disease* is a popular medical book written for a general readership, and a panicked readership in particular. The findings from clinical corporate-medical research on panic disorder, which Sheehan names the "anxiety disease," are combined with the story of Maria, a woman suffering from the anxiety disease, and Adam, her boyfriend. Each chapter, a mix of story, scientific tables and statistics, and clinical case histories, begins with a quote from a repertoire of figures in Western arts and sciences: Shakespeare, Dickinson, Horace, Kierkegaard, Pavlov, Cervantes. A quote from Percy Bysshe Shelley opening the first chapter reads simply, *"For there are . . . . sufferings which have no tongue"* (p. 3).

Set within a contemporary scientific discourse of genetic transmission and biochemical disorder, Maria's story is staged as a mythic-historical narrative of struggle and liberation: "This book is about Maria's people— their plight, their descent into terror, their peculiar experiences. It is also about the beginnings of the liberation of these people. And their journey to freedom" (p. 7). Maria's plight is her experience of panic attacks and the disruption of a heterosexual narrative promising normal love and familial reproduction. In the opening scene of the book, a romantic birthday dinner with Adam at an expensive restaurant is ruined by Maria's uncontrollable panic and flight to the women's room. After a tirade of accusation against Maria's "neurotic hypochondriacal fears," Sheehan narrates Adam's parting shot to a disconsolate Maria: "[H]ow . . . . could she ever expect to have kids and take care of them and raise them, if she went on with this nonsense?" (p. 6).

The deterioration of the heterosexual promise in the face of panic doesn't reverse itself until Adam, in Chapter 17, comes across an article in a science magazine titled "Panic Attacks Can Kill." The information in this article—that people with panic "as a group died off at a faster rate and at an earlier age than the matched normal group"—finally convinces a skeptical Adam to help Maria (pp. 104–5). He goes to the library at a nearby medical school, searches the computer databases and gets printouts of the most interesting articles on panic. A newly informed Adam at last brings Maria to a doctor who understands panic disorders. She learns of the biochemical basis of panic and meets the real hero of her story—pharmaceutical medication. Her "journey to freedom" is now phrased in the medical discourse of a four-target plan for recovery. The first step is "Target 1: Biological," where a choice is made between available drug treatments to control the "metabolic core" of the disease (pp. 118–29).

Sheehan is a doctor and clinical researcher who understands with remarkable clarity that "the boundary between science fiction and social reality is an optical illusion" (Haraway 1985, p. 66). Sheehan operates this illusive boundary through the textual construction of Maria, a fully fictional character whose features are drawn from the disassembly/reassembly of clinical details, stories, and symptoms experienced by "real" people and (re)constructed into the book's narrative oscillations between medical monograph and Harlequin romance. Maria is a curious artifact of social realities imploding into science fictions, a cyborg-subject produced within the marketable formulas of heterosexual romance, medical crisis, and successful pharmaceutical cure. She is a "composite" of truthful clinical facts recombined into a fiction whose truth is no less scientific because she never really existed at all.

II. Interlude: Constructing the Sociological Text as a Social Problem

The composition is the thing seen by every one living in the living they are doing, they are the composing of the composition that at the time they are living is the composition of the time in which they are living. It is that that makes living a thing they are doing.
—Gertrude Stein, "Composition as Explanation'

What are my methods? My method is my style. I presume . . . . that method is not simply procedure, but "criticism and composition are . . . . inseparable."
—Avery Gordon, *Ghostly Memories*

The composition of a sociological text, including the one you hold in your hands, demands a more or less conscious negotiation through the charged terrain of language and the disciplinary regimes of institutions (university, publisher, academic journal, research organization) committed to regulating what may count as sociological discourse. I use the word "composition" as a tactical prod, a tiny explosion of expectation, to evoke the question of the relationship between sociological practices and "artistic" or "creative" forms: Composing is the province of those who would produce music or poetry or a painted canvas; those who would produce sociology research, analyze, theorize, model, calculate, factor, regress, correlate, or write, decidedly, sociology.

But as writer and filmmaker Trinh Minh-ha notes, "by writing one situates oneself vis-à-vis both society and the nature of literature, that is to say, the tools of creation" (1989, p. 20). A sociologist, asked about the relationship between creation and society, might entertain the problem as an engaging sociological question, but not recognize it as a relationship performed with every production of a sociological text. The composition of sociology as *not* literature, as writing if you will but certainly *not* within the opaque field of creative fictions, is a construction of the discipline that suppresses its very potent, problematic ties with literary practice, magically disappearing the epistemological and methodological *(k)nots* between sociology and writing, between sociological texts and a socially created, creative language that has become the object—as well as the self-reflexive location—of contemporary philosophical elaborations and political struggle (Gordon 1990). Far from achieving an indifferent distance from these struggles or a convincing autonomy of theoretical and research practices from the messy matters of language and literature, sociology requires that fiction repeatedly return as an insistent and useful "other" against which sociology constructs its identity, without which it could (k)not "constitute the authority of the discipline" to represent social realities, problems, changes, or truths (p. 17).

"Why (k)not sociology?" he asked somewhat irritably, anxious about the analysis of his latest regression. "Because sociology is already (k)not its self," she replied, impatient with offering (seemingly) parenthetical supplements to the central matters of "real" social research. Because the *separation* between social facts (history) and creative imaginings (story) is a persistent and often brutal cultural fiction, authorized through Western practices of enlightened reason and reproduced in most positivist or humanist understandings of social science, that would construct the "real" difference between facts and fictions through an oppositional and exclusive hierarchy, through a thoroughly fictitious exiling of story from the realm of sociology. This is *not* to say there are *no* differences between the making of facts and fictions, but rather that the differences between them "can articulate on a different set of principles, one which may be said to stand outside the hierarchical realm of facts" (Trinh Minh-ha 1989, p. 121). A different practice, then, a different politics of difference that refuses, *not* the possibility of social and historical truth-making, but the sanctioned habit of "consuming truth as fact." A practice that affirms the historical power of story to effect truths that effect (social) movement. That recognizes the structural possibility of a story, of a "composing on life," to make the formal suggestion that "structure should remain an unending question" (pp. 148, 143). This is a story telling of the moving, material powers of fiction. Why (k)not sociology?

The recognition of sociology as a writing practice, as an institutionally regulated and nonetheless *composed* instance of the possible relations between society and textual creation, opens the sociological text toward a more critical, creative relation to the process of its own production, a more in-formed, and formally reflexive, relation to its own possible practices of representation.

Both Trinh's and Gordon's critiques can be situated within convergent, contemporary feminist challenges to the forms of truth, theory, and textual representation that circulate as the master discourses of the social sciences. Within sociology, Dorothy Smith's work interrogates the operations of power, or relations of ruling, producing the textual representations of social "facts" and theory (1987, 1990). The "objectivity" of sociological facts constructed by material, but masked, procedures of conceptual abstraction, produces sociological texts that work as a kind of "virtual reality," suppressing the necessarily situated and social character of all claims to knowledge (Smith 1990, p. 62). By virtue of this suppression, the sociological and theoretical text stakes its claim to represent true, real, and general knowledge. Smith imagines a more embodied measure for the "representational adequacy" of "existence claims" embedded in all sociological theorizings: "A relation of adequacy is one in which *the structure of the object of study determines the structure of the theory*" (1990, p. 48, emphasis added). Certainly for a theorist of panic, Smith's reformulation invites a radical recomposition of possible theoretical structures!

Also within sociology, Patricia Hill Collins (1990) relocates and rehistoricizes the site, the sound, the forms in which social theorizing is practiced in the everyday lives and "subjugated knowledges" of African-American women. Systematically excluded from most academic institutions, marked by an official history of violent silence, black women's rich legacy of thought and intellectual achievements is identified by Collins—not only in the un-remembered, remarkable writings of black women who did successfully work within scholarly discourses—but also in the alternative institutional and community sites where black women activists, writers, artists, singers, poets and musicians have historically "hammered out a Black women's standpoint" (p. 15).

The contemporary politics of some recent black feminist thought and writings by women of color converge around a move to "occupy theorizing space," that "forbidden territory" from which women of color have been marginalized or disqualified (Anzuldua 1990, p. xxv). But the occupation is also, and necessarily, a transformation, a refusal of the sedimented constructions of theory conceived and regulated through racist, antiwomen, colonial, and imperializing discursive forms. To occupy theorizing space is to remake that space differently through practices of language that can recognize and explore the complex relations between analysis and emotion, between theory and bodies inscribed within very present histories of domination. In the opening pages of *Making Face, Making Soul/Haciendo Caras*, editor Gloria Anzuldua introduces this way a collection of critical, creative writings by women of color:

> "Face" is the surface of the body that is the most noticeably inscribed by social structures, marked with instructions on how to be mujer, macho, working class, Chicano. As mestizas—biologically and/or culturally mixed—we are "written" all over, or should I say, carved and tattooed with the sharp needles of experience. (1990, p. xv)

"Making face" in the face of such material inscriptions of experience is a *gesto subversivo*, a subversive gesture of challenge, questioning, of social and self-creation. It marks a challenge that also writes itself in/as the body of the text:

> Montage and fragmented discourse. Let the reader beware . . . . s/he must do the work of piecing the text together. . . . . [T]he method of organizing the book was largely that of poetic association, another way of organizing experience, one that reflects our lives. (p. xvii)

The body in theory . . . . a reflexive foregrounding of the matter of bodies and language, bodies in language . . . . a strategic intervention in the normal operations of theory . . . . a political pleasure in the (de)constructions and (re)constructions of partial, sensible, poetic, erotic texts as forms of social theory in practice.

> "Writing the body" is that abstract-concrete, personal-political realm of excess not fully contained by writing's unifying structural forces. Its physicality (vocality, tacticity, touch, resonance), or edging and margin, exceeds the rationalized "clarity" of communicative structures. (Trinh Minh-ha 1990, p. 44)

Writing the body, as theory and practice, has emerged in recent years as a convergent and diverse effort among feminist theorists, fiction-writers, and philosophers.[3] The effort, far from representing a common body of writing or producing a common representation of the body, has emphasized the politically significant, poetically resonant fact of the social constructed-ness of women bodies (en)gendered through different historical, racial, imaginary, cultural inscriptions. Rather than reifying a single representation of "the" Body of Woman, the project effectively documents the importance of language and representational practices in constructing women's embodied experiences, and the possibility of (re)constructing bodies and experiences through radically different forms of representation.

Insisting on the artifactuality of embodiment, the materiality of the body as a "making," the practice of women bodies writing becomes recognizable and theorizable as a material site of remaking, of becoming embodied differently. Writing for and about a lesbian body, Teresa de Lauretis explains this transformative and textual desire:

> The struggle with language to rewrite the body beyond its precoded, conventional representations is not and cannot be a reappropriation of the body as it is, domesticated, maternal . . . . but is a struggle to . . . . recre-

ate the body other-wise, to see it perhaps as monstrous, or grotesque, or mortal, or violent, and certainly also sexual. (1990, p. 29)

Of those who would misunderstand "writing the body" as a representation of authentic or unmediated experience, Trinh Minh-ha cautions,

[F]or them writing the body means writing *closer* to the body, which is understood as being able to express itself directly without any social mediation. The biological remains here conveniently separate from the sociohistorical, and the question "where does the social stop in the biological?" and vice versa, is not dealt with. (1989, p. 41)

Where *does* the social stop in the biological? Is there any piece, any process of the body that cultural mediations of meaning, social structures of feeling and power, cannot touch? And transform? How do writing and representation matter to the materiality of bodies? The questions seem urgent—the answers quite uncertain, and certainly difficult to speak: "To be lost, to encounter impasse, to fall, and to desire both fall and impasse, isn't this what happens to the body in theory?" (p. 42).

Refusing the head as the only intelligent bodily member . . . . recognizing the mind-full abstractions of theory as a material site of social violence (Wittig 1980; de Lauretis 1987) . . . . embracing the hand, the neck, the fingers, a foot as sentient fragments of fleshy knowledge, as pieces to decompose and recompose into playful, political, and deadly serious retheorizings of the social spaces that we do and that we might inhabit . . . . is not, then, a relinquishing of theoretical territory but "a way of making theory in gender, of making of theory a politics of everyday life" (Trinh Minh-ha 1989, p. 44). Recent writings of women of color, lesbians, feminist anthropologists, sociologists, and poststructuralists point toward the possibilities of differently writing, differently (re)constructing the significance of embodied differences, pursuing in a range of voices and with a diversity of other weapons the potential for languages and collective representations that speak our different demands and desires. The place of social theory becomes a place of potent stories telling (of) possible pasts, futures, and presents in-between . . . . giving words to worlds unwritten, disappeared from sight, when peoples are systematically denied participation or power in the story called History.

Critical feminist efforts to investigate the embodied effects of language-making and representational practices have sometimes generated alliances with constructionist theory, finding there a useful theoretical frame for thinking about gender and power. But the version of constructionist method elaborated by Ibarra and Kitsuse (this volume) finds little affinity with feminist projects to construct the social science text as a site where language meets flesh and makes, there, some difference in writing.

Conceiving the construction of social problems as a "language game" in which members contest for and create meanings, Ibarra and Kitsuse attempt to clarify the rules by which constructionist sociologists should play the social problems game. Conducting their own theoretical practice as something of a language game, Ibarra and Kitsuse perform a linguistic move—substituting the concept "condition-category" for the earlier term "putative condition"—in an effort to advance a general theory of social problems. The theoretical point and methodological rule clarified by this linguistic change reads as follows: A constructionist approach to the social problems process should not itself make or evaluate claims about the sociohistorical circumstances, objective conditions, or moral force fields (i.e., claimants' "condition-categories") in which a social problem putatively emerges, but rather should analyze the dynamics of the language game, the vernacular resources, and rhetorical conventions by which members' claims are constituted. For a constructionist to do otherwise is to make the mistake of "going native," falling for the "seductive" common sense of regarding members' "condition-categories" as "referents for independently documentable social conditions," and forgetting that these categories are "first and foremost units of language."[4]

Let me briefly reconstruct several claims (some explicit, some implicit, all moral) made by Ibarra and Kitsuse:

1.   Language is form and content. The two are analytically separable. The constructionist should analyze forms of language and not examine the content to which language attempts to refer.

2.   Although members' language refers to sociohistorical conditions, constructionist theorists (who now know that the "correspondence theory of meaning" is a positivist and objectivist illusion) should not understand that language as corresponding to documentable, verifiable, or potentially "true" social conditions. However, the constructionist theorists' language, when referring to members' discursive activity, should be understood as corresponding to that activity and can, with theoretical confidence, meaningfully claim that members' activity does *not* correspond to socio-historical conditions relevant to the social constructionist's analysis.

3.   Social members engage in the *practical and moral* project of constructing social problems, while constructionists should engage in the (not practical and not moral) *theoretical* project of reconstructing the vernacular claims of members.

4.   In reconstructing the claims-making activity of members, the con-

structionist theorist should never privilege the validity of claims made in scientific-objective discourse. However, the discourse of the constructivist theorist should itself be constructed in a scientific-objective language that is precise, disinterested, sober, technical, neither excessively poetic nor political, that is, in the "styleless" style of science.[5]

Ibarra and Kitsuse's story of the constructionist approach to social problems is a contested story, making contestable claims. The contest, I would claim, is playing out within sociohistorical conditions and a moral economy of forces that partially construct the claims of members about social problems, the claims of constructionists about members' activities, and the claims of constructionists about their own activities. Social constructionists should be attentive to the effects of these forces on both members and themselves. Furthermore, I would claim, the contest is both ABOUT language and IN language. It is a struggle for and over meaning, including the meaning of "language." Language and meaning make simultaneously formal and substantive claims. The struggle over meaning and its forms is located within substantive struggles over history, power, politics, and morals. A theoretical language like Ibarra and Kitsuse's, which presumes and reproduces forms of exclusive, hierarchical opposition between the meanings of form/content, language/sociohistorical conditions, theory/practice, and social constructionists/social members, should wonder how these historical, highly politicized meanings came to be so constructed.

Finally, the contest between different stories about what constructionism means is BOTH an unstable, artful, and indeterminate game, AND at the same time a contest already constructed by institutional, linguistic, historical, and political forces. These forces give some bodies in the game a powerful position, while other bodies are lucky to get a team jersey with their name on it. I mean to say there are powerful stakes in this contested game and powerful structures already reproducing the rules. Whether or not these stakes and these structures are noticed has everything to do with how the game gets played.

"[T]he strict constructionist never leaves language," Ibarra and Kitsuse claim. Where then precisely does that leave him? Where is language? Does any theorist ever leave it? The opening section of this essay never leaves language in its attempt to construct a historical story of panic disorder and the clinical, cultural, and technological conditions that shape both the naming and the experience of panic. Where does this story leave Ibarra and Kitsuse's claims? How would the story read differently if it strictly played a language game constructed by Ibarra and Kitsuse's rules? What happens to a story of the social problem of panic when the theoretical playing field excludes sociological claims about contemporary conditions of transnational capital, medical technologies, military strategies, gendered experience, and technological change? What can't be said when the meaning of social theory is separated from the practical matters of everyday lives—or when the problem of dis-ease is separated from the desire for cure? Who gets tongue-tied when the social theorist remembers language only to forget history? How to hear some bodies' claims that *language is a social problem*?

These questions, theoretically speaking, touch the ear of a cyborg sleeping dreamless, slightly anxious on the edge of Xanax waning, a trace of terror slightly bared beneath the techno-comfort of an even pulse, panic-eased. "Cyborg politics is the struggle for language and the struggle against perfect communication, against the one code that translates all meaning perfectly" (Haraway 1985, p. 95). So let me make myself perfectly unclear: Writing the panicked body is for me nothing more or less than a profoundly constructionist project, a project in and about language and the shifting sociohistorical constructions of dis-ease, of power, of medical discourse, of subjectivities, of terror and of sociological texts telling stories of social problems and possible cures. And all this without ever leaving language. And all this without ever leaving, or wanting to, the pursuit in language of possible truths—whose power and sanction would lie neither in the evidence of objective conditions, nor in the essence of subjective knowledge—but in a provisional, partial in-between of accuracy where the story is true "because it partakes in the setting into motion of forces that lie dormant in us" (Trinh Minh-ha 1989, p. 148). To effectively represent such truthful stories as themselves sociological and constructed, informed by the demands of careful research and formed by the material fields of meaningful writing is, at this moment, a profound social and sociological problem.

III. In-Conclusions: Panic Diary

Let me tell you a story.

In the fall of 1987, I participated in a clinical study on panic disorder conducted at Massachusetts General Hospital (MGH) and sponsored by Upjohn Co., makers of Xanax. I did not volunteer for the program because I had panic disorder. I participated because I once had panic disorder, and had found a cure in part by asking questions about the dominant social construction of panic as a biochemical disorder. I had become a panic theorist. The following story is a piece of panic theory, written during a four-month period of fieldwork at MGH.[6] Like the story of Maria in *The Anxiety Disease* (Sheehan 1986), this text is composed of facts and fictions. Unlike her story, the boundaries between fact and fiction are not (re)constructed in order to persuade the reader to take a pill, but rather to sufficiently disorder the reader into wondering how a pill could truly cure such a story.

September 1987. I participate in a clinical research program on panic disorder at Massachusetts General Hospital. As a volunteer research subject, I agree to take an unidentified drug (either Xanax, Tofranil, or a placebo) and to attend the clinic for regular check-ups over a four-month period. During my first visit I am given one week's supply of pills, and a "Patient Diary" published by Upjohn Co. It reads:

> INSTRUCTIONS: Please fill out a page in the diary each evening after taking your last capsule. Since it is very important that you do not miss even one capsule, if you get in the habit of filling out your diary regularly, it may help you to remember your medication.
> —Upjohn Co., Patient Diary

Wednesday, September 23, 1987, 11:30 p.m. And what would I forget? A patient diarist, I remember this evening this morning's scene: I am in the Exam Room alone and waiting. I have just been diagnosed with panic disorder. I have just been accepted into a clinical research program on panic disorder. I am now a subject of research. The Research Assistant Joe enters the Exam Room and introduces the woman with him: Dina. Her hair is thick black turning early to silver-gray. She wears a blouse, skirt, and sandals, bare-legged. Joe says, "We're going to do an EKG. You'll need to take off your blouse and brassiere. If you prefer, I can leave." I say, smiling, "I'd prefer if you'd leave." Joe leaves.

> You don't give a damn if he never comes around again. You never want to see him again. Fuck his round face and his blonde hair and his five feet ten inches tall lean body. Fuck him in shit. Fuck him in piss. *You walk two miles until the town ends and you cross into a field and keep walking.* Fuck his "good guy" manner fuck him with a needle fuck his filthy toes *and you cross a black tar road and crawl under a barbed wire fence and climb a low green hill* and his red tongue fuck that lousy cynicism that's totally fake fuck his sexual uptightness fuck everything he's ever done fuck everything he's ever said. *At the top of the hill it is windy you see green fields and the town far away* everything he's ever said is false stick it in a barrel and send it to me. *At the top of the hill you take off your clothes and run back and forth in cold grass.* Fuck him in my blood. (Acker 1978, p. 149)

Alone with Dina I take off my shirt, my bra, my shoes, and my nylon stockings. I leave on my black skirt. I put on a blue paper smock, open down the front. Dina rolls clean white paper the length of the brown leather exam table. I lie down on the paper, bare-legged. Dina holds a tube of gel and applies a cold, small gob on my right ankle. She applies a cold gob on my left ankle. She turns over my right arm and applies a cold gob to my right wrist. I raise my left arm toward her across my chest so she won't have to reach. She applies a cold gob of gel to my left wrist. She pulls back the blue paper and applies four cold gobs of gel in a half-circle below my left breast. She applies one cold gob below my right breast. She says, "This is an old machine, so we have to connect you at the ankles and wrists, too. I'm going to attach these straps to your legs and arms. I have to pull them pretty tight. Just tell me if it hurts."

> 7:30 a.m. This hurts. I awake and search, barely slept, for a place in the waking noise and sleepy rush to connect with feeling for you—CRASH. Body broken (but let's not break up we say) and I am returned to my self barely and alone. This hurts. I lie quite alone.

Dina wraps the white rubber strap around my right ankle. She pulls it tight. She wraps the second strap around my left ankle and pulls tight. Does it hurt yet? Her face is freckled slightly and pale, her black hair thick turning early to silver-gray. She wraps the third strap around my right wrist. I raise my left arm toward her across my chest so she won't have to reach. She wraps the fourth strap around my left wrist. She pulls tight. She says, "I'm going to do the first reading just from your ankles and wrists for thirty seconds." She attaches the first wire to my right ankle. She attaches the second wire to my left ankle. She attaches the third wire to my right wrist. I raise my left arm toward her across my chest so she won't have to reach. She attaches the fourth wire to my left wrist. I ask, "Will this be sending electricity through my body?" Dina says, "No. This will just measure the electricity going through you already."

> 4:00 a.m. We are in a restaurant. It is like a diner and late night. We are walking down the aisle when a very large, very densely built man comes from behind and takes my left wrist. He is threatening me. With my right hand, I scratch my nails deep across the top of his hand. I am not yet afraid. You say to me—you cannot believe I really scratched him—you say that your mother taught you never to do that. Now I am scared. The man follows us down the aisle. He grabs me. He sticks a blunt knife through my hand. Enormous pain. We are standing before a booth with red seats. You are sitting down. You do not help me at all. The man sticks a second knife through my thigh. I am so scared and in pain. No one is coming to help me and I feel this man gripping my body in total control I cannot run.

I hear Dina turn a knob. I stare at the wall to my left. It is white mostly. Her face was slightly freckled, her thick black hair soft going to silver-gray early. Her hands were cold and gentle.

The menu distracted her. She ordered a double Scotch, straight. . . . . And then it happened: her heart started beating faster. At first Maria thought it must be the thrill of the occasion. . . . . Her heart accelerated so fast she could feel the pounding in her chest. She thought Adam must notice. Then the flushing sensation. She couldn't breathe properly. Her throat tightened. Beads of sweat broke out on her forehead; a rushing sensation rose from her stomach up through her chest, then came a sinking sensation in the bottom of her stomach. Everything became detached. She felt dizzy, lightheaded, and then that panicky feeling—that mental panic. (Sheehan 1986, p. 5)

I hear a click. Dina says, "Now I'm just going to attach this cup here," and presses a small rubber cup attached to a wire below my left breast. The gel has slid down my left side and the cup does not stick. She applies another cold gob of gel beneath my left breast. The cup sticks. I hear Dina click a knob on, then off. She moves the cup three times in a half-circle below my left breast. Click on, click off. Click on, click off. Click on. Does it hurt yet? Her hands are cold and gentle.

Until recently, the root of panic disorder was assumed to be strictly psychological. . . . . Traditional psychoanalytic theory held that the attacks were the result of accumulated anxiety over unconscious conflicts and that, as the anxiety built, it must erupt in the form of an attack. Today, researchers are looking to the body, not just the mind, for clues to the mysteries of panic attacks and panic disorder. It seems to run in families, and this may provide support for those who believe the condition is triggered by physical, perhaps inheritable, problems. (Upjohn 1986, p. 6)

Click off. Dina moves the rubber cup below my right breast. "Okay," she says, "now we're going to take a reading for a full sixty seconds." I turn my head to the left and stare at the wall mostly white.

Her hands 1 were going around and around 2 a frying pan, scraping flecks 3 of black into cold, greasy dishwater. 4 The timid, tucked-in look of the scratching 5 toe—that was what Pauline was doing the first time 6 he saw her in Kentucky. 7 The tenderness welled up 8 in him, and he sank to his knees, 9 his eyes on the foot 10 of his daughter. Crawling on all fours 11 toward her, he raised 12 his hand and caught the foot 13 in an upward stroke. 14 Pecola lost her balance and 15 was about to career to the floor. 16 Cholly raised his other hand to her 17 hips to save her from falling. He put 18 his head down and nibbled at the back 19 of her leg. His mouth trembled at the firm 20 sweetness of the flesh. 21 He closed his eyes, letting his fingers 22 dig into her waist. 23 The rigidness of her shocked 24 body, the silence of her 25 stunned throat, was better than Pauline's easy laughter 26 had been. The confused 27 mixture of his memories of 28 Pauline and the doing of a wild 29 and forbidden thing excited 30 him, and a bolt of desire ran down 31 his genitals, giving it 32 length, and softening the lips 33 of his anus. 34 Surrounding all this lust 35 was a border of politeness. 36 He wanted to fuck 37 her—tenderly. 38 But the tenderness would 39 not hold. The tightness 40 of her vagina was more than he could 41 bear. His soul seemed to slip down 42 to his guts and fly out 43 into her, and the gigantic 44 thrust he made into her 45 then provoked the only 46 sound she 47 made—a hollow 48 suck of 49 air in the back 50 of her 51 throat. Like the rapid loss of air from a circus balloon. He was conscious of her wet, soapy hands on his wrists, 52 the fingers clenching, but whether her grip was from a hopeless but stubborn struggle to be free, 53 or from some other emotion, he could not tell. Removing himself from her was so painful 54 to him he cut it short and snatched his genitals out of her vagina. 55 She appeared to have fainted. 56 Cholly stood up and could see only her greyish panties, so sad and limp around her ankles. 57 Again the hatred mixed with tenderness. 58 The hatred would not let him pick her up. 59 The tenderness forced him to cover her 60. (Morrison 1970, pp. 128–29)

Dina turns off the machine. She removes the cup from below my right breast. She removes the first rubber strap from my right ankle. She removes the second rubber strap from my left ankle. She removes the third rubber strap from my right wrist. I raise my left arm toward her across my chest so she won't have to reach. She removes the fourth rubber strap from my left wrist. I ask, "Do you do this all day?" She answers, "No. Just when there's a woman patient who asks for me."

So when the child regained consciousness, she was lying on the floor under a heavy quilt, trying to connect the pain between her legs with the face of her mother looming over her (Morrison 1970, p. 129). Something down breaks deep and I am wet all over. Dear Daddy I remember naked in a loft Lower East Side New York and raining on the Lower East Side wet and you naked daddy save me from the story dear papa naked I leave you in the rain and hop in a car. Three brown women, big, friendly, we ride across wet bridges away from the Lower East Side. Quite a passage. Wet. Weeping. Down deep and wild. Regain consciousness on kitchen floor— quilted mama face looming pain—between legs and floored mama—face looming pain consciousness—face between legs mama—loom connection —face pain.

Holding a small square of clean white gauze Dina wipes the gel from my right ankle. She uses two gauze squares to wipe off my left ankle. She wipes the gel on my right wrist with one gauze square. I raise my left arm toward her across my chest so she won't have to reach. She uses one gauze square to wipe the gel from my left wrist. She uses one gauze square to wipe below my left breast. She uses one gauze square to wipe below my right breast. She says, "Here's some more if you want to clean yourself off better." She places several clean white gauze squares on the exam table next to my right shoulder.

Whatever the causes, panic attacks and anticipatory anxiety can have serious consequences when untreated. . . . . In their desperate attempts to
quell the attacks and the anticipatory anxiety, some develop pathological
dependency. They are unable to cope with feared situations without constant companionship. With all its complications, panic disorder in the
United States is estimated to cost billions of dollars annually in health care
expenses, disability benefits, and lost wages. As the disorder is more
widely recognized, studied and treated, more precise cost figures will
become available. (Upjohn 1986, p. 7)

I sit up. Dina walks to the sink and begins washing the four white rubber
straps. I take one gauze square and wipe below my left breast. It takes
three gauze squares to clean off all the gel. I ask, "Can I get dressed
now?" Dina answers, "Sure. It's all over."

I come across you, out of time we meet. You are with her, spending time
together. I feel her soft razor-edged blondness her black beauty, neck bare.
I feel your blonde hair. I feel you spending time with her. I stand before
you, barely there. You ask, "Who are you?" I am no body. I am breathless.
It's all over. I leave you. Wind rises from my gut explodes through my
chest, up my neck, in my throat I am gasping in storm without air. I am no
body. We are out of time. Out of breath. I leave you. I walk two miles until
the town ends and cross into a field and keep walking. I cross a black tar
road and crawl under a barbed wire fence and climb a low green hill. At
the top of the hill it is windy. At the top of the hill I crawl under blowing
trees to brown dirt rooting down I vomit you, vomit your blonde hair,
vomit your piss, vomit your shit, vomit your tongue. I search through my
vomit, your shit, my vomit, your tongue, my vomit, your piss, your
blonde hair. I am searching for some body. In the dirt I see a gleam, a glass
shard dime-sized clear and hard. I see a glass shard—just in time.

I rise to my knees.
I extend my tongue.
You place the shard upon my tongue.

I bow my head, sucking gently. I see brown dirt, orange vomit, blonde
hair, green shit, yellow piss, pink tongue. I suck gently until I taste salty
red wound melt. My tongue returns. I swallow hard. Warmth in my
throat, down my neck, rolling through my chest, in my gut. Then the
burn, a clear spine of flame from my throat to my belly, burning. I am here.
I am remembered. You return. I am home. I am some body burning pain
edged with fire a warm blood flows in me I feel you at last we are together
again. Some body has come home. I am weeping, I am on my knees, I am
ecstatic. My tongue returns, "Never leave me, please don't ever leave me
again I love you hold me love me hold me never leave me again. I love you
when I want put my head on someone's shoulder I will love you forever."

I stand up. I put on my bra and shirt, then my stockings and shoes. Dina
is washing her hands in the sink. She dries her hands with a paper

towel, then throws it in the blue metal trash can. Then she walks to the brown leather exam table and pulls off the white paper, crumples it, then throws it in the blue metal trash can.

Dear Mary, you strike me with your look, I am thrown. Two women out of time. My eye sees you and I fear. You are threat to me in this time our animal being run down to whimper. An animal threat, your soft razor-edged blondeness, curved arm muscle and neck bare. I see you woman and whimper with the threat of striking look bright light red lips blonde hair going to black, beauty you hit me. I run scared. (I am a deer.)

And he whistles at your bare
neck fine ass passing him
street-wise. He whimpers in quiet
animal tongue, "Slut'
or "I love you."

Your fine muscle tone tightens and voice gone to nothing you pass by an animal whimper, rage. But you will die for his desire, slut, I love you, and cut me as you slow summer seduce him street-wise. Your razor-edged blondeness rakes across my bare neck, across this lying body. (You are a deer?) You dance tight ass for his sweet bondage, slut, who cuts me up?

Dear Mary, fuck him in my blood.

I put on my bra, then my shirt, then my stockings and shoes. Does it hurt yet you—touch me, touch my left breast do—you know how I long a woman—at my left breast you cup—me, mostly white I am—hurting, bare-legged and electric black gone—early to silver-gray. I put on my bra, then my shirt, then my stockings and shoes. It's all over. You are the first woman Dina ever to make love with me last. Does it hurt yet? Do the straps pull too tight?

The American Psychiatric Association diagnostic manual indicates that one predisposition to panic disorder may be childhood separation anxiety (excessive anxiety concerning separation from people, places or things to whom a child is attached).

Dina leaves the Exam Room.

In contrast, biological theories propose that a physical defect in the regulation of the autonomic nervous system exists. (Upjohn 1986, p. 8)

Dina leaves the Exam Room. She closes the door behind her. On the back of the door hangs a live body. From a hook on the back of the door, from a coat hanger rising from her back, hangs a live woman body. She is laughing. From the back of the door hangs a live woman half-body laughing with both hands she is rubbing wild and furious in round brown-nipple circles laughing her breasts. She is trying to come. Her mouth is open and laughter coming out shaking her breasts she rubs in wild circles her brown nipples. She is laughing.

> The future is hopeful. . . . . Old views are being revised; the idea that [panic disorder] is an illness rather than a state of mind or a response to stress is gaining more credibility. This model offers new hope. . . . . There is little doubt that in the near future this model will help us better to unravel the mysteries of [panic disorder] and will lead us to a better under-standing of its causes. . . . . [A]bove all, it will guide us to newer, safer, more rapid and effective treatments. We have already come a long way in controlling it. The rest is only a matter of time. (Sheehan 1986, pp. 182–83)

She is not mad. She has no body below her breasts. She is trying to come. I am watching. I am laughing. I am not mad. My mouth is open and I am trying to come. I was waking. I am remembered. It is wild. It was morning. I rise. I am in the Exam Room, alone and waiting. In the Exam Room, laughing mad, and learning to pass the time.

Notes

1. Foucault's words, perhaps more curious than comforting, are from Philip Horvitz, "Don't Cry for Me, Academia," interview with Michel Foucault, *Jimmy and Lucy's House of K* (Berkeley), no. 2, August 1985, quoted in Treichler (1988, p. 68). The context of Foucault's comment was an exchange about the threat of AIDS. According to Treichler, for Foucault "the 'tragedy' of AIDS was not intrin-sically its lethal character, but rather that a group that has risked so much—gays—are looking to standard authorities—doctors, the church—for guidance in a time of crisis" (p. 68).
2. This section of the text draws on Aihwa Ong's ethnographic research as reported in her essay "The Production of Possession: Spirits and the Multina-tional Corporation in Malaysia" (1988). In the interests of style and brevity, I have (reductively!) paraphrased her analysis. I take full responsibility for this interpretation, but want to clearly acknowledge that the substance and structure of my text closely follow Ong's work.
3. I am thinking here of the various writings of Hélène Cixous, Luce Irigaray, Frigga Haug, Trinh Minh-ha, Jane Gallop, Kathy Acker, Nicole Brossard, Gloria Anzuldua, Avital Ronell, Monique Wittig. This is far from an inclusive list, and not all of these authors have themselves used this expression to describe their work. While there is tremendous diversity among the writings of these women, I read them all as engaging in formal, feminist, and materialist efforts to articu-late the body in and as language-making.
4. Only practitioners of an abstract theory of language could deploy the racially-coded danger of "going native" and the gender-coded threat of "seduc-tion" with the kind of theoretical innocence displayed here by Ibarra and Kit-

suse. What are the dirty dangers of noticing that "units of language" are sedimented with historically and politically charged meanings?

5. In describing Ibarra and Kitsuse's own practice of language I am borrowing the adjectives they use to describe the "styleless" scientific style that can lend the authority of "objectivity" to claimants' discourse. The authors do not remark that their own discourse is a perfect exemplar of this claims-making style.

6. The decision to enter a field under false pretenses (throughout the fieldwork I presented myself as currently suffering from panic disorder) is fraught with methodological, political, and ethical questions. It is not my purpose here to raise these questions in their complexity, but to remind readers of the possibility that the investigation of certain institutional settings and fieldwork situations becomes impossible *without* the use of "masquerade." The fact that I entered, as a researcher, a research setting under false pretenses may be particularly disturbing to some readers/researchers. I admit to my fantasy that social and scientific research would be far more useful and accurate if more research subjects were also taking notes and publishing their findings. One of the most significant findings of my "masquerade" was, simply, that it is possible to successfully simulate panic disorder within a medical-scientific setting where all diagnosis, research, and treatment of panic is premised on a biochemical model of disorder. Biochemical research on panic disorder remains curiously beholden to the symptomatic storytellings of those who say (how) they suffer.

References

Acker, Kathy. 1978. *The Adult Life of Toulouse Lautrec by Henri Toulouse Lautrec.* New York: Turtle Press.

Alarcon, Norma. 1990. "The Theoretical Subject(s) of *This Bridge Called My Back* and Anglo-American Feminism." Pp. 356–69 in *Making Face, Making Soul: Haciendo Caras,* edited by Gloria Anzuldua. San Francisco: Aunt Lute Foundation Books.

Anzuldua, Gloria. 1990. "En Rapport, In Opposition: Cobrando cuentas a las nuestras." Pp. 142–48 in *Making Face, Making Soul: Haciendo Caras,* edited by Gloria Anzuldua. San Francisco: Aunt Lute Foundation Books.

Ballenger, J.C., J. Gorman, A. Fyer, et al. 1986. "Alprazolam in Panic Disorder and Agoraphobia: Results from a Multicenter Trial." *Archives of General Psychiatry* 45:413–22.

Bordo, Susan. 1988. "Anorexia Nervosa: Psychopathology as the Crystallization of Culture." Pp. 87–118 in *Feminism and Foucault,* edited by Irene Diamond and Lee Quinby. Boston: Northeastern University Press.

Cixous, Hélène and Catherine Clément. 1986. *The Newly-Born Woman.* Translated by Betsy Wing. Minneapolis: University of Minnesota Press.

Collins, Patricia H. 1990. *Black Feminist Thought.* Boston: Unwin Hyman.

Davis, Angela. 1990. "Sick and Tired of Being Sick and Tired: The Politics of Black Women's Health." Pp. 53–65 in *Women, Culture, Politics,* edited by Angela Davis. New York: Vintage Books.

de Lauretis, Teresa. 1987. *Technologies of Gender: Essays on Theory, Film, and Fiction.* Bloomington: Indiana University Press.

———. 1990. "Sexual Indifference and Lesbian Representation." Pp. 17–39 in *Performing Feminisms: Feminist Critical Theory and Theatre*, edited by Sue-Ellen Case. Baltimore: Johns Hopkins University Press.

Delaporte, François. 1986. *Disease and Civilization: The Cholera in Paris, 1832*. Cambridge, MA: MIT Press.

Foucault, Michel. [1963] 1975. *The Birth of the Clinic: An Archaeology of Medical Perception*. New York: Vintage Books.

———. 1977. *Discipline and Punish*. New York: Pantheon.

———. 1978. *The History of Sexuality*, Vol. I. New York: Vintage Books.

———. 1982. "The Subject and Power." Pp. 208–26 in *Michel Foucault: Beyond Structuralism and Hermeneutics*, by Paul Rabinow and Hubert L. Dreyfus. Chicago: University of Chicago Press.

———. 1984a. "Nietzsche, Genealogy, History." Pp. 76–100 in *The Foucault Reader*, edited by Paul Rabinow. New York: Pantheon.

———. 1984b. "Polemics, Politics, and Problemizations: An Interview with Michel Foucault." Pp. 381–90 in *The Foucault Reader*, edited by Paul Rabinow. New York: Pantheon.

Gordon, Avery. 1990. *Ghostly Memories: Feminist Rituals of Writing the Social Text*. Ph.D. dissertation, Boston College.

Haraway, Donna. 1981. "The High Cost of Information in Post-World War II Evolutionary Biology: Ergonomics, Semiotics, and the Sociobiology of Communication Systems." *The Philosophical Forum* 13(2–3):244–78.

———. 1985. "A Manifesto for Cyborgs: Science, Technology, and Socialist Feminism in the 1980s." *Socialist Review* 80:65–107.

hooks, bell. 1981. *Ain't I A Woman: Black Women and Feminism*. Boston: South End Press.

———. 1990. *Yearning: race, gender, and cultural politics*. Boston: South End Press.

Klein, Donald. 1981. "Anxiety Reconceptualized." Pp. 235–63 in *Anxiety: New Research and Changing Concepts*, edited by D. Klein and J. Rabbin. New York: Raven Press.

———. 1984. "Psychopharmacological Treatment of Panic Disorder." *Psychosomatics* 25 (supplement):32–36.

Klerman, Gerald. 1988. "Overview of the Cross-National Collaborative Panic Study." *Archives of General Psychiatry* 45:407–12.

LaPiere, Richard T. 1938. *Collective Behavior*. New York: McGraw-Hill.

Liebowitz, M., J. Gorman, A. Fyer, et al. 1986. "Possible Mechanisms for Lactate's Induction of Panic." *American Journal of Psychiatry* 143:495–501.

Martin, Biddy. 1988. "Feminism, Criticism, and Foucault." Pp. 3–20 in *Feminism and Foucault: Reflections on Resistance*, edited by Irene Diamond and Lee Quinby. Boston: Northeastern University Press.

McDougall, William. 1920. *The Group Mind*. New York: G.P. Putnam's Sons.

Mohanty, Chandra T., A. Russo, and L. Torres. 1991. *Third World Women and the Politics of Feminism*. Bloomington: Indiana University Press.

Moraga, Cherrie, and G. Anzuldua (eds.). 1981. *This Bridge Called My Back: Writings by Radical Women of Color*. Watertown, MA: Persephone Press.

Morrison, Toni. 1970. *The Bluest Eye*. New York: Simon and Schuster.

National Institute of Mental Health (NIMH). 1989. *Panic Disorder in the Medical*

Setting, by Wayne Katon. DHHS Pub. No. (ADM) 89–1629. Washington, DC: Supt. of Documents, U.S. Government Printing Office.

O'Neill, John. 1989. "AIDS as a Globalizing Panic." Pp. 77–86 in *PUBLIC³/Carnal Knowledge*. Toronto: Public Access Collective.

Ong, Aihwa. 1987. *Spirits of Resistance and Capitalist Discipline: Factory Women in Malaysia*. Albany: State University of New York Press.

———. 1988. "The Production of Possession: Spirits and the Multinational Corporation in Malaysia." *American Ethnologist* 15(1):28–42.

Orr, Jackie. 1990. "Theory on the Market: Panic, Incorporating." *Social Problems* 37(4):460–84.

Pfohl, Stephen. 1990. "Welcome to the PARASITE CAFE: Postmodernity as a Social Problem." *Social Problems* 37(4):421–42.

Sandoval, Chela. 1990. "Feminism and Racism: A Report on the 1981 National Women's Studies Association Conference." Pp. 55–71 in *Making Face, Making Soul: Haciendo Caras*, edited by Gloria Anzuldua. San Francisco: Aunt Luce Foundation Books.

Scheper-Hughes, Nancy and Margaret Lock. 1991. "The Message in the Bottle: Illness and the Micropolitics of Resistance." *Journal of Psychohistory* 18(4):409–32.

Schultz, Duane. 1964. *Panic Behavior*. New York: Random House.

Sheehan, David V. 1982. "Current Concepts in Psychiatry: Panic Attacks and Phobias." *New England Journal of Medicine* 307(3):156–58.

———. 1986. *The Anxiety Disease*. New York: Bantam Books.

Showalter, Elaine. 1985. *The Female Malady*. New York: Pantheon Books.

Smith, Dorothy. 1987. *The Everyday World As Problematic: A Feminist Sociology*. Boston: Northeastern University Press.

———. 1990. *The Conceptual Practices of Power: A Feminist Sociology of Knowledge*. Boston: Northeastern University Press.

Stein, Gertrude. 1945. *Selected Writings of Gertrude Stein*. New York: Random House.

Strauss, Anselm. 1944. "The Literature on Panic." *Journal of Abnormal and Social Psychology* 39:317–28.

Taylor, C., J. Sheikh, A. Fyer, et al. 1986. "Ambulatory Heart Rate Changes in Patients with Panic Attacks." *American Journal of Psychiatry* 143(4):478–82.

Treichler, Paula. 1988. "AIDS, Homophobia, and Biomedical Discourse: An Epidemic of Signification." P. 68 in *AIDS: Cultural Analysis/Cultural Activism*, edited by D. Crimp. Cambridge, MA: MIT Press.

Trinh Minh-ha. 1989. *Woman, Native, Other: Writing Postcoloniality and Feminism*. Bloomington: Indiana University Press.

Upjohn Company. 1982. *The Upjohn Company Annual Report 1981*. Kalamazoo, MI: Author.

———. 1985. *The Upjohn Company Annual Report 1984*. Kalamazoo, MI: Author.

———. 1986. "What You Should Know About Panic Disorder." Pamphlet. Kalamazoo, MI: Author.

Wittig, Monique. 1980. "The Straight Mind." *Feminist Issues* 1(1):103–11.

Representational Challenges

21

Constructionism and Practices of Objectivity

Lawrence E. Hazelrigg

During the 1830s a heated debate engaged two of Britain's most eminent comparative anatomists, Robert Edmond Grant and Richard Owen. The ostensive focus of their disagreement consisted in a few very' small fossilized jawbones, the now mostly forgotten "Stonesfield jaws," which had been extracted earlier in the century from some Stonesfield slate near Oxford. Owen knew the bones to be from a marsupial and therefore mammalian creature. Grant knew them to be from a reptilian creature. Much turned on the difference—not merely the proper identity of a theretofore unknown creature but indeed the integrity of an entire network of correlated dates, sites, and developmental relations. If Owen should be right, the creature existed where previously mammals had not been able to exist, the (Jurassic) "age of reptiles." If Grant should be right, the standard stratigraphy of fossil evidences would remain intact, but at least one species of reptile had teeth of a sort (i.e., incisors and multicusped molars) previously known to be one of the distinctive markers of mammalian creatures.[1]

Who was right, Grant or Owen? By the early 1840s the standard journals had declared in favor of Owen's marsupial. Although Grant and many of his allies refused to concede, the majority of scientists involved in the debate agreed with Owen. Later in the century the animal became neither marsupial nor reptilian but the representative of a new order of mammals. Even this later determination was partial to Owen over Grant, however. The revised standard account attributed Owen's success in seeing a mammal of some sort to his keener insight, his superior procedures, and (to borrow a locution from a still later day) his better "feeling for the organism."

So who *was* right, Grant, Owen, or the subsequent emendation of Owen? The question calls up another: Which standpoint shall we take? The conflicting claims were built of a number of smaller, more particular disputes—for instance, about the teeth, about the stratigraphy of the embedding slate, about probable respiratory mechanics of the creature, and so on. But in addition, a much larger struggle was being waged in the debate over this short handful of bones. Grant's claim was informed by a more internationalist, more "secularist" natural science, which, after Lamarck, Geoffroy, and Cuvier, knew that species were arrayed in progressive series of development toward perfection. Owen, on the other hand, was paladin to the ruling Anglican and corporate interests of English natural science, which saw threat in the "radical" implications of Lamarckian progressivism. Personal standing was at stake for the disputants, in organizations such as the Geological Society and the Zoological Society as well as in various less formal circles. And national pride was on the line; while London was playing catch-up in matters of natural science to the Paris of Cuvier, Geoffroy, and company, any claim that appeared merely to emulate French science, as Grant's did to a large section of his audience, was met with considerable resistance. In this mix of interests, preferences, and convictions, the standpoint taken by Owen prevailed.

One might well object, of course, that the preceding sketch of an answer to the question Who was right? is given in terms of standpoints largely coined from social-political-economic interests. It is perhaps all to the good as a sociocultural explanation why one claim prevailed over another. It does not tell us, however, what kind of animal Grant and Owen were quarreling about. We need an objective description, an objective identification, of the nature of the beast. For only on that basis can we objectively decide whether Grant or Owen, or neither, was right; and without that, we cannot know, in our sociocultural explanation, which of the various social-political-economic interests were biasing, how much they were biasing, in what direction, with what consequence, and so forth. Indeed, the critic might well contend, make whatever sociocultural explanation you like of Grant's claim, of Owen's claim, and of the settlement in support of Owen; the question still remains, Who was right? What kind of animal was it?

I begin with this vignette from the annals of paleozoology because it illustrates rather well an apparent conflict between the operations of a constructionist approach to competing claims about the facts of a case and an objectivist expectation that beneath any competing claims about the facts of a case there is one and only one set of the *real* facts (because, in any given instance, there is one and only one *case*, the facts of which are inherent), and the real facts surely ought to be ascertainable under objective description. The constructionist approach, much like a sociology-of-knowledge approach, which focuses on "claims of knowledge" relative to "existential conditions" (cf. Knorr-Cetina 1989), wants to concentrate inquiry on competing claims, claimants, and claims-making processes, without prejudicing the inquiry by invoking an objec-

tive description of the focal object of the various claims. Initial proponents of constructionism within social problems theory, Spector and
Kitsuse ([1977] 1987) most notably, signalled that intent by adopting the
locution, "putative conditions," when referring to the focal object of
claims-making activity. The intent was to hold in abeyance the question
of objective description. In a stronger version of constructionism the
intent has been not merely to hold the question of objective description
in abeyance but, further, to argue that *any* objective description is itself
just another claim and should not be privileged over others by virtue of
its more or less successful effort to monopolize the mantle of "the objective description." Indeed, to return to the Stonesfield jaws for a moment, there is good reason to think that Grant and Owen each genuinely
believed that his was the objective description. Like all of us, each was
an actor of invested interests. But those interests in each case included
"the interest in truth," and there is no good reason to think that either
man was deliberately playing a paleontological equivalent of the shell
game. Conspirators there are. But conspiracy theories are usually quite
unnecessary.

The question of objective description has a way of circling back into
the picture, however, "even" into the constructionist picture. Rarely,
after all, does one hear a self-proclaimed constructionist announce that
her or his description of the various claims, claimants, and claims-
making activities under address is *not* objective—in other words, that
the proffered description is "merely another subjective opinion" about
matters at hand. But the point is not simply that constructionism, too,
knows the benefits of "ontological gerrymandering," as critics such as
Woolgar and Pawluch (1985) have rightly argued. One could easily imagine that a constructionist investigator should be uncommonly explicit
about gerrymandering moves—that is, about the sort of boundary work
by which people, including those whose occupation is science, establish
the borders of an object, the line between the theoretical and the practical, the qualification of one claim as objective knowledge and another as
error or subjective opinion or myth, and so forth.

My aim in this chapter is to examine the question why objectivism and
objectivity have been such an issue for constructionism. In particular, I
want to bring into account the underlying notion that "objective description" can be avoided, and that it is beneficial to do so. This volume's
featured essay by Ibarra and Kitsuse argues that constructionism, at
least in social problems theory [in Schneider's (1985) sense of theory *of*
social problems], must forgo interest in explaining how the existential
conditions of claimants figure in the production of claims, lest inquiry
into the claims and claims-making activity be prejudiced by objective
description. I believe that is a rather high price to pay, especially consid-

ering the purchase. My chief concern here is with that transaction, its motivations, its desirability, indeed its possibility.

Gerrymandering Representation

At the risk of some redundancy, let me rehearse very briefly the circumstances that have brought Ibarra and Kitsuse to their current recommendation. Assume a distinction between the perspective of the sociological analyst-observer (hereafter, "observer") and the perspective of the ordinary participant-member (hereafter, "member").[2] The observer should of course strive to be neutral toward members' perspectives, allowing any and all of them into the picture without prejudgment. The observer should focus neutrally on members' perspectives and activities (including vernacular languaging) as they construct moral objects as social problems, without taking a stand on the question whether, how, and to what extent the members' constructions are adequate (valid, accurate, appropriate, etc.) to the conditions in, of, and under which the constructions are made.

All of this would appear to be quite straightforward and sensible. But enacting the prescriptions without lapsing into the seemingly intractable problems of ontological gerrymandering has proven to be extremely difficult at best—especially when, as Ibarra and Kitsuse point out, the constructionist observer includes any focus on what the members' claims-making activities are "about" (i.e., an "external referent" of the claims). Ibarra and Kitsuse appreciate the promise of constructionism's negative critique of objectivism—namely, that objectivism is prejudicial because it fails to extend sociocultural explanation to the reality that it claims to know as objective fact *tout court*[3]—and they want to redeem the promise, the benefits, of that critique. In order to do so, they conclude, the intractable problems of ontological gerrymandering must be circumvented, and this means that the constructionist observer's perspective must be devoid of attention to how members' constructions (definitions, claims, moral objects as social problems, etc.) are produced by the circumstances in which the constructions "emerge." Properly engaged, in other words, the constructionist observer of the Stonesfield jaws episode would be entirely unconcerned both with the object about which Grant and Owen were quarreling *and* with the sociocultural circumstances of that object and of Grant's and Owen's querulous claims-making activities, which yielded two alternative constructions.

The recommendation seems rather extreme. Certainly it is legitimate to focus one's attention on members' perspectives and activities (discursive and otherwise)[4] as they go about whatever it is they are doing, including the construction of moral objects as social problems (and/or the construction of problems in a Meadian sense). But is it desirable to calibrate that focus without making any assumptions about members' object-world or the circumstances in, of, and under which they produce their constructions? For that matter, is it possible?

Social problems theory is not the only venue of struggles with these ethnographic issues. Anthropologists have debated them increasingly during the last two decades, sometimes in ways that demonstrate quite clearly what is at stake.[5] While this is not the place to review all of that large and diverse literature, some important insights can be drawn from it nonetheless, and I shall try to explicate a few of them by trading chiefly on an argument recited by Sperber in his once controversial essays *On Anthropological Knowledge* ([1982] 1985). In particular, I want to use a piece of his argument as a device for clarifying dimensions of issues involved in the "constructionism versus objectivism" debate, and in Ibarra and Kitsuse's recommendation.

Sperber says that in certain situations ethnographers can (and have) become confused about the object of their investigations and proceed to build interpretations as if they, the observers, were in the midst of an epiphany of the object. What is more, the situations of confusion are systematically identifiable in terms of the ethnographer's focus of attention, as depicted schematically in Figure 1.

In Situation 1 the observer interprets her or his representations of Other's representations of Other's own behavior and existential conditions (institutional circumstances, etc.). This situation Sperber regards as rather straightforward and nonproblematic, at least in principle. In Situation 2 the observer interprets his or her representations of Other's own behavior and existential conditions. Here, too, the situation is straightforward and nonproblematic, at least in principle. But ethnographers sometimes become confused within this second situation and tacitly assume that they are interpreting Other's behaviors and existential conditions (signified in the figure by the broken line). "It is hard," Sperber says, "not to mistake the object of the representations interpreted for the object of the interpretation" ([1982] 1985, p. 21). Thus, whereas in Situation 1 interpretation is "obviously" of a representation (the point being that because anthropologists traditionally conducted ethnography in settings that posed obvious translations problems, the ethnographer was keenly aware that Other's representations were being represented), in Situation 2 it is easy to imagine that Other's behaviors and existential conditions body forth on their own, without "benefit" of observer's representations of them.

Some interesting parallels can be drawn between Sperber's treatment of ethnographic activity and the "strict constructionist" concerns about

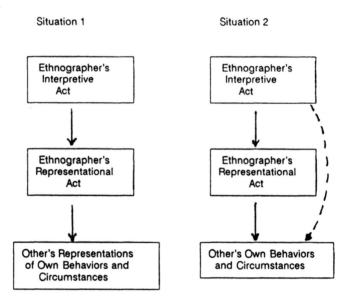

Figure 1.   Two Ethnographic Situations

avoiding ontological gerrymandering.[6] Situation 1 appears to be parallel to the constructionist recommendation that attention should be focused only on Other's representations of Other's world, activities, and so on. Situation 2, according to the recommendation, should be avoided entirely, for it introduces observer prejudice of Other's representations; it is the unwanted objectivism.

But a couple of questions come to mind. First, isn't the unwanted objectivism Sperber's *mistaken* Situation 2? The fault of objectivism is its presumption, usually tacit, that the observer's standpoint is identified with "the standpoint of the object"—in other words, that the object just as it is in itself shows itself just as it is to the properly situated (i.e., objective) observer, and that sociocultural explanation (representation, etc.) of that object-showing-itself is entirely superfluous.[7] This is indeed a prejudicial position. Sperber's point is that "even" in Situation 2 the observer is constructing the object as well as the explanation of it.

Second, if Situation 1 is acceptable to the strict constructionist, why isn't Situation 2 (correctly understood)? Or more to the point of Ibarra and Kitsuse's recommendation, why is it necessary to forswear Situation 2 in order to proceed successfully with Situation 1? Again, the recommended answer emphasizes the avoidance of prejudicial evaluations, implicit if not explicit, of Other's representations (and the avoidance of gerrymandering). But there is reason to suspect that this answer and the recommended program behind it are formulated as a *mistaken* Situation 1, analogous to Sperber's case of mistaken Situation 2. If the recommendation is to avoid any attention to how members' constructions are produced by and in members' existential circumstances (i.e., correlations between Situations 1 and 2), so as to avoid prejudicing what would otherwise not be prejudged, then the implication would appear to be that Other's representations allow of a quality of access that is not possible for Other's existential conditions. In other words, the recommended program tacitly assumes that the observer makes no representations of Other's representations, that Other's representations are apprehended objectively (or if represented, represented neutrally, and therefore in effect not really represented at all).[8] Absent that assumption, the issue of prejudice simply doesn't differentiate the two situations. But on what grounds can one assume that Other's representations are available to "objective description" (i.e., objectivism's claim), if Other's existential conditions are not? Or to put the point differently, while it could be argued that conducting inquiry within both Situations 1 and 2 simultaneously would increase the risk of prejudicial representations by the observer, I see no reason to believe that eschewing Situation 2 would leave inquiry in Situation 1 free of the risk of prejudgments.

Is it possible to conduct inquiry in Situation 1 while entirely avoiding Situation 2? I suppose it is—in the same sense, for example, that one can study gardeners' claims about "planting by the moon" without caring whether lunar properties or events make any difference whatsoever in horticultural yields. Holding one's doubts harmless (to say nothing of one's facts and unreflected biases) may well be ultimately as impossible as jumping out of one's skin; nevertheless, there is something to be said in favor of trying to comprehend Other's world in Other's own terms ("assuming the gaze of the member"), even though the effort itself is productive of a "new" or later reality of situated actions in the ongoingness of history. But where does one draw the line between Other's representations and Other's existential conditions? Eschewing the focus of Situation 2 presupposes that members' claims and the circumstances in and by which those claims are produced can be segregated well enough to insure that the observer's representations of members' claims are not influenced by those productive circumstances. While the expectation may seem feasible when considered abstractly, it would be a rather tall order concretely, especially since members' claims are produced in and by organized activities (claims-making activities) that are integral to their existential conditions.[9]

Even if one could achieve a sufficiently clean segregation between members' claims and claims-making activities, on one side, and all other activities integral to their existential conditions, on the other, one should still acknowledge the boundary work involved in representing members' claims as a reality objectively grasped. Certainly I can investigate members' claims without caring about "the true identity" of the referent of those claims. The putative rewards of planting by the moon, for instance, or the putative animal of Grant's and Owen's competing claims, need not be decided one way or the other in my investigation. But I should recognize that avoiding that decision (i.e., avoiding an objective description of the rewards or the animal) is purchased by boundary work that shifts the focus of objective description from the referent of the claims to the claims themselves and their production. Of course, one should also recognize that boundary work is always provisional, in all senses of the word. Boundary work provides a featured landscape, perspective(s), horizon(s), and so on (though not from nothing or de novo); and boundary work is more or less temporary, even when it appears from within to be the last word. Attempting to avoid assumptions about or attention to the circumstances in and by which the claims are produced changes none of that, frees no investigation from the boundary work of objective description, but only substitutes one objective description for another.

That being the case, however, one must ask, What exactly is "objective description," and why should one seek to avoid it even at the cost proposed by Ibarra and Kitsuse?

The Conditions of Objective Description

Objectivism would treat the ethnographic observer's representations as neutral media—that is, as if in one-to-one correspondence with Other's representations and/or existential conditions. There is, of course, no way to judge the assumed correspondence except by adding another layer of observer's representations, ad infinitum. The authority of "objective description," as it is conventionally understood and practiced (i.e., "the standpoint of the object") is then brought into play—when it can be made to work—in order to staunch the "regress," that is to say, staunch the ongoing productivity of representation. Constructionism's critique of this operation is correct: The decisive reality (objectivism's objective reality) is exempted from sociocultural explanation. This does not mean that observer's representations are therefore worthless, however. If science cannot tell stories, then it can do nothing. But the stories it tells are constructed, and in the very same sense that constructionism has members engaged in the construction of claims.

The doctrine of objectivism has long monopolized the constitution of the conditions of objectivity—of what will count as "objective description," of "being objective," and so forth. Curiously enough, as I tried to argue on an earlier occasion (Hazelrigg 1986), constructionists are often complicit in that monopolization. Objectivism's objectivity is an ideal goal—Novick's "noble dream"—which could be achieved, if it could, only through the complete effacement of the observer, or at least through the complete neutralization of observer's representational work. To be objective is to be identified with the (alleged) standpoint of the object as such, not with one's own, necessarily partial standpoint. It may be, as Nagel (1986) has allowed, that while not everything is something from no point of view, some things are, and when those things are known as such they are known objectively. In one sense, the point is incontrovertible: Even to imagine a world otherwise is more than extremely difficult, it is impossible. But what exactly *is* this "view from nowhere," objectivism's principal condition of objectivity? Is it an effect of the sociality of seeing, thinking, saying, judging, making? Or is it, as objectivism claims, a necessary precondition of seeing an object-just-as-it-is-in-itself, independent of the heterogeneous character of sociality? In other words, what is the human practice accomplished in "the view from nowhere," in "the standpoint of the object," in "being objective'?

To repeat: According to objectivism, an object is known objectively or under objective description when it is (re-)presented from no point of view (or from neutral point of view, where "neutral" means independent of, uninfluenced by, the bias of observer's contingency). The crucial assumption in this claim holds that the act of representation (or description) is not productive beyond "the purely linguistic act" of (re-)presenting the object in words. But in fact representation is as productive as any other human activity, and that productivity extends all the way to the object world (i.e., to the so-called extralinguistic reality, which is anything but devoid of language; cf. Hazelrigg 1989, part 2). A representation or description is a socially situated product that, if successful (persuasive), establishes the identity of the object, its integrity of being, for and within the productive situation. Short of that condition, the object would always be destined to remain just beyond the reach of language—as "the *real* object," "the extralinguistic object" (remember the perpetual regress of judging the fit of words to world always only by more words)—and thus *the entirety* of human being's "objective world" would be locked away in a Kantian domain of "alien causes" (i.e., causes that could never be part of the social world, and thus never known). Objectivism seeks to shut down the regress, and thereby retain at least some of its "objective world" to the capacity of knowable causes, by importing a description that, even though produced in and as socially situated action, is held immune to sociocultural explanation.

Does acknowledgment of the productivity of representation (description, interpretation, etc.) mean the loss of objectivity or objective description? Hardly. It does, however, make any principle of objectivity (and correspondingly, any principle of subjectivity) an unexceptional product of sociality, of socially situated action.[10] If I describe X as p and you do not agree (or, more carefully, I persuade no community of hearers to the correctness or validity or truth of my predication), then my description is not an objective description. It is *my* description, not *ours*, and from your point of view it is likely to be judged an opinion informed by my point of view, my interests, my biases, or perhaps simply my failure to follow proper procedure. If, on the other hand, you and I, or a community of hearers, agree that X is p, we agree in *our* description of the object, and the description is likely to be accorded the mantle (for us) of objectivity. We agree that you and I do know not merely one and the same description but one and the same object. And indeed we do.

The point is, objective description is always a socially situated accomplishment of agreement in the practice of world—in what counts as correct seeing, as proper procedure, as evidence, as knowledge versus opinion versus myth, and so on.[11] Some things are precisely what they are from no point of view because we share the point of view from which they are what they are. Either we recognize no alternative point(s) of view or, more likely, we regard all alternatives as inferior (biased, mythic, error, etc.). Modern science, and more especially modern natural science, has been unprecedentedly successful in the effort to universalize certain shared points of view—beyond class, beyond nation, beyond gender, indeed beyond any "merely social" difference.[12]

Constructionism acknowledges the productivity of members' representations. That is, after all, the burden of attention to members' claims and claims-making activities, the recommended value of "assuming the gaze of the other" (or trying to understand Other's world in Other's own terms), and the intended point of the "putative condition" locution. But constructionists have often been much less inclined to acknowledge the productivity of *observer's* representations. Otherwise, there would be no point to their avowed eschewal of objective description (though not of objectivism). Otherwise, avoidance of ontological gerrymandering would not appear to be a meaningful goal. Otherwise, the extraordinary restriction that Ibarra and Kitsuse recommend would not appear to purchase benefits commensurate with the cost.

How might we account for the inconsistency in a constructionism that acknowledges the productivity of members' representations but not of observer's—indeed, that wants to deny to observer the powers of productivity insistently accorded members? What motivates the restriction? Here, too, some lessons from anthropology's recent record are instructive.

Objectivity and Power

Recall that while Ibarra and Kitsuse want to avoid all opportunity of objective description of the circumstances in and by which members' claims are produced, they say nothing about the corresponding risks of bias in observer's representations of members' representations. Presumably that is because the on-going productivity of representation ceases just long enough for the observer to hear in a neutral way exactly what the members mean when they say their claims. In other words, the observer can achieve an objective description (in objectivism's sense) of members' meanings, though not of their conditions of being. Presumably, in turn, *that* is because observer and members "speak the same language" (where "language" consists somehow only in meanings and not in conditions of human being).

For anthropology's tradition of ethnography the case was somewhat different, inasmuch as the observer could not so easily assume that hearing Other speak was immediately comparable to hearing one's own voice. In ethnography's modal circumstance of "culture contact," the task of fitting words to words was problematic, and the value of objectivity (à la objectivism) made heavy demands on the character of observer's representations of Other's representations. As Sperber notes, ethnographers typically responded to those demands by cultivating "native informants" as facilitators of ethnography's requisitely neutral or objective description of Other's representations as well as of Other's existential conditions (Sperber [1982] 1985, pp. 22–23). Increasingly, however, during the 1950s and 1960s, ethnography, a product of European and Euroamerican culture, caught sight of itself in the common etymological root of "cultivation" and "colonization." This new self-recognition was unsettling.

Objectivity had been assumed to afford a sort of assurance that one's representations, when objective, would be morally neutral or, sometimes even better, always on the side of the angels. It was thought crucial to the authority of anthropological science, both in general and most especially in ethnography's modal circumstance, either to avoid all moral judgment (thus maintaining the supposed separation of "the epistemic" from "the ethical," "the theoretical" from "the practical," etc.) or to offer only benign judgments, judgments that would improve Other's conditions of being (thus maintaining an engaged objectivity of *positive* knowledge—"better living through science"). But ethnography's recognition of its inherent complicity in a cultural imperialism was an acknowledgment both that its representations of Other were unavoidably an exercise in differentials of power (and neither morally neutral nor free of epistemic prejudgment) *and* that even under its best intentions (e.g., to bring home objective descriptions of an undisturbed Otherness, or to contribute benefits to the Other) its representations often had malignant effects, at home as well as away. In the "culture shock" of this new self-recognition, ethnography became rather nervous about the exercise of power that is inherent in the productivity of representation. Ethnographers began to eschew the "harsh" vocabulary of objective description and representation, in favor of a "softer" vocabulary of invocation—of "invoking Other's voice," of letting the ethnographic object body forth in its own self-contained measure.

Rejection of the doctrine of objectivism became confused, under stimulus of a sort of intellectualist flight from power, as rejection of any principle of objectivity. The standard ideology of modern science admits of only one kind of power, an allegedly self-contained epistemic power.[13] Since objective description necessarily involves the productivity of representation, the powerfulness of which is not confined to the "strictly epistemic" but includes an inherence of prejudgmental evaluation (an irreducible condition of sociality), objective description must be avoided if one wants to invoke members' claims nonprejudicially. This is the position taken by Ibarra and Kitsuse. Just as they would exclude all objective description or representation of the circumstances in and by which members' claims are produced, so too, for the same reason, they would exclude all objective description or representation of members' claims. They would rather "assume the gaze of the members," that is, only invoke members' claims. Invocation is meant to do what objectivism's objective description was supposed to do but does not and cannot—avoid the productivity of representation. Neither can invocation. A conversation is produced (and is productive) on *all* sides, although not necessarily equally so.

Strict constructionism is right to insist that *any* objective description is just another claim. But an objective description is also a social fact, a product forged in the practices of sociality, and as such it exerts very considerable force because (or insofar as) it exists as a piece of the world with which members-observers contend. To recognize that its reality consists in agreement in practices of the world (i.e., in objectification) does not in any way diminish its reality. Nor is it beyond the pale of sociocultural explanation. Moreover, inquiry (description, representation, explanation) cannot begin without some range of agreements in practice—agreed practices of some part of the world's furniture, etc.— even though the agreed practices, the objects, *are* socially produced, made. To that extent, prejudgment is unavoidable, necessary, and provisional.

But What About the Bones?

Ibarra and Kitsuse's recommendation illustrates rather well that, and why, constructionism tends to succumb to its nemesis, objectivism. The tendency occurs for a couple of reasons. The first has to do with concerns about power and knowledge. Constructionism turns away from objective description because it wants to avoid observer effects, the risk that observer's point of view will contaminate, distort, or prejudge the object that is to be described, represented, interpreted. But its recommended procedure, whether called "invoking Other's voice" or "assuming the gaze of the members," amounts to what objectivism only pretended to do; and constructionism's version of the pretense is no better than objectivism's.

The second reason has to do with "the *real* object." When all is said and done, constructionism finds it difficult not to agree with objectivism in the claim that, while conversations and everything else of the social world may be social facts, bones are not. Or not primarily. *Representations* of bones are social facts, and in that sense bones may *become* social facts; but before they become represented objects, and beneath the represented objects when they do become that, they are just bones. In other words, a constructionist can be as willing as an objectivist to say, "Make whatever sociocultural explanation of Grant's and Owen's competing claims you believe appropriate, valid, accurate, truthful; there is still the question what kind of animal deposited those bones." The intent of this question is objectivism's objective description.

Constructionism has some difficulty in maintaining consistency with regard to when its central principle, the constructedness of reality, applies and when it does not. On the one hand, it insists that members' claims are constructed realities, that members' representations are both produced and productive; on the other hand, it grows nervous at the thought that observer's claims are no less constructed, that observer's representations are both produced and productive. By the same token, even as constructionism insists on the constructedness of members' social facts, *and* argues (against objectivism) that observer's attempt at an objective description of members' social facts is prejudgmental and thus should be avoided, it tends to agree with objectivism that bones—that is, the physical or material object, in the sense of classical (Feuerbachian) materialism—are just bones. The agreement rests in the assumption that because physicality is (allegedly) outside "the social" (or "logically prior to the social"), the physical objectness of the bones, and of the animal that deposited them, was not and is not constructed. Despite its apparent concerns about ontological gerrymandering, constructionism finds it easy to agree with objectivism in the claim that whereas contracts, group solidarity, beliefs, conflicts, meanings, and the like, are social products, made reality, the sheer physicality of certain objects ("naturally occurring objects") is not. This tendency to agreement extends, moreover, to the (usually subtle) conviction that while the former products (contracts, etc.) are indeed real, because they are *social* products (i.e., human-made) they are of a lesser degree or sort of reality, by comparison to the latter, "the *real* (physical) object." Thus, the persistent question: Who was right, Grant or Owen, or neither?

Notes

1. My account is based on Desmond (1984); see also Desmond (1982).
2. Qualify them respectively as "theoretical" and "practical" perspectives, if you like, although so doing can lead to unnoticed confusions down the road.
3. The bias shows, for instance, in my repetition (above) of the vocabulary of distinction between the *ordinary* participant-member" ("ordinary actor," "ordinary language," etc.) and the "scientific analyst-observer," who, when acting as such, is no longer "ordinary."
4. By "discursive" I mean most importantly a self-consciously reflexive language-use. It should carry no implication to the effect that other activities (nondiscursive activities) are ever devoid of language.
5. In addition to Geertz's (1973, 1988) well-known essays, for example, see Strathern (1980), Fabian (1983), and several of the papers in Clifford and Marcus (1986); and regarding struggles over "the objectivity question" in historiography, see Novick (1988). Goffman's work is also highly relevant, of course, especially his *Frame Analysis* (1974), wherein he negotiates with the reflexivity of studied actions, resourceful rules, boundary work, and the like (cf. Hazelrigg 1992).
6. Granted, Sperber's distinction between "representation" and "interpretation" is problematic. It suggests the objectivist claim that one must "get the facts of the case right" (neutral representation) before commencing the biasing work of interpretation (What do the facts mean?), but Sperber acknowledges that representational work is no more immune to prejudice than is interpretive work. While Sperber defends his distinction illustratively by the example of translating one language into another, the defense fails at least to the extent that "representing Other's language correctly" always already involves "interpreting meanings" (deciding where one word or meaning ends and another begins, etc.). The white spaces of this page are integral to the meanings you make of it, even though the white spaces are probably not consciously intended by you in quite the same way as are the black spaces.
7. And not only explanation, of course; justification comes under objectivism's move as well. "There is a major folk theory," as Lakoff nominates it, "according to which being objective is being fair, and human judgment is subject to error or likely to be biased. Consequently, decisions concerning people should be made on 'objective' grounds as often as possible. It is the major way that people who make decisions avoid blame" (1987, p. 184).

8. As Sperber notes, anthropologists have hardly been immune to this short-circuiting—despite what I said earlier about the "obvious" work of translation facing the ethnographer of an "exotic" culture: "Ethnographers maintain a fiction according to which all the representations synthesized in their interpretations are genuine and truthful descriptions kindly provided by the people whom they call, off-handedly and rather naively, 'informants'" (Sperber [1982] 1985, p. 22). The standard assumption is that the performance of words is meant always only, or primarily, as conveyance of information (cf. Favret-Saada [1977] 1980, pp. 9, 25–28).

9. The "vernacular resources" at hand in claims-making activities, although we tend to valorize them separately as "cognitive structures" (symbolic forms, classificatory schemes, etc.), are embodied social structures that provide the terrain on which simplistic architectures of "base and superstructure" (i.e., "exististic conditions and representations," etc.) can be fashioned.

10. Critics who charge that this argument must mean that all points of view (all truths, moralities, etc.) are equally valid fail to note the next question: "Equally valid" from which/whose point of view? The charge continues to presuppose objectivism's framing, in which some anonymous authority judges as if from a God's-eye point of view (or from object's point of view). Traditionally, of course, that is what most claims-making activity has been about, at root: who succeeds in capturing the God's-eye (or object's) point of view, making it their own without seeming to, winning at least acquiescence in it or, better, the legitimacy of a matter-of-fact rightness that the losers of the contest will then defend in acts of loyalty to a "we" (solidarity, communal faith, patriotism, etc.). Lest there be misunderstanding of my point, I am *not* disparaging that process as a process of solidarity. At some general abstract level—theorized in the Rousseauist notion of noncontractual conditions of contract, for instance—sociality *is* that process of solidarity. But the tradition of a God's-eye (or object's) point of view, and contests for control of it, are not ordained by any metaphysical necessity.

11. I should emphasize that the agreement is not "merely in words" (in the sense of the "purely linguistic act," which always leaves in remainder what it depends on but can never breach, the "extralinguistic object"). It is, when it is, an agreement in the practice of an object world, which is also to say a practice of subject (or "subjective positions").

12. Which is not to say that the shared points of view, "even" in natural science, have been classless, genderless, and so forth. The shared point of view that becomes the view from nowhere has surely never been randomly selected from all actual points of view.

13. This remains largely so, despite the weight of arguments by critics such as Thomas Kuhn, Bruno Latour, and Andrew Pickering.

References

Clifford, James and George E. Marcus (eds.). 1986. *Writing Culture*. Berkeley: University of California Press.

Desmond, Adrian. 1982. *Archetypes and Ancestors*. London: Blond and Briggs.

———. 1984. "Interpreting the Origin of Mammals." *Zoological Journal of the Linnaean Society* 82:7–16.

Fabian, Johannes. 1983. *Time and the Other*. New York: Columbia University Press.

Favret-Saada, Jeanne. [1977] 1980. *Deadly Words*. Translated by Catherine Cullen. Cambridge: Cambridge University Press.

Geertz, Clifford. 1973. "Thick Description." Pp. 3–30 in *The Interpretation of Cultures*, edited by Clifford Geertz. New York: Basic Books.

————. 1988. *Works and Lives: The Anthropologist as Writer*. Stanford: Stanford University Press.

Goffman, Erving. 1974. *Frame Analysis*. Cambridge, MA: Harvard University Press.

Hazelrigg, Lawrence. 1986. "Is There a Choice between 'Constructionism' and 'Objectivism'?" *Social Problems* 33:S1–S13.

————. 1989. *Claims of Knowledge*. Gainesville: University Presses of Florida.

————. 1992. "Reading Goffman's Framing as Provocation of a Discipline." *Human Studies* 15:239–64.

Knorr-Cetina, Karin. 1989. "Spielarten des Konstruktivismus." *Sozial Welt* 40:86–96.

Lakoff, George. 1987. *Women, Fire, and Dangerous Things*. Chicago: University of Chicago Press.

Nagel, Thomas. 1986. *The View from Nowhere*. New York: Oxford University Press.

Novick, Peter. 1988. *That Noble Dream: The "Objectivity Question" and the American Historical Profession*. Cambridge: Cambridge University Press.

Schneider, Joseph W. 1985. "Social Problems Theory: The Constructionist View." *Annual Review of Sociology* 11:209–29.

Spector, Malcolm and John I. Kitsuse. [1977] 1987. *Constructing Social Problems*. Hawthorne, NY: Aldine de Gruyter.

Sperber, Dan. [1982] 1985. *On Anthropological Knowledge*. Cambridge: Cambridge University Press.

Strathern, Marilyn. 1980. "No Nature, No Culture: The Hagen Case." Pp. 174–222 in *Nature, Culture and Gender*, edited by C. P. MacCormack and M. Strathern. Cambridge: Cambridge University Press.

Woolgar, Steve and Dorothy Pawluch. 1985. "Ontological Gerrymandering: The Anatomy of Social Problems Explanations." *Social Problems* 32:214–27.

22

Moral Mimesis and Political Power: Toward a Rhetorical Understanding of Deviance, Social Control, and Civic Discourse

Richard Harvey Brown

The Sea of Faith
Was once, too, at the full . . . .
But now I only hear
Its melancholy, long, withdrawing roar . . . .
—Matthew Arnold, *Dover Beach*

We need a redescription of liberalism as the hope that culture as a whole
can be "poeticized" rather than as the Enlightenment hope that it can be
"rationalized" or "scientized." That is, we need to substitute the hope that
chances for fulfillment of idiosyncratic fantasies will be equalized for the
hope that everyone will replace "passion" or fantasy with "reason."
—Richard Rorty, *Contingency, Irony, and Solidarity*

My project here is to uncover some rhetorics of moral representation by
which people encode what is taken as good, normal, or permissible
without negative sanction. I assume that in these rhetorics there is a
radical entanglement between "poetic" and "political" practices—that
is, between the formalization of moral discourses, the privileges of their
practitioners, and political and economic power. By untangling these
relationships, we can gain insights into the ways in which morality and
deviance not only have been fashioned through conscious acts, but also
how they have been imposed historically, structurally, and discursively.
Such a move would also help link micro- and macrolevels within sociological discourse. I believe this extends the work of Ibarra and Kitsuse
and relates it to a larger literature and project.

Rhetorical analysis can contribute to this project by revealing homolo-
gies between stylistic and social practices. It can treat truth and persuasion, and morality and politics, within a single framework. Thus rhetorical analysis may help us understand how the representation of morality

re-creates and transmits forms of power, and how power shapes and deploys forms of morality and its violations. Through rhetorical awareness and criticism, moral norms are relocated in the act of symbolic construction, and no longer are regarded as sacred or natural facts that symbols subserviently convey. Moral norms are not viewed merely as objective products, but also as symbolic processes that are inherently persuasive. Humans enact morality not merely by legislating it rationally, but also by performing it rhetorically. In this view, elaborated also by Ibarra and Kitsuse, ethics are not based on some extralinguistic rationality, because rationality itself is demystified and reconstituted as a historical construction and deployment by human rhetors. Logic, reason, and ethics all are brought down from their absolute, preexistent heights into the creative, contextual web of history and action (Brown 1987, pp. 64–79).

Dominant moral discourses define which experiences and statements are to be taken as good or evil, normal or deviant, legal or illegal, courteous or rude. Such categories and distinctions come to be ordered as a hierarchy of values. The allocating of persons and practices into subordinate categories within these moral hierarchies also constitutes them as subordinate persons and practices in the social hierarchy. Thus, categories of moral value, hierarchies of social worth, and structures of domination tend to converge. In this view, social conflict is composed of multiple continuous jurisdictional disputes over the boundaries and interpretation of the relevant categories, and jurisprudential disputes over who and what shall be their incumbents. Hence the dominance of one moral discourse or one set of categories and the dominance of certain political positions and social groups are entangled.

To understand such interchanges between political and moral representation, the key question no longer is *what* the universal good or evil is. Instead, the focus is on *how* morality and its violation are constructed, both textually and socially, in specific historical contexts. In this view, representations of moral conduct become true descriptions not by correspondence to their noumenal objects, but by conformity to orthodox practices of writing and reading the social text.

Morality normally appears to inhere in actions and not in the categorial discourse that constitutes such actions as actions and as the *sorts* of actions that they are taken to be. The "naturalism" of morality, however, is not because our words reflect a reality external to discourse, but because the discursive construction of that reality is operating so transparently that it goes unnoticed. But every representation is always a representation from some point of view, within some frame of vision. Thus, in this perspective, the dominant morality is the one that has "made it" socially and, thence, which denies the necessary partiality of its own modes of representation. Moral mimesis is therefore inherently ideological when naturalized, because it thereby excludes from consciousness the possibility of alternative valid versions of things as they are. Thus, to reveal the practices by which things take on meaning and value is to disclose the ideology that is encoded in the "modes of production" of moral norms—those processes of human inscription that are collapsed into and held captive by a static moral code that is the product of these very processes.

Like means of economic production, the modes of morality production also tend to be concentrated in the hands of a few. Of course, language, the principal such mode, is universally available to all socialized members of any community. But moral norms are not produced through any speech, performance, or image-making whatever, but mainly through those discourses that have achieved hegemonic legitimacy. Schizophrenic paralogia, coke talk, or racetrack gossip at most create only very local realities shared by a politically impotent few.

I attempt here to develop these ideas into a more general framework for assessing relations between moral mimesis and political power or, more strongly, moral mimesis as political power. Many microprocessual studies of moral discourse and deviance have been done by ethnographers and sociolinguists, and numerous researchers have investigated macrostructural aspects of legitimation and domination. My aim in the present essay is to conjoin these two levels and discourses, and to show how the interactionist approach can be fruitfully applied at the macrosocietal level. For this project, I conjoin ideas on racism and stigma developed by Herbert Blumer, with perspectives on knowledge/power developed by Michel Foucault. My chief examples are of slavery, and of relations between moral representation of cultures and ideological legitimation of states. I try to show how the authority of states is achieved by the suppression of cultural difference. In early processes of state formation, such cultural violence may take the form of "ethnocide," the elimination of entire cultures, sometimes through the physical elimination of their bearers. Other states, though founded in conquest, may later order different cultures within them through systems of distinction and hierarchy. India provides an example, with parallels between its colonial and postcolonial periods. If a critical rhetorical or social constructionist approach can address both microprocessual as well as macrostructural phenomena, it may also be a fitting mode of civic discourse for constructing both life world and system in modern societies.

Moral Representation as Ideological Legitimation

Sociologists of deviance and critics of ideology have shown how naming is a form of social control. To be called a son and not a lover implies a different role and identity, different rights and duties, different norms and sanctions. Such categories and their use as labels not only *describe* a prevailing reality. Insofar as societies are discursively enacted, they also *constitute* that social reality. Membership categories are not discovered as manifestations of a predefined social reality, but are apprehended in and through the very process by which they are deployed.

Such naming not only is a way to get others to do what one wants; it also gets them to *be* what one wants. To describe a membership category is to attribute a moral character to its incumbents. If, on occasion, Mary dresses gaudily, steals, and takes money from her boyfriends, she is rendered "the kind of person" who could do that sort of thing. People project attributes and expectable actions onto Mary that constitute and essentialize her as, say, a "loose woman," despite her unique circumstances and biography. In short, once cast into a category, the incumbents are conventionally regarded as being governed not by experiential contingencies, but by maxims of conduct inherent in the categories themselves. Thus, classifications—such as true or false, good or bad, legal or criminal, sane or mad—also are definitions of personhood, hierarchies of value, and forms for power.

Put slightly differently, certain traits and not others are invested with social significance and attributed to or claimed by persons whose personal or group identity is thereby constituted. In this way, a set of logical distinctions becomes homologous to a hierarchy of social distinctions. This hierarchy is not only a system of signification, but also a structure of domination. A key instrument of this process of description/domination is the "list"—a set of elements selected and assembled to form a coherent moral gestalt. Thus unified, the listed features constitute a generic description and render the category available for application. However, the boundaries and contents of these social categories are inherently contestable. This is because every listing is accompanied by the problem of translating it into practical applications—that is, in each case of use, the behavior to which listed items refer needs to be specified, and this process in principle can be negotiated. Hence, legitimated domination always is inherently open to righteous defiance. Indeed, such defiance can even reinforce the system of domination, as long as it is articulated in the categories of the regnant code.

Because categories are used not as mere labels but as methods for organizing perceptions, knowledge, and moral relationships, modification of the category in which a person is placed alters the meaning of his or her behavior. For example, a Mexican peasant woman may say to her husband when he comes home drunk and smelling of another woman, "What kind of *father* are you!?" to which he may reply, "I am a *man!*" Everyday moral judgments thus cannot be adequately explained in terms of universal moral codes. One also has to look at specific instances of application. To ignore these enactments is ideological, since it leads us to incorporate our own position into a definition of what is moral that presumes to be nonlocal. Instead of attempting to say what morality is in general terms, if we look at moral reasoning itself in concrete social and historical settings we discover that it is eminently practical, and that practical reasoning is always morally organized (Jayyusi 1984, p. 201; see Sacks 1963).

These processes of naming by which persons form images of themselves as members of a certain group are reciprocal and collective: In characterizing others as different, one also characterizes one's own group as different from them. "This is equivalent to placing the two groups in relations to each other or defining their positions vis-à-vis each other" (Blumer 1988, p. 198).

This relational and structural character of group relations and prejudices can be highlighted by thinking of various personal feelings not as psychological attitudes but as expressions of the position of one's own group in relation to others. For example, the feelings of snobbism or superiority in one group place members of subordinate groups *below*; feelings of alienation place other groups *beyond*; feelings of moral right in relation to group privileges place others *outside*; feelings of fear place others too close. This structural aspect of moral ideas is captured in the universal attribute of subordinated groups, that these "others" are all right "in their place" (p. 199). This was recognized explicitly by one member of the ruling group in South Africa some decades ago:

> No one ever dreams, in the ordinary course, of the employment of white unskilled labour. . . . [I]t is rigidly tabooed. It is socially discountenanced. It is condemned outright as calculated to lower the general standard and status of the whites in the eyes of the Blacks, and so to menace that prestige which is the only real support of the white man's presence in the county. (*The Chinese Labour Question* 16/17, quoted by Meer 1987, p. 61)

In sum, notions of cultural difference readily become systems of judgment by which one group marks off and dominates or resists others. These ideas and practices are discursive. That is, "through talk, tales, stories, gossip, anecdotes, messages, pronouncements, news accounts, orations, sermons, preachments, and the like, definitions are presented and feelings are expressed . . . . and a sense of group position is set" (Blumer 1988, pp. 202–3).

Moral Classification and Social Stratification Among Peoples

This relation between moral classification and social stratification can be seen in writings on cultural differences within and between societies and civilizations throughout the ages. Much of this writing is devoted to assigning specific cultures or cultural traits to their proper category, such as Greek versus barbarian, Christian versus infidel, civilized versus primitive, or modern versus traditional. While writers may disagree as to the nature and boundaries of particular categories, nearly all believe that such categories and their members exist and can be identified. My question is how power relations infuse such categories and how instances of difference are adjudicated (Root 1989).

Within the colonial situation, for example, the system of judgment produces differences that become visible as such within the system of power. In such a system, each instance of difference is fitted into a hierarchy of values that has been established in advance. Differences are recognized as traits that mark the culture as infidel or savage or otherwise in need of Christian, or Chinese, or Islamic civilization or assistance. Thus, the system of judgment is legitimated by the politically generated empirical evidence, and the political system is legitimated by the logical cohesion of the system of judgment (Root 1989). An example is provided by Lord Frederick Lugard, Governor of British Nigeria:

> As Roman imperialism laid the foundation of modern civilization, and led the wild barbarians of these islands [Britain] along the path of progress. So in Africa today we are repaying the debt, and bringing to the dark places of the earth—the abode of barbarism and cruelty—the torch of culture and progress, while ministering to the material needs of our own civilization. . . . . [W]e hold these countries because it is the genius of our race to colonize, to trade, and to govern. (1922, in Carnoy 1974, front piece)

In this manner, cultural difference becomes political deviance, and cultural representation becomes ideological legitimation. The genius of the British, the barbarism and cruelty of the Africans, the use of an essentializing "the" for groups, the invocation of the idea of progress, the analogic parallel (civilizing ancient Romans are to barbarian early British as civilizing contemporary British are to barbarian contemporary Africans)—all this turns logical distinctions into moral hierarchies and orders them into a temporal development crowned by British rule.

These ideological functions are not contrary to the "truth value" of the cultural markings. On the contrary, the more that such markings are generated in consistency with the accepted system of representation that guarantees their truth, the more they are seen as natural and inhering in the persons or practices so marked. The classifications and their members, or the stigmas and the persons who bear them, may be so fully enmeshed that the acts and functions of labeling go unnoticed. The artifactuality of the classification system is reduced to the factuality of its contents, and these facts are viewed as mere things rather than as things made. By such processes of objectification, the moral hierarchy of classifications becomes less available to people's awareness. This enhances its ideological power, as is suggested by the naturalization of apartheid in South Africa in terms of the supposedly biological category of race:

> Colour . . . . is in the natural order of things, the actual, the only, and the ultimate arbiter and determinant of the white man's role and its limitations in South Africa. The white who attempts to ignore that declasses himself. He degenerates socially ipso facto. He is ostracized. He sinks and loses self-respect. (T. G. 13, 1908, p. 16, quoted by Meer 1987, p. 62)

Not only does the dominant group dominate by marking off the dominated as different and thereby inferior; they also must mark themselves as different and thereby superior. That is, they must continually construct authority internally, or else become subject to the same negative labeling that marks their subordinates. This also means that any trait or behavior can readily come to be identified as deviant or treasonous, and that any member of the dominant group or any internal minority or social group can suddenly seem dangerous to the authorities (Root 1989).

State Morality and Cultural Violence

These cognitive, moral, and political processes go on within states as well as between colonizers and colonized. Indeed, both colonists and state builders within new nations operate at a critical ideological juncture, for nowhere are the notions of normal, familiar action and given systems of difference in greater jeopardy than at the external frontier of the empire or the internal frontier of the state. It is here that the conquerors confront not only unfamiliar Others but also unfamiliar selves. Thus, the process of state formation may be seen as a kind of internal colonization, ethnocide, and maintenance of authority by dominant groups through labeling and suppression. An example is provided by Las Sietes Partides, 1252–1284, a document of the early reconquest of Spain:

> Men sometimes become insane and lose their prudence and understanding, as, for instance, where unfortunate persons, and those who despair of everything, renounce the faith of Our Lord Jesus Christ, and become Moors . . . . they are guilty of a very great wickedness and treason. . . . . Where fore we order that all those who are guilty of this wickedness shall lose all their possessions, ... and, in addition . . . . shall be put to death. (cited by Root 1989)

A similar process of making/labeling went on in the Soviet Union, where it often was a cynically plotted strategy as much as an unconsciously naturalized process. For example, the dissident writer Petor Grigorinko compares the vocabularies of criminality and of insanity as media for the construction and control of deviance:

> If you say to the interrogator that there is no freedom of the press in the USSR, that means that you are a slanderer, a criminal. If you say the same thing to a doctor-psychiatrist he says that this is delirium, a mental illness. If you say to the interrogator that elections should be made elections . . . . that means you are a criminal. . . . . If you repeat the same thing to a psychiatrist he will ascribe to you "concepts of reforms." . . . . And so you have a whole clump of symptoms of schizophrenia. In order to be cured of such "illnesses," you have to renounce your own convictions. . . .And if you are unwilling to thus recuperate, you will be subjected to an indefinitely long "treatment"—lifelong. This gives you something to think about. (1982)

Although there have been many grounds for stigmatization and suppression in the Soviet Union and elsewhere, many of the dissidents cum mental patients have been ethnic protesters and cultural nationalists. Thus, we might even say that states and civilizations, when they are "successful," are ethnocidal. This means that what would appear as cultural differences within a society are violently obliterated as a way (or precondition) of consolidating the authority of the state. Since the essence of the state is dominion over the diverse,

> The State endeavors to become and proclaims itself to be the totality of the social body and the master of its various organs. . . . . As the embodiment of the One, the state refuses the Many and is horrified of difference. (Clastres 1977)

It could even be said that the state "creates" difference by making it a symbolic public reality. That is, the state itself is constructed through reproducing cultural difference as cultural deviance.

The qualities that might mark a group as deviant are labile, and can shift from one group to another or be invoked alternately for the same group by different institutions of control. For example, as Root (1989) noted in documents of imperial Spain, a single negative quality could be used in one text to define Muslims, in another to define Castilian peasants, in another to define unruly women, in still another to define Mexican idolaters, and on and on as more deviants were revealed as such to the authorities. Indeed, the categories used to marginalize various groups in Spain were easily shifted to refer to a specifically Mexican type of deviance or effluvia from within Spain itself, the deviance that is the result of treason or betrayal. Similarly, in contemporary Western societies, the idea of the primitive has authorized the control of societies outside the West and of women and minorities within it (Torgovnick 1990; Street 1975). For example, explorers, novelists, and anthropologists employed the same metaphors and polar opposition to contrast the virgin, exotic, primitives of the New World with literate, hierarchical, commercial, property-owners of the old, much as women had been compared to men within European society itself.

This labeling process also goes on between states, and is applied to cultural violence itself. For example, what the United States calls a "peace-keeping mission" is called a "military intervention" by its rivals. Such differences between nations can be created by highlighting extreme moments of violence, such as the sacrifice of humans by Aztecs or, conversely, the massacres or enslavements of entire villages by Spaniards. These extreme moments of violence are made to appear either as typical or as aberrational, depending on the rhetorical resources of the groups trying to impose or evade a negative label. For example, whereas Spaniards have tended to see the Aztecs as inherently violent, they generally have viewed their own colonial enterprise as an orderly business punctuated by some regrettable (and aberrant) instances. Among competing colonizers, however, the "aberrant" and the "normal" are likely to be reversed. For example, the *Leyenda Negra*, or Black Legend, of Spanish atrocities in the New World became a way for English imperialists to distinguish their supposedly benign project from the destructive one of the Spanish. Similarly, parallels between the cultural oppression of colonization and the cultural oppression of state formation are likely to be overlooked by leaders of newly independent nations and their sympathizers.

States and Slavery

The transmission of ideologies of racism and slavery between Islamic and Christian European peoples also illustrates the transferability of discourses of domination from one culture or population to another. Both Christianity and Islam arose in relatively color-blind environments, and both affirmed theologically the unity of mankind. Yet both produced slave-holding societies that shared remarkably similar discourses of domination (Davis 1984, p. 39; Lewis 1990).

Black Africans, Ibn Khaldun said, "have little [that is essentially] human and have attributes that are quite similar to those of dumb animals." Magdisi referred to the despised Zanj as "people of black color, flat noses, kinky hair, and little under-standing or intelligence." In fact, the Arabic word for slave, *abd*, came to mean only a black, whether slave or free. In 1855 Arabs of Western Arabia rebelled against their Ottoman overlords because the latter banned the slave trade. Shaykh Jamal, the ruler of Mecca, denounced the ban "as contrary to the holy law of Islam. Because of this anti-Islamic act . . . . the Turks had become apostates and heathens" and therefore subject to legal killing or enslavement (Lewis 1990). As late as 1960, Muslims on pilgrimage to Mecca were reported to sell African slaves on arrival, "using them as living traveler's cheques" (Sir Ernest Henry Shackleton, quoted in Davis 1984, p. 317; also see Miers 1975).

The European slave trade had its origins in the traffic by light-skinned Arabs, Berbers, and Persians of sub-Saharan Africans. More curious, and less easy to explain, is the remarkable parallelism between medieval Islamic and later Western racist discourse. For example, Bernard Lewis (1990) quotes depictions of the Zanj by Muslim writers from the eighth to the fifteenth centuries that characterized Africans as ugly, stupid, dishonest, frivolous, foul smelling, filled with music and rhythm, inclined to simple piety, and dominated by animal lust. In his study of the stereotyped "Sambo personality" of *American* slavery, Stanley Elkins (1976) noted exactly the same features. Two quotations may illustrate this similarity of characterization, one from Ibn Butlan, the other from Thomas Jefferson:

> The blacker they are the uglier their faces. . . . . Dancing and rhythm are ingrained in them . . . . [T]hey can endure hard work . . . . but the smell of their armpits. (Ibn Butlan, quoted in Davis 1990, p. 38)
> They [have] a very strong and disagreeable odor. . . . . [They] proceed from want of forethought. . . . . [T]hey are more ardent after their female. . . . . Their griefs are transient. . . . . [They] participate more of sensation than reflection. . . . . Comparing them to the whites . . . . in reason [they are] much inferior. . . . . In music they are more generally gifted. (Jefferson 1964, pp. 133–35)

How might we explain this remarkable parallelism? One source might be cultural borrowing—from European scholars who learned the Greek and Latin classics in the Middle East, to European slave merchants and their apologists who had direct dealings with Arab slave traders. Another, more sociological account is provided by Stanley Elkins. Elkins compared Africans in slavery in America to free African groups in Africa, and both of these to Jews who were alternately free and later enslaved by Nazis in Europe. He found that neither the free Africans nor the free Jews displayed the "Sambo personality" of the racist stereotype, whereas both Africans and Jews in slavery did so, despite the great difference between these two cultural groups on other dimensions. Thus, it seems that the discourse and practice of slavery itself creates the "Sambo personality," both as a stereotype held by slaveholders to legitimate their domination, and as a tactic of adaptation used by the oppressed to survive psychically and to limit exploitation.

Other studies that support Elkins's contentions are by John Ogbu (1978), who compares various minorities in terms of their castelike position, which promotes feelings of inferiority and discourages political participation. Ogbu studied caste systems in Japan, New Zealand, Great Britain, South Africa, India, and the United States, and found that such excluded minorities were herded into menial jobs and did poorly in school and on IQ and other standardized tests. One group Ogbu writes about is the Burakumin, a pariah class in Japan. The Burakumin were emancipated in 1871, but they remain severely disadvantaged, working at menial jobs and performing poorly in school. Burakumin who have come to the Unites States, however, do as well as other Japanese. The reason, Ogbu says, is that they are not overwhelmed by the feelings of powerlessness and inferiority that generally hold back castelike groups.

Ogbu also points to the example of black West Indians, who have been found to rise much faster in the United States than American blacks. Ogbu also examines West Indians in Britain, where they do not do nearly as well as in the United States. In America, says Ogbu, West Indians act like Asians, where in Britain they are more like American blacks, with lower IQ scores and higher rates of unemployment, crime, and illegitimacy. The difference is that West Indians in Britain

> regard themselves as British subjects, not as immigrants, and when they encounter discrimination they do not react the way an immigrant does. An immigrant doesn't mind weeping the streets, because he thinks the future will be better, if not for himself then for his children. (quoted by Matusow 1989, p. 289)

Low-income West Indians or Burakumin in the United States see themselves as better off than they were back home, and they adopt the discourse of equality and achievement of their new context. By contrast, American blacks have no "back home"; thus they compare themselves unfavorably with middle-class whites, and tend to adopt the very racist discourses that have contributed to their subordination. In sum, stigmas parallel group domination, and castelike positions may have parallel moral vocabularies from one country or historical period to another.

Critical Rhetoric, Relativism, and Civic Discourse

If we take the rhetorical approach seriously, it would seem that everything available to human understanding is constructed through lan-

guage and that, indeed, in Derrida's famous phrase, "there is nothing
outside the text" (1974). Such a position radically undermines moral
discourses, since these are almost invariable anchored in some extralinguistic foundation, be it God, the ancestors, conscience, or a world of
facts. Moreover, the rhetorical perspective would seem also to subvert
its own epistemological warrant, since social science explanations would
seem to have no status more privileged than any other. This also would
appear to vitiate any claim to criticality, because the moral position of
social analysis seems to be relativized along with everything else. Thus,
scholars of the linguistic turn often withdraw into conservatism or even
nihilism, retreat into an eleatory estheticism, or surrender to an anarchism of "anything goes" (e.g., respectively Lyotard or Derrida, Baudrillard, and Feyerabend).

Thus the practical scope of rhetoric seems limited to a politics of resistance, since rhetorical deconstruction relativizes the grounds, goals, or
even stable meaning of any positive social historical project. As Lyotard
suggested,

> The real political task today . . . . is to carry forward the resistance that
> writing offers to established thought, to what has already been done, to
> what everyone thinks, to what is well known, to what is widely recog-
> nized, to what is 'readable,' to everything which can change its form and
> make itself acceptable to opinion in general. (1988, p. 302)

After rhetorical criticism has done its work of resistance, however, we
still are faced with the challenge of establishing moral authority and
inventing positive values as central elements of any polity. In addition to
a postmodern hermeneutic of suspicion (Ricoeur 1983, 1986) then, we
also need a "hermeneutic of affirmation." This positive task is to imagine
more adequate narratives for our political community, and to show how
academic writing can help create these narratives. Such an affirmative
hermeneutic rejects realist, positivist, and foundationalist views of language, ethics, and reality, but finds in rhetoric or deconstruction a potential affirmation of the human authorship of social reality and a possible antidote for discourses of elitism, technical exclusivity, or political
domination. For example, rhetorical deconstruction can demystify elite
technical discourses and thus make them available to popular understanding and moral interpretation.

Interpretive openness and moral sensibility through critical rhetorical
methods are possible only within the context of certain social and historical conditions.Thus the reform of inquiry into social problems requires
more than the replacement of positivistic constructions with rhetorical
deconstructions or reconstructions. More importantly, it requires a new

vision and new practices of the public space. Traditional social science gave an implicit account of the public space and a model of the ideal citizen. Disciplined inquiry into the laws of society provided an ideal of general political discussion; the scholar's suspension of self-interest provided a model of the citizen, who would make judgments about the social whole according to general reason instead of partisan passions. In short, ideals implicit in social science became interwoven with the very fabric of the liberal polity. Science, in the words of Walter Lippmann, was "the discipline of democracy."

For these reasons, however brilliantly positivism or foundationalism have been criticized by academics, they remain powerful supports for institutions and practices that few of us are willing to abandon: academic freedom, professional judgment, civil liberties, and due process of law (Peters 1990). As a child of liberalism and the Enlightenment, social science has been a major ideological force in the victory of civility over violence, reason and evidence over passion and prejudice, clear communication over cloudy commitment. Thus, we should not dismiss positivist social science too blithely, nor imagine that all one needs is a more congenial vocabulary. Instead, if we are to make social constructionism and deconstructive social theory consequential in the public and political arenas, we must consider their ramifications outside the halls of academe. Despite its profound achievements, foundationalism has become philosophically untenable and liberalism politically exhausted. What, then, can be a substitute way of conceiving the moral nature and political functions of social science? Clearly, any response entails relativism and, with this, the fear that usually accompanies the view of the world as uncertain. Acceptance of rhetoric, social constructionism, and relativity undermines absolutisms and invites a broader tolerance for alternative perspectives. In an increasingly diverse and conflictual world, the need for such an openness of discourse is greater than ever. But politics is also about closure, and power about exclusion. We still need moral criteria to make and measure actions and decisions. Whose discourse and which moral criteria shall we use? Does not rhetorical theory relativize any possible moral political practice?

Several answers to the fear of relativism can be made. First, fewer atrocities in the history of the world have happened as a result of excessive tolerance than as a result of absolutism. Which is worse, the possibility that evil will be tolerated in the name of cultural relativism, or the promise that future atrocities will be justified by some group's assurance that they are absolutely right? Whereas tyranny is or depends on absolutism, in a democratic polity we are and must be relativists in practice because we exercise judgments as citizens in shaping or finding ethical truth. Democratic practice requires prudent judgment, and such judgment presupposes rhetorical reflection on political experience that is inherently contingent.

Relativism does not entail a society without standards. Rather, the conjoining of rhetoric and epistemology helps us to recognize when, where, and how the standards are to be cooperatively established, constantly renewed, and periodically reshaped. Hence, unlike absolutism, relativism is reflective about its own limits. This can be shown through the work of Alisdair MacIntyre. MacIntyre deplores the multiplicity of incommensurable local discourses that characterize our postmodern condition. Insofar as incommensurability reigns, a community beyond the local must remain a distant and perhaps impossible dream. But is the picture really as bleak as MacIntyre paints it? Incommensurability is largely a product of people's certainty about their own version of truth and their own particular vocabulary and grammar (MacIntyre 1981, pp. 69ff., 1988, pp. 326–48). For most practical purposes, however, such competing advocates do not need to persuade one another. Instead, they must only gain the adherence of a relevant audience—one usually composed of *others* who are affected by the matter at hand but whose values are still open to discussion and debate. Protesters, as MacIntyre notes in *After Virtue* (1981, p. 66), talk past one another, as one side grounds arguments in "rights" and the other in "law." But they do not talk past those who will decide the outcome of the controversy. This public assesses the coherence and fidelity of the rival stories told by these factions and makes decisions usually for good reasons (Fisher 1992, p. 204).

This sort of reasonableness will not satisfy those who demand consensus based on strict logical computation. But it does comply with another notion of rationality, the idea of rationality as a social process, of rationality as the civic intelligence that is displayed when people are open to argument and willing and able to take good reasons into account. Thus the fear of relativism can be partly allayed by shifting from a conception of truth as discovery or product, toward a view of truth as invention or process. In their different ways, this shift characterizes the writings of Walter Fisher (1987, 1992), Jurgen Habermas (1983), Chaim Perelman (1969), and Richard Rorty (1979, 1982, 1989). For example, Rorty has argued that it "is the vocabulary of practice rather than of theory, of action rather than contemplation, in which one can say something useful about truth" (1982, p. 162). Rorty establishes the centrality of language, allowing the "text" and conversation to become loci of inquiry. He thereby orients us toward communicative *process* with respect to the practical life of a civic or scholarly community. In this sense, pragmatism does not collapse into relativism, but "the pragmatist knows no better way to explain his convictions than to remind his interlocutor of the position they both are in, the contingent starting points they both share, the floating, ungrounded conversations of which they are both members" (Rorty 1982, pp. 173–74; cf. Cheney 1987). Even if we accept Rorty's deconstruction of epistemology, and of ethics as well, the consequences of such a move are open. And, for better or worse, it does make it harder to isolate any general or transcultural standards of judgment (Hacking 1986; Rabinow 1986, p. 236).

Michel Foucault explored this problem by showing how Western notions of reason, ethics, and identity are historically embedded in institutionalized patterns of discourse. Thus, despite pressures from the French Left, Foucault was reluctant to designate utopian goals or even a particular social arrangement as *the* ideal implied by his historical and social criticism. Instead, Foucault argued for an institutionalized social criticism. In his historical genealogies of major institutions of society, such as mental health, criminal justice, and the human sciences, and in his later analyses of power (1977, 1980), Foucault sought to expose various modes of domination. Foucault conceived of power as interactive and enabling, and best understood through analysis of both resistance and empowerment. In this sense, Foucault promoted a critique of knowledge/power that would treat it *in action,* for that is the only place it truly exists (Foucault 1980; see Dallmayr 1984; Cheney 1987). Thus Foucault also responds to relativism by focusing on the *how* rather than the *what* of truth or virtue, and he implies a form of knowledge/power that may be more open and democratic than existing ones.

Kenneth Burke also speaks of critical rhetoric as a civic discourse. Unlike most literary theorists, Burke never separated action from contemplation, willing from imagining, or poetry from power. Instead, Burke held that all intellectual activity (even the most theoretical sort that disdains politics) is itself a kind of praxis, first and foremost an *act* (Lentricchia 1983, p. 87; Cheney 1987). Burke thereby helps us to recover the classical relationship of *theory* and *praxis* through a realization of criticism's practical power. By concerning itself with the ways we make and change allegiances to key symbols of authority such as family, employer, religion, or nation, rhetorical criticism participates in the ongoing moral and practical recreation of society. As early as 1937, Burke acknowledged this dimension of his activity:

Our own program, as literary critic, is to integrate technical criticism with social criticism . . . . by taking the allegiance to the symbol of authority as our subject. We take this as our starting point and "radiate" from it. Since the symbols of authority are radically linked with [social and material] relationships, this point of departure automatically involves us in socioeconomic criticism. And since the whole purpose of a "revolutionary" critic is to contribute to a change in allegiance to the symbols of authority, we maintain our role as "propagandist" by keeping this subject ever uppermost in our concerns. (1937, Vol. 2, pp. 234–35)

More specifically, as Cheney has noted, what Burke seeks is a continual shift toward humane symbols of authority, as devices "for spreading the areas of allegiance" (Burke 1935, p. 89). Such symbols must enlist our sympathies and hopes by articulating ideals "which we should like to share" (1937, Vol. 2, p. 78). Consequently, for Burke the ideal society is one of *communion*, where the reciprocity of identification is maximized, where all have a "common stake in both cooperative and symbolic networks" (pp. 247–48), where "we the people" means the entire human race (1935). With the broadening of loyalties, a new kind of transcendence might be achieved in which opposing groups would stress and enhance their similarities and not their differences. This is the locus of social praxis for Burke—one in which ethics and politics meet on rhetorical ground (Cheney 1987).

To the extent that modern social science ignores this critical perspective and remains linguistically unreflective, it becomes part of society's mechanisms for legitimation, marginalization, and punishment. In reproducing prevailing discursive practices, an unreflective social science helps to fix persons, objects, and relations in the categories already established through institutionalized social control (Cohen 1985). By contrast, a rhetorically reflexive social science would make it evident that objects, norms, persons, and events are inseparable from the processes of representation by which they are formed. The activities of the imagination that produce facts and meanings are not simply acts of a disembodied cogito; instead, they are historically developed practices that reside in the very style in which statements are made, in the grammatical and narrative structures that compose even the discourses of science. The *what* of any system of knowledge and value is radically entangled in the *how* of its writing and speaking. For this reason, the text that is self-conscious about its own rhetorical structure is the exemplar of a nondelusional mode of writing for social scientists and, by extension, for citizens as well (Shapiro 1989, pp. 7–8; Klumpp and Hollihan 1989, p. 94).

These observations also suggest that critical rhetorical practice has an uneasy relation to its own institutionalization. This is because rhetorical criticism is transgressive, more profane than pious. It demands a generalized displacement and rearticulation of established discourses or disciplines, not a quarantined place at their margins (LaCapra 1987, p. 236). Thus the relativity of rhetorical deconstruction and its ambiguous relation to practice does not imply the endless proliferation of variety, but the agonistic elimination of error, the marginalization of trivial contentions, and the clarification of fundamental and irreducible differences. It is not a "liberal toleration of opposing views from a neutral ground, but transformation, conversion, or at least, the kind of communication which clarifies exactly what is at stake in any critical conflict" (Mitchell 1982, pp. 613–14; see Farrell 1976; Johnstone 1980). Critical rhetoric is our self-consciousness through civic discourse.

Accordingly, we need to reconstrue the discourse on social problems from explanation and verification to a conversation of scholars and citizens who seek to guide and persuade themselves and each other. Moral and civic truth are no longer seen as fixed entities discovered according to a metatheoretical blueprint of linearity or hierarchy; instead, they are invented within an ongoing self-reflective community in which "critic," "social scientist," and "citizen" become relatively interchangeable (Burke 1984; Rorty 1979). Critique of theory, method, and practice remain permanently immanent precisely because they cannot be universalized. We too are required to acknowledge the permanent immanence of our own role and identity, our rhetorical constitution of ourselves as subjects and of our fields as disciplinary objects. And then we are obliged to maintain and apply this consciousness and practice of rhetorical awareness to our common civic life.

I believe that this is how rhetorical, deconstructive discourse can be a discourse of both resistance and of affirmation. What is affirmed is the will toward knowledge and experience of the good, and this affirmation is contained in the practice of resistance, including resistance to either complacent self-endorsement or nihilistic "anything goes." Resistance will always have to be specific and contingent upon the cultural field within which it operates. It cannot be defined simply in terms of negativity or nonidentity, a la Adorno, nor will the litanies of a totalizing, collective project suffice. At the same time, the very notion of resistance may itself be problematic in its simple opposition to affirmation. After all, there are affirmative forms of resistance and resisting forms of affirmation. The space of fruitful tensions between a hermeneutics of suspicion and a hermeneutics of affirmation is always shifting. But this problem need not and should not keep us from making moral judgments.

Indeed, critical rhetoric can be a particularly suited mode of making such judgments in contemporary civic life. As noted, this is implied even while denied in the work of Alisdair MacIntyre (1988, 1981). MacIntyre described our condition as one bereft of a shared moral discourse because our social and cognitive world have been fragmented into a congeries of incommensurate claims. According to MacIntyre, moral and cognitive traditions compete with one another and cannot be reconciled as parts of a single bigger picture that could be impartially assembled, since there is no standpoint for morality and reason outside society and history. Hence, in our own age, when taken-for-granted norms of truth and virtue have been subverted by their very proliferation, we must ask, Whose justice? and which rationality will we accept? Yet contrary to his own exposition of the relativization of reason (and abandoning his earlier fruitful work on narrative), MacIntyre returns to blind logic and uncritical hermeneutics as the neutral arbiters of choices *between* traditions. Malgre MacIntyre, however, rhetoric is "the art that induces choice-making, given competing possibilities. It is also an art of address, that is, a way of engaging others persuasively" (Peters, Lyne, and Hariman 1991, p. 83). The conditions that MacIntyre describes are exactly those which call for rhetorical engagement, since it is most of all in conditions of challenge and conflict that adherents of a tradition need to address and persuade others both within and outside their own tradition. Instead of locating himself in the lineage of Aristotle and Augustine, MacIntyre might do better to claim the Sophists, Vico, and even the despised Nietzsche as his forebears. Each of them rejected universalizing reason as does MacIntyre, but unlike MacIntyre, each sought in rhetoric a way to cope. Vico, for example, spoke of prudence in civic life:

> As human affairs are governed by chance and choice . . . . , those who solely have [lawlike] truth in view only with difficulty understand the paths which these affairs take and, with still greater difficulty, their goals. The impudent scholars [such as Descartes or Hobbes] who go directly from the universally true to the singular, rupture the interconnection of life. The wise men, however, ... make a detour, as it is not possible to attain [practical wisdom] by a direct road; and the thoughts which *these* conceive promise to remain useful for a long time, at least insofar as nature permits. ([1744] 1972, p. 34)

The impudent scholars remove reason and decision-making from the practical moral contexts in which they are derived and to which they are applied. By contrast, for Vico knowledge and decision-making must be located in specific situations that are assessed prudentially in terms of the paths that these affairs take and, with more difficulty, their goals. Indeed, as many thinkers have shown, even the most scientific and abstract rationality can be put to use in specific situations only by reflective judgments that interpret the local situation and its particular requirements (e.g., Kant 1952; Makkreel 1980; Polanyi 1958; Garfinkel 1967; Cicourel 1986). These prudential forms of decision-making are inherently problematic because they refer to human situations that are characterized by chance and choice. Thus, contrary to the assumption of propagandists for universally applicable intellectual technologies, a prudent civic narration would not attempt to prescribe definitive rules for applying any theory to any practical situation (Douglas 1988; MacIntyre 1981). Instead, it would construe public discourse and decision-making as practical (rhetorical, moral, political) activities that draw on accumulated cultural wisdom.

We need neither to suppress nor to overcome the tensions of rhetorical deconstruction. Instead, we should heighten these tensions, continually rediscover and refocus them in criticism and in practice. This is our contribution as scholars to civic discourse. This is our obligation. This is our hope.

References

Arnold, Matthew 1908. "Dover Beach." In *The Poems of Matthew Arnold, 1840– 1866*. London: J. M. Dent.

Blumer, Herbert. 1988. "Race Prejudice as a Sense of Group Position." Pp. 196– 207 in *Social Order and the Public Philosophy: An Analysis and Interpretation of the Work of Herbert Blumer*, edited by Stanford M. Lyman and Arthur J. Vidich. Fayetteville: University of Arkansas Press.

Brown, Richard Harvey. 1987. *Society as Text. Essays on Rhetoric, Reason, and Reality*. Chicago: University of Chicago Press.

Burke, Kenneth. 1935. "Revolutionary Symbolism in America." Pp. 87–94 in *American Writers' Congress*, edited by H. Hart. New York: International Publishers.

———. 1937. *Attitudes Toward History*. New York: The New Republic.

———. 1984. *Permanence and Change: An Anatomy of Purpose*. Berkeley: University of California Press.

Carnoy, Martin. 1974. *Education as Cultural Imperialism*. New York: David McKay.

Cheney, George. 1987. "On Communicative Praxis and the Realization of Our Discipline's Potential." Paper presented to the Speech Communication Association, Columbus, Ohio.

Cicourel, Aaron V. 1986. "Social Measurement as the Creation of Expert Systems." Pp. 246–70 in *Metatheory in Social Science*, edited by Donald W. Fiske and Richard A. Shivider. Chicago: University of Chicago Press.

Clastres, Pierre. 1977. *Society Against the State* (La Societé contre l'Etat) . Translated by Robert Hurley. New York: Urizen Books

Cohen, Stanley. 1985. *Visions of Social Control: Crime, Punishment, and Classification*. New York: Basil Blackwell.

Dallmayr, Fred R. 1984. *Polis and Praxis: Exercises in Contemporary Political Theory*. Cambridge, MA: MIT Press.

Davis, David Brion. 1984. *Slavery and Human Progress*. New York: Oxford University Press.

Derrida, Jacques. 1974. *Of Grammatology*. Baltimore: John Hopkins University Press.

Douglas, Jack. 1988. *The Myth of the Welfare State*. New Brunswick, NJ: Transaction.

Elkins, Stanley. 1976. *Slavery: A Problem in American Intellectual and Institutional Life*. Chicago: University of Chicago Press.

Farrell, Thomas B. 1976. "Knowledge, Consensus, and Rhetorical Theory," *Quarterly Journal of Speech* 62(1, February):1–14.

Fisher, Walter R. 1987. *Human Communication as Narration: Toward a Philosophy of Reason, Value, and Action*. Columbia: University of South Carolina Press.

————. 1992. "Narration, Reason, and Community." Pp. 199–218 in *Writing the Social Text: Poetics and Politics in Social Science Discourse*, edited by Richard Harvey Brown. New York and Berlin: Aldine de Gruyter.

Foucault, Michel. 1977. *Power/Knowledge: Selected Interviews and Other Writings, 1972–1977*. Edited by Colin Gordon. New York: Pantheon.

Garfinkel, Harold. 1967. *Studies in Ethnomethodology*. Englewood Cliffs, NJ: Prentice-Hall.

Grigorinko, Petro. 1982. *Memoirs*. Translated by Thomas P. Whitney. London: Collins.

Habermas, Jurgen. 1983. "Modernity—An Incomplete Project." Pp. 3–15 in *The Anti-Aesthetic: Essays on Postmodern Culture*, edited by Hal Foster. Port Townsend, WA: Bay Press.

Hacking, Ian. 1986. "Making Up People." Pp. 222–36 in *Reconstructing Individualism: Autonomy, Individuality, and the Self in Western Thought*, edited by T. C. Heller, M. Sosna, and D. E. Wellberg. Stanford: Stanford University Press.

Jayyusi, Lena. 1984. *Categorization and the Moral Order*. Boston: Routledge and Kegan Paul.

Jefferson, Thomas. 1964. *Notes on the State of Virginia*. New York: Harper and Row.

Johnstone, Christopher Lyle. 1980. "An Aristotelian Trilogy: Ethics, Politics, and the Search for Moral Truth." *Philosophy and Rhetoric* 13(1, Winter):1–24.

Kant, Immanuel. 1952. *Critique of Judgment*. Oxford: Clarendon Press.

Klumpp, James F. and Thomas Hollihan. 1989. "Rhetorical Criticism as Moral Action," *Quarterly Journal of Speech* 75:84–97.

LaCapra, Dominik. 1987. "Criticism Today." Pp. 235–55 in *The Aims of Representation: Subject/Text/History*, edited by Murry Krieger. New York: Columbia University Press.

Lentricchia, Frank. 1983. *Criticism and Social Change*. Chicago: University of Chicago Press.

Lewis, Bernard. 1990. *Race and Slavery in the Middle East: An Historical Inquiry*. New York: Oxford University Press.

Lyotard, Jean-François. 1988. *The Postmodern Condition: A Report on Knowledge*. Minneapolis: University of Minnesota Press.

MacIntyre, Alisdair. 1981. *After Virtue: A Study in Moral Theory*. Notre Dame, IN: University of Notre Dame Press.

————. 1988. *Whose Justice? Which Rationality?* Notre Dame, IN: University of Notre Dame Press.

Makkreel, Rudolf A. 1980. "Vico and Some Kantian Reflections on Historical Judgment." *Man and World* 13:99–120.

Matusow, Barbara. 1989. "Alone Together." *Washingtonian* (November).

Meer, Fatima. 1987. "Indians within Apartheid: Indentured Labor and Group Formation in South Africa." Pp. 49–68 in *Migration and Modernization: The Indian Diaspora in Comparative Perspective*, Vol. 39, edited by Richard Harvey Brown and George V. Coelho. Williamsburg, VA: Studies in Third World Societies.

Miers, Suzanne. 1975. *Britain and the Ending of the Slave Trade*. New York: Africana.

Mitchell, T. J. 1982. "Critical Inquiry and the Ideology of Pluralism." *Critical Inquiry* 8(3, Summer):604–18.

Ogbu, John. 1978. *Minority Education and Caste: The American System in Cross Cultural Perspective*. New York: Academic Press.

Perelman, Chaim and Lucie Olbrechts-Tyteca. 1969. *The New Rhetoric: A Treatise on Argumentation*. Notre Dame, IN: University of Notre Dame Press.

Peters, John D. 1990. "Rhetorics Revival, Positivism's Persistence: Social Science, Clear Communication, and the Public Space." Pp. 224–31 in *The Postmodern Turn in Sociological Theory*, edited by Richard Harvey Brown. Special number of *Sociological Theory* 8(2).

Peters, John D., John R. Lyne, and Robert Hariman. 1991. "Review of Alisdair MacIntyre's Whose Justice? Which Rationality?" *Quarterly Journal of Speech* 77(1, February):82–84.

Polanyi, Michael. 1958. *Personal Knowledge: Toward a Post-Critical Philosophy*. Chicago: University of Chicago Press.

Rabinow, Paul. 1986. "Representations Are Social Facts: Modernity and Postmodernity in Anthropology." Pp. 194–233 in *Writing Culture: The Poetics and Politics of Ethnography*, edited by James Clifford and George Marcus. Berkeley: University of California Press.

Ricoeur, Paul. 1983. *Time and Narrative*, Vol. 1. Translated by Kathleen McLaughlin and David Pellaner. Chicago: University of Chicago Press.

―――. 1986. *Lectures on Ideology and Utopia*. Edited by George H. Taylor, New York: Columbia University Press.

Root, Deborah. 1989. "Colonial Authority and the Production of Difference: Notes on the Spanish Conquest of Mexico." Paper presented to the conference on Writing the Social Text, University of Maryland, College Park, Maryland, November.

Rorty, Richard. 1979. *Philosophy and the Mirror of Nature*. Princeton, NJ: Princeton University Press.

―――. 1982. *Consequences of Pragmatism*. Minneapolis: University of Minnesota Press.

―――. 1989. *Contingency, Irony, and Solidarity*. New York: Cambridge University Press.

Sacks, Harvey. 1963. "Sociological Description." *Berkeley Journal of Sociology* 8:1–16.

Shapiro, Michael J. 1989. *The Politics of Representation: Writing Practices in Biography, Photography, and Policy Analysis.* Madison: University of Wisconsin Press.
Street, Brian V. 1975. *The Savage in Literature: Representation of "Primitive" Society in English Fiction 1858–1920.* London: Routledge and Kegan Paul.
Torgovnick, Marianna. 1990. *Gone Primitive: Savage Intellects, Modern Lives.* Chicago: University of Chicago Press.
Vico, Giambattista. [1744] 1972. *The New Science of Giambattista Vico.* Translated by Thomas Goddard Bergin and Max Harold Frisch. Ithaca, NY: Cornell University Press.

Note

Some paragraphs of this essay also appear in my article "Cultural Representation and Ideological Domination," *Social Forces* 71, 3, March 1993.

23

How Come Prose? The Writing of Social Problems

Laurel Richardson

How and for whom we write social problems has consequences for us as theorists, the discipline of sociology, and larger publics. *How* we are expected to write affects *what* we can write about. The *form* in which we write social problems shapes its *content*. Little attention, however, has been directed to conventional constructionist writing. Virtually absent is any analysis of the basic writing form through which claims are made and knowledge delimited, namely, the deployment of *prose* as the unheralded literary form in which to report "findings."

For nearly a decade, I have been exploring alternative forms of staging sociological texts. My purposes have been several: to discover the norms; to write more interesting sociology; and to reach diverse audiences (cf. Richardson 1990). In this paper, after briefly discussing some postmodernist writing issues, I will discuss one alternative way of staging findings, *poetic representation*, and conclude with an extended example. My intent is not to argue that poetic representation is the only or even the best way to represent everything sociological; but I do claim that poetic representation is both a framework and a method for seeing through and beyond sociological naturalisms. If we are to reconsider the constructionist's project, we might well begin with its immersion in and dependence upon science-writing conventions.

Positioning

Peter Ibarra and John Kitsuse (in this volume) conclude their discussion of an interactionist agenda for the study of social problems by drawing the reader's attention to the "rhetorical forms, in the social problems process . . . . discursive practices through which the claims are constituted." They propose,

> Our task as theorists is to note the differences in meaning and conse-
> quence that the strategic uses of vernacular forms can have for the shape of
> the social problems process. . . . . [T]he study of the vernacular constitu-
> ents of social problems provides us with new ways of conceiving our
> project . . . . as well as indicating to us . . . . the theoretical language we
> employ to reconstruct those social interactions we have called "claims-
> making activities."

My theoretical positioning is that of a feminist-postmodernist- inter-
pretivist. The core of that position is the *doubt* that any discourse has a
privileged place, any method/theory a universal and general claim to
authoritative knowledge. Truth claims are suspected of masking and
serving particular interests in local, cultural, and political struggles.
Wherever truth is claimed so is power; the claim to truth is a claim to
power. Once the veil of privileged truth is lifted, the opportunities for
rethinking how we think and who can think and what we can think are
legion; also comes the possibility of alternative criteria for evaluating
sociological production. Moral implications, practical applications, esthetic pleasure, fun, performativity, credibility become other possible
criteria for choosing one discourse over another. Interpretivists can with
philosophical impunity interrupt their own discursive spaces, reflect on
their modes of production and their power interests, and explore writ-
ing/performing/teaching/sharing sociology *both* as a "science" *and* as a
public or esthetic or practical or morally charged discourse.

In the representation of social problems, interpretivists (like other
academics) use rhetorical conventions that have gone mostly unexamined, but that serve to venerate the claims-making activities of the
researcher/theorist. In order to undertake a "reconstruction" of how
constructionists "do" social problems, it is necessary for us to "deconstruct" our own writing vernaculars, our formulas, our tropes, our metaphors, our unheralded devices through which we constitute the social
problems world.

Language is a constitutive force, creating a particular view of reality.
This is as true of writing as it is of speaking, and as true of science as it is of
poetry. Producing "things" always involves value—what to produce,
what to name the productions, and what the relationship between the
producers and the named things will be. Writing "things" is no exception.
Writing always involves what Roland Barthes calls "the ownership of the
means of enunciation" (quoted in Shapiro 1985–86, p. 195). A disclosure
of writing practices is thus always a disclosure of forms of power (Derrida
1982). No textual staging is ever innocent (including this one).

Social problems writing, like all other forms of writing, is a sociohistorical construction that depends upon literary devices (e.g., narra-

tive, metaphor, imagery, invocations to authority, and appeals to audiences) not just for adornment, but for *cognitive* meaning. The truth value of social problems writing depends upon a deep epistemic code regarding how knowledge *in general* is figured. Imminent in the prefiguring are metaphors so entrenched and familiar that they do their partisan work in the guise of neutrality, passing as literal (Derrida 1982). For example, the grammatical split between subject and object goes wholly unnoticed as metaphor for the separation of "real" subjects and objects, for "objectivity," and a static world, fixed in time and space. The temporal and human practices that reified the objects are rendered invisible, irrelevant. The technical mechanisms of explanation are quarantined from the human processes of interpretation. The actual linguistic practices in which the researcher/writer is engaged are hidden; but they are not eradicated.

Poetic Representation

A deep and totally unnoticed trope used by social problems theorists is prose to stage their arguments and to report their findings. In this essay, I have myself used the prose trope and will for the next several pages. Its conventions allow me to stage my arguments in a way that is familiar to the reader, which is my goal in this part of the paper. The reader is not distracted by a different genre, and I am aided in my argument by the invisible power inherent in the adoption of conventional writing (essayic prose.) Those conventions are particularly helpful in making abstract arguments, which I am rhetorically interested in doing before I violate those conventions.

In conventional social problems writing not only are the arguments written in prose, the findings are as well. I wish to challenge, however, the ossification whereby prose is reified as the only way in which to write "findings." In what follows, I consider the production and writing of findings from the sociological interview, a fairly standard method of the social constructionist.

In the routine work of the sociological interviewer, the interview is tape-recorded, transcribed as prose, and then cut, pasted, edited, trimmed, smoothed, and snipped, just as if it were a literary text, which it is, albeit usually without explicit acknowledgment or recognition of such by its sociological constructor. Normatively, underlying this process is the belief that the purpose of the text is to convey information, as though information consists of facts or themes or notions that exist independently of the context in which they were told, as if the story we have recorded, transcribed, edited, and rewritten as snippets is the true one: a "science" story. Using standard writing conventions, including the use of prose, conceals the hand print of the sociologist who produced the written text.

Ironically, prose might not be the most "accurate" (i.e., "valid" and "scientific") way to "report" speech. According to the oral historian Dennis Tedlock, when people talk, whether as conversants, storytellers, informants, or interviewees, their speech is closer to poetry than it is to sociological prose (1983, p. 109). Nobody talks in "prose." Everybody— literate and nonliterate, adult and child, male and female—speaks using a poetical device, the pause. Indeed, in American speech, estimates are that about half of the time we are speaking, we are not; we are pausing (p. 198). And some 25 percent of pauses cannot be explained by physiological needs for breath or grammatical demands for closure, such as at the ends of sentences or clauses (p. 198). Unlike prose, poetry writes in pauses through the conventions of line breaks, and spaces between lines and between stanzas and sections; a poem, therefore, more closely mimics actual speech by building its text upon both sounds and silence.

Most importantly, poetry and its related genres are both written and oral traditions. They can be read or performed. Drama (cf. Ellis and Bochner 1991; McCall and Becker 1990; Richardson and Lockridge 1991; Richardson forthcoming), "ethnographic fiction" (cf. Ellis 1989; Krieger 1983; Stewart 1989), responsive reading (cf. Richardson 1992a), and poetry bring social theoretic understandings "live" to different audiences: poetry bars, theatres, policymaking settings, literary conventions, street scenes, and mass media.

I have used poetic representation to "report" the "findings" of an interview I had with Louisa May. One evening, as part of a larger project on the "social problem" of the "life experiences" of "unwed mothers," I completed a five-hour interview with Louisa May. I transcribed the tape into thirty-six pages of prose, and then shaped the transcript into a three-page poem. In so doing, I have drawn upon both scientific and literary criteria. In fashioning the poem, I used only her words, tone, and diction, but relied upon poetic devices such as repetition, off-rhyme, meter, and pauses to convey her narrative. The speech style is Louisa May's, the word are hers, but the poetic representation is my construction. I have chosen which themes to emphasize and how to stage the narrative. In doing so, I am doing what I and other social researchers do in social research—guide, organize, and write *as if* we are giving "voice" to those whom we interview, rather than to our own complex relationships with the material.

The way in which I have constructed the poem inscribes the interactional nature of the interview, and that the "talk" is one that has been produced in a particular kind of speech context—the sociological interview. I am the implied listener throughout the poem; when Louisa May speaks to me about the interview process itself, her words are italicized. The poem "shows" the sociological buttress to the "conversation," reminding the reader that this is a recording of a particular kind of speech performance. Louisa May's story arises in the context of an interview; the context is written into the poem. Because an interview is a jointly constructed text arising from the intersection of two subjectivities in a particular social context (see especially Mischler 1986; Richardson 1992b), framing the "findings" as though they are independent of the method in which they were produced is falsifying, although a standard claims-making procedure.

Because "Louisa May's Story of Her Life" has been constructed as a poem, listeners/readers are not deluded into thinking that the one and only true story about her has been written; rather, the facticity of its constructedness is ever present. Because the poetic form plays with connotative structures and literary devices to convey meaning, moreover, poetic representations of "findings" have a greater likelihood of engaging readers in reflexive analyses of their own interpretive labors of the researcher's interpretive labors of the speaker's interpretive labors. The construction of "text" is thus positioned as joint, prismatic, open, and partial.

I have presented "Louisa May" to diverse audiences. The responses have been uniformly strong, sometimes heated. Inadvertently, the "genre-breaking" writing displayed foundational, unexamined assumptions regarding the nature of "theory," "data," "findings," "authority," and "authorship." Poets theorize about the social construction of "normality," genre boundaries, and authorship. Women's studies audiences theorize the poem as a method for revealing "findings" as masculinist—with poetry "feminizing" the product and its production. General audiences have used "Louisa May" as a springboard for discussing what constitutes a "family problem." Oral historians have seen the poetic representation as a method for capturing "essence," which is lacking in their own conventions. Social workers and policymakers claim the poem has altered their stereotypical thinking. Some social scientists, and even some with constructionist and postmodernist leanings, have challenged the "validity" of the poem, demanded to see the transcript (although not to hear the tape) see a videotape, or talk directly to Louisa May—all possible grounds for establishing validity that do not privilege a written document. I have been variously accused of exploiting Louisa May, of fabricating her, and of being her. I doubt if these accusations would have been made by poets or sociologists or feminists had I written conventionally.

For social problems readers, in addition, the poem may seem to lack

certain sociological data. But this poem is based on Louisa May's sense
of what is relevant, not the sociologist's; it is her narrative. For example,
Louisa May did not talk about her education or occupation in the original interview; those were not relevant themes to her and therefore they
are not written into the poem. If readers feel uneasy about Louisa May
because they lack knowledge of her socioeconomic status, I submit this
uneasiness reflects the readers' unexamined assumptions. If they wonder, for example, how Louisa May supports herself and her daughter,
are they tapping into their stereotypes about *unwed* mothers? Would
they wonder about "support" if Louisa May were married or were Louis
M.? If they feel they cannot understand her unless they know about her
educational level, are they telling us about the place of education in their
own lives? More generally, have the categories of sociology been so
reified that even interpretivists feel they have to refract a person's life
through a sociologically prescribed lens?

Here is "Louisa May's Story of Her Life," a poetic representation, a
transcript masquerading as a poem/a poem masquerading as a transcript. I welcome your response/reading.

Louisa May's Story of Her Life

i

The most important thing
to say   is that
I grew up in the South.
Being southern shapes
aspirations   shapes
what you think you are
and what you think you're going to be.
   *(When I hear myself, my Ladybird
   kind of accent on tape. I think, OH Lord,
   You're from Tennessee.)*
No one ever suggested to me
that anything
might happen *with* my life.
I grew up poor in a rented house
in a very normal sort of way
on a very normal sort of street
with some very nice middle-class friends
      (Some still to this day)
and so I thought I'd have a lot of children.
I lived outside.

Unhappy home. Stable family, till it fell apart.
The first divorce in Milfrount County.
So, that's how that was worked out.

ii

Well, one thing that happens
growing up in the South
is that you leave. I
always knew I would
    I would leave.
        (I don't know what to say . . . .
        I don't know what's germane.)
My high school sweetheart and I married,
went north to college.
        I got pregnant and miscarried,
and I lost the child.
        (As I see it now it was a marriage
        situation which got increasingly horrendous,
        where I was under the most stress
        and strain without any sense
        of how to extricate myself.)
It was purely chance
that I got a job here,
and Robert didn't.
I was mildly happy.
After fourteen years of marriage,
That was the break.
We divorced.
A normal sort of life.

iii

So, the doctor said, "You're pregnant."
I was forty-one. John and I
had had a happy kind of relationship,
not a serious one.
But beside himself with fear and anger,
awful, rageful, vengeful, horrid,
Jody May's father said,
'Get an abortion."
I told him,
'I would never marry you.
I would never marry you.
I would never.
'I am going to have this child.
I am going to.

I am. I am.

'Just Go Away!'

But he wouldn't. He painted the nursery.
He slept on the floor. He went to therapy.
We went to LaMaze.

> *(We ceased having a sexual relationship directly*
> *after I had gotten pregnant and that has never again*
> *entered the situation.)*

He lives one hundred miles away now.
He visits every weekend.
He sleeps on the floor.
We all vacation together.
We go camping.

I am not interested in a split family,
her father taking her on Sundays.
I'm not interested in doing so.

So, little Jody May always has had a situation which is normal.

Mother—bless her—the word "married" never crossed her lips.
> *(I do resent mother's stroke. Other mothers have their mother.)*

So, it never occurs to me really that we are unusual in any way.

No, our life really is very normal. I own my house.
I live on a perfectly ordinary middle-class street.

So, that's the way that was worked out.

iv

She has his name. If she wasn't going to have a father,
I thought she should have a father, so to speak.

We both adore her.
John says Jody May saved his life.

OH, I do fear that something will change—

v

> *(Is this helpful?)*

This is the happiest time in my life.

I am an entirely different person.

With no husband in the home there is less tension.
And I'm not talking about abnormal families here.
Just normal circumstances. Everyone comes home tired.

I left the South a long time ago.
I had no idea how I would do it.

So, that's the way that worked out.
> *(I've talked so much my throat hurts.)*

References

Derrida, Jacques. 1982. *Margins of Philosophy.* Translated by Alan Bass. Chicago: University of Chicago.

Ellis, Carolyn. 1989. "What Are You Feeling? Issues in the Introspective Method." Paper presented at the American Sociological Association Meetings, San Francisco, CA.

Ellis, Carolyn and Art Bochner. 1992. "Telling and Performing Personal Stories: The Constraint of Choice in Abortion." Pp. 79–101 in *Investigating Subjectivity: Research on Lived Experience,* edited by Carolyn Ellis and Michael G. Flaherty. Newbury Park, CA: Sage.

Krieger, Susan. 1983. *The Mirror Dance: Identity in a Woman's Community.* Philadelphia: Temple University Press.

McCall, Michael M. and Howard S. Becker. 1990. "Performance Science." *Social Problems* 32:117–32.

Mischler, Elliot G. 1986. *Research Interviewing.* Cambridge, MA: Harvard University Press.

Richardson, Laurel. 1990. *Writing Strategies: Reaching Diverse Audiences.* Newbury Park, CA: Sage.

———. 1992a. "Resisting Resistance Narratives: A Representation for Communication." *Studies in Symbolic Interaction* 13:77–82.

———. 1992b. "The Consequences of Poetic Representation: Writing the Other, Re-Writing the Self." Pp. 124–41 in *Investigating Subjectivity: Research on Lived Experience,* edited by Carolyn Ellis and Michael G. Flaherty. Newbury Park, CA: Sage.

———. Forthcoming. "The Case of the Skipped Line: Poetics, Dramatics, and Transgressive Validity." *The Sociological Quarterly.*

Richardson, Laurel and Ernest Lockridge. 1991. "The Sea Monster: An Ethnographic Drama." *Symbolic Interaction* 14(3):335–41.

Shapiro, Michael. 1985–86. "Metaphor in the Philosophy of the Social Sciences." *Cultural Critique:*191–214.

Stewart, John O. 1989. *Drinkers, Drummers and Decent Folk: Ethnographic Narratives of Village Trinidad.* Albany: State University of New York.

Tedlock, Dennis. 1983. *The Spoken Word and the Work of Interpretations.* Philadelphia: University of Pennsylvania Press.

Conclusion

24

Social Constructionism and Its Critics: Assessing Recent Challenges

Gale Miller and James A. Holstein

Recent challenges by social critics and poststructuralists raise fundamental questions about the usefulness of social constructionism for analyzing contemporary social life and problems. As the essays in Part II illustrate, social criticism and poststructuralism have many variants and raise diverse questions regarding social problems and the constructionist perspective. Moreover, some theorists intentionally blend aspects of the perspectives, while others import analytic resources and concerns from one to the other without explicitly recognizing the resulting conflation. This produces a somewhat confusing set of claims and critiques that sometimes only obliquely address issues central to the constructionist program.

We conclude this volume with a discussion of several of the current debates about social problems theory, raising three questions that intersect the major approaches to the field: (1) Is a general theory of social problems warranted? (2) Should social problems theorists be claims-makers? (3) How should social problems theory be written? While they do not exhaust the issues that might be raised about social constructionism and social problems theory, these questions elucidate fundamental challenges faced by contemporary social problems theorists. They also indicate the extent to which social problems theorists have rejected the structural functionalist assumptions that dominated the field less than twenty years ago. Put in Pollner's (1991) terms, the field has become epistemologically unsettled.

The questions involve important choices and, perhaps, dilemmas for students of social problems, including those who describe themselves as "only doing research." Most importantly, the questions highlight the variety of ways in which theoretical matters are embedded in all studies of social problems. Theoretical choices are made in formulating studies, carrying them out, and writing about them. Potential dilemmas emerge when social problems theorists choose to combine aspects of differing perspectives, or commit themselves to projects that do not fit neatly within their theoretical frameworks. For example, how do some poststructuralist theorists reconcile the nonemancipatory themes in poststructuralism with their desire to use their writings to facilitate the development of *the just society?*

We do not believe that social constructionist, critical, and poststructuralist standpoints can or should be "reconciled" in order to create a unified, comprehensive, or triangulated theory. Social problems theory is not advanced by creating "one big, happy, eclectic family" within which there is no disagreement or conflict. Nor do we claim that we can demonstrate that one standpoint has more explanatory power, is more humane, or, by some other absolute standard, is better than others. We do believe, however, that recent critical and poststructuralist challenges represent promising opportunities to reconsider the assumptions, distinctions, and categories on which social constructionism and social problems theory rest.

The challenges also suggest ways of enriching the constructionist program. For example, an especially promising area of theoretical development may be Foucauldian studies of discourse, knowledge, and power. Social constructionists would do well to consider how aspects of Foucault's (1973, 1977, 1978) studies of the clinical gaze, panopticon, and sexuality may be used to extend the constructionist project. Constructionism might be enhanced by analyzing the discursive and epistemic contexts within which social problems movements and rhetorics emerge, and the technologies associated with them. Leslie Miller's (in this volume) analysis of gendered silence as claims-making is also an important example of how such studies might be conducted.

Similarly, Douglas's (1986) approach to institutional thinking (which is informed by Foucauldian studies) promises much for the development of social constructionism. She analyzes institutional thinking as the ways in which social issues and problems are constituted and responded to within culturally shared and institutionally standardized discourses. Studies of institutional thinking might focus on the cultural and institutional constraints within which claims-makers work in rhetorically assigning aspects of everyday life to social problems categories and justifying their calls for social action. Douglas's analysis also challenges social constructionists to reconsider their assumptions about human agency and the ways in which institutional discourses "think" and "speak" for us.

Our assessments of the social problems debates reflect our orientation to social problems theory. Clearly, we are sympathetic to social constructionism, and believe that some recent criticisms are unjustified and that others are overstated. But we also find much to appreciate in the diverse responses found in this volume. Thus, the discussions that follow emphasize both the merits of the social constructionist project and how it might be extended to take account of recent criticisms. We begin with the most far-reaching challenge, that is, whether a general theory of social problems is warranted.

Is a General Social Problems Theory Warranted?

A major difference between current debates about social problems theory and early debates between social constructionists and structural functionalists involves the debaters' orientations to the development of a general theory of social problems. While they disagreed about its proper content and focus, both constructionists and functionalists agreed that the development of a general theory was a worthy goal. The assumption is central to Spector and Kitsuse's ([1977] 1987) specification of the claims-making approach, which they argued would make sociological studies of social problems distinctive and produce generalizable data. Ibarra and Kitsuse's (in this volume) refocusing of the perspective on condition-categories and their call for ethnographies of moral discourse also involve the assumption that a general theory of social problems is attainable and warranted.

The general theories envisioned by social constructionists and structural functionalists are quite different, however. The functionalist project involves developing a grand theory of social organization and process that encompasses a "middle-range" theory (Merton 1957) of social problems. Further, structural functional theory is intended to produce knowledge that may be used to predict, if not control, behavior. Most generally construed, the social constructionist project promises only a theory of social problems claims-making and/or moral discourses. The project's focus is on describing and comparing the ways in which social problems and their concrete instances are interpretively and rhetorically accomplished. While social constructionists have analyzed the social conditions associated with successful and unsuccessful social problems movements, they do not use their studies to predict and control behavior.

Nonetheless, some critics of constructionism challenge the longstanding assumption that such a general theory of social problems is warranted. In part, the challenges raise issues about the language used by constructionists to explain and justify their project. We believe that both Spector and Kitsuse's ([1977] 1987) initial formulation of the project and Ibarra and Kitsuse's respecification of it may be too rigidly tied to the analysis of public rhetoric. They implicitly suggest that there is only one proper (scientific and sociological) way of conceptualizing and studying social problems. Social constructionists might be better served by a constructionist framework that allows for diverse theoretical interests in social problems claims-making, interpretive practice, and condition-categories. A more general framework and less restrictive language would remind both constructionist writers and their readers of the definitional boundaries and domain assumptions within which the project is being pursued.

But some challenges to social constructionism go well beyond this issue. They question the need for the *field* of social problems theory, although the challengers do not necessarily reject continued studies of aspects of everyday life that are typically treated under the social problems rubric. One suggestion is to analyze social problems as aspects of capitalism and patriarchy. Another approach at least partially dismisses a general theory of social problems as a modernist goal.

Social Problems as Aspects of Capitalism and Patriarchy

Social critics' rejection of the constructionists' attempt to develop a general theory of social problems is related to their concern for more comprehensive theories of contemporary society. Thus, social critics wish to eliminate constructionist and other theories of social problems, and replace them with more general and encompassing theories of capitalism and patriarchy. They argue that such theories facilitate social change by showing that inequality, racism, sexism, and similar problems are endemic to capitalism and patriarchy. Social critics' theories also counter the "bad faith" associated with dominant ideologies, which assume that the social conditions that presently exist are inevitable and that we must accept them.

For example, Agger (in this volume) argues that a general theory of social problems is unwarranted because inequality and oppression are fundamental aspects of "fast capitalism" (Agger 1989), and should be analyzed as such. He contends that such a broad-based critical theory would show that constructionists' assumption that social problems are inevitable aspects of all societies is unwarranted. Agger emphasizes the possibility for emancipation from social problems through radical social change, a possibility that he states is discouraged by constructionists' narrow focus on claims-making activities and condition-categories. Agger suggests that the constructionist project is based on and perpetuates a conservative, professional, and scientistic ideology that justifies the status quo.

We agree with Agger's claim that a social problems theory that treats social problems as real social and material conditions is redundant with other materialist frameworks. Such analyses are pervasive in mainstream and radical sociologies. But the distinctiveness and importance of the social constructionist perspective is that it challenges, and is an alternative to, such forms of sociological realism. It shares with ethnomethodology the assumption that social realities are accomplished through interactional and interpretive practices. Thus, constructionist analyses of social problems cannot be subsumed within more general, realist theories of society.

We also believe that two of Agger's other criticisms of social constructionism are unwarranted. From the social constructionist perspective, conditions of life do not exist separate from persons' interpretations of them. Rather, people only recognize and act toward them by first constituting them as kinds of conditions, such as instances of inequality or oppression. Thus, social constructionists do take account of the conditions of life by showing how the conditions are interpretively constituted as practical matters that warrant public attention and concern. Constructionists' studies of claims-making and condition-categories are also a way of calling attention to and countering the "bad faith" assumptions that social critics analyze as aspects of dominant ideologies. Put simply, if social problems are social constructions, then they are not inevitable aspects of social life.

Second, we disagree with Agger's claim that social constructionists assume that social problems are universal. Agger's claim rests on the assumption that constructionists study "real" social conditions and what is interpretively made of them—a sort of contextual constructionism (Best 1989). Ibarra and Kitsuse and other more radical constructionists emphasize that the social constructionist project is about moral discourses and how social problems conditions are constituted within them. Thus, the perspective may be applied to interpretive practices in diverse settings without assuming that social conditions associated with capitalism are universal. Indeed, one way in which the constructionist project may be extended is through the examination of the diverse moral discourses analyzed in anthropological studies of non-Western societies. Such studies would broaden the perspective by pointing to the variety of moral discourses within which the conditions of life may be constituted.

Smith (in this volume) also challenges social constructionists' interest in developing a general theory by analyzing claims-making as an aspect of public discourse and relations of ruling. She contrasts social problems claims-making with the various local sites and actualities of everyday life within which inequality and oppression are experienced by marginalized groups and individuals. According to Smith, constructionists are unable to see and analyze how social problems are aspects of lived experience because they have defined their project to only focus on events occurring within the public domain. Constructionists also ignore how social problems claims and persons' lives are shaped by public textually mediated discourse.

Smith's criticism of social constructionists for overemphasizing the "public" claims-making of organized movements and groups is well founded. Social problems claims-making is a pervasive aspect of contemporary life and social relations, and much of it is ignored by constructionists. We also agree that Smith's (1987) "institutional ethnography" research strategy is one way of analyzing the relationship between lived experience and public discourses about social problems. But it is also possible to address Smith's concerns and extend the social constructionist project in other ways, such as by elaborating on Emerson and Messinger's (1977) ethnomethodologically informed micropolitics of trouble perspective.

The perspective focuses on the ways in which persons define aspects of their own and others' everyday lives as troublesome and construct remedies to them. It also considers how definitions of trouble emerge, are reconsidered, and are often transformed when third parties (such as social workers, physicians, psychiatrists, and attorneys) are consulted or intervene to remedy persons' troubles. At this point, "private" troubles become "public" issues, and social constructionists may study the practical consequences of public discourses (including textually mediated discourse) about social problems for persons' everyday lives. Analyzing the micropolitics of trouble is also a way of describing the social organization of power relations.

Social Problems Theory as Modernist

Poststructuralist critics take an ostensibly different tack in criticizing social constructionism. Some suggest that trying to develop a general theory of social problems is an inappropriate modernist enterprise because it assumes that those aspects of everyday life that constructionists call claims-making and condition-categories are adequately explained by a single, social scientific perspective. Poststructuralists argue that social scientists' perspectives should not be privileged over others. They also challenge constructionists' claims that constructionist analyses are non-evaluative. Finally, the constructionist perspective is considered modernist because it de-emphasizes how analysts' understandings of and orientations to their topics are related to such social positionings as gender, race, and social class.

Spector and Kitsuse's ([1977] 1987) initial specification of the social constructionist project is clearly modernist (Troyer, in this volume). As noted above, they imply that there is only one proper way of conceptualizing and studying social problems. We agree with Pfohl's criticism of Ibarra and Kitsuse's emphasis on decontextualizing and cataloging social problems rhetorics. The practical uses and meanings of such rhetorics are best revealed by analyzing them within the diverse contexts of everyday life. Special attention should focus on how discourse is reflexively embedded in social context. That is, analysis should attend to how the practical meanings of rhetorical claims are defined by their contexts and how their use shapes the contexts within which they are defined.

But we also have some serious reservations about the ways in which poststructuralists' perspectives are being introduced into social problems theory. Our concern partly involves poststructuralists' tendency to combine aspects of social criticism with poststructuralist themes. While synthesis is often useful, the practical result of blending critical and poststructural assumptions in social problems theory has too often been mystification, rather than clarification and insight. We believe that the development of poststructuralist social problems theory requires that poststructuralists seriously examine (perhaps deconstruct) the assumptions associated with their analyses, including the ways in which they sometimes assume that there is an intrinsically meaningful world separate from discourse, and their assumption of an authentic human experience that can be understood and represented through poststructuralist perspectives, methodologies, and writing practices.

Another reservation involves poststructuralists' rejection of general theories as totalizing, and their call for the development of narratives that are partial and provisional. For poststructuralists, such narratives do not privilege sociologists' constructions of social reality, but allow for others' deconstruction of sociological narratives and make room for dialogues between sociologists and the persons about whom sociologists write. Poststructuralists' claims about others' theories and their narratives become problematic, however, when we consider the unexplicated assumptions and theory associated with the claims.

Assumptions and theory are unavoidable aspects of all interpretive communities. They constitute the domains within which community members may "see," speak of, or write about social reality. Fish argues against the distinction between totalizing and nontotalizing theories:

[I]t seems to me that all thought is totalizing in that its successive incarnations always deliver a fully articulated world, a world without gaps or spots of unintelligibility. (This doesn't mean that everything is understood, but that even what is puzzling and mysterious is so in ways specific to some elaborated system of thought.) It follows then that the differences between ways of thinking (forms of belief) can never be characterized as the difference between closed and open structures, but between structures that are differently (if temporarily) closed; flexibility or openness is not a possible mode of cognitive performance for human beings . . . . , it cannot be a program a human performer might self-consciously enact. (1989, p. 16)

The distinction between totalizing and nontotalizing theory is best understood as a rhetorical resource that poststructuralists and others use to constitute themselves as members of a distinctive interpretive community. To speak or write of social problems is to constitute and work within an interpretive framework that may be considered a general theory. For example, we may analyze Pfohl's response to Ibarra and Kitsuse as a world-making activity within which the social construction-ist project is constituted as an exclusionary interpretive framework that reconstructs others in its own terms, downgrades the lived experiences of others, and fails to acknowledge the partiality and provisional status of its own knowledge.

Pfohl constructs this vision by constituting and privileging an inter-pretive frame that treats knowledge as related to (if not a direct product of) a limited set of social positions. The approach is openly evaluative, prefers knowledge produced through transferential acts between "us" and "them," and calls attention to its own partiality and provisional status. Pfohl also insists that lived experience and knowledge are en-meshed in contradiction and irony. It is within the interpretive context of such a general theory of social organization, lived experience, and knowledge that Pfohl is able to justify an approach to social problems that treats them as diverse and localized phenomena that cannot be adequately explained by a general theory of claims-making.

Our point is not to call Pfohl or other poststructuralists' motives or theoretical competence into question. Rather, we wish to highlight the choice that social problems theorists face. It is not between totalizing and nontotalizing theories. Rather, the choice determines the interpre-tive worlds within which social problems theorists do their work.

Social Problems Theory as Claims-Making?

One of the issues on which social critics and many poststructuralists agree is their rejection of strict constructionists' desire to avoid claims-making. Spector and Kitsuse ([1977] 1987) argue that the development of a distinctive and sociological approach to social problems demands that social problems theorists resist the temptation to make social problems claims. Ibarra and Kitsuse's updating of the perspective also involves the assumption (claim) that sociologists of social problems should study (not make) claims about social problems conditions. Social critics and many poststructuralists offer two major explanations for their assertion that social problems claims-making is an important and warranted aspect of social problems theorizing.

First, they argue that the purpose of social problems theory is to foster social change. This may be accomplished by changing persons' orientations to aspects of their everyday lives, including their acceptance of unequal and oppressive social conditions as normal or unchangeable conditions. Critical and some poststructuralist theorists make such conditions visible and matters for public debate and intervention by analyzing them as social problems. For example, studies of the invisible work of mothers are claims-making activities because they call attention to the unrecognized ways in which women's work in their families is shaped by the (sometimes oppressive) demands of such extrafamilial institutions as schools and employers (Smith and Griffith 1990; Griffith and Smith 1990). Thus, achieving gender equality partly involves changing invisible inequities in families and the exploitative demands made by extrafamilial institutions on families.

Although they orient to and use it differently, social critics and post-structuralists assume that all knowledge is political. The assumption is related to their argument that social problems theory should involve claims-making. For example, some argue that our understandings of social reality are inextricably intertwined with our social positions, and the practical experiences and concerns associated with them. Social position is related to sociologists' professionally sanctioned and institutionalized orientations to knowledge. One such orientation is the detached attitude associated with science, and central to the constructionist approach to social problems. It involves observing, describing, and analyzing public debates without "taking sides."

Social critics and some poststructuralists consider constructionism an ideology that justifies the status quo, regardless of social constructionists' motives or personal orientations to political issues. They argue that constructionism perpetuates the belief that "factual" and "objective" knowledge is apolitical, and unrelated to the practical circumstances of analysts' lives. Further, constructionism ignores "invisible" conditions that are not matters of public recognition and debate, making no demands on persons to engage in the debates under study. Finally, Gordon (in this volume) contends that social constructionism is an ideology that justifies a managerial orientation that involves monitoring powerless groups and individuals, describing them as social problems, and taking actions to manage their behavior.

We agree that knowledge is value laden, and political. We also believe that persons' understandings of social reality are related to their practical concerns and experiences and, therefore, to their social positions. Thus, it is not surprising that social constructionism emerged within academic institutions, and the questions that it emphasizes are often literally academic. The same can also be said of social criticism and poststructuralism. We do not believe, however, that these assumptions are necessarily inconsistent with the constructionist perspective, although the language used by constructionists often allows for other interpretations.

Specifically, social constructionists insist on taking a detached attitude toward claims-making in order to generate a particular type of "disinterested" description, but they do not necessarily claim that other approaches to knowledge are invalid. Constructionist approaches and topics are simply different from those of the conventional social sciences, and of advocates for social change. As Ibarra and Kitsuse show, two issues that may be studied from a detached standpoint involve the structure of social problems rhetorics and how claims-makers express and reproduce culture. Such issues are unlikely to be emphasized by sociologists interested in persuading others that aspects of everyday life are social problems.

Thus, we reject the claim that the purpose of social problems theory must be social change. It is merely one of several concerns to which social problems theory may be directed. We also question whether explicit claims-making is always an effective way of furthering the political interests of social critics and poststructuralists. Critics of social constructionism often assume that there is a linear relationship between social problems claims-making and social change. The assumption diverts attention from the practical constraints faced by claims-makers in directly pressing their claims (a phenomenon that is examined in constructionist studies of claims-making), and from ironic aspects of social change.

For example, explicit claims-making frequently requires that sociologists engage in ongoing debates that are already structured within culturally standardized discourses, limiting the options available to sociologists in making further claims. An alternative strategy is to undermine others' claims by analyzing how they are socially constructed. Smith's (1974, 1978, 1984) ethnomethodologically informed analyses of psychiatric, documentary, and textually mediated discourses are examples of such an approach to social criticism. The studies challenge professionally and organizationally sanctioned realities by showing how mental illness designations and other "factual" claims are social accomplishments.

Some social critics' and poststructuralists' dismissals of social constructionism as conservative and managerialist are overstated. While it is not a politically radical perspective, social constructionist studies may be useful to sociologists and others interested in advancing radical positions. Of course, they may also be useful to those pursuing conservative ends. Similarly, Gordon's charge that social constructionism is managerialist caricatures constructionism and attributes to it a practical agenda that is not part of the analytic program. As Foucault (1977) states, institutional oversight and control of outcast and marginalized groups involves both legitimating discourses and technologies of social control. We agree that Foucault's analysis has important implications for aspects of the human sciences (such as psychiatry, behaviorism, and criminology), but see no evidence that social constructionism is organized as a discourse and technology of control.

How Should Social Problems Be Written?

While the claims-making issue has been an aspect of debates in social problems theory for years, the issue of how social problems theory should be written is more recent. It is associated with some theorists' interest in aspects of poststructuralism and the rhetoric of inquiry. Both orientations emphasize the ways in which theoretical and empirical realities are textually organized and produced. Poststructuralist and other theorists challenge social constructionist writing practices in three major and interrelated ways.

First, they question the appropriateness of objectivist writing in a postmodern society filled with diverse perspectives and voices, images of social reality, and combinations of seemingly contradictory orientations and styles. Poststructuralists portray constructionists' objectivism as a modernist and elitist approach that casts writers as aloof and objective observers of a unitary social reality. Thus, while constructionists deny that they are experts on "real" social problems, they write in ways that cast themselves as detached experts on claims-making practices and social problems rhetorics. Constructionists seem to violate one of their own principles when they write as if the objects of their analyses exist independent of their rhetoric.

The second criticism involves social constructionists' failure to inform their readers about their social positions and to discuss how their positioning shapes their orientations to social problems. The criticism is similar to Gouldner's (1970) argument that sociological writing is unreflexive. Unlike Gouldner, however, some poststructuralist social problems theorists define reflexive writing as the offering of confessionlike statements about their social positions and orientations to issues. Such writing is also intended to overcome the subject-object distinction that is central to conventional writing practices in sociology, including social constructionism.

Finally, poststructuralists raise questions about the ways in which constructionists constitute the subjects of their analyses. The subjects are claims-makers and others involved in public debates about social problems. For poststructuralists, such an approach to others degrades their concerns, abilities, and experiences by removing their claims-making activities from the larger contexts of their lives. As Pfohl states in this volume,

> As respectful of members' linguistic productions as an analyst may be, by simply recognizing members as "figures" differentiated from an "otherwise" unproblematic or unnoticed social background s/he is (for better and/or worse) reducing somebody else's lived bodily experience to an ideally "downgraded" categorization.

We would not deny that constructionism's aims and writing practices are elitist, particularly if we define elitism as an interest in understanding aspects of social life differently than those engaged in it. For example, Ibarra and Kitsuse's focus on social problems rhetorics makes a largely taken-for-granted aspect of everyday life into an analytic topic. Adopting a "detached" standpoint toward the subjects and objects of their studies may also be described as elitist. The analyst is an uninvolved, objective observer and describer of a unitary social reality, while the others constituted in constructionist writings are nothing more than social problems claims-makers.

While we agree that social constructionism may be construed as an elitist project, we find the alternatives to it problematic. One alternative is a reflexive writing style that reminds writers and readers of some of the writers' social positionings, asserting that the positionings are important contexts for understanding the meaning of writers' claims. As in Pfohl's and Orr's essays in this volume, this writing style is often associated with the claim that the surreal is real. Two aspects of this approach are troublesome.

First, such writing replaces detached constructionists who seem to be uninvolved in the worlds that they analyze with highly involved poststructuralists around whom the world is centered. In an effort to relativize and take responsibility for their claims, such reflexive writers "downgrade" others' concerns and experiences by recasting (constituting) them as meaningful only in relation to the writers' concerns and experiences. A second concern involves the audiences for such writing. As Michalowski (in this volume) concludes, the reflexive writing style is itself elitist, because it is unlikely to be understood or appreciated by readers who have not been initiated into the poststructuralist interpretive community. Indeed, one practical consequence of such writing has been to produce an interpretive community that is more exclusive than the social constructionist community.

A second alternative to social constructionists' writing practices is to experiment with nonrealist alternative writing forms, such as poetry (Richardson, in this volume). The approach is not writer-focused because it involves working with others to express their practical concerns and experiences in new ways. Such writing is also frequently intended for nonsociological audiences, and is presented as a topic for discussion, not the final word of a sociological expert on the subject. While it overcomes the elitism associated with constructionist and some forms of reflexive writing, this approach raises serious questions about social problems theorists' contribution to understanding contemporary social life.

It suggests that social problems theorists' proper role is to act as advisors to others who have stories to tell, as editors of their representations of social reality, and as circulators of their reconstituted stories. Such a conceptualization of the work not only runs counter to central assumptions of the social constructionist project, but also undermines social criticism and some poststructuralist perspectives. Certainly, there is room in social problems theory for alternative approaches, but we agree with Hilbert's (1990) suggestion that advocates of such approaches not reject all analysis. They should consider how recent developments in interpretive analysis complement their approach. For example, they might ask "how actors can have points-of-view at all, how there could be anything for them to have points-of-view about, how these two converge in ongoing social practices, and so on" (Hilbert 1990, p. 134).

Conclusion

Perhaps the most important message conveyed by this volume is that social problems theory is in flux. Matters that theorists have treated as settled are being raised and debated within new intellectual contexts. There is little reason to believe that the controversies will subside, or that differences will be reconciled. While the essays in this volume are diverse and often critical, they convince us that social constructionism will respond to the recent challenges, to be transformed and enriched as it does.

References

Agger, Ben. 1989. *Fast Capitalism*. Urbana: University of Illinois Press.

Best, Joel. 1989. "Afterward." Pp. 243–54 in *Images of Issues*, edited by Joel Best. Hawthorne, NY: Aldine de Gruyter.

Douglas, Mary. 1986. *How Institutions Think*. Syracuse, NY: Syracuse University Press.

Emerson, Robert M. and Sheldon L. Messinger. 1977. "The Micro-Politics of Trouble." *Social Problems* 25:121–35.

Fish, Stanley. 1989. *Doing What Comes Naturally*. Durham, NC: Duke University Press.

Foucault, Michel. 1973. *The Birth of the Clinic*. New York: Pantheon.

―――. 1977. *Discipline and Punish*. New York: Pantheon.

―――. 1978. *The History of Sexuality*, Vol. 1. New York: Random House.

Gouldner, Alvin W. 1970. *The Coming Crises of Western Sociology*. New York: Equinox Books.

Griffith, Alison I. and Dorothy E. Smith. 1990. "What Did You Do in School Today'." Pp. 3–24 in *Perspectives on Social Problems*, Vol. 2, edited by Gale Miller and James A. Holstein. Greenwich, CT: JAI Press.

Hilbert, Richard. 1990. "The Efficacy of Performance Science." *Social Problems* 37:133–35.

Merton, Robert K. 1957. *Social Theory and Social Structure*. New York: The Free Press.

Pollner, Melvin. 1991. "Left of Ethnomethodology." *American Sociological Review* 56:370–80.

Smith, Dorothy. 1974. "The Social Construction of Documentary Reality." *Sociological Inquiry* 44:257–68.

―――. 1978. " 'K is Mentally Ill." *Sociology* 12:23–53.

―――. 1984. "Textually Mediated Social Organization." *International Social Science Journal* 36:59–75.

―――. 1987. *The Everyday World as Problematic*. Boston: Northeastern University Press.

Smith, Dorothy E. and Griffith, Alison I. 1990. " Coordinating the Uncoordinated." Pp. 25–44 in *Perspectives on Social Problems*, Vol. 2, edited by Gale Miller and James A. Holstein. Greenwich, CT: JAI Press.

Spector, Malcolm and John I. Kitsuse. [1977] 1987. *Constructing Social Problems*. Hawthorne, NY: Aldine de Gruyter.

Index

of reflexivity, 206
social problem analysis in, 294,
295–298, 321–322
of social problems work, 152–155
Society for the Study of Social
Problems and mainstream, 291
SSSP (Society for the Study of Social
Problems)
analysis of social problems and,
281–282
postmodernism and, 297
social constructionism and, 118–
119
social problems theory and, 292
sociology and, mainstream, 291
State, 507–511 (*See also* New Left;
Radical Right)
State-sponsored style, 366
Strict constructionism
Best's view of, 242
contextual constructionism and, 10,
11, 122–123
emergence of, 132–133
objectivist constructionism and, 134
ontological gerrymandering and,
134–135
possibility of, 136–138
price of, 136–138
problems of, 143–144
satanism and, 130–131
"Vernacular Constituents of Moral
Discourse" and, 130
Structural functionalism, 7, 284–285
Structuralism, 265–267, 394
Subcultural style, 53, 366, 369
Subject-object question, 391–393
Subordinate style, 369–370
Symbolic interactionism, 380
Sympathetic counterrhetorics, 70–71

Tactical criticism, 44–45
Telling anecdote, 45
Textual analysis, 63, 103–104
Theatrical style, 52, 76
Theoretical project, 29–30, 384
Ticking time bomb metaphor, 47–48

Topical constructionism
Constructing Social Problems as, 202–
204
description of, 201
goals of, 245
Ibarra and Kitsuse's view of, 242
Total administration, 287
Totalizing theory, 541–542
Troubles-telling, 17, 178, 186, 356–357

Underdog skills, 367–370
Unreason, rhetoric of, 34, 40–41,
70
Unsympathetic counterrhetorics, 45–
47, 71
Unwarranted social problems, 12

Values, 66–68
"Vernacular Constituents of Moral
Discourse" (Ibarra and Kitsuse)
broadening subject matter of social
problems and, 48–53
claims-making styles and, 106–107,
112–113, 328
condition-categories and, 30–33,
105, 122–123, 140
damaging rhetorical device in, 143–
144
deconstruction and, 105–106, 111
discourse in social problems analysis and, 306–308
epistemology and, 307, 308–309
feminism's criticism of, 310–312,
314–315, 318
membership and, 97–98, 107–112
membership differentiation and,
307–309
mundane and, 95–96
naturalism and, cautious, 98–100
normative constructionists and,
302–305
positioning and, theoretical, 523–
524
postmodernism and, 123–125
preface to, 25–30
problems plaguing, 142–143

CPSIA information can be obtained at www.ICGtesting.com
Printed in the USA
LVOW06s1716291013

359125LV00019B/1304/P